LEADERSHIP

ESSENTIAL WRITINGS BY OUR GREATEST THINKERS

No Man's Land:
Preparing for War and Peace in Post-9/11 America

Soldier's Heart:
Reading Literature Through Peace and
War at West Point

Willing Obedience:
Citizens, Soldiers, and the Progress of Consent
in America, 1776–1898

A NORTON ANTHOLOGY

LEADERSHIP

ESSENTIAL WRITINGS BY OUR GREATEST THINKERS

EDITED BY

ELIZABETH D. SAMET

W. W. NORTON & COMPANY · NEW YORK · LONDON

Since this page cannot legibly accommodate all the copyright notices,
pages 708–15 constitute an extension of the copyright page.

For information about permission to reproduce selections from this book,
write to Permissions, W. W. Norton & Company, Inc.,
500 Fifth Avenue, New York, NY 10110

For information about special discounts for bulk purchases, please contact
W. W. Norton Special Sales at specialsales@wwnorton.com or 800-233-4830

Manufacturing by RR Donnelley, Harrisonburg
Book design by JAM Design
Production manager: Devon Zahn

Library of Congress Cataloging-in-Publication Data

Leadership : essential writings by our greatest thinkers :
a Norton anthology / edited by Elizabeth D. Samet. — 1st ed.
    pages cm
Includes index.
ISBN 978-0-393-23969-0 (hardcover)
1. Leadership. I. Samet, Elizabeth D., editor.
HM1261.L4144 2015
303.3'4—dc23
                          2015000741

W. W. Norton & Company, Inc.
500 Fifth Avenue, New York, N.Y. 10110
www.wwnorton.com

W. W. Norton & Company Ltd.
Castle House, 75/76 Wells Street, London W1T 3QT

1 2 3 4 5 6 7 8 9 0

Whither wilt thou lead me?

—WILLIAM SHAKESPEARE, *Hamlet*

Contents

Contents Organized by Field of Interest

SCIENCE, TECHNOLOGY, NATURE, ENVIRONMENT

CULTURE, ARTS, LETTERS

EDUCATION AND TRAINING

FAMILY, SOCIETY, CIVILIZATION

WAR AND PEACE

INTROSPECTION AND MOTIVATION

Editor's Note

Correspondence and conversations with a delightfully eclectic group of thinkers have informed the selections in this book as well as my thinking about various facets of leadership, especially the relationship of reading to its cultivation. I have numerous West Point students, friends, and colleagues—past and present—to thank, especially Damon Durall, Mark Gagnon, Tony Hartle, Harry Jones, Rick Kerin, Tom Kolditz, Scott Krawczyk, Rick McPeak, Sean Morrow, Suzanne Nielsen, Karin Roffman, Geri Smith, Peter Stromberg, Nick Utzig, and Laura Vidler. Virtual and actual exchanges with far-flung scholars, soldiers, and a variety of professionals were also immensely helpful along the way. In particular I would like to thank Joseph Badaracco, Daniel Donoghue, Paul Edgar, David Fivecoat, Stephen Greenblatt, Mark Hertling, Suzanne Koon, Jonathan Lewis, Donna Orwin, Frank Rotondo, Haun Saussy, Anna Simons, Sandra Sucher, Anne Taranto, and Rosanna Warren.

My thanks, as well, to the readers who gave such trenchant, spirited responses to the initial proposal for this anthology: JoAnn Barbour (doctoral program in Leadership Studies, Gonzaga University), Joseph Cerami (Bush School of Government and Public Service, Texas A&M University), Alexander B. Horniman (Darden School of Business, University of Virginia), Matthew J. Sowcik (Jay S. Sidhu School of Business and Leadership, Wilkes University), and Jeffrey D. Zacko-Smith (International Center for Studies in Creativity, Buffalo State College).

It has been a great pleasure to work with everyone at Norton. Julia Reidhead is an editor distinguished by precision, kindness, and a sense of calm and common sense that should be the envy of any leader. Emily Stuart's contributions have been many and invaluable; her patience and good humor are always most welcome.

A version of the introduction to "Abraham Lincoln: Artist of Judgment" originally appeared on *Bloomberg View* (July 1, 2013), and parts of the introductions to "Artists of Delay" and "Taking Responsibility" appeared in different form in *Portland Magazine* (Autumn 2012).

The editorial opinions expressed in this book are my own and do not necessarily represent those of West Point, the Department of the Army, or the Department of Defense.

INTRODUCTION:
A Crisis of Leadership

Call it a crisis of leadership.

—PROPOSITION JOE, *The Wire*,
season 3, episode 10

THE CASE OF STRINGER BELL

In the so-called Third Golden Age of Television, there has perhaps been no show more gilded by critical acclaim than *The Wire*, which ran on HBO for five seasons (2002–8). *The Wire* is a Baltimore story—an urban story—premised on the alarming interconnectedness of all things. Commentators have compared the series to works of Dickens and Dostoyevsky, but its creator David Simon imagined *The Wire* as a tragedy on ancient models that lifted "wholesale from Aeschylus, Sophocles, Euripides to create doomed and fated protagonists who confront a rigged game and their own mortality." "But instead of the old gods," Simon explained in a 2007 interview with Nick Hornby in *The Believer*, "*The Wire* is a Greek tragedy in which postmodern institutions are the Olympian forces."

Those institutions, which overlap with and mimic one another in surprising ways, include unions, schools, political machines, the police force, the prison system, and the criminal underworld. One of the questions *The Wire* forces viewers to ask is whether it is still possible for any leader to control these new-model "Olympian forces," or whether the postmodern behemoth has outstripped the capacities of any one person, or group of people, to alter its course. Thus *The Wire* presents us with a tragedy of dysfunction in which we watch leaders operating on scales large and small. Some enjoy fleeting successes, but most are doomed by hypocrisy, moral compromise, viciousness, and greed.

One of the most intriguing figures offered for our contemplation in *The Wire* is Stringer Bell, the right-hand man of the gangster Avon Barksdale, who runs the drug trade on the city's west side and whose invisibility to the police force has been ensured by Bell's prudence and the ruthless discipline he has inculcated in the soldiers, corner boys, and hoppers who work for him. There are, for example, no cell phones in this organization. Instead, using a complex system of pagers, pay phones, and codes, its various members manage for years to conceal their operations from the law. When Barksdale eventually goes to jail, despite such precautions, Bell recognizes the fragility of even the best-run criminal enterprise and begins the work of transformation.

There are some hiccups: meetings with his middle managers don't always go according to *Robert's Rules of Order*, despite the fact that Bell's lieutenant carries a copy around with him. And that same assistant has to be reprimanded on one occasion for dutifully recording the minutes of a criminal conspiracy. Nevertheless, Bell's system starts to work when he persuades his dealers to think profit, not territory. While Barksdale is serving his sentence, Bell forms an alliance—"the co-op"—with the city's other drug lords and starts investing his growing profits in real estate. Shaped by an introductory macroeconomics course he takes at a local community college as well as by his reading of Adam Smith's *The Wealth of Nations* and Tom Peters's *Liberation Management*, Bell's dream is to leave drugs behind altogether and move entirely into legitimate business.

It is Barksdale's release from jail that threatens everything Bell has built. The two men now inhabit different worlds. While Barksdale, preoccupied with restoring his reputation on the street, launches a war with an up-and-coming gangster to avenge his honor, Bell worries about maintaining profits. As he tells his old friend after the latter shows off a grenade he has just added to his arsenal, Barksdale thinks only of honor, corners, and the now, but he thinks of business, the world, and the future. All of Bell's efforts to transform the organization are thwarted by his inability to change the ethos of its newly returned leader and of all those members who readily follow Barksdale into war. In a pivotal episode, Bell's erstwhile rival and temporary ally, Proposition Joe, tells Bell that the co-op is ready to throw him out: "The feeling is it ain't right for you to sit at the head of the table," Joe explains, "when you can't call off your dog. Call it a crisis of leadership." That crisis soon ends in mutual betrayal and Bell's death. Searching the dead man's apartment, Jimmy McNulty, the detective who has been hunting him for years, gazes at the books on the shelves and realizes that he knew the man he had been chasing not at all.

The Wire's dramatization of organizational dysfunction and failed leadership reveals the spirit of the age. Crises of leadership are the order of the day at the beginning of the twenty-first century: our institutions seem to be in serial meltdown. Hardly a day passes without an exposé of incompetence or corruption in the private or public sector. But if we live in a world of crisis, we also live in a world that romanticizes crisis—that finds in it fodder for an addiction to the twenty-four-hour news cycle, multiple information streams, and constant stimulation.

Crises, we have long believed, call forth great leaders: "These are times in which a Genious would wish to live," Abigail Adams wrote to her son John Quincy in 1780: "It is not in the still calm of life, or the repose of a pacific station, that great characters are formed. Would Cicero have shone so distinguished an orator, if he had not been roused, kindled and enflamed by the Tyranny of Catiline, Millo, Verres and Mark Anthony." Yet it was Abigail's husband, John, who cautioned against the dangers of waiting for someone to rescue us, of depending on "a succession" of extraordinary men to preserve our liberties and save us from tyrants. A savior like George Washington, Adams insisted, appears on the scene perhaps only once in "two or three ages." There would be little improvement in social and political organization, John Adams insisted, until the people learn to "consider themselves as the fountain of power, and until they shall know how to manage it wisely and honestly." And in the great rescuer's absence, the false prophets, the smooth operators, the gangsters, and the demagogues, together with all those who resist the tyranny of the system in small yet principled ways, carry on.

THINGS THAT DON'T FIT

"It can be subversive, constructive, deconstructive . . . whatever," the lieutenant colonel suggested in the message inviting me to conduct a leader professional development seminar with the officers in his battalion. The subject? Disobedience. (His choice.) I liked him already. Most of the battalion's officers had served combat tours in Iraq or Afghanistan. Now they had acclimated themselves to their assignment to the Old Guard, the regiment that conducts funerals at Arlington National Cemetery and performs various ceremonial and security details in the Washington, D.C., area.

Leader professional development sessions—LPDs—are common throughout the army, where they often entail the presentation of "lessons learned" from recent combat experience or a group discussion of an assigned book, perhaps from the U.S. Army Chief of Staff's Professional Reading List. Paul, the battalion commander who had invited me to visit, has an expansive vision of leader development: the activities he designed were not meant to train specific areas of competence, he explained, but to build competence for a lifetime of service: "I think the most valuable thing I can do is expand an officer's ability to perceive, appreciate, and solve problems," he wrote. "But I can't begin to guess what problems they will have to solve. They might be tactical or strategic. They might be technical or social. [These officers] might be looking down the barrel of a gun, or they might be in an office and have some time to deliberate with a group of smart people. So I've tried to give them the very best across a spectrum."

Paul's program of events was wonderfully eclectic. There were case studies drawn from history and from the recent experience of some of the battalion's officers. There were expeditions: after camping overnight near the place where George Washington crossed the Delaware in 1776, Paul led his officers across the river in rafts at dawn before running the ten miles to Trenton along the Continental Army's line of march. There were theoretical discussions: for example, on the ideas of Carl von Clausewitz, the author of the landmark treatise *On War*.

There was also a category called "Things That Don't Fit into the Other Categories." That's where I fit in. Paul had read something I had written about the tension in our history between liberty and the very un-American virtue of obedience, and he was interested in delving into cultural assumptions: "Obedience (and lack of it) is something we deal in every day," he explained. "But we never pick it up and look at it."

So that day we picked it up and looked at it—from every possible angle. We explored issues of duty, autonomy, loyalty, resistance, and ethical responsibility. The texts I assigned as homework are not typically found on army professional reading lists: Thoreau's *Civil Disobedience*; a chapter from Herman Melville's *White-Jacket*, a novel about life in the antebellum navy; a few of Ambrose Bierce's satirical Civil War stories; and a selection from *Army Life in a Black Regiment*, Thomas Wentworth Higginson's account of his time in command of former slaves in Civil War South Carolina. We also watched *Paths of Glory*, Stanley Kubrick's film about a French army mutiny during World War I.

Not everyone was immediately comfortable: after all, these officers hadn't been spending much time with English professors. But soon their reflections on combat were texturing our exchanges about the readings in front of us, enriching stories familiar to me and enlarging their thinking about lived experience. The different settings and periods depicted helped to defamilarize ideas they had been steeped in, thereby illuminating issues afresh. Situations in which these officers, wrapped up in the urgency of the moment, found themselves every day, began to look a lot different when they involved a soldier in a Western Front trench, a sailor on a nineteenth-century man-o'-war, or a civilian sitting in the Concord jail. At the end of the day a few officers, having noted my comment about liking to read one of Bierce's stories with plebes (West Point's first-year students), approached me. Describing themselves as former plebes, they told me that this was precisely the kind of endeavor they had so valued while students but had found too little opportunity to engage in since.

Through his leader development program Paul had provided the time and

space for speculative discussion that is difficult to come by in a practitione
life. These sessions were free of the pressure—inherent in so many high-stres
environments—of coming up with a finite set of lessons, an answer, a blue-
print, a plan. Instead, these were ideas that would linger, evolve, or perhaps be
forgotten for a time only to resurface later when they formed a point of inter-
section with some new experience. Paul's theory of leader development was
influenced by past mentors but also by his concern for the long-term health of
his officers and for the institution to which they had committed themselves.
In a crisis—a war that has strained the army in so many ways—Paul's sense
of urgency led him to think strategically.

BEYOND THE MILITARY LEADER

I work in an organization geared to crisis, but its most successful leaders deal
with emergencies in the calmest possible way. Military culture, in which hierarchy is explicit, extremity often the norm, presents what might be thought of
as an intensified version of dynamics that operate in a range of institutions,
industries, and professions, all of which have their own pecking orders, crises, and organizational idiosyncrasies. I have talked with various audiences—
generals, health-care providers, students at an all-girls prep schools, sheriffs
who came to class packing heat—about the ways in which literature can help
to illuminate such phenomena and to foster the creative imagination, mental
discipline, and improvisational skills essential for strategic leadership.

The inescapable backdrop for my thinking about leadership—and for
this book—is the series of wars in which the United States has been engaged
since almost the beginning of the twenty-first century. That enterprise at once
crystallized and confused so many things a lot of people in uniform and out
thought they understood about developing leaders. For me, it reaffirmed in
any number of ways the great value literature offers to anyone serious about
the project of taking responsibility for other people and the organizations
of which they are a part, about helping them to realize their full potential,
about leading them anywhere (sometimes into hazardous places), and about
preparing them to endure the aftermath of any trial.

That is the spirit in which I hope readers will take up this book, which is
designed to accommodate students and novices embarking on their careers
as well as mature professionals. Questions at the end of each section can help
seminar leaders structure discussions, but the book also supports the solitary
or casual reader who may wish, for example, to read a selection at a time and
in no particular order. It offers a resource with which leaders in a time of
crisis might practice through reading literature the deep attention, sustained
contemplation, and introspection that the most pressing problems demand.

"One of the most universal cravings of our time," the historian and polit-

.l scientist James M. Burns began his seminal 1978 book *Leadership*, "is a .unger for compelling and creative leadership." Burns argued, "The crisis of leadership today is the mediocrity and irresponsibility of so many men and women in power. . . . The fundamental crisis underlying mediocrity," he continued, "is intellectual. If we know all too much about leaders, we know far too little about *leadership*." Burns called for a revival of a once-vital study of leadership that had languished in the modern world.

In 1978, Burns looked around to discover no philosophical study, no "school of leadership." Today, nearly forty years on, we have entered a period that might be called, like the golden age of ancient Chinese philosophy, the era of "One Hundred Schools of Thought" about leadership. Books on leadership abound: they range from theoretical examinations to breezy memoirs to self-help formulas for success. Most studies of leadership draw heavily on the social sciences. This book offers not an alternative but a complement to those investigations, and it shares with them a desire to help leaders better serve their institutions by better understanding themselves and their environments. In a world perpetually embroiled in emergency, literature offers something potentially enduring. What was relevant yesterday in that headline-screaming way is irrelevant today. "Literature," on the other hand, as the poet Ezra Pound once proposed, "is news that STAYS news."

ORGANIZATION OF THIS BOOK

This anthology is divided into two kinds of sections: chapters and albums. The chapters trace a narrative arc predicated on some fundamental assumptions. Newcomers to any organization, institution, or community must first understand the system if they hope to become effective participants and leaders. After **studying the system**, the natural impulse is to imitate what one sees. Unconsciously, at first, and then consciously, we engage in the project of identifying and **emulating heroes**. The next, more sophisticated step is to grow beyond those models—to risk change, innovation, deviation from the norm when circumstances demand a new course. **Risking revision** is another essential step on the road to mastery, for leaders come closest to **knowing the way** when they accept the idea that mastery is less a state of arrival than a condition of perpetual growth and development.

The next several chapters shift focus slightly to address some essential activities and challenges leaders must navigate, and which are perhaps made especially complex in today's technology-dominated global culture: **cultivating trust**, **negotiating world and self**, **taking responsibility**, and **learning from failure**. Of course, sometimes leading involves **resisting the system** altogether: dissonant voices can expose systemic flaws that even the most well-intentioned leaders cannot see. On occasion, a rebellious follower must learn how to become a leader. Resistance is often characterized by inflamed, even violent, passions. Emotions are also a fundamental part of the healthiest organizations and institutions, where they help to forge sympathetic communities and build a shared sense of mission. But **disciplining desire** is among leaders' most difficult problems: they must understand and manage not only their followers' legitimate as well as destructive desires but also the double edge of their own internal drives and ambitions.

The short albums that punctuate these chapters highlight a set of attributes that leaders (both admirable and reprehensible) have demonstrated over the centuries: the capacity for **deep attention**, a sense of timing and the knowledge of when to **delay** decisions, an ability to **persuade**—occasionally to **con**—others, the exercise of superior **judgment**, the ability to weave effective personal and organizational **stories**, and a recognition, achieved through introspection and reflection, of when to **let go**.

Any comprehensive discussion of leadership explores both good and bad examples: leaders who had triumphant, disastrous, or wildly uneven careers. The texts assembled here are not offered as formulas for success, even if there is much to admire in these pages; emulation, after all, is but an imperfect strategy. Many selections depict desperate moments, ethical quandaries, and imperfect solutions to vexing problems. Nor do the authors collected here tend to make definitive moral judgments on the leaders or actions they describe: even the fables and parables are open to various interpretations. Rather, the argument of this book is that the work of understanding, analyzing, interpreting, comparing, contrasting, synthesizing, and reflecting—the work that serious literature compels a reader to perform—can help awaken leaders and keep them ever sharp.

LEADERSHIP

ESSENTIAL WRITINGS BY OUR
GREATEST THINKERS

STUDYING THE SYSTEM

Our little systems have their day.

—ALFRED, LORD TENNYSON,
In Memoriam

To contribute meaningfully to any institution or organization, to say nothing of leading it effectively, one must work to understand its systems and structures, as well as the various smaller communities and associations operating within it. This is true equally of an investment bank, a charitable foundation, a university, and an automaker. Even organizations belonging to the same overarching enterprise—two schools, perhaps, or two manufacturers—may nevertheless have radically different internal processes, assumptions, and expectations.

Anthropologists propose that culture reveals itself in various ways: in habits and behaviors, practices and rituals, manners and customs, beliefs, values, symbols, and heroes. Following Edgar Schein, management theorists often speak of three core levels of organizational culture. In *Organizational Culture and Leadership* Schein offers the following taxonomy: "(1) visible artifacts; (2) espoused beliefs, values, rules, and behavioral norms; and (3) tacit, taken-for-granted, basic underlying assumptions." Until "you dig down to the level of the basic assumptions," Schein argues, "you cannot really decipher artifacts, values, and norms."

Prospective leaders must understand not only the individual facets of a given organization but also the ways in which people interact with, and are transformed by, the institutions in which they operate. To what extent have individuals within a given organization apparently adapted to larger norms and expectations? How much autonomy have employees actually retained?

Does a given corporation compel apparent uniformity by subtle or explicit means? Does it foster independence and idiosyncrasy while preserving commonality?

Rigid hierarchies were once the order of the day, but in recent years there has been a new focus on issues of autonomy and individual voice as many leaders seek to flatten organizational structures because they believe corporate success depends on flourishing individuals. For example, Tony Hsieh, CEO of the online retailer Zappos and author of the book *Delivering Happiness: A Path to Profits, Passion, and Purpose*, is recognized for cultivating a company culture promoting happiness and employee satisfaction. Among the company's ten "Family Core Values" are "4. Be Adventurous, Creative, and Open-Minded" and "5. Pursue Growth and Learning."

In order to ensure the survival of institutions and businesses in times of regulatory, economic, geopolitical, or other uncertainty, leaders sometimes attempt to change culture with mixed results. Soon after being named the CEO of Yahoo, for example, Marissa Mayer placed a ban on telecommuting. She was criticized in the media not simply for rescinding the company's work-from-home policy but also for allowing the news to be communicated through a leaked Human Resources memo. As the president of New York University, John Sexton has overseen a 3-billion-dollar campaign, turned the institution into a global brand with campuses in various countries, and doubled undergraduate applications. Nevertheless, as Rachael Aviv documented in "The Imperial Presidency" (*The New Yorker* [September 9, 2013]), Sexton received a vote of no-confidence in 2013 from four of the school's faculties, who complained about NYU's apparent corporatization and lack of shared governance.

To understand the nuances of the culture in which a leader finds herself, she must become, to borrow a term from anthropology, a "participant-observer": a kind of ethnographer who learns the intricacies of an organization by studying it as if it were a new culture. The selections that follow explore a variety of cultures. We begin in the distant time of Bessie Head's "The Deep River: A Story of Ancient Tribal Migration," a fictional exploration of the mythic origins of Botswana's Batalaote tribe, during a period in which society had but one face and one will: that of its chief. We move to the world of the Brazilian jungle in the 1930s, in the excerpt from "Men, Women, and Chiefs," a chapter from *Tristes Tropiques* (*Sad Tropics*), in which the social anthropologist Claude Lévi-Strauss examines what the nomadic Indian band, "if considered as an elementary social structure, has to teach us about the origins and function of power" within society at large.

The next two selections, by a historian and a poet respectively, emerge from Western antiquity. Thucydides's account of the speech of Pericles, the great Athenian statesman, suggests what it might mean for a culture to know itself thoroughly and to adhere to its underlying values and assumptions even in adversity. Virgil, the great poet of Rome's Augustan Age, shows us the industry of an exiled people establishing a new society under the leadership of their queen, Dido. Both Thucydides and Virgil are concerned with the founding and definition of cultural, social, and political institutions. In the next selection, the contemporary American poet Rosanna Warren meditates on a scene in Virgil's epic, in which the hero's father, Anchises, prophesies Rome's future greatness and the human cost that will attend it.

The selections from the political philosopher Friedrich Engels and the novelist Herman Melville reveal the ways in which modern industrial society brings human beings into a potentially new relationship with one another, one characterized less by kinship and social ties than by alienation and urban dislocation. First, Engels offers his view of the modes whereby authority works. Next, Melville presents us with an allegory in which human interdependence is symbolized by the rope fastening two sailors together while they are engaged in the dangerous business of cutting blubber away from a captured whale. The excerpt from Jane Jacobs's *The Death and Life of Great American Cities* offers a late twentieth-century critique of urban planning. Rejecting the "romantic . . . search for the salves of society's ills in slow-moving rustic surroundings, or among innocent, unspoiled provincials," as "a waste of time," Jacobs insists that the "answers to . . . the great questions that worry us today" can be found only in the "lively, diverse, intense" life of cities. In George Orwell's essay "Shooting an Elephant," we encounter elements of colonial society. Drawing on his experience as a minor functionary in the British administration of Burma, Orwell reflects on the ways in which the machinations of imperialism deform both the colonizer and the colonized. Finally, in "Remaining Awake Through a Great Revolution," Martin Luther King Jr. outlines a psychology of "geographical oneness" for the modern age.

RECOMMENDED READING AND VIEWING

Battleship Potemkin (1925), directed by Sergei Eisenstein
Fyodor Dostoyevsky, *Memoirs from the House of the Dead* (1861–62)
Edward Gibbon, *The History of the Decline and Fall of the Roman Empire* (1776–88)
Mary Kingsley, *Travels in West Africa* (1897)
Rory Stewart, *The Places in Between* (2004)

Bessie Head
(1937–1986)

BESSIE HEAD'S WRITING reveals a sensitivity to the political struggles of late twentieth-century South Africa and a sense of deep time—of the myths that are the wellspring of modern social structures. Born in a mental asylum to a white mother and a black father, Head was raised by adoptive parents of mixed race during the dominance of the Afrikaner Nationalist Party and the rise of apartheid. Head traced her own political awakening to an encounter with the writings of Mohandas Gandhi (whose speech on nonviolence can be found in "Resisting the System") as well as with her move to Cape Town, where in addition to serving as a court reporter, she founded *The Citizen*, a newspaper dedicated to fighting apartheid. The next phase of her life brought her to Botswana, where hospitalization for mental illness was followed by a highly productive period during which she published fiction and nonfiction, including the hybrid work *A Question of Power* (1974). Head was an influence on, among others, the American Nobel Laureate Toni Morrison, who cites Head, together with other writers of the Négritude Movement, as pioneers who "did not explain their black world. Or clarify it. Or justify it. White writers had always taken white centrality for granted," she explains in Carolyn C. Denard's *Toni Morrison: Conversations*: "They inhabited their world in a central position and everything nonwhite was 'other.' These African writers took their blackness as central and the whites were the 'other.'" Like Chinua Achebe, Wole Soyinka, and Ngugi wa Thiong'o, Bessie Head chronicles the cataclysms of Africa in the twentieth century. Sometimes, as in the case of "The Deep River," she sheds light on the present by means of a mythological lens. This short story dramatizes the moment of crisis when the members of a tribe heretofore accepting of total submission to the one will of their chief first "awoke and showed their individual faces." Questions emerge about the destructive role of rumor and the precariousness of reputation as well as about the proper relationship between private attachment and public responsibility.

The Deep River: A Story of Ancient Tribal Migration
from *The Collector of Treasures and Other Botswana Village Tales* (1977)

Long ago, when the land was only cattle tracks and footpaths, the people lived together like a deep river. In this deep river which was unruffled by conflict or a movement forward, the people lived without faces, except for their chief, whose face was the face of all the people; that is, if their chief's name was Monemapee, then they were all the people of Monemapee. The Talaote tribe have forgotten their origins and their original language during their journey southwards—they have merged and remerged again with many other tribes—and the name, Talaote, is all they have retained in memory of their history. Before a conflict ruffled their deep river, they were all the people of Monemapee, whose kingdom was somewhere in the central part of Africa.

They remembered that Monemapee ruled the tribe for many years as the hairs on his head were already saying white! by the time he died. On either side of the deep river there might be hostile tribes or great dangers, so all the people lived in one great town. The lands where they ploughed their crops were always near the town. That was done by all the tribes for their own protection, and their day-to-day lives granted them no individual faces either for they ploughed their crops, reared their children, and held their festivities according to the laws of the land.

Although the people were given their own ploughing lands, they had no authority to plough them without the chief's order. When the people left home to go to plough, the chief sent out the proclamation for the beginning of the ploughing season. When harvest time came, the chief perceived that the corn was ripe. He gathered the people together and said:

'Reap now, and come home.'

When the people brought home their crops, the chief called the thanksgiving for the harvest. Then the women of the whole town carried their corn in flat baskets, to the chief's place. Some of that corn was accepted on its arrival, but the rest was returned so that the women might soak it in their own yards. After a few days, the chief sent his special messenger to proclaim that the harvest thanksgiving corn was to be pounded. The special messenger went around the whole town and in each place where there was a little hill or mound, he climbed it and shouted:

'Listen, the corn is to be pounded!'

So the people took their sprouting corn and pounded it. After some days the special messenger came back and called out:

'The corn is to be fermented now!'

A few days passed and then he called out:

'The corn is to be cooked now!'

So throughout the whole town the beer was boiled and when it had been strained, the special messenger called out for the last time:

'The beer is to be brought now!'

On the day on which thanksgiving was to be held, the woman all followed one another in single file to the chief's place. Large vessels had been prepared at the chief's place, so that when the women came they poured the beer into them. Then there was a gathering of all the people to celebrate thanksgiving for the harvest time. All the people lived this way, like one face, under their chief. They accepted this regimental levelling down of their individual souls, but on the day of dispute or when strife and conflict and greed blew stormy winds over their deep river, the people awoke and showed their individual faces.

Now, during his lifetime Monemapee had had three wives. Of these marriages he had four sons: Sebembele by the senior wife; Ntema and Mosemme by the second junior wife; and Kgagodi by the third junior wife. There was a fifth son, Makobi, a small baby who was still suckling at his mother's breast by the time the old chief, Monemapee, died. This mother was the third junior wife, Rankwana. It was about the fifth son, Makobi, that the dispute arose. There was a secret there. Monemapee had married the third junior wife, Rankwana, late in his years. She was young and beautiful and Sebembele, the senior son, fell in love with her—but in secret. On the death of Monemapee, Sebembele, as senior son, was installed chief of the tribe and immediately made a blunder. He claimed Rankwana as his wife and exposed the secret that the fifth son, Makobi, was his own child and not that of his father.

This news was received with alarm by the people as the first ripples of trouble stirred over the even surface of the river of their lives. If both the young man and the old man were visiting the same hut, they reasoned, perhaps the old man had not died a normal death. They questioned the councillors who knew all secrets.

'Monemapee died just walking on his own feet,' they said reassuringly.

That matter settled, the next challenge came from the two junior brothers, Ntema and Mosemme. If Sebembele were claiming the child, Makobi, as his son, they said, it meant that the young child displaced them in seniority. That they could not allow. The subtle pressure exerted on Sebembele by his junior brothers and the councillors was that he should renounce Rankwana and the child and all would be well. A chief lacked nothing and there were many other women more suitable as wives. Then Sebembele made the second blunder. In a world where women were of no account, he said truthfully:

'The love between Rankwana and I is great.'

This was received with cold disapproval by the councillors.

'If we were you,' they said, 'we would look for a wife somewhere else. A ruler must not be carried away by his emotions. This matter is going to cause disputes among the people.'

They noted that on being given this advice, Sebembele became very quiet, and they left him to his own thoughts, thinking that sooner or later he would come to a decision that agreed with theirs.

In the meanwhile the people quietly split into two camps. The one camp said:

'If he loves her, let him keep her. We all know Rankwana. She is a lovely person, deserving to be the wife of a chief.'

The other camp said:

'He must be mad. A man who is influenced by a woman is no ruler. He is like one who listens to the advice of a child. This story is really bad.'

There was at first no direct challenge to the chieftaincy which Sebembele occupied. But the nature of the surprising dispute, that of his love for a woman and a child, caused it to drag on longer than time would allow. Many evils began to rear their heads like impatient hissing snakes, while Sebembele argued with his own heart or engaged in tender dialogues with his love, Rankwana.

'I don't know what I can do,' Sebembele said, torn between the demands of his position and the strain of a love affair which had been conducted in deep secrecy for many, many months. The very secrecy of the affair seemed to make it shout all the louder for public recognition. At one moment his heart would urge him to renounce the woman and child, but each time he saw Rankwana it abruptly said the opposite. He could come to no decision.

It seemed little enough that he wanted for himself—the companionship of a beautiful woman to whom life had given many other attractive gifts; she was gentle and kind and loving. As soon as Sebembele communicated to her the advice of the councillors, she bowed her head and cried a little.

'If that is what they say, my love,' she said in despair, 'I have no hope left for myself and the child. It were better if we were both dead.'

'Another husband could be chosen for you,' he suggested.

'You doubt my love for you, Sebembele,' she said. 'I would kill myself if I lose you. If you leave me, I would kill myself.'

Her words had meaning for him because he was trapped in the same kind of anguish. It was a terrible pain which seemed to paralyse his movements and thoughts. It filled his mind so completely that he could think of nothing else, day and night. It was like a sickness, this paralysis, and like all ailments it could not be concealed from sight; Sebembele carried it all around with him.

'Our hearts are saying many things about this man,' the councillors said among themselves. 'They were saying that he was unmanly; that he was unfit to be a ruler; that things were slipping from his hands. Those still sympathetic approached him and said:

'Why are you worrying yourself like this over a woman, Sebembele? There are no limits to the amount of wives a chief may have, but you cannot have that woman and that child.'

And he only replied with a distracted mind: 'I don't know what I can do.'

But things had been set in motion. All the people were astir over events; if a man couldn't make up his mind, other men could make it up for him.

Everything was arranged in secret and on an appointed day Rankwana and the child were forcibly removed back to her father's home. Ever since the controversy had started, her father had been harassed day and night by the councillors as an influence that could help to end it. He had been reduced to a state of agitated muttering to himself by the time she was brought before him. The plan was to set her up with a husband immediately and settle the matter. She was not yet formally married to Sebembele.

'You have put me in great difficulties, my child,' her father said, looking away from her distressed face. 'Women never know their own minds and once this has passed away and you have many children you will wonder what all the fuss was about.'

'Other women may not know their minds . . .' she began, but he stopped her with a raised hand, indicating the husband who had been chosen for her. In all the faces surrounding her there was no sympathy or help, and she quietly allowed herself to be led away to her new home.

When Sebembele arrived in his own yard after a morning of attending to the affairs of the land, he found his brothers, Ntema and Mosemme, there.

'Why have you come to visit me?' he asked, with foreboding. 'You never come to visit me. It would seem that we are bitter enemies rather than brothers.'

'You have shaken the whole town with your madness over a woman,' they replied mockingly. 'She is no longer here so you don't have to say any longer "I-don't-know-what-I-can-do". But we still request that you renounce the child, Makobi, in a gathering before all the people, in order that our position is clear. You must say: "That child Makobi is the younger brother of my brothers, Ntema and Mosemme, and not the son of Sebembele who rules".'

Sebembele looked at them for a long moment. It was not hatred he felt but peace at last. His brothers were forcing him to leave the tribe.

'Tell the people that they should all gather together,' he said. 'But what I say to them is my own affair.'

The next morning the people of the whole town saw an amazing sight which stirred their hearts. They saw their ruler walk slowly and unaccompanied through the town. They saw him pause at the yard of Rankwana's father. They saw Sebembele and Rankwana's father walk to the home of her new husband where she had been secreted. They saw Rankwana and Sebembele walk together through the town. Sebembele held the child Makobi in his arms. They saw that they had a ruler who talked with deeds rather than words. They saw that the time had come for them to offer up their individual faces to the face of this ruler. But the people were still in two camps. There was a whole section of the people who did not like this face; it was too out-of-the-way and shocking; it made them very uneasy. Theirs was not a tender, compassionate, and romantic world. And yet in a way it was. The arguments in the other camp which supported Sebembele had flown thick and fast all this time, and they said:

'Ntema and Mosemme are at the bottom of all this trouble. What are they after for they have set a difficult problem before us all? We don't trust them. But why not? They have not yet had time to take anything from us. Perhaps we ought to wait until they do something really bad; at present they are only filled with indignation at the behaviour of Sebembele. But no, we don't trust them. We don't like them. It is Sebembele we love, even though he has shown himself to be a man with a weakness . . . '

That morning, Sebembele completely won over his camp with his extravagant, romantic gesture, but he lost everything else and the rulership of the kingdom of Monemapee.

When all the people had gathered at the meeting place of the town, there were not many arguments left. One by one the councillors stood up and condemned the behaviour of Sebembele. So the two brothers, Ntema and Mosemme, won the day. Still working together as one voice, they stood up and asked if their senior brother had any words to say before he left with his people.

'Makobi is my child,' he said.

'Talaote,' they replied, meaning in the language then spoken by the tribe—'all right, you can go.'

And the name Talaote was all they were to retain of their identity as the people of the kingdom of Monemapee. That day, Sebembele and his people packed their belongings on the backs of their cattle and slowly began the journey southwards. They were to leave many ruins behind them and it is said that they lived, on the journey southwards, with many other tribes like the Baphaleng, Bakaa, and Batswapong until they finally settled in the land of the Bamangwato. To this day there is a separate Botalaote ward in the capital village of the Bamangwato, and the people refer to themselves still as the people of Talaote. The old men there keep on giving confused and contradictory accounts of their origins, but they say they lost their place of birth over a woman. They shake their heads and say that women have always caused a lot of trouble in the world. They say that the child of their chief was named, Talaote, to commemorate their expulsion from the kingdom of Monemapee.

FOOTNOTE

The story is an entirely romanticized and fictionalized version of the history of the Botalaote tribe. Some historical data was given to me by the old men of the tribe, but it was unreliable as their memories had tended to fail them. A re-construction was made therefore in my own imagination; I am also partly indebted to the London Missionary Society's *'Livingstone Tswana Readers', Padiso III*, school textbook, for those graphic paragraphs on the harvest thanksgiving ceremony which appear in the story.

B. HEAD.

Claude Lévi-Strauss
(1908–2009)

CLAUDE LÉVI-STRAUSS WAS a social anthropologist who founded the school of structuralism, which, building on the work of the linguists Ferdinand de Saussure and Roman Jakobson, influenced not only anthropology but also other social sciences and the humanities. After attending one of Jakobson's lectures in New York City, Lévi-Strauss came to a realization that "kinship system is a language," as he wrote in *Structural Anthropology* (1963). Positing that all objects have not only functional but communicative significance, he adapted the methods of structural linguistics to the study of culture, which he regarded, despite its diverse manifestations across time and place, as structured by universal myths. His four-volume *Mythologiques* (1964–71), a major exposition of this theory, analyzed hundreds of myths in order to illuminate elemental structures across cultures. Trained as a philosopher rather than an ethnographer, Lévi-Strauss did limited fieldwork. Although subsequently criticized by some for his methods and conclusions, Lévi-Strauss, as Edward Rothstein noted in a *New York Times* obiturary, is credited with transforming and enriching Western attitudes toward primitive societies with his accounts of the complexity and imaginative richness of what was once referred to as the "savage mind." In the 1930s, while working as a professor of sociology at the University of São Paulo, Brazil, Lévi-Strauss spent time with various Indian tribes. That work informed the autobiographical *Tristes Tropiques* (*Sad Tropics*), published in 1955. The book earned its author international acclaim. In the chapter "Men, Women, and Chiefs," excerpted here, Lévi-Strauss reflects on the political influence of chiefs in two nomadic tribes. In particular, he considers the perhaps counterintuitive fact that the chief is a unifier: "the cause of the group's wish to constitute itself as a group," rather "than the effect of the need, felt by an already-existing group, for a central authority." Lévi-Strauss explores the interplay of knowledge, generosity, and authority within this close-knit subsistence society. (The following selection is translated by John Russell.)

Men, Women, and Chiefs
from *Tristes Tropiques* (1955)

Why, therefore, do the Nambikwara divide themselves into bands at all? Economically speaking, they could hardly do otherwise than break up into small groups, given their extreme poverty in natural resources and the large area of ground which is needed, in the dry season, to keep even one Indian alive. The problem is not why, but how, they should so divide themselves. Initially there is a small group of acknowledged leaders who constitute the nucleus around which each band forms itself. On the ability of the leader to consolidate his position and keep his followers in their place will depend the importance of his band and the quasi-permanence of its character throughout the dry season. Political power does not seem to result from the community's needs; rather does the little community derive its characteristics—form, size, origins even— from the potential leader who existed before the group came into being.

·   ·   ·

The exceptional qualities manifested by both these chiefs derived from the manner of their designation—for political power is not hereditary among the Nambikwara. When a chief grows old, falls ill, or feels that he can no longer shoulder his heavy burdens, he himself chooses his successor: 'That one shall be chief . . . ' But this autocracy is more apparent than real. We shall see later on how slender is the chief's authority; and in this matter, as in others, the final decision would seem to be preceded by an appeal to public opinion, so that the heir finally appointed is the man most acceptable to the majority. But the choice of the new chief is not dictated entirely by the wishes or preferences of the group; the leader-designate must be willing to take on the job and, not uncommonly, he answers with a violent: 'No, I don't want to be chief!' A second choice must then be made. There does not, in fact, seem to be any great competition for power, and the chiefs whom I knew were more likely to complain of their heavy burdens and manifold responsibilities than to talk with pride of the chief's lofty position. What, in fact, are the chief's privileges, and what are his obligations?

Around the year 1560 Montaigne met, in Rouen, three Brazilian Indians who had been brought back by some early navigator. What, he asked one of them, were the privileges of a chief ('king' was what he said) in their country? The Indian, himself a chief, said: 'He's the first man to march off to war.' Montaigne tells this story in his *Essays* and marvels at the proud definition. It was a matter, for me, of intense astonishment and admiration that I received the same reply, nearly four centuries later. The civilized countries do not show anything like the same constancy in their political philosophy! Striking as it is, the formula is not so fraught with meaning as the choice of the word for 'chief' in Nambikwara language. *Uilikandé* seems to mean 'the one who unites' or 'the one who binds together', and it suggests that the Indian mentality is aware of the phenomenon which I have already underlined: that the chief is rather the cause of the group's wish to constitute itself as a group, than the effect of the need, felt by an already-existing group, for a central authority.

Personal prestige and the ability to inspire confidence are the foundations of power in Nambikwara society. Both are indispensable to the man who will be their guide in the adventurous, nomadic life of the dry season. For six or seven months the chief will be entirely responsible for the leadership of his band. He it is who organizes their departure, chooses their itinerary, and decrees where and for how long they will stop. He decides on the expeditions—hunting, fishing, collecting, scavenging—and he deals with relations with neighbour-bands. When the chief of a band is also the chief of a village (by this I mean a semi-permanent installation for use during the rainy season) his obligations go further. He determines the time and the place for the sedentary life. He supervises the gardens and says what crops are to be planted. More generally, he adapts his band's activities to the needs and possibilities of the season.

Where these manifold functions are concerned it should be said at once that the chief cannot seek support either in clearly defined powers or in a publicly recognized authority. Consent lies at the origins of power, and consent also confers upon power its legitimacy. Bad conduct (from the Indians' point of view, needless to say) or marks of ill will on the part of one or two malcontents may throw the chief's whole programme out of joint and threaten the well-being of his little community. Should this happen, the chief has no powers of coercion. He can disembarrass himself of undesirable elements only in so far as all the others are of the same mind as himself. And so he needs to be clever: and his cleverness is not so much that of an all-powerful sovereign as that of a politician struggling to maintain an uncertain majority. Nor does it suffice for him merely to keep his group together. They may live in virtual isolation during the nomadic season, but they never forget that neighbour-groups are not far away. The chief must not merely do well: he must try, and his group will expect him to try, to do better than the others.

How does the chief fulfil his obligations? The first and the main instrument of his power is his generosity. Generosity is among most primitive peoples, and above all in America, an essential attribute of power. It has a role to play even in those elementary cultures where the notion of property consists merely in a handful of rudely fashioned objects. Although the chief does not seem to be in a privileged position, from the material point of view, he must have under his control surplus quantities of food, tools, weapons, and ornaments which, however trifling in themselves, are none the less considerable in relation to the prevailing poverty. When an individual, a family, or the band as a whole, wishes or needs something, it is to the chief that an appeal must be made. Generosity is, therefore, the first attribute to be expected of a new chief. It is a note which will be struck almost continuously; and from the nature, discordant or otherwise, of the sound which results the chief can judge of his standing with the band. His 'subjects' make the most of all this: of that there can be no doubt. The chiefs were my best informers; and as I knew the difficulties of their position I liked to reward them liberally. Rarely, however, did any of my presents remain in their hands for more than a day or two. And when I moved on, after sharing for several weeks the life of any particular band, its members rejoiced in the acquisition of axes, knives, pearls, and so forth from my stores. The chief, by contrast, was generally as poor, in material terms, as he had been when I arrived. His share, which was very much larger than the average allowance, had all been extorted from him. This often reduced the chief to a kind of despair. A chief who can say 'No' in such situations is like a Prime Minister, in countries subject to parliamentary democracy, who can snap his fingers at a vote of confidence. A chief who can say: 'I'll give no more! I've been generous long enough! Let someone else take a turn!' must really be sure of his authority if he is not to provoke a moment of grave crisis.

Ingenuity is generosity transposed to the level of the intellect. A good chief gives proofs of his initiative and skill. He it is who prepares the poison for the arrows. He, likewise, who constructs the ball of wild rubber which is used on Nambikwara sports days. He must also be able to sing and dance, with a repertory large enough to amuse the band at any time and distract them from the monotony of their everyday life. These functions might easily make of him something of a shaman, and some chiefs do, in fact, combine the roles of warrior and witch-doctor. But mysticism in all its forms remains well in the background of Nambikwara life, and the gift of magic, when present, is merely one of the secondary attributes of command. It is more common for one person to assume the temporal and another the spiritual power. In this the Nambikwara differ from their neighbours, the Tupi-Kawahib, whose chiefs are also shamans much given to premonitory dreams, visions, trances, and the dissociation of personality.

But the skill and ingenuity of the Nambikwara chief are none the less astonishing for being directed towards a more positive outlet. He must have a minute knowledge of the territories frequented by his band and by its neighbours; the hunting-grounds must have no secrets from him, and he must know just when each clump of wild fruit-trees will be ripe for plucking. Thus instructed, he can work out a rough itinerary for each of his neighbour-bands, whether friendly or hostile; and, as he needs to be constantly on the move, reconnoitring or exploring, he may well seem to be not so much leading his band as circling rapidly round it.

Apart from one or two men who have no real authority, but are prepared to collaborate if paid to do so, the passivity of the band is in striking contrast to the dynamism of its leader. It is as if, having handed over to him certain advantages, they expect him to take entire charge of their interests and their security. This attitude was well displayed in the episode which I have already described of the journey on which, when we lost our way and had not enough food, the Indians lay down on the ground instead of going off to look for some, leaving it to the chief and his wives to remedy the situation as best they could.

. . .

I went to the ends of the earth in search of what Rousseau called 'the barely perceptible advances of the earliest times'. Beneath and beyond the veil of the all-too-learned laws of the Bororo and the Caduveo I had gone in search of a state which, to quote once again from Rousseau, 'no longer exists, perhaps may never have existed, and probably will never exist'. 'And yet,' he goes on, 'without an accurate idea of that state we cannot judge properly of our present situation.' Myself luckier than he, I thought that I had come upon that state in a society then nearing its end. It would have been pointless for me to wonder whether or not it was a vestigial version of what Rousseau had in mind; whether traditional or degenerate, it brought me into contact with one of the most indigent of all conceivable forms of social and political organization. I had no need to go into its past history to discover what had maintained it at its rudimentary level—or what, as was more likely, had brought it thus far down. I had merely to focus my attention on the experiment in sociology which was being carried out under my nose.

But that 'experiment' eluded me. I had been looking for a society reduced to its simplest expression. The society of the Nambikwara had been reduced to the point at which I found nothing but human beings.

Thucydides
(ca. 460–400 BCE)

GENERAL, STATESMAN, EXILE, survivor, Thucydides made his most lasting contribution in the form of his history, *The Peloponnesian War*. As the classicist M. I. Finley writes in an introduction to the Penguin Classics edition, "That war lives on not so much for anything that happened or because of any of the participants, but because of the man who wrote its history, Thucydides the Athenian. No other historian can match this achievement; no other war, or for that matter no other historical subject, is so much the product of its reporter." Following Herodotus (a selection from whose work can be found in "Learning from Failure"), Thucydides recognized, as Finley notes, that "it was possible to analyse the political and moral issues of the time by a close study of events, of the concrete day-to-day experiences of society, thereby avoiding the abstractions of the philosophers on the one hand and the myths of the poets on the other." Thucydides was both a chronicler of, and a combatant in, the war between Athens and Sparta (431–404 BCE), which transformed the political landscape of the ancient world. His history provides an invaluable guide to the period and to some of its central figures, especially the formidable Athenian leader Pericles (ca. 495–429 BCE). A year into the war, the Athenians, in despair over a second Spartan invasion and the ravages of the plague, sent emissaries to Sparta to sue for peace. In the speech reproduced here, Pericles insists that the survival of a city requires individual sacrifice for the collective good. A year before, he had warned the Athenians, "people do not have the same feelings when they are persuaded to go to war as when they are actually engaged in it, and change their resolve with changing events." In this speech, Pericles alludes to that earlier moment and attempts to remind his fellow citizens of the enduring keys to their success: the political value of Athenian democracy and the practical strength of the city's naval supremacy. He also emphasizes the need to grapple with certain inescapable strategic realities of maintaining of an empire. Less celebrated perhaps than the so-called Funeral Oration, which influenced Abraham Lincoln's Gettysburg Address, this speech reveals Pericles's gifts as a strategic thinker as well as the integrity for which Thucydides praises him: "when Pericles was in power, his popularity, his intellect, his conspicuous imperviousness to bribes gave him free rein to bridle the majority. He was not led by it, he led it, because he was not always trying to acquire power improperly, by saying just anything to please the people; he could contradict them and even make them angry, because his prestige gave him power. Indeed, whenever he saw that they were rashly about to do something flagrantly premature, he would give a speech and whip them into a panic; but when they were irrationally frightened, he would restore their confidence. In its rhetoric, Athens was becoming a democracy; in practice it was the domain of its foremost man." (The following selection is translated by Walter Blanco.)

Pericles Reminds the Athenians Who They Are
from *The Peloponnesian War*

I expected that these signs of your anger would be directed against me, and I know the reasons for them. That is why I have called for this assembly—to refresh your memories and to reproach *you* should it turn out that you are misguided in being angry at me or in giving way to your misfortunes. I believe that a city that is on the whole well governed benefits individual citizens more than one in which individual citizens do well while the city collectively staggers and falls. A man who does very well for himself will ultimately be ruined by the destruction of his city; but he has a much better chance of surviving his own bad luck in a successful city. Since, then, a city is able to carry individual misfortunes—something a single individual cannot do for the city—wouldn't it be better for all of us to defend her instead of what you are doing now? For, driven to distraction by the calamities in your homes, you are casting aside the safety of the whole and are holding me, who counseled war, and yourselves, who agreed with me, responsible. When you get angry at me, it is at the sort of man who, as well as any other, knows what must be done and how to put it into words, a man who is both patriotic and uninterested in money. The man who has ideas but can't teach them might as well not have any at all. The one who has both abilities but is disloyal won't say what is good for the city. If he is also patriotic but can be bought off, he will sell it all for the right price. So if you considered me to have these abilities to even a slightly greater degree than others when you were persuaded to go to war, it would be unfair for me now to bear the blame for having done you wrong.

It is, surely, folly for those who have a choice and who are in other respects well off to go to war. If, however, they either had to immediately give in and submit to their neighbors or prevail by taking risks, then the one who fled danger is more blameworthy than the one who stood his ground. I remain the same; I have not changed my position. It is you who have changed. What has happened is that you listened to me when you were unharmed and have changed your minds now that you are in a bad way. Your irresolution makes the policy I advocated seem wrong, because grief has taken hold of your objectivity and you are yet to see the realization of its benefits, and because the great change that has befallen you in a short time has weakened your determination to persevere in your decision. The will is enslaved by sudden and unexpected events, events completely beyond our calculation. More than anything else, the plague has done this to you. Nevertheless, you live in a great city and have been brought up with habits corresponding to its greatness. You must willingly hold out in the greatest misfortunes and not tarnish the city's reputation. (After all, people think it is equally right to condemn whoever falls short of his reputation out of cowardice and to hate whoever reaches for a reputation he doesn't deserve out of arrogance.) You must put aside your private sorrow and strive to save the state.

Now as to the war effort, that it would be onerous and that we would still not win—you must be satisfied from the speeches I frequently gave on other occasions that your fears about that were unfounded. But I want to make this clear too. It has to do with the greatness of your empire. I think you never had any idea of it before, and I never revealed it in my previous speeches. Nor would I now, since it involves a claim that is a bit boastful, if I didn't see you so unreasonably frightened out of your wits. You see, you think that you just rule over your allies. But I tell you that of the two realms open to man's use, the land and the sea, you are the lords and masters of all of the latter—of as much as you now control and of as much more as you may want, because given your current naval resources, there is no one, not the Great King or any other people on earth, who can stop you from sailing where you please. Thus this sea power is a far greater thing than your lands and your farms, whose loss you think is so terrible. We ought not to trouble ourselves about them or take them any more seriously than gardens or the ornaments of wealth in comparison with this power. And freedom—we must know that if we cling to our freedom and win through to safety, we will easily recover these trifles, but that if you submit to others, even what you already have will tend to wither away. We must not be inferior to our fathers in both realms, land and sea—our fathers, who did not inherit them from others but who took them, won through, and handed them down to you. It is more disgraceful to be stripped of what you have than to be unlucky about getting what you want, so go and grapple with your enemies not just with spirit, but with a spirit of contempt. A lucky stupidity breeds boastfulness in cowards; contempt belongs to those who can trust in their strategy to triumph over their enemies, as you can. When the chances are even on both sides, intelligence makes for a surer daring when combined with a sense of superiority. Intelligence trusts less to hope, which is powerful only in desperate straits, than to a strategy based on facts, and this is the source of a firm foreknowledge.

It is right that you uphold the honor the city gets from its empire—honor in which we all take pride—and that you either not run away from the effort involved or stop pursuing the honor. You must also stop thinking that you are fighting about just one thing: freedom versus slavery. It is also about the loss of the empire and about the danger you are in from being hated because of that empire. You can no longer detach yourselves from it, just in case anyone, from fear of the present crisis, makes a manly virtue of staying home and minding his own business. You hold your empire like a tyranny by now. Taking it is thought to have been criminal; letting it go would be extremely dangerous. The do-nothings I referred to would quickly destroy a city, either by influencing others or by somehow going off and living on their own. An easygoing man is only protected if he marches beside a man of action. The safety of slavery is convenient in a subject city, but not in an imperial one.

Don't be led astray by these citizens, and don't be angry with me, with whom you joined in voting for war, just because our enemies attacked and did what they naturally would when you refused to submit to them. Over and above what we foresaw has come this plague, the only thing that has occurred that has been, in fact, beyond our expectation. I know that it is largely because of this that I am hated, unjustly I believe—unless, of course, you have an equally unexpected success and then give me credit for it. No, we must bear acts of god with fortitude and acts of war with courage. This attitude used to be part of the ethos of this city; don't let it come to an end in you. Bear in mind that we have the highest reputation in the whole world for not giving in to misfortune, for having lost the greatest number of lives and endured the greatest hardships in war, and for having acquired the greatest power so far. And even if we eventually have to relinquish some of that power (for after all, there is a natural tendency for all things to decay), we will have left behind the memory that we were the Greeks who ruled over the greatest number of Greeks, that we fought the greatest wars against enemies coming singly and together, and that we inhabited what was in every way the greatest and the richest city on earth. True enough, the do-nothing will disapprove of this; but the man of action will want to emulate it, and those who do not equal our achievements will envy us. To be hated and envied for a time is the lot of everyone who dares to rule over others, but whoever incurs envy in a great cause has made the right choice. Hatred can't survive for long, and present splendor is passed on as eternally remembered fame. It is your duty to throw yourselves into achieving the glory to come and avoiding disgrace in the here and now. Do not negotiate with the Spartans. Do not show that you are disheartened by your present suffering. For city and citizen alike, those whose minds are least saddened by misfortune, and who take action against it, are the strongest.

Virgil
(70–19 BCE)

BORN IN MANTUA, Publius Vergilius Maro grew to adulthood during the political upheavals of first-century BCE Rome: the end of the Republic, the career of Julius Caesar and the civil wars that followed his assassination in 44 BCE, and the ascendancy of the ultimate victor in those wars: Caesar's adopted nephew Octavian, later called Augustus Caesar. Augustus initiated what the eighteenth-century historian Edward Gibbon named the *Pax Romana*, a period of relative peace that followed so many years of civil unrest and fostered a great flowering of literary culture perhaps best embodied by Horace, the master of the lyric ode, and Virgil, whose career culminated in the *Aeneid*, an epic poem that revealed him to be a poet's poet—a master of meter. When Virgil died at fifty-one, the manuscript was still incomplete, but the emperor himself reversed the poet's instructions that it be destroyed. The *Aeneid* is at once an expression of the power of Augustan Rome and an ambivalent accounting of the private and communal costs of founding nations and securing empires. Tracing the mythical origins of Rome back to Aeneas and a band of refugees who escaped from the burning city of Troy, Virgil, as the literary critic David Quint explains in *Epic and Empire*, transforms a tale of losers into an epic of winners. The following passage, excerpted from the poem's first book, takes up the story after the Trojans have landed on the coast of Africa. On a reconnaissance patrol with his trusted friend Achates, Aeneas encounters his mother, the goddess Venus, disguised as a young huntress. Venus informs her son that he has landed in the Punic kingdom, the leader of which is, like him, an exile: Queen Dido escaped from the menaces of her wicked brother and sailed her fleet of refugees to Carthage. *"Dux femina facti,"* Venus tells Aeneas in one of the poem's best-remembered lines: "The leader of the exploit was a woman." In lines omitted here, Aeneas regales Venus with an account of his own hardships. Then, having inadvertently revealed her divinity on turning to go, the goddess surrounds Aeneas and Achates with a protective cloud so that they can safely approach the city walls. The narrative resumes with a description of the bustling city. Later, Aeneas will fall in love with Dido and she with him, but he will be forced to abandon her in order to fulfill the destiny of founding his own city in Italy, in the process displacing the native inhabitants of that land. Thus abandoned, Dido ultimately commits suicide and delivers a harrowing curse on Aeneas. That curse the so-called Punic curse—had a very real significance to Augustan Romans, for whom the memory of the Punic Wars, culminating in the Carthaginian General Hannibal's devastating victory at Cannae, was still fresh. (The following selections from book 1 of the *Aeneid* are translated by Robert Fagles.)

Dux Femina Facti: Dido Builds Carthage
from *Aeneid*

What you see is a Punic kingdom, people of Tyre
and Agenor's town, but the border's held by Libyans
hard to break in war. Phoenician Dido is in command,
she sailed from Tyre, in flight from her own brother.
Oh it's a long tale of crime, long, twisting, dark,
but I'll try to trace the high points in their order . . .

  "Dido was married to Sychaeus, the richest man in Tyre,
and she, poor girl, was consumed with love for him.
Her father gave her away, wed for the first time,
a virgin still, and these her first solemn rites.   10
But her brother held power in Tyre—Pygmalion,
a monster, the vilest man alive.
A murderous feud broke out between both men.
Pygmalion, catching Sychaeus off guard at the altar,
slaughtered him in blood. That unholy man, so blind
in his lust for gold he ran him through with a sword,
then hid the crime for months, deaf to his sister's love,

his heartbreak. Still he mocked her with wicked lies,
with empty hopes. But she had a dream one night.
The true ghost of her husband, not yet buried,   20
came and lifting his face—ashen, awesome in death—
showed her the cruel altar, the wounds that pierced his chest
and exposed the secret horror that lurked within the house.
He urged her on: 'Take flight from our homeland, quick!'
And then he revealed an unknown ancient treasure,
an untold weight of silver and gold, a comrade
to speed her on her way.
                      "Driven by all this,
Dido plans her escape, collects her followers
fired by savage hate of the tyrant or bitter fear.
They seize some galleys set to sail, load them with gold—   30
the wealth Pygmalion craved—and they bear it overseas
and a woman leads them all. Reaching this haven here,
where now you will see the steep ramparts rising,
the new city of Carthage—the Tyrians purchased land as
large as a bull's-hide could enclose but cut in strips for size
and called it Byrsa, the Hide, for the spread they'd bought.

            .   .   .

                      Meanwhile the two men
are hurrying on their way as the path leads,
now climbing a steep hill arching over the city,
looking down on the facing walls and high towers.   40
Aeneas marvels at its mass—once a cluster of huts—
he marvels at gates and bustling hum and cobbled streets.
The Tyrians press on with the work, some aligning the walls,
struggling to raise the citadel, trundling stones up slopes;
some picking the building sites and plowing out their boundaries,
others drafting laws, electing judges, a senate held in awe.
Here they're dredging a harbor, there they lay foundations
deep for a theater, quarrying out of rock great columns
to form a fitting scene for stages still to come.
As hard at their tasks as bees in early summer,   50
they work the blooming meadows under the sun,
they escort a new brood out, young adults now,
or press the oozing honey into the combs, the nectar
brimming the bulging cells, or gather up the plunder
workers haul back in, or close ranks like an army,

driving the drones, that lazy crew, from home.
The hive seethes with life, exhaling the scent
of honey sweet with thyme.
                                    "How lucky they are,"
Aeneas cries, gazing up at the city's heights,
"their walls are rising now!" And on he goes,   60
cloaked in cloud—remarkable—right in their midst
he blends in with the crowds, and no one sees him.

    Now deep in the heart of Carthage stood a grove,
lavish with shade, where the Tyrians, making landfall,
still shaken by wind and breakers, first unearthed that sign:
Queen Juno had led their way to the fiery stallion's head
that signaled power in war and ease in life for ages.
Here Dido of Tyre was building Juno a mighty temple,
rich with gifts and the goddess' aura of power.
Bronze the threshold crowning a flight of stairs,   70
the doorposts sheathed in bronze, and the bronze doors
groaned deep on their hinges.
                                    Here in this grove
a strange sight met his eyes and calmed his fears
for the first time. Here, for the first time,
Aeneas dared to hope he had found some haven,
for all his hard straits, to trust in better days.
For awaiting the queen, beneath the great temple now,
exploring its features one by one, amazed at it all,
the city's splendor, the work of rival workers' hands
and the vast scale of their labors—all at once he sees,   80
spread out from first to last, the battles fought at Troy,
the fame of the Trojan War now known throughout the world,
Atreus' sons and Priam—Achilles, savage to both at once.
Aeneas came to a halt and wept, and "Oh, Achates,"
he cried, "is there anywhere, any place on earth
not filled with our ordeals? There's Priam, look!
Even here, merit will have its true reward . . .
even here, the world is a world of tears
and the burdens of mortality touch the heart.
Dismiss your fears. Trust me, this fame of ours   90
will offer us some haven."
                                    So Aeneas says,
feeding his spirit on empty, lifeless pictures,
groaning low, the tears rivering down his face

as he sees once more the fighters circling Troy.
Here Greeks in flight, routed by Troy's young ranks,
there Trojans routed by plumed Achilles in his chariot.
Just in range are the snow-white canvas tents of Rhesus—
he knows them at once, and sobs—Rhesus' men betrayed
in their first slumber, droves of them slaughtered
by Diomedes splattered with their blood, lashing   100
back to the Greek camp their high-strung teams
before they could ever savor the grass of Troy
or drink at Xanthus' banks.
                             Next Aeneas sees
Troilus in flight, his weapons flung aside,
unlucky boy, no match for Achilles' onslaught—
horses haul him on, tangled behind an empty war-car,
flat on his back, clinging still to the reins, his neck
and hair dragging along the ground, the butt of his javelin
scrawling zigzags in the dust.
                        And here the Trojan women
are moving toward the temple of Pallas, their deadly foe,   110
their hair unbound as they bear the robe, their offering,
suppliants grieving, palms beating their breasts
but Pallas turns away, staring at the ground.
                         And Hector—
three times Achilles has hauled him round the walls of Troy
and now he's selling his lifeless body off for gold.
Aeneas gives a groan, heaving up from his depths,
he sees the plundered armor, the car, the corpse
of his great friend, and Priam reaching out
with helpless hands . . .
                   He even sees himself
swept up in the melee, clashing with Greek captains,   120
sees the troops of the Dawn and swarthy Memnon's arms.
And Penthesilea leading her Amazons bearing half-moon shields—
she blazes with battle fury out in front of her army,
cinching a golden breastband under her bared breast,
a girl, a warrior queen who dares to battle men.
                       And now
as Trojan Aeneas, gazing in awe at all the scenes of Troy,
stood there, spellbound, eyes fixed on the war alone,
the queen aglow with beauty approached the temple,
Dido, with massed escorts marching in her wake.
Like Diana urging her dancing troupes along   130

the Eurotas' banks or up Mount Cynthus' ridge
as a thousand mountain-nymphs crowd in behind her,
left and right—with quiver slung from her shoulder,
taller than any other goddess as she goes striding on
and silent Latona thrills with joy too deep for words.
Like Dido now, striding triumphant among her people,
spurring on the work of their kingdom still to come.
And then by Juno's doors beneath the vaulted dome,
flanked by an honor guard beside her lofty seat,
the queen assumed her throne. Here as she handed down   140
decrees and laws to her people, sharing labors fairly,
some by lot, some with her sense of justice, Aeneas
suddenly sees his men approaching through the crowds,
Antheus, Sergestus, gallant Cloanthus, other Trojans
the black gales had battered over the seas
and swept to far-flung coasts.
                             Aeneas, Achates,
both were amazed, both struck with joy and fear.
They yearn to grasp their companions' hands in haste
but both men are unnerved by the mystery of it all.
So, cloaked in folds of mist, they hide their feelings,   150
waiting, hoping to see what luck their friends have found.
Where have they left their ships, what coast? Why have they come?
These picked men, still marching in from the whole armada,
pressing toward the temple amid the rising din
to plead for some good will.
                             Once they had entered,
allowed to appeal before the queen   the eldest,
Prince Ilioneus, calm, composed, spoke out:
"Your majesty, empowered by Jove to found
your new city here and curb rebellious tribes
with your sense of justice—we poor Trojans,   160
castaways, tossed by storms over all the seas,
we beg you: keep the cursed fire off our ships!
Pity us, god-fearing men! Look on us kindly,
see the state we are in. We have not come
to put your Libyan gods and homes to the sword,
loot them and haul our plunder toward the beach.
No, such pride, such violence has no place
in the hearts of beaten men.
                             "There is a country—
the Greeks called it Hesperia, Land of the West,

an ancient land, mighty in war and rich in soil.   170
Oenotrians settled it; now we hear their descendants
call their kingdom Italy, after their leader, Italus.
Italy-bound we were when, surging with sudden breakers
stormy Orion drove us against blind shoals and from the South
came vicious gales to scatter us, whelmed by the sea,
across the murderous surf and rocky barrier reefs.
We few escaped and floated toward your coast.
What kind of men are these? What land is this,
that you can tolerate such barbaric ways?
We are denied the sailor's right to shore—   180
attacked, forbidden even a footing on your beach.
If you have no use for humankind and mortal armor,
at least respect the gods. They know right from wrong.
They don't forget.
                    "We once had a king, Aeneas . . .
none more just, none more devoted to duty, none
more brave in arms. If Fate has saved that man,
if he still draws strength from the air we breathe,
if he's not laid low, not yet with the heartless shades,
fear not, nor will you once regret the first step
you take to compete with him in kindness.   190
We have cities too, in the land of Sicily,
arms and a king, Acestes, born of Trojan blood.
Permit us to haul our storm-racked ships ashore,
trim new oars, hew timbers out of your woods, so that,
if we are fated to sail for Italy—king and crews restored—
to Italy, to Latium we will sail with buoyant hearts.
But if we have lost our haven there, if Libyan waters
hold you now, my captain, best of the men of Troy,
and all our hopes for Iulus have been dashed,
at least we can cross back over Sicilian seas,   200
the straits we came from, homes ready and waiting,
and seek out great Acestes for our king."

    So Ilioneus closed. And with one accord
the Trojans murmured Yes.
                            Her eyes lowered,
Dido replies with a few choice words of welcome:
"Cast fear to the winds, Trojans, free your minds.
Our kingdom is new. Our hard straits have forced me
to set defenses, station guards along our far frontiers.

Who has not heard of Aeneas' people, his city, Troy,
her men, her heroes, the flames of that horrendous war?   210
We are not so dull of mind, we Carthaginians here.
When he yokes his team, the Sun shines down on us as well.
Whatever you choose, great Hesperia—Saturn's fields—
or the shores of Eryx with Acestes as your king,
I will provide safe passage, escorts and support
to speed you on your way. Or would you rather
settle here in my realm on equal terms with me?
This city I build—it's yours. Haul ships to shore.
Trojans, Tyrians: they will be all the same to me.
If only the storm that drove you drove your king   220
and Aeneas were here now! Indeed, I'll send out
trusty men to scour the coast of Libya far and wide.
Perhaps he's shipwrecked, lost in woods or towns."

Rosanna Warren
(b. 1953)

IN "POETRY READING" Rosanna Warren distills Virgil's epic world into
the intimate confines of the lyric poem. She takes as her point of departure
an episode recorded in Aelius Donatus's *Life of Virgil*, in which the poet
recites several books from the *Aeneid* for the imperial family. Warren's
poem begins *in medias res*, with Virgil at that moment in the sixth book
where Aeneas, having made his catabasis, or descent into the underworld,
encounters the ghost of his father Anchises, who delivers a prophecy of
Rome's future greatness: its legions, its monuments, its laws, its power.
Also included, however, is a foretelling of the death of Augustus's nephew,
the young and popular Marcellus, once the heir apparent, who had succumbed to a fever at the age of nineteen. In this private moment with the
imperial family, Warren discloses the double edge of imperial greatness.
The closing allusion to "the gate of false dreams," through which Aeneas
ascends on departing the underworld, calls our attention to the vicissitudes of power and to the tragedy of the powerful when they come face to
face with the limits of their control over the course of human events. The
Latin epigraph *"manibus date lilia plenis,"* spoken by Anchises in his grief
over Marcellus's fate, may be translated: "Give me lilies with full hands."
History is a frequent subject for Warren, the Hanna Holborn Gray Distinguished Service Professor at the University of Chicago, who received
a B.A. in painting from Yale University and an M.A. from the Writing

Seminars at Johns Hopkins University. She is a consummate poet, translator, and literary critic whose work reflects deep learning, rich imagination, and a scrupulous ear for the nuances of cultures ancient and modern. Her books include *Each Leaf Shines Separate*, *Stained Glass*, which was named a Lamont Poetry Selection by the Academy of American Poets, *Departure*, and *Ghost in a Red Hat*. Her numerous awards include a Guggenheim Fellowship, a Pushcart Prize, the Witter Bynner Poetry Prize, and the Sara Teasdale Award in Poetry.

Poetry Reading

from *Departure* (2003)

manibus date lilia plenis (Aeneid VI)

It is a promise they hold in their hands.
Feathers waver in the ghostly crests.
Rome is an iron glint in the eyes,
a twitch at sword hilt. Down the long avenue
through silted shadow and pale leaking light
stalks the future. Power,
whispers the father, power bounded
only by the edge of earth, the rim of heaven.
The arts of peace, the rule of law:
the Capitol, aqueducts, legions, circuses.
Disorder chained in the temple. Abundant calm.
In such love you have given yourself.

But who is that young one, pallid
in armor with darkened brow
and night coming on at his heels,
scent of crushed lilies, a bruise—

Here the reading breaks off.
The emperor's sister falls into hysterical tears,
patrons and literati disband.
Servants clear away wine-cups, platters of cake.

And Aeneas climbs back into daylight
through the gate of false dreams.

Friedrich Engels
(1820–1895)

THE LESS CELEBRATED half of that pivotal nineteenth-century partnership of political thinkers, Marx and Engels, Friedrich Engels made his own seminal contributions to the theories of communism and socialism. Born to a Prussian textile manufacturer in the Rhineland city of Barmen, Engels at first followed the path his father set for him by learning the textile business in the port city of Bremen. It was here, and subsequently in Berlin, that Engels, circulating among a group of leftist intellectuals, steeped himself in radical writing, banned poets, and the philosophy of G. W. F. Hegel. He also worked as a journalist. Ultimately, however, Engels moved to Manchester, England, to manage a factory at the behest of his father, and it was this experience that helped him to formulate his political ideology, first expressed in *The Condition of the Working Class in England* (1845). Engels met Marx in Paris a short time later, and together they wrote *The Communist Manifesto*, an incendiary call to arms with transnational implications published in 1848, the year of failed revolutions across Europe—a defeat of democratic impulses that also affected Herman Melville, at work in America on his novel *Moby-Dick*. Marx and Engels subsequently settled in England, where Engels helped Marx to write his monumental *Das Kapital*. After Marx's death in 1883, Engels continued to edit his friend's papers, thereby helping to shape his enduring legacy. "On Authority," written in 1872, and published two years later, is representative of late Engels and, as Robert C. Tucker notes, forms a part of his quarrel with the Anarchists. Engels conducts a series of thought experiments in this piece in order to prove his contention that no social organization—even (perhaps especially) a revolutionary one—can entirely do away with authority.

On Authority
from *Almanacco Repubblicano* (1874)

A number of Socialists have latterly launched a regular crusade against what they call the *principle of authority*. It suffices to tell them that this or that act is *authoritarian* for it to be condemned. This summary mode of procedure is being abused to such an extent that it has become necessary to look into the matter somewhat more closely. Authority, in the sense in which the word is used here, means: the imposition of the will of another upon ours; on the other hand, authority presupposes subordination. Now, since these two words sound bad and the relationship which they represent is disagreeable to the subordinated party, the question is to ascertain whether there is any way of dispensing with it, whether—given the conditions of present-day society—we could not create another social system, in which this authority would be given no scope any longer and would consequently have to disappear. On examining the economic, industrial and agricultural conditions which form the basis of present-day bourgeois society, we find that they tend more and more to replace isolated action by combined action of individuals. Modern industry with its big factories and mills, where hundreds of workers supervise complicated machines driven by steam, has superseded the small workshops of the separate producers; the carriages and wagons of the highways have been substituted by railway trains, just as the small schooners and sailing feluccas have been by steam-boats. Even agriculture falls increasingly under the dominion of the machine and of steam, which slowly but relentlessly put in the place of the small proprietors big capitalists, who with the aid of hired workers cultivate vast stretches of land. Everywhere combined action, the complication of processes dependent upon each other, displaces independent action by individuals. But whoever mentions combined action speaks of organisation; now, is it possible to have organisation without authority?

Supposing a social revolution dethroned the capitalists, who now exercise their authority over the production and circulation of wealth. Supposing, to adopt entirely the point of view of the anti-authoritarians, that the land and the instruments of labour had become the collective property of the workers who use them. Will authority have disappeared or will it only have changed its form? Let us see.

Let us take by way of example a cotton spinning mill. The cotton must pass through at least six successive operations before it is reduced to the state of thread, and these operations take place for the most part in different rooms. Furthermore, keeping the machines going requires an engineer to look after the steam engine, mechanics to make the current repairs, and many other labourers whose business it is to transfer the products from one room to another, and so forth. All these workers, men, women and children, are obliged to begin and finish their work at the hours fixed by the authority of the steam, which cares nothing for individual autonomy. The workers must, therefore, first come to an understanding on the hours of work; and these hours, once they are fixed, must be observed by all, without any exception. Thereafter particular questions arise in each room and at every moment concerning the mode of production, distribution of materials, etc., which must be settled at once on pain of seeing all production immediately stopped; whether they are settled by decision of a delegate placed at the head of each branch of labour or, if possible, by a majority vote, the will of the single individual will always have to subordinate itself, which means that questions are settled in an authoritarian way. The automatic machinery of a big factory is much more despotic than the small capitalists who employ workers ever have been. At least with regard to the hours of work one may write upon the portals of these factories: *Lasciate ogni autonomia, voi che entrate!*[1] If man, by dint of his knowledge and inventive genius, has subdued the forces of nature, the latter avenge themselves upon him by subjecting him, in so far as he employs them, to a veritable despotism independent of all social organization. Wanting to abolish authority in large-scale industry is tantamount to wanting to abolish industry itself, to destroy the power loom in order to return to the spinning wheel.

Let us take another example—the railway. Here too the co-operation of an infinite number of individuals is absolutely necessary, and this co-operation must be practised during precisely fixed hours so that no accidents may happen. Here, too, the first condition of the job is a dominant will that settles all subordinate questions, whether this will is represented by a single delegate or a committee charged with the execution of the resolutions of the majority of persons interested. In either case there is very pronounced authority. Moreover, what would happen to the first train dispatched if the authority of the railway employees over the Hon. passengers were abolished?

But the necessity of authority, and of imperious authority at that, will nowhere be found more evident than on board a ship on the high seas. There, in time of danger, the lives of all depend on the instantaneous and absolute obedience of all to the will of one.

When I submitted arguments like these to the most rabid anti-authoritarians the only answer they were able to give me was the following: Yes, that's true, but here it is not a case of authority which we confer on our delegates, *but of a commission entrusted*! These gentlemen think that when they have changed the names of things they have changed the things themselves. This is how these profound thinkers mock at the whole world.

We have thus seen that, on the one hand, a certain authority, no matter how delegated, and, on the other hand, a certain subordination, are things which, independently of all social organisation, are imposed upon us together with the material conditions under which we produce and make products circulate.

We have seen, besides, that the material conditions of production and circulation inevitably develop with large-scale industry and large-scale agriculture, and increasingly tend to enlarge the scope of this authority. Hence it is absurd to speak of the principle of authority as being absolutely evil, and of the principle of autonomy as being absolutely good. Authority and autonomy are relative things whose spheres vary with the various phases of the development of society. If the autonomists confined themselves to saying that the

1 "Leave, ye that enter in, all autonomy behind!"

social organisation of the future would restrict authority solely to the limits within which the conditions of production render it inevitable, we could understand each other; but they are blind to all facts that make the thing necessary and they passionately fight the word.

Why do the anti-authoritarians not confine themselves to crying out against political authority, the state? All Socialists are agreed that the political state, and with it political authority, will disappear as a result of the coming social revolution, that is, that public functions will lose their political character and be transformed into the simple administrative functions of watching over the true interests of society. But the anti-authoritarians demand that the authoritarian political state be abolished at one stroke, even before the social conditions that gave birth to it have been destroyed. They demand that the first act of the social revolution shall be the abolition of authority. Have these gentlemen ever seen a revolution? A revolution is certainly the most authoritarian thing there is; it is the act whereby one part of the population imposes its will upon the other part by means of rifles, bayonets and cannon—authoritarian means, if such there be at all; and if the victorious party does not want to have fought in vain, it must maintain this rule by means of the terror which its arms inspire in the reactionaries. Would the Paris Commune have lasted a single day if it had not made use of this authority of the armed people against the bourgeois? Should we not, on the contrary, reproach it for not having used it freely enough?

Therefore, either one of two things: either the anti-authoritarians don't know what they are talking about, in which case they are creating nothing but confusion; or they do know, and in that case they are betraying the movement of the proletariat. In either case they serve the reaction.

Herman Melville
(1819–1891)

ONE OF THE examples Engels uses to illustrate the enduring necessity for authority is that of "a ship on the high seas." It is precisely this construct, of course, that so appealed to Herman Melville in his own meditations on the sources of authority and influence and the various abuses of power to which individuals are subjected. Melville was deeply familiar with the sea. Family poverty exposed him to a variety of milieus, including the seafaring life that became a favorite setting for his subsequent fiction. Brutal experiences on naval and whaling ships were transmuted into the worlds of his novels and stories, which use the microcosm of the ship at sea as an experimental space in which political and social phenomena are played out. The passage excerpted here comes from the chapter in

Moby-Dick (1851) that describes "cutting-in," the process by which the blubber is stripped from a captured whale as it lies by the side of the ship. Tied to his friend Queequeg, one of the ship's harpooners, Ishmael, the novel's narrator, becomes directly responsible for—and simultaneously dependent on—the fate of the other man, balancing himself on the perilously slippery hide of the whale into which he is cutting. Ishmael thus finds himself bound in the arbitrary relation to another human being that is symptomatic of the age of industrialization and urbanization. Many readers express frustration at the long technical passages in *Moby-Dick*, but this section provides an occasion for Melville to explore the ways in which human beings are enmeshed, whether they like it or not, in the same network of human connection. After the failure of *Moby-Dick*, reviled on its first publication, and of several subsequent works of fiction, Melville supported his family with a job as a customs inspector in New York City. From the customs house on Pearl Street he could gaze at the sea. Today Melville's reputation rests chiefly on *Moby-Dick*, which was rediscovered in the 1920s by critics who admired its hybrid genre, invention, and daring experimentation.

The Monkey-Rope

from *Moby-Dick* (1851)

It was a humorously perilous business for both of us. For, before we proceed further, it must be said that the monkey-rope was fast at both ends; fast to Queequeg's broad canvas belt, and fast to my narrow leather one. So that for better or for worse, we two, for the time, were wedded; and should poor Queequeg sink to rise no more, then both usage and honor demanded, that instead of cutting the cord, it should drag me down in his wake. So, then, an elongated Siamese ligature united us. Queequeg was my own inseparable twin brother; nor could I any way get rid of the dangerous liabilities which the hempen bond entailed.

So strongly and metaphysically did I conceive of my situation then, that while earnestly watching his motions, I seemed distinctly to perceive that my own individuality was now merged in a joint stock company of two; that my free will had received a mortal wound; and that another's mistake or misfortune might plunge innocent me into unmerited disaster and death. Therefore, I saw that here was a sort of interregnum in Providence; for its even-handed equity never could have sanctioned so gross an injustice. And yet still further pondering—while I jerked him now and then from between the whale and ship, which would threaten to jam him—still further pondering, I say, I saw that this situation of mine was the precise situation of every mortal that breathes; only, in most cases, he, one way or other, has this Siamese connexion with a plurality of other mortals. If your banker breaks, you snap; if your apothecary by mistake sends you poison in your pills, you die. True, you may say that, by exceeding caution, you may possibly escape these and the multitudinous other evil chances of life. But handle Queequeg's monkey-rope heedfully as I would, sometimes he jerked it so, that I came very near sliding overboard. Nor could I possibly forget that, do what I would, I only had the management of one end of it.[1]

Jane Jacobs
(1916–2006)

APPRAISING THE DEATH and Life of Great American Cities in the New York Times in 1961, the urban studies professor Lloyd Rodwin wrote, "Jane Jacobs achieves a brashly impressive tour de force in her reinterpretation of the problems and needs of the contemporary metropolis." Jacobs's "attack on current city planning and rebuilding" met with strong criticism, especially from those who, like Rodwin, claimed that she did not understand the theories she sought to debunk. Nevertheless, her work profoundly changed our understanding of American cities. In Jacobs's New York Times obituary Douglas Martin argued that the book "rocked the planning and architectural establishment and continues to influence a third generation of students who can still find the book in college bookstores." Martin ranks The Death and Life of Great American Cities with Rachel Carson's Silent Spring, Betty Friedan's The Feminine Mystique, and the work of Ralph Nader, Paul Goodman, and Malcolm X, as the most provocative American writing of the 1960s. Born in the coal mining town of Scranton, Pennsylvania, Jacobs elected to join the workforce rather than attend college. Moving to New York City, she held a number of jobs while embarking on a career in journalism. With the encouragement of her husband, an architect, she began to write books as well. She would later become an editor at *Architecture* magazine. An activist as well as a writer, Jacobs joined protests against various urban planning projects. Above all, she championed learning through observation: "The way to get at what goes on in the seemingly mysterious and perverse behavior of cities is," she wrote in The Death and Life of Great American Cities, "to look closely,

---

1 The monkey-rope is found in all whalers; but it was only in the Pequod that the monkey and his holder were ever tied together. This improvement upon the original usage was introduced by no less a man than Stubb, in order to afford to the imperilled harpooneer the strongest possible guarantee for the faithfulness and vigilance of his monkey-rope holder. [Melville's note.]

and with as little previous expectation as is possible, at the most ordinary scenes and events, and attempt to see what they mean and whether any threads of principle emerge among them." Many of the "ordinary scenes and events" Jacobs observed took place in her own neighborhood, Manhattan's Greenwich Village. The following excerpt comes from the introduction to her vital book.

Understanding the City
from *The Death and Life of Great American Cities* (1961)

This book is an attack on current city planning and rebuilding. It is also, and mostly, an attempt to introduce new principles of city planning and rebuilding, different and even opposite from those now taught in everything from schools of architecture and planning to the Sunday supplements and women's magazines. My attack is not based on quibbles about rebuilding methods or hairsplitting about fashions in design. It is an attack, rather, on the principles and aims that have shaped modern, orthodox city planning and rebuilding.

In setting forth different principles, I shall mainly be writing about common, ordinary things: for instance, what kinds of city streets are safe and what kinds are not; why some city parks are marvelous and others are vice traps and death traps; why some slums stay slums and other slums regenerate themselves even against financial and official opposition; what makes downtowns shift their centers; what, if anything, is a city neighborhood, and what jobs, if any, neighborhoods in great cities do. In short, I shall be writing about how cities work in real life, because this is the only way to learn what principles of planning and what practices in rebuilding can promote social and economic vitality in cities, and what practices and principles will deaden these attributes.

There is a wistful myth that if only we had enough money to spend—the figure is usually put at a hundred billion dollars—we could wipe out all our slums in ten years, reverse decay in the great, dull, gray belts that were yesterday's and day-before-yesterday's suburbs, anchor the wandering middle class and its wandering tax money, and perhaps even solve the traffic problem.

But look what we have built with the first several billions: Low-income projects that become worse centers of delinquency, vandalism and general social hopelessness than the slums they were supposed to replace. Middle-income housing projects which are truly marvels of dullness and regimentation, sealed against any buoyancy or vitality of city life. Luxury housing projects that mitigate their inanity, or try to, with a vapid vulgarity. Cultural centers that are unable to support a good bookstore. Civic centers that are avoided by everyone but bums, who have fewer choices of loitering place than others. Commercial centers that are lackluster imitations of standardized suburban chain-store shopping. Promenades that go from no place to nowhere and have no promenaders. Expressways that eviscerate great cities. This is not the rebuilding of cities. This is the sacking of cities.

Under the surface, these accomplishments prove even poorer than their poor pretenses. They seldom aid the city areas around them, as in theory they are supposed to. These amputated areas typically develop galloping gangrene. To house people in this planned fashion, price tags are fastened on the population, and each sorted-out chunk of price-tagged populace lives in growing suspicion and tension against the surrounding city. When two or more such hostile islands are juxtaposed the result is called "a balanced neighborhood." Monopolistic shopping centers and monumental cultural centers cloak, under the public relations hoohaw, the subtraction of commerce, and of culture too, from the intimate and casual life of cities.

That such wonders may be accomplished, people who get marked with the planners' hex signs are pushed about, expropriated, and uprooted much as if they were the subjects of a conquering power. Thousands upon thousands of small businesses are destroyed, and their proprietors ruined, with hardly a gesture at compensation. Whole communities are torn apart and sown to the winds, with a reaping of cynicism, resentment and despair that must be heard and seen to be believed. A group of clergymen in Chicago, appalled at the fruits of planned city rebuilding there, asked,

> Could Job have been thinking of Chicago when he wrote:
>
>> Here are men that alter their neighbor's landmark . . . shoulder the poor aside, conspire to oppress the friendless.
>>
>> Reap they the field that is none of theirs, strip they the vineyard wrongfully seized from its owner . . .
>>
>> A cry goes up from the city streets, where wounded men lie groaning . . .

If so, he was also thinking of New York, Philadelphia, Boston, Washington, St. Louis, San Francisco and a number of other places. The economic rationale of current city rebuilding is a hoax. The economics of city rebuilding do not rest soundly on reasoned investment of public tax subsidies, as urban renewal theory proclaims, but also on vast, involuntary subsidies wrung out of helpless site victims. And the increased tax returns from such sites, accruing to the cities as a result of this "investment," are a mirage, a pitiful gesture against the ever increasing sums of public money needed to combat disintegration and instability that flow from the cruelly shaken-up city. The means to planned city rebuilding are as deplorable as the ends.

Meantime, all the art and science of city planning are helpless to stem decay—and the spiritlessness that precedes decay—in ever more massive swatches of cities. Nor can this decay be laid, reassuringly, to lack of opportunity to apply the arts of planning. It seems to matter little whether they are applied or not. Consider the Morningside Heights area in New York City. According to planning theory it should not be in trouble at all, for it enjoys a great abundance of parkland, campus, playground and other open spaces. It has plenty of grass. It occupies high and pleasant ground with magnificent river views. It is a famous educational center with splendid institutions— Columbia University, Union Theological Seminary, the Juilliard School of Music, and half a dozen others of eminent respectability. It is the beneficiary of good hospitals and churches. It has no industries. Its streets are zoned in the main against "incompatible uses" intruding into the preserves for solidly constructed, roomy, middle- and upper-class apartments. Yet by the early 1950's Morningside Heights was becoming a slum so swiftly, the surly kind of slum in which people fear to walk the streets, that the situation posed a crisis for the institutions. They and the planning arms of the city government got together, applied more planning theory, wiped out the most run-down part of the area and built in its stead a middle-income cooperative project complete with shopping center, and a public housing project, all interspersed with air, light, sunshine and landscaping. This was hailed as a great demonstration in city saving.

After that, Morningside Heights went downhill even faster.

Nor is this an unfair or irrelevant example. In city after city, precisely the wrong areas, in the light of planning theory, are decaying. Less noticed, but equally significant, in city after city the wrong areas, in the light of planning theory, are refusing to decay.

Cities are an immense laboratory of trial and error, failure and success, in city building and city design. This is the laboratory in which city planning should have been learning and forming and testing its theories. Instead the practitioners and teachers of this discipline (if such it can be called) have ignored the study of success and failure in real life, have been incurious about the reasons for unexpected success, and are guided instead by principles derived from the behavior and appearance of towns, suburbs, tuberculosis sanatoria, fairs, and imaginary dream cities—from anything but cities themselves.

If it appears that the rebuilt portions of cities and the endless new developments spreading beyond the cities are reducing city and countryside alike to a monotonous, unnourishing gruel, this is not strange. It all comes, first-, second-, third- or fourth-hand, out of the same intellectual dish of mush, a mush in which the qualities, necessities, advantages and behavior of great cities have been utterly confused with the qualities, necessities, advantages and behavior of other and more inert types of settlements.

There is nothing economically or socially inevitable about either the decay of old cities or the fresh-minted decadence of the new unurban urbanization. On the contrary, no other aspect of our economy and society has been more purposefully manipulated for a full quarter of a century to achieve precisely what we are getting. Extraordinary governmental financial incentives have been required to achieve this degree of monotony, sterility and vulgarity. Decades of preaching, writing and exhorting by experts have gone into convincing us and our legislators that mush like this must be good for us, as long as it comes bedded with grass.

Automobiles are often conveniently tagged as the villains responsible for the ills of cities and the disappointments and futilities of city planning. But the destructive effects of automobiles are much less a cause than a symptom of our incompetence at city building. Of course planners, including the highwaymen with fabulous sums of money and enormous powers at their disposal, are at a loss to make automobiles and cities compatible with one another. They do not know what to do with automobiles in cities because they do not know how to plan for workable and vital cities anyhow—with or without automobiles.

The simple needs of automobiles are more easily understood and satisfied than the complex needs of cities, and a growing number of planners and designers have come to believe that if they can only solve the problems of traffic, they will thereby have solved the major problem of cities. Cities have much more intricate economic and social concerns than automobile traffic. How can you know what to try with traffic until you know how the city itself works, and what else it needs to do with its streets? You can't.

IT MAY BE that we have become so feckless as a people that we no longer care how things do work, but only what kind of quick, easy outer impression they give. If so, there is little hope for our cities or probably for much else in our society. But I do not think this is so.

Specifically, in the case of planning for cities, it is clear that a large number of good and earnest people do care deeply about building and renewing. Despite some corruption, and considerable greed for the other man's vineyard, the intentions going into the messes we make are, on the whole, exemplary. Planners, architects of city design, and those they have led along with them in their beliefs are not consciously disdainful of the importance of knowing how things work. On the contrary, they have gone to great pains to learn what the saints and sages of modern orthodox planning have said about how cities *ought* to work and what *ought* to be good for people and businesses in them.

They take this with such devotion that when contradictory reality intrudes, threatening to shatter their dearly won learning, they must shrug reality aside.

.   .   .

Since theoretical city planning has embraced no major new ideas for considerably more than a generation, theoretical planners, financers and bureaucrats are all just about even today.

And to put it bluntly, they are all in the same stage of elaborately learned superstition as medical science was early in the last century, when physicians put their faith in bloodletting, to draw out the evil humors which were believed to cause disease. With bloodletting, it took years of learning to know precisely which veins, by what rituals, were to be opened for what symptoms. A superstructure of technical complication was erected in such deadpan detail that the literature still sounds almost plausible. However, because people, even when they are thoroughly enmeshed in descriptions of reality which are at variance with reality, are still seldom devoid of the powers of observation and independent thought, the science of bloodletting, over most of its long sway, appears usually to have been tempered with a certain amount of common sense. Or it was tempered until it reached its highest peaks of technique in, of all places, the young United States. Bloodletting went wild here. It had an enormously influential proponent in Dr. Benjamin Rush, still revered as the greatest statesman-physician of our revolutionary and federal periods, and a genius of medical administration. Dr. Rush Got Things Done. Among the things he got done, some of them good and useful, were to develop, practice, teach and spread the custom of bloodletting in cases where prudence or mercy had heretofore restrained its use. He and his students drained the blood of very young children, of consumptives, of the greatly aged, of almost anyone unfortunate enough to be sick in his realms of influence. His extreme practices aroused the alarm and horror of European bloodletting physicians. And yet as late as 1851, a committee appointed by the State Legislature of New York solemnly defended the thoroughgoing use of bloodletting. It scathingly ridiculed and censured a physician, William Turner, who had the temerity to write a pamphlet criticizing Dr. Rush's doctrines and calling "the practice of taking blood in diseases contrary to common sense, to general experience, to enlightened reason and to the manifest laws of the divine Providence." Sick people needed fortifying, not draining, said Dr. Turner, and he was squelched.

Medical analogies, applied to social organisms, are apt to be farfetched, and there is no point in mistaking mammalian chemistry for what occurs in a city. But analogies as to what goes on in the brains of earnest and learned men, dealing with complex phenomena they do not understand at all and trying to make do with a pseudoscience, do have point. As in the pseudoscience of bloodletting, just so in the pseudoscience of city rebuilding and planning, years of learning and a plethora of subtle and complicated dogma have arisen on a foundation of nonsense. The tools of technique have steadily been perfected. Naturally, in time, forceful and able men, admired administrators, having swallowed the initial fallacies and having been provisioned with tools and with public confidence, go on logically to the greatest destructive excesses, which prudence or mercy might previously have forbade. Bloodletting could heal only by accident or insofar as it broke the rules, until the time when it was abandoned in favor of the hard, complex business of assembling, using and testing, bit by bit, true descriptions of reality drawn not from how it ought to be, but from how it is. The pseudoscience of city planning and its companion, the art of city design, have not yet broken with the specious comfort of wishes, familiar superstitions, oversimplifications, and symbols, and have not yet embarked upon the adventure of probing the real world.

George Orwell
(1903–1950)

NOVELIST, ESSAYIST, JOURNALIST, political observer, George Orwell held a deep mistrust of ideologies and -isms of all kinds. That mistrust characterizes his writings on politics and society, the most well known of which are the allegorical fiction *Animal Farm* (1945) and the dystopian novel *1984* (1949). Orwell's early recognition of his "facility with words and a power of facing unpleasant facts" led him to expose himself to a broad range of hardships: In a 2012 *Vanity Fair* piece Christopher Hitchens describes Orwell as having taken up "the task of amateur anthropologist, both in his own country and overseas" in the 1930s. These expeditions included working as a dishwasher in Paris and fighting against the Fascists in Spain. The first experience, during which he almost died of pneumonia in the poor ward of a public hospital, produced *Down and Out in Paris and London* (1933), a riveting and devastating exploration of life at the margins of society. The latter experience, in which he nearly died of a bullet to the neck, produced *Homage to Catalonia* (1938), an account of his service with Republican forces. George Orwell was born Eric Blair in India, where his father was a British civil servant. After attending school in England, he returned to South Asia to serve with the Imperial Police in Burma. In this job, which he held from 1922 to 1927, Orwell cultivated his insights on, and hatred for, colonial oppression. Published about a decade later, in 1936, "Shooting an Elephant" is representative of its author's ability to dissect the insidious tyrannies of political organizations. Orwell's honesty about his own failures as well as those of colonial rule make this an especially penetrating analysis of the system's brutality, a word Hitchens defines in *Why Orwell Matters* as "the coarsening effect that this exercise of cruelty produces in the strong."

Shooting an Elephant
from *New Writing 2* (1936)

In Moulmein, in Lower Burma, I was hated by large numbers of people—the only time in my life that I have been important enough for this to happen to me. I was sub-divisional police officer of the town, and in an aimless, petty kind of way anti-European feeling was very bitter. No one had the guts to raise a riot, but if a European woman went through the bazaars alone somebody would probably spit betel juice over her dress. As a police officer I was an obvious target and was baited whenever it seemed safe to do so. When a nimble Burman tripped me up on the football field and the referee (another Burman) looked the other way, the crowd yelled with hideous laughter. This happened more than once. In the end the sneering yellow faces of young men that met me everywhere, the insults hooted after me when I was at a safe distance, got badly on my nerves. The young Buddhist priests were the worst of all. There were several thousands of them in the town and none of them seemed to have anything to do except stand on street corners and jeer at Europeans.

All this was perplexing and upsetting. For at that time I had already made up my mind that imperialism was an evil thing and the sooner I chucked up my job and got out of it the better. Theoretically—and secretly, of course—I was all for the Burmese and all against their oppressors, the British. As for the job I was doing, I hated it more bitterly than I can perhaps make clear. In a job like that you see the dirty work of Empire at close quarters. The wretched prisoners huddling in the stinking cages of the lock-ups, the grey, cowed faces of the long term convicts, the scarred buttocks of the men who had been flogged with bamboos—all these oppressed me with an intolerable sense of guilt. But I could get nothing into perspective. I was young and ill-educated and I had had to think out my problems in the utter silence that is imposed on every Englishman in the East. I did not even know that the British Empire is dying, still less did I know that it is a great deal better than the younger empires that are going to supplant it. All I knew was that I was stuck between my hatred of the empire I served and my rage against the evil-spirited little beasts who tried to make my job impossible. With one part of my mind I thought of the British Raj as an unbreakable tyranny, as something clamped down, *in saecula saeculorum*, upon the will of prostrate peoples; with another part I thought that the greatest joy in the world would be to drive a bayonet into a Buddhist priest's guts. Feelings like these are the normal by-products of imperialism; ask any Anglo-Indian official, if you can catch him off duty.

One day something happened which in a roundabout way was enlightening. It was a tiny incident in itself, but it gave me a better glimpse than I had had before of the real nature of imperialism—the real motives for which despotic governments act. Early one morning the sub-inspector at a police station the other end of the town rang me up on the phone and said that an elephant was ravaging the bazaar. Would I please come and do something about it? I did not know what I could do, but I wanted to see what was happening and I got on to a pony and started out. I took my rifle, an old .44 Winchester and much too small to kill an elephant, but I thought the noise might be useful *in terrorem*. Various Burmans stopped me on the way and told me about the elephant's doings. It was not, of course, a wild elephant, but a tame one which had gone "must". It had been chained up as tame elephants always are when their attack of "must" is due, but on the previous night it had broken its chain and escaped. Its mahout, the only person who could manage it when it was in that state, had set out in pursuit, but he had taken the wrong direction and was now twelve hours' journey away, and in the morning the elephant had suddenly reappeared in the town. The Burmese population had no weapons and were quite helpless against it. It had already destroyed somebody's bamboo hut, killed a cow and raided some fruit-stalls and devoured the stock; also it had met the municipal rubbish van, and, when the driver jumped out and took to his heels, had turned the van over and inflicted violence upon it.

The Burmese sub-inspector and some Indian constables were waiting for me in the quarter where the elephant had been seen. It was a very poor quarter, a labyrinth of squalid bamboo huts, thatched with palm-leaf, winding all over a steep hillside. I remember that it was a cloudy stuffy morning at the beginning of the rains. We began questioning the people as to where the elephant had gone, and, as usual, failed to get any definite information. That is invariably the case in the East; a story always sounds clear enough at a distance, but the nearer you get to the scene of events the vaguer it becomes. Some of the people said that the elephant had gone in one direction, some said that he had gone in another, some professed not even to have heard of any elephant. I had almost made up my mind that the whole story was a pack of lies, when we heard yells a little distance away. There was a loud, scandalised cry of "Go away, child! Go away this instant!" and an old woman with a switch in her hand came round the corner of a hut, violently shooing away a crowd of naked children. Some more women followed, clicking their tongues and exclaiming; evidently there was something there that the children ought not to have seen. I rounded the hut and saw a man's dead body sprawling in the mud. He was an Indian, a black Dravidian coolie, almost naked, and he could not have been dead many minutes. The people said that the elephant had come suddenly upon him round the corner of the hut, caught him with its trunk, put its foot on his back and ground him into the earth. This was the rainy season and the ground was soft, and his face had scored a trench a foot deep and a couple of yards long. He was lying on his belly with arms crucified and head sharply twisted to one side. His face was coated with mud, the eyes wide open, the teeth bared and grinning with an expression of unendurable agony. (Never tell me, by the way, that the dead look peaceful. Most of the corpses I have seen looked devilish.) The friction of the great beast's foot had stripped the skin from his back as neatly as one skins a rabbit. As soon as I saw the dead man I sent an orderly to a friend's house nearby to borrow an elephant rifle. I had already sent back the pony, not wanting it to go mad with fright and throw me if it smelled the elephant.

The orderly came back in a few minutes with a rifle and five cartridges, and meanwhile some Burmans had arrived and told us that the elephant was in the paddy fields below, only a few hundred yards away. As I started forward practically the whole population of the quarter flocked out of their houses and followed me. They had seen the rifle and were all shouting excitedly that I was going to shoot the elephant. They had not shown much interest in the elephant when he was merely ravaging their homes, but it was different now that he was going to be shot. It was a bit of fun to them, as it would be to an English crowd; besides, they wanted the meat. It made me vaguely uneasy. I had no intention of shooting the elephant—I had merely sent for the rifle to defend myself if necessary—and it is always unnerving to have a crowd following you. I marched down the hill, looking and feeling a fool, with the rifle over my shoulder and an ever-growing army of people jostling at my heels. At the bottom, when you got away from the huts, there was a metalled road and beyond that a miry waste of paddy fields a thousand yards across, not yet ploughed but soggy from the first rains and dotted with coarse grass. The elephant was standing eighty yards from the road, his left side towards us. He took not the slightest notice of the crowd's approach. He was tearing up bunches of grass, beating them against his knees to clean them and stuffing them into his mouth.

I had halted on the road. As soon as I saw the elephant I knew with perfect certainty that I ought not to shoot him. It is a serious matter to shoot a working elephant—it is comparable to destroying a huge and costly piece of machinery—and obviously one ought not to do it if it can possibly be avoided. And at that distance, peacefully eating, the elephant looked no more dangerous than a cow. I thought then and I think now that his attack of "must" was already passing off; in which case he would merely wander harmlessly about until the mahout came back and caught him. Moreover, I did not in the least want to shoot him. I decided that I would watch him for a little while to make sure that he did not turn savage again, and then go home.

But at that moment I glanced round at the crowd that had followed me. It was an immense crowd, two thousand at the least and growing every minute.

It blocked the road for a long distance on either side. I looked at the sea of yellow faces above the garish clothes—faces all happy and excited over this bit of fun, all certain that the elephant was going to be shot. They were watching me as they would watch a conjuror about to perform a trick. They did not like me, but with the magical rifle in my hands I was momentarily worth watching. And suddenly I realised that I should have to shoot the elephant after all. The people expected it of me and I had got to do it; I could feel their two thousand wills pressing me forward, irresistibly. And it was at this moment, as I stood there with the rifle in my hands, that I first grasped the hollowness, the futility of the white man's dominion in the East. Here was I, the white man with his gun, standing in front of the unarmed native crowd—seemingly the leading actor of the piece; but in reality I was only an absurd puppet pushed to and fro by the will of those yellow faces behind. I perceived in this moment that when the white man turns tyrant it is his own freedom that he destroys. He becomes a sort of hollow, posing dummy, the conventionalised figure of a sahib. For it is the condition of his rule that he shall spend his life in trying to impress the "natives" and so in every crisis he has got to do what the "natives" expect of him. He wears a mask, and his face grows to fit it. I had got to shoot the elephant. I had committed myself to doing it when I sent for the rifle. A sahib has got to act like a sahib; he has got to appear resolute, to know his own mind and do definite things. To come all that way, rifle in hand, with two thousand people marching at my heels, and then to trail feebly away, having done nothing—no, that was impossible. The crowd would laugh at me. And my whole life, every white man's life in the East, was one long struggle not to be laughed at.

But I did not want to shoot the elephant. I watched him beating his bunch of grass against his knees, with that preoccupied grandmotherly air that elephants have. It seemed to me that it would be murder to shoot him. At that age I was not squeamish about killing animals, but I had never shot an elephant and never wanted to. (Somehow it always seems worse to kill a *large* animal.) Besides, there was the beast's owner to be considered. Alive, the elephant was worth at least a hundred pounds; dead, he would only be worth the value of his tusks—five pounds, possibly. But I had got to act quickly. I turned to some experienced-looking Burmans who had been there when we arrived, and asked them how the elephant had been behaving. They all said the same thing: he took no notice of you if you left him alone, but he might charge if you went too close to him.

It was perfectly clear to me what I ought to do. I ought to walk up to within, say, twenty-five yards of the elephant and test his behaviour. If he charged I could shoot, if he took no notice of me it would be safe to leave him until the mahout came back. But also I knew that I was going to do no such thing. I was a poor shot with a rifle and the ground was soft mud into which one would sink at every step. If the elephant charged and I missed him,

I should have about as much chance as a toad under a steam-roller. But even then I was not thinking particularly of my own skin, only the watchful yellow faces behind. For at that moment, with the crowd watching me, I was not afraid in the ordinary sense, as I would have been if I had been alone. A white man mustn't be frightened in front of "natives"; and so, in general, he isn't frightened. The sole thought in my mind was that if anything went wrong those two thousand Burmans would see me pursued, caught, trampled on and reduced to a grinning corpse like that Indian up the hill. And if that happened it was quite probable that some of them would laugh. That would never do. There was only one alternative. I shoved the cartridges into the magazine and lay down on the road to get a better aim.

The crowd grew very still, and a deep, low, happy sigh, as of people who see the theatre curtain go up at last, breathed from innumerable throats. They were going to have their bit of fun after all. The rifle was a beautiful German thing with cross-hair sights. I did not then know that in shooting an elephant one should shoot to cut an imaginary bar running from ear-hole to ear-hole. I ought therefore, as the elephant was sideways on, to have aimed straight at his ear-hole; actually I aimed several inches in front of this, thinking the brain would be further forward.

When I pulled the trigger I did not hear the bang or feel the kick—one never does when a shot goes home—but I heard the devilish roar of glee that went up from the crowd. In that instant, in too short a time, one would have thought, even for the bullet to get there, a mysterious, terrible change had come over the elephant. He neither stirred nor fell, but every line of his body had altered. He looked suddenly stricken, shrunken, immensely old, as though the frightful impact of the bullet had paralysed him without knocking him down. At last, after what seemed a long time—it might have been five seconds, I dare say—he sagged flabbily to his knees. His mouth slobbered. An enormous senility seemed to have settled upon him. One could have imagined him thousands of years old. I fired again into the same spot. At the second shot he did not collapse but climbed with desperate slowness to his feet and stood weakly upright, with legs sagging and head drooping. I fired a third time. That was the shot that did for him. You could see the agony of it jolt his whole body and knock the last remnant of strength from his legs. But in falling he seemed for a moment to rise, for as his hind legs collapsed beneath him he seemed to tower upwards like a huge rock toppling, his trunk reaching skyward like a tree. He trumpeted, for the first and only time. And then down he came, his belly towards me, with a crash that seemed to shake the ground even where I lay.

I got up. The Burmans were already racing past me across the mud. It was obvious that the elephant would never rise again, but he was not dead. He was breathing very rhythmically with long rattling gasps, his great mound of a side painfully rising and falling. His mouth was wide open—I could see far down into caverns of pale pink throat. I waited a long time for him to die, but his breathing did not weaken. Finally I fired my two remaining shots into the spot where I thought his heart must be. The thick blood welled out of him like red velvet, but still he did not die. His body did not even jerk when the shots hit him, the tortured breathing continued without a pause. He was dying, very slowly and in great agony, but in some world remote from me where not even a bullet could damage him further. I felt that I had got to put an end to that dreadful noise. It seemed dreadful to see the great beast lying there, powerless to move and yet powerless to die, and not even to be able to finish him. I sent back for my small rifle and poured shot after shot into his heart and down his throat. They seemed to make no impression. The tortured gasps continued as steadily as the ticking of a clock.

In the end I could not stand it any longer and went away. I heard later that it took him half an hour to die. Burmans were arriving with dahs and baskets even before I left, and I was told they had stripped his body almost to the bones by the afternoon.

Afterwards, of course, there were endless discussions about the shooting of the elephant. The owner was furious, but he was only an Indian and could do nothing. Besides, legally I had done the right thing, for a mad elephant has to be killed, like a mad dog, if its owner fails to control it. Among the Europeans opinion was divided. The older men said I was right, the younger men said it was a damn shame to shoot an elephant for killing a coolie, because an elephant was worth more than any damn Coringhee coolie. And afterwards I was very glad that the coolie had been killed; it put me legally in the right and it gave me a sufficient pretext for shooting the elephant. I often wondered whether any of the others grasped that I had done it solely to avoid looking a fool.

Martin Luther King Jr.
(1929–1968)

BORN IN ATLANTA to a family tradition of ministry, Martin Luther King Jr. absorbed a philosophy of political and social engagement from his father and grandfather, both of whom were pastors at the Ebenezer Baptist Church and were also involved in the NAACP. King himself was ordained in 1947, and graduated from Morehouse College the following year. He studied subsequently at the Crozer Theological Seminary in Pennsylvania and earned a doctorate in systematic theology from Boston University in 1955. Throughout his career King remained dedicated to the principles of nonviolence—a philosophy influenced by the writings of Henry David Thoreau and Mohandas Gandhi, and one that became increasingly difficult to maintain during the turbulent 1960s, with the rise of the black power movement. King began his activist work soon after becoming the pastor of the Dexter Avenue Baptist Church in Montgomery, Alabama, where he assumed leadership of the Montgomery Improvement Association and the boycott of city buses. Here he was arrested for the first time, and he continued to preach and practice nonviolent protest in the years that followed, in Birmingham, Selma, Albany, and elsewhere, as he led and participated in sit-ins, marches, and other acts of civil disobedience amid church bombings in the South and race riots in the North. He was involved in the founding of two organizations, the Southern Christian Leadership Conference (SCLC) and the Student Nonviolent Coordinating Committee (SNCC), which played vital roles in the civil rights movement. King traveled to India in 1959 to learn more about the teachings of Gandhi, and he returned to the United States to continue his work, gathering the support of the labor movement and various communities along the way. A year after the March on Washington in 1963, where he delivered his "I Have a Dream" speech, King won the Nobel Peace Prize. In his acceptance speech he affirmed his belief in the worth of nonviolence and refused "to accept the view that mankind is so tragically bound to the starless midnight of racism and war that the bright daybreak of peace and brotherhood can never become a reality." King's opposition to the Vietnam War was of a piece with his code of nonviolence, but it earned him enemies in certain quarters and prompted the surveillance of J. Edgar Hoover's FBI. King was assassinated in Memphis, Tennessee, where he had traveled in support of a sanitation workers' strike, by a white segregationist named James Earl Ray on April 5, 1968. The following sermon was delivered on March 31, 1968, less than a week before his murder, at Washington's National Cathedral. In it, King invoked Washington Irving's character Rip Van Winkle, who slept through the American Revolution, to illustrate the radical change of the civil rights revolution.

Remaining Awake Through a Great Revolution
Delivered at the National Cathedral, Washington, DC
(March 31, 1968)

I need not pause to say how very delighted I am to be here this morning, to have the opportunity of standing in this very great and significant pulpit. And I do want to express my deep personal appreciation to Dean Sayre and all of the cathedral clergy for extending the invitation.

It is always a rich and rewarding experience to take a brief break from our day-to-day demands and the struggle for freedom and human dignity and discuss the issues involved in that struggle with concerned friends of goodwill all over our nation. And certainly it is always a deep and meaningful experience to be in a worship service. And so for many reasons, I'm happy to be here today.

I would like to use as a subject from which to preach this morning: "Remaining Awake Through a Great Revolution." The text for the morning is found in the Book of Revelation. There are two passages there that I would like to quote, in the sixteenth chapter of that book: "Behold I make all things new; former things are passed away."

I am sure that most of you have read that arresting little story from the pen of Washington Irving entitled "Rip Van Winkle." The one thing that we usually remember about the story is that Rip Van Winkle slept twenty years. But there is another point in that little story that is almost completely over-looked. It was the sign in the end, from which Rip went up in the mountain for his long sleep.

When Rip Van Winkle went up into the mountain, the sign had a picture of King George the Third of England. When he came down twenty years later the sign had a picture of George Washington, the first president of the United States. When Rip Van Winkle looked up at the picture of George Washington—and looking at the picture he was amazed—he was completely lost. He knew not who he was.

And this reveals to us that the most striking thing about the story of Rip Van Winkle is not merely that Rip slept twenty years, but that he slept through a revolution. While he was peacefully snoring up in the mountain a revolution was taking place that at points would change the course of history—and Rip knew nothing about it. He was asleep. Yes, he slept through a revolution. And one of the great liabilities of life is that all too many people find themselves living amid a great period of social change, and yet they fail to develop the new attitudes, the new mental responses, that the new situation demands. They end up sleeping through a revolution.

There can be no gainsaying of the fact that a great revolution is taking place in the world today. In a sense it is a triple revolution: that is, a techno-logical revolution, with the impact of automation and cybernation; then there is a revolution in weaponry, with the emergence of atomic and nuclear weap-ons of warfare; then there is a human rights revolution, with the freedom explosion that is taking place all over the world. Yes, we do live in a period where changes are taking place. And there is still the voice crying through the vista of time saying, "Behold, I make all things new; former things are passed away."

Now whenever anything new comes into history it brings with it new challenges and new opportunities. And I would like to deal with the chal-lenges that we face today as a result of this triple revolution that is taking place in the world today.

First, we are challenged to develop a world perspective. No individual can live alone, no nation can live alone, and anyone who feels that he can live alone is sleeping through a revolution. The world in which we live is geographically one. The challenge that we face today is to make it one in terms of brotherhood.

Now it is true that the geographical oneness of this age has come into being to a large extent through modern man's scientific ingenuity. Modern man through his scientific genius has been able to dwarf distance and place time in chains. And our jet planes have compressed into minutes distances that once took weeks and even months. All of this tells us that our world is a neighborhood.

Through our scientific and technological genius, we have made of this world a neighborhood and yet we have not had the ethical commitment to make of it a brotherhood. But somehow, and in some way, we have got to do this. We must all learn to live together as brothers or we will all perish together as fools. We are tied together in the single garment of destiny, caught in an inescapable network of mutuality. And whatever affects one directly affects all indirectly. For some strange reason I can never be what I ought to be until you are what you ought to be. And you can never be what you ought to be until I am what I ought to be. This is the way God's universe is made; this is the way it is structured.

John Donne caught it years ago and placed it in graphic terms: "No man is an island entire of itself. Every man is a piece of the continent, a part of the main." And he goes on toward the end to say, "Any man's death diminishes me, because I am involved in mankind, and therefore never send to know for whom the bell tolls; it tolls for thee." We must see this, believe this, and live by it if we are to remain awake through a great revolution.

Secondly, we are challenged to eradicate the last vestiges of racial injustice from our nation. I must say this morning that racial injustice is still the black man's burden and the white man's shame.

It is an unhappy truth that racism is a way of life for the vast majority of white Americans, spoken and unspoken, acknowledged and denied, subtle and sometimes not so subtle—the disease of racism permeates and poisons a whole body politic. And I can see nothing more urgent than for America to work passionately and unrelentingly—to get rid of the disease of racism.

Something positive must be done. Everyone must share in the guilt as individuals and as institutions. The government must certainly share the guilt; individuals must share the guilt; even the church must share the guilt.

We must face the sad fact that at eleven o'clock on Sunday morning when we stand to sing "In Christ There Is No East or West," we stand in the most segregated hour of America.

The hour has come for everybody, for all institutions of the public sector and the private sector to work to get rid of racism. And now if we are to do it we must honestly admit certain things and get rid of certain myths that have constantly been disseminated all over our nation.

One is the myth of time. It is the notion that only time can solve the problem of racial injustice. And there are those who often sincerely say to the Negro and his allies in the white community, "Why don't you slow up? Stop pushing things so fast. Only time can solve the problem. And if you will just be nice and patient and continue to pray, in a hundred or two hundred years the problem will work itself out."

There is an answer to that myth. It is that time is neutral. It can be used either constructively or destructively. And I am sorry to say this morning that I am absolutely convinced that the forces of ill will in our nation, the extreme rightists of our nation—the people on the wrong side—have used time much more effectively than the forces of goodwill. And it may well be that we will have to repent in this generation. Not merely for the vitriolic words and the violent actions of the bad people, but for the appalling silence and indifference of the good people who sit around and say, "Wait on time."

Somewhere we must come to see that human progress never rolls in on the wheels of inevitability. It comes through the tireless efforts and the persistent work of dedicated individuals who are willing to be co-workers with God. And without this hard work, time itself becomes an ally of the primitive forces of social stagnation. So we must help time and realize that the time is always ripe to do right.

Now there is another myth that still gets around: it is a kind of overreliance on the bootstrap philosophy. There are those who still feel that if the Negro is to rise out of poverty, if the Negro is to rise out of the slum conditions, if he is to rise out of discrimination and segregation, he must do it all by himself. And so they say the Negro must lift himself by his own bootstraps.

They never stop to realize that no other ethnic group has been a slave on American soil. The people who say this never stop to realize that the nation made the black man's color a stigma. But beyond this they never stop to realize the debt that they owe a people who were kept in slavery two hundred and forty-four years.

In 1863 the Negro was told that he was free as a result of the Emancipation Proclamation being signed by Abraham Lincoln. But he was not given any land to make that freedom meaningful. It was something like keeping a person in prison for a number of years and suddenly discovering that that person is not guilty of the crime for which he was convicted. And you just go up to him and say, "Now you are free," but you don't give him any bus fare to get to town. You don't give him any money to get some clothes to put on his back or to get on his feet again in life.

Every court of jurisprudence would rise up against this, and yet this is the very thing that our nation did to the black man. It simply said, "You're free," and it left him there penniless, illiterate, not knowing what to do. And the irony of it all is that at the same time the nation failed to do anything for the black man, though an act of Congress was giving away millions of acres of land in the West and the Midwest. Which meant that it was willing to under-gird its white peasants from Europe with an economic floor.

But not only did it give the land, it built land-grant colleges to teach them how to farm. Not only that, it provided county agents to further their exper-tise in farming; not only that, as the years unfolded it provided low interest rates so that they could mechanize their farms. And to this day thousands of these very persons are receiving millions of dollars in federal subsidies every year not to farm. And these are so often the very people who tell Negroes that they must lift themselves by their own bootstraps. It's all right to tell a man to lift himself by his own bootstraps, but it is a cruel jest to say to a bootless man that he ought to lift himself by his own bootstraps.

We must come to see that the roots of racism are very deep in our country, and there must be something positive and massive in order to get rid of all the effects of racism and the tragedies of racial injustice.

There is another thing closely related to racism that I would like to men-tion as another challenge. We are challenged to rid our nation and the world of poverty. Like a monstrous octopus, poverty spreads its nagging, prehen-sile tentacles into hamlets and villages all over our world. Two-thirds of the people of the world go to bed hungry tonight. They are ill-housed; they are ill-nourished; they are shabbily clad. I've seen it in Latin America; I've seen it in Africa; I've seen this poverty in Asia.

I remember some years ago Mrs. King and I journeyed to that great coun-try known as India. And I never will forget the experience. It was a marvelous experience to meet and talk with the great leaders of India, to meet and talk with and to speak to thousands and thousands of people all over that vast country. These experiences will remain dear to me as long as the cords of memory shall lengthen.

But I say to you this morning, my friends, there were those depressing moments. How can one avoid being depressed when he sees with his own eyes evidence of millions of people going to bed hungry at night? How can one avoid being depressed when he sees with his own eyes God's children sleeping on the sidewalks at night? In Bombay more than a million people sleep on the sidewalks every night. In Calcutta more than six hundred thousand sleep on the sidewalks every night. They have no beds to sleep in; they have no houses to go in. How can one avoid being depressed when he discovers that out of India's population of more than five hundred million people, some four hun-dred and eighty million make an annual income of less than ninety dollars a year. And most of them have never seen a doctor or a dentist.

As I noticed these things, something within me cried out, "Can we in America stand idly by and not be concerned?" And an answer came: "Oh no!" Because the destiny of the United States is tied up with the destiny of India and every other nation. And I started thinking of the fact that we spend in America millions of dollars a day to store surplus food, and I said to myself, "I know where we can store that food free of charge—in the wrinkled stomachs of millions of God's children all over the world who go to bed hungry at night." And maybe we spend far too much of our national budget establishing military bases around the world rather than bases of genuine concern and understanding.

Not only do we see poverty abroad, I would remind you that in our own nation there are about forty million people who are poverty-stricken. I have seen them here and there. I have seen them in the ghettos of the North; I have seen them in the rural areas of the South; I have seen them in Appalachia. I have just been in the process of touring many areas of our country and I must confess that in some situations I have literally found myself crying.

I was in Marks, Mississippi, the other day, which is in Whitman County, the poorest county in the United States. I tell you, I saw hundreds of little black boys and black girls walking the streets with no shoes to wear. I saw their mothers and fathers trying to carry on a little Head Start program, but they had no money. The federal government hadn't funded them, but they were trying to carry on. They raised a little money here and there; trying to get a little food to feed the children; trying to teach them a little something.

And I saw mothers and fathers who said to me not only were they unemployed, they didn't get any kind of income—no old-age pension, no welfare check, no anything. I said, "How do you live?" And they say, "Well, we go around, go around to the neighbors and ask them for a little something. When the berry season comes, we pick berries. When the rabbit season comes, we hunt and catch a few rabbits. And that's about it."

And I was in Newark and Harlem just this week. And I walked into the homes of welfare mothers. I saw them in conditions—no, not with wall-to-wall carpet, but wall-to-wall rats and roaches. I stood in an apartment and this welfare mother said to me, "The landlord will not repair this place. I've been here two years and he hasn't made a single repair." She pointed out the walls with all the ceiling falling through. She showed me the holes where the rats came in. She said night after night we have to stay awake to keep the rats and roaches from getting to the children. I said, "How much do you pay for this apartment?" She said, "A hundred and twenty-five dollars." I looked, and I thought, and said to myself, "It isn't worth sixty dollars." Poor people are forced to pay more for less. Living in conditions day in and day out where the whole area is constantly drained without being replenished. It becomes a kind of domestic colony. And the tragedy is, so often these forty million people are invisible because America is so affluent, so rich. Because our expressways carry us from the ghetto, we don't see the poor.

Jesus told a parable one day, and he reminded us that a man went to hell because he didn't see the poor. His name was Dives. He was a rich man. And there was a man by the name of Lazarus who was a poor man, but not only was he poor, he was sick. Sores were all over his body, and he was so weak that he could hardly move. But he managed to get to the gate of Dives every day, wanting just to have the crumbs that would fall from his table. And Dives did nothing about it. And the parable ends saying, "Dives went to hell, and there were a fixed gulf now between Lazarus and Dives."

There is nothing in that parable that said Dives went to hell because he was rich. Jesus never made a universal indictment against all wealth. It is true that one day a rich young ruler came to him, and he advised him to sell all, but in that instance Jesus was prescribing individual surgery and not setting forth a universal diagnosis. And if you will look at that parable with all of its symbolism, you will remember that a conversation took place between heaven and hell, and on the other end of that long-distance call between heaven and hell was Abraham in heaven talking to Dives in hell.

Now Abraham was a very rich man. If you go back to the Old Testament, you see that he was the richest man of his day, so it was not a rich man in hell talking with a poor man in heaven; it was a little millionaire in hell talking with a multimillionaire in heaven. Dives didn't go to hell because he was rich; Dives didn't realize that his wealth was his opportunity. It was his opportunity to bridge the gulf that separated him from his brother Lazarus. Dives went to hell because he was passed by Lazarus every day and he never really saw him. He went to hell because he allowed his brother to become invisible. Dives went to hell because he maximized the minimum and minimized the maximum. Indeed, Dives went to hell because he sought to be a conscientious objector in the war against poverty.

And this can happen to America, the richest nation in the world—and nothing's wrong with that—this is America's opportunity to help bridge the gulf between the haves and the have-nots. The question is whether America will do it. There is nothing new about poverty. What is new is that we now have the techniques and the resources to get rid of poverty. The real question is whether we have the will.

In a few weeks some of us are coming to Washington to see if the will is still alive or if it is alive in this nation. We are coming to Washington in a Poor People's Campaign. Yes, we are going to bring the tired, the poor, the huddled masses. We are going to bring those who have known long years of hurt and neglect. We are going to bring those who have come to feel that life is a long and desolate corridor with no exit signs. We are going to bring children and adults and old people, people who have never seen a doctor or a dentist in their lives.

We are not coming to engage in any histrionic gesture. We are not coming to tear up Washington. We are coming to demand that the government address itself to the problem of poverty. We read one day, "We hold these truths to be self-evident, that all men are created equal, that they are endowed by their Creator with certain inalienable Rights, that among these are Life, Liberty, and the pursuit of Happiness." But if a man doesn't have a job or an income, he has neither life nor liberty nor the possibility for the pursuit of happiness. He merely exists.

We are coming to ask America to be true to the huge promissory note that it signed years ago. And we are coming to engage in dramatic nonviolent action, to call attention to the gulf between promise and fulfillment; to make the invisible visible.

Why do we do it this way? We do it this way because it is our experience that the nation doesn't move around questions of genuine equality for the poor and for black people until it is confronted massively, dramatically in terms of direct action.

Great documents are here to tell us something should be done. We met here some years ago in the White House conference on civil rights. And we came out with the same recommendations that we will be demanding in our campaign here, but nothing has been done. The President's commission on technology, automation and economic progress recommended these things some time ago. Nothing has been done. Even the urban coalition of mayors of most of the cities of our country and the leading businessmen have said these things should be done. Nothing has been done. The Kerner Commission came out with its report just a few days ago and then made specific recommendations. Nothing has been done.

And I submit that nothing will be done until people of goodwill put their bodies and their souls in motion. And it will be the kind of soul force brought into being as a result of this confrontation that I believe will make the difference.

Yes, it will be a Poor People's Campaign. This is the question facing America. Ultimately a great nation is a compassionate nation. America has not met its obligations and its responsibilities to the poor.

One day we will have to stand before the God of history and we will talk in terms of things we've done. Yes, we will be able to say we built gargantuan bridges to span the seas, we built gigantic buildings to kiss the skies. Yes, we made our submarines to penetrate oceanic depths. We brought into being many other things with our scientific and technological power.

It seems that I can hear the God of history saying, "That was not enough! But I was hungry, and ye fed me not. I was naked, and ye clothed me not. I was devoid of a decent sanitary house to live in, and ye provided no shelter for me. And consequently, you cannot enter the kingdom of greatness. If ye do it unto the least of these, my brethren, ye do it unto me." That's the question facing America today.

I want to say one other challenge that we face is simply that we must find an alternative to war and bloodshed. Anyone who feels, and there are still a lot of people who feel that way, that war can solve the social problems facing mankind is sleeping through a great revolution. President Kennedy said on one occasion, "Mankind must put an end to war or war will put an end to mankind." The world must hear this. I pray God that America will hear this before it is too late, because today we're fighting a war.

I am convinced that it is one of the most unjust wars that has ever been fought in the history of the world. Our involvement in the war in Vietnam has torn up the Geneva Accord. It has strengthened the military-industrial complex; it has strengthened the forces of reaction in our nation. It has put us against the self-determination of a vast majority of the Vietnamese people, and put us in the position of protecting a corrupt regime that is stacked against the poor.

It has played havoc with our domestic destinies. This day we are spending five hundred thousand dollars to kill every Vietcong soldier. Every time we kill one we spend about five hundred thousand dollars while we spend only fifty-three dollars a year for every person characterized as poverty-stricken in the so-called poverty program, which is not even a good skirmish against poverty.

Not only that, it has put us in a position of appearing to the world as an arrogant nation. And here we are ten thousand miles away from home fighting for the so-called freedom of the Vietnamese people when we have not even put our own house in order. And we force young black men and young white men to fight and kill in brutal solidarity. Yet when they come back home that can't hardly live on the same block together.

The judgment of God is upon us today. And we could go right down the line and see that something must be done—and something must be done quickly. We have alienated ourselves from other nations so we end up morally and politically isolated in the world. There is not a single major ally of the United States of America that would dare send a troop to Vietnam, and so the only friends that we have now are a few client-nations like Taiwan, Thailand, South Korea, and a few others.

This is where we are. "Mankind must put an end to war or war will put an end to mankind," and the best way to start is to put an end to war in Vietnam, because if it continues, we will inevitably come to the point of confronting China which could lead the whole world to nuclear annihilation.

It is no longer a choice, my friends, between violence and nonviolence. It is either nonviolence or nonexistence. And the alternative to disarmament, the alternative to a greater suspension of nuclear tests, the alternative to strengthening the United Nations and thereby disarming the whole world, may well be a civilization plunged into the abyss of annihilation, and our earthly habitat would be transformed into an inferno that even the mind of Dante could not imagine.

This is why I felt the need of raising my voice against that war and working wherever I can to arouse the conscience of our nation on it. I remember so well when I first took a stand against the war in Vietnam. The critics took me on and they had their say in the most negative and sometimes most vicious way.

One day a newsman came to me and said, "Dr. King, don't you think you're going to have to stop, now, opposing the war and move more in line with the administration's policy? As I understand it, it has hurt the budget of your organization, and people who once respected you have lost respect for you. Don't you feel that you've really got to change your position?" I looked at him and I had to say, "Sir, I'm sorry you don't know me. I'm not a consensus leader. I do not determine what is right and wrong by looking at the budget of the Southern Christian Leadership Conference. I've not taken a sort of Gallup Poll of the majority opinion." Ultimately a genuine leader is not a searcher for consensus, but a molder of consensus.

On some positions, cowardice asks the question, is it expedient? And then expedience comes along and asks the question, is it politic? Vanity asks the question, is it popular? Conscience asks the question, is it right?

There comes a time when one must take the position that is neither safe nor politic nor popular, but he must do it because conscience tells him it is right. I believe today that there is a need for all people of goodwill to come with a massive act of conscience and say in the words of the old Negro spiritual, "We ain't goin' study war no more." This is the challenge facing modern man.

Let me close by saying that we have difficult days ahead in the struggle for justice and peace, but I will not yield to a politic of despair. I'm going to maintain hope as we come to Washington in this campaign. The cards are stacked against us. This time we will really confront a Goliath. God grant that we will be that David of truth set out against the Goliath of injustice, the Goliath of neglect, the Goliath of refusing to deal with the problems, and go on with the determination to make America the truly great America that it is called to be.

I say to you that our goal is freedom, and I believe we are going to get there because however much she strays away from it, the goal of America is freedom. Abused and scorned though we may be as a people, our destiny is tied up in the destiny of America.

Before the Pilgrim fathers landed at Plymouth, we were here. Before Jefferson etched across the pages of history the majestic words of the Declaration of Independence, we were here. Before the beautiful words of the "Star-Spangled Banner" were written, we were here.

For more than two centuries our forebears labored here without wages. They made cotton king, and they built the homes of their masters in the midst of the most humiliating and oppressive conditions. And yet out of a bottomless vitality they continued to grow and develop. If the inexpressible cruelties of slavery couldn't stop us, the opposition that we now face will surely fail.

We're going to win our freedom because both the sacred heritage of our nation and the eternal will of the almighty God are embodied in our echoing demands. And so, however dark it is, however deep the angry feelings are, and however violent explosions are, I can still sing "We Shall Overcome."

We shall overcome because the arc of the moral universe is long, but it bends toward justice.

We shall overcome because Carlyle is right—"No lie can live forever."

We shall overcome because William Cullen Bryant is right—"Truth, crushed to earth, will rise again."

We shall overcome because James Russell Lowell is right—as we were singing earlier today,

> Truth forever on the scaffold,
> Wrong forever on the throne.
> Yet that scaffold sways the future.
> And behind the dim unknown stands God,
> Within the shadow keeping watch above his own.

With this faith we will be able to hew out of the mountain of despair the stone of hope. With this faith we will be able to transform the jangling discords of our nation into a beautiful symphony of brotherhood.

Thank God for John, who centuries ago out on a lonely, obscure island called Patmos caught vision of a new Jerusalem descending out of heaven from God, who heard a voice saying, "Behold, I make all things new; former things are passed away."

God grant that we will be participants in this newness and this magnificent development. If we will but do it, we will bring about a new day of justice and brotherhood and peace. And that day the morning stars will sing together and the sons of God will shout for joy. God bless you.

DISCUSSION QUESTIONS

1. *The social and political organizations described in this section likely differ in substantial ways from those with which most readers are familiar. What are*

some of the most important similarities and divergences you perceive between the communities depicted in these readings and your own?

2. *What are the foundations of authority, power, legitimacy, and influence described in these readings?*

3. *How have industrialization, urbanization, and technology complicated social and political relations?*

4. *What are the defining characteristics, values, and assumptions of your organization or institution?*

5. *Is an overview of the history of your organization or institution part of the orientation program for new personnel? Should it be?*

EMULATING HEROES

Emulation is the very nerve of human society.

—WILLIAM JAMES,
Talks to Teachers on Psychology, chap. 7

Heroes are among the most revealing features of any culture, be it national or local, public or private: conspicuous models whose exploits are discussed in contexts ranging from informal lunchroom conversations to official histories. These figures may be the stuff of legend (John Henry, the prodigious steel driver of American folklore, for instance), or of fact grown into myth (England's Elizabeth I, whose powerful rhetoric can be found in "Artists of Delay" and "Negotiating World and Self"). Sometimes heroes are known to millions, sometimes to only a few, yet their deeds make up an elemental part of any group's larger story, and their examples are held up in all sorts of situations to awaken a desire in others to equal or perhaps excel their accomplishments.

Naturally mimetic creatures, we emulate models presented to us in life and art and tend likewise to be flattered and gratified when others copy us. Emulation is customarily regarded as an elemental link in the chain of social relations, intimately bound up with imitation and ambition. Yet slavish imitation can limit potential, while a figure of influence, like the hypnotist Svengali in George du Maurier's novel *Trilby* (1894), may exert excessive control over the development of another. Philosophers from Aristotle to Adam Smith have regarded emulation as a motor of human action. For Aristotle, "emulation" is a virtuous emotion that finds its opposite in "envy." The first reading in this section, the story of Nathan and Mithridanes from Giovanni Boccaccio's *Decameron*, is catalyzed by envy, emulation's dark flip side. Mithridanes's obsession with outshining Nathan's reputation for generosity is so pernicious that he is prepared to go to criminal lengths to achieve his aim.

In the next reading Miguel de Cervantes offers the seriocomic portrait of Don Quijote, simultaneously elevated and ruined by his reading of chivalric tales, which have awakened in him a monomaniacal desire to emulate the knights-errant of old. We at once admire Quijote's seemingly inextinguishable idealism and laugh at the serial misadventures occasioned by his misunderstandings. The potential of reading to awaken a virtuous emulation has long been a preoccupation of theorists, educators, and political censors alike. And they have offered various theories to account for the effect that books have on the young. The neo-Confucianists of early modern Japan argued for the role of classic texts in cultivating "luminous virtue." Aristotle saw at least a part of poetry's value in its presentation of men as they might be as opposed to how they are, whereas Plato made the case for censorship by warning of the power of literary models to encourage imitation of the wrong kinds of behavior.

In book 3 of Plato's *Republic* Socrates acknowledges the power and beauty of Homer and other poets but also insists on "supervision," as Paul Shorey translates the Greek, to ensure a literary curriculum "suited to the ears of boys and men who are destined to be free and to be more afraid of slavery than of death." Citing the poetic representation (found in Homer and Aeschylus) of Achilles's claim that he would rather be a poor tenant farmer on earth than a king of heroes in Elysium, Socrates wonders if any man whose encounter with poetry leaves him with a belief "in the reality of the underworld and its terrors . . . will be fearless of death and in battle will prefer death to defeat and slavery?"

In his autobiographical *Confessions* the eighteenth-century French political philosopher Jean-Jacques Rousseau provides a dramatic testament to the power of reading as a stimulant to, in his case, republican virtue. Having exhausted his mother's collection of novels, Rousseau reports—here translated by J. M. Cohen—first encountering Plutarch's lives of Greek and Roman statesmen and commanders at the age of seven: "I became indeed that character whose life I was reading; the recital of his constancy or his daring deeds so carrying me away that my eyes sparkled and my voice rang."

Rousseau encountered in Plutarch the story of Mucius Scaevola, "the left-handed," a defender of the early Roman republic. Scaevola earned his nickname when, after being captured during a failed coup he thrust his hand into an open flame and glared at his enemy "with a steadfast and undaunted countenance" while his arm burned. "One day when I was reading the story of Scaevola over the table," Rousseau confesses, "I frightened them all by putting out my hand and grasping a chafing-dish in imitation of my hero." Rousseau's political inspiration, symbolized by his rash seizing of the hot chafing-dish on the dinner table, suggests the transports to which a reader might be brought by stories of virtuous action.

As this vignette suggests, emulation, like several of the concepts explored in this anthology, is double-edged. The third reading in this section, from Joseph Roth's *The Radetsky March*, offers the portrait of a soldier, the so-called "Hero of Solferino," who essentially refuses to be emulated and goes so far as to have his exploits expunged from the schoolbooks of the Austro-Hungarian Empire. Sadly, however, his shadow, hanging over his family's ambitions and fortunes, continues to dictate the fate of his intimidated grandson. Carolyn Heilbrun's "Once upon a Time" presents us with a rather different situation: someone whose encounter with imperfect, ultimately unsuitable models exposes the limits of emulation as a means of human growth and development. This recognition leads Heilbrun to define herself against her models in a process of healthy maturation. In Jorge Luis Borges's story "The Dead Man," we encounter a story that shares some features with that of Nathan and Mithridanes but presents us with the deadly consequences of unsophisticated, almost instinctive emulation coupled with a failure to understand what it is that we desire. Finally, in Janet Flanner's meditation on the legacy of the dancer Isadora Duncan we encounter the phenomenon of an artist who animated an entire cultural movement by inspiring "people who had never been inspired in their lives before" and attracting untold numbers of conscious and unconscious imitators.

RECOMMENDED READING

Ambrose Bierce, "One Kind of Officer," from *Tales of Soldiers and Civilians* (1891)
Charles Dickens, *Great Expectations* (1860)
Antonia Fraser, *The Warrior Queens* (1989)
Patricia Highsmith, *The Talented Mr. Ripley* (1955)
Plutarch, *Julius Caesar* (first century CE)

Giovanni Boccaccio
(1313–1375)

BORN IN OR near Florence, Italy, Giovanni Boccaccio resisted the pressures his father placed on him to pursue a career in banking or the law. After moving to Naples, Boccaccio, turning instead to the study of literature, found encouragement and happiness in the Neapolitan court, then a flourishing center of humanism. Boccaccio's Italian contemporaries, including Dante and Petrarch, were engaged in no less a project than attempting to revive Italian arts and letters and to restore national culture to its erstwhile greatness. Petrarch served as a mentor to Boccaccio and urged him to begin writing in Latin as well as in the Italian vernacular. Boccaccio produced reference works and supported a project to translate Homer's epics into Latin. It was another influence altogether, however, that spurred him to write his masterpiece, the *Decameron*. The Black Death, which killed one third of the population of Europe from 1348 to 1351, provides the catastrophic backdrop to the work. The book has a "frame narrative," which means that its individual stories are situated within a particular dramatic situation: ten young women and men escape from Florence for ten days and exchange stories as the plague ravages the world around them. The hundred tales reveal the influence of oral and folk traditions; different cultures and religions are represented, an indication of the influence of global trade. The tale included here, the third story of the tenth and final day of the young people's sojourn, is told by Philostrato about a man named Nathan, famed through Cathay (or China) for his liberality, and his rival Mithridanes, whose desire to excel Nathan in generosity turns, in his own words, to "despicable envy." (The following selection is translated by Guido Waldman.)

Nathan and Mithridanes

from *Decameron* (ca. 1348–49)

If we may rely on the evidence of certain Genoese and others who have visited those parts, it is an undoubted fact that in Cathay there was once upon a time a man of noble stock and incomparable wealth called Nathan. His residence stood by a road almost inevitably travelled by anyone going from the West to the Orient or returning to the West. He was of a generous, lavish disposition and was anxious that nobody should be in any doubt about this, so he had himself built in the shortest possible time one of the most beautiful, vast, and luxurious palaces ever seen—there being no shortage of skilled craftsmen in the area—and had it sumptuously furnished with everything required for the proper entertainment of gentlemen. He maintained an ample household in excellent array and would offer hospitality and entertainment and the most festive of welcomes to whoever passed his way; and so assiduously did he pursue this commendable practice that he acquired a reputation not merely in the East but throughout most of the West. He reached a ripe old age, never wearying in his lavish hospitality, and eventually his fame reached the ears of a young man called Mithridanes.

Now Mithridanes, who lived no great distance away, recognized that he was quite as wealthy as Nathan and became jealous of Nathan's reputation and sheer goodness; he determined to obliterate or at any rate overshadow such munificence by outdoing it. He built himself a palace similar to Nathan's and stopped at nothing in the generosity he lavished upon those who came his way. Assuredly he achieved a great reputation in no time at all.

Now one day, as the young man happened to be on his own in his palace courtyard, a little old woman came in through one of the gates and asked for alms and received them. Then she returned to him, coming through the second gate, and received more alms. So she proceeded until she had entered by twelve of the gates. When she came back to him through the thirteenth gate, Mithridanes said to her: 'How importunate you are, my good woman!' though he still gave her alms.

On hearing this, the little old woman exclaimed: 'Ah for Nathan, such a wonderfully generous man *he* is! His palace, like this one, has thirty-two gates, and I went in through each one and asked him for alms; he never took note of me, or gave any sign of doing so, and always made me a gift. Here I come in by only thirteen of the gates when I'm picked on and taken to task.' This said, she left and never returned.

These words of the old woman sent Mithridanes into a towering rage: this endorsement of Nathan's reputation was, he felt, a slight upon his own. 'Oh what a curse this is!' said he. 'How am I ever to equal Nathan, let alone achieve my aim to surpass him in the greatest acts of generosity when even in the most trifling ones he leaves me miles behind? The fact is it's all a waste of effort if I don't remove him from this earth. And as old age is not carrying him off, I'll simply have to see to it myself with my own hands.'

Stung to this decision, he leapt up and, keeping his proposal to himself, took horse with but a small escort and reached Nathan's domain after a three-days' journey. He instructed his company to pretend that they were not associated with him and did not know him; they were to find their own accommodation and await his further orders. It was towards sundown that he had arrived and was left on his own; not far from the gorgeous palace he came across Nathan all by himself; he was simply dressed and out for a stroll, and Mithridanes did not recognize him. 'Can you tell me', he asked him, 'where Nathan lives?'

'My boy, there's not a man in these parts who is better able to tell you this than I am', said Nathan good-humouredly. 'If you like, I'll show you the way.'

The young man said there was nothing he would like better but he would prefer, if possible, not to be seen or recognized by Nathan. 'Leave it to me', said Nathan, 'if that's what you would like.'

So Mithridanes dismounted and accompanied Nathan to his fine palace, Nathan making the most agreeable conversation on the way. Once arrived, Nathan ordered one of his attendants to take charge of the young man's mount, and as he did so he had a word in his ear, telling him, 'Don't you or anyone else in my household tell the young man that I am Nathan.' And this was done. They entered the palace and he brought Mithridanes into a splendid room where he would be seen by no one but those he had placed at his service. He paid him every attention and himself kept him company.

While Mithridanes treated him with filial respect as they consorted together, he did make bold to ask him who he was. 'I'm a humble servant of Nathan', the other replied. 'I'm an old man now but I've been with him since I was a boy, and never received any preferment from him. So although the whole world speaks highly of him, I personally cannot bring myself to do so.'

These words encouraged Mithridanes in the hope of being able to give effect to his evil purpose with somewhat greater deliberation and security. Nathan asked him most politely who he was and what brought him here; he offered to be of service to him in any way he might with his help and advice. Mithridanes hesitated at first to reply, but eventually decided to take him into his confidence; after beating about the bush for a good while he asked him to keep his secret, and to give him the benefit of his aid and counsel; then he told him all about himself and what motive and purpose it was that had brought him here.

What the young man told him of his brutal resolution left the older man profoundly shaken, but after only the shortest pause he answered steadfastly: 'Your father possessed true nobility and you wish to live up to his standards, Mithridanes, for you have set yourself a lofty goal, to treat everyone with generosity. As for the jealousy you feel towards Nathan and his qualities, I find it highly praiseworthy; if there were only more jealousy of this sort, the world would cease to be so beggarly a place and would change for the better in no time. The plan you have divulged to me will of course be kept secret; I can't offer you much help towards its fulfillment, but I have some useful advice: here it is. You see that little copse over there, about half a mile off: Nathan goes there practically every morning all by himself for a good leisurely stroll. What can be easier for you than to meet him there and dispose of him as you will? If you kill him, you should leave the wood by the path you can see there to the left, not by the one you took coming here, if you want to avoid any obstacle on your way home. It's a slightly more tangled path but it brings you out closer to home and is safer for you.'

Equipped with this information, after Nathan had left and his companions had joined him, Mithridanes surreptitiously advised them where they were to meet him on the morrow. Now when the new day dawned, Nathan, still being of the same mind in which he had offered his advice to Mithridanes, made his way alone to the copse where he was to die.

Mithridanes remained as resolute as ever. He got up, took his bow and his sword, the only weapons he had by him, mounted his horse, and made for the wood; from a distance he espied Nathan walking there all on his own. As he had decided, before attacking him, that he would like to have a good look at him and hear him speak, he galloped up to him, seized him by his turban, and cried: 'Old man, you're dead!'

To which Nathan's only response was: 'Well, I've deserved it.'

Once he had heard his voice and looked him in the face, Mithridanes recognized him for the very man who had welcomed him so kindly, offered him such easy companionship, and given him such trustworthy advice. His passion subsided, his anger turned to shame, and he threw down the sword he had drawn in order to run him through. He dismounted and fell, weeping, at Nathan's feet: 'Your kindness to me, dearest father, is too inescapably obvious', he cried; 'I can see just what tact you employed in coming here to yield me up your life, on which I had no just claim though I apprised you myself of my designs upon it. But God has shown greater concern than I have for where my duty lay and has opened my eyes just when I stood most in need of it, for they have been blinded by despicable envy. So I acknowledge that I'm fit to be punished for my wickedness, and all the more so in view of your readiness to satisfy my wish. Take your revenge on me, then, in whatever way you deem suitable.'

Nathan raised Mithridanes to his feet, then hugged and kissed him tenderly. 'No matter how you describe your enterprise, my son—call it evil or not as you will—there is no case for either seeking or granting pardon: you did not undertake it out of hatred but in order to be held in greater esteem. So have no fear of me; let me assure you that there is no man alive who loves you half as much as I do, for I appreciate the nobility of your spirit—baser mortals are concerned only to amass wealth while your wish is to spread it around. Don't be ashamed of your decision to kill me in order to enhance your fame: believe me, I am not surprised. How have the greatest emperors, the mightiest monarchs increased their dominions and thus their renown? By pursuing virtually one policy, and one alone: slaughter. They have killed men by the score, not merely one man as you aimed to do, and they have spread fire across the land, razed cities to the ground. So if you meant to murder only me in order to enhance your reputation, you have done nothing all that remarkable—it happens every day.'

Mithridanes did not seek to excuse his ill-conceived purpose but spoke highly of Nathan's well-meaning extenuation; in the course of their conversation he remarked on his astonishment at the way Nathan had fallen in with his design and given him advice as to its execution.

'Well', said Nathan, 'you're not to be surprised at my decision or at my advice: ever since I became master of my own will and determined to do precisely what it has been your ambition to achieve, nobody has ever come to my house and failed to be satisfied in that which he requested of me, to the limits of my power. You came, hankering for my life. When I heard you asking for it, I promptly decided to make you a gift of it so that you should not be the one and only person to leave here with your wish unfulfilled; to ensure that you obtained it, I gave you such advice as seemed to me serviceable if you were to have my life without forfeiting your own. I do urge you once more, then, take my life if you would like it, give yourself this satisfaction; I cannot think of a better way to expend it. I've had the use of it for eighty years, for my pleasure and comfort. In the normal course of nature I know that it will be left to me only a little while longer, as is the situation for other men and generally for all things. And it is far better, in my view, to give it away, as I have always given away and lavished what I treasure, rather than clinging on to it until Nature robs me of it against my will. A hundred years is a small enough gift to make; how much less is the gift of the six or eight years remaining to me? Do take it, therefore, if such is your pleasure; in all my years I've never yet come across anyone who has required it and I don't know when I ever shall if you don't take it, you who have sought it. Besides, even if I did find someone else who was after my life, I know that the longer I hold on to it, the smaller will be its value. So before it becomes any more worthless, take it, I beseech you.'

Mithridanes was utterly shamefaced. 'Your life is so precious, God forbid that I should even covet it, as I have been doing, let alone wrest it from you! Far from shortening the number of your years, I would gladly add some of mine to them if I could.'

'You'd like to add to mine?' put in Nathan at once. 'You'd be making me do to you what I've never done yet to a soul, taking something that belongs to you—I've never taken anything from anyone.'

'Oh but yes!' cried Mithridanes.

'Very well, then. Here's what you must do; you're to stay here in my house, young man that you are, and be called Nathan. I shall go to your house and will always be known as Mithridanes.'

'I shouldn't think twice about taking up your offer', said Mithridanes, 'if I had your capabilities; but I have not the smallest doubt that whatever I did would only diminish your reputation as Nathan, and it is not my intention to spoil for another that which I cannot make a success of myself. So I'll not accept it.'

After much agreeable discussion of this kind the two of them, at Nathan's invitation, returned to the palace, where the old man entertained the younger one with every attention for several days; he devoted all his shrewdness and wisdom to encouraging Mithridanes in his lofty ideal. When Mithridanes was ready to return home with his company, Nathan, having made it abundantly clear to him that he was never to be outdone in generosity, gave him leave to go.

Miguel de Cervantes
(1547–1616)

DON QUIJOTE IS one of literature's most popular creations; the work that bears his name is often referred to as the first instance of a new genre now so familiar: the novel. The first part was published in 1605, the second ten years later. It is a self-referential work that calls attention repeatedly to its own status as a fiction. Its inventiveness and energy have in the years since its publication influenced, implicitly or explicitly, numerous works including Francis Beaumont's *The Knight of the Burning Pestle*, Charlotte Lennox's *The Female Quixote*, Dostoyevsky's *The Idiot*, Flaubert's *Madame Bovary*, Salman Rushdie's *The Moor's Last Sigh*, a ballet by George Balanchine, an opera by Jules Massenet, and the Broadway musical *The Man of La Mancha*. Cervantes lived a varied life: student, soldier, prisoner, tax collector. Born near Madrid, where his father was a barber-surgeon, he studied with the humanist Juan López. He also lived in Rome. Cervantes survived the Battle of Lepanto (1571) and other military actions against the Ottomans, only to be captured by the Barbary pirates. He was imprisoned for five years in Algiers before being ransomed and returned in 1580 to Madrid, where he turned to literature and occasional government service, and served a stint in prison. Cervantes's forays into drama are largely forgotten, but his great novel endures, a testament to its turbulent historical moment. His portrait of a man obsessed with tales of chivalry, his idealism repeatedly buffeted by the real, asks us to think about what it means to model one's life on those of heroes. We admire this "quixotic" figure even as we see his aspirations repeatedly end in failure. The passage included here, recounting Don Quijote's attack on windmills he mistakes for giants, is one of the book's best-known examples of its protagonist's project "to fulfill what he'd read in his books." (The following selection is translated by Burton Raffel.)

Tilting at Windmills
from *Don Quijote* (1605)

Just then, they came upon thirty or forty windmills, which (as it happens) stand in the fields of Montiel, and as soon as Don Quijote saw them he said to his squire:

"Destiny guides our fortunes more favorably than we could have expected. Look there, Sancho Panza, my friend, and see those thirty or so wild giants, with whom I intend to do battle and to kill each and all of them, so with their stolen booty we can begin to enrich ourselves. This is noble, righteous warfare, for it is wonderfully useful to God to have such an evil race wiped from the face of the earth."

"What giants?" asked Sancho Panza.

"The ones you can see over there," answered his master, "with the huge arms, some of which are very nearly two leagues long."

"Now look, your grace," said Sancho, "what you see over there aren't giants, but windmills, and what seem to be arms are just their sails, that go around in the wind and turn the millstone."

"Obviously," replied Don Quijote, "you don't know much about adventures. Those are giants—and if you're frightened, take yourself away from here and say your prayers, while I go charging into savage and unequal combat with them."

Saying which, he spurred his horse, Rocinante, paying no attention to the shouts of Sancho Panza, his squire, warning him that without any question it was windmills and not giants he was going to attack. So utterly convinced was he they were giants, indeed, that he neither heard Sancho's cries nor noticed, close as he was, what they really were, but charged on, crying:

"Flee not, oh cowards and dastardly creatures, for he who attacks you is a knight alone and unaccompanied."

Just then the wind blew up a bit, and the great sails began to stir, which Don Quijote saw and cried out:

"Even should you shake more arms than the giant Briareus himself, you'll still have to deal with me."

As he said this, he entrusted himself with all his heart to his lady Dulcinea, imploring her to help and sustain him at such a critical moment, and then, with his shield held high and his spear braced in its socket, and Rocinante at a full gallop, he charged directly at the first windmill he came to, just as a sudden swift gust of wind sent its sail swinging hard around, smashing the spear to bits and sweeping up the knight and his horse, tumbling them all battered and bruised to the ground. Sancho Panza came rushing to his aid, as fast as his donkey could run, but when he got to his master, found him unable to move, such a blow had he been given by the falling horse.

"God help me!" said Sancho. "Didn't I tell your grace to be careful what you did, that these were just windmills, and anyone who could ignore that had to have windmills in his head?"

"Silence, Sancho, my friend," answered Don Quijote. "Even more than other things, war is subject to perpetual change. What's more, I think the truth is that the same Frestón the magician, who stole away my room and my books, transformed these giants into windmills, in order to deprive me of the glory of vanquishing them, so bitter is his hatred of me. But in the end, his evil tricks will have little power against my good sword."

"God's will be done," answered Sancho Panza.

Then, helping his master to his feet, he got him back up on Rocinante, whose shoulder was half dislocated. After which, discussing the adventure they'd just experienced, they followed the road toward Lápice Pass, for there, said Don Quijote, they couldn't fail to find adventures of all kinds, it being a well-traveled highway. But having lost his lance, he went along very sorrowfully, as he admitted to his squire, saying:

"I remember having read that a certain Spanish knight named Diego Pérez de Vargas, having lost his sword while fighting in a lost cause, pulled a thick bough, or a stem, off an oak tree, and did such things with it, that day, clubbing down so many Moors that ever afterwards they nicknamed him Machuca [Clubber], and indeed from that day on he and all his descendants bore the name Vargas y Machuca. I tell you this because, the first oak tree I come to, I plan to pull off a branch like that, one every bit as good as the huge stick I can see in my mind, and I propose to perform such deeds with it that you'll be thinking yourself blessed, having the opportunity to see them, and being a living witness to events that might otherwise be unbelievable."

"It's in God's hands," said Sancho. "I believe everything is exactly the way your grace says it is. But maybe you could sit a little straighter, because you seem to be leaning to one side, which must be because of the great fall you took."

"True," answered Don Quijote, "and if I don't say anything about the pain it's because knights errant are never supposed to complain about a wound, even if their guts are leaking through it."

"If that's how it's supposed to be," replied Sancho, "I've got nothing to say. But Lord knows I'd rather your grace told me, any time something hurts you. Me, I've got to groan, even if it's the smallest little pain, unless that rule about knights errant not complaining includes squires, too."

Don Quijote couldn't help laughing at his squire's simplicity, and cheerfully assured him he could certainly complain any time he felt like it, voluntarily or involuntarily, since in all his reading about knighthood and chivalry he'd never come across anything to the contrary. Sancho said he thought it was dinner-time. His master replied that, for the moment, he himself had no need of food, but Sancho should eat whenever he wanted to. Granted this permission, Sancho made himself as comfortable as he could while jogging along on his donkey and, taking out of his saddlebags what he had put in them, began eating as he rode, falling back a good bit behind his master, and from time to time tilting up his wineskin with a pleasure so intense that the fanciest barman in Málaga might have envied him. And as he rode along like this, gulping quietly away, none of the promises his master had made were on his mind, nor did he feel in the least troubled or afflicted—in fact, he was thoroughly relaxed about this adventure-hunting business, no matter how dangerous it was supposed to be.

In the end, they spent that night sleeping in a wood, and Don Quijote pulled a dry branch from one of the trees, to serve him, more or less, as a lance, fitting onto it the spearhead he'd taken off the broken one. Nor did Don Quijote sleep, that whole night long, meditating on his lady Dulcinea—in order to fulfill what he'd read in his books, namely, that knights always spent long nights out in the woods and other uninhabited places, not sleeping, but happily mulling over memories of their ladies.

Joseph Roth
(1894–1939)

JOSEPH ROTH, BORN in 1894 in Galicia—now in Russia but at the time part of the Austro-Hungarian Empire—served in the army during World War I and worked as a journalist in addition to writing novels. Along with Robert Musil and Stefan Zweig, Roth was one of the great chroniclers of the fall of the old order in Europe after the Great War. His journalism is masterful and sensitive in its observations on interwar Europe. Fleeing Hitler's Berlin in 1933, Roth ended up in Paris, where as a refugee he continued to resist fascism and where he died of tuberculosis on the eve of World War II. Roth's masterpiece, *The Radetsky March* (1932), tells the story of three generations of the Trotta family during the dissolution of the Habsburg Empire: a Slovenian infantry lieutenant who becomes a hero after saving the life of the emperor at the Battle of Solferino and thereafter feels "condemned" by the unaccustomed glow of imperial favor "to wear another man's boots for the rest of life"; his son, prevented by his father from joining the army, who has a career as a civil servant; and his grandson, who grows up in the shadow of the Hero of Solferino's portrait and dreams of future glory. The novel turns on the cruel irony that the third-generation Trotta must carry the burden of a once-famous grandfather who has become obscure in all but the minds of his own family because of his insistence that his name be expunged from the history books, where it had been placed to inspire "the patriotic sentiments of each new generation." Like *Don Quijote*, Roth's novel invites us to consider the role of reading in the development of heroes and leaders. (The following selection is translated by Jaochim Neugroschel.)

The Hero of Solferino
from *The Radetsky March* (1932)

The Trottas were not an old family. Their founder's title had been con-
ferred on him after the battle of Solferino. He was a Slovene and chose
the name of his native village, Sipolje. Though fate elected him to perform an
outstanding deed, he himself saw to it that his memory became obscured to
posterity.

As infantry lieutenant, he was in command of a platoon at Solferino. The
fighting had been in progress for half an hour. He watched the white backs
of his men three paces in front of him. The front line was kneeling, the rear
standing. They were all cheerful and confident of victory. They had eaten their
bellyful and drunk brandy at the expense, and in honor, of their Emperor,
who had been in the field since the previous day. Here and there a man fell,
leaving a gap. Trotta leaped into every breach, firing the orphaned rifles of
the dead and wounded; he would close up the thinned-out line or extend it;
he cast his hyper-perceptive eye in many directions and strained after sounds
on all sides. Amid the clatter of rifles his quick ears picked up his captain's
intermittent, clear orders. His eyes pierced the grayish-blue haze in front of
the enemy's lines. He fired with sure aim and every shot went home. His men
sensed his glance, his hand, heard his voice and they felt safe.

The cease fire order trickled along the front line, which stretched farther
than the eye could see. Here and there a ramrod continued its clatter, a shot
rang out, belated and solitary. The haze between the lines lifted a little, suddenly giving way to the silvery midday warmth of an overcast, stormy sun.
Between the lieutenant and the backs of his platoon, the Emperor arrived,
escorted by two staff officers. He was in the act of raising to his eyes a field
glass handed to him by one of the escorts. Trotta was aware of the significance of the gesture. Even if it were assumed that the enemy was retreating,
the rear guard would nevertheless still be facing the Austrian army and the
raising of a field glass might be interpreted as a challenge: and the challenger
was the young Emperor. Trotta's heart pounded. Terror of the unthinkable,
boundless calamity which might annihilate him, his regiment, the army, the
State—the very world—sent burning shivers down his spine. The ancient
grudge of infantry subalterns against staff officers, with their ignorance of
the bitter realities of the front, inspired the action which stamped Trotta's
name indelibly on the history of his regiment. With both hands he gripped
the monarch's shoulders to push him down. No doubt the lieutenant's grasp
was too rough. The Emperor fell at once. The escorts flung themselves on the
falling man. That same instant a shot pierced Trotta's left shoulder—a shot
aimed at the Emperor's heart. Trotta fell as the Emperor rose. Everywhere

along the whole front the confused and irregular clatter of timid and newly awakened gunfire resounded. The Emperor, warned impatiently by his escort to leave the danger zone, nevertheless bent over the prostrate lieutenant to inquire, in accordance with Imperial duty, the name of the unconscious man who was unable to hear him. An army surgeon, an ambulance orderly, and two stretcher-bearers came running, backs bent, heads lowered. The staff officers pulled the Emperor down, then flung themselves on the ground beside him. "Here—the lieutenant," the Emperor called up to the breathless military surgeon.

Meanwhile the fire had died down again. Then, while a substitute cadet arrived to take over the platoon and announced in his shrill treble, "I'm taking over," while Francis Joseph and his escort rose, ambulance orderlies carefully strapped the lieutenant to a stretcher and all retired in the direction of regimental headquarters, where a snow-white tent spread over the nearest dressing station.

Trotta's left collarbone had been shattered. The ball lodged directly beneath the shoulderblade was removed under the eyes of the Supreme War Lord and amid the inhuman cries of the sufferer, whom pain had resuscitated.

A month later Trotta was healed. He returned to his South Hungarian garrison, promoted to Captain with the most distinguished of all decorations: the Order of Maria Theresa; the prefix "von" was added to his name. Thenceforward he was called Captain Joseph Trotta von Sipolje.

As if his old life had been replaced by a strange new one, manufactured to order in some workshop, he would recite to himself every night before going to sleep and every morning after waking his new rank and his new status; he would stand in front of the mirror to make certain that his face and appearance were unchanged. Despite the clumsy heartiness of comrades seeking to bridge this sudden gulf opened by incomprehensible fate, and his own vain attempt to encounter all men as unconstrainedly as before, the titled Captain seemed in danger of losing his equilibrium. He felt condemned to wear another man's boots for the rest of his life, walking on slippery ground and pursued by secret murmurings—the object of uncertain glances. His grandfather had been a smallholder; his father an assistant paymaster, then sergeant-major of the gendarmery on the southern frontiers of the monarchy. Having lost an eye in a tussle with Bosnian border smugglers, old Trotta was now pensioned off as an invalid and was caretaker in the park at Schloss Laxenburg. There he fed the swans, trimmed the hedges, and in spring protected the laburnum and later the elder from pilfering hands; on mild spring nights he would root out homeless pairs of lovers from the benevolent shelter of dark park benches.

The rank and status of a plain infantry lieutenant had been natural and fitting enough to the son of a noncommissioned officer. But his own father felt a sudden chasm between himself and the titled Captain who moved in the strange, almost unearthly radiance of Imperial favor as if through a golden cloud. The measured affection which the young man offered the old seemed to call for a different manner, a new relationship between father and son. It was five years since the Captain had seen his father. Nevertheless, every other week when, in accordance with established routine he took his turn on the rounds, he had written the old man a short letter by the dim gusty light of guardroom candles—after he had inspected the sentries, and entered the times for relieving them, and had scribbled his bold, forceful *None* under the heading UNUSUAL INCIDENTS, thus denying even the remotest possibility of such occurrences. His letters were all the same, like army orders or regulation forms. They were written on yellowish, fibrous foolscap sheets, beginning "Dear Father" to the left, spaced four digits off the top margin and two off the side. They all gave the same brief intimation that the writer was in very good health, continued in the hope that the recipient was likewise, ended in the same formula, inscribed with flourishes in a fresh paragraph to the right on an exact diagonal with the beginning "Your truly respectful and grateful son, Joseph Trotta, lieutenant."

But how, now that his new rank no longer required him to go on the old rounds, was he to adapt the official letter form, designed to meet every requirement of the military curriculum; how was he to insert among the standard phrases extraordinary descriptions of circumstances which had become extraordinary and which he himself had scarcely managed to grasp? On that quiet evening when for the first time since his recovery Captain Trotta sat down at the table, much notched and scarred by the idle knives of bored privates, he realized that he would never get beyond the opening "Dear Father." So he leaned his sterile pen against the inkwell; nipped off an end of guttering wick as though expecting some happy inspiration from the soft light of the candle, some suitable turn of phrase, and drifted by degrees into vague recollections of childhood, his village, his mother, his military school. He observed the immense shadows cast by small objects on the bare blue walls; the gently curved shimmering outline of his sword hanging from its hook by the door, its dark ribbon tucked into the hilt. He listened to the ceaseless rain outside drumming on leaded window frames; and rose at last, having decided to go and see his father the following week, after the customary audience of thanks with the Emperor for which he was to be detailed in the next few days.

A week later, he took a cab to see his father at Schloss Laxenburg, immediately following the audience which had lasted a bare ten minutes—ten minutes of Imperial graciousness, ten or twelve inquiries read from a dossier to which it had been his duty, standing stiffly at attention, to fire the reply, "Yes, Your Majesty."

He found the old gentleman in his shirtsleeves sitting in the kitchen of his quarters at a plain deal table covered with a dark-blue cloth edged in scarlet, a large cup of steaming, fragrant coffee in front of him. His notched cherry-wood stick swung by its crook from the edge of the table. A creased leather pouch stuffed with shag lay half open beside the long white clay pipe which was stained a brownish-yellow, the colour matching his father's bristling mustache. Captain Joseph Trotta von Sipolje stood among these frugal, modest comforts like some military god in his gleaming officer's sash and lacquered helmet which generated a kind of black sunshine of its own; in smooth, finely polished riding boots with glittering spurs, two rows of bright, almost blazing buttons on his coat; and blessed with the superterrestrial effulgence of the Order of Maria Theresa. Thus the son approached his father, who rose slowly, as if to foil the young man's magnificence by the slowness of his greeting. Captain Trotta kissed his father's hand, bent his head to receive the paternal kiss on cheek and forehead.

"Sit down," said the old man.

The Captain unbuckled a portion of his glory and sat down.

"Congratulations," said his father, using the ordinary harsh German of army Slavs. His consonants rumbled like thunderbolts, the final syllables laden with small weights. Only five years previously he had addressed his son in Slavonic dialect, although the young man had merely a smattering of it and never used a word of dialect himself. However, to address his son in his mother tongue on this day, his son who by the grace of fortune and the Emperor had been removed so far from him, would have struck the old man an impertinence not to be risked. The Captain, in the meantime, was watching his father's lips, ready to welcome the first sound of Slavonic like long-lost, familiar sounds of home.

"Congratulations, congratulations," the Sergeant-major thundered again. "It wasn't so easy to get on in my time. In my day Radetzky gave us a rough time."

It really is all over, thought the Captain. A leaden mound of military grades divided him from his father. "Do you still drink *rakija*, Father?" he asked, to acknowledge the last vestiges of kinship and intimacy. They drank, clinked glasses, drank again; after every glass his father groaned, gave himself up to endless coughing fits, turned purple, spat, then gradually subsided and began to tell anecdotes of his own days in active service, all with the unmistakable intention of belittling his son's career and merit. At last the Captain rose, kissed his father's hand, received his father's kiss on cheek and forehead, buckled on his sword, put on his shako, and left—aware that he had seen the last of his father in this life.

It was indeed the last time. He wrote the usual letters to the old man, but no other visible tie remained between them. Captain Trotta was severed from the long line of his Slavonic peasant forebears. With him fresh stock came into being. The years turned full circle, one by one, like smoothly running wheels. In accordance with his rank, Trotta married the no-longer-very-young niece of his colonel, daughter of a district commissioner. She brought him a dowry, and bore him a son. He settled down to enjoy the even tenor of a healthy military existence. He served in a small garrison, rode each morning into the barrack square, played chess with the notary in the same café every afternoon, grew into his rank, position, dignity, and reputation. He possessed an average talent for strategy, of which he demonstrated adequate proof at maneuvers each summer. He was a good husband, suspicious of women, was anything but a gambler, surly but just with subordinates, grimly opposed to all forms of deceit, unmanly conduct, cowardly safety, idle praise, ambitious self-seeking. He was as simple and blameless as his conduct sheet, and only the rage which occasionally shook him might have indicated to the observer of human nature that even in the soul of Captain Trotta black precipices loomed where storms sleep, and the unknown voices of nameless ancestors.

He was no great reader, Captain Trotta, and secretly pitied his growing son, who was beginning to have to cope with pencil, slate, sponge, ruler, and arithmetic; and for whom the inevitable reading books were lined up. As yet the Captain was convinced that one day his boy would be a soldier. It had never entered his mind that, from the battle of Solferino until the extinction of their line, a Trotta could follow any other calling. Had he had two, three, four sons (his wife was sickly, in constant need of medicines and doctors, and pregnancies were a hazard for her), they would all have become soldiers. That was how Captain Trotta felt in those days. There was talk of another war, and he was prepared for it. Indeed, it seemed almost certain to him that he was destined to die in battle. His unshaken simplicity accepted death in the field as the necessary consequence of a soldier's good name. Until one day when, out of idle curiosity, he picked up his son's first reader. The child was just five and had a tutor who, reflecting the mother's ambition, was acquainting him far too early with the exigencies of school. The Captain read the morning prayer in verse—it had been the same for decades and he remembered it well. He read "The Four Seasons," "The Fox and the Hare," "The King of Beasts." Then he turned to the table of contents, where he found the title of a piece which concerned him personally: "Francis Joseph I at the Battle of Solferino." As he read it he had to find a chair. "At the battle of Solferino," the paragraph began, "our King and Emperor, Francis Joseph encountered extreme danger." Trotta himself came into it—but how transfigured! "Our monarch," it said,

> had ventured so far forward among the enemy in the heat of battle that suddenly he found himself surrounded by enemy cavalry. At this moment of supreme danger a young lieutenant, mounted on a foaming chestnut horse, galloped into the fray; waving his sword. What blows he inflicted on the backs and heads of the enemy horsemen.

And further:

> An enemy lance pierced the young hero's breast, even though most of the enemy had been killed. With his drawn sword in his hand, our young and fearless monarch had no difficulty in fending off their ever-weakening attacks. On that occasion all the enemy cavalry were taken. The young lieutenant—his name was Joseph von Trotta—was awarded the highest distinction our fatherland can give its heroes, the Order of Maria Theresa.

Clutching the reader, Captain Trotta went to the little orchard behind his house where his wife spent her time on mild afternoons. With blanched lips and in a very low voice, he asked her if she was acquainted with the outrageous story. She nodded smiling. "It's a pack of lies," yelled the Captain, and he flung the book down onto the damp ground. "It's for children," his wife replied gently. He turned his back on her. Rage shook him like a hurricane shaking a feeble shrub. He hurried back indoors, his heart pounding. It was time for his game of chess. He took down his sword from its hook, buckled it on with a vicious jerk, and left the house with long, uncontrolled strides. Anyone who saw him might have thought he was out to slaughter five dozen enemies. Without uttering a word, he sat in the café, four deep furrows drawn across his pale, narrow forehead under the rough cropped hair. When he had lost his second game, he knocked the rattling chessmen aside with an angry gesture and said to his opponent, "I need your advice." Silence. "I've been grossly misrepresented," he began again, looking straight into the notary's flashing spectacles. But he realized that words were failing him. He should have brought the reader. With the odious object in his hands, things might have been easier to explain.

"What kind of misrepresentation?" asked the notary.

"I have never served with the cavalry," Captain Trotta felt himself constrained to begin, though he himself was aware that such a beginning was unintelligible. "And those unscrupulous compilers of school books have the temerity to say that I came galloping on a chestnut—'foaming chestnut horse,' to save the Emperor's life."

The notary understood. He knew the piece from his son's books. "Captain," he said, "you're taking it too seriously. Remember, it's for children." Trotta stared at him in horror. At that moment he felt the whole world was in league against him: the writers of school books, the notary, his wife, his son, his son's tutor. "All historical events," continued the notary, "are modified for consumption in schools. And quite right too. Children need examples which they can understand, which impress them. They can learn later what actually occurred."

"Bring me my bill," the Captain roared and rose. He went to the barracks, surprised Lieutenant Amerling (the officer on duty) with a young lady in the assistant paymaster's office, did the rounds himself, summoned the sergeant-major, ordered the NCO on duty to report for punishment, turned the company out for fatigue rifle drill in the square. The men obeyed him, frightened and confused. There were a few absentees in each platoon who could not be found. Captain Trotta ordered their names to be called. "All absentees for fatigue drill tomorrow," the Captain told the lieutenant. The privates panted at their drill. Ramrods clattered, rifle straps flew, sweaty palms slapped around the cool metal barrels, the heavy butts grounded on soft, dull clay.

"Load," ordered the Captain. The air vibrated with the rattle of blank cartridges. "Half an hour's salute drill," ordered the Captain. In ten minutes he changed his mind. "To prayers—kneel!" Appeased, he heard the thud of bony knees on clay, gravel, sand. He was Captain still and master of his company. He'd show these schoolbook hacks.

That night he avoided the mess, ate nothing, went to bed, and slept heavily without dreaming. Next day, at the officers' roll call, he rapped out his complaint to the colonel briefly and clearly. It was transmitted. And the martyrdom of Captain Joseph Trotta, Knight of Sipolje, champion of truth, began. Six weeks elapsed before the war office informed him that the complaint he submitted had been forwarded to the Ministry of Culture and Education; many more weeks passed before, one morning, the Minister's reply came. It read as follows:

Dear Sir,

In reply to your complaint with reference to reading lesson No. 15 in the authorized reading primer for Austrian elementary and secondary schools, composed in accordance with the Act of July 21, 1864, and edited by Professors Weidner and Srdehy, the Minister of Education most respectfully calls your attention to the fact that all pieces containing reading matter of historical significance, and in particular those which concern the august person of His Majesty the Emperor Francis Joseph, or indeed any other member of the Supreme Imperial House, have been adapted in accordance with the provisions of the edict of March 21, 1840, to suit the capacities of pupils for the best possible furtherance of all educational ends.

The said reading lesson No. 15 to which you draw the attention of the Ministry had already been submitted to the personal inspection of His Excellency the Minister of Culture, and by him approved as suitable for use in schools.

It is the heartfelt aim both of our higher- and lower-grade education authorities to set before the pupils of the Monarchy deeds of valor of all arms in such a fashion as may seem adaptable to the child's character and imagination, and to the patriotic sentiments of each new generation, without sacrificing veracity in the incidents described; yet at the same time eschewing a bare, dry style of narrative, devoid of imaginative stimulus or lacking incentive to patriotic feelings. In consequence of the above and other similar considerations, the undersigned most respectfully begs that you withdraw the complaint you have laid before us.

This document bore the signature of the Minister of Culture and Education. The colonel handed it to the Captain with a fatherly admonition to forget the whole thing.

Trotta received it without a word. A week later he had petitioned in the proper quarter for a private audience with His Majesty, and one morning three weeks later he stood in the Burg face to face with the Supreme War Lord.

"Look here, my dear Trotta," said the Emperor, "it's a bit awkward, but you know, neither of us shows up too badly in the story. Forget it."

"Your Majesty," replied the Captain, "it's a lie."

"A great many lies are told," agreed the Emperor.

"I can't forget it, Your Majesty," gulped out the Captain.

The Emperor moved closer to him. He was not much taller than Trotta. Their eyes met.

"My ministers," said Francis Joseph, "know what they're doing, and I am obliged to rely on them. Do you understand, my dear Captain Trotta?" Then, after a silence, "We'll do something about it, you'll see."

The audience was at an end.

Although his father was still alive, Trotta did not go to Laxenburg. He returned to his garrison and sent in his papers. They retired him as Major. He moved to his father-in-law's small estate in Bohemia. But Imperial favor had not deserted him: a few weeks later he received the information that the Emperor had seen fit to bestow on the son of the man who had saved his life five thousand gulden out of the privy purse, for purposes of study. At the same time Trotta was raised to the rank of Baron.

Baron Joseph Trotta von Sipolje received these Imperial favors with an ill grace as though they were insults. The campaign against Prussia was fought and lost without him. He nursed a grudge. His temples were touched with silver, his eyes grew dull, his gait slow, his hand heavy and his tongue ever more silent. Though he was a man in the prime of life, he seemed to be ageing rapidly. He had been driven out of his paradise of simple faith in Emperor and virtue, truth and righteousness, and, fettered in suffering silence, he may well have recognized that the stability of the world, the power of the law, and the splendour of royalty are maintained by guile. Following a casually uttered wish of the Emperor, reading lesson no. 15 was expunged from the schoolbooks of the monarchy. The name of Trotta was now known only to the unpublished annals of his regiment.

THE MAJOR CONTINUED to vegetate, obscure subject of ephemeral fame, like a fleeting shadow which is sent into the bright world of the living by some hidden agency.

He pottered on his father-in-law's estate with watering can and garden shears; and, like his father in the grounds of Laxenburg, the Baron trimmed hedges and mowed lawns. In spring he protected the laburnum and later the elder from pilfering hands. He replaced the rotten palings in the wooden fences with smoothly planed new ones, busied himself with household gear, harnessed his own bays, renewed rusty locks on gates and doors, wedged new, carefully whittled slats into sagging hinges, stayed out in the woods for days on end, shot small game and slept in the gamekeeper's hut. He tended poultry, crops, manure, fruit and espalier bloom, looked after groom and coachman. Stingy and suspicious, he made purchases fishing for coins with his fingertips in a skimpy leather purse which he thrust back quickly into his breast pocket. He became an insignificant Slavonic peasant. Occasionally the old rage would overpower him, shaking him as a hurricane shakes a feeble shrub. Then he would belabor the groom or the horse's flanks, bang doors into the locks which he himself had mended, threaten the farmhands with murder and destruction, push his dinner plate away with a growl and refuse to eat.

With him lived his sickly wife, in a separate room; his son, whom he saw only at mealtimes and whose school reports came twice a year for his inspection, evoking no word of praise or blame; his father-in-law, who gaily squandered his pension, had a weakness for young ladies, and stayed in town for weeks on end, though he was always in fear of his daughter's husband. A small, gnarled, Slavonic peasant, this Baron Trotta. He still wrote to his father twice a month, late at night by flickering candlelight on yellowish fibrous foolscap, the heading "Dear Father" to the left spaced four digits from the top and two from the side margin. He rarely received a reply. Indeed, the Baron sometimes thought of paying his father a visit. He had long been homesick for the caretaker, for the frugal, modest comforts, the stringy shag, the home-distilled *rakija*. But the son disliked spending as much as did his father, grandfather, great-grandfather before him. He now felt closer to the pensioner than on that day years ago when, in the fresh glamour of his nobility, he had sat beside him drinking *rakija* in the narrow blue kitchen.

He never mentioned his origins to his wife. He felt that embarrassed pride would come between the daughter of a fairly old family of civil servants and a Slavonic sergeant-major.

One day, on a fine March morning, as the Baron stumped over frozen clods to see his steward, a farmhand came to him with a letter from the authorities in charge of Schloss Laxenburg. The pensioner was dead, had quietly passed away at the age of eighty-one. All Trotta said was, "Go to the Baroness. Ask her to have my trunks packed. I am going to Vienna this evening."

He went on to his steward's house, inquired after the spring sowings and discussed the weather. He gave orders for three new plows to be bought, for the veterinary surgeon to come on Monday and for the midwife that same day to attend a pregnant farmgirl. As he left he remarked, "My father has died. I shall be away in Vienna for three days." And he went, raising a negligent finger.

His trunk was packed, the horses harnessed to the carriage; it was an hour's drive to the station. Having gulped down soup and meat, he said to his wife, "I can't manage any more. My father was a good man. You never met him." Was it an epitaph? Or a lamentation?

"You're to come with me," he told his startled son. His wife rose to pack the boy's things. While she busied herself in the rooms above, Trotta said, "Now you'll see your grandfather." His son trembled and lowered his eyes.

When they arrived, the Sergeant-Major had been laid out. The corpse, with three glittering medals on its chest, its great bristly mustache, lay on a bier in the old man's living room. It was guarded by church candles six feet high and attended by two fellow pensioners in dark-blue uniforms. An Ursuline nun prayed in the corner by the single window, its curtains drawn. The pensioners stood at attention as Trotta entered. He was wearing his major's uniform with the Order of Maria Theresa. He knelt; his son, too, fell to his knees at the feet of the dead man, the soles of those great boots thrusting themselves into his young face. For the first time in his life Baron Trotta felt a tiny sharp pain somewhere in the region of his heart. His small eyes remained dry. A sensation of awkward piousness made him mutter three paternosters. Then he got to his feet, bent over the dead man, kissed the great mustache, and waved his hand at the pensioners. "Come," he said to his son.

"Did you see him?" he asked outside.

"Yes," said the boy.

"He was only a sergeant-major in the gendarmery," his father said, "I saved the Emperor's life at the battle of Solferino. That was how we got the baronetcy."

The boy said nothing.

The pensioner was buried in the little cemetery at Laxenburg in the military section. Six comrades in dark-blue uniforms bore the coffin from chapel to grave. Major Trotta in full-dress uniform and wearing his shako kept one hand on his son's shoulder the whole time. The boy sobbed. The solemn noise of the military band, the priest's monotonous, dreary sing-song which became audible with every break in the music, the drifting incense—it all choked the boy with a pain he could not understand. And the gun salute fired over the grave by a demi-platoon made him tremble with its reverberating finality. Martial greetings sped the old man's soul on its way to heaven, vanished forever from the earth.

Father and son returned home. The Baron said nothing all the way back. Only as they were getting off the train and into the carriage which was waiting for them behind the station garden did the Major say "Never forget your grandfather."

The Baron resumed his daily routine. The years slipped by. The Sergeant-Major's was not the last corpse he had to see underground. He buried first his wife's father, then, a few years later, his wife who had died quickly, unobtrusively, and without farewells after severe inflammation of the lungs. He sent his son to a boarding school in Vienna, having decreed that he should never become a regular soldier. He remained alone on the estate in the spacious white house still quick with the breath of the dead. He spoke only to the gamekeeper and steward, the groom and coachman. His rages became less and less frequent, but the servants were always aware of the weight of his hard peasant fist, and his wrathful silence lay like a yoke across the necks of all his dependents. Apprehensive silence, like the calm before a storm, preceded him.

Twice a month his son's dutiful letters arrived; once a month he answered in a couple of short sentences on scrappy strips of paper, torn from the margins of the letters he had received. Once a year, on August 18th, the Emperor's birthday, he went in uniform to the nearest garrison town. Twice a year his son visited him, for the Christmas and summer vacations. Each Christmas Eve the boy received three hard silver gulden, for which he had to sign a receipt and which he was never allowed to take away with him. The gulden were put away that same night into a cashbox in the old man's safe. The school reports were kept with them. These spoke of his son's sturdy industry, his middling but always adequate capacities. The boy received not a single toy, no pocket money, not one book apart from the statutory schoolbooks. Yet he seemed to lack nothing. He possessed a neat, matter of fact, honest intelligence. His limited imagination made him wish for nothing more than to get through his school days as quickly as possible.

When he was eighteen, his father said on Christmas Eve, "This year you are not having three gulden. You can take nine out of the cashbox and sign a receipt for them. Be careful with women, most of them have got some sort of disease." And after a silence, "I've decided you're to go in for law. It will take you two years. There's no hurry for your military service. We can put that off until you're qualified."

The young man received his nine gulden as obediently as his father's wish. He seldom went after a woman, choosing with great caution, and he still had six gulden in hand when he came home for the summer vacation. He asked his father's permission to invite a friend. "All right," said the Major with some surprise. The friend arrived without much luggage but with a well-stocked paint box, which displeased the master of the house. "So he paints?" the old man asked.

"Yes, very well indeed," said his son Franz.

"Tell him not to mess up the house. He can paint the landscape."

The visitor did his painting out of doors but not of the landscape. He was painting a portrait, from memory, of the Baron. Every day at mealtimes he memorized his host's features. "What's he staring at me for?" Trotta asked. Both young men blushed and looked at the tablecloth.

Nevertheless, the portrait was finished, framed, and presented to the old man before they left. He examined it with deliberation, smiling, turning it around as if looking for details on the reverse which had been omitted from the front; he held it up to the window, then at arm's length; looked at himself in the mirror, compared himself with the portrait, and said at last, "Where shall we hang it?"

It was his first pleasure in many years. "You can lend your friend money if he needs it," he said quietly to Franz. "Be good to each other."

This likeness was the first and remained the only one ever taken of old Trotta. Later it hung in his son's study, and excited his grandson's imagination.

Meanwhile for the next few weeks it kept the Major in exceptionally good spirits. He hung it first on one wall then on another; examined with flattered satisfaction his bony jutting nose, pale, clean-shaven skin, tight-set lips, high cheekbones rising like hills under the small dark eyes; the low, heavily wrinkled forehead, thatched with a downward sloping crop of bristling close-cut hair. Only now was he getting to know his own face and sometimes he would hold silent conversation with it. It aroused in him thoughts he had never known and elusive memories—quickly fading shades of melancholy. He had needed this portrait to make him aware of his premature old age and his great solitude; they leapt out at him from the painted canvas, this old age and solitude. "Has it always been like this?" he asked himself.

Now and then he would make an unplanned visit to his wife's grave, look at the gray plinth and the chalky-white cross, read the dates of her birth and death and reckon that she had died too early, and admit that he could not recall her. He had forgotten, for instance, her hands. "Bitter tincture of iron" came to mind, a remedy she had taken for many years. Her face? If he shut his eyes he could still summon it, but it soon faded into the reddish twilight.

He grew gentle in the house and on the farm, sometimes stroked a horse or smiled at cows, treated himself to a glass of schnapps more often, and one day wrote a short letter to his son in addition to the usual monthly slip. People began to smile at him and he nodded pleasantly. Summer came, the vacation brought Franz and his painter friend. The old man took them to the inn in town, drank a few glasses of *slivovitz* and ordered an excellent meal for the young men.

His son passed his law finals, came home more often, began to look about the estate, and one day felt moved to give up law and manage it. The Major said, "It's too late for that. You're not cut out for farming and estate managing. You'll make a good civil servant. That's all." So the matter was settled. His son became a civil servant, assistant district commissioner in Austrian Silesia. Though the name of Trotta had vanished from authorized schoolbooks, it remained in the secret archives of higher bureaucrats, and those five thousand gulden allotted from the Emperor's privy purse assured Assistant District Commissioner Trotta of constant and benevolent supervision and protection from anonymous high places. His promotion was rapid. Two years before he was nominated Chief District Commissioner, the Major died.

He left a surprising will. Being assured, he wrote, that his son had no gift for agriculture, and since he hoped that the Trottas, indebted as they were to His Majesty the Emperor's continuing favor, might attain new honors and dignities and live more happily than he, the testator, had ever done, he had decided, in memory of his father, to bequeath the estate made over to him by his late lamented father-in-law, together with all its movable and immovable chattels, to the administrators of the pensioner's fund at Laxenburg. The sole proviso was that the authorities of this beneficiary should accord the testator a plain headstone in the cemetery where they had buried his late father and, if convenient, in close proximity to his grave. He, the testator, requested a very simple funeral. All residuary moneys, five thousand florins with interest accrued, deposited in the Ephrussi bank in Vienna, as also any unallotted gold, silver, or copper coins found in his house after decease, together with the ring, watch, and chain of his late wife to go to the testator's only son, Baron Franz Trotta von Sipolje.

A Viennese military band, a company of foot soldiers, a representative of the Knights of the Order of Maria Theresa, some officers sent by the South Hungarian regiment whose modest hero he had been, all pensioners able to march, two officials from the Court and Cabinet Chancellory, a staff officer from the Military and Privy Cabinet, and an NCO bearing the Order of Maria Theresa on a black tasseled cushion, formed the official cortège. His son, Franz, walked apart, thin, black, solitary. The band played the same march they had played at his grandfather's funeral. On this occasion the salvos over the grave were louder and their reverberations greater. His son shed no tears. No one wept for the dead man. Everything remained contained and ceremonious. No graveside speeches. In close proximity to the sergeant-major of the gendarmery lay Major Baron Trotta von Sipolje, the champion of truth. They gave him a plain, military headstone on which, in small black letters beneath name, rank, and regiment, was engraved the proud addition, HERO OF SOLFERINO.

Little remained of the dead man but this stone, a faded glory, and the portrait. Thus in spring does a peasant tread the furrow, and later, in summer the traces of his feet are obscured by the fullness of the wheat he has sown. That same week Royal Chief District Commissioner Trotta von Sipolje received a letter of condolence from His Majesty in which two separate mentions were made of the "ever unforgettable services" rendered by the blessed deceased.

·   ·   ·

The portrait hung in the District Commissioner's study facing the window, so high up that hair and forehead were almost obscured in the brown shadows under the old wooden ceiling. This fading shape and his grandfather's vanished fame filled the grandson with constant curiosity. Sometimes on quiet afternoons, the windows open, the dappled green shadow of chestnut trees from the park filling the room with the heady peace of summer afternoons when the District Commissioner was out of town on government business and old Jacques shuffled down distant stairs like a ghost in felt slippers collecting clothes to brush, boots to polish, ashtrays, silver candlesticks, and standard lamps—on such afternoons Carl Joseph would stand up on a chair to get a closer view of his grandfather's portrait. It disintegrated into deep shadows and bright highlights, into brush strokes and dots, the contours lost behind an intricate web of painted canvas, a hard iridescence of cracking oil paint. Carl Joseph climbed down from his chair. The reflections of leaves spotted his grandfather's brown coat. Brush strokes and dots rearranged themselves into the familiar yet unfathomable face. The eyes resumed their customary distant gaze, staring into the shadows of the ceiling. Every summer the grandson communed mutely with his grandfather. But the dead man revealed nothing. And the boy learned nothing. From year to year the portrait appeared to grow dimmer and more remote, as if the hero of Solferino were dying over again, slowly drawing his memory back into himself, as if the day must come when an empty canvas would stare down on his descendants from its black frame.

Carolyn G. Heilbrun
(1926–2003)

CAROLYN HEILBRUN, A graduate of Wellesley College and Columbia University, went on to become a literature professor at the latter, where she fought zealously against the discrimination she believed to be hampering women's progress at the university. In 1957, she published a landmark essay, "The Character of Hamlet's Mother," in which she argued for renewed attention to the neglected figure of Gertrude in Shakespeare's tragedy. Increasingly, her work focused on women's contributions to literature and culture, and she became the first director of Columbia's Institute for Research on Women and Gender (now Women, Gender, and Sexuality), which promotes feminist scholarship. Heilbrun published numerous articles and books and eventually became the president of the Modern Language Association. In 1995, she published a biography of *Ms.* magazine founder Gloria Steinem. Heilbrun was also a prolific writer of mysteries, published under the name Amanda Cross. Revered by some colleagues, mistrusted by others, she was never afraid to speak her mind: "When I spoke up for women's issues," she explained in a 1992 interview in the *New York Times Magazine*, "I was made to feel unwelcome in my own department, kept off crucial committees, ridiculed, ignored. . . . . In life, as in fiction, women who speak out usually end up punished or dead." Heilbrun's memoir *When Men Were the Only Models I Had* chronicles the difficulties of carving out a career in the absence of female models: "So guys it had to be. They filled my imagination; they occupied the room in my mind devoted to hope, ambition, emulation." The three literary luminaries Heilbrun admired—Clifton Fadiman, Jacques Barzun, and Lionel Trilling—were nevertheless fundamentally incomplete models, and she offers a rich concept of heroes as something not merely to emulate but also "to struggle against."

Once upon a Time

from *When Men Were the Only Models I Had* (2001)

> *The critic of the opposite sex will be*
> *genuinely puzzled and surprised by an attempt to*
> *alter the current scale of values, and will see in it not merely*
> *a difference of view, but a view that is weak, or trivial,*
> *or sentimental, because it differs from their own.*
> VIRGINIA WOOLF, *"Women and Fiction"*

ONCE UPON A TIME there were three men who exemplified, without knowing it, my ideal life. All of them became famous as writers, influential thinkers, and public figures. Their names are Clifton Fadiman, Lionel Trilling, and Jacques Barzun. They met in college, they remained aware of one another—as friends or, if less than friends, companions and fellow crusaders on behalf of similar ideals. What I recount here is only part of their story, a small part of their significance, their accomplishments. They, however, were a large part of my story, and the place they occupied in my life is what I have set out to convey here. Although one of them never knew of my existence, the second ignored it, and the third treated me with formal kindness, without them I would have had no concrete model in my youth of what I wanted to become.

Indeed, until I was past forty they remained my guides. It is hardly too much to say they were my motivation, my inspiration, my fantasy. Theirs was the universe in which I wished to have my being. When I first encountered them, however, the fact that no woman could have her being in the world where they prevailed evaded my consciousness; the impossibility of that particular dream did not present itself to me as an inexorable fact. Like women before me, I hoped against all evidence that I, an exception, might join that blessed circle. Had it not been for the women's movement of the twentieth century's last three decades, I would have had to choose, as women in academia and elsewhere had long chosen, between my inevitable exclusion from this brilliant, beckoning world or my half-life as an "exceptional" woman— never a full member of these men's fellowship but clinging to the edges of it.

Fadiman, Trilling, and Barzun were, when it came to women, men of their time, at least in their published sentiments. All three of them witnessed the early years of the women's movement, although Trilling died soon after the explosive beginnings of modern feminism. Yet neither Barzun, who has lived into the twenty-first century, nor Fadiman, who missed that turning point by only half a year, took serious notice of women's new place in their universe. The question for me now, in the light of the failure of even these two to change profoundly, is why did I revere only men then, and why those three? Why do I remember my veneration of them as the single most compelling passion of my youth?

Lovers are supposed to serve as milestones, as markers on the road to maturity or old age; if not lovers, then jobs, children, marriage, adventures of one kind or another. But for me Fadiman, Trilling, Barzun are the markers; they were the significant events. Oddly, even when I finally understood that I could never be a colleague in their eyes, my admiration for them, my devotion to them, if qualified, did not abate. Even today, I remember my preoccupation with their world, or what I glimpsed of it, exactly as if these three men had been a palpable part of my life rather than actors in my dream—a dream not of romance but of vocation.

"HOW DO YOU feel writing about guys?" a friend asked me when I told her about this book. It was a fair question. At the start of my professional life I had written about guys—Edward, Richard, and David Garnett, as well as Christopher Isherwood. True, a woman, Constance Garnett, had been included in my Garnett family history, but through no venture of mine: she simply belonged there, with her group of guys. But thereafter I wrote only of women, their writings, their lives, their status in the world, earlier and now.

Yet, before that time, of course I wrote about guys, and thought about guys, and read as a guy: what else was possible? If I wanted a prototype, an example of the sort of career and accomplishment I sought, where was there to look except at men? True, at Columbia where I studied and taught, as at most other universities, there were a few women professors, but they tended toward type. As we callow students saw it then, they were unmarried, hence unloved—that they might have loved women did not so much as occur to us—and while that fact alone did not disturb me, who had few illusions even then about marriage as the only suitable destiny for women, the sense of their incompleteness was palpable. If we assumed that their apparent unfulfillment arose from their single state, we had no other terms in which to describe what we observed. Now, I can perceive that the wound those women displayed did indeed have to do with deprivation of their womanhood, but not sexually or maternally. The deprivation arose from their having, of necessity, determined not to act or write as women. They had become what I would later call honorary men; they presented themselves and their ideas in male attire. One did not choose them as models; the aura of deficiency was too tangible.

So guys it had to be. They filled my imagination; they occupied all the room in my mind devoted to hope, ambition, emulation. And, what is more, they continued to hold sway over me even after feminism had rescued me both from the hope of becoming one of the boys and from the realization of that role's high cost. When it had become possible to be a woman among women, to have women friends and colleagues, to speak, teach, read, and write as women, their magic still prevailed.

Having placed these men and their accomplishments as the exemplars of my aspirations, I was asked if I ever desired them sexually, ever had fantasies about them in that role. Strangely enough, I never did, either at first encountering them, or in the years since. Those casting a disbelieving eye at this response have asked why not? There are a number of possible reasons. I never at any time in my life was attracted to older men; every man for whom I felt desire was close to my own age; these men were over twenty years my senior. Also, if the longing for a nurturing father explains a woman's passion for older men, having had a supportive father all my early life perhaps enabled me to escape this route toward infatuation. Another possible reason: I was married, and not, as they say, on the hunt. Not long after beginning my graduate studies, I had a child and, soon after, two more. A life as busy as mine hardly left time for sex, let alone sexual fantasies. (I have since learned that this configuration of time and sex under those circumstances is far from universally true; nonetheless, it was true for me.) The main reason, however, is simplest of all: I needed them as exemplars, not as lovers. Freud had written that men experience ambition and the erotic as separate desires; women experience only erotic desire. For me, in this case (*pace* Freud), it was with those men only the ambitious desire that operated.

But surely I felt affection for them, however expressed or experienced? Not even that. They were beyond affection from such as me: admiration was what they deserved and what they got. What made their gift to me greater, I now believe, than any with which they endowed their male followers was the fact that I knew I could not become like them. When the women's movement finally freed me from the choice between playing at being male or remaining outside the boundaries of male accomplishment, I combined what I had learned from them with the pleasure of thinking and writing as a woman. The male acolytes merely imitated their models and, I suspect, inevitably fell short. For my three guys were not readily imitated, and in the nick of time I was enabled to understand this and not to try to become them, in however pale or awkward a replication.

I HAD WANTED to be a doctor for most of my childhood; specifically, I wanted to be like Banting and discover the equivalent of insulin. At college, an aptitude test revealed my capacities for the law. But women were not welcome in either of these spheres in the 1940s, and it was literature—reading—that occupied and restored me, though it took me a while to admit this, despite the fact that I had been enthralled by books as long as I could remember. (I'm always amazed today to discover that perfectly bright children, even those with highly educated parents, have not yet learned to read fluently even by the age of eight. Probably the regime in schools has changed, or perhaps television, computers, video games render reading inessential.) For me, as for so many then, there was reading and there was life, and they neither competed with nor noticeably affected one another. Fadiman, in *Reading I've Liked*, would insist that "commuters' wives—there are tens of thousands of them—were not really in any active sense doing any reading at all. They were taking their daily novel in a numbed or somnambulistic state. They were using books not for purposes of entertainment, but as an anodyne, a time-killer, a life-killer."

I shall consider this condemnation later, in the light of Fadiman's prevailing and consistent scorn for women in his literary world, but for now let me say that, whether or not this kind of reading is true of "commuters' wives," it was not true of me. Nor do I think it is true of many child readers: we read, I think, to peek outside the boundaries of our world, eventually to step outside those boundaries, but not by means of fantasy or mainly for escape. Rather, I think, with the intentions of explorers, psychologists, and archaeologists, children seek not anodynes but more examples of a moral language than a child's life can give them. I fear that the moral ideas—in the largest sense of moral—that children today receive from videos, television, and computer games are hardly concerned with truth, trust, courtesy, or personal courage in any subtle sense. But, being old, I try to refuse the temptation to damn the occupations of youth—a temptation neither Trilling nor Fadiman resisted; Barzun has contented himself with damning most of the twentieth century and trying to rescue the English language and the ideals of art from decimation.

And so, like many young people who "live in books," I got a job in publishing, about which the less said the better, although publishing in those days had not yet become the property of corporations mainly producing almost anything but books. Then one day in 1949 my husband and I were in Chicago; having already visited the site where he had attended midshipman's school in World War II, we went to look at the University of Chicago. We sat on the grass in the "midway" between the Gothic buildings, and I became convinced that I must go back to school and study literature. We lived in New York, which meant, at least to me in those days, Columbia. I had no intention of continuing for a Ph.D. I would get an M.A. I was merely putting my toe in.

In that first year at Columbia, I attended many lectures, though not the ones I signed up for; no notice was taken of any student apart from his or her appearance in a seminar. My seminar was in Modern Studies, the term then encompassing the years from 1890 to 1950—a rough demarcation. The professor was William York Tyndall, a man frightened of women and devoted to Joyce with a passion equaled only by those dedicated to Freud. Tyndall barely tolerated women students or women writers: recently, I was amused to come across this recollection in a book by Herbert Marder, who was also a graduate student of his:

> [I] decided to work on Virginia Woolf, "women and fiction"—it was then an uncluttered field, without the sludge that encrusted Yeats and Eliot. My adviser at Columbia [Tyndall] said: "Not much mileage in feminism these days. Virginia Woolf was not a political animal. She was a lady, you know—disliked workingmen, Negroes, and Jews."
>
> "There are subversive, radical ideas all over her books," I said.
>
> He puffed decisively on his unlit pipe. "E. M. Forster says she was a snob and proud of it—true Brit. Could generate some heat. I think you should go ahead." So it was settled.

Tyndall, however, was not as adamant on the question of women as was Trilling. Later, I would learn that he and Trilling had been classmates at Columbia, and that Tyndall deeply resented Trilling's greater fame. In Tyndall's seminar I joined in the general fascination with Joyce, and in fact did admire some of his stories, and the first half, together with the Ithaca chapter, of *Ulysses*. I played at analyzing Joyce as others play at bridge or chess. Occasionally I wondered why we worked so hard to find out what Joyce had put into his book on purpose to puzzle us, but I hardly mentioned this doubt, even to myself.

The only part of the studies for my master's degree that enthralled me and that would, as a direct result, commit me to doctoral studies was Lionel Trilling's lectures. He spoke as a prophet—no less dramatic a word will suffice. He made acceptable what we believed, but had thought improper to believe. When, for example, he described how Hyacinth in Henry James's *Princess Casamassima* learned the profound pleasure to be taken in large rooms with high ceilings—a pleasure that those who were both poor and revolutionary had told him contained no virtue—we too suddenly admitted the attraction of space and elegance, if not luxury. Hyacinth kills himself because of his inability to resolve the terrible dilemma that had also tortured me and, I suspect, many others: that art was worth experiencing, that the greatest art did not come from the purest minds, that the rich exploited the poor but at the same time made art possible. If all this was too much for Hyacinth, it was also profoundly distressing to me.

I had grown up liberal in my inclinations despite my politically conservative parents. Hyacinth, lonely like me, like me split in his deepest loyalties, revealed to me, through Trilling's analysis, that the essence of literature was in the tensions of the thinking life. Trilling himself embodied tension, though I could not, in those early days, have so identified the energy that flowed from him. It was only twenty-five years after his death that I would learn of what pulled him, first this way, then that, and of the impossibility of reconciling those conflicts. I remember him saying—or perhaps I read it as I began to read everything he had published—how Freud knew that we paid for everything life gave us with more than equal coin. Long before I came to distrust some of Trilling's obiter dicta, I had learned to distrust Freud, because of his views of women and because of the Freudian psychoanalysts I had come to know. Yet, even distrusting Freud, I agreed with him that tragedy is what most marks us if we are thinkers—a central concept of Trilling's worldview.

Never once in anything he said did Trilling admit women to the fellowship of learning. Men were what it was all about, men struggling for some assurance—these were the actors in Trilling's drama. Trilling readily published comments like this:

> Truth, we feel, must *somewhere* be embodied in man. Ever since the nineteenth century, we have been fixing on one kind of person or another, one group of people or another, to satisfy our yearning—the peasant and the child have served our purpose; so has woman; so has the worker; for the English, there has been a special value in Italians and Arabs. (*Gathering of Fugitives*, Trilling's emphasis)

Even if Trilling was using "man" to mean humankind, it is still noticeable that on his list of individual subcategories of human beings (exotics, naifs, all of them), we find "woman"—exotic, naive, other—always an object, never the subject.

Usually when Trilling said "we" he meant men like himself, or younger men learning from him. Some years later, Trilling would take a lot of flak for his use of "we," his assumption that anyone reading him was part of his "we." I never was part of "we," and even in my earliest times of infatuation I knew it to be an impossibility. Later, wistfully, I wondered, though not with much hope, if I could somehow persuade Trilling to include women in his intellectual community. I think I always sensed that this was as probable as persuading Orthodox Jews or Muslims to admit women on an equal basis to their religious life.

It astonishes me now to recognize that almost from the beginning I wanted to confront him, to force him to recognize that I, a woman, was, at the least, not prevented from embodying truth, even if I could not embody it for him. It is clear to me now, and was clear then, that when he spoke of woman or others as embodying truth, it was to deny the possibility of their doing so; his only question was where should "man" look for confirmation. I never confronted him, but it was because of the power he had seized over me, and because of the quality of mind and the persuasiveness he demonstrated in his lectures, that I decided to go on for the doctorate. Perhaps, I must have thought—indeed, I remember thinking—one day he will confirm my right to be a part of the struggle he embodied, of the yearning he expressed.

I would, however, soon have to face the truth that there was no chance of women entering into his union of thinkers. Long before the question of admitting women to Columbia College came to be seriously considered, Trilling declared—and his announcements were always widely quoted—no women at Columbia: he liked the idea of a men's college. It was reported that he even opposed a woman's presence at college faculty meetings.

IN THE EARLY 1950s, the most important event in my years as a graduate student occurred: I was persuaded by a fellow graduate student—a future professor of literature, although he never went on to get his doctorate (which, particularly if one was a published poet, was not absolutely required in those halcyon days)—to apply for admission to the by then famous Trilling-Barzun seminar. Admittance was strictly limited: the seminar was intended to be small, cohesive, and hardworking. I was accepted into the seminar, as was my friend. There was at least one other woman in the group. I tried once, when she and I met many years later, to ask her how many women members there had been, but she flatly dismissed the question by saying she didn't share my interest in such matters; she remains to this day an unflinching deplorer of feminism.

The seminar was carefully structured by its two instructors. I recall this with amusement when I read of seminars these days where the reading list, the schedule, and the conduct of the class are all under the direction of the students; Trilling did not live to know this, and by the time this fashion took hold Barzun was long gone from the university. We read a book each week, and each week one of us wrote a paper discussing that book from any angle we chose.

My book was *Jane Eyre*. It is strange to remember that in 1953 not much notice was taken of *Jane Eyre*. No books by women were studied in the honors courses; yet Trilling and Barzun included Brontë in their seminar, the only woman on the list. I wrote a paper on the contemporary critical reception of the book, a subject often repeated once feminist criticism entered the academy, but I had then launched myself on a maiden voyage, having simply chosen a topic that seemed to provide an opportunity for both research and interpretation. The practice in the seminar, a method firmly established, no excuses accepted, was for the writer of that week's essay to leave a copy of the paper in the library for the other students to read and to give a copy to each of the instructors. We were true library workers in those days. There were few paperback books, no copy machines: one took notes on reserved books and typed papers with carbons. Did we leave a carbon copy in the library, give one of the exalted men a carbon? Did we type out two clean copies, one for each of them? I can recall only that Barzun liked my paper and Trilling didn't, but that hardly registered; they discussed it as though my opinions and ideas mattered. Even more astonishing, they each annotated each paper, making comments in the margin, as no other paper I wrote in graduate school was ever marked, perhaps ever read. The respect they showed for us was invigorating, and full of the promise of what an academic life might afford. Once, I remember, Trilling responded to something I had said or written, and I must have looked troubled. "Did I traduce you?" I remember him asking.

From that seminar I came away with another vision of what I might find in the life of the mind: friendship, intimacy as it existed between Trilling and Barzun, for they were, famously, friends. By "intimacy," I meant a mutual trust, consultations, laughter, conversation, perhaps private or personal, but not necessarily so, above all the knowledge that they were part of the same group; they were "we." Recently I have learned more of that friendship—I did not earlier even know that they had both attended Columbia College—and discovered that it was indeed, as I had imagined it, a close professional companionship such as I would one day know with female colleagues and the occasional male. Did I dream then that I might one day be their friend? I doubt it, except perhaps as an idle fantasy.

Perhaps I hoped to be a disciple. Trilling had disciples, young men whom he honored, supported, took pleasure in; no woman ever played that role in his life. Barzun did not, I think, have disciples in that sense, neither men nor women, but he continued to welcome women into his graduate seminars in history. Barzun, unlike Trilling, did not strike one as a lovable man. This was odd, since Trilling was also obviously distant and disdainful; one sensed, however, that once one was accepted into his affections he could be lovable. Barzun was always kind, but distant, cool—qualities I eventually came to attribute to his Frenchness; but of that, more anon.

Oddly enough from my point of view, a number of Trilling's "disciples" went on to teach, as I did, at Columbia, to gain tenure, as I did, and to be my colleagues. They all idealized him and referred to him often, long after, so I thought, what he had stood for had ceased to be appropriate. None of his disciples could touch him; indeed, I soon determined that their having idolized him had limited them in their achievements and in their dispositions. Even those who did not teach seemed to betray something essential in Trilling: Norman Podhoretz, for example, became a neoconservative whose opinions seemed altogether foreign to Trilling's as I read him.

I remember reading in Trilling's essay on George Orwell in *The Opposing Self* his account of a discussion about Orwell with a student, and the student's remarking that Orwell was "virtuous." This seemed to Trilling exact and profound, as indeed it was. Yet I often thought, in later years, that these younger men, Trilling's disciples, like Trilling himself, could not recognize virtue in a woman or in any but a certain kind of man. I well remember Trilling sadly remarking about Victorian men—he may have been quoting Chesterton—that, since there had for so long been no wars, men were not risking their lives in battle while women were risking their in childbirth; this was a failure of their manhood. Long before feminism I disliked having a woman's life defined exclusively by childbirth. But that was what women were for: I read Chesterton who averred that when women ceased to have children there would be no reason for their existence. Trilling might not have put it quite that definitively, but he was prepared to deny women "the peculiar reality of the moral life." "They seldom exist as men exist—as genuine moral destinies," he famously wrote in his 1957 introduction to *Emma*. Nor was that all. "It is the presumption of our society that women's moral life is not as men's," he declared—and certainly "we" women could hardly deny the point at that time. While I longed to convince him of women's "genuine moral destinies," that wish quickly became less a hope than a dream. Trilling's views on women were unchangeable, and in fact never changed.

What he and Barzun, however, could and did teach me in those student years was that to be highly intelligent, persuasive, and knowledgeable as a thinker and writer, it was essential to write readable, clear, elegant prose and to avoid jargon. "Jargon" was their favorite pejorative term; its misuse arose from the inclusion in prose for a general audience of the specific, technical terms of a particular discipline. When it came to writing, even all those years before incomprehensible "theory" took over, Barzun and Trilling taught us how to write without shame or condescension for an audience as intelligent as we, though not perhaps as professionally trained.

They wrote as I wanted to write, but they were not my first or only models in that important skill. My first exemplar in writing was Clifton Fadiman, whose precise but unpedantic prose I had encountered while still in high school. Fadiman had been at Columbia College with Barzun and Trilling—he was born in 1904, Trilling in 1905, Barzun in 1907—and when I was fifteen, he showed me how one might write intelligently while avoiding the traps of excessive erudition and garbled syntax. Fadiman wrote as though he wanted to entertain the reader, and perhaps, by chance, persuade him (there were no "or hers" for Fadiman or Trilling) of the delights of intellect.

LOOKING BACK NOW I can see that these three men identified for me what I aspired to. What other model had I? Rereading their works today has enabled me to identify the distinct aspects of these men's lives and ideas that I early intuited but could not then have accurately delineated. In writing of them here, I am not attempting biographies, and shall use only published, public materials. I wish only to capture, if I can, that ideal of the life of the mind they represented, and the way that model was eventually translatable to a female possibility. All were, as I wished to be and in a sense became, reformers, seeking to change those aspects of society they saw as limiting and diluting. Two of the three men—Fadiman and Trilling—were, like me, Jewish and suffered from that condition in pre–World War II academia. Barzun, born in France, was also, to some slight extent at least, an outsider. I knew none of this when I first encountered them.

Because they all attended Columbia College, because two of them remained at Columbia throughout their professional lives, they provide me, who also devoted my professional life to that institution, an opportunity to construe their accomplishments in the particular conditions and profound limitations Columbia offered. For Columbia produced these three men, two of whom became part of Columbia's establishment, as in turn it produced me, who became a feminist.

It is worth reemphasizing that none of these men was feminist; Barzun alone seemed capable of respecting female accomplishment and eschewing stereotyped views of women. Trilling frankly admitted no interest in teaching women or in considering their destinies beyond the domestic sphere. Fadiman's many anthologies and introductions hardly indicated any devotion to questions of female destiny; indeed, women writers, as we shall see, were his favorite target when he was scattering literary scorn. Yet these three men, all unconsciously, made my professional life possible by representing both what I wished to join and what I needed to struggle against. Since there was no woman inviting me to the destiny I sought, these three stood in such a woman's place. One male model might have become the unwilling mentor of a confused young woman. Because there were three of them, I avoided that trap—the betrayal of the mentor—and scattered my hopes among the triad.

They knew each other well; me they scarcely knew at all.

NOW, MIDWAY THROUGH my seventies, I find myself thinking back, remembering the time when only men seemed able to represent the life a woman not attracted by conventional female destinies might aspire to. I find it possible to keep distinct my views of these men at the time when they held the greatest sway over my mind—the 1950s and '60s but at the same time I have discovered the urge to ponder their lives beyond those years, when their influence on my thought did not abate even as my judgment of their ideas became more critical, more confrontational. I want to follow them into the time when the modern feminist movement made feasible a career few in the earlier decades could have imagined possible. What were they writing and propounding in those years?

During the heady beginnings of the feminist movement, when being a woman seemed to encourage rather than limit my professional accomplishment, had that revolution which altered my life in any way affected the thought and the writings of my three models? And if it did affect them, how, and to what extent? Trilling was dead at seventy, but Fadiman worked well into his nineties, and Barzun, now in his nineties, has never ceased to publish and to think. What were they thinking in the late years—what had Trilling been thinking before his death? Did they think about women at all, and was I able to follow their interpretations of modern life half as fervently as I had done at the time of my earliest professional aspirations?

Jorge Luis Borges
(1899–1986)

JORGE LUIS BORGES, known the world over for his labyrinthine, allegorical fictions, was a complex amalgam of South American culture and European education. Born in Buenos Aires, Argentina, and caught in Europe at the outbreak of World War I, Borges attended schools in Switzerland, where he studied French, German, and Latin to complement his native Spanish and the English he had learned from his father. After the war, his family moved to Spain, where Borges joined the Ultraists, a group of writers committed to experimental poetry. When he returned to Argentina in 1921, he founded an offshoot of the group and took up a job as a librarian. A vocal opponent of Juan Perón and the Fascist party, Borges was fired. After Perón's fall, Borges taught at the University of Buenos Aires and became the director of the National Library. Michael Greenberg, writing in the *New York Review of Books* (January 9, 2014), regards Borges's subsequent support for the brutal military dictatorships of Jorge Rafael Videla and Augusto Pinochet in the 1970s as "an act of despair" at Argentina's descent into fascism under Perón. Borges experimented with many different genres, including fantasy, science fiction, and the detective story. In "The Dead Man," which comes from his collection *The Aleph and Other Stories* (1949), Borges tells the story of Benjamin Otálora, "a sad sort of hoodlum whose only recommendation was his infatuation with courage." Can that ever be, we might ask, recommendation enough? Otálora's career begins in the tormenting shadow of Azevedo Bandeira, a bandit with a reputation as someone who outdoes everyone at every "deed of manly strength or courage." (The following section is translated by Andrew Hurley.)

The Dead Man
from *The Aleph* (1949)

That a man from the outskirts of Buenos Aires, a sad sort of hoodlum whose only recommendation was his infatuation with courage, should go out into the wilderness of horse country along the Brazilian frontier and become a leader of a band of smugglers—such a thing would, on the face of it, seem impossible. For those who think so, I want to tell the story of the fate of Benjamin Otálora, whom no one may remember anymore in the neighborhood of Balvanera but who died as he lived, by a bullet, in the province of Rio Grande do Sul. I do not know the full details of his adventure; when I am apprised of them, I will correct and expand these pages. For now, this summary may be instructive:

IN 1891, BENJAMIN OTÁLORA is nineteen years old—a strapping young man with a miserly brow, earnest blue eyes, and the strength and stamina of a Basque. A lucky knife thrust has revealed to him that he is a man of courage; he is not distressed by the death of his opponent, or by the immediate need to flee the country. The ward boss of his parish gives him a letter of introduction to a man named Azevedo Bandeira, over in Uruguay Otálora takes ship;

the crossing is stormy, creaking; the next day finds him wandering aimlessly through the streets of Montevideo, with unconfessed and perhaps unrecognized sadness. He doesn't manage to come across Azevedo Bandeira. Toward midnight, in a general-store-and-bar in Paso del Molino, he witnesses a fight between two cattle drovers. A knife gleams; Otálora doesn't know whose side he should be on, but he is attracted by the pure taste of danger, the way other men are attracted by gambling or music. In the confusion, he checks a low thrust meant for a man in a broad-brimmed black hat and a poncho. That man later turns out to be Azevedo Bandeira. (When Otálora discovers this, he tears up the letter of introduction, because he'd rather all the credit be his alone.) Though Azevedo Bandeira is a strong, well-built man, he gives the unjustifiable impression of being something of a fake, a forgery. In his face (which is always too close) there mingle the Jew, the Negro, and the Indian; in his air, the monkey and the tiger; the scar that crosses his face is just another piece of decoration, like the bristling black mustache.

Whether it's a projection or an error caused by drink, the fight stops as quickly as it started. Otálora drinks with the cattle drovers and then goes out carousing with them and then accompanies them to a big house in the Old City—by now the sun is high in the sky. Out in the back patio, the men lay out their bedrolls. Otálora vaguely compares that night with the previous one; now he is on terra firma, among friends. He does, he has to admit, feel a small twinge of remorse at not missing Buenos Aires. He sleeps till orisons, when he is awakened by the same *paisano* who had drunkenly attacked Bandeira. (Otálora recalls that this man has been with the others, drunk with them, made the rounds of the city with them, that Bandeira sat him at his right hand and made him keep drinking.) The man tells him the boss wants to see him. In a kind of office that opens off the long entryway at the front of the house (Otálora has never seen an entryway with doors opening off it), Azevedo Bandeira is waiting for him, with a splendid, contemptuous red-haired woman. Bandeira heaps praise on Otálora, offers him a glass of harsh brandy, tells him again that he looks like a man of mettle, and asks him if he'd like to go up north with the boys to bring a herd back. Otálora takes the job; by dawn the next morning they are on their way to Tacuarembó.

That is the moment at which Otálora begins a new life, a life of vast sunrises and days that smell of horses. This life is new to him, and sometimes terrible, and yet it is in his blood, for just as the men of other lands worship the sea and can feel it deep inside them, the men of ours (including the man who weaves these symbols) yearn for the inexhaustible plains that echo under the horses' hooves. Otálora has been brought up in neighborhoods full of cart drivers and leather braiders; within a year, he has become a gaucho. He learns to ride, to keep the horses together, to butcher the animals, to use the rope that lassos them and the bolas that bring them down, to bear up under weariness, storms, cold weather, and the sun, to herd the animals with whistles and shouts. Only once during this period of apprenticeship does he see Azevedo Bandeira, but he is always aware of his presence, because to be a "Bandeira man" is to be taken seriously—in fact, to be feared—and because no matter the deed of manly strength or courage they see done, the gauchos say Bandeira does it better. One of them says he thinks Bandeira was born on the other side of the Cuareim, in Rio Grande do Sul; that fact, which ought to bring him down a notch or two in their estimation, lends his aura a vague new wealth of teeming forests, swamps, impenetrable and almost infinite distances.

Gradually, Otálora realizes that Bandeira has many irons in the fire, and that his main business is smuggling. Being a drover is being a servant; Otálora decides to rise higher—decides to become a smuggler. One night, two of his companions are to cross the border to bring back several loads of brandy; Otálora provokes one of them, wounds him, and takes his place. He is moved by ambition, but also by an obscure loyalty. *Once and for all* (he thinks) *I want the boss to see that I'm a better man than all these Uruguayans of his put together.*

Another year goes by before Otálora returns to Montevideo. They ride through the outskirts, and then through the city (which seems enormous to Otálora); they come to the boss's house; the men lay out their bedrolls in the back patio. Days go by, and Otálora hasn't seen Bandeira. They say, timorously, that he's sick; a black man takes the kettle and *mate* up to him in his room. One afternoon, Otálora is asked to carry the things up to Bandeira. He feels somehow humiliated by this, but derives some pride from it, too.

The bedroom is dark and shabby. There is a balcony facing west, a long table with a gleaming jumble of quirts and bullwhips, cinches, firearms, and knives, a distant mirror of cloudy glass. Bandeira is lying on his back, dozing and moaning some; a vehemence of last sunlight spotlights him. The vast white bed makes him seem smaller, and somehow dimmer; Otálora notes the gray hairs, the weariness, the slackness, and the lines of age. It suddenly galls him that it's this old man that's giving them their orders. One thrust, he thinks, would be enough to settle *that* matter. Just then, he sees in the mirror that someone has come into the room. It is the redheaded woman; she is barefoot and half dressed, and staring at him with cold curiosity. Bandeira sits up; while he talks about things out on the range and sips *mate* after *mate*, his fingers toy with the woman's hair. Finally, he gives Otálora leave to go.

Days later, they receive the order to head up north again. They come to a godforsaken ranch somewhere (that could be anywhere) in the middle of the unending plains. Not a tree, not a stream of water soften the place; the sun beats down on it from first light to last. There are stone corrals for the stock, which is long-horned and poorly. The miserable place is called *El Suspiro*—The Sigh.

Otálora hears from the peons that Bandeira will be coming up from Montevideo before long. He asks why, and somebody explains that there's a foreigner, a would-be gaucho type, that's getting too big for his britches. Otálora takes this as a joke, but he's flattered that the joke is possible. He later finds out that Bandeira has had a falling-out with some politico and the politico has withdrawn his protection. The news pleases Otálora.

Crates of firearms begin to arrive; a silver washbowl and pitcher arrive for the woman's bedroom, then curtains of elaborately figured damask; one morning a somber-faced rider with a thick beard and a poncho rides down from up in the mountains. His name is Ulpiano Suárez, and he is Azevedo Bandeira's *capanga*, his foreman. He talks very little, and there is something Brazilian about his speech when he does. Otálora doesn't know whether to attribute the man's reserve to hostility, contempt, or mere savagery, but he does know that for the plan he has in mind he has to win his friendship.

At this point there enters into Benjamin Otálora's life a sorrel with black feet, mane, and muzzle. Azevedo Bandeira brings the horse up with him from the south; its bridle and all its other gear is tipped with silver and the bindings on its saddle are of jaguar skin. That extravagant horse is a symbol of the boss's authority, which is why the youth covets it, and why he also comes to covet, with grudge-filled desire, the woman with the resplendent hair. The woman, the gear, and the sorrel are attributes (adjectives) of a man he hopes to destroy.

Here, the story grows deeper and more complicated. Azevedo Bandeira is accomplished in the art of progressive humiliation, the satanic ability to humiliate his interlocutor little by little, step by step, with a combination of truths and evasions; Otálora decides to employ that same ambiguous method for the hard task he has set himself. He decides that he will gradually push Azevedo Bandeira out of the picture. Through days of common danger he manages to win Suárez' friendship. He confides his plan to him, and Suárez promises to help. Many things happen after this, some of which I know about: Otálora doesn't obey Bandeira; he keeps forgetting, improving his orders, even turning them upside down. The universe seems to conspire with him, and things move very fast. One noon, there is a shoot-out with men from Rio Grande do Sul on the prairies bordering the Tacuarembó. Otálora usurps Bandeira's place and gives the Uruguayans orders. He is shot in the shoulder, but that afternoon Otálora goes back to *El Suspiro* on the boss's sorrel and that afternoon a few drops of his blood stain the jaguar skin and that night he sleeps with the woman with the shining hair. Other versions change the order of these events and even deny that they all occurred on a single day.

Though Bandeira is still nominally the boss, he gives orders that aren't carried out; Benjamin Otálora never touches him, out of a mixture of habit and pity.

The last scene of the story takes place during the excitement of the last night of 1894. That night, the men of *El Suspiro* eat fresh-butchered lamb and drink bellicose liquor. Somebody is infinitely strumming at a milonga that he has some difficulty playing. At the head of the table, Otálora, drunk, builds exultancy upon exultancy, jubilation upon jubilation; that vertiginous tower is a symbol of his inexorable fate. Bandeira, taciturn among the boisterous men, lets the night take its clamorous course. When the twelve strokes of the clock chime at last, he stands up like a man remembering an engagement. He stands up and knocks softly on the woman's door. She opens it immediately, as though she were waiting for the knock. She comes out barefoot and half dressed. In an effeminate, wheedling voice, the boss speaks an order:

"Since you and the city slicker there are so in love, go give him a kiss so everybody can see."

He adds a vulgar detail. The woman tries to resist, but two men have taken her by the arms, and they throw her on top of Otálora. In tears, she kisses his face and his chest. Ulpiano Suárez has pulled his gun. Otálora realizes, before he dies, that he has been betrayed from the beginning, that he has been sentenced to death, that he has been allowed to love, to command, and win because he was already as good as dead, because so far as Bandeira was concerned, he was already a dead man.

Suárez fires, almost with a sneer.

Janet Flanner
(1892–1978)

THE AMERICAN JOURNALIST Janet Flanner lived and worked for much of her life in Paris. A longtime contributor to *The New Yorker*, Flanner published a "Letter from Paris" column in the magazine from 1925 to 1975 under the pen name "Genêt." In addition to portraits of American expatriates and European luminaries, Flanner offered American readers a window onto the cosmopolitan French capital as well as the larger social, culture, and political issues preoccupying Europe. Flanner's dispatches were later published in a multivolume collection: the volume *Paris Journal, 1944–1965* earned her a National Book Award in 1966. In this piece, first published in 1927, Flanner portrays the American dancer Isadora Duncan, the "mother of modern dance." According to Flanner, Duncan was the best-known American in Paris in the 1920s and one of the major global celebrities of the early twentieth century: "She was the last of the trilogy of great female personalities our century cherished," wrote Flanner, the other two being the actors Eleonora Duse and Sarah Bernhardt. The dance critic

Deborah Jowitt notes in *Time and the Dancing Image* (1988) that Duncan's "audacity" and revolutionary advocacy for "simplicity and organic design when public taste decreed elaboration in both decoration and decorum" influenced "innovators" in a variety of fields, including poetry, theater, sculpture, painting, fashion, and design.

Isadora (1878–1927)
from *Paris Was Yesterday, 1925–1939* (1972)

In the summer of 1926, like a ghost from the grave, Isadora Duncan began dancing again in Nice. Two decades before, her art, animated by her extraordinary public personality, came as close to founding an aesthetic renaissance as American morality would allow, and the provinces especially had a narrow escape. But in the postwar European years her body, whose Attic splendor once brought Greece to Kansas and Kalamazoo, was approaching its half-century mark. Her spirit was still green as a bay tree, but her flesh was worn, perhaps by the weight of laurels. She was the last of the trilogy of great female personalities our century cherished. Two of them, Duse and Bernhardt, had already gone to their elaborate national tombs. Only Isadora Duncan, the youngest, the American, remained wandering the foreign earth.

No one had taken Isadora's place in her own country and she was not missed. Of that fervor for the classic dance which she was the first to bring to a land bred on "Turkey in the Straw," beneficial signs remained from which she alone had not benefited. Eurythmic movements were appearing in the curriculums of girls' schools. Vestal virgins formed a frieze about the altar fire of Saint Marks-in-the-Bouwerie on Sabbath afternoons. As a cross between gymnasiums and God, Greek-dance camps flourished in the Catskills, where under the summer spruce, metaphysics and muscles were welded in an Ilissan hocus-pocus for the female young. Lisa, one of her first pupils, was teaching in the studio of the Théâtre des Champs-Élysées. Isadora's sister Elizabeth, to whom Greek might still be Greek if it had not been for Isadora, had a toga school in Berlin. Her brother Raymond, who operated a modern craft school in Paris, wore sandals and Socratic robes as if they were a family coat of arms. Isadora alone had neither sandals nor school. Most grandiose of all her influences, Diaghilev's Russian Ballet—which ironically owed its national rebirth to the inspiration of Isadora, then dancing with new terpsichorean ideals in Moscow—was still seasoning as an exotic spectacle in London and Monte Carlo. Only Isadora, animator of all these forces, had become obscure. Only she, with her heroic sculptural movements, had dropped by the wayside, where she lay inert like one of those beautiful battered pagan tombs that still line the Sacred Way between Eleusis and the city of the Parthenon.

As an artist, Isadora made her appearance in our plain and tasteless republic before the era of the half-nude revue, before the discovery of what is now called our Native Literary School, even before the era of the celluloid sophistication of the cinema, which by its ubiquity does so much to unite the cosmopolitanism of Terre Haute and New York. What America now has, and gorges on in the way of sophistication, it then hungered for. Repressed by generations of Puritanism, it longed for bright, visible, and blatant beauty presented in a public form the simple citizenry could understand. Isadora appeared as a half-clothed Greek. . . .

A Paris *couturier* once said woman's modern freedom in dress is largely due to Isadora. She was the first artist to appear uncinctured, barefooted, and free. She arrived like a glorious bounding Minerva in the midst of a cautious corseted decade. The clergy, hearing of (though supposedly without ever seeing) her bare calf, denounced it as violently as if it had been golden. Despite its longings, for a moment America hesitated, Puritanism rather than poetry coupling lewd with nude in rhyme. But Isadora, originally from California and by then from Berlin, Paris, and other points, arrived bearing her gifts as a Greek. She came like a figure from the Elgin marbles. The world over, and in America particularly, Greek sculpture was recognized to be almost notorious for its purity. The overpowering sentiment for Hellenic culture, even in the unschooled United States, silenced the outcries. Isadora had come as antique art and with such backing she became a cult.

Those were Isadora's great years. Not only in New York and Chicago but in the smaller, harder towns, when she moved across the stage, head reared, eyes mad, scarlet kirtle flying to the music of the "Marseillaise," she lifted from their seats people who had never left theater seats before except to get up and go home. Whatever she danced to, whether it was France's revolutionary hymn, or the pure salon passion of Chopin's waltzes, or the unbearable heat of Brahms' German mode, she conspired to make the atmosphere Greek, fusing *Zeitgeists* and national sounds into one immortal Platonic pantomime.

Thus she inspired people who had never been inspired in their lives before, and to whom inspiration was exhilarating, useless, and unbecoming. Exalted at the concert hall by her display of Greek beauty, limbs, and drapes which though they were two thousand years old she seemed to make excitingly modern, her followers, dazzled, filled with Phidianisms, went home to Fords, big hats, and the theory of Bull Moose, the more real items of their progressive age.

Dancing appeals less to the public than the other two original theatrical forms, drama and opera (unless, like the Russian Ballet, dancing manages to partake of all three). Nevertheless, Isadora not only danced but was demanded all over America and Europe. On the Continent she was more widely known than any other American of that decade, including Woodrow Wilson and excepting only Chaplin and Fairbanks, both of whom, via a strip of celluloid, could penetrate to remote hamlets without ever leaving Hollywood. But Isadora went everywhere in the flesh. She danced before kings and peasants. She danced from the Pacific to London, from Petrograd to the Black Sea, from Athens to Paris and Berlin.

She penetrated to the Georgian states of the Caucasus, riding third-class amid fleas and disease, performing in obscure halls before yokels and princes whom she left astonished, slightly enlightened, and somehow altered by the vision. For thirty years her life was more exciting and fantastic than anything Zola or Defoe ever fabricated for their heroines. Her companions were the great public talent of our generation—Duse, D'Annunzio, Bakst, Bernhardt, Picabia, Brancusi, Anatole France, Comtesse Anna de Noailles, Sardou, Ellen Terry.

Three of the greatest sculptors of her day at this time took Isadora's body as a permanent model and influence on their work though, alas, left no record in marble. Maillol alone made over five hundred drawings of Isadora dancing to Beethoven's Seventh Symphony; Rodin followed her all over Europe and literally made thousands of drawings, many still in the Musée Rodin in Paris. One of his most beautiful *gouaches*, now in the Metropolitan Museum, is *La Naissance d'un Vase Grecque*, in which he used Isadora's torso as his inspiration. Bourdelle also used Isadora as the main typical figure in his Théâtre des Champs-Élysées frescoes. These artists made the likeness of Isadora's limbs and the loveliness of her small face immortal. This was the great, gay, successful period of life. Her friends ran the gamut from starving poets down to millionaires. She was prodigal of herself, her art, illusions, work, emotions, and everybody's funds. She spent fortunes. After the war was over in France, her Sunday-night suppers in the Rue de la Pompe were banquets where guests strolled in, strolled out, and from low divans supped principally on champagne and strawberry tarts, while Isadora, barely clad in chiffon robes, rose when the spirit moved her to dance exquisitely. Week after week came obscure people whose names she never even knew. They were like moths. She once gave a house party that started in Paris, gathered force in Venice, and culminated weeks later on a houseboat on the Nile. She was a nomad de luxe.

In order to promulgate her pedagogic theories of beauty and education for the young, she legally adopted and supported some thirty or forty children during her life, one group being the little Slavs who afterward danced in Soviet Russia. During her famous season at the New York Century Theatre where she gave a classic Greek cycle, *Oedipus Rex, Antigone,* and the like, she bought up every Easter lily in Manhattan to decorate the theater the night she opened in Berlioz's *L'Enfance du Christ*, which was her Easter program. The lilies, whose perfume suffocated the spectators, cost two thousand dollars. Isadora had, at the moment, three thousand dollars to her name. And at midnight, long after all good lily-selling florists were in bed, she gave a champagne supper. It cost the other thousand.

Isadora, who had an un-American genius for art, for organizing love, maternity, politics, and pedagogy on a great personal scale, had also an un-American genius for grandeur.

After the lilies faded, Isadora and her school sat amid their luggage on the pier where the ship was about to sail for France. They had neither tickets nor money. But they had a classic faith in fate and a determination to go back to Europe, where art was understood. Just before the boat sailed, there appeared a schoolteacher. Isadora had never seen her before. The teacher gave Isadora the savings of years and Isadora sailed away. Herself grand, she could inspire grandeur in others, a tragic and tiring gift. There were always schoolteachers and lilies in Isadora's life.

Those three summer programs which Isadora gave in 1926 at her studio in Nice were her last performances on earth. At the end of the next summer she was dead. One of the soirées was given with the concordance of Leo Tecktonius, the pianist, and the other two with Jean Cocteau, who accompanied her dancing with his spoken verse. In all three performances her art was seen to have changed. She treaded the boards but little, she stood almost immobile or in slow splendid steps with slow splendid arms moved to music, seeking, hunting, finding. Across her face, tilting this way and that, fled the mortal looks of tragedy, knowledge, love, scorn, pain. Posing through the works of Wagner, through the tales of Dante, through the touching legend of St. Francis feeding crumbs and wisdom to his birds, Isadora was still great. By an economy (her first) she had arrived at elimination. As if the movements of dancing had become too redundant for her spirit, she had saved from dancing only its shape.

In one of her periodic fits of extravagant poverty and although needing the big sum offered, she once refused to dance in Wanamaker's Auditorium, disdaining for her art such a "scene of suspenders." She refused to appear in certain Continental theaters because they contained restaurants where dining might distract the spectators from her art. She early refused (though she and family were starving in Berlin) to dance at the Wintergarten for one thousand gold marks a night because there were animal acts on the bill. During the worst of her final financial predicaments in Paris, when few theaters were offering her anything at all, she refused to dance at the Théâtre des Champs-Élysées because it was a music hall. Yet her image in sculpture adorned the theater's façade, where Bourdelle had chiseled her likeness for all times and passers-by. She talked vaguely of consenting to dance in Catalonia. To anyone who knew her it seemed natural that Isadora would like to dance in a castle in Spain.

The lack of money, which never worried Isadora as much as it anguished her devoted friends, became more acute during the last years of her life. Nevertheless she refused a legacy of over a quarter of a million francs from the estate of her stormy young husband, Yessenine, the Russian revolutionary poet whom she had married late and unhappily. At the worst of her final picturesque poverty, when, as Isadora gallantly declared, she hardly knew where the next bottle of champagne was coming from (champagne was the only libation she loved), it was decided by her friends that she should write her memoirs. At this time she was living in a small studio hotel in the Rue Delambre, behind the Café du Dôme in Paris. Isadora's handwriting was characteristic; it was large, handsome, illegible, with two or three words to a line and four or five lines to a page. During her authorship the scantly scribbled pages accumulated like white leaves, left to drift over her littered studio floor. Then, as in all the frequent crises in her life, her friends rallied around her with scenes, jealousies, memories, quarrels, recriminations, good cases of wine, fine conversation, threats of farewell, new leases of affection—all the dramatics of loyalty, disillusion, hero worship, duty, fatigue, patience, and devotion which animated even her Platonic associations—all the humorous and painful disorders which genius, as if to prove its exceptional chemistry, catalyzes in commoner lives. The book, called *My Life*, finally appeared posthumously. It was to have furnished money for her to live.

As her autobiography made clear, an integral part of Isadora's nature died young when her two adored little children, Deirdre and Patrick, were tragically drowned in 1913 at Neuilly; the automobile in which they were waiting alone slipped its brakes and plunged into the Seine. The children had been the offspring of free unions, in which Isadora spiritedly believed. She believed, too, in polyandry and that each child thus benefited eugenically by having a different and carefully chosen father. She also attributed the loss of her third child, born the day war was declared, to what she called the curse of the machine. At the wild report that the Germans were advancing by motor on Paris, the old Bois de Boulogne gates were closed, her doctor and his automobile, amidst thousands of cars, were caught behind the grill, and by the time he arrived at her bedside it was too late. The child had been born dead. "Machines have been my enemy," she once said. "They killed my three children. Machines are the opposite of, since they are the invention of, man. Perhaps a machine will one day kill me."

In a moment of melancholy her friend Duse prophesied that Isadora would die like Jocasta. Both prophecies were fulfilled. On August 13, 1927, while driving on the Promenade des Anglais at Nice, Isadora Duncan met her death. She was strangled by her colored shawl, which became tangled in the wheel of the automobile.

A few days later in Paris great good-natured crowds had gathered in the Rue de Rivoli to watch the passing of the American Legion, then holding their initial postwar jollification and parade in France. By a solemn chance, what the crowd saw first, coming down the flag-strewn, gaily decorated thoroughfare, was the little funeral cortege of Isadora Duncan, treading its way to the cemetery of Père-Lachaise. Her coffin was covered by her famous purple dancing cape serving as a pall. On the back of the hearse, her family, though unsympathetic to her radical views, had loyally placed her most imposing floral tribute, a great mauve wreath from the Soviet Union with a banner that read "*Le Cœur de Russie Pleure Isadora.*" Though she had once rented the Metropolitan Opera House to plead the cause of France before we went into the war, though she had given her Neuilly château as a hospital, though she had been a warm and active friend to France, the French government sent nothing. Nor did her great French friends, who had once eagerly drunk her fame and champagne, walk behind dead Isadora.

Of all the famous personages she had loved and known and who had hailed her genius and hospitality, only two went to Passy, where she lay in state, to sign the mourners' books—Yvette Guilbert and the actor Lugné-Poë. Hundreds of others scrawled their signatures on the pages, but they were casuals, common, loyal, unknown. Since Isadora was an American, it was regrettable that both the Paris American newspapers, the Paris *Herald* and the Chicago *Tribune*, busy doubtless with the gayer Legion matters, did not send reporters to follow her funeral cortege to its destination. Thus Americans next morning read that Isadora was followed to her grave by a pitiful handful. Only five carriages made up the official procession; but four thousand people—men, women, old, young, and of all nationalities—waited in the rain for the arrival of her body at Père-Lachaise.

Of earthly possessions, Isadora had little enough to leave. Still she had made a will—and forgot to sign it.

All her life Isadora had been a practical idealist. She had put into practice certain ideals of art, maternity, and political liberty which people prefer to read as theories on paper. Her ideals of human liberty were not unsimilar to those of Plato, to those of Shelley, to those of Lord Byron, which led him to die dramatically in Greece. All they gained for Isadora were the loss of her passport and the presence of the constabulary on the stage of the Indianapolis Opera House, where the chief of police watched for sedition in the movement of Isadora's knees.

Denounced as a Russian Bolshevik sympathizer, Isadora said she never even received a postal card from the Soviet government to give her news of her school which she housed in its capital. For Isadora had a fancy for facts. As she once told Boston it was tasteless and dull, so, when they were feting her in triumph in Moscow, she told the Communists she found them bourgeois. She had a wayward truthful streak in her and a fancy for paradox. "Everything antique Greek," she once said to an American woman friend, "is supposed to be noble. Did you ever notice how easily the Greeks became Roman?"

Great artists are tragic. Genius is too large, and it may have been grandeur that proved Isadora's undoing—the grandeur of temporary luxury, the grandeur of permanent ideals.

She was too expansive for personal salvation. She had thousands of friends. What she needed was an organized government. She had had checkbooks. Her scope called for a national treasury. It was not for nothing that she was hailed by her first name only, as queens have been, were they great Catherines or Marie Antoinettes.

As she stepped into the machine that was to be her final enemy, Isadora's last spoken words were, by chance, "*Je vais à la gloire!*"

DISCUSSION QUESTIONS

1. *What kinds of leaders and models do these readings suggest are the most likely to attract imitators?*

2. *The concept of the "role model" is ubiquitous in our culture. To what extent are leaders responsible for being role models? To what extent are they accountable for the behavior of the imitators they attract? In what circumstances are role models useful? Irrelevant? Dangerous?*

3. *Now that you have considered several readings about the project of emulation, can you determine what causes a healthy concern for reputation to turn into a counterproductive obsession?*

4. *What kinds of leaders does your organization hold up as worthy of emulation?*

5. *How does one develop his or her own independent style?*

ALBUM
Artists of Deep Attention

Do external things distract you?

—MARCUS AURELIUS,
Meditations, 2.7

Sound bite, Snapchat, meme, text, and tweet—we have grown to love the ephemeral, disappearing morsel while we resist anything that demands excessive patience or an extended commitment of attention. We live in the age of multitasking. Multiple, often competing streams of information, to which we are tethered by habit or necessity, exercise the faculty of hyper attention even as they erode the capacity for deep attention. As studies at MIT, Stanford, and elsewhere have shown, our commitment to multitasking has produced some unexpected consequences.

One study conducted in the Stanford Memory Lab by Clifford Nass, Eyal Ophir, and Anthony D. Wagner revealed "systematic differences in information processing styles between chronically heavy and light media multitaskers." In fact, the researchers reported in the *Proceedings of the National Academy of Sciences* in 2009, "heavy media multitaskers are more susceptible to interference from irrelevant environmental stimuli and from irrelevant representations in memory. This led to the surprising result that heavy media multitaskers performed worse on a test of task-switching ability, likely due to reduced ability to filter out interference from the irrelevant task set." Multitasking, then, does not seem to make us more agile or to improve our memory. It turns out that the most confident multitaskers are the least successful managers of competing activities.

In our general celebration of hyper attention and our addiction to speed and immediate sensory gratification, deep attention seems to have fallen out of fashion even as the increasingly complex problems we face continue to demand it. Thus the voices of the various "slow movements" that have emerged in recent decades—from Cittaslow to Carlo Petrini's Slow Food Movement to the World Institute of Slowness, founded by Geir Berthelsen—are driven not simply by nostalgia but by a recognition that slowing down is something we cannot do without. The adherents of these movements express a yearning for the cultivation of a kind of deep attention and focus that seems to be disappearing from our world.

It would be foolhardy to deny the value of rapid decision-making, yet we tend to forget how long it takes to master such speed. The twenty-first-century cult of busyness and the attendant drama of urgency—the notion that only crisis carries meaning—has eclipsed in many organizations the value of moving slowly in order to separate the information from the noise, the essence from the distractions.

One way to cultivate such attention is through education. For example, Jennifer L. Roberts, an art historian at Harvard University, asks all her students—novice undergraduates as well as experienced graduate students—to write a long research paper on one work of art. Roberts insists that the first step in the process be a three-hour session of looking at the object. Roberts explains in "The Power of Patience" (*Harvard Magazine* [November–December 2013]) that this is meant to seem "a painfully long time. . . . The time span is explicitly designed to seem excessive." Students initially tend to "resist" the assignment, finding it difficult to imagine that even careful observation could take so long. In a world characterized by its haste, however, Roberts demonstrates the constructive value of prolonged immersion: "What this exercise shows students is that just because you have *looked* at something doesn't mean that you have *seen* it. Just because something is available instantly to vision does not mean that it is available instantly to consciousness. Or, in slightly more general terms: access is not synonymous with learning. What turns access into learning is time and strategic patience."

In the album that follows, the reader will find portraits of artists of deep attention: individuals who seem able to bring their powers of concentration to bear even in the midst of confusion and to sustain those powers despite inevitable distractions. The readings cut across periods, traditions, and genres to offer up examples of deep concentrators at work: the Roman philosopher Seneca meditates on noise; Augustine portrays Ambrose reading; the American Civil War general Horace Porter describes his boss, Ulysses S. Grant, writing dispatches in the field; the Zen tale "A Cup of Tea" offers a master's advice to a would-be disciple; the American poet Wallace Stevens invites us to consider the world with a "mind of winter"; and the novelist Georges Simenon brings to life the formidable Inspector Maigret, who approaches the work of solving crimes by soaking up the world around him "like a sponge."

RECOMMENDED READING

Arthur Conan Doyle, *A Study in Scarlet* (1887)
Stephen Jay Gould, *The Richness of Life* (2007)
Pico Iyer, "A Chapel Is Where You Can Hear Something Beating Below Your Heart," *Portland Magazine* (May–June 2011)
Oliver Sacks, *The Man Who Mistook His Wife for a Hat* (1985)
Jonathan Spence, *The Memory Palace of Matteo Ricci* (1984)

Seneca
(ca. 3 BCE–65 CE)

SENECA'S TRAGEDIES INFLUENCED Renaissance dramatists, while his moral epistles awakened the imaginations of the essayists Michel de Montaigne and Francis Bacon with their anti-Ciceronian plain style—a style the critic Phillip Lopate characterizes as the model from which "came modern prose: quick, pungent, ironic, self-questioning, reflective of mental process" (*The Art of the Personal Essay*). Born in Spain at the beginning of the first century, Lucius Annaeus Seneca moved to Rome in order to study philosophy and rhetoric. There he achieved success in writing and oratory while also committing himself to Stoicism, a philosophy counseling the impassive acceptance of pain and pleasure. It was a school of thought to which the Roman emperor Marcus Aurelius, whose *Meditations* are excerpted in this anthology, also subscribed. Seneca attained a certain celebrity in Rome, but he was temporarily banished by Claudius on suspicion of adultery with the emperor's niece. Later recalled to fulfill the thankless task of serving as Nero's tutor, Seneca, together with a soldier named Burrus, in essence ruled Rome as regent during the emperor's minority. But when Nero grew into his monstrous, murderous majority, he exiled Seneca and instructed him to commit suicide. Seneca obeyed, exemplifying the Stoicism that had not, according to some critics, consistently distinguished his life. In the letter reproduced here Seneca describes a capacity for "forcing my mind to focus on itself." (The unidentified quotation, "Everything was settled in the calm repose of night," can be found in Virgil and Ovid, but its origins are earlier. The following letter is translated by Elaine Fantham.)

On Noise
from *Moral Epistles*

'll be damned if silence is as necessary as it seems for a man withdrawn for study! Here a mixed hubbub surrounds me on all sides. I am living over a public bath. Just imagine all the varieties of cries that can fill the ears with loathing; when the tougher fellows are exercising and thrusting arms heavy with lead, when they are either straining or imitating those under strain, I hear their grunts, and whenever they let out the breath they have been holding, I hear their whistles and bitter panting: when I come upon some feeble fellow content with the common-or-garden massage, I hear the crack of hands slapping the shoulders, which changes pitch as it hits them flat or hollowed. But if the umpire of the ballgame joins in and begins to count the balls, that is the end. Now listen to the brawler and the thief caught in the act, and the man who likes the sound of his own voice in the bath. Then add those who leap into the pool with a great splash, as well as those whose voices, if nothing else, are loud and clear. Imagine the depilator suddenly emitting his thin, shrill cry, calculated to make him more conspicuous, constantly uttering and never silent except when he is plucking the underarms and forcing the other man to cry out instead. Now I hear the different cries of the cake-seller and the sausage-seller and pastrycook and all the hawkers from the snack-bars selling their wares with a special distinct intonation.

You must be saying: 'You are a man of iron, or stone-deaf, if your mind is firm among such assorted and clashing cries, although constant greeting drives our Chrysippus to death.' But by Jove, I no more care about that din than about beating waves, or a waterfall, although I have heard that this was the single reason for a certain tribe moving their city, that they could not bear the crash of the Nile cataracts. In fact a human voice seems to distract me more than thudding, since the former attracts the attention whereas the latter just fills and beats on the ears. Among the noises which resound all about me without distracting me I count passing wagons and the tenant carpenter and the neighbouring ironworker, or the fellow who practises his trumpet and pipes at the Sweating Fountain, and does not sing but just shouts out. But sound is still more of a nuisance when it is intermittent than when it is continuous. However, I have so hardened myself by now against all these disturbances that I can even hear the coxswain calling out the rhythm to oarsmen in his most disagreeable voice. In fact I am forcing my mind to focus on itself and not be distracted by outside events; let everything be echoing outside, so long as there is no disruption within me, while desire and fear are not quarrelling with each other, while greed and extravagance are not in conflict and neither is bothering the other. For what good is silence in the whole neighbourhood if your emotions are in uproar?

Everything was settled in the calm repose of night.

This is false; there is no calm repose except when reason has settled it; night causes disturbance, rather than removes it, and merely changes our worries. In fact the dreams of sleepers are as troublesome as their days. The real calm is when a good state of mind unfolds.

Look at the man who seeks his sleep in the silence of a spacious home, when the whole crowd of slaves have fallen silent and those coming near keep on tip-toe so that no sound can trouble his ears. To be sure, he tosses this way and that trying to catch a light sleep from the midst of his distress: he thinks he has heard even what he does not hear. What do you think is to blame? It is his mind that is disturbing him, that must be appeased, the conflict of his mind that must be quelled. There is no reason to think him calm just because his body is in repose. Sometimes rest itself is restless. This is why we must be roused to action and kept busy by the performance of skilled arts whenever this sloth which cannot bear itself puts us in a bad state. When great generals see their troops are prone to mutiny they control them by some task and keep them busy with exercises: there is never leisure for them to riot when they are kept busy, and nothing is more sure than that the failings of leisure are dispelled by activity. Often we seem to have gone into retreat out of weariness with public affairs and distaste at our unwanted eminence, but in the hiding-place where fear and exhaustion has thrust us ambition sometimes revives. It did not fade because it was forcibly cut out, but out of mere weariness or irritation at hostile circumstances. The same is true of self-indulgence, which sometimes seems to have lapsed, but then harasses men set on pursuing thrift and in their austerity seeks out pleasures which it had not really condemned but simply left behind. It does this all the more violently because it is more surreptitious. All faults are milder when they are open to view; even diseases are on their way to healing, when they break out of hiding and expose their strength. So you might be sure that avarice and ambition and other sicknesses of the human mind are most destructive when they ebb in a pretence of health.

We seem at leisure, and we are not. For if we are genuinely at leisure, if we have sounded the retreat, if we despise mere show, as I said just now, nothing will distract us, no chorus of men or birds will interrupt our thoughts when they are good and sound and resolved. It is a flighty mind which has not yet with-drawn into itself, that is aroused by speech and external events. It must contain some anxiety and some element of fear to make it alert, and as Virgil puts it:

> Then although no spears alarmed me, or clustering
> Greeks in opposing ranks, each breeze and every sound
> Now terrified me, fearing on tenterhooks,
> Alike for my companion and him I bore.

The former Aeneas is a wise man whom no whirring spears, no weapons jostling among a massed horde, no crash of the city's collapse terrifies. This other is inexperienced, fearing for his possessions, panicked at every crackle, a man who hears each sound as threatening and is cast down by it, whom the lightest movements panic; it is his burdens that make him scared. Choose any of those lucky men who carry or drag behind them many pieces of baggage, and you will see him 'fearing for his companion and him he bears . . .'. So recognize that you are settled when no shouting will affect you, no voice will shatter you, whether it wheedles or threatens, or raises meaningless din with its hollow sound.

What does this mean? Isn't it sometimes more comfortable to be free of abuse? Yes, I admit it. So I shall move out of this place. I wanted to test it and put myself on trial. What need to suffer any longer, since Ulysses found such an easy cure for his comrades against even the Sirens? Keep well.

Augustine
(354–430)

CANONIZED IN 1298, St. Augustine found his spiritual vocation in his early thirties, when he decided to surrender a secular career in 386. He was baptized by St. Ambrose the following year and (unwillingly) ordained in 391. Within five years, he had become Bishop of Hippo (present-day Annaba), a post he held until he died in the midst of the city's sacking by the Vandals. Augustine was born in Algeria, which was then the Roman province of Numidia. His parents were farmers, his mother a Christian and his father a pagan. Augustine triumphed over a poor education by studying on his own and becoming an accomplished reader of Latin, especially the works of Cicero and Virgil. He then became a teacher of literature and public speaking in Carthage, Rome, and Milan, but his ambitions for high office in the imperial administration were thwarted by the presence in his life of an unsuitable mistress with whom he had a child and to whom he remained faithful for fifteen years. His abandonment of her is one of the many acts detailed in *Confessions*, which is regarded as one of the great spiritual autobiographies of the Christian tradition. This apologia and Augustine's other rich and varied writings have influenced writers as diverse as Dante and Flannery O'Connor. In the passage that follows, Augustine illuminates his mentor Ambrose's extraordinary powers of concentration and capacity for total immersion in his books. (The following selection from book 4 is translated by Henry Chadwick.)

Ambrose Reading
from *Confessions* (ca. 397)

Ambrose himself I thought a happy man as the world judges things, for he was held in honour by the great and powerful. Only his celibacy seemed to me painful. But I had no notion nor any experience to know what were his hopes, what struggles he had against the temptations of his distinguished position, what consolations in adversities, and the hidden aspect of his life—

what was in his heart, what delicious joys came as he fed on and digested your bread. He for his part did not know of my emotional crisis nor the abyss of danger threatening me. I could not put the questions I wanted to put to him as I wished to do. I was excluded from his ear and from his mouth by crowds of men with arbitrations to submit to him, to whose frailties he ministered. When he was not with them, which was a very brief period of time, he restored either his body with necessary food or his mind by reading. When he was reading, his eyes ran over the page and his heart perceived the sense, but his voice and tongue were silent. He did not restrict access to anyone coming in, nor was it customary even for a visitor to be announced. Very often when we were there, we saw him silently reading and never otherwise. After sitting for a long time in silence (for who would dare to burden him in such intent concentration?) we used to go away. We supposed that in the brief time he could find for his mind's refreshment, free from the hubbub of other people's troubles, he would not want to be invited to consider another problem. We wondered if he read silently perhaps to protect himself in case he had a hearer interested and intent on the matter, to whom he might have to expound the text being read if it contained difficulties, or who might wish to debate some difficult questions. If his time were used up in that way, he would get through fewer books than he wished. Besides, the need to preserve his voice, which used easily to become hoarse, could have been a very fair reason for silent reading. Whatever motive he had for his habit, this man had a good reason for what he did.

Horace Porter
(1837–1921)

HORACE PORTER, SON of the governor of Pennsylvania, graduated from West Point on the eve of the Civil War in 1860, almost twenty years behind his future commander, Ulysses S. Grant. Porter served in a number of posts before joining Grant's staff, and he served as his aide-de-camp for the latter part of the war. Porter continued to work with Grant after the war and during the latter's troubled presidency before going to work for the railroads. He also served as U.S. ambassador to France. Porter was instrumental in the construction of Grant's tomb in New York City, and he published his memoir of the war days, *Campaigning with Grant*, in 1897. "The object aimed at in this narrative," Porter wrote in his preface, "is to recount the daily acts of General Grant in the field, to describe minutely his personal traits and habits, and to explain the motives which actuated him in important crises." War reminiscences were a popular genre in the nineteenth century. In the excerpts below, Porter recounts his first meeting with Grant during the battles for Chattanooga, Tennessee, in the fall of 1863. He then goes on to describe the general's habits of mind, specifically his unusual powers of concentration and his method of writing orders—orders always composed with an eye, as Grant explained in his own memoirs, to stating their meaning "so plainly that there could be no mistaking it."

Ulysses S. Grant at Work
from Campaigning with Grant (1897)

Early on the morning of the 24th the party set out from headquarters, and most of the day was spent in examining our lines and obtaining a view of the enemy's position. At Brown's Ferry General Grant dismounted and went to the river's edge on foot, and made his reconnaissance of that important part of the line in full view of the enemy's pickets on the opposite bank, but, singularly enough, he was not fired upon.

Being informed that the general wished to see me that evening, I went into the room he was occupying at headquarters, and found two of his staff-officers seated near him. As I entered he gave a slight nod of the head by way of recognition, and pointing to a chair, said rather bluntly, but politely, "Sit down." In reply to a question which he asked, I gave him some information he desired in regard to the character and location of certain heavy guns which I had recently assisted in putting in position on the advanced portion of our lines, and the kind and amount of artillery ammunition. He soon after began to write despatches, and I arose to go, but resumed my seat as he said, "Sit still." My attention was soon attracted to the manner in which he went to work at his correspondence. At this time, as throughout his later career, he wrote nearly all his documents with his own hand, and seldom dictated to any one even the most unimportant despatch. His work was performed swiftly and uninterruptedly, but without any marked display of nervous energy. His thoughts flowed as freely from his mind as the ink from his pen; he was never at a loss for an expression, and seldom interlined a word or made a material correction. He sat with his head bent low over the table, and when he had occasion to step to another table or desk to get a paper he wanted, he would glide rapidly across the room without straightening himself, and return to his seat with his body still bent over at about the same angle at which he had been sitting when he left his chair. Upon this occasion he tossed the sheets of paper across the table as he finished them, leaving them in the wildest disorder. When he had completed the despatch, he gathered up the scattered sheets, read them over rapidly, and arranged them in their proper order. Turning to me after a time, he said, "Perhaps you might like to read what I am sending." I thanked him, and in looking over the despatches I found that he was ordering up Sherman's entire force from Corinth to within supporting distance, and was informing Halleck of the dispositions decided upon for the opening of a line of supplies, and assuring him that everything possible would be done for the relief of Burnside in east Tennessee. Directions were also given for the taking of vigorous and comprehensive steps in every direction throughout his new and extensive command. At a late hour, after having given further directions in regard to the contemplated movement for the opening of the route from Bridgeport to Chattanooga, and in the mean time sending back to be foraged all the animals that could be spared, he bid those present a pleasant good night, and limped off to his bedroom.

I cannot dwell too forcibly on the deep impression made upon those who had come in contact for the first time with the new commander, by the exhibition they witnessed of his singular mental powers and his rare military qualities. Coming to us crowned with the laurels he had gained in the brilliant campaign of Vicksburg, we naturally expected to meet a well-equipped soldier, but hardly anybody was prepared to find one who had the grasp, the promptness of decision, and the general administrative capacity which he displayed at the very start as commander of an extensive military division, in which many complicated problems were presented for immediate solution.

.   .   .

The general had occupied himself continually during this anxious and exciting period in giving specific instructions by wire and messengers to meet the constantly changing conditions which were taking place from day to day and from hour to hour in the theater of military operations; and no despatches were ever of greater importance than those which were sent from headquarters at this time. His powers of concentration of thought were often shown by the circumstances under which he wrote. Nothing that went on around him, upon the field or in his quarters, could distract his attention or interrupt him. Sometimes, when his tent was filled with officers, talking and laughing at the top of their voices, he would turn to his table and write the most important communications. There would then be an immediate "Hush!" and abundant excuses offered by the company; but he always insisted upon the conversation going on, and after a while his officers came to understand his wishes in this respect, to learn that noise was apparently a stimulus rather than a check to his flow of ideas, and to realize that nothing short of a general attack along the whole line could divert his thoughts from the subject upon which his mind was concentrated. In writing his style was vigorous and terse, with little of ornament; its most conspicuous characteristic was perspicuity. General Meade's chief of staff once said: "There is one striking feature about Grant's orders: no matter how hurriedly he may write them on the field, no one ever has the slightest doubt as to their meaning, or ever has to read them over a second time to understand them." The general used Anglo-Saxon words much more frequently than those derived from the Greek and Latin tongues. He had studied French at West Point, and picked up some knowledge of Spanish during the Mexican war; but he could not hold a conversation in either language, and rarely employed a foreign word in any of his writings. His adjectives were few and well chosen. No document which ever came from his hands was in the least degree pretentious. He never laid claim to any knowledge he did not possess, and seemed to feel, with Addison, that "pedantry in learning is like hypocrisy in religion—a form of knowledge without the power of it." He rarely indulged in metaphor, but when he did employ a figure of speech it was always expressive and graphic, as when he spoke of the commander at Bermuda Hundred being "in a bottle strongly corked," or referred to our armies at one time moving "like horses in a balky team, no two ever pulling together." His style inclined to the epigrammatic without his being aware of it. There was scarcely a document written by him from which brief sentences could not be selected fit to be set in mottos or placed upon transparencies. As examples may be mentioned: "I propose to move immediately upon your works"; "I shall take no backward steps"; the famous "I propose to fight it out on this line if it takes all summer," and, later in his career, "Let us have peace"; "The best means of securing the repeal of an obnoxious law is its vigorous enforcement"; "I shall have no policy to enforce against the will of the people"; and "Let no guilty man escape." He wrote with the first pen he happened to pick up, and never stopped to consider whether it was sharp-pointed or blunt-nibbed, good or bad. He was by no means as particular in this regard as General Zachary Taylor, of whom an old army rumor said that the only signature he ever made which was entirely satisfactory to him was written with the butt-end of a ramrod dipped in tar. General Grant's desk was always in a delirious state of confusion, pigeonholes were treated with a sublime disregard, and he left his letters piled up in apparently inextricable heaps; but, strange to say, he carried in his mind such a distinct recollection of local literary geography as applied to his writing-table that he could go to it and even in the dark lay his hand upon almost any paper he wanted. His military training had educated him to treat purely official documents with respect, and these were always handed over to Colonel Bowers, the adjutant-general, to be properly filed; but as to his private letters, he made his coat-pockets a general depository for his correspondence until they could hold no more, and then he discharged their contents upon his desk in a chaotic mass. The military secretaries made heroic struggles to bring about some order in this department, and generally saw that copies were kept of all letters of importance which the chief wrote. Whatever came from his pen was grammatically correct, well punctuated, and seldom showed an error in spelling. In the field he never had a dictionary in his possession, and when in doubt about the orthography of a word, he was never known to write it first on a separate slip of paper to see how it looked. He spelled with heroic audacity, and "chanced it" on the correctness. While in rare instances he made a mistake in doubling the consonants where unnecessary, or in writing a single consonant where two were required, he really spelled with great accuracy. His pronunciation was seldom, if ever, at fault, though in two words he had a peculiar way of pronouncing the letter *d:* he always pronounced corduroy "corjuroy," and immediately "immejetly."

A Cup of Tea, from *Zen Flesh, Zen Bones*
(1957)

"A CUP OF TEA" and two other vignettes reproduced in this anthology originally come from *101 Zen Stories* (1939), a collection of Chinese and Japanese Zen teachings from across the centuries. These stories, many of which were translated from the late thirteenth-century Japanese *Shaseki-shu,* or *Collection of Stone and Sand*, were subsequently assembled, together with anecdotes and koans from various sources and periods, in the influential compilation *Zen Flesh, Zen Bones*. In its illustration of contemplation, deep concentration, and mental focus, "A Cup of Tea" is a typical Zen story. Zen (or "Ch'an" in China) Buddhism is a meditative practice aimed at self-discovery. As Joel Kupperman explains in *Classic Asian Philosophy*, the stories in *Zen Flesh, Zen Bones* "dramatize (rather than explain) the philosophical element" of Zen; they are designed to offer a mode of living. Kupperman cautions against attempting to interpret Zen writing by searching for Western parallels: "Asian philosophy fitted to a Western template," he writes, "will emerge as a crude caricature." Instead, a Western reader might look to "A Cup of Tea" and other Zen stories and koans as offering a distinctive mode for contemplating the world and the human being's place within it.

A Cup of Tea

NAN-IN, a Japanese master during the Meiji era (1868–1912), received a university professor who came to inquire about Zen.

Nan-in served tea. He poured his visitor's cup full, and then kept on pouring.

The professor watched the overflow until he no longer could restrain himself. "It is overfull. No more will go in!"

"Like this cup," Nan-in said, "you are full of your own opinions and speculations. How can I show you Zen unless you first empty your cup?"

Wallace Stevens
(1879–1955)

ONE OF THE most important, influential practitioners of American modernist poetry, Wallace Stevens was born in Reading, Pennsylvania, and attended Harvard University for three years until his family could no longer pay his tuition. From Harvard, Stevens went to New York City, where he worked for a time as a newspaper reporter before attending law school. He continued to work for a series of law and insurance firms even as he invested in his poetry. In 1923, he published his first volume, *Harmonium*, which showcased his facility with imagery and the influence of East Asian poetry. While working throughout his life for the Hartford Accident and Indemnity Company, Stevens continued to pursue his poetic career, which culminated in a Pulitzer Prize in 1955 for *The Collected Poems of Wallace Stevens*. "The Snow Man," first published in *Harmonium*, demands we perceive the natural world through the "mind of winter" before investing the scene with the imaginative associations habitual to human beings. To merge with the purely objective consciousness of a snow man—to achieve a state of emptiness akin to Buddhist "no-mind"—requires the deepest attention. "Poetry," Stevens wrote in his notebooks, "has to be something more than a conception of the mind. It has to be a revelation of nature. Conceptions are artificial. Perceptions are essential."

The Snow Man
from *Harmonium* (1923)

One must have a mind of winter
To regard the frost and the boughs
Of the pine-trees crusted with snow;

And have been cold a long time
To behold the junipers shagged with ice,
The spruces rough in the distant glitter

Of the January sun; and not to think
Of any misery in the sound of the wind,
In the sound of a few leaves,

Which is the sound of the land
Full of the same wind
That is blowing in the same bare place

For the listener, who listens in the snow,
And, nothing himself, beholds
Nothing that is not there and the nothing that is.

Georges Simenon
(1903–1989)

GEORGES SIMENON PUBLISHED his first novel in 1923. Between that year and his death sixty-six years later, he wrote more than four hundred more. Simenon divided his output into two categories: pulp and serious fiction. The latter he called *romans durs*, or hard novels. Yet it is the former—and the character of Inspector Jules Maigret, who appears in most of them— for which he is best known throughout the world. Inspector Maigret, who rises over the course of the novels to the rank of superintendent in the Paris police force, has had an active life in television and film, where he has been played over the years by the likes of Jean Gabin and Michael Gambon. Simenon's novels are also greatly admired by writers. Ernest Hemingway wrote in *True at First Light*, "If you are to be rained in while camped in Africa there is nothing better than Simenon and with him I did not care how long it rained . . . I would read happily, transferring all my problems to Maigret." And it is the way in which Maigret handles problems that proves the great fascination of the novels. As various critics have noted, Simenon mysteries are unconventional in their attention to character rather than plot. Everyone in these novels is curious to know the great Maigret's "method," but as the detective himself readily admits, he has no method, at least not in the conventional sense: he moves through his world "like a sponge" absorbing himself in whatever strange milieu he must, listening to its rhythms, watching its patterns, and feeling his way toward possible motives. Maigret is calm—almost placid—but occasionally he grows frustrated with the unexpected twist that is a part of every case. Routinely, he is forced to revise his theories in the light of new evidence and to anticipate the unfolding of events. The following excerpts, drawn from five of the seventy-five Maigret novels, document the inspector's supple mind and infinite patience. He is a sublime artist of deep attention. (Translators of the novels excerpted here are as follows: *Maigret and the Millionaires* [Jean Stewart], *Maigret in Court* [Robert Brain], *Inspector Cadaver* [Helen Thomson], *The Bar on the Seine* and *The Hotel Majestic* [David Watson].)

The Method of Inspector Maigret

MAIGRET AND THE MILLIONAIRES (1958)

"The most frustrating cases are those that seem so run-of-the-mill that at first you don't think they're important. It's like those illnesses that sneak up on you, beginning with vague discomfort. When you finally take them seriously, it's often too late."

Maigret had once said this to Inspector Janvier one evening when they were returning together to the Quai des Orfèvres over the Pont-Neuf.

MAIGRET IN COURT (1960)

Maigret had no wish to spend the afternoon sitting motionless in the crowd, in the humid heat, listening to witnesses who, from now on, would spring no more surprises. He had heard these witnesses, all of them, in the quiet of his office. Most of them he had seen in their homes, in their proper surroundings, as well.

The Assize Court had always constituted the most unpleasant, most depressing part of his functions, and each time he had the same feeling of misery.

Was not everything distorted there? Not through any fault of the judges, the jury, the witnesses, nor on account of the criminal code or the procedure, but because human beings were suddenly reduced, if one can so put it, to a few words, a few sentences.

He had sometimes discussed it with his friend Pardon, the local G.P. with whom he and his wife had got into the habit of dining once a month.

Once when his surgery had been full all day, Pardon had displayed a touch of discouragement, almost of bitterness.

'Twenty-eight patients in the afternoon alone! Hardly time to let them sit down, ask them a few questions. What is it you feel? Where does it hurt? How long has it been going on? The others are waiting, staring at the padded door, and wondering if their turn will ever come. Show me your tongue! Take off your clothes! In most cases an hour wouldn't be sufficient to find out everything one should know. Each patient is a separate case, and yet I have to work on the conveyor-belt system . . .'

Maigret had then told him of the end-result of his own work, in other words the Assize Court, since most investigations anyway come to their conclusion there.

'Historians,' he had remarked, 'scholars, devote their entire lives to the study of some figure of the past on whom there already exist numerous works. They go from library to library, from archives to archives, search for the least item of correspondence in the hope of grasping a little more of the truth . . .

'For fifty years or more they've been studying Stendhal's letters to get a clearer idea of his character . . .

'Isn't a crime almost always committed by someone out of the ordinary, in other words less easy to comprehend than the man in the street? They give me a few weeks, sometimes only a few days, to steep myself in a new atmosphere, to question ten, twenty, fifty people I knew nothing at all about till then, and, if possible, to sift out the true from the false.

'I've been reproached for going myself onto the scene instead of sending my detectives. You wouldn't believe it, but it's a miracle that I'm still allowed this privilege!

'The examining magistrate, following on from me, had hardly any more scope and he only sees people, detached from their private lives, in the neutral atmosphere of his office.

'All he has in front of him, in fact, are men already reduced to mere diagrams.

'He also has only a limited time at his disposal; hounded by the press, by public opinion, his initiative restricted by a maze of regulations, submerged by administrative formalities which occupy most of his time, what is he likely to find out?

'If it is mere disincarnate beings who leave his office, what is left for the Assizes, and on what basis are the jury going to decide the fate of one or more of their own kindred?

'It's no longer a question of months or weeks, scarcely of days. The number of the witnesses is reduced to the minimum, as are the questions that are put to them.

'They come and repeat before the court a condensed version, a *digest*, as people say nowadays, of everything they have said beforehand.

'The case is merely sketched in with a few strokes, the people concerned are no more than outlines, caricatures almost . . .'

Hadn't he had that feeling once again this morning, even when he was giving his own evidence?

The press would report that he had spoken *at length* and perhaps be surprised at it. With any other judge than Xavier Bernerie, it was true, he would have been allowed only a few minutes to speak, whereas he had stayed in the witness-box for almost an hour.

He had done his best to be precise, to communicate a little of what he himself felt to those who listened to him.

INSPECTOR CADAVER (1944)

Many a time at the Police Judiciaire, his colleagues had joked about his going off into one of these reveries, and he also knew that people used to talk about this habit of his behind his back.

At such moments, Maigret seemed to puff himself up out of all proportion and become slow-witted and stodgy, like someone blind and dumb who is unaware of what is going on around him. Indeed, if anyone not forewarned was to walk past or talk to Maigret when he was in one of these moods, he would more than likely take him for a fat idiot or a fat sleepyhead.

"So, you're concentrating your thoughts?" said someone who prided himself on his psychological perception.

And Maigret had replied with comic sincerity:

"I never think."

And it was almost true. For Maigret was not thinking now, as he stood in the damp, cold street. He was not following through an idea. One might say he was rather like a sponge.

It was Sergeant Lucas who had described him thus, and he had worked constantly with Maigret and knew him better than anyone.

"There comes a time in the course of an investigation," Lucas had said, "when the *patron* suddenly swells up like a sponge. You'd think he was filling up."

THE BAR ON THE SEINE (1931)

He had handled hundreds of cases in his time, and he knew that they nearly always fell into two distinct phases. Firstly, coming into contact with a new environment, with people he had never even heard of the day before, with a little world which some event had shaken up. He would enter this world as a stranger, an enemy; the people he encountered would be hostile, cunning or would give nothing away. This, for Maigret, was the most exciting part. He would sniff around for clues, feel his way in the dark with nothing to go on. He would observe people's reactions—any one of them could be guilty, or complicit in the crime.

Suddenly he would get a lead, and then the second period would begin. The inquiry would be underway. The gears would start to turn. Each step in the inquiry would bring a fresh revelation, and nearly always the pace would quicken, so the final revelation, when it came, would feel sudden.

The inspector didn't work alone. The events worked for him, almost independently of him. He had to keep up, not be overtaken by them.

THE HOTEL MAJESTIC

He had had to take off his overcoat, because of the heat in the basement, but he hadn't abandoned his bowler or his pipe. Thus accoutred, he wandered peacefully along the corridors, with his hands behind his back, stopping from time to time by one of the glass partitions, rather as if he were inspecting an aquarium.

The huge basement, with its electric lights burning all day long, did in fact strike him as being very like an oceanographical museum. In each glass cage there were creatures, varying in number, darting to and fro. You could see them constantly appearing and disappearing, heavily laden, carrying saucepans or piles of plates, setting service-lifts or goods-lifts in motion, forever using the little instruments which were the telephones.

"What would someone from another planet make of it all? . . ."

.   .   .

Between one and three o'clock, the pace was at its most hectic, everything happening so fast that it was like seeing a film run off in fast motion.

"Excuse me . . . Sorry . . ."

People were constantly bumping into the superintendent, who continued his walk unperturbed, stopping and starting, asking a question now and then.

How many people had he talked to? At least twenty, he reckoned. The head chef had explained to him how the kitchens were run.

.   .   .

All these seemingly complicated operations were in fact quite simple. The large dining-room of the Majestic, where two or three hundred people would then be having lunch, was immediately over the kitchens, so most of the service-lifts went there. Each time one of them came down again, the sound of music was wafted down with it.

Some of the guests had their meals in their rooms, however, and there was a waiter on each floor. There was also a grill-room on the same floor as the basement, where there was dancing in the afternoons from about five o'clock.

The men from the Forensic Laboratory had come for the body, and two specialists from the Criminal Records Office had spent half an hour working on locker 89 with cameras and powerful lights, looking for fingerprints.

None of this seemed to interest Maigret. They would be sure to inform him of the result in due course.

Looking at him, you would have thought he was making an amateurish study of how a grand hotel functions.

DISCUSSION QUESTIONS

1. *How realistic a goal is deep attention in a hyperconnected world?*

2. *What problems in your own, or your institution's, history might have been solved had they been approached with greater patience and more prolonged attention?*

3. *What are some practical techniques for cultivating the habit of deep attention in yourself and in the members of your organization?*

RISKING REVISION

Does change terrify you? Yet what can come into being without change? What after all is dearer, or more proper to Nature? Can you have your bath, without change passing upon the firewood? or nourishment, without change passing upon the viands? Can any serviceable thing be accomplished without change? Do you not see that change within yourself is of a piece with this, and equally indispensable to Nature?

—MARCUS AURELIUS,
Meditations, 7.18

Change, as Marcus Aurelius long ago recognized, is inevitable. It presents exhilarating opportunities, but it also disturbs the equilibrium of creatures naturally craving the comfort of routine and stability. Change comes from without, but it can also come from within those leaders who accept its necessity and harness its energy. Leaders who do this well—leaders who respond swiftly to external change or anticipate such change with their own innovation—show themselves capable of seeing things afresh and imagining new paradigms. Such leaders prove willing to risk revision not only of their own habits and techniques but also of the direction of entire fields.

Ours is a technologically saturated age preoccupied with "the speed of change." Future leaders are trained to operate in dynamic environments. The acronym VUCA, which signifies the volatility, uncertainty, complexity, and ambiguity of a given situation, originated in the military but has now spread to business and other organizational cultures. Prevailing attitudes toward change are largely structured by computing and the Internet. The series of *Shift Happens (Did You Know?)* videos created by Scott McLeod and Karl Fisch have popularized the notion that "we live in exponential times" with their illustrations of the rapid spread of information technology throughout the world. The principle of "technological singularity" proposes that machines will one day outstrip human ability to control them. Today this idea is popularly associated with the artificial intelligence theorist Ray Kurzweil, but the concept emerged as early as the nineteenth-century Industrial Revolution. In an 1863 letter to the editor of New Zealand's *Christchurch Press*, the Victorian writer Samuel Butler declared war on the machines that he understood as threatening to rob human beings of moral and physical autonomy:

> Day by day, however, the machines are gaining ground upon us; day by day we are becoming more subservient to them; more men are daily bound down as slaves to tend them, more men are daily devoting the energies of their whole lives to the development of mechanical life. The upshot is simply a question of time, but that the time will come when the machines will hold the real supremacy over the world and its inhabitants is what no person of a truly philosophic mind can for a moment question.

One need not deplore the march of industry—or, with the Luddites, smash the machines—to acknowledge the ways its enhancement of certain human capabilities entails the transformation, even weakening, of other habits of mind. Any successful innovator must reckon honestly with those alterations. Stepping outside our own age, as some of the following readings allow us to do, reveals that some of the most insightful thinking about change is rather old.

Although we are fond of saying that digital technology has radically reshaped the world's circuitry, we are by no means the first era to believe itself one of cataclysmic change. Other technologies have transformed the landscape and caused similar revolutions in daily life as well as in our humanity's metaphysical conception of it: the technology of writing, the printing press, the steam engine, the airplane, to enumerate but a few. Philosophies of change likewise have an ancient provenance. We might think of the pre-Socratic thinkers Empedocles and Heraclitus, both of whom imagined a world in constant flux. Empedocles theorized a universe in which elements, dominated by the opposed forces of Love and Strife, "never cease changing place continually, now being all united by Love into one, now each borne apart by the hatred engendered of Strife, until they are brought together in the unity of the all, and become subject to it." In the fragments that survive of his work, rendered here in Arthur Fairbanks's translation, Empedocles goes on to explain: "Thus inasmuch as one has been wont to arise out of many and again with the separation of the one the many arise, so things are continually coming into being and there is no fixed age for them; and farther inasmuch as they [the elements] never cease changing place continually, so they always exist within an immovable circle." For his part, Heraclitus envisioned cosmos as continuum, a theory embodied in his celebrated claim that one can never step in the same river twice.

In ancient Chinese thought we find an accepting attitude toward change in the Taoist notion, articulated by Lao Tzu in the *Tao Te Ching*, that one might seek enlightenment in contemplation of the constant unfolding of the universe's "ten thousand things." As Stephen Greenblatt documented in *The Swerve*, his 2011 Pulitzer Prize–winning study, an analogous theory is expressed in the work of the Roman philosopher Lucretius, whose meditations on constant change, articulated in *De Rerum Natura* (*On the Nature of Things*), so strongly influenced subsequent thinkers ranging from the Renaissance poet Edmund Spenser to Isaac Newton. Spenser proposed in the so-called "Mutabilitie Cantos," a coda to his epic *The Faerie Queene*, a law of nature in which everything was "eterne in mutabilitie," eternally in flux, while Newton traced his own thinking about gravity to the "swerve" (*clinamen*), Lucretius's term for the unpredictable atomic motion out of which life and death unfold. Modern physicists may argue over whether the universe will continue its accelerated expansion forever or reverse itself in the far future and begin to contract, yet no one imagines it to be standing still.

Leaders and organizations, then, can change in response to external threats or initiate change in order to realize individual and corporate potential. Leaders may be charged with shepherding organizations through periods of turbulence or with being stewards in times of relative stability. They will have to consider whether the most enduring changes come from above or below and how to implement new ideas in a potentially resistant organization accustomed to doing things a certain way.

The readings in this section address various aspects of change: internal and external change, growth and deterioration, development and repair, innovation and revolution. Change entails risk and demands courage, but "movement," as Brad Pitt's Gerry Lane, the zombie-hunting protagonist of the 2013 film *World War Z*, declares, "is life." Machiavelli argues for the virtue of adaptability in a leader. Atul Gawande and Alexander Wolff discuss the necessity for professionals—surgeons and coaches—to continue to improve by revising their approaches and rejecting comfortable habits. In the short stories "An Old and Established Name" and "Electrification" we encounter individuals utterly resistant to change, while in Kai Bird and Martin Sherwin's portrait of J. Robert Oppenheimer, the head of the Manhattan Project, we find the example of someone leading an entire team into the unknown. Finally, Ovid and La Fontaine illuminate aspects of innovation and change through the genres of the myth and fable, respectively.

RECOMMENDED READING

John Colapinto, "Mother Courage," *The New Yorker* (December 20, 2001)
Roland Huntsford, *The Last Place on Earth* (1979)
Tony Kushner, *Angels in America: A Gay Fantasia on National Themes* (1991)
Lauren Slater, "Dr. Daedalus," *Harper's Magazine* (July 2001)
Gordon Wood, *The Radicalism of the American Revolution* (1991)

Niccolò Machiavelli
(1469–1527)

AS A CITIZEN of Florence, Niccolò Machiavelli lived in a European commercial and cultural center with deep republican roots. He was a career civil servant, whose portfolio was foreign policy, and his work took him on several diplomatic missions. In 1512, the republic, menaced by foreign mercenaries and the power of the Medici family, fell: Machiavelli's own attempts to defend the city with a homegrown militia failed in the face of trained Spanish troops. The Medici imprisoned and tortured Machiavelli for a time but ultimately released him to retirement and the composition of *Il Principe*, or *The Prince*, as it is known in English, and *Discourses on the First Ten Books of Titus Livius*. Both books were published posthumously, in 1532 and 1531, respectively. The latter book, from which this passage is drawn, is a commentary on the ancient Roman historian Livy, whose republican sympathies Machiavelli much admired. Although *The Prince* is the more sensational text, Machiavelli's *Discourses* could be said to offer more sustained and developed insights into his political philosophy. In this chapter Machiavelli explores the necessity for leaders to change their style to suit the times in which they find themselves. (The following selection is translated by Christian E. Detmold.)

Whoever Desires Constant Success Must Change His Conduct with the Times
from *Discourses on the First Ten Books of Titus Livius* (1531)

I have often reflected that the causes of the success or failure of men depend upon their manner of suiting their conduct to the times. We see one man proceed in his actions with passion and impetuosity; and as in both the one and the other case men are apt to exceed the proper limits, not being able always to observe the just middle course, they are apt to err in both. But he errs least and will be most favored by fortune who suits his proceedings to the times, as I have said above, and always follows the impulses of his nature. Every one knows how Fabius Maximus conducted the war against Hannibal with extreme caution and circumspection, and with an utter absence of all impetuosity or Roman audacity. It was his good fortune that this mode of proceeding accorded perfectly with the times and circumstances. For Hannibal had arrived in Rome whilst still young and with his fortunes fresh; he had already twice routed the Romans, so that the republic was as it were deprived of her best troops, and greatly discouraged by her reverses. Rome could not therefore have been more favored by fortune, than to have a commander who by his extreme caution and the slowness of his movements kept the enemy at bay. At the same time, Fabius could not have found circumstances more favorable for his character and genius, to which fact he was indebted for his success and glory. And that this mode of proceeding was the result of his character and nature, and not a matter of choice, was shown on the occasion when Scipio wanted to take the same troops to Africa for the purpose of promptly terminating the war. Fabius most earnestly opposed this, like a man incapable of breaking from his accustomed ways and habits; so that, if he had been master, Hannibal would have remained in Italy, because Fabius failed to perceive that the times were changed. But Rome was a republic that produced citizens of various character and dispositions, such as Fabius, who was excellent at the time when it was desirable to protract the war, and Scipio, when it became necessary to terminate it. It is this which assures to republics greater vitality and more enduring success than monarchies have; for the diversity of the genius of her citizens enables the republic better to accommodate herself to the changes of the times than can be done by a prince. For any man accustomed to a certain mode of proceeding will never change it, as we have said, and consequently when time and circumstances change, so that his ways are no longer in harmony with them, he must of necessity succumb. Pietro Soderini, whom we have mentioned several times already, was in all his actions governed by humanity and patience. He and his country prospered so long as the times favored this mode of proceeding; but when afterwards circumstances arose that demanded a course of conduct the opposite to that of patience and humanity, he was unfit for the occasion, and his own and his country's ruin were the consequence. Pope Julius II acted throughout the whole period of his pontificate with the impetuosity and passion natural to his character; and as the times and circumstances well accorded with this, he was successful in all his undertakings. But if the times had changed so that different counsels would have been required, he would unquestionably have been ruined, for he could not have changed his character or mode of action.

That we cannot thus change at will is due to two causes; the one is the impossibility of resisting the natural bent of our characters; and the other is the difficulty of persuading ourselves, after having been accustomed to success by a certain mode of proceeding, that any other can succeed as well. It is this that causes the varying success of a man; for the times change, but he does not change his mode of proceeding. The ruin of states is caused in like manner, as we have fully shown above, because they do not modify their institutions to suit the changes of the times. And such changes are more difficult and tardy in republics; for necessarily circumstances will occur that will unsettle the whole state, and when the change of proceeding of one man will not suffice for the occasion.

Lao She
(1899–1966)

BORN TO A poor Manchu family, probably in Beijing, Lao She (Shu Qing-chun) left China for England in 1924. He wrote several novels there while teaching Mandarin at the University of London. In England he also found a lasting influence in the work of Charles Dickens. In 1930, Lao She returned to China to continue his writing career. His literary stature grew at home, and the 1945 English translation of his novel *The Rickshaw Boy* (1937), inexact though it may have been, established his reputation in the West. He visited the United States in 1946. Lao She reportedly drowned himself after being humiliated and beaten by Red Guards during the Cultural Revolution. In 1978, his name and work were rehabilitated by the Communist Party. (The following selection is translated by William A. Lyell.)

An Old and Established Name
(1936)

After Manager Qian left, Xin Dezhi—the senior apprentice who now had quite a hand in the operation of the Fortune Silk Store—went for several days without eating a decent meal. Manager Qian had been universally recognized as a skilled old hand in the silk business just as the Fortune Silk Store was universally recognized as an old and established name. Xin Dezhi had been trained for the business under the hands of Manager Qian. However, it wasn't solely personal feeling that made Xin Dezhi take it so hard when Manager Qian left, nor was his agitation due to any personal ambition that might have been stimulated by the vague possibility that he himself might become the new manager. He really couldn't put his finger on the reason for all the anxiety that he felt; it was as though Manager Qian had taken away with him something or other that would be forever difficult to recover.

When Manager Zhou arrived to take things over, Xin Dezhi realized that his anxiety had not been unfounded. Previously he had only felt *sorrow* at the departure of the old manager, but now he felt downright *fury* at the arrival of the new one. Manager Zhou was a hustler. The Fortune Silk Store—an old and established name of years standing!—now demeaned itself into employing every kind of trick to rope in customers. Xin Dezhi's mouth hung so far open in dismay that his face began to look like a dumpling that had split apart while boiling. An old hand, an old and established name, old rules—all had vanished along with Manager Qian, perhaps never to return again. Manager Qian had been very honest and gentlemanly, so much so, in fact, that the Fortune

Silk Store lost money. The owners, for their part, weren't all that impressed by Manager Qian's upright demeanor; they were only concerned with having dividends to split up at the end of the year. Hence, they had let him go.

For as long as anyone could remember, the Fortune Silk Store had maintained an air of cultured elegance—a simple sign with the name of the store in black characters against a gold background, green fittings in the shop itself, a black counter with blue cloth cover, large square stools sheathed in blue woolen cloth, and fresh flowers always set out on the tea table. For as long as anyone could remember, except for hanging out four lanterns with big red tassels upon the occasion of the Lantern Festival, the Fortune Silk Store had never exhibited a trace of that vulgar ostentation so prevalent among ordinary merchants. For as long as anyone could remember, the Fortune had never engaged in such base practices as haggling with customers, letting the customer pay to the nearest dollar, pasting advertisements all over the place, or running two-week sales. What the Fortune Silk Store sold was its old and established name. For as long as anyone could remember, the Fortune had never set free cigarettes out on the counter as a come-on to customers; nor had any of the apprentices in the shop ever spoken in loud tones; the only sound in the store had been the gentle gurgle of the manager's water pipe intermingled with his occasional coughing.

As soon as Manager Zhou walked through the door, Xin Dezhi saw only too clearly that these precedents, as well as many other old and valuable customs, were all going to come to an end. There was something improper about the new manager's eyes. He never lowered his eyelids, but rather swept the whole world with his vision as if he were searching out a thief. Manager Qian, on the other hand, had always sat on a stool with his eyes closed, and yet if any of the apprentices did the slightest thing wrong, he knew about it immediately.

Just as Xin Dezhi had feared, within a few days Manager Zhou had transformed the Fortune into something akin to a carnival sideshow. In front of the main entrance the new manager set up a garish sign bearing the words GIANT SALE. Each word was five feet square! Then he installed two bright gaslights whose flames lit up faces in such a way as to turn them green. As if all this weren't enough, he had a drum and bugle set up by the main entrance, which made a din from dawn until the third watch at night. Four apprentices in red hats stood at the door and roamed up and down the sidewalk passing out handbills to anyone who came within their reach.

But Manager Zhou still wasn't satisfied. He appointed two clerks to the specific task of providing customers with cigarettes and tea; even someone who was buying only half a foot of plain cloth would be dragged to the back counter and given a cigarette. Soldiers, street-cleaners, and waitresses stood about firing up their tobacco until the shop was so smoked up that it looked like a Buddhist temple lost in incense fumes. Manager Zhou even went a step further; if a customer bought one foot of material, he'd give him an extra one free and throw in a foreign doll for the kids. And now all the apprentices were expected to joke and make small talk with the customers. If the customer wanted something that the store didn't have, then the apprentice wasn't to tell him right out that the store didn't have it, but was rather expected to drag out something else and force the customer to take a look at it. Any order over ten dollars would be delivered by one of the apprentices, and Manager Zhou bought two broken-down bicycles for that purpose.

Xin Dezhi longed to find some place where he could have a good cry. In fifteen or sixteen years of faithful service he had never even imagined (much less expected to see) the Fortune Silk Store coming to such a pass. How could he look people in the face? In the past who on the whole street had not held the Fortune Silk Store in great respect? When an apprentice hung out the lantern which served as the store's sign at night, even the policemen on the beat would treat him with special regard. And remember that year when the soldiers came! To be sure, during the pillaging, the Fortune had been cleaned out just like the other stores, but the doors and the signs saying *We Never Go Back on Our Prices* had not been torn away, as had been the case with some of the neighboring shops. Yes, that golden plaque bearing the inscription *Fortune Silk Store* had a certain awe-inspiring dignity about it.

Xin Dezhi had already lived in the city now for twenty-some years and fifteen or sixteen of them had been spent in the Fortune. In fact, it was his second home. His way of speaking, his very cough, and the style of his long blue gown had all been given to him by the Fortune Silk Store. The store had given him his personal pride and he, in turn, was proud of the store. Whenever he went out to collect bills, people would invite him in for a cup of tea. For although the store was a business, it treated its steady customers as friends. Often Manager Qian would even participate in the weddings and funerals of his regular customers. The Fortune Silk Store was a business conducted with "gentlemanly style." The more prestigious people in the neighborhood could often be found sitting and chatting on the bench in front of the main entrance. Whenever there were parades or any lively doings on the streets, the women in his customers' families would contact Manager Qian and he would arrange good seats at his store from which they could observe all of the excitement. This past glorious history of the shop was ever in Xin Dezhi's heart. And now?

It wasn't that he didn't know that the times had changed. For instance, a number of old and established shops on both sides of the Fortune had already tossed their rules to the winds (the newer shops were not worth worrying about because they had never had any traditions to begin with). He realized all this. But it was precisely because the Fortune had remained doggedly faithful to its traditions that he loved it all the more, was all the more proud of it. It was as though the Fortune Silk Store were the only bolt of real silk in a pile of synthetics. If even the Fortune hit the skids, then the world would surely come to an end. Damn! He had to admit it—now the Fortune was just like all the others, if not worse.

In the past, his favorite object of contempt had always been the Village Silk Shop across the street. The manager over there was always shuffling around with a cigarette dangling from lips that occasionally opened wide enough to reveal gold-capped front teeth. The manager's wife was forever carrying little children on her back, in her arms, and seemingly even in her pockets. She scurried in and out of the shop all day clucking and cackling in a southern dialect so that Xin Dezhi couldn't make out what she was jabbering about. When the couple had a good spat, they always picked the shop to have it in; when they beat the children or breastfed a baby, they always picked the shop to do it in. You couldn't tell whether they were doing business or putting on a circus over there. However, one thing was certain: the manager's wife had her breasts forever on display in the shop with a baby or two hanging from them. He had no idea as to where in the world they had dug up the clerks that worked there. They all wore shoddy shoes, but for the most part dressed in silk. Some of them had Sun-Brand Headache Salve plastered conspicuously on their temples; some had their hair so slicked down that the tops of their heads looked like the bottoms of large lacquerware spoons; and some of them wore gold-rimmed glasses. Besides all these specifics, the place had a generally contemptible air about it: they had GIANT SALES from one end of the year to the other; they always had gaudy gaslights hung out in front of the store; and they were forever playing a phonograph full blast in order to attract business. Whenever a customer bought two dollars' worth of goods, the manager would, with his own hands offer him a sweet sesame cake; if the customer didn't accept it, he might even shove it right into his mouth. Nothing in the shop had a fixed price and the rate of exchange that was given for foreign currency often fluctuated. Xin Dezhi had never deigned to look directly at the three words on the shop's sign; moreover, he had never gone over there to buy anything. He had never imagined that such a business firm could even exist on this earth, much less have the nerve to be located right across the street from the Fortune Silk Store! But strange to say, the Village Silk Shop had prospered, while the Fortune had gone downhill day after day. He hadn't been able to figure out what the reason was. It certainly couldn't be that there was an inexorable law that required that a business be run completely divorced from any code of ethics before it could make money. If this were really the case, then why should stores bother to train apprentices? Couldn't any old lout do business just as long as he were alive and kicking? It couldn't be this way! It just couldn't! At least he had always been sure that the Fortune would never be like that.

How could he have foreseen that after Manager Zhou's arrival, his beloved Fortune would also hang out gaslights so that its lights combined with those of the Village Silk Shop lit up more then half the block? Yes, they were two of a kind now! The Fortune and the Village a pair!—he must be dreaming! But it wasn't a dream and even Xin Dezhi had to learn to do things in Manager Zhou's way. He had to chitchat with the customers, offer them cigarettes, and then inveigle them into going to the back counter for a cup of tea. He was forced to haul out ersatz goods and pass them off as genuine; he had to learn to wait until a customer became insistent before giving him an honest length of material. He had to learn tricks to be employed in measuring the cloth—he was even expected to use his finger on the sly to pinch back a bit of the cloth before cutting it! How much more could he take?

But most of the apprentices seemed happy with doing things the new way. If a woman came in, it was all they could do to keep themselves from completely surrounding her; they just itched to haul out every piece of goods in the store for her inspection. Even if she bought only two feet of dust-cloth it was all they could do to keep themselves from escorting her home. The manager loved this kind of thing. He wanted to see the clerks turn head over heels and do acrobatics when the customers came in; he would have liked it even better if they had been able to fly around the customers in mid-air.

Manager Zhou and the boss of the Village Silk Shop became fast friends. Sometimes the two of them would even make up a foursome with the people from the Heaven Silk Store and have a round of mah-jongg. The Heaven was another silk store on the same street that had been in business now for four or five years. In times gone by, Manager Qian had always ignored the Heaven; hence the Heaven had made it a point to go into direct competition with the Fortune and even boasted that they wouldn't be satisfied until they had put it out of business. Manager Qian had never picked up the gauntlet, but occasionally he used to observe: "*We* do business on our old and established name." The Heaven was the kind of store that had a Giant Anniversary Sale three hundred and sixty-five days a year. And now even the people from the Heaven were coming over to play mah-jongg! When they did, Xin Dezhi, of course, utterly ignored them.

Whenever he had a little spare time, he would sit behind the counter and stare vacantly at the racks of materials. Originally all the goods on the racks had been covered up with white cloth. Now, ceiling to floor, all the rolls of material were exposed to full view in all their varied colors so that they might serve as an attraction to the customers. It was such a dazzling sight that it made one's eyes blur just to look at it. In his heart, Xin Dezhi knew that the Fortune Silk Store had already ceased to exist. And yet, after the first business third had passed, he could not help but admire Manager Zhou. Because when it came time to balance the books, although Zhou hadn't made a great deal of money, yet he hadn't lost any either. He had pulled the Fortune out of the red. Manager Zhou smiled at everyone and explained: "You have to bear in mind that this is only my first third. I still have a lot of plans up my sleeve for the future that I haven't even tried yet. Furthermore, think of my initial outlay in advertising displays and gas lights. All of that took money you know. So . . . (Whenever he felt full of himself in conversation, he'd take a *so* . . . and tack it on the end of whatever he was saying.) Later on we won't even have to use those advertising displays. We'll have newer and more economical ways of making ourselves known. Then there'll be a profit to show. So. . . ." Xin Dezhi could plainly see that there was no turning back for Manager Zhou. The world had really changed. After all, Manager Zhou was on very good terms with people from the Heaven and the Village, and both of those businesses had prospered.

Just after the books were balanced, there was a great deal of commotion in town about searching out and boycotting Japanese goods. And yet, as if possessed, Manager Zhou started laying in all the Japanese goods he could get his hands on, and even though student investigating teams were already on the streets, he displayed Japanese goods right out in the open. Then he issued an order: "When a customer comes in, show him the Japanese goods first. None of the other places dare to sell them, so we might as well make hay while the sun shines. If a farmer comes in, tell him straight out that it is Japanese cloth; they'll buy it anyway. But if someone from the city comes in, then say it's German material."

When the investigating students arrived, Manager Zhou's face butterflied into smiles as he offered them cigarettes and tea. "The Fortune Silk Store swears by its good name that it will not sell Japanese goods. Look over there, gentlemen. Those goods by the door are German materials along with some local products. Inside the store we have nothing but Chinese silks and satins. Our branch store in the south sends them up to us."

The students began to eye some of the printed materials with suspicion. Manager Zhou smiled and shouted, "Bring me that piece of leftover Japanese material that we have in back." When the cloth had been brought to him, he grabbed the leader of the investigating students by the sleeve and said, "Sir, I swear that this is the only piece of Japanese goods that we have left. It's the same material that the shirt you're wearing is made from. So . . ." He turned his head around and ordered, "All right, let's throw this piece of Japanese material out into the street." The leader of the investigating students looked at his own shirt and, not daring to raise his head, led the rest of the students out the door.

Manager Zhou made quite a bit of money from these Japanese materials, which could at any time turn into German, Chinese, or English goods. If a customer who knew his materials threw a piece of goods right down on the floor in front of Manager Zhou's face, the latter would issue an order to one of the apprentices: "Bring out the *real* Western goods. Can't you tell we have an intelligent man here who knows his materials?" Then he'd say to the customer: "You know what you want. You wouldn't take that even if I gave it to you free! So . . ." Thus he'd tie up another sale. By the time that the whole transaction was completed, it would be all the customer could do to tear himself away from the congenial company of Manager Zhou. Xin Dezhi came to the realization that if you plan to make money in business, you have to be a combination magician and burlesque comedian. Manager Zhou was really something, all right. And yet, Xin Dezhi didn't feel like working at the Fortune anymore. For the more he came to admire Manager Zhou, the worse he felt. Lately even his food all seemed to go down the wrong way. If he were ever again to enjoy a good night's sleep, he would have to leave his beloved Fortune Silk Store.

But before he had found a good position someplace else, Manager Zhou left. The Heaven Silk Store had need of just such talents, and Manager Zhou himself was anxious to make the change: he felt that the stick-in-the-mud traditions of the Fortune were so deeply rooted that he would never really be able to display his talents fully here.

When Xin Dezhi saw Manager Zhou off, it was as though he were seeing away a great burden that had been pressing on his heart. On the basis of his fifteen or sixteen years of service, Xin Dezhi felt that he had the right to talk things over with the owners of the store, although he could not be sure that his words would carry any real weight. However, he did know which of them were basically conservative and had a good idea as to how to influence them. He began to propagandize for Manager Qian's return and even got Qian's old friends to help. He didn't say that everything that Manager Qian had done was right, but would merely observe that each of the two managers had his good points and that these points ought to be combined harmoniously. One could not rigidly stick to old customs, but neither would it do to change too radically. An old and established name was worth preserving, but new business methods ought also be studied and applied. One ought to lay equal emphasis upon preserving the name *and* making a profit—he knew that this line of argument would be potent in persuading the owners.

But in his heart of hearts, he really had something quite different in mind. He hoped that when Manager Qian returned, everything that had been lost would come back with him and the Fortune Silk Store would once again be the *old* Fortune Silk Store; otherwise, as far as he was concerned, it would be nothing. He had it all figured out: they would get rid of the gaslights, the drum and bugle, the advertisements, handbills, and cigarettes; they would cut down on personnel as much as possible, and thus possibly save quite a bit on operating expenses. Moreover, without advertising the fact, they would sell low, use a long foot in measuring, and stock honest-to-goodness materials. Could the customers all be such asses that they wouldn't see the advantages of doing business at the Fortune?

And in the end Manager Qian actually did return. Now the only gaslights left on the street were those of the Village Silk Shop. The Fortune had recovered its former air of austere simplicity—although, in order to welcome Manager Qian back, they had gone so far as to hang out four lanterns decorated with tassels.

The day that the Fortune put out its lanterns of welcome, two camels appeared before the door of the Heaven Silk Store. The camels' bodies were completely draped in satin sash, and flashing, colored electric lights were installed on the humps. On both sides of the camels, stands were set up to sell chances at ten cents each. Whenever at least ten people had bought tickets, a drawing would be held. If lucky, one had hopes of winning a fashionable piece of silk. With this sort of thing going on the area around the Heaven Silk Store soon became something of a country fair, so crowded you could scarcely budge in the press. Because, you see, it *was* true that every once in a while somebody really *did* emerge from the crowd, all smiles, with a piece of fashionable silk tucked under his arm.

Once again the bench in front of the Fortune was covered with a piece of blue woolen cloth. Once again Manager Qian sat within the shop, eyelids drooping. Once again the clerks sat quietly behind the counters. Some of them toyed quietly with the beads of an abacus; others yawned leisurely. Xin Dezhi didn't say anything, but in his heart he was really worried. Sometimes it would seem ages and ages before a single customer appeared. Occasionally someone would glance in from the outside as if he were about to enter, but then he would glance at the small golden plaque and head over in the direction of the Heaven Silk Store. Sometimes a customer would actually come in and look at materials, but upon discovering that one couldn't bargain over the price, would walk out again empty-handed. There were still a few of the old reliables who came regularly to buy a little something or other, but sometimes they merely stopped by to have a chat with Manager Qian. They'd usually sigh a bit over the poverty of the times, have a few cups of tea, and then leave without buying anything. Xin Dezhi loved to listen to them talk, for it would remind him of the good times the store had once known in the past. But even he knew that the past cannot be easily recovered. The Heaven Silk Store was the only one on the whole street that was really doing any business.

At the end of a season, the Fortune had to cut back again on personnel. With tears in his eyes, Xin Dezhi told Manager Qian: "I can do five clerks' work all by myself. What's there to worry about?" Manager Qian took courage and chimed in: "What do we have to be afraid of?" And that night Xin Dezhi slept a very sweet sleep, fully prepared to do the work of five clerks on the very next day.

Yet after a year, the Fortune Silk Store was bought out by the Heaven.

Mikhail Zoschenko
(1895–1958)

MIKHAIL ZOSCHENKO WAS born in St. Petersburg. After serving in World War I, he joined the Red Army in 1918. For the next several decades Zoschenko enjoyed a successful literary career; his humorous style proved immensely popular with Russian readers. Always alert to the costs of what his translator Robert Chandler calls "grand visions of progress," such as Communism itself, Zoschenko focused on small subjects in order to "capture the texture of everyday life in Soviet Russia," with all its monumental indignities. In 1946, Zoschenko was expelled from the Communist Party and declared an "enemy of Soviet literature." The brief sketch "Electrification" (1924) typifies its author's method of social critique.

Electrification
(1924)

What, brothers, is today's most fashionable word?

Today's most fashionable word of all is, of course, 'electrification'.

Lighting up Soviet Russia with light, without doubt, is a matter of massive importance. No one can argue with that. But it does, for the time being, have its downside. I'm not saying, comrades, that it costs too much. It costs money—that's all. No, I'm saying something different.

What I'm saying is this:

I was living, comrades, in a huge building. The whole of this building ran on paraffin. Some of us had lamps, some—cans of oil with a wick. The poorest had to make do with church candles. Life wasn't easy.

And then they start to install light.

First it's the house manager. Lights up his room—and that's that. A quiet fellow, doesn't let on what he's thinking. Though he wanders about a bit strangely and keeps absent-mindedly blowing his nose.

But he doesn't let on what he's thinking.

Then in comes my dear wife, Yelizaveta Ignatyevna Prokhorova. Says we should illuminate the apartment.

'Everyone,' she says, 'is installing light. The director himself has installed light,' she says.

So—of course—we do the same.

Light is installed, the apartment illuminated—heavens above! What foulness and filth!

Till then, you went to work in the morning, you came back in the evening, you drank down your tea and you went to bed. You never saw a thing with just paraffin. But now, with illumination—you see wallpaper flapping off the wall, and somebody's beaten-up slipper lying about on the floor. You see a bedbug trotting along, trying to get away from the light. An old rag here, a gob of spit there, a flea frisking about . . .

Heavens above! It's enough to make you call the night watchman. Such a sight is sad to see.

In our room, for instance, we had a sofa. I'd always thought it wasn't a bad sofa—even quite a good sofa! In the evenings I used to sit on it. But now with this electricity—heavens above! Some sofa! Bits sticking up, bits hanging down, bits falling out. How can I sit on such a sofa? My soul protests.

No, I think, I don't live in luxury. Everything's revolting to look at. And everything I do goes wrong.

Then I see dear Yelizaveta Ignatyevna. She looks sad. She's muttering away to herself, tidying things up in the kitchen.

'What,' I ask, 'are you so sad about, dear wife?'

She shrugs her shoulders.

'I had no idea, my dear man,' she says, 'what a shabby life I've been living.'

I look at our bits and pieces. Not so great, I think. Foulness and filth. Rags of one kind and rags of another kind. All flooded with light and staring you in the eye.

So I start to get a bit down in the mouth, you might say, when I come back home in the evenings.

I come in. I switch on the light. I briefly admire the lamp, then bury my nose in the pillow.

Then I think again. I get my pay. I buy whitewash, I mix it up—and I set to work. I tear off wallpaper, I stamp out bedbugs, I sweep away cobwebs. I sort out the sofa. I paint, I adorn—my soul sings and rejoices.

I did well. But not that well. It was in vain, dear brothers, that I blew all that money. My wife cut the wires.

'Light,' she says, 'makes life seem horribly shabby. Why,' she says, 'shine light on our poverty? The bedbugs will die of laughter.'

I beg her. I argue arguments with her. No use.

'You can move,' she says, 'to another apartment. I don't want,' she says, 'to live with light. I've no money,' she says, 'to renovate and renew.'

But how could I move, comrades, after spending a fortune on whitewash? I gave in.

Light's all very well, brothers, but it's not easy to live with.

Atul Gawande
(b. 1965)

A GENERAL AND endocrine surgeon at Boston's Brigham and Women's Hospital and a public health researcher, Atul Gawande writes eloquently about medicine and culture. A professor at the Harvard School of Public Health and Harvard Medical School, Gawande is also a staff writer at *The New Yorker* and the author of the bestselling books *Complications, Better*, and *The Checklist Manifesto*. The recipient of a MacArthur Fellowship, Gawande has also been numbered among the hundred most influential thinkers by *Time* and *Foreign Policy*. In his books and essays Gawande illuminates with precision and empathy various aspects of medical culture and the ways in which human beings, driven by an amalgam of passion and reason, often act in contradictory ways. In this piece Gawande focuses on the behavior of surgeons and their general reluctance to have their work observed by someone else even if such a process might promote growth and improvement: "Human beings resist exposure and critique; our brains are well defended." Having investigated the role of coaches in the careers of athletes, musicians, and teachers, Gawande decides to take on a coach of his own. In the process he discovers shortcomings in his surgical technique and explains the role of his coach in helping him to overcome blind spots: "The sort of coaching that fosters effective innovation and judgment," he concludes, "not merely replication of technique, may not be so easy to cultivate." Gawande's recognition that the willingness to take on coaches depends on how cultures "regard failure" has significant implications for practitioners who also lead cultures, especially for those responsible for getting maximum performance from those who have already reached a very high level of achievement.

Personal Best
from *The New Yorker* (October 3, 2011)

I've been a surgeon for eight years. For the past couple of them, my performance in the operating room has reached a plateau. I'd like to think it's a good thing—I've arrived at my professional peak. But mainly it seems as if I've just stopped getting better.

During the first two or three years in practice, your skills seem to improve almost daily. It's not about hand-eye coördination—you have that down halfway through your residency. As one of my professors once explained, doing surgery is no more physically difficult than writing in cursive. Surgical mastery is about familiarity and judgment. You learn the problems that can occur during a particular procedure or with a particular condition, and you learn how to either prevent or respond to those problems.

Say you've got a patient who needs surgery for appendicitis. These days, surgeons will typically do a laparoscopic appendectomy. You slide a small camera—a laparoscope—into the abdomen through a quarter-inch incision near the belly button, insert a long grasper through an incision beneath the waistline, and push a device for stapling and cutting through an incision in the left lower abdomen. Use the grasper to pick up the finger-size appendix, fire the stapler across its base and across the vessels feeding it, drop the severed organ into a plastic bag, and pull it out. Close up, and you're done. That's how you like it to go, anyway. But often it doesn't.

Even before you start, you need to make some judgments. Unusual anatomy, severe obesity, or internal scars from previous abdominal surgery could make it difficult to get the camera in safely; you don't want to poke it into a loop of intestine. You have to decide which camera-insertion method to use—there's a range of options—or whether to abandon the high-tech approach and do the operation the traditional way, with a wide-open incision that lets you see everything directly. If you do get your camera and instruments inside, you may have trouble grasping the appendix. Infection turns it into a fat, bloody, inflamed worm that sticks to everything around it—bowel, blood vessels, an ovary, the pelvic sidewall—and to free it you have to choose from a variety of tools and techniques. You can use a long cotton-tipped instrument to try to push the surrounding attachments away. You can use electrocautery, a hook, a pair of scissors, a sharp-tip dissector, a blunt-tip dissector, a right-angle dissector, or a suction device. You can adjust the operating table so that the patient's head is down and his feet are up, allowing gravity to pull the viscera in the right direction. Or you can just grab whatever part of the appendix is visible and pull really hard.

Once you have the little organ in view, you may find that appendicitis was the wrong diagnosis. It might be a tumor of the appendix, Crohn's disease, or an ovarian condition that happened to have inflamed the nearby appendix. Then you'd have to decide whether you need additional equipment or personnel—maybe it's time to enlist another surgeon.

Over time, you learn how to head off problems, and, when you can't, you arrive at solutions with less fumbling and more assurance. After eight years, I've performed more than two thousand operations. Three-quarters have involved my specialty, endocrine surgery—surgery for endocrine organs such as the thyroid, the parathyroid, and the adrenal glands. The rest have involved everything from simple biopsies to colon cancer. For my specialized cases, I've come to know most of the serious difficulties that could arise, and have worked out solutions. For the others, I've gained confidence in my ability to handle a wide range of situations, and to improvise when necessary.

As I went along, I compared my results against national data, and I began beating the averages. My rates of complications moved steadily lower and lower. And then, a couple of years ago, they didn't. It started to seem that the only direction things could go from here was the wrong one.

Maybe this is what happens when you turn forty-five. Surgery is, at least, a relatively late-peaking career. It's not like mathematics or baseball or pop music, where your best work is often behind you by the time you're thirty. Jobs that involve the complexities of people or nature seem to take the longest to master: the average age at which S. & P. 500 chief executive officers are hired is fifty-two, and the age of maximum productivity for geologists, one study estimated, is around fifty-four. Surgeons apparently fall somewhere between the extremes, requiring both physical stamina and the judgment that comes with experience. Apparently, I'd arrived at that middle point.

It wouldn't have been the first time I'd hit a plateau. I grew up in Ohio, and when I was in high school I hoped to become a serious tennis player. But I peaked at seventeen. That was the year that Danny Trevas and I climbed to the top tier for doubles in the Ohio Valley. I qualified to play singles in a couple of national tournaments, only to be smothered in the first round both times. The kids at that level were playing a different game than I was. At Stanford, where I went to college, the tennis team ranked No. 1 in the nation, and I had no chance of being picked. That meant spending the past twenty-five years trying to slow the steady decline of my game.

I still love getting out on the court on a warm summer day, swinging a racquet strung to fifty-six pounds of tension at a two-ounce felt-covered sphere, and trying for those increasingly elusive moments when my racquet feels like an extension of my arm, and my legs are putting me exactly where the ball is going to be. But I came to accept that I'd never be remotely as good as I was when I was seventeen. In the hope of not losing my game altogether, I play when I can. I often bring my racquet on trips, for instance, and look for time to squeeze in a match.

One July day a couple of years ago, when I was at a medical meeting in Nantucket, I had an afternoon free and went looking for someone to hit with. I found a local tennis club and asked if there was anyone who wanted to play. There wasn't. I saw that there was a ball machine, and I asked the club pro if I could use it to practice ground strokes. He told me that it was for members only. But I could pay for a lesson and hit with him.

He was in his early twenties, a recent graduate who'd played on his college team. We hit back and forth for a while. He went easy on me at first, and then started running me around. I served a few points, and the tennis coach in him came out. You know, he said, you could get more power from your serve.

I was dubious. My serve had always been the best part of my game. But I listened. He had me pay attention to my feet as I served, and I gradually recognized that my legs weren't really underneath me when I swung my racquet up into the air. My right leg dragged a few inches behind my body, reducing my power. With a few minutes of tinkering, he'd added at least ten miles an hour to my serve. I was serving harder than I ever had in my life.

Not long afterward, I watched Rafael Nadal play a tournament match on the Tennis Channel. The camera flashed to his coach, and the obvious struck me as interesting: even Rafael Nadal has a coach. Nearly every élite tennis player in the world does. Professional athletes use coaches to make sure they are as good as they can be.

But doctors don't. I'd paid to have a kid just out of college look at my serve. So why did I find it inconceivable to pay someone to come into my operating room and coach me on my surgical technique?

WHAT WE THINK of as coaching was, sports historians say, a distinctly American development. During the nineteenth century, Britain had the more avid sporting culture; its leisure classes went in for games like cricket, golf, and soccer. But the aristocratic origins produced an ethos of amateurism: you didn't want to seem to be trying too hard. For the Brits, coaching, even practicing, was, well, unsporting. In America, a more competitive and entrepreneurial spirit took hold. In 1875, Harvard and Yale played one of the nation's first American-rules football games. Yale soon employed a head coach for the team, the legendary Walter Camp. He established position coaches for individual player development, maintained detailed performance records for each player, and pre-planned every game. Harvard preferred the British approach to sports. In those first three decades, it beat Yale only four times.

The concept of a coach is slippery. Coaches are not teachers, but they teach. They're not your boss—in professional tennis, golf, and skating, the athlete hires and fires the coach—but they can be bossy. They don't even have to be good at the sport. The famous Olympic gymnastics coach Bela Karolyi couldn't do a split if his life depended on it. Mainly, they observe, they judge, and they guide.

Coaches are like editors, another slippery invention. Consider Maxwell Perkins, the great Scribner's editor, who found, nurtured, and published such writers as F. Scott Fitzgerald, Ernest Hemingway, and Thomas Wolfe. "Perkins has the intangible faculty of giving you confidence in yourself and the book you are writing," one of his writers said in a *New Yorker* Profile from 1944. "He never tells you what to do," another writer said. "Instead, he suggests to you, in an extraordinarily inarticulate fashion, what you want to do yourself."

The coaching model is different from the traditional conception of pedagogy, where there's a presumption that, after a certain point, the student no longer needs instruction. You graduate. You're done. You can go the rest of the way yourself. This is how élite musicians are taught. Barbara Lourie Sand's book *Teaching Genius* describes the methods of the legendary Juilliard violin instructor Dorothy DeLay. DeLay was a Perkins-like figure who trained an amazing roster of late-twentieth-century virtuosos, including Itzhak Perlman, Nigel Kennedy, Midori, and Sarah Chang. They came to the Juilliard School at a young age—usually after they'd demonstrated talent but reached the limits of what local teachers could offer. They studied with DeLay for a number of years, and then they graduated, launched like ships leaving drydock. She saw her role as preparing them to make their way without her.

Itzhak Perlman, for instance, arrived at Juilliard, in 1959, at the age of thirteen, and studied there for eight years, working with both DeLay and Ivan Galamian, another revered instructor. Among the key things he learned were discipline, a broad repertoire, and the exigencies of technique. "All DeLay's students, big or little, have to do their scales, their arpeggios, their études, their Bach, their concertos, and so on," Sand writes. "By the time they reach their teens, they are expected to be practicing a minimum of five hours a day." DeLay also taught them to try new and difficult things, to perform without fear. She expanded their sense of possibility. Perlman, disabled by polio, couldn't play the violin standing, and DeLay was one of the few who were convinced that he could have a concert career. DeLay was, her biographer observed, "basically in the business of teaching her pupils how to think, and to trust their ability to do so effectively." Musical expertise meant not needing to be coached.

Doctors understand expertise in the same way. Knowledge of disease and the science of treatment are always evolving. We have to keep developing our capabilities and avoid falling behind. So the training inculcates an ethic of perfectionism. Expertise is thought to be not a static condition but one that doctors must build and sustain for themselves.

Coaching in pro sports proceeds from a starkly different premise: it considers the teaching model naïve about our human capacity for self-perfection. It holds that, no matter how well prepared people are in their formative years, few can achieve and maintain their best performance on their own. One of these views, it seemed to me, had to be wrong. So I called Itzhak Perlman to find out what he thought.

I asked him why concert violinists didn't have coaches, the way top athletes did. He said that he didn't know, but that it had always seemed a mistake to him. He had enjoyed the services of a coach all along.

He had a coach? "I was very, very lucky," Perlman said. His wife, Toby, whom he'd known at Juilliard, was a concert-level violinist, and he'd relied on her for the past forty years. "The great challenge in performing is listening to yourself," he said. "Your physicality, the sensation that you have as you play the violin, interferes with your accuracy of listening." What violinists perceive is often quite different from what audiences perceive.

"My wife always says that I don't really know how I play," he told me. "She is an extra ear." She'd tell him if a passage was too fast or too tight or too mechanical—if there was something that needed fixing. Sometimes she has had to puzzle out what might be wrong, asking another expert to describe what she heard as he played.

Her ear provided external judgment. "She is very tough, and that's what I like about it," Perlman says. He doesn't always trust his response when he listens to recordings of his performances. He might think something sounds awful, and then realize he was mistaken: "There is a variation in the ability to listen, as well, I've found." He didn't know if other instrumentalists relied on coaching, but he suspected that many find help like he did. Vocalists, he pointed out, employ voice coaches throughout their careers.

The professional singers I spoke to describe their coaches in nearly identical terms. "We refer to them as our 'outside ears,' " the great soprano Renée Fleming told me. "The voice is so mysterious and fragile. It's mostly involuntary muscles that fuel the instrument. What we hear as we are singing is not what the audience hears." When she's preparing for a concert, she practices with her vocal coach for ninety minutes or so several times a week. "Our voices are very limited in the amount of time we can use them," she explains. After they've put in the hours to attain professional status, she said, singers have about twenty or thirty years to achieve something near their best, and then to sustain that level. For Fleming, "outside ears" have been invaluable at every point.

SO OUTSIDE EARS, and eyes, are important for concert-calibre musicians and Olympic-level athletes. What about regular professionals, who just want to do what they do as well as they can? I talked to Jim Knight about this. He is the director of the Kansas Coaching Project, at the University of Kansas. He teaches coaching—for schoolteachers. For decades, research has confirmed that the big factor in determining how much students learn is not class size or the extent of standardized testing but the quality of their teachers. Policymakers have pushed mostly carrot-and-stick remedies: firing underperforming teachers, giving merit pay to high performers, penalizing schools with poor student test scores. People like Jim Knight think we should push coaching.

California researchers in the early nineteen-eighties conducted a five-year study of teacher-skill development in eighty schools, and noticed something interesting. Workshops led teachers to use new skills in the classroom only ten per cent of the time. Even when a practice session with demonstrations and personal feedback was added, fewer than twenty per cent made the change. But when coaching was introduced—when a colleague watched them try the new skills in their own classroom and provided suggestions—adoption rates passed ninety per cent. A spate of small randomized trials confirmed the effect. Coached teachers were more effective, and their students did better on tests.

Knight experienced it himself. Two decades ago, he was trying to teach writing to students at a community college in Toronto, and floundering. He studied techniques for teaching students how to write coherent sentences and organize their paragraphs. But he didn't get anywhere until a colleague came into the classroom and coached him through the changes he was trying to make. He won an award for innovation in teaching, and eventually wrote a Ph.D. dissertation at the University of Kansas on measures to improve pedagogy. Then he got funding to train coaches for every school in Topeka, and he has been expanding his program ever since. Coaching programs have now spread to hundreds of school districts across the country.

There have been encouraging early results, but the data haven't yet been analyzed on a large scale. One thing that seems clear, though, is that not all coaches are effective. I asked Knight to show me what makes for good coaching.

We met early one May morning at Leslie H. Walton Middle School, in Albemarle County, Virginia. In 2009, the Albemarle County public schools created an instructional-coaching program, based in part on Knight's methods. It recruited twenty-four teacher coaches for the twenty-seven schools in the semi-rural district. (Charlottesville is the county seat, but it runs a separate school district.) Many teacher-coaching programs concentrate on newer teachers, and this one is no exception. All teachers in their first two years are required to accept a coach, but the program also offers coaching to any teacher who wants it.

Not everyone has. Researchers from the University of Virginia found that many teachers see no need for coaching. Others hate the idea of being observed in the classroom, or fear that using a coach makes them look incompetent, or are convinced, despite assurances, that the coaches are reporting their evaluations to the principal. And some are skeptical that the school's particular coaches would be of any use.

To find its coaches, the program took applications from any teachers in the system who were willing to cross over to the back of the classroom for a couple of years and teach colleagues instead of students. They were selected for their skills with people, and they studied the methods developed by Knight and others. But they did not necessarily have any special expertise in a content area, like math or science. The coaches assigned to Walton Middle School were John Hobson, a bushy-bearded high-school history teacher who was just thirty-three years old when he started but had been a successful baseball and tennis coach, and Diane Harding, a teacher who had two decades of experience but had spent the previous seven years out of the classroom, serving as a technology specialist.

Nonetheless, many veteran teachers—including some of the best—signed up to let the outsiders in. Jennie Critzer, an eighth-grade math teacher, was one of those teachers, and we descended on her first-period algebra class as a small troupe—Jim Knight, me, and both coaches. (The school seemed eager to have me see what both do.)

After the students found their seats—some had to search a little, because Critzer had scrambled the assigned seating, as she often does, to "keep things fresh"—she got to work. She had been a math teacher at Walton Middle School for ten years. She taught three ninety-minute classes a day with anywhere from twenty to thirty students. And she had every class structured down to the minute.

Today, she said, they would be learning how to simplify radicals. She had already put a "Do Now" problem on the whiteboard: "Simplify $\sqrt{36}$ and $\sqrt{32}$." She gave the kids three minutes to get as far as they could, and walked the rows of desks with a white egg timer in her hand as the students went at it. With her blond pigtails, purple striped sack dress, flip-flops, and painted toenails, each a different color, she looked like a graduate student headed to a beach party. But she carried herself with an air of easy command. The timer sounded.

For thirty seconds, she had the students compare their results with those of the partner next to them. Then she called on a student at random for the first problem, the simplified form of $\sqrt{36}$. "Six," the girl said.

"Stand up if you got six," Critzer said. Everyone stood up.

She turned to the harder problem of simplifying $\sqrt{32}$. No one got the answer, $4\sqrt{2}$. It was a middle-level algebra class; the kids didn't have a lot of confidence when it came to math. Yet her job was to hold their attention and get them to grasp and apply three highly abstract concepts—the concepts of radicals, of perfect squares, and of factoring. In the course of one class, she did just that.

She set a clear goal, announcing that by the end of class the students would know how to write numbers like $\sqrt{32}$ in a simplified form without using a decimal or a fraction. Then she broke the task into steps. She had the students punch $\sqrt{32}$ into their calculators and see what number they got (5.66). She had them try explaining to their partner how whole numbers differed from decimals. ("Thirty seconds, everyone.") She had them write down other numbers whose square root was a whole number. She made them visualize, verbalize, and write the idea. Soon, they'd figured out how to find the factors of the number under the radical sign, and then how to move factors from under the radical sign to outside the radical sign.

Toward the end, she had her students try simplifying $\sqrt{20}$. They had one minute. One of the boys who'd looked alternately baffled and distracted for the first half of class hunched over his notebook scratching out an answer with his pencil. "This is so easy now," he announced.

I told the coaches that I didn't see how Critzer could have done better. They said that every teacher has something to work on. It could involve student behavior, or class preparation, or time management, or any number of other things. The coaches let the teachers choose the direction for coaching. They usually know better than anyone what their difficulties are.

Critzer's concern for the last quarter of the school year was whether her students were effectively engaged and learning the material they needed for the state tests. So that's what her coaches focussed on. Knight teaches coaches to observe a few specifics: whether the teacher has an effective plan for instruction; how many students are engaged in the material; whether they interact respectfully; whether they engage in high-level conversations; whether they understand how they are progressing, or failing to progress.

Novice teachers often struggle with the basic behavioral issues. Hobson told me of one such teacher, whose students included a hugely disruptive boy. Hobson took her to observe the boy in another teacher's classroom, where he behaved like a prince. Only then did the teacher see that her style was the problem. She let students speak—and shout, and interrupt—without raising their hands, and go to the bathroom without asking. Then she got angry when things got out of control.

Jennie Critzer had no trouble maintaining classroom discipline, and she skillfully used a variety of what teachers call "learning structures"—lecturing, problem-solving, coöperative learning, discussion. But the coaches weren't convinced that she was getting the best results. Of twenty kids, they noticed, at least four seemed at sea.

Good coaches know how to break down performance into its critical individual components. In sports, coaches focus on mechanics, conditioning, and strategy, and have ways to break each of those down, in turn. The U.C.L.A. basketball coach John Wooden, at the first squad meeting each season, even had his players practice putting their socks on. He demonstrated just how to do it: he carefully rolled each sock over his toes, up his foot, around the heel, and pulled it up snug, then went back to his toes and smoothed out the material along the sock's length, making sure there were no wrinkles or creases. He had two purposes in doing this. First, wrinkles cause blisters. Blisters cost games. Second, he wanted his players to learn how crucial seemingly trivial details could be. "Details create success" was the creed of a coach who won ten N.C.A.A. men's basketball championships.

At Walton Middle School, Hobson and Harding thought that Critzer should pay close attention to the details of how she used coöperative learning. When she paired the kids off, they observed, most struggled with having a "math conversation." The worst pairs had a girl with a boy. One boy-girl pair had been unable to talk at all.

Élite performers, researchers say, must engage in "deliberate practice"—sustained, mindful efforts to develop the full range of abilities that success requires. You have to work at what you're not good at. In theory, people can do this themselves. But most people do not know where to start or how to proceed. Expertise, as the formula goes, requires going from unconscious incompetence to conscious incompetence to conscious competence and finally to unconscious competence. The coach provides the outside eyes and ears, and makes you aware of where you're falling short. This is tricky. Human beings resist exposure and critique; our brains are well defended. So coaches use a variety of approaches—showing what other, respected colleagues do, for instance, or reviewing videos of the subject's performance. The most common, however, is just conversation.

At lunchtime, Critzer and her coaches sat down at a table in the empty school library. Hobson took the lead. "What worked?" he asked.

Critzer said she had been trying to increase the time that students spend on independent practice during classes, and she thought she was doing a good job. She was also trying to "break the plane" more—get out from in front of the whiteboard and walk among the students—and that was working nicely. But she knew the next question, and posed it herself: "So what didn't go well?" She noticed one girl who "clearly wasn't getting it." But at the time she hadn't been sure what to do.

"How could you help her?" Hobson asked.

She thought for a moment. "I would need to break the concept down for her more," she said. "I'll bring her in during the fifth block."

"What else did you notice?"

"My second class has thirty kids but was more forthcoming. It was actually easier to teach than the first class. This group is less verbal." Her answer gave the coaches the opening they wanted. They mentioned the trouble students had with their math conversations, and the girl-boy pair who didn't talk at all. "How could you help them be more verbal?"

Critzer was stumped. Everyone was. The table fell silent. Then Harding had an idea. "How about putting key math words on the board for them to use—like 'factoring,' 'perfect square,' 'radical'?" she said. "They could even record the math words they used in their discussion." Critzer liked the suggestion. It was something to try.

For half an hour, they worked through the fine points of the observation and formulated plans for what she could practice next. Critzer sat at a short end of the table chatting, the coaches at the long end beside her, Harding leaning toward her on an elbow, Hobson fingering his beard. They looked like three colleagues on a lunch break—which, Knight later explained, was part of what made the two coaches effective.

He had seen enough coaching to break even their performance down into its components. Good coaches, he said, speak with credibility, make a personal connection, and focus little on themselves. Hobson and Harding "listened more than they talked," Knight said. "They were one hundred per cent present in the conversation." They also parcelled out their observations carefully. "It's not a normal way of communicating—watching what your words are doing," he said. They had discomfiting information to convey, and they did it directly but respectfully.

I asked Critzer if she liked the coaching. "I do," she said. "It works with my personality. I'm very self-critical. So I grabbed a coach from the beginning." She had been concerned for a while about how to do a better job engaging her kids. "So many things have to come together. I'd exhausted everything I knew to improve."

She told me that she had begun to burn out. "I felt really isolated, too," she said. Coaching had changed that. "My stress level is a lot less now." That might have been the best news for the students. They kept a great teacher, and saw her get better. "The coaching has definitely changed how satisfying teaching is," she said.

I DECIDED TO try a coach. I called Robert Osteen, a retired general surgeon, whom I trained under during my residency, to see if he might consider the idea. He's one of the surgeons I most hoped to emulate in my career. His operations were swift without seeming hurried and elegant without seeming showy. He was calm. I never once saw him lose his temper. He had a plan for every circumstance. He had impeccable judgment. And his patients had unusually few complications.

He specialized in surgery for tumors of the pancreas, liver, stomach, esophagus, colon, breast, and other organs. One test of a cancer surgeon is knowing when surgery is pointless and when to forge ahead. Osteen never hemmed or hawed, or pushed too far. "Can't be done," he'd say upon getting a patient's abdomen open and discovering a tumor to be more invasive than expected. And, without a pause for lament, he'd begin closing up again.

Year after year, the senior residents chose him for their annual teaching award. He was an unusual teacher. He never quite told you what to do. As an intern, I did my first splenectomy with him. He did not draw the skin incision to be made with the sterile marking pen the way the other professors did. He just stood there, waiting. Finally, I took the pen, put the felt tip on the skin somewhere, and looked up at him to see if I could make out a glimmer of approval or disapproval. He gave me nothing. I drew a line down the patient's middle, from just below the sternum to just above the navel.

"Is that really where you want it?" he said. Osteen's voice was a low, car-engine growl, tinged with the accent of his boyhood in Savannah, Georgia, and it took me a couple of years to realize that it was not his voice that scared me but his questions. He was invariably trying to get residents to think—to think like surgeons—and his questions exposed how much we had to learn.

"Yes," I answered. We proceeded with the operation. Ten minutes into the case, it became obvious that I'd made the incision too small to expose the spleen. "I should have taken the incision down below the navel, huh?" He grunted in the affirmative, and we stopped to extend the incision.

I reached Osteen at his summer home, on Buzzards Bay. He was enjoying retirement. He spent time with his grandchildren and travelled, and, having been an avid sailor all his life, he had just finished writing a book on nineteenth-century naval mapmaking. He didn't miss operating, but one day a week he held a teaching conference for residents and medical students. When I explained the experiment I wanted to try, he was game.

He came to my operating room one morning and stood silently observing from a step stool set back a few feet from the table. He scribbled in a notepad and changed position once in a while, looking over the anesthesia drape or watching from behind me. I was initially self-conscious about being observed by my former teacher. But I was doing an operation—a thyroidectomy for a patient with a cancerous nodule—that I had done around a thousand times, more times than I've been to the movies. I was quickly absorbed in the flow of it—the symphony of coördinated movement between me and my surgical assistant, a senior resident, across the table from me, and the surgical technician to my side.

The case went beautifully. The cancer had not spread beyond the thyroid, and, in eighty-six minutes, we removed the fleshy, butterfly-shaped organ, carefully detaching it from the trachea and from the nerves to the vocal cords. Osteen had rarely done this operation when he was practicing, and I wondered whether he would find anything useful to tell me.

We sat in the surgeons' lounge afterward. He saw only small things, he said, but, if I were trying to keep a problem from happening even once in my next hundred operations, it's the small things I had to worry about. He noticed that I'd positioned and draped the patient perfectly for me, standing on his left side, but not for anyone else. The draping hemmed in the surgical assistant across the table on the patient's right side, restricting his left arm, and hampering his ability to pull the wound upward. At one point in the operation, we found ourselves struggling to see up high enough in the neck on that side. The draping also pushed the medical student off to the surgical assistant's right, where he couldn't help at all. I should have made more room to the left, which would have allowed the student to hold the retractor and freed the surgical assistant's left hand.

Osteen also asked me to pay more attention to my elbows. At various points during the operation, he observed, my right elbow rose to the level of my shoulder, on occasion higher. "You cannot achieve precision with your elbow in the air," he said. A surgeon's elbows should be loose and down by his sides. "When you are tempted to raise your elbow, that means you need to either move your feet"—because you're standing in the wrong position—"or choose a different instrument."

He had a whole list of observations like this. His notepad was dense with small print. I operate with magnifying loupes and wasn't aware how much this restricted my peripheral vision. I never noticed, for example, that at one point the patient had blood-pressure problems, which the anesthesiologist was monitoring. Nor did I realize that, for about half an hour, the operating light drifted out of the wound; I was operating with light from reflected surfaces. Osteen pointed out that the instruments I'd chosen for holding the incision open had got tangled up, wasting time.

THAT ONE TWENTY-MINUTE discussion gave me more to consider and work on than I'd had in the past five years. It had been strange and more than a little awkward having to explain to the surgical team why Osteen was spending the morning with us. "He's here to coach me," I'd said. Yet the stranger thing, it occurred to me, was that no senior colleague had come to observe me in the eight years since I'd established my surgical practice. Like most work, medical practice is largely unseen by anyone who might raise one's sights. I'd had no outside ears and eyes.

Osteen has continued to coach me in the months since that experiment. I take his observations, work on them for a few weeks, and then get together with him again. The mechanics of the interaction are still evolving. Surgical performance begins well before the operating room, with the choice made in the clinic of whether to operate in the first place. Osteen and I have spent time examining the way I plan before surgery. I've also begun taking time to do something I'd rarely done before—watch other colleagues operate in order to gather ideas about what I could do.

A former colleague at my hospital, the cancer surgeon Caprice Greenberg, has become a pioneer in using video in the operating room. She had the idea that routine, high-quality video recordings of operations could enable us to figure out why some patients fare better than others. If we learned what techniques made the difference, we could even try to coach for them. The work is still in its early stages. So far, a handful of surgeons have had their operations taped, and begun reviewing them with a colleague.

I was one of the surgeons who got to try it. It was like going over a game tape. One rainy afternoon, I brought my laptop to Osteen's kitchen, and we watched a recording of another thyroidectomy I'd performed. Three video pictures of the operation streamed on the screen—one from a camera in the operating light, one from a wide-angle room camera, and one with the feed from the anesthesia monitor. A boom microphone picked up the sound.

Osteen liked how I'd changed the patient's positioning and draping. "See? Right there!" He pointed at the screen. "The assistant is able to help you now." At one point, the light drifted out of the wound and we watched to see how long it took me to realize I'd lost direct illumination: four minutes, instead of half an hour.

"Good," he said. "You're paying more attention."

He had new pointers for me. He wanted me to let the residents struggle thirty seconds more when I asked them to help with a task. I tended to give them precise instructions as soon as progress slowed. "No, use the DeBakey forceps," I'd say, or "Move the retractor first." Osteen's advice: "Get them to think." It's the only way people learn.

And together we identified a critical step in a thyroidectomy to work on: finding and preserving the parathyroid glands—four fatty glands the size of a yellow split pea that sit on the surface of the thyroid gland and are crucial for regulating a person's calcium levels. The rate at which my patients suffered permanent injury to those little organs had been hovering at two per cent. He wanted me to try lowering the risk further by finding the glands earlier in the operation.

Since I have taken on a coach, my complication rate has gone down. It's too soon to know for sure whether that's not random, but it seems real. I know that I'm learning again. I can't say that every surgeon needs a coach to do his or her best work, but I've discovered that I do.

COACHING HAS BECOME a fad in recent years. There are leadership coaches, executive coaches, life coaches, and college-application coaches. Search the Internet, and you'll find that there's even Twitter coaching. ("Would you like to learn how to get new customers/clients, make valuable business contacts, and increase your revenue using Twitter? Then this Twitter coaching package is perfect for you"—at about eight hundred dollars for a few hour-long Skype sessions and some e-mail consultation.) Self-improvement has always found a ready market, and most of what's on offer is simply one-on-one instruction to get amateurs through the essentials. It's teaching with a trendier name. Coaching aimed at improving the performance of people who are already professionals is less usual. It's also riskier: bad coaching can make people worse.

The world-famous high jumper Dick Fosbury, for instance, developed his revolutionary technique—known as the Fosbury Flop—in defiance of his coaches. They wanted him to stick to the time-honored straddle method of going over the high bar leg first, face down. He instinctively wanted to go over head first, back down. It was only by perfecting his odd technique on his own that Fosbury won the gold medal at the 1968 Mexico City Olympics, setting a new record on worldwide television, and reinventing high-jumping overnight.

Renée Fleming told me that when her original voice coach died, ten years ago, she was nervous about replacing her. She wanted outside ears, but they couldn't be just anybody's. "At my stage, when you're at my level, you don't really want to go to a new person who might mess things up," she said. "Somebody might say, 'You know, you've been singing that way for a long time, but why don't you try this?' If you lose your path, sometimes you can't find your way back, and then you lose your confidence onstage and it really is just downhill."

The sort of coaching that fosters effective innovation and judgment, not merely the replication of technique, may not be so easy to cultivate. Yet modern society increasingly depends on ordinary people taking responsibility for doing extraordinary things: operating inside people's bodies, teaching eighth graders algebraic concepts that Euclid would have struggled with, building a highway through a mountain, constructing a wireless computer network across a state, running a factory, reducing a city's crime rate. In the absence of guidance, how many people can do such complex tasks at the level we require? With a diploma, a few will achieve sustained mastery; with a good coach, many could. We treat guidance for professionals as a luxury—you can guess what gets cut first when school-district budgets are slashed. But coaching may prove essential to the success of modern society

There was a moment in sports when employing a coach was unimaginable—and then came a time when not doing so was unimaginable. We care about results in sports, and if we care half as much about results in schools and in hospitals we may reach the same conclusion. Local health systems may need to go the way of the Albemarle school district. We could create coaching programs not only for surgeons but for other doctors, too—internists aiming to sharpen their diagnostic skills, cardiologists aiming to improve their heart-attack outcomes, and all of us who have to figure out ways to use our resources more efficiently. In the past year, I've thought nothing of asking my hospital to spend some hundred thousand dollars to upgrade the surgical equipment I use, in the vague hope of giving me finer precision and reducing complications. Avoiding just one major complication saves, on average, fourteen thousand dollars in medical costs—not to mention harm to a human being. So it seems worth it. But the three or four hours I've spent with Osteen each month have almost certainly added more to my capabilities than any of this.

Talk about medical progress, and people think about technology. We await every new cancer drug as if it will be our salvation. We dream of personalized genomics, vaccines against heart disease, and the unfathomed efficiencies from information technology. I would never deny the potential value of such breakthroughs. My teen-age son was spared high-risk aortic surgery a couple of years ago by a brief stent procedure that didn't exist when he was born. But the capabilities of doctors matter every bit as much as the technology. This is true of all professions. What ultimately makes the difference is how well people use technology. We have devoted disastrously little attention to fostering those abilities.

A determined effort to introduce coaching could change this. Making sure that the benefits exceed the cost will take work, to be sure. So will finding coaches—though, with the growing pool of retirees, we may already have a ready reserve of accumulated experience and know-how. The greatest difficulty, though, may simply be a profession's willingness to accept the idea. The prospect of coaching forces awkward questions about how we regard failure. I thought about this after another case of mine that Bob Osteen came to observe. It didn't go so well.

THE PATIENT WAS a woman with a large tumor in the adrenal gland atop her right kidney, and I had decided to remove it using a laparoscope. Some surgeons might have questioned this decision. When adrenal tumors get to be a certain size, they can't be removed laparoscopically—you have to do a traditional, open operation and get your hands inside. I persisted, though, and soon had cause for regret. Working my way around this tumor with a ten-millimetre camera on the end of a foot-and-a-half-long wand was like trying to find my way around a mountain with a penlight. I continued with my folly too long, and caused bleeding in a blind spot. The team had to give her a blood transfusion while I opened her belly wide and did the traditional operation.

Osteen watched, silent and blank-faced the entire time, taking notes. My cheeks burned; I was mortified. I wished I'd never asked him along. I tried to be rational about the situation—the patient did fine. But I had let Osteen see my judgment fail; I'd let him see that I may not be who I want to be.

This is why it will never be easy to submit to coaching, especially for those who are well along in their career. I'm ostensibly an expert. I'd finished long ago with the days of being tested and observed. I am supposed to be past needing such things. Why should I expose myself to scrutiny and fault-finding?

I have spoken to other surgeons about the idea. "Oh, I can think of a few people who could use some coaching" has been a common reaction. Not many say, "Man, could I use a coach!" Once, I wouldn't have, either.

Osteen and I sat together after the operation and broke the case down, weighing the decisions I'd made at various points. He focussed on what I thought went well and what I thought didn't. He wasn't sure what I ought to have done differently, he said. But he asked me to think harder about the anatomy of the attachments holding the tumor in.

"You seemed to have trouble keeping the tissue on tension," he said. He was right. You can't free a tumor unless you can lift and hold taut the tissue planes you need to dissect through. Early on, when it had become apparent that I couldn't see the planes clearly, I could have switched to the open procedure before my poking around caused bleeding. Thinking back, however, I also realized that there was another maneuver I could have tried that might have let me hold the key attachments on tension, and maybe even freed the tumor.

"Most surgery is done in your head," Osteen likes to say. Your performance is not determined by where you stand or where your elbow goes. It's determined by where you decide to stand, where you decide to put your elbow. I knew that he could drive me to make smarter decisions, but that afternoon I recognized the price: exposure.

For society, too, there are uncomfortable difficulties: we may not be ready to accept—or pay for—a cadre of people who identify the flaws in the professionals upon whom we rely, and yet hold in confidence what they see. Coaching done well may be the most effective intervention designed for human performance. Yet the allegiance of coaches is to the people they work with; their success depends on it. And the existence of a coach requires an acknowledgment that even expert practitioners have significant room for improvement. Are we ready to confront this fact when we're in their care?

"Who's that?" a patient asked me as she awaited anesthesia and noticed Osteen standing off to the side of the operating room, notebook in hand.

I was flummoxed for a moment. He wasn't a student or a visiting professor. Calling him "an observer" didn't sound quite right, either.

"He's a colleague," I said. "I asked him along to observe and see if he saw things I could improve."

The patient gave me a look that was somewhere between puzzlement and alarm.

"He's like a coach," I finally said.

She did not seem reassured.

Alexander Wolff
(b. 1957)

ALEXANDER WOLFF IS a longtime staff writer for *Sports Illustrated*, the author of several books, and the winner of numerous awards for his writing about basketball and other sports. In this piece Wolff focuses on a pivotal season in the career of UCLA men's basketball coach John Wooden (1910–2010), known as "the Wizard of Westwood." Wolff examines the phenomenon of Wooden's mid-course correction, when, in 1964, the coach "questioned himself" and grew from a good coach into a truly great one by reevaluating his principles in the light of the particular strengths and weaknesses of his players. Wooden grew up on an Indiana farm his parents lost in 1924; there he learned the value of hard work and dedication. A three-time All-American, an English major who initially thought he wanted to be an engineer, Wooden was a man of complexity and remarkable reserves. He passed up a chance to play professional basketball to coach and teach English at high schools in Indiana. He had one losing season in his career: his first, at a high school in Dayton, Kentucky. After World War II, during which he served as a physical education instructor in the navy, Wooden moved to the college level, ultimately going to UCLA in 1948. At the time the team did not even have a home court. Wooden retired from UCLA in 1975, after twenty-seven years, with a record of 620–147, four perfect seasons, and ten National Championships. Key to Wooden's ultimate success was his courting of confrontation and his realization that learning must occur after you "know it all." One of Wooden's most successful players, Bill Walton, said of his coach's trademark emphasis on detail, that he set the conditions "so that anything in our control would never fail us."

Birth of a Dynasty
from *Sports Illustrated* (March 19, 2007)

UCLA Basketball today seems shot full of the John Wooden magic. This season's Bruins, who are 26–5 and considered a strong title contender heading into the NCAA tournament, wear facsimiles of classic UCLA uniforms and share the commitment to defense that produced 10 national championships in the 1960s and '70s. A pilgrim to Pauley Pavilion might easily believe the UCLA dynasty began with a simple wave of the Wizard's wand, but in fact, Wooden spent 16 years in Westwood unable to elevate the program much beyond mediocrity. He questioned himself and tinkered, and ultimately came wisdom—and then victory on a scale unlikely ever to be matched.

The old coach, 96 now, is such a passionate collector and spouter of aphorisms that it's easy to regard them as quaint. But one sign that Wooden hung on the wall of his office serves as a worthy caption for the first of UCLA's title teams, the 1963–64 Bruins, who went undefeated without a starter taller than 6'5": when you're through learning, you're through. Keep that in mind as you read their story.

UCLA had enjoyed only four winning seasons in the previous 20 years when 37-year-old John Wooden took over as the Bruins' coach in 1948, so the team's accomplishments in his first season—most important, beating Cal for the Pacific Coast Conference title after being picked to finish last—delighted the campus. Over the next 14 seasons the Bruins racked up winning records every time out. Still, it wasn't until Wooden was 53 that a team of his won a national title. The first three times his Bruins qualified for the NCAA tournament—in '50, '52 and '56—they failed to win their opening game. Today the chat boards and talk show hosts would have taken him down a decade before he had bagged his first title.

Wooden believes that "six or seven" of those early teams could have won a national championship—"not should have," he wrote in his autobiography, *They Call Me Coach*, "but could have." All they lacked were luck and timing. In 1952, the day before the start of the NCAA tournament, starter Don Bragg stumbled coming out of the shower and broke his toe. The only player in Wooden's first 15 years in Westwood to later stick as a pro, Willie Naulls, happened to play between '53 and '56, precisely when Bill Russell reigned at San Francisco. No sooner had Russell left than UCLA's football team was discovered to have been part of a leaguewide pay-for-play scandal, and the school's three-year probation was applied to all sports. After which came Cal and its Hall of Fame coach, Pete Newell; though Wooden beat Newell seven straight times at one point, the Golden Bears turned the tables beginning in '57, eventually taking eight straight from the Bruins and winning an NCAA title along the way.

So, despite UCLA's relative success, Wooden took heed of another sign on his office wall, the one that read, IT'S WHAT YOU LEARN AFTER YOU KNOW IT ALL THAT COUNTS. From studying Newell he learned the virtues of patience and simplicity. He sat in on a psychology class and decided that he didn't want yes-men as assistants. Sometimes he even courted conflict with players because he believed a worthwhile lesson might emerge from the clash. He asked other coaches to scout his team and share their critiques. And he would spend each off-season poring over the meticulous records he kept of his practices, wondering what he might do differently.

In the spring of 1960, after a 14–12 season that would turn out to be his worst at UCLA, Wooden reassessed everything. He concluded that his teams tended to fade late in the season and wondered if he worked the players too hard in practice. Moreover, when he substituted, the reserves didn't mesh well with the starters. A single tweak to his practice plan—he began to rotate reserves among the first five more often in scrimmages—solved both problems. Two years later the Bruins reached the national semifinals, where they suffered a controversial last-minute charging call and a two-point loss to eventual champion Cincinnati.

Preposterous as it may sound, winning per se was never Wooden's main emphasis, even as the Bruins reached that doorstep. As Doug McIntosh, a reserve on the 1964 team, says, "The word win never escaped his lips. Literally. He just asked us to play to our potential."

The great lesson from the Cincinnati game, Wooden says, was simply this: "I learned we could play with the best." The next season UCLA finished 20–9, but six of those losses were by four points or fewer. Wooden sensed an imminent turn in the program's fortunes. In January 1963, on the flight home from two close losses at Washington, he whipped off some doggerel for Pete Blackman, a recent Bruins player and fellow poetry aficionado. It included a lengthy lamentation on the shortcomings of his team, but ended with these lines:

> I want to say—yes, I'll foretell
> Eventually, this team will jell
> And when they do, they will be great
> A championship will be their fate.
> With every starter coming back,
> Yes, Walt and Gail and Keith and Jack,
> And Fred and Freddie and some more
> We could be champs in sixty-four.

"Freddie" was guard Freddie Goss, who wound up sitting out the 1963–64 season as a redshirt. The "some more" turned out to be two small-town sophomores, McIntosh, a white center from Lily, Ky., and Kenny Washington, a black guard from segregated schools in Beaufort, S.C. Each was perfectly suited to be a reserve and seemed to save his finest contributions for the biggest games. And then there were Walt and Gail and Keith and Jack and Fred.

To be sure, guards Walt Hazzard and Gail Goodrich and forward Jack Hirsch had been high school players of distinction in their respective high schools in Philadelphia, Los Angeles and Van Nuys, Calif. But all were seemingly one-dimensional: Hazzard, a passer; Goodrich, a shooter; and Hirsch, a defender. Goodrich accepted a scholarship as a Polytechnic High junior when, at 5'8" and 120 pounds, he correctly intuited that he wasn't likely to get an offer much better than UCLA's. At first he was wary of Hazzard, who had the ball most of the time, but Goodrich soon realized that if he moved to an open spot, Hazzard would find him—for Hazzard loved to deliver the ball as much as Goodrich longed to launch it. "I defy you to find two finer guards who ever played on the same team," says Hirsch. "They averaged 43 a game between them, and we had no shot clock or three-pointer."

HIRSCH WAS A player unlike any Wooden had encountered, on or off the court. Hirsch was a poker-playing sharpie who had grown up in Brooklyn, learning the subtleties of basketball on the playgrounds of Bedford-Stuyvesant. His father had become wealthy from a chain of bowling alleys, and when the family moved to the West Coast, Jack brought along a knack, at 6'3", for stealing rebounds from, and improvising shots over, taller players. "I was two or three years ahead of these other guys as far as how the game should be played," says Hirsch, whose dad promised to quit a five-packs-a-day smoking habit if his son played at UCLA. "Wooden adapted to me as much as I did to him. Everyone else was afraid of him. But even though he seemed to hold my life in his hands, I knew I could always go back to playing cards. He's admitted his stubbornness kept him from winning sooner, and I was one of the people who opened his eyes because of how crazy I was."

As for center Fred Slaughter and forward Keith Erickson, neither went to UCLA on a full basketball scholarship. But that was a reflection of their versatility, not their ability. Slaughter had been a sprinter in high school in Topeka, Kans.—he ran the 100 yards in 9.9 seconds—and had a choice of colleges at which to run. He ultimately accepted the Bruins' offer of a scholarship split between track and basketball. Erickson had grown up just down the freeway from the Westwood campus, in El Segundo, but had never seen a Bruins basketball game until he played in one. No other school had offered him a ride for basketball, and UCLA's deal was half for hoops and half for baseball; though volleyball, which he would play in the '64 Tokyo Olympics, was the sport in which he first displayed his astonishing jumping ability.

When practice began in October 1963 the players scaled three flights of stairs to what was known as the B.O. Barn, the cramped and fetid men's gym on campus where the basketball court shared space with wrestling mats and gymnastics equipment. Chalk drifting over from the pommel horses had to be swept off the court before practice; two managers pushed mops while Wooden walked in front of them, backward and crouched over, dribbling water out of a bucket as if, he says, he were "feeding the chickens back on the farm." The B.O. Barn once accommodated 2,400 spectators, but in 1955 fire marshals prohibited crowds of more than 1,300. For the program to pay for itself, the players had to become vagabonds. So for home games that season the Bruins bused to the L.A. Sports Arena, which was virtually on the USC campus; the Long Beach Arena, 25 miles away; and even the gym at a community college in Santa Monica. The Bruins would essentially play 30 road games.

With their raw athletes, split scholarships and three-ring practices in that hoops hayloft, the 1963–64 Bruins were less a basketball team than a rarefied phys-ed class, with Wooden the gym teacher. He was then known as Johnny, a transplanted Hoosier whose superbly conditioned teams played the pell-mell Midwestern style but weren't regarded as very sophisticated defensively.

Only later, after UCLA's first several titles, would Wooden begin to dominate the recruiting scene, picking and choosing among the top players in the nation. In fact, the coach disliked recruiting, and only welcomed out-of-state players if someone else initiated the contact. McIntosh would have attended Tennessee, but the coach there, a Purdue alum like Wooden, resigned suddenly and was happy to steer his recruit to a fellow Boilermaker. Hazzard arrived thanks to a connection twice removed: He was recommended by Naulls, who from the Philly playgrounds knew Woody Sauldsberry, Hazzard's distant cousin. Meanwhile, Hazzard recommended Washington, who played pickup ball in Philly while spending summers visiting a sister; Washington had arrived in Los Angeles unseen by any UCLA coach—and two inches shorter and 40 pounds lighter than advertised—after cowering in the back of a Greyhound for three days.

Washington emerged from that bus into a dreamland, the polar opposite of the Jim Crow south. "At first you say, 'No, it can't be,' " he recalls. "And then you see this university, this microcosm of the world, and say, 'Well, why not?' " Those first couple of years he would write buddies back home, telling them they wouldn't believe what he'd seen: guys flooding dormitory floors to slide around on them, and putting matches to their farts, and drinking beer. And this guy Hirsch, who drove his own red Pontiac Grand Prix, called the coach "John" or "J-Dub" or "Woody" to his face.

"Yes, buses were being burned by the side of the road," Washington says of the harassment of Freedom Riders in the early '60s. "But [African-Americans] had faith, because if the whole country were like that, we'd still be in chains. And then I'd see this man who practiced what he preached, and that was like beauty. [Wooden] had structure, a philosophy based on fairness. He was a small-town person, too. The same things his father taught him, my father taught me. I felt like a foster child."

"We all came by accident," says Hirsch, whose father, failing to hold up his end of the pact he had made with his son, died of lung cancer just months after the championship season ended. "But we had great quickness, great hands, great communication, great chemistry."

"We used to talk about how we were the all-American team, a group of guys from such diverse backgrounds, yet on the court were a perfect mesh,"

Slaughter says. "Two black, two white, one Jewish, who after games would go in our separate directions. But game time, practice time, ride-the-bus time, we were pretty well matched. We liked to protect each other. We liked to do our jobs. And we just enjoyed playing for the man."

Once a year Wooden made it a point to poll his players, asking them who they thought should be starting. He did this to test his own judgment, and to have something with which he might shoo away a parent disgruntled over a son's playing time. Wooden had never before, and would never again, find such unanimity on this question as he did during the 1963–64 season.

SHORTLY AFTER HE announced his retirement in 1975, in the aftermath of his final title run, Wooden confided to a young alumnus that he had blundered badly early in his career by associating too much with yes-men. "Whatever you do in life, surround yourself with smart people who'll argue with you," he said. Wooden didn't mention any names, but he was tipping his hat to one smart, argumentative assistant coach in particular.

Jerry Norman had played on three of Wooden's early teams, and he had the kind of contrarian spirit that both drives coaches nuts and steals their hearts. He was an instigator, but instigators are also initiators—and in athletics the initiators tend to seize opportunity. "Very headstrong, set in his ways, and profane," Wooden called Norman in his autobiography. "Jerry gave me fits. I don't believe I ever had a boy more strong-willed, more sure of himself and more outspoken." Wooden kicked him off the team for two weeks during the 1950–51 season. Yet after Norman did turns in the service and as a coach for Wooden's brother Maurice, the principal at West Covina (Calif.) High, his old college coach brought him back, first to run the freshman team and then, in 1963, to serve as a varsity assistant. "I guess I wanted a rebel," Wooden wrote, "someone who would stand up to me."

Like his boss, Norman had been influenced by UCLA's nemesis, Pete Newell, who retired as Cal coach in 1960. Newell believed that a team controlling the tempo controlled the game. Accordingly, over the 1962–63 season, the Bruins had looked to push the pace at every opportunity. In their next-to-last game, a 51–45 win over Stanford for the conference title, they'd used a full-court, man-to-man press to that end. They forced almost 20 turnovers, Norman says, but still scored only 51 points.

After UCLA lost to Arizona State in the Bruins' NCAA tournament opener, Norman caucused with his boss. He argued that a full-court, man-to-man defense forces the opponent to advance the ball with the dribble, which chews up time. If the Bruins really wanted to hasten changes in possession and shorten each possession, the team needed a zone press, with the kinds of traps that only a foolish dribbler would try to slalom through. Opponents would have to advance the ball by passing, and human nature being what it is, those passes would eventually become hurried and careless. UCLA's quick hands, long arms and sprinters' speed would lead to deflections and interceptions, and soon the ball would be headed the other way. The Bruins would score, and the way they'd score—suddenly and as a result of turnovers—would sow, as Wooden later put it, "disharmony and disunity" on the opposing team.

There was more. Force a turnover as a result of a zone press, Norman argued, and the five UCLA players would be spread across the breadth and most of the length of the floor—the better to take advantage of Hazzard's skill in transition. Size may be an advantage in basketball, but it dissipates when spread over the court. And if the Bruins opened a lead with a flurry of baskets, their opponents would have to adopt a faster tempo to catch up, playing right into UCLA's hands. "I laid out the rationale," says Norman, who had used a 2-2-1 zone press successfully as coach of the Bruins' freshman team. "We had no size, and we played in a conference in which teams liked to walk the ball up the floor. The idea wasn't to steal the ball, remember. That would be an ancillary benefit. It was to increase tempo."

Wooden was skeptical. He had used a zone press effectively in his first college job, at Indiana State, but he feared that players had become too skilled to be flummoxed by one. It wasn't Norman who ultimately won over Wooden so much as the presence of Erickson, whose lateral quickness, sense of timing and gambler's sangfroid made him the perfect safetyman at the back of the 2-2-1. Cal coach Rene Herrerias would liken him to "a 6'5" Bill Russell," and Wooden came to call Erickson the finest athlete he had ever coached.

Wooden eventually concluded that he had erred in not using a zone press earlier. "When I came to UCLA, I expected to use it more often, and a number of years I had the personnel for it," he says. From 1957 through '59 he had coached Rafer Johnson, the Olympic decathlon champion-to-be, and kicked himself for not recognizing in Johnson another ideal backliner for the 2-2-1. "I tried it for a while and gave up on it," Wooden adds, reproaching himself. "And as a coach, you know, you preach patience."

The zone press, Wooden came to realize, had additional virtues. It built morale and promoted cohesion. And just as a lumbering team was vulnerable to it, a bunch of big galoots couldn't really make it work.

At the front of the press Wooden deployed Goodrich, who despite his wraithlike physique had huge hands and a 37-inch sleeve length, and the 6'5" Slaughter, who was fast enough to sprint back and set up if an opponent broke into the forecourt, but whose broad 235 pounds made breaking the press even more of a challenge. "They had a poor little person trying to throw the ball in, trying to see around me," Slaughter recalls. "And please, don't try to throw a long pass. While I was running and jumping at the front of the press, Keith was running and jumping at the back."

If Erickson picked off the most passes, the ensuing baskets usually came as a result of the decisions by Hazzard, who lined up with Hirsch near midcourt and, just as Norman envisioned, tended to wind up with the ball in the open floor. "Walt and Gail never called a play for the rest of us," Erickson says. "Much to our chagrin and to their credit. But we were best when we were running, so we didn't really need plays." The Glue Factory, one wag called the Bruins' press. Another called it Arranged Chaos. Asked what it was like to face the 2-2-1, USC coach Forrest Twogood responded with a question of his own. "Have you ever been locked up in a casket for six days?" he said. "That's how it feels."

THE BRUINS DROPPED a hint of what was in store just before Christmas, when they took out unbeaten Creighton and muscular Paul Silas. But it would be six days later, against No. 3 Michigan in the L.A. Classic, when UCLA conclusively demonstrated how speed could trump size. The Wolverines called their frontline of Bill Buntin, Oliver Darden and Larry Tregoning the Anvil Chorus, and guard Cazzie Russell was an All-America and future collegiate player of the year. Hirsch nonetheless locked up Russell, Slaughter shut down the 6'7", 250-pound Buntin, and the Bruins won 98–80, improving their record to 8–0. Harry Combes, coach of the Illinois team the Bruins would beat the next night for the tournament title, called it "the best performance in a single game I've ever seen by a college team." Nonetheless, it wasn't until January, after Georgia Tech beat Kentucky and the Bruins rang up 121 points against Washington State, that UCLA ascended to No. 1 in the polls. A team unmentioned in *SI*'s preseason Top 20 suddenly found itself lording over the sport.

In each of their 30 games, the Bruins used the zone press to deliver at least one game-altering spurt, a period of two or three minutes in which UCLA outscored its opponent by 10 or more points. These Bruin Blitzes, as they came to be known, usually took place before the end of the first half. In a few instances—such as a 100–88 win over Stanford, in which Erickson's three steals spurred an 18–3 run that put UCLA up 77–65—opponents didn't get blown away until the second half. But those decisive runs always came.

UCLA's confidence flowed from its coach. "A couple of times when we were way down, I remember looking over at him with his legs crossed and program rolled up," Slaughter recalls, "and I'd think, Hey, if he's not worried, I'm not worried." Sometime in February, Slaughter remembers, he picked up an out-of-town paper and read speculation that the Bruins might go undefeated. It hadn't occurred to him. "We were too busy having fun," Slaughter says, "and beating the crap out of everyone."

If a lightness persisted among the players, it's because their success seemed so unexpected and sudden. The fans embraced the lark of it, wearing their red we try harder buttons from Avis's popular ad campaign. Just the same, this wasn't a case of a team that would only appreciate what it accomplished with the passage of time. "As it was unfolding," says reserve forward Rich Levin, one of five end-of-the-benchers who called themselves the Mop-Up Squad, "we knew it was special."

In their first game of the NCAA tournament, in the West Regional in Corvallis, Ore., the Bruins trailed Seattle late before Goodrich bailed them out, finding Washington for a layup and free throw, then scoring on a layup himself off a steal in a 95–90 victory. The next night UCLA fell behind San Francisco early, trailing by 13 in the first half. The blitz came like the cavalry, "right at the end of the game," Erickson remembers, delivering the Bruins to the Final Four in Kansas City, Mo.

There they drew a virtual home team, Kansas State. "They're up five with seven minutes to play," Hirsch recalls, "and their best player takes a 15-footer. The ball is in the net, and somehow comes out. I grab the ball, throw it down to Gail for a layup, and we're down three. If that ball goes in, with no shot clock. . . ." He lets you imagine the consequences. "It's as if God said, 'This team is going undefeated.'"

UCLA drew even at 75 with four minutes left, and then another K-State shot went in and out. This time the blitz had been modest, 11 points in three minutes, but it was enough to make UCLA a 90–84 winner and set up a title-game matchup with Duke. Like Hirsch, Wooden knew that as superbly as his team had performed all season, fate seemed to be playing an ever larger role. "Somehow we keep our poise and get out of the jams we get ourselves into," Wooden said on the eve of the final. "Now we have to do it one more time."

Skeptics remained. "There is no way for UCLA to beat Duke," wrote Dick Wade of *The Kansas City Star*. "The Blue Devils simply have too much— height, shooting ability, rebounding ability and defense." At least Wade had been smart enough to preface his prediction with this: "If you're silly enough to apply logic to basketball."

Logic fled the arena late in the first half, shortly after Erickson had picked up his third foul with UCLA trailing 30–27. Here came the blitz by which all others would be measured. Hirsch made three steals. Goodrich scored eight points. Washington, playing before his dad for the first time, knocked down two jumpers. And Erickson, disregarding the fouls, blocked several shots. Twice Duke called timeout, but to no avail. By the time the Bruins' run had ended—after one Blue Devil turned to Slaughter and said, "Hey, can you guys slow down?"—UCLA had scored 16 unanswered points in slightly more than 2 1/2 minutes to take a 43–30 lead. Off the bench, McIntosh and Washington would combine for 23 rebounds; Duke's two 6'10" frontliners, Hack Tison and

Jay Buckley, would get only 10 between them. UCLA forced 29 turnovers and coasted, 98–83, to finish 30–0. "Don't let it change you," Wooden told his players in the locker room. "You are champions and must act like champions."

Five times during that season the Bruins scored more than 100 points; only six times did they win by five or fewer. Over the ensuing months Wooden would field some 700 inquiries from coaches asking how the press worked. He has always called that first title team the one that came "as close to reaching its potential as a team could come," and given his definition of success, that is the highest praise he could deliver.

"PEOPLE SAY HE didn't have the horses before us," says Hirsch. "No—he didn't win because he wasn't a great coach. He was a good coach who filled in all the blanks."

Wooden agrees. "We'd have had a little better chance in earlier years," he says, "if I'd have known a little more."

Who knew? The Wizard of Westwood was really the Master of the Midcourse Correction. The 1963–64 title team stands as both a summation of everything he had learned to that time and a grand experiment in the coaching arts that he would apply to win nine more championships. Precept after precept was tonged and tempered in the crucible of that season: The game rewards quickness above all, victory begins with defense and, perhaps most important of all, it's what you learn after you know it all that counts.

Kai Bird and Martin J. Sherwin
(b. 1951)   (b. 1937)

THE TITLE OF Kai Bird and Martin J. Sherwin's Pulitzer Prize–winning biography *American Prometheus: The Triumph and Tragedy of J. Robert Oppenheimer* (2005) suggests something of the ambiguity of their subject's life. Prometheus delivered the gift of fire to humankind by stealing it from the gods on Olympus; for his pains he was nailed in perpetuity to a mountain where each day an eagle feasted on his liver and each night the organ grew back. The physicist Oppenheimer (1904–1967), who studied quantum theory at Cambridge University in England and at Germany's Göttingen University after graduating from Harvard, would come to be known as "the father of the atom bomb." General Leslie Groves brought Oppenheimer into the Manhattan Project in 1941. The chapter of *American Prometheus* reproduced here chronicles Oppenheimer's leadership of the program at Los Alamos, highlighting not only his scientific insight but also his ability to build a team out of eccentric, prickly geniuses and somehow to navigate the inevitable collisions between military and scientific cultures in the laboratory. Oppenheimer also never lost sight of the ethical implications of nuclear weaponry. Indeed, his postwar resistance to the development of the hydrogen bomb, together with his past affiliation with various left-wing political movements, resulted in the loss of his security clearance in 1953, at the height of the nation's anti-Communist fervor. In the 1960s, in an NBC documentary on the Trinity test, an emotional Oppenheimer said of that first explosion of the atom bomb, "We knew the world would not be the same. A few people laughed, a few people cried. Most people were silent. I remembered the line from the Hindu scripture, the *Bhagavad Gita*; Vishnu is trying to persuade the prince that he should do his duty, and to impress him, takes on his multi-armed form and says, 'Now I am become death, the destroyer of worlds.' I suppose we all thought that, one way or another."

Robert Oppenheimer at Los Alamos

from *American Prometheus: The Triumph and Tragedy of J. Robert Oppenheimer* (2006)

*My feeling about Oppenheimer was, at that time, that this was a man who is angelic, true and honest and he could do no wrong. . . .
I believed in him.*

—ROBERT WILSON

Everyone sensed Oppie's presence. He drove himself around The Hill in an Army jeep or in his own large black Buick, dropping in unannounced on one of the laboratory's scattered offices. Usually he'd sit in the back of the room, chain-smoking and listening quietly to the discussion. His mere presence seemed to galvanize people to greater efforts. "Vicki" Weisskopf marveled at how often Oppie seemed to be physically present at each new breakthrough in the project. "He was present in the laboratory or in the seminar room when a new effect was measured, when a new idea was conceived. It was not that he contributed so many ideas or suggestions; he did so sometimes, but his main influence came from his continuous and intense presence, which produced a sense of direct participation in all of us." Hans Bethe recalled the day Oppie dropped in to a session on metallurgy and listened to an inconclusive debate over what type of refractory container should be used for melting plutonium. After listening to the argument, Oppie summed up the discussion. He didn't directly propose a solution, but by the time he left the room the right answer was clear to all.

By contrast, General Groves' visits were always interruptions—and sometimes comically disruptive. One day, Oppie was showing Groves around a lab when the general put his considerable weight on one of three rubber tubes funneling hot water into a casing. As McAllister Hull recalled for the historian Charles Thorpe, "It [the rubber tube] pops off the wall and a stream of water just below the boiling point shoots across the room. And if you've ever seen a picture of Groves, you know what it hit." Oppenheimer looked over his soaking-wet general and quipped, "Well, just goes to show the incompressibility of water."

Oppie's interventions sometimes proved to be absolutely essential to the success of the project. He understood that the single major impediment to building a usable weapon quickly was the meager supply of fissionable material. And so he was constantly looking for ways to accelerate the production of these materials. Early in 1943, Groves and his S-1 Executive Committee had settled on gaseous diffusion and electromagnetic technologies to separate out enriched fissionable uranium for the Los Alamos bomb lab. At the time, another possible technology, based on liquid thermal diffusion, had been rejected as unfeasible. But in the spring of 1944, Oppenheimer read some year-old reports about liquid thermal diffusion and decided that this had been a mistake. He thought this technology represented a relatively cheap path to providing partially enriched uranium for the electromagnetic process. So in April 1944, he wrote Groves that a liquid thermal diffusion plant might serve as a stopgap measure; its production of even slightly enriched uranium could then be fed to the electromagnetic diffusion plant and thereby accelerate production of fissionable material. It was his hope, he wrote, "that the production of the Y-12 [electromagnetic] plant could be increased by some 30 to 40 percent, and its enhancement somewhat improved, many months earlier than the scheduled date for K-25 [gaseous diffusion] production."

After sitting on Oppie's recommendation for a month, Groves agreed to explore it. A plant was rushed into production, and by the spring of 1945 it was producing just enough extra partially enriched uranium to guarantee a sufficient amount of fissionable material for one bomb by the end of July 1945.

Oppenheimer had always possessed a high degree of confidence in the uranium gun-design program—whereby a "slug" of fissionable material would be fired into a target of additional fissionable matter, creating "criticality" and a nuclear explosion. But in the spring of 1944, he suddenly faced a crisis that threatened to derail the entire effort to design a plutonium bomb. While Oppenheimer had authorized Seth Neddermeyer to conduct explosive experiments aimed at creating an implosion design bomb—a loosely packed sphere of fissionable material that could be instantly compressed to reach criticality—he had always hoped that a straightforward gun assembly would prove viable for the plutonium bomb. In July 1944, however, it became clear from tests performed on the first small supplies of plutonium that an efficient plutonium bomb could not be triggered within the "gun-barrel" design. Indeed, any such attempt would undoubtedly lead to a catastrophic pre-detonation inside the plutonium "gun."

One solution might have been to separate further the plutonium materials in an attempt to make a more stable element. "One could have separated out those bad plutonium isotopes from the good ones," John Manley explained, "but that would have meant duplicating everything that had been done for uranium isotope separation—all those big plants—and there was just no time to do that. The choice was to junk the whole discovery of the chain reaction that produced plutonium, and all of the investment in time and effort of the Hanford [Washington] plant, unless somebody could come up with a way of assembling the plutonium material into a weapon that would explode."

On July 17, 1944, Oppenheimer convened a meeting in Chicago with Groves, Conant, Fermi and others, to resolve the crisis. Conant urged that they aim merely to build a low-efficiency implosion bomb based on a mixture of uranium and plutonium. Such a weapon would have had an explosive equivalent of only several hundred tons of TNT. Only after successfully testing such a low-efficiency bomb, Conant said, would the lab have the confidence to proceed with a larger weapon.

Oppenheimer rejected this notion on the grounds that it would lead to unacceptable delays. Despite having been skeptical about the implosion idea when it was first broached by Serber, Oppenheimer now marshaled all his persuasive powers to argue that they gamble everything on an implosion-design plutonium bomb. It was an audacious and brilliant gamble. Since the spring of 1943, when Seth Neddermeyer had volunteered to experiment with the concept, little progress had been made. But in the autumn of 1943, Oppenheimer brought the Princeton mathematician John von Neumann to Los Alamos, and von Neumann calculated that implosion was possible, at least theoretically. Oppenheimer was willing to bet on it.

The next day, July 18, Oppenheimer summarized his conclusions for Groves: "We have investigated briefly the possibility of an electromagnetic separation. . . . It is our opinion that this method is in principle a possible one but that the necessary developments involved are in no way compatible with present ideas of schedule. . . . In the light of the above facts, it appears reasonable to discontinue the intensive effort to achieve higher purity for plutonium and to concentrate attention on methods of assembly which do not require a low neutron background for their success. At the present time the method to which an overriding priority must be assigned is the method of implosion."

Oppenheimer's assistant, David Hawkins, later explained, "The implosion was the only real hope [for a plutonium bomb], and from current evidence not a very good one." Neddermeyer and his men in the Ordnance Division were making very little progress on the implosion design. Neddermeyer, shy and retiring, liked to work alone, and methodically. He later admitted that Oppenheimer "became terribly impatient with me in the spring of 1944. . . . I think he felt very badly because I seemed not to push things as for war research but acted as though it were just a normal research situation." Neddermeyer was also one of the few men on the mesa who seemed immune to Oppie's charms. In his frustration, Oppie uncharacteristically began to lose his temper. "Oppenheimer lit into me," Neddermeyer recalled. "A lot of people looked up to him as a source of wisdom and inspiration. I respected him as a scientist, but I just didn't look up to him that way. . . . He could cut you cold and humiliate you right down to the ground. On the other hand, I could irritate him." Stoked by this personality conflict, the crisis over the implosion design came to a head late that summer when Oppenheimer announced a major reorganization of the lab.

Early in 1944, Oppenheimer had persuaded an explosives expert from Harvard, George "Kisty" Kistiakowsky, to move to Los Alamos. Kistiakowsky was opinionated and strong-willed. Inevitably, he had numerous run-ins with his ostensible superior, Captain "Deke" Parsons. Neither did Kistiakowsky get along with Neddermeyer, who seemed to him far too lackadaisical in his approach. Early in June 1944, Kistiakowsky wrote Oppenheimer a memo threatening to resign. In response, Oppenheimer swiftly called Neddermeyer in and told him that Kistiakowsky was replacing him. Angry and hurt, Neddermeyer walked out. Although he would feel an "enduring bitterness," he nevertheless was persuaded to remain in Los Alamos as a senior technical adviser. Acting decisively, Oppenheimer had announced this change without first consulting Captain Parsons. "Parsons was furious," recalled Kistiakowsky. "He felt that I had bypassed him and that was outrageous. I can understand perfectly how he felt, but I was a civilian, so was Oppie, and I didn't have to go through him."

Parsons chafed at what he considered a loss of control over his Ordnance Division, and in September he sent Oppie a memorandum proposing to give himself broad decision-making powers over all aspects of the implosion bomb project. Oppenheimer gently but firmly refused: "The kind of authority which you appear to request from me is something I cannot delegate to you because I do not possess it. I do not, in fact, whatever protocol may suggest, have the authority to make decisions which are not understood and approved by the qualified scientists of the laboratory who must execute them." As a military man, Navy Captain Parsons wanted the authority in order to short-circuit the debates among his scientists. "You have pointed out," Oppenheimer wrote him, "that you are afraid your position in the laboratory might make it necessary for you to engage in prolonged argument and discussion in order to obtain agreement upon which the progress of the work would depend. Nothing that

I can put in writing can eliminate this necessity." The scientists had to be free to argue—and Oppenheimer would arbitrate disputes only for the purpose of reaching some kind of collegial consensus. "I am not arguing that the laboratory should be so constituted," he told Parsons. "It is in fact so constituted."

In the midst of this ongoing crisis associated with the design of the plutonium bomb, Isidor Rabi paid one of his periodic visits to Los Alamos. He later remembered a gloomy session with a number of top scientists on the project as they talked of the urgency they felt about finding a way to make the plutonium bomb work. The conversation soon turned to the enemy: "Who were the German scientists? We knew them all," Rabi recalled. "What were they doing? We went over the whole thing again and looked at the history of our own development and tried to see where they could have been cleverer, where they might have had better judgment and avoided this error or that error. . . . We finally arrived at the conclusion that they could be exactly up to us, or perhaps further. We felt very solemn. One didn't know what the enemy had. One didn't want to lose a single day, a single week. And certainly, a month would be a calamity." As Philip Morrison summed up their attitude in mid-1944, "The only way we could lose the war was if we failed in our jobs."

Despite the reorganization, by late 1944 Kistiakowsky's group had still not managed to manufacture shaped explosives (called lenses) that would precisely crush a loosely packed, grapefruit-sized sphere of plutonium symmetrically into a sphere the size of a golf ball. Without such lenses, an implosion bomb seemed impractical. Captain Parsons was so pessimistic that he went to Oppenheimer and proposed that they abandon the lenses and try instead to create a non-lens type of implosion. In January 1945, the issue was hotly debated between Parsons and Kistiakowsky in the presence of both Groves and Oppenheimer. Kistiakowsky insisted that implosion could not be achieved without the lenses, and he promised that his men would soon be able to make them. In a decision critical to the success of the plutonium bomb, Oppenheimer backed him. During the next few months, Kistiakowsky and his team managed to perfect the implosion design. By May 1945, Oppenheimer felt fairly confident that the plutonium gadget would work.

Bomb-building was more engineering than theoretical physics. But Oppenheimer was as singularly adept at marshaling his scientists to overcome technical and engineering obstacles as he had been at stimulating his students to new insights at Berkeley. "Los Alamos might have succeeded without him," Hans Bethe later said, "but certainly only with much greater strain, less enthusiasm, and less speed. As it was, it was an unforgettable experience for all the members of the laboratory. There were other wartime laboratories of high achievement. . . . But I have never observed in any one of these other groups quite the spirit of belonging together, quite the urge to reminisce about the days of the laboratory, quite the feeling that this was really the great time of their lives. That this was true of Los Alamos was mainly due to Oppenheimer. He was a leader."

IN FEBRUARY 1944, a team of British scientists led by the German-born Rudolf E. Peierls arrived in Los Alamos. Oppenheimer had first met this brilliant but unassuming theoretical physicist in 1929, when both men were studying under Wolfgang Pauli. Peierls had emigrated from Germany to England in the early 1930s, and in 1940 he and Otto R. Frisch had written the seminal paper "On the Construction of a Superbomb," which had persuaded both the British and American governments that a nuclear weapon was feasible. During the next several years, Peierls worked on all aspects of Tube Alloys, the British bomb program. In 1942 and again in September 1943, Prime Minister Winston Churchill sent Peierls to America to help expedite work on the bomb. Peierls visited Oppenheimer in Berkeley and was "very impressed with his command of things. . . . He was the first person I met on that trip who had thought about the weapon itself and the implications of the physics of what would be going on."

Dr. Peierls spent only two and a half days on his first visit to Los Alamos. But Oppenheimer reported to Groves that they had agreed the British team could contribute substantially to studying the hydrodynamics of implosion. A month later, Peierls moved back to Los Alamos for the duration of the war. He admired how articulate and quick Oppenheimer was to understand anyone— but he particularly admired the way "he could stand up to General Groves."

As Peierls and his team settled into Los Alamos in the spring of 1944, Oppenheimer decided to give Peierls the job ostensibly held by Edward Teller. The mercurial Hungarian physicist was supposed to be working on a complicated set of calculations necessary for the implosion bomb. But Teller wasn't performing. Obsessed with the theoretical challenges posed by a "Super" thermonuclear bomb, Teller had no interest in a fission bomb. After Oppenheimer decided in June 1943 that wartime exigencies dictated a low priority for the Super, Teller became increasingly uncooperative. He seemed oblivious to any responsibility to contribute to the war effort. Always loquacious, he talked incessantly about a hydrogen bomb. Neither could he contain his resentment at having to work under Bethe. "I was not happy about having him as my boss," Teller recalled. To be sure, his resentment was fueled by Bethe's criticisms. Every morning Teller would have a bright new idea about how to make an H-bomb work—and overnight Bethe would prove it cockeyed. After one particularly trying encounter with Teller, Oppie quipped to Charles Critchfield, "God protect us from the enemy without and the Hungarians within."

Oppenheimer, understandably, became increasingly annoyed by Teller's behavior. One day that spring, Teller walked out of a meeting of section leaders and refused to do some calculations Bethe needed for his work on the implosion project. Extremely angry, Bethe complained to Oppie. "Edward essentially went on strike," Bethe recalled. When Oppenheimer confronted him about the incident, Teller finally asked to be relieved of all responsibility for work on the fission bomb. Oppenheimer agreed, and wrote General Groves that he wished to replace Teller with Peierls: "These calculations were originally under the supervision of Teller, who is, in my opinion and Bethe's, quite unsuited for this responsibility. Bethe feels that he needs a man under him to handle the implosion program."

Feeling slighted, Teller let it be known that he was thinking of leaving Los Alamos altogether. No one would have been surprised if Oppenheimer had let him go. Everyone thought of Teller as a "prima donna"; Bob Serber called him "a disaster to any organization." But instead of firing him, Oppenheimer gave Teller what he wanted, freedom to explore the feasibility of a thermonuclear bomb. Oppenheimer even agreed to give him a precious hour of his time once a week just to talk about whatever was on Teller's mind.

Not even this extraordinary gesture satisfied Teller, who thought that his friend had become a "politician." Oppie's colleagues wondered why he bothered with Teller. Peierls considered Teller "somewhat wild; he can back an idea for a time and then it turns out to be nonsense." Oppenheimer could be impatient with fools; but he was aware that Teller was no fool. He tolerated him because, in the end, he might contribute something to the project. When, later that summer, he hosted a reception for Churchill's special representative, Lord Cherwell (Frederic A. Lindemann), Oppenheimer realized afterwards that he had inadvertently left Rudolf Peierls off the invitation list. The next day he apologized to Peierls and then quipped, "It could have been worse—it could have been Teller."

IN DECEMBER 1944, Oppenheimer urged Rabi to make another visit to Los Alamos. "Dear Rab," he wrote, "We have been wondering for some time when you could come out again. The crises here are so continuous that it is hard to find one time which would be better or worse than another from our point of view." Rabi had just been awarded the Nobel Prize in physics in recognition for "his resonance method for recording the magnetic properties of atomic nuclei." Oppie congratulated him: "It is nice to have the prize go to a man who is out of his adolescence rather than just entering it."

Swamped with administrative work, Oppenheimer still found time to write the occasional personal letter. In the spring of 1944, he wrote to a family of German refugees whose escape from Europe he had facilitated. They were utter strangers, but in 1940 he had given the Meyers family—a mother and four daughters—a sum of money to pay their expenses to the United States.

Four years later, the Meyers repaid Oppenheimer and proudly informed him that they had become American citizens. He wrote back that he understood the "pride" they felt, and he thanked them for the money: "I hope it has not been a hardship for you. . . ." He then offered to return the money if they had any further need for it. (Years later, one of the Meyers daughters wrote in gratitude: "[I]n 1940 you brought us all over and we could save our lives.") For Oppenheimer, the rescue of the Meyerses from the Nazi contagion was important in several respects. It was in the first instance a politically noncontroversial extension of his antifascist activism—and that felt good. Secondly, while a small act of generosity, it was nevertheless a profound and welcome reminder of why he was racing to build a horrific weapon.

And racing he was. Restlessness was part of his character—or so thought Freeman Dyson, a young physicist who came to know and admire Oppenheimer after the war. But Dyson also saw restlessness as Oppie's tragic flaw: "Restlessness drove him to his supreme achievement, the fulfillment of the mission of Los Alamos, without pause for rest or reflection."

"Only one man paused," Dyson wrote. "The one who paused was Joseph Rotblat from Liverpool. . . ." A Polish physicist, Rotblat had been stranded in England when the war broke out. He was recruited by James Chadwick into the British bomb project and by early 1944 found himself in Los Alamos. One evening in March 1944, Rotblat experienced a "disagreeable shock." General Groves came for dinner at the Chadwicks' and in the course of casual banter over the dinner table, he said, "You realize of course that the main purpose of this project is to subdue the Russians." Rotblat was shocked. He had no illusions about Stalin—the Soviet dictator had, after all, invaded his beloved Poland. But thousands of Russians were dying every day on the Eastern Front and Rotblat felt a sense of betrayal. "Until then I had thought that our work was to prevent a Nazi victory," he later wrote, "and now I was told that the weapon we were preparing was intended for use against the people who were making extreme sacrifices for that very aim." By the end of 1944, six months after the Allies had landed on the beaches of Normandy, it was clear that the war in Europe would soon be over. Rotblat saw no point in continuing to work on a weapon that was no longer needed to defeat the Germans. After saying good-bye to Oppenheimer at a going-away party, he left Los Alamos on December 8, 1944.

IN THE AUTUMN of 1944, the Soviets received the first of many intelligence reports directly from Los Alamos. The spies overlooked by Army counterintelligence included Klaus Fuchs, a German physicist with British citizenship, and Ted Hall, a precociously brilliant nineteen-year-old with a Harvard B.S. in physics. Hall arrived in Los Alamos in late January 1944, while Fuchs came in August as part of the British team led by Rudolf Peierls.

Fuchs, born in 1911, was raised in a German Quaker family. Studious and idealistic, he joined the German socialist party, the SPD, while studying at the University of Leipzig in 1931—the same year his mother committed suicide. In 1932, alarmed by the growing political strength of the Nazis, Fuchs broke with the socialists and joined the Communist Party, which was more actively resisting Hitler. In July 1933, he fled Hitler's Germany and became a political refugee in England. Over the next few years, his family was decimated by the Nazi regime. His brother escaped to Switzerland, leaving behind a wife and child who later died in a concentration camp. His father was sent to prison for "anti-government agitation," and in 1936 his sister Elizabeth killed herself after her husband was arrested and sent to a concentration camp. Fuchs had every reason to hate the Nazis.

In 1937, after earning a doctorate in physics in Bristol, Fuchs won a postgraduate fellowship to work with Oppenheimer's former professor Max Born, who by then was teaching at Edinburgh. After the war began, Fuchs was interned in Canada as an enemy alien, and Professor Born helped to obtain his release by attesting that Fuchs was "among the two or three most gifted theoretical physicists of the young generation." He and thousands of other anti-Nazi German refugees were released at the end of 1940; Fuchs was given permission to return to his work in England. Although the British Home Office knew all about his communist past, by the spring of 1941 Fuchs was working with Peierls and other British scientists on the highly classified Tube Alloys project. In June 1942, Fuchs received British citizenship—by then, he was already passing information to the Soviets about the British bomb program.

When Fuchs arrived in Los Alamos, neither Oppenheimer nor anyone else had any suspicion that he was a Soviet spy. After he was arrested in 1950, Oppie told the FBI that he had thought Fuchs was a Christian Democrat, and certainly not a "political fanatic." Bethe considered Fuchs one of the best men in his division. "If he was a spy," Bethe told the FBI, "he played his role beautifully. He worked days and nights. He was a bachelor and had nothing better to do, and he contributed very greatly to the success of the Los Alamos project." Over the next year, Fuchs passed detailed written information to the Soviets about the problems and advantages of the implosion-type bomb design over the gun method. He was unaware that the Soviets were getting confirmation of his information from another Los Alamos resident.

By September 1944, Ted Hall was working on the calibration tests needed for the implosion-design bomb. Oppenheimer heard that Hall was one of the best young technicians on the mesa when it came to creating a test implosion. An extremely bright man, Hall that autumn was sitting on the edge of an intellectual precipice. He was a socialist in outlook, an admirer of the Soviet Union, but not yet a formal communist, and neither was he disgruntled or unhappy with his work or his station in life. No one recruited him. But all that year he had listened to "older" scientists—in their late twenties and early thirties—talk about their fear of a postwar arms race. On one occasion, sitting at the same Fuller Lodge dinner table with Niels Bohr, he heard Bohr's concerns for an "open world." Prompted by his con- clusion that a postwar U.S. nuclear monopoly could lead to another war, in October 1944 Hall decided to act: ". . . it seemed to me that an American monopoly was dangerous and should be prevented. I was not the only scientist to take that view."

While on a fourteen-day leave from Los Alamos, Hall boarded a train to New York City and simply walked into a Soviet trade office and gave a Soviet official a handwritten report on Los Alamos. It described the laboratory's purpose and listed the names of the leading scientists working on the bomb project. In the months that followed, Hall managed to pass the Soviets much additional information, including critical information on the design for the implosion bomb. Hall was the perfect "walk-in" spy; he knew what the Russians needed to know about the atomic bomb project; he needed nothing himself and expected nothing. His sole purpose was to "save the world" from a nuclear war that he believed was inevitable if the United States emerged from the war with an atomic monopoly.

Oppenheimer knew nothing about Hall's espionage activities. But he did know that a group of twenty or so scientists, some of them group leaders, had begun meeting informally once a month to talk about the war, politics and the future. "It used to be in the evenings," recalled Rotblat, "usually at somebody's house like the Tellers', someone who had fairly large rooms. People would meet to discuss the future of Europe, the future of the world." Among other issues, they talked about the exclusion of Soviet scientists from the project. According to Rotblat, Oppenheimer came to at least one of their meetings and Rotblat said later, "I always thought he was a soul mate in the sense that we had the same humanitarian approach to problems."

BY LATE 1944, a number of scientists at Los Alamos began to voice their growing ethical qualms about the continued development of the "gadget." Robert Wilson, now chief of the lab's experimental physics division, had "quite long discussions with Oppie about how it might be used." Snow was still on the ground when Wilson went to Oppenheimer and proposed holding a formal meeting to discuss the matter more fully. "He tried to talk me out of it," Wilson later recalled, "saying I would get into trouble with the G-2, the security people."

Despite his respect, even reverence, for Oppie, Wilson thought little of this argument. He told himself, "All right. So what? I mean, if you're a good pacifist, then clearly you are not going to be worried about being thrown in jail or whatever they would do—have your salary reduced or horrible things like that." So Wilson told Oppenheimer that he hadn't talked him out of at least having an open discussion about an issue that was obviously of great importance. Wilson then put up notices all over the lab announcing a public meeting to discuss "The Impact of the Gadget on Civilization." He chose this title because earlier, at Princeton, "just before we'd come out, there'd been many sanctimonious talks about the 'impact' of something else, with all very scholarly kinds of discussions."

To his surprise, Oppie showed up on the appointed evening and listened to the discussion. Wilson later thought about twenty people attended, including such senior physicists as Vicki Weisskopf. The meeting was held in the same building that housed the cyclotron. "I can remember," Wilson said, "it being very cold in our building. . . . We did have a pretty intense discussion of why it was that we were continuing to make a bomb after the war had been [virtually] won."

This may not have been the only occasion when the morality and politics of the atomic bomb were discussed. A young physicist working on implosion techniques, Louis Rosen, remembered a packed daytime colloquium held in the old theater. Oppenheimer was the speaker and, according to Rosen, the topic was "whether the country is doing the right thing in using this weapon on real live human beings." Oppenheimer apparently argued that as scientists they had no right to a louder voice in determining the gadget's fate than any other citizen. "He was a very eloquent and persuasive guy," Rosen said. The chemist Joseph O. Hirschfelder recalled a similar discussion held in Los Alamos' small wooden chapel in the midst of a thunderstorm on a cold Sunday evening in early 1945. On this occasion, Oppenheimer argued with his usual eloquence that, although they were all destined to live in perpetual fear, the bomb might also end all war. Such a hope, echoing Bohr's words, was persuasive to many of the assembled scientists.

No official records were kept of these sensitive discussions. So memories prevail. Robert Wilson's account is the most vivid—and those who knew Wilson always thought him a man of singular integrity. Victor Weisskopf later recalled having political discussions about the bomb at various times with Willy Higinbotham, Robert Wilson, Hans Bethe, David Hawkins, Phil Morrison and William Woodward, among others. Weisskopf recalled that the expected end of the war in Europe "caused us to think more about the future of the world after the war." At first, they simply met in their apartments, and pondered questions such as "What will this terrible weapon do to this world? Are we doing something good, something bad? Should we not worry about how it will be applied?" Gradually, these informal discussions became formal meetings. "We tried to organize meetings in some of the lecture rooms," Weisskopf said, "and then we ran into opposition. Oppenheimer was against that. He said that's not our task, and this is politics, and we should not do this." Weisskopf recalled a meeting in March 1945, attended by forty scientists, to discuss "the atomic bomb in world politics." Oppenheimer again tried to discourage people from attending. "He thought we should not get involved in questions about the use of the bomb. . . ." But, contrary to Wilson's memory, Weisskopf later wrote that "the thought of quitting did not even cross my mind."

Wilson believed it would have reflected badly on Oppenheimer if he had chosen not to appear. "You know, you're the director, a little bit like a general. Sometimes you have got to be in front of your troops, sometimes you've got to be in back of them. Anyway, he came and he had very cogent arguments that convinced me." Wilson wanted to be convinced. Now that it seemed so clear that the gadget would not be used on the Germans, he and many others in the room had doubts but no answers. "I thought we were fighting the Nazis," Wilson said, "not the Japanese particularly." No one thought the Japanese had a bomb program.

When Oppenheimer took the floor and began speaking in his soft voice, everyone listened in absolute silence. Wilson recalled that Oppenheimer "dominated" the discussion. His main argument essentially drew on Niels Bohr's vision of "openness." The war, he argued, should not end without the world knowing about this primordial new weapon. The worst outcome would be if the gadget remained a military secret. If that happened, then the next war would almost certainly be fought with atomic weapons. They had to forge ahead, he explained, to the point where the gadget could be tested. He pointed out that the new United Nations was scheduled to hold its inaugural meeting in April 1945—and that it was important that the delegates begin their deliberations on the postwar world with the knowledge that mankind had invented these weapons of mass destruction.

"I thought that was a very good argument," said Wilson. For some time now, Bohr and Oppenheimer himself had talked about how the gadget was going to change the world. The scientists knew that the gadget was going to force a redefinition of the whole notion of national sovereignty. They had faith in Franklin Roosevelt and believed that he was setting up the United Nations precisely to address this conundrum. As Wilson put it, "There would be areas in which there would be no sovereignty, the sovereignty would exist in the United Nations. It was to be the end of war as we knew it, and this was a promise that was made. That is why I could continue on that project."

Oppenheimer had prevailed, to no one's surprise, by articulating the argument that the war could not end without the world knowing the terrible secret of Los Alamos. It was a defining moment for everyone. The logic—Bohr's logic—was particularly compelling to Oppenheimer's fellow scientists. But so too was the charismatic man who stood before them. As Wilson recalled that moment, "My feeling about Oppenheimer was, at that time, that this was a man who is angelic, true and honest and he could do no wrong. . . . I believed in him."

Ovid
(43 BCE–17 CE)

THE POET KNOWN as Ovid was born Publius Ovidius Naso during the Roman civil wars. Having received his education at Rome, he traveled throughout Greece and, after a rather brief career in public service, decided to devote himself to poetry. He had written his first book, *Amores*, before the age of twenty. Later works, including *Fasti*, a poem about the rituals, festivals, and cults of Rome; and *Metamorphoses*, were interrupted when Augustus exiled the poet to Tomi, a remote frontier town on the Black Sea. The reasons for Ovid's exile are a little vague: the formal charges concerned his poem *Ars Amatoria*, the frank, satirical, and often ribald nature of which offended the emperor; and some unspecified error, perhaps involvement in a scandal touching the imperial family. He was never recalled to Rome and died in Tomi. *Metamorphoses*, a wonderful, witty poem of shape-shifting that begins with the creation and ends with the poet's prediction of his own apotheosis, is distinguished by its intricate narrative structure, its delight in the foibles and instability of humans and gods alike, and its insightful psychology. Ovid drew on Greek and Roman sources for his myths, and his versions were well known throughout the Middle Ages and the Renaissance, when they proved a source of inspiration to Shakespeare. The two myths included here follow the fate of the inventor Daedalus, who designs an ingenious method of escape for himself and his son from the isle of Crete, where he was imprisoned in the very labyrinth he had once been commissioned to build—locked away by King Minos as retribution for revealing its secret and allowing its original inmate, the man-eating Minotaur, to escape. In his book *The Icarus Deception: How High Will You Fly?* business writer Seth Godin argues that the tragedy of the Icarus story has been generally misunderstood: it is not the hubris of flying too high but the tendency to fly too low that constitutes its tragedy. Other poetic treatments of this myth that provide instructive comparisons with Ovid's include W. H. Auden's "Musée des Beaux Arts," William Carlos Williams's "Landscape with the Fall of Icarus," Carol Frost's "Icarus in Winter," and Jack Gilbert's "Failing and Flying." The second myth provides a lesser-known coda to the bold inventor's story. (The following selections are translated by Charles Martin.)

Daedalus and Icarus

from *Metamorphoses*

Meanwhile, detesting Crete and his long exile,
and longing to return to his own nation,
Daedalus found that an escape by sea
was closed to him:
          "Though he may bar the earth
and seas," he said, "without a doubt, the sky
above is open; that is how we'll go:
Minos rules everything except the air."
   He spoke and turned his mind to arts unknown,
and changed the face of nature, for he placed
a row of feathers in ascending order,   10
smallest to largest, so you would have thought
that they had all grown that way on a slope;
thus antic panpipes with unequal reeds
will rise above each other; these were bound
together in the middle with flaxen thread
and then joined at the quills with molded wax;
and finally, he bent them just a bit,
so they resembled bird's wings.
                    Icarus,
his boy, was standing close by, unaware
of any danger in the things he handled;   20
he smiled as he snatched at wisps of feathers blown
from his father's workbench by a passing breeze,
or left a thumbprint in the golden wax
and playfully got in his father's way.
   The wondrous work continued nonetheless,
and when he'd put the final touches to it,
the artisan himself hung poised between
the wings upon his shoulders in midair,
and offered these instructions to his son;
   "Listen to me: keep to the middle course,   30
dear Icarus, for if you fly too low,
the waves will weight your wings down with their moisture;
and if you fly too high, flames will consume them;
stay in the middle and don't set your course
by gazing at the stars: ignore Boötes,
the Dipper, and Orion's unsheathed sword;

keep to my path and follow where I lead you."
And while he was instructing him in flight,
he fit the untried wings to the boy's shoulders.

    And as he works and as he warns the boy,   40
the old man's cheeks are dampened by his tears;
the father's hands are trembling as he gives
his son a not-to-be-repeated kiss,
and lifts off on his wings into the air;
he flies ahead, afraid for his companion,
just like a bird who leads her young in flight
from their high nest, and as he flies along,
exhorts the boy to follow in his path,
instructing him in their transgressive art,
as he employs his wings in flight and watches   50
his fledgling Icarus attempt his own.

    Some fisherman whose line jerks with his catch,
some idle shepherd leaning on his crook,
some plowman at his plow, looks up and sees
something astonishing, and thinks them gods,
who have the power to pass through the air.

    Now on their left, they had already passed
the Isle of Samos, Juno's favorite,
Delos and Paros too; and on their right,
Lebinthos and Calymne, honey-rich,   60
when the boy audaciously began to play
and driven by desire for the sky,
deserts his leader and seeks altitude.

    The sun's consuming rays, much nearer now,
soften the fragrant wax that bound his wings
until it melts.

          He agitates his arms,
but without wings, they cannot grip the air,
and with his father's name on them, his lips
are taken under by the deep blue sea
that bears his name, even to the present.   70

    And his unlucky father, now no more
a father, cries out, "Icarus, where are you,
where, in what region, shall I look for you?"

    And then he saw the feathers on the waves
and cursed his arts; he built his son a tomb
in the land that takes its name from Icarus.

Daedalus and Perdix[1]

As he entombs his child's pathetic corpse,
he is observed, from where a rank ditch drips,
by a chatty partridge, who chirps cheerfully
and makes his wing tips flutter in applause:
a novel and unprecedented bird,
and one who'd only lately been transformed,
O Daedalus, because of a misdeed
that, for a long time, will be held against you.
    For, as it happened, the inventor's sister,
quite unaware of what the Fates intended,   10
entrusted her own son to his instruction,
a likely lad of twelve, who had a mind
with the capacity for principles and precepts;
and from his observation of the spines
of fishes, which he'd taken as his model,
incised a row of teeth in an iron strip
and thereby managed to invent the saw.
Likewise, he was the first to bind two arms
of iron at a joint, so one is fixed
and the other, as it moves, inscribes a circle.   20
    Daedalus envied him, and headlong hurled
this lad of precepts from a precipice,
the steep acropolis Minerva loves,
and lying, said the lad had slipped and fallen.
    But Athena, who takes care of clever people,
snatched him from harm, changed him to a bird,
and covered him with feathers in midair.
His former brilliance, like his former name,
he kept, although the former was transformed
into the swiftness of his wings and feet.   30
    Although a bird, she does not soar aloft,
and does not build her nest high up in trees
or on lofty peaks; she flies close to the ground
and lays her eggs in hedges; remembering
that fall of long ago, she fears the heights.

---

1 *Perdix* is the word Greeks had for partridge.

Jean de La Fontaine
(1621–1695)

JEAN DE LA Fontaine was in his thirties by the time he embarked on a literary career. The son of a ducal park ranger in Château-Thierry, a position to which he eventually succeeded, La Fontaine spent much of his life in Paris, trying first the priesthood and then the law. In the capital he had a series of patrons and joined a circle of writers that included Jean Racine, Nicolas Boileau, and Molière. He is perhaps best known for his collection of fables, published in a series of twelve volumes appearing periodically from 1668 to 1694. Composed in technically accomplished verse, the fables follow the method of Aesop while also incorporating Eastern traditions. La Fontaine enriched the genre of the conventional animal fable. As John Hollander notes in his introduction to Norman R. Shapiro's translation of the complete fables, La Fontaine imparted a particular sophistication to the form: possessing an epic structure in twelve volumes, his fables initiated a "great transformation" of the genre in France. Offering social and political commentary, mirroring the age's mores and manners, these fables also do the transhistorical work customary to the genre by employing archetypal flora and fauna. In "The Oak and the Reed" La Fontaine offers an allegory of flexibility: the oak, sturdy and strong but unyielding, compares notes with the reed, apparently flimsy yet never breaking. (The following selection, from the first volume, is translated by Elizur Wright).

The Oak and the Reed
from *Fables* (1668)

The oak one day addressed the reed:—
"To you ungenerous indeed
Has nature been, my humble friend,
With weakness aye obliged to bend.
The smallest bird that flits in air
Is quite too much for you to bear;
The slightest wind that wreathes the lake
Your ever-trembling head does shake.
  The while, my towering form
  Dares with the mountain top
  The solar blaze to stop,
  And wrestle with the storm.

What seems to you the blast of death,
　To me is but a zephyr's breath.
Beneath my branches had you grown,
　That spread far round their friendly bower,
Less suffering would your life have known,
　Defended from the tempest's power.
　Unhappily you oftenest show
　　In open air your slender form,
　Along the marshes wet and low,
　　That fringe the kingdom of the storm.
　　To you, declare I must,
　　Dame Nature seems unjust."
Then modestly replied the reed:
"Your pity, sir, is kind indeed,
But wholly needless for my sake.
The wildest wind that ever blew
Is safe to me compared with you.
I bend, indeed, but never break.
Thus far, I own, the hurricane
Has beat your sturdy back in vain;
But wait the end." Just at the word,
The tempest's hollow voice was heard.
The North sent forth her fiercest child,
Dark, jagged, pitiless, and wild.
The oak, erect, endured the blow;
The reed bowed gracefully and low.
But, gathering up its strength once more,
In greater fury than before,
　　　The savage blast
　　　Overthrew, at last,
　That proud, old, sky-encircled head,
Whose feet entwined the empire of the dead!

DISCUSSION QUESTIONS

1. *What do these readings suggest about the relationship between change and personal success? About change and organizational success?*

2. *Why are some individuals—Xin Dezhi, the senior apprentice in Lao She's story, for example—more resistant to change than others? How does one persuade another of the value of change?*

3. *How do these readings help you to distinguish enduring, productive innovation from fad or novelty?*

4. *Under what circumstances might stability be more important than innovation?*

5. *How does your organization foster innovation? Is it willing to risk near-term turbulence for long-term gains?*

KNOWING THE WAY

The fox knows many things, but the hedgehog knows one great thing.

—ARCHILOCHUS (attributed)

The medieval Japanese *Heike monogatari* (*The Tales of the Heike*) contains the story of Taira no Tadanori, a general in the twelfth century Genpei War between the Taira and Genji clans. We encounter Tadanori soon after his fortunes have turned. Fleeing the capital for the last time, he stops with an armed retinue before the locked gates of the poet Shunzei's house. Reassuring his frightened servants that this fearsome warrior means no harm, Shunzei receives Tadanori, who had been his student until forced to abandon his formal studies because of the war. Tadanori, reaching into his armor for a scroll, asks the poet to fulfill, in Burton Watson's translation, his "lifelong hopes" by including one of his poems in an imperial anthology. Moved by Tadanori's "deep concern for the art of poetry" even in the midst of a civil war his side is losing, Shunzei assures the general that he will give his poems the most serious consideration.

"Perhaps I will find rest beneath the waves of the western ocean," a joyful Tadanori replies; "perhaps my bones will be left to bleach on the mountain plain. Whatever may come, I can now take leave of this uncertain world without the least regret. And so I say good-bye!" The weeping poet watches the general ride away and imagines that he can hear him reciting poetry long after he has disappeared from view.

Shunzei does include one of Tadanori's poems in the anthology, although he is compelled to list its author, who is now an enemy of the state, as "unknown." Tadanori, meanwhile, meets his end at the Battle of Ichi-no-tani, his identity revealed to his enemy by means of a signed poem fastened to his quiver of arrows: "When they heard Tadanori's name," the episode concludes, "Taira and Genji warriors alike exclaimed, 'What a pity! A man skilled both in arms and the practice of poetry, a true commanding general!' And there were none who did not wet their sleeve with tears."

The tale of Tadanori illuminates several aspects of the concept of knowing the way. His frustration at having to suspend his studies suggests the time and patient labor required to achieve mastery, while his continued pursuit of a poetic career reveals something important about his priorities, which he refuses to surrender entirely to the exigencies of the day. What was important to Tadanori in peace remains so in war, even if he can no longer devote himself to his art. The fact that the poem he carries with him into battle proves the instrument of his unmasking at his death—verse as identity disc or dog tag—symbolizes the enduring value of his artistry. He is "a true commanding general," his enemies acknowledge, because of his proficiency in both war and poetry. Tadanori's concept of mastery involves disciplined devotion but not, it would seem, a ruthlessly single-minded economy of effort. His is the spirit of the polymath, not the utilitarian.

Mastery requires all of the attributes examined thus far in this anthology: the capacity for studying systems and cultures; an ability to follow and then depart from exemplary models; the cultivation of patience and deep attention; the willingness to risk revising oneself and one's organization. These are habits of successful leaders but only because they are habits of self-aware and resilient individuals. Utilitarian mastery of skills without any grounding in a knowledge of self and world produces inchoate leaders. A more comprehensive leadership accommodates both application and study—the charting of a course between the Scylla of exclusive practice and the Charybdis of abstract theory.

There are periods in history when the cult of theory or the cult of experience seems to have the upper hand: at the beginning of the twenty-first century the latter arguably appears to be ascendant. Practical experience seems to be at once the guarantee of authenticity and the harbinger of future success. One way to think about mastery might be to imagine it as the artful combination of theoretical knowledge and practical experience in the cultivation of exquisite judgment. The sixteenth-century French philosopher Michel de Montaigne spent a lifetime in pursuit of the self-knowledge that would teach him, as he wrote in an essay "On Books," "how to live and die well." When he was thirty-eight, Montaigne dedicated himself to this pursuit by retreating to a room at the top of a tower on his estate. There, surrounded by his books, he wrote the essays—they eventually ran to three volumes—that made him a household word in France and throughout the world. Montaigne was defiantly a man of letters, but he was likewise committed to the value of experience: "Knowledge and truth can lodge within us without judgement," he warned (translated here by M. A. Screech); "judgement can do so without them: indeed, recognizing our ignorance is one of the surest and most beautiful witnesses to our judgement that I can find."

Achieving mastery of this sort requires a balance between academic knowledge and practical experience, as Francis Bacon's essay "Of Studies" advises. As the selections from Lao Tzu, Marcus Aurelius, Sun Tzu, Tolstoy, and the anonymous Zen story "A Taste of Banzo's Sword" all suggest, it requires, too, the maintenance of principles; an acceptance of the limits of one's control; and, when appropriate, a neglect of one's own perceived dignity. Furthermore, as the examples of Dido, Omar Bradley, Clausewitz's military genius, and the chefs David Pasternack and Barbara Lynch (the subjects of "Gone Fishing" and "A Woman's Place Is Running the Kitchen," respectively) attest, it demands an admixture of skill, technical knowledge, strategic vision, and the simultaneous possession of facts and imagination. Finally, mastery is enhanced by an ability, expressed by the speaker of Robert Frost's "Oven Bird," to listen well.

FURTHER READING AND VIEWING

Mary Oliver, "Building the House," *Winter Hours: Prose, Prose Poems, and Poems* (1999)
Antoine de Saint-Exupéry, *Wind, Sand and Stars* (1939)
Jonathan A. Spence, *Emperor of China: Self-Portrait of K'ang-Hsi* (1974)
The Twilight Samurai (2002), directed by Yôji Yamata
T. H. White, *The Once and Future King* (1958)

Lao Tzu
(ca. sixth–third century BCE)

A TOUCHSTONE OF ancient Chinese thought and the foundational text of Taoism, the *Tao Te Ching*, or "Book of the Way and its Virtue," offers what David Hinton, a distinguished translator of the major works of Chinese poetry and philosophy, calls a wellspring of "spiritual ecology." Widely and diversely translated for over two millennia, it is a text that remains full of "dark ambiguities and evocative silences." And it is attributed to an equally mysterious figure: Lao Tzu. Legend has it that Lao was a near contemporary of Confucius (551–479 BCE), but his biography is essentially unknown. Part of the tradition called "Masters Literature," which includes works by Confucius, Mencius, Chuang Tzu, and other sages, the *Tao Te Ching* articulates central tenets of ancient Chinese thought: the

Way is the natural course of everything in the cosmos, while Virtue or Integrity is the motive force that allows all beings to flourish. Didactic yet mystical, contradictory and indirect, the text nevertheless presents, as Hinton writes, "a voice that is consistent and compassionate." Harking back to a Paleolithic culture in which human beings dwell within, rather than attempting to control, nature, the *Tao Te Ching* portrays the world as having suffered, in Hinton's words, a "fundamental rupture between human being and natural process." This aspect of the text has relevance for our own era's environmental disasters and the problem of global warming, as human societies and governments decide what they wish their relationship to the planet to be. Three selections are presented here: the first two from the section of the text called "the Way," the third from the section entitled "Integrity," or the manifestation of the way in the world. All evoke at once the mystical and the practical, urging a restraint, discipline, and self-containment productive of harmonious dwelling. All are infused with what scholars regard as Master Lao's fundamental care for social justice.

Tao Te Ching

15
Ancient masters of Way
all subtle mystery and dark-enigma vision:
they were deep beyond knowing,

so deep beyond knowing
we can only describe their appearance:

perfectly cautious, as if crossing winter streams,
and perfectly watchful, as if neighbors threatened;
perfectly reserved, as if guests,
perfectly expansive, as if ice melting away,
and perfectly simple, as if uncarved wood;
perfectly empty, as if open valleys,
and perfectly shadowy, as if murky water.

Who's murky enough to settle slowly into pure clarity,
and who still enough to awaken slowly into life?

If you nurture this Way, you never crave fullness.
Never crave fullness
and you'll wear away into completion.

30
If you use the Way to help a ruler of people
you never use weapons to coerce all beneath heaven.
Such things always turn against you:

fields where soldiers camp
turn to thorn and bramble,
and vast armies on the march
leave years of misery behind.

The noble prevail if they must, then stop:
they never press on to coerce the world.

Prevail, but never presume.
Prevail, but never boast.
Prevail, but never exult.
Prevail, but never when there's another way.
This is to prevail without coercing.

Things grown strong soon grow old.
This is called *losing the Way:*
Lose the Way and you die young.

49
A sage's mind is never his own:
he makes the hundred-fold people's mind his mind.

I treat the noble with nobility
and the ignoble too:
such is the nobility of Integrity.
I treat the sincere with sincerity
and the insincere too:
such is the sincerity of Integrity.

A sage dwells within all beneath heaven
at ease, mind mingled through it all.
The hundred-fold people devote their eyes and ears,
but a sage inhabits it all like a child.

Marcus Aurelius
(121–180)

IT WAS THE 2000 motion picture *Gladiator* that gave us the popular-culture image of the Roman emperor Marcus Aurelius, played with stately dignity by Richard Harris, as the wise emperor who dies too soon and whose descendants preside over the death throes of the empire. In that film, Marcus muses, "How will the world speak my name in years to come? Will I be known as the philosopher? The warrior? The tyrant? Or will there be a more golden sounding to my name? Will I be the Emperor who gave Rome back her freedom?" Today Marcus is known above all for his *Meditations*, a touchstone of Stoic philosophy. In the original Greek, these observations bore the title "To Himself," which, as the classicist Bernard Knox observes in *The Norton Book of Classical Literature*, properly describes this "book of self-exhortation; when Marcus writes 'you' he means himself. It is a remarkable document. The ruler of a world empire who had to deal not only with hard-fought campaigns on the threatened Balkan frontier but also with the ravages of a devastating plague here jots down his inmost thoughts as he steels himself for the daily struggle with the problems of a world in crisis." Admired by Edward Gibbon, the eighteenth-century author of the monumental history *Decline and Fall of the Roman Empire*, Marcus was also a great favorite with the Victorians, including Walter Pater and Matthew Arnold. The latter wanted to make the Roman's name as familiar to readers as that of Socrates because of the wisdom imparted by the *Meditations*, especially on the subject of what Arnold called "the ground-motives of human action." Arnold concludes an essay on Marcus with the following encomium: "We see him wise, just, self-governed, tender, thankful, blameless; yet, with all this, agitated, stretching out his arms for something beyond." The selections that follow center on the internal focus required by the individual who would master the inevitable vicissitudes of human nature. Like Lao Tzu, Marcus urges on himself a self-knowledge acquired through patience, understanding, and discipline. (The following selections are translated by Jeremy Collier.)

Meditations

2.5

Take care always to remember that you are a man and a Roman; and let every action be done with perfect and unaffected gravity, humanity, freedom, and justice. And be sure you entertain no fancies, which may give check to these qualities. This is possible, if you will but perform every action as though it were your last; if your appetites and passions do not cross upon your reason; if you keep clear of rashness, and have nothing of insincerity and self-love to infect you, and do not complain of your destiny. You see what a few points a man has to gain in order to attain to a godlike way of living; for he that comes thus far, performs all which the immortal powers will require of him.

2.7

Do not let accidents disturb, or outward objects engross your thoughts, but keep your mind quiet and disengaged, that you may be at leisure to learn something good, and cease rambling from one thing to another. There is likewise another sort of roving to be avoided; for some people are busy and yet do nothing; they fatigue and wear themselves out, and yet aim at no goal, nor propose any general end of action or design.

2.13

Nothing can be more unhappy than the curiosity of that man that ranges everywhere, and digs into the earth, as the poet says, for discovery; that is wonderfully busy to force by conjecture a passage into other people's thoughts, but does not consider that it is sufficient to reverence and serve the divinity within himself. And this service consists in this, that a man keep himself pure from all violent passion, and evil affection, from all rashness and vanity, and from all manner of discontent towards gods or men. For as for the gods, their administration ought to be revered upon the score of excellency; and as for men, their actions should be well taken for the sake of common kindred. Besides, they are often to be pitied for their ignorance of good and evil; which incapacity of discerning between moral qualities is no less a defect than that of a blind man, who cannot distinguish between white and black.

5.5

Wit and smartness are not your talent. What then? There are a great many other good qualities in which you cannot pretend nature has failed you; improve them as far as you can, and let us have that which is perfectly in your power. You may if you please behave yourself like a man of gravity and good faith, endure hardship, and despise pleasure; want but a few things, and complain of nothing; you may be gentle and magnanimous if you please, and have nothing of luxury or trifling in your disposition. Do not you see how much you may do if you have a mind to it, where the plea of incapacity is out of place? And yet you do not push forward as you should do. What then! Does any natural defect force you to grumble, to lay your faults upon your constitution, to be stingy or a flatterer, to seek after popularity, boast, and be disturbed in mind? Can you say you are so weakly made as to be driven to these practices? The immortal gods know the contrary. No, you might have stood clear of all this long since; and after all, if your parts were somewhat slow, and your understanding heavy, your way had been to have taken the more pains with yourself, and not to have lain fallow and remained content with your own dulness.

Sun Tzu
(ca. sixth–third century BCE)

LIKE MACHIAVELLI'S THE PRINCE, Sun Tzu's *The Art of War* has been transmuted into a practical handbook of strategic lessons for executives, leaders, and managers. As Thomas Cleary puts it in the introduction to his translation, it is a "most revered" primer for success, especially in an era of globalization. It is also associated in popular culture with the most ruthless bankers and traders: "The public is out there throwing darts at a board, sport," declares the proudly greedy Gordon Gekko in *Wall Street* (1987). "I don't throw darts at a board. I only bet sure things. Read Sun Tzu's *The Art of War.* 'Every battle is won before it is ever fought.' Think about it." Eminently quotable and frequently decontextualized, *The Art of War* is far more elusive than the Gordon Gekkos of the world would like us to believe. The work attributed to Sun Tzu—or Master Sun—is sometimes obscured by the commentaries often published alongside the primary text. Read on its own, as here in John Minford's translation, *The Art of War* offers an incisive portrait of authority's workings, the variability of human nature, and the effects of discipline on both leader and led. One must look to the great historian Sima Qian to find any biographical details about Sun Tzu; there are no other references to him. He may have been a military adviser to the king of Wu during the Warring States period; by the Han Dynasty (206 BCE–220 BC), he was well known as a sage whose work offered a counterpoint to that of Confucius. The following excerpt comes from the end of chapter 12, "Attack by Fire," which describes the attributes necessary in the enlightened ruler and the effective general.

The Ruler and the General
from *The Art of War*

To win victory,
    To complete an objective,
    But not to follow through,
    Is a disastrous
    Waste.

Hence the saying
    "The enlightened ruler
    Considers deeply;
    The effective general
    Follows through."

Never move
    Except for gain;
Never deploy
    Except for victory;
Never fight
    Except in a crisis.

A ruler
    Must never
    Mobilize his men
    Out of anger;
    A general
    Must never
    Engage battle
    Out of spite.

Move
    If there is gain;
Halt
    If there is no gain.

Anger
    Can turn to
    Pleasure;
Spite
    Can turn to
    Joy.

But a nation destroyed
> Cannot be
> Put back together again;
> A dead man
> Cannot be
> Brought back to life.

So the enlightened ruler
> Is prudent;
The effective general
> Is cautious.
This is the Way
> To keep a nation
> At peace
> And an army
> Intact.

Christine de Pizan
(ca. 1364–ca. 1431)

BORN IN ITALY, Christine de Pizan spent the majority of her life in France, where her father, a physician and an astrologer, served at the Parisian court of Charles V. When the premature death of her husband forced Christine to earn an income, she put her fine education to work as the first woman to become a professional writer in Europe. A contemporary of Petrarch, Boccaccio, and Chaucer, Christine responded to a world characterized by tremendous upheaval, including the plague and the Hundred Years' War. The selection reproduced here is one of the tales in her best-known work, *The Book of the City of Ladies* (1405), an allegory in which the narrator, guided by three goddesses—Reason, Rectitude, and Justice—builds a city of worthy women stone by stone by mining myth and history for tales about women of learning and abilities: from ancient queens to some of Christine's remarkable contemporaries. It opens with the character "Christine," weary of reading weighty tomes of scholarship and turning to lighter fare only to encounter a slanderous attack against women. Putting the book aside, she begins to "wonder why on earth it was that so many men, both clerks and others, have said and continue to say and write such awful, damning things about women and their ways . . . It is all manner of philosophers, poets and orators too numerous to mention, who all seem to speak with one voice and are unanimous in their view that female nature is wholly given up to vice." The ensuing book is offered as a corrective. It was widely read throughout Europe; an English translation circulated at the Tudor court. Yet Christine's reputation suffered over time, and it was not until the late nineteenth and early twentieth centuries that interest in this long-neglected writer was revived. Christine focuses here on Dido, the wise queen who built a nation at Carthage. Dido's story is also treated in "Studying the System," in the passage from Virgil's *Aeneid*. (The following selection from book 1 is translated by Rosalind Brown-Grant.)

About the Good Sense and Cleverness of Queen Dido
from *The Book of the City of Ladies* (1405)

As you yourself pointed out earlier, good judgement consists of weighing up carefully what you wish to do and working out how to do it. To prove to you that women are perfectly able to think in this way, even about the most important matters, I'll give you a few examples of some high-born ladies, the first of whom is Dido. As I'll go on to tell you, this Dido, whose name was originally Elissa, revealed her good sense through her actions. She founded and built a city in Africa called Carthage and was its queen and ruler. It was In the way that she established the city and acquired the land on which it was built that she demonstrated her great courage, nobility and virtue, qualities which are indispensable to anyone who wishes to act prudently.

This lady was descended from the Phoenicians, who came from the remotest regions of Egypt to settle in Syria where they founded and built several fine towns and cities. Amongst these people was a king named Agenor, who was a direct ancestor of Dido's father. This king, who was called Belus, ruled over Phoenicia and conquered the kingdom of Cyprus. He had only two children: a son, Pygmalion, and a daughter, Dido.

On his deathbed, Belus ordered his barons to honour his children and be loyal to them, making them swear an oath that they would do so. Once the king was dead, they crowned his son Pygmalion and married the beautiful Elissa to a duke named Acerbas Sychaea, or Sychaeus, who was the most powerful lord in the country after the king. This Sychaeus was a high priest in the temple dedicated to Hercules, whom they worshipped, as well as being an extremely wealthy man. He and his wife loved each other very deeply and led a happy life together. But King Pygmalion was an evil man, the cruellest and most envious person you ever saw, whose greed knew no bounds. Elissa, his sister, was all too aware of what he was like. Seeing how rich her husband was and how well known for his fabulous wealth, she advised Sychaeus to be on his guard against the king and to put his treasure in a safe place where her brother couldn't lay his hands on it. Sychaeus followed his wife's advice but failed to watch his own back against possible attack from the king as she had told him to do. Thus it happened that, one day, the king had him killed in order to steal his great riches from him. Elissa was so distraught at his death that she nearly died of grief. For a long time, she gave herself over to weeping and wailing for the loss of her beloved lord, cursing her brute of a brother for having ordered his murder. However, the wicked king, whose wishes had been thwarted since he had only managed to recover a tiny part of Sychaeus's wealth, bore a deep grudge against his sister, whom he suspected of having hidden it all away.

Realizing that her own life was in danger, Elissa's good sense told her to leave her native land and live elsewhere. Her mind made up, she carefully considered all that she needed to do and then steeled herself to put her plans into effect. This lady knew very well that the king did not enjoy the full support of his barons or his subjects because of his great cruelty and the excessive burdens he imposed on them. She therefore rallied to her cause some of the princes, townspeople and even the peasants. Having sworn them to secrecy, she outlined her plans to them in such persuasive terms that they declared their loyalty to her and agreed to go with her.

As quickly and as quietly as she could, Elissa had her ship prepared. In the dead of night, she set sail with all her treasure and her many followers aboard, urging the sailors to make the ship go as fast as possible. Yet this lady's cleverness didn't end there. Knowing that her brother would send his men after her as soon as he learnt of her flight, she had great chests, trunks and boxes secretly filled up with heavy, worthless objects to make it look as if they contained treasure. The idea was that she would give these chests and boxes to her brother's men if they would only leave her alone and let her continue on her course. It all happened just as she planned, for they had not long been at sea when a whole host of the king's men came racing after her to stop her. In measured tones, she pointed out to them that as she was only setting out on a pilgrimage, they should allow her to sail on unhindered. However, seeing that they remained unconvinced by her explanation, she declared that if it was her treasure her brother was after, she would be prepared to give it to him, even though he had no right to interfere with her wishes. The king's men, who knew that this was his sole desire, forced her to part with it as that way they could do the king's bidding and she could appease her brother. With a sad face, as if it cost her dear, the lady made them load up all the chests and boxes on to their ships. Thinking that they had done well and that the king would be delighted with the news, his men immediately went on their way.

Uttering not a single word of protest, the queen's only thoughts were of setting sail once more. They journeyed on, by day and night, until they came to the island of Cyprus, where they stopped for a short while to refresh themselves. As soon as she had made her sacrifices to the gods, the lady went back to the ship, taking with her the priest from the temple of Jupiter and his family. This priest had predicted that a lady would come from the land of the Phoenicians and that he would leave his country to join her. Casting off again, they left the island of Crete behind them and passed the island of Sicily on their right. They sailed along the whole length of the coast of Massylia until they finally arrived in Africa, where they landed. No sooner had they docked than the people living there rushed down to see the ship and to find out where those aboard were from.

When they saw the lady and realized that she and her people had come in peace, they went and brought them food in abundance. Elissa talked to them in a very friendly way, explaining to them that she had heard such good things about their country that she wished to make her home there, if they had no objections. They replied that they were happy for her to do so. Insisting that she didn't want to establish a large colony on this foreign soil, the lady asked them to sell her a piece of land by the coast which was no bigger than what could be covered by the hide of a cow. Here she would build some dwellings for herself and her people. They granted her wishes and, as soon as the terms of the deal had been agreed upon, her cleverness and good sense came to the fore. Taking the cowhide, the lady had it cut into the tiniest strips possible, which were then tied together to form a rope. This rope was laid out on the ground by the seashore where it enclosed a huge plot of land. Those who had sold her the land were amazed and stunned by her cunning ruse, yet they had to abide by the deal they had struck with her.

So it was that this lady took possession of all this territory in Africa. On her plot of land, a horse's head was discovered. This head, along with the movements and noises of the birds in the sky, they interpreted as prophetic signs that the city which they were about to found would be full of warriors who would excel themselves in the pursuit of arms. The lady immediately sent all over for workmen and spent her wealth freely to pay for their labour. The place which she had built was a magnificent and mighty city called Carthage, the citadel and main fortress of which were called Byrsa, which means "cowhide".

Just as she was beginning to build her city, she received news that her brother was coming after her and her followers for having made a fool of him and tricked him out of his treasure. She told his messengers that she had most definitely given the treasure to the king's men for them to take back to him, but that perhaps it was they who had stolen it and replaced it with worthless objects instead. It was possibly even the gods who had decided to metamorphose the treasure and stop the king from having it because of the sin he had committed in ordering her husband's murder. As for her brother's threats, she had faith that, with the help of the gods, she could defend herself against him. Elissa therefore assembled all her fellow Phoenicians together and told them that she wanted no one to stay with her against their will nor suffer any harm for her sake. If any or all of them wanted to return home, she would reward them for their hard work and let them go. They all replied with one voice that they would live and die by her side, and would never leave her even for a single day.

The messengers departed and the lady worked as fast as she could to finish the city. Once it was completed, she established laws and rules for her people to live an honest and just existence. She conducted herself with such wisdom and prudence that her fame spread all over the world and talk of her was on everyone's lips. Thanks to her bold and courageous actions and her judicious rule, she became so renowned for her heroic qualities that her name was changed to Dido, which means *"virago"* in Latin: in other words, a woman who has the virtue and valour of a man. She lived a glorious life for many years, one which would have lasted even longer had Fortune not turned against her. As this goddess is wont to be envious of those she sees prosper, she concocted a bitter brew for Dido to drink, which I'll tell you about all in good time.

Francis Bacon
(1561–1626)

AS THE BIOGRAPHERS Lisa Jardine and Alan Stewart put it in their introduction to *Hostage to Fortune: The Troubled Life of Francis Bacon*, this Elizabethan and Jacobean figure—scholar, lawyer, attorney general, lord chancellor, and occasional prisoner of the state—lived "a life of virtue and mischief." A progressive advocate for science and experimentation; a believer in man's potential for progress; the author of a utopian work, *New Atlantis*, as well as a collection of essays on civil and moral themes written in the Senecan style, Bacon balanced his public role with a commitment to the retired life of contemplation, befitting the period's "Great Renewal of Learning." The essays, Jardine and Stewart propose, present a "succinct distillation of the kind of day-to-day counsel and self-fashioning which . . . occupied Bacon full-time." Bacon envisioned *Essays Civil and Moral*, published in 1597, as "the fruits of both" the "contemplative and active" halves of his life, as he wrote in the revised edition of 1612. Modeled, at least in part, on those of Montaigne, they were quite popular in the seventeenth century and remain intelligent guides to the relationship between the life of the mind and that of the world. In the essay "Of Studies" Bacon recommends a judicious combination of learning and practical experience in public life. Expertise comes from both sources, and only the fool would dismiss one in favor of the other: "Crafty men contemn studies, simple men admire them, and wise men use them."

Of Studies

from *Essays Civil and Moral* (1597)

Studies serve for delight, for ornament, and for ability. Their chief use for delight, is in privateness and retiring; for ornament, is in discourse; and for ability, is in the judgment and disposition of business. For expert men can execute, and perhaps judge of particulars, one by one; but the general counsels, and the plots and marshalling of affairs, come best from those that are learned. To spend too much time in studies is sloth; to use them too much for ornament, is affectation; to make judgment wholly by their rules, is the humour of a scholar. They perfect nature, and are perfected by experience: for natural abilities are like natural plants, that need proyning by study; and studies themselves do give forth directions too much at large, except they be bounded in by experience. Crafty men contemn studies, simple men admire them, and wise men use them; for they teach not their own use; but that is a wisdom without them, and above them, won by observation. Read not to contradict and confute; nor to believe and take for granted; nor to find talk and discourse; but to weigh and consider. Some books are to be tasted, others to be swallowed, and some few to be chewed and digested; that is, some books are to be read only in parts; others to be read, but not curiously; and some few to be read wholly, and with diligence and attention. Some books also may be read by deputy, and extracts made of them by others; but that would be only in the less important arguments, and the meaner sort of books; else distilled books are like common distilled waters, flashy things. Reading maketh a full man; conference a ready man; and writing an exact man. And therefore, if a man write little, he had need have a great memory; if he confer little, he had need have a present wit: and if he read little, he had need have much cunning, to seem to know that he doth not. Histories make men wise; poets witty; the mathematics subtile; natural philosophy deep; moral grave; logic and rhetoric able to contend. *Abeunt studia in mores:* [*Studies pass into the character.*] Nay there is no stond or impediment in the wit, but may be wrought out by fit studies: like as diseases of the body may have appropriate exercises. Bowling is good for the stone and reins; shooting for the lungs and breast; gentle walking for the stomach; riding for the head; and the like. So if a man's wit be wandering, let him study the mathematics; for in demonstrations, if his wit be called away never so little, he must begin again. If his wit be not apt to distinguish or find differences, let him study the schoolmen; for they are *cymini sectores*. If he be not apt to beat over matters, and to call up one thing to prove and illustrate another, let him study the lawyers' cases. So every defect of the mind may have a special receipt.

Mark Singer and Marnie Hanel
(b. 1950)   (b. 1982?)

A *NEW YORKER* staff writer since 1974, Mark Singer has written on a broad range of subjects (including a dentist suspected of cheating at marathons, the lost crew of a Mexican fishing boat, and the long-defunct *New York Herald Tribune*), in a range of journalistic forms, notably the profile: the brilliant magician Ricky Jay, for example; the masterful film director Martin Scorsese, and, the subject of "Gone Fishing," David Pasternack, winner of a James Beard Award and "the chef and co-creator" of the Manhattan restaurant Esca. Singer's journalism has been collected in several volumes, among them *Character Studies*. In the introduction to that book he likens the reporter's role to that of a cultural anthropologist. Singer measures success by the thoroughness with which he is able to disappear into the scene so that his subject behaves as if he were not being observed at all. In this selection he follows Pasternack from the fishing boat to the kitchen; in each venue Pasternack reveals an utter devotion to craft and a comprehensive knowledge of its various aspects, from filleting a fish to coaching his staff during the lunch rush. In a 2007 *New York Times* review of Esca, Frank Bruni asked: "Given all the talk about horse whisperers and dog whisperers, it's impossible not to wonder: is Dave Pasternack a fish whisperer"?

Marnie Hanel's profile of Boston chef Barbara Lynch in the *New York Times Magazine* explores Lynch's approach to leadership, teaching, and mentoring within the male-dominated world of professional kitchens. In addition to writing for the *New York Times Magazine*, Hanel, a Morehead scholar at the University of North Carolina at Chapel Hill and a graduate of the Columbia School of Journalism, writes for VanityFair.com, *Departures*, *W*, and *Marie Claire*. Hanel's Twitter profile announces that she writes "about the wonderful, wild way we live," and her profile of Lynch explores with gusto both the intense, often chaotic world of restaurant kitchens as well as the aura of calm and confidence that Lynch's generosity and technical mastery impart to those who work in her restaurants. Hanel notes that Lynch was nominated for the 2014 James Beard Foundation

Outstanding Restaurateur Award. Lynch has since won that award; she is only the second woman to have done so.

Gone Fishing

from *The New Yorker* (September 5, 2005)

A poll that I recently conducted among several of David Pasternack's friends and colleagues yielded a nearly unanimous result. The question was: if Dave were a fish, what kind would he be? The answer was: a tuna. One respondent, Artie Hoernig, a commercial fisherman who also operates a retail fish market and restaurant in Island Park, New York, was more specific. "Absolutely a bluefin tuna," he said, referring to a species that I'd heard Pasternack characterize as "like a freight train swimming in the ocean." A minority opinion from his father, Mel ("striped bass—wild, big, good fighter"), dovetailed with Dave's own measured self-appraisal: "Half tuna, half striper, I guess. Tuna for the thrill of the chase, the hunt. I love to catch a tuna. And striped bass is the king of the fish inshore. It's our native fish, and I grew up catching 'em, you know." He went on, "Basically, I've fished my whole life. I started fishing with my father when I was about five, in Jamaica Bay, off of Floyd Bennett Field, in Brooklyn. Snapper, bluefish, blowfish, flounder. I fished regularly with a guy named Captain Lou. I always fished with older guys. It was, like, somebody would introduce me and they'd take me under their wing. People don't necessarily do that anymore, which is too bad, because that's how you learn—'You're tying it *that* way? No, you tie it *that* way.' If you wanna catch a lot of fish, you've gotta take an aggressive approach. And what's the point of fishing if you don't wanna catch 'em?"

Pasternack is the chef and co-creator of Esca, a five-year-old fish restaurant on West Forty-third Street, in Manhattan. His recipes are unaffectedly refined, and he defines his culinary creativity in elliptical, prosaic terms: "It's passion, plus knowing when something needs a little something"—the emblem of a cook, or, for that matter, any artist who knows what to put in and what to leave out. A focussed, sensible fellow, he understands the fish business better than just about anyone, in ways intuitive, visceral, and pragmatic. Before dawn one spring morning at the Fulton Fish Market, as we were admiring a machete-wielding Ecuadorean who, with the celerity of a Jedi, was quartering and trimming a mattress-sized yellowfin tuna, Pasternack noticed a neatly pressed silver-haired gent standing nearby. He said to me softly, "A good old-fashioned 'made' guy. Nice guy. But he's notorious. The market was run by 'em for years, until they passed the RICO laws and then these guys were supposed to be banned. I'm surprised to see him here, even though he owns the business. And if you print the name of the business I'll have no glass left in my windows."

Local climate and geography have surprisingly little bearing upon the experience of eating in New York. The foods most closely identified with the city at street level—pizza, pastrami, pretzel, dim sum, falafel—all made their way here on immigrant tides. And the past decade has witnessed an exoticism that often seems more than a little forced. When a phenomenon like Jean-Georges Vongerichten creates an empire in Manhattan, his ambition— which presumes, of course, that a critical mass of people will ante up the equivalent of a mortgage payment for a meal—reflects a high-wire determination to move far beyond his Alsatian roots. (French-Thai fusion! Malay-Thai street food!) Pasternack happens to be Jewish and Esca happens to be resolutely Italian (if unlike any other Italian restaurant in the city). Whatever. Compared with New York's other celebrated chefs, he has stayed unusually close to home; Esca is, among other things, the direct consequence of his years of experience with a rod and reel. Pasternack lives in Long Beach and, for a while, had a habit of schlepping to Esca, on the Long Island Rail Road, plastic garbage bags containing fish that he'd caught the previous day. "But I'd be exhausted by the time I made the walk from Penn Station," he said. So he persuaded his wife, Donna Peltz, to make deliveries in their 1988 Toyota sedan, which she did until two years ago, when he decided that he could justify investing in a truck. No other restaurant in the city—not now and presumably not ever—offers year-round wild game that has been personally bagged by the chef.

Before Esca ("bait," in Italian), Pasternack worked for two decades in a succession of mostly French-themed New York restaurants, bistros, and brasseries, and before that he attended culinary school at Johnson & Wales, in Providence, Rhode Island. During his year and a half in Providence, he drove every weekend to his home town, Rockville Centre, a Nassau County suburb only a few miles inland (or only a madeleine-like sea breeze) from the South Shore of Long Island. Then, after he found work and began living in Manhattan, he stayed connected to the old neighborhood by renting a room or an apartment close to the beach. As often as he could manage, he spent his days off fishing, in the bays and inlets and in the wide-open Atlantic, from the Rockaways to Montauk Point. He took stripers, tuna, flounder, fluke, sea bass, porgies, cod, weakfish, bluefish, mackerel, the inadvertent shark—in his concise inventory, "whatever swam." Though there's no mistaking Pasternack for a literary type, spending time with him got me thinking about the way a chef's evolution can mirror that of a novelist. In the same way that a fiction writer can rely upon the dictum "write about what you know," Pasternack, as much as a New York-born-and-bred chef can, has thrived by cooking best what he knows best.

IN THE DIFFERENTIATION between executive chefs, celebrity chefs, and working chefs, Pasternack is plainly in his element in the third category. He doesn't have a cell phone or respond to e-mail, but he's easy to get hold of. His office, in effect, is the same spot in the kitchen where he cuts fish, orders supplies, conceives menus, plates food, and supervises his staff. He's at Esca five, sometimes six days a week, typically from 10 a.m. to 11 p.m. Though he rents a pied-à-terre on the East Side, most nights he takes the train home to Long Beach, where he and Donna live with their year-old daughter, Ruby, in a red brick and rose stucco bungalow with a detached garage. My first glimpse inside the garage was a moment of recognition: suspended from the rafters were two punching bags. Days when Pasternack is neither working nor fishing, he likes to ride his bicycle along the Long Beach boardwalk—it extends nearly two and a half miles—and then spend a half hour thumping the heavy bags. On or off the job, whether he's giving instructions in Spanglish to a fish cleaner ("Antonio, you're gonna take this *abajo* and this *abajo* and you're gonna keep 'em *separado*, O.K.?") or butchering a side of veal or setting the hook in a fish that's on the line, he has the authority of a nimble middle-weight, at once firmly grounded and light on his feet. He's five nine, with powerful arms and shoulders and a creeping waistline. At forty-one, he looks his age. He has short light-brown hair that's receding and thinning at the crown, a nose you notice, broad cheeks, a strong jaw, blue-gray eyes, and often a slightly weary demeanor. His smile is wry and asymmetrical, listing toward starboard. About every third day, he's clean-shaven.

The kitchen at Esca is relatively small—two levels, six hundred square feet in all—but for the twenty or so prep cooks, line cooks, runners, and dishwashers who circulate during peak hours, it probably feels less crowded than others they've worked in, because the boss isn't inclined toward histrionics or harangues. He speaks in a low, even register, with an inflection and delivery that are pure South Shore, which is basically blue-collar Brooklynese that's moved farther out on Long Island. "St. Francis said you have to speak in the vernacular, and that's Dave," Mel Pasternack, a semi-retired trial attorney, told me. "When he talks to a fishmonger, he speaks fishspeak."

"The fish business is very complicated, very complicated," Dave says when the conversation turns to catch limits, size limits, quotas for different species in different jurisdictions, and the vagaries of a marketplace in which the law of supply and demand regularly conflicts with conservation laws that often strike commercial fishermen as impractical and convoluted. In general, his sympathies lie with the fishermen. Which is to say that Pasternack is a resourceful guy who has cultivated mutually beneficial relationships with certain other guys: "My striped-bass guy called this morning. . . . I was talking to a guy who just came back from Florida. He was snook fishing every day. . . .

Whenever Mike goes cod fishing, I'm his guy. . . . The way they ship stuff now is pretty amazing. Here, try this opah. It's also called moonfish. Fatty, right? A lot of natural fat to it. Kinda has that tuna texture? With a completely different flavor. Very buttery, almost swordfishy. Opah comes from somewhere in the Pacific. I can speak to a guy, he'll call me at eleven or twelve o'clock, the fish'll be here when I get here the next morning. . . . A lot about buying fish is spontaneity. A guy called me yesterday and told me what he had and what he recommended. You'd have to be an idiot to buy what he didn't recommend. I talked to a guy this morning, he was unloading a boat of monkfish. I bought some of the monkfish livers from him, to make pâté. He also had big jumbo scallops. And I bought a box of blackfish from him. . . . I called my crab guy last week. To find out when he's gonna have blue claws and softshells. He told me to call him back in a month. I call guys all the time."

The great majority of restaurants in the city, from cozy to corporate, buy all their fish through a single supplier. Pasternack deals with at least fifty: brokers; wholesalers; gill-netters; dredgers; and pinhook, or rod-and-reel, anglers. On any given day, salmon might arrive from Alaska; abalone and black cod from British Columbia; giant clams from Puget Sound; mahogany clams, sea urchins, and diver scallops from Maine; spot prawns from Santa Barbara; pink snapper and John Dory from New Zealand; yellowtail from Japan or California; red snapper, pompano, mahi-mahi, and grouper from the Gulf of Mexico; sardines from Portugal or California; scorpionfish, branzino, orata, and calamari from the Mediterranean; red mullet from Senegal; Arctic char from Iceland; octopus from South Carolina, Portugal, or Thailand; halibut, hake, skate, monkfish, fluke, flounder, kingfish, weakfish, sea bass, striped bass, scallops, sole, and tuna from up and down the East Coast; oysters from Long Island, Rhode Island, Maine, the Canadian Maritimes. Almost all of it is wild, and none of it has ever been frozen, nor will it be. (The freezer at Esca, no larger than a domestic fridge, is reserved for pasta and desserts.) The fish travel by truck, express mail, air freight, courier, U.P.S. Some arrive at the kitchen still flopping.

Pasternack speaks almost daily with Rod Mitchell, the owner of Browne Trading Company, in Portland, Maine, where hundreds of boats a month unload at the Portland Fish Exchange, the largest display fish auction in the country. Mitchell, who has been described as the "fish purveyor to the stars" but prefers to call himself a "fish picker," combines his talent for scrutinizing individual fish with a global overview of the seafood trade, and he regards Pasternack as an ideal customer. "Dave's quest is to have as many different kinds of fish as he can and still be able to sell them all," he told me. "He wants to know every kind of fish that he can get his hands on. If I mention something he hasn't heard of before, he says, 'Send it.' He can get something new and taste it raw, and he knows exactly what to do with it. I'm about to send him a new fish from Brazil, pintado. It's also called a tigerfish.

Amazing-looking. It makes you imagine that it could walk. It has no scales, and its skin is colored like a tiger's. It's never been imported to the United States before. It's a fish we found at a seafood exposition in Brussels. The minute I saw it, I thought of Dave."

Every weekday, Pasternack dispatches a buyer, Roberto Nuñez, and a driver ("Tony, the truck guy") to the Fulton Fish Market. About once a week, he shows up at the Fulton market for the pre-dawn rounds (a ritual that, lamentably, will soon be drained of its echt-Manhattan flavor, when the market relocates to Hunts Point, in the Bronx). Pasternack moves briskly from stall to stall, with an open mind and the confidence that if he doesn't see what he likes ("Some weeks the market's good, some weeks it has shit") he'll find something else somewhere else that will excite him. Certain dishes appear on the Esca menu three hundred and sixty-three days a year: Sicilian fish stew, Amalfitano fish soup, linguine with mahogany clams, spaghetti with a whole lobster, squid-ink pasta with cuttlefish, fritto misto, marinated anchovies and sardines, grilled octopus. But the guiding principle is that everything is provisional—dependent upon the quality of the available ingredients and upon Pasternack's sensibility ("There is no system; it's more about mood")—and that, of course, there are always plenty more fish in the sea.

INVARIABLY, WHEN I'VE dropped by Esca to see Pasternack, I've found him just inside the open doorway of the kitchen, on the ground-floor level, armed with a very sharp knife. The first fish I watched him perform surgery on was a forty-pound halibut that had recently been swimming in the vicinity of Portland. His workstation—situated to afford an unobstructed view of the line cooks and prep cooks at the grill, sauté, and pasta stations, and to allow him to inspect every dish before it leaves the kitchen—is two and a half feet deep and nine feet wide, sufficient to accommodate the occasional four-hundred-pound tuna. His knife was German, with a twelve-inch blade, one of a dozen of varying sizes that he keeps in a plastic tray within easy reach. "I sharpen my knives every Saturday," he said. "Nobody touches my knives. Not even my wife. They're sacred."

Downstairs, the halibut had already been scaled, gutted, and shorn of its dorsal and pelvic fins. It took Pasternack about a minute to remove the first fillet, drawing the knife handle toward him in sure, even strokes, with his left hand, as he proceeded along the spine. He lifted and flipped the fish, reinserted the knife laterally, just behind the pectoral fin, cut to the caudal fin, and severed the second fillet. He separated the flesh from the skin of both fillets as cleanly and economically as if he were peeling apples. The carcass was headed for the soup kettle, but not quite yet. "The head's gonna be my lunch," he said as he harvested two plum-sized lumps of cheek meat. Then he began trimming the fillets. "Pretty nice halibut," he said. "This time of year they can be on the spawn. The meat can be a little milky." Not in this instance, however. From each fillet he cut out the bloodline, a dark-meat layer that extends lengthwise below the dorsal fin, and sectioned the collar into strips for fritto misto. "You know, this is a fish that you're paying six and a half dollars a pound for. You're gonna lose at least thirty-five or forty per cent. So you've got to utilize the whole animal. That's where your knife really makes all the difference." The halibut's primary destiny was to be carved into seven-ounce serving portions, poached, and accompanied by smashed fava beans from Pennsylvania and a vinaigrette made with ramps from upstate New York. Twenty-seven dollars, à la carte.

Esca has seating for sixty—a hundred and ten in pleasant weather, when an outdoor patio is opened—and on a normal day each table fills four times. Pasternack fillets and slices fish throughout the morning and during lunch, breaks for a couple of hours in midafternoon, and then resumes until seven o'clock. He multitasks in a self-assured manner—announces orders to the line cooks; talks on the phone; consults with the front-of-the-house managers, nodding when he hears that there's someone in the dining room whom he should meet and greet; gives instructions to the kitchen runners, who shuttle one aluminum tray after another laden with freshly gutted fish—all the while wielding knives with the same rhythmic, delicate precision. How often does he cut himself? "Only when somebody asks me that question. No, actually, not that much. But I'm due." A wall phone with an extra-long cord rings at all hours, and Pasternack usually answers it himself, always with the same greeting: "Kitchen."

Between the moment he first looks at a fish and the moment he finishes filleting it, he often changes his mind about what he's going to do with it. If it's perfectly fresh yet doesn't look perfect (it hasn't been bled properly; it's bruised; it was caught in a net and drowned and the flesh is now too opaque; spawning season is under way and the texture seems a bit flabby or "funky"), it won't be right for the house specialty, crudo—sashimi-sized slices of raw fish that have been accented with sea salt, olive oil, and lemon juice, or with other condiments. But it would still be fine grilled or pan-seared or sautéed. I once asked him to try to articulate the process of creating a new dish. What, precisely, is he thinking when he combines raw fluke with sea beans, radish, and salt? Geoduck (a.k.a. giant clam crudo) with sugar-baby watermelon or artichoke? "I don't know, man," he replied. "It's a very hard question to answer. I think it's more experience than anything else. Experience dictates that you understand certain things about certain ingredients at certain times of year. You look in the fridge and you have to be able to work with what you have, in season. But it can't be arbitrary. That's the problem with a lot of these young cooks. They don't yet get the idea of how flavors can work, how you have to take into consideration acidity, texture, the properties of various oils. They think they're being creative but they're pushing the envelope too much. People like Daniel Boulud and Thomas Keller, what makes them so good is that their food is creative but they know the boundaries."

I suppose it's odd to say that I've been struck by Pasternack's empathy for fish, given his recurring role in their demise, but he nevertheless seems intent upon doing honor to the deceased, characteristically by doing no more than necessary to evoke essential flavors and unembellished subtleties. Not that he's unwilling to call a fish a fish. One day, as I watched him reduce an eight-pound mahi-mahi to about thirty bites of crudo, he showed me its pearly, iridescent pale-pink flesh and said, "You don't always see it this color. Sometimes the meat's a little grayer." On the other hand, mahi-mahi is "a very stupid fish. You catch one and you leave him in the water and all the others'll follow and you can catch 'em all. Not very smart. Good eating, though."

Next, he went to work on a Pacific sturgeon, scraping away a yellow adipose layer that looked like chicken fat. "Atlantic sturgeon is a protected species," he said. "This fish was caught in the Columbia River, in Washington. It's called a bullet because of the shape. Actually, they're always a little dirty. But this is one of my personal favorites. Really fatty, like eating a piece of pork."

From time to time, I would prompt him with fish names and he would respond with an off-the-cuff Pasternackian taxonomy.

Flounder: "The quintessential Long Island fish. In New England, they've got scrod. Maine, they've got haddock. Long Island, it's flounder. I was born to flounder fish. I fished for them in Jamaica Bay, South Bay, Hewlett Harbor, under the Meadowbrook Bridge, Island Park, East Rockaway. It was a really abundant fish. But the flounder haven't coöperated in the last couple of years."

Cod: "Cod is God. The Spaniards came here in search of cod. Italians, the same thing. It's a great, versatile fish. Unfortunately, none of them seem to make that right turn at Montauk anymore."

Porgy: "Ghetto fish. It's a fish that's usually associated with minorities. A great fish. But not considered your mainstream white-bread fish. I grill it. Sweet meat. Phenomenal skin."

Hake: "In the cod family but sweeter, softer in texture than cod, not as rich; half the price of cod. I like it roasted, because it can get really caramelized on the outside without doing anything. It's just got a lot of natural sugars."

Bluefish: "Godzilla. The other quintessential Long Island fish. Pound for pound, the hardest-fighting fish there is. Ferocious, eats anything, bites anything that gets in its way. Powerful, elusive. You could stick a beer can on a hook with bait inside and the fish'll bite the beer can."

PASTERNACK'S FIRST RESTAURANT job was more turf than surf. At fourteen, he bused tables in a Rockville Centre steak house whose charms included the bookies who hung out at the bar and the pictures of photo finishes that hung on the walls. Not until his mid-twenties, while cooking at La Reserve, an old-school French place near Rockefeller Center, did he commit to the notion that this was what he would do with his life. By then, he'd gone to college for a year; spent a winter cooking in Vermont and a couple of years at Provence, in Greenwich Village; earned a diploma from Johnson & Wales; and worked in a hotel kitchen in Dallas long enough (less than a week) to recognize that he belonged back in New York. He left La Reserve after three years, following the death of André Gaillard, the French-Vietnamese chef who had hired him, and for the next five years stayed in motion as a line cook or sous-chef in a number of busy, trendy restaurants: Bouley, Steak Frites, Prix Fixe, and Sam's (where he met Donna Peltz, who was tending bar). He was in his early thirties and feeling that he was spinning his wheels when Terrance Brennan, a former sous-chef at Le Cirque who had also been at Prix Fixe, asked him to come to Picholine, a year-old bistro near Lincoln Center. Brennan had a clear idea of what he wanted Picholine to be and the good sense to give Pasternack plenty of latitude. When Ruth Reichl, in a 1996 review in the *Times*, awarded the restaurant three stars, it was understood that Pasternack, the chef de cuisine, deserved much of the credit. One of his signature dishes was seared sturgeon with caviar sauce; the fish was served with a reduction of shallots, white wine, champagne vinegar, tarragon, and peppercorns whisked with a beurre blanc, to which malossol caviar was added at the last moment. Typical of Pasternack's cooking style at Picholine, it was labor-intensive (that is, French) in a way that his style at Esca is decidedly not.

While at Prix Fixe, he'd become friendly with Susan Cahn, whose family owned Coach Farms, and who often worked at their goat-cheese stand in the Union Square farmers' market. Through her, he met her husband-to-be, Mario Batali, who was then merely a robustly talented chef, not yet a food-culture demigod and conglomerateur. Batali and his partner Joe Bastianich, who between them had interests in five Manhattan restaurants (this was 1999; they're now up to ten), dined frequently at Picholine. They could see that Pasternack was crazy about fish yet otherwise demonstrably sane, and, conveniently, they had an available location, Fricco Bar, an underperforming trattoria on Forty-third Street west of Ninth Avenue.

"Joe and Mario kept coming into Picholine and saying, 'Come on, let's do something,'" Pasternack recalled. "They asked me what I wanted to do. I said a seafood restaurant, Provençal style. I wanted to call it Rascasse. That's the name of a very important fish in the whole Mediterranean culture. Bony, spiny, gnarly, a basic ingredient in bouillabaisse, *zuppa di pesce*, fritto misto. Joe said, 'Can you make it Italian?' I said, 'A good cook is a good cook. I can do it Chinese if you need to.' He said, 'Let's make a deal.'"

That fall, Pasternack accompanied Batali and Bastianich on a ten-day excursion to Italy. Starting out in Venice, they ate and drank their way up the Adriatic coast, toward Trieste and Istria, in northern Croatia. (On a subsequent trip, Batali and Pasternack and Simon Dean, who became a manager of and partner in Esca, spent a week in Amalfi, Sorrento, and Naples.) "We met my buddies who were fishmongers and restaurateurs," Bastianich, who owns vineyards in

Friuli and Tuscany and is the co-author of a book on Italian regional wines, told me. "We found out that everyone was eating raw fish. We had thought we were going to come back with ideas along the lines of what you would consider classic Venetian-style food—risottos and *brodetto di pesce*. Crudo was a revelation."

They tasted, among other things, raw scampi, orata, branzino, lobster, scallops, and sole—briny, sweet, chewy, buttery, and enhanced only by lemon, olive oil, and sea salt. Immediately, they knew that the Esca kitchen would become a testing laboratory for crudo—a term that Bastianich more or less coined. (The word *crudo* means "uncooked," but when it appears on a menu in Italy it typically refers to prosciutto.)

"Joe conceptualized the idea behind our crudo selections," Batali told me. "And Dave's taken the ball and run around the bases several times with it. A month before we opened, we were in the kitchen, trying this and that. Dave did a crudo that was a giant sea scallop with tangerine oil, pink peppercorns, and some Sicilian sea salt. And it was a giant moment. It was: Holy shit, this is gonna be a great restaurant."

This is, perhaps, benignly revisionist history. According to Pasternack, none of them had quite foreseen that crudo would become the hallmark of Esca, or anticipated that the restaurant would generate such instant enthusiasm. "The crudo appetizers at Esca are the freshest, most exciting thing to happen to Italian food in recent memory," William Grimes wrote in the *Times*. Nor could Pasternack have predicted that his handiwork would inspire so much mimicry. "Imitated by many, copied by few," he likes to say about the post-Esca proliferation of crudo, which has become appetizer fare in such unlikely locales as Cleveland, Denver, and St. Louis.

Each day, Esca offers a dozen or so wallet-lightening crudo options. Thirty dollars, for instance, will bankroll a tasting selection that amounts to two bites each of, say, pink snapper with black lava sea salt, weakfish with a thin sliver of preserved blood-orange rind, opah with baby fennel and wild-fennel pollen, yellowtail with Gaeta-olive aioli, kingfish with pickled fiddlehead, and fluke with sea beans and radish. "Raw fish makes a statement about quality," Pasternack told me. "People don't eat raw fish at just any restaurant." And he draws a firm distinction between crudo and ordinary American sushi and sashimi. "I always liked sushi—and I lived above a sushi place for four years—but I thought it always tasted the same. Place A was the same as Place B as Place C."

One night last spring, I observed Pasternack adroitly handling a crudo crisis that materialized as he was preparing a guest-chef banquet at the James Beard House, in Greenwich Village. (In 2004, the James Beard Foundation honored him as the New York chef of the year.) Pasternack and his crew had come expecting to serve dinner to seventy-two, but, at the last minute, the Beard House staff had allowed an extra table of eight. Not counting the oysters that were served before everyone was seated, the menu included two crudo courses. The first of these consisted of two morsels of black sea bass garnished with lemon juice, sea salt, pepper, and a sprig of salad burnet, a green that looks like parsley and tastes like cucumber. The bass had been cut by Pasternack that morning, and now eighty plates were lined up in the kitchen—eight of them empty. A loaves-and-fishes moment, of sorts. Somehow he discerned sixteen pieces of bass that could be halved, a sleight-of-knife executed so that no one in the dining room would notice. As he drizzled olive oil over each portion, he said, "How was that for creative management?" A faint smile. "They'll go home. They just won't necessarily go home full."

"For a lot of American chefs, it's hard to understand how simple things are in Italy," Batali said. "That was our idea, both with the crudo and with how Esca presents fish in general. It's all in the ingredients. When Dave talks about the difference between the fluke in Sheepshead Bay and the fluke from some other part of Long Island, you know that in fact one does taste different from the other. Dave has a real understanding of what the Italians call *materia prima*— the raw ingredients—and making them available for the palate to explore."

It hasn't proved to be a professional or interpersonal liability that Pasternack's instinctive Italian sensibility doesn't extend to actually speaking the language (though he possesses a sizable vocabulary of kitchen nouns and adjectives). One of the waitresses at the Beard House addressed him in Italian throughout the evening; he would occasionally nod, and nothing was apparently lost in translation. In the area of Long Island where he grew up there is a great deal of cultural overlap between Italian-Americans and Jews. For whatever reason—and probably not merely because in the twenty-eight years since his bar mitzvah he has consumed immeasurable quantities of pork and shellfish—his diction, body language, and general affinities make him come across like a bit player in "GoodFellas," so much so that he's occasionally prone to identity confusion. A few years ago, for an appearance with Bryant Gumbel on "The Early Show," he prepared a crudo that consisted of ivory salmon, fresh soybeans, lemon juice, sea salt, and olive oil. Gumbel asked, "How important is it what kind of oil you use on these fish?"

"Oil is essential," Pasternack replied. "When we talk about oil, we talk only about extra-virgin olive oil. Because it's like the Japanese put the soy sauce, us Italians, we put the olive oil."

When he got home, his father, who had been watching, called and said, "What's with this 'us Italians' business? We're Jewish. Remember?"

"My wife's half Italian," Dave replied.

"Davey," Mel Pasternack felt constrained to point out, "you don't inherit that."

A SPRING WEEKDAY, shortly after noon. In the Esca dining room—pale-yellow walls; brown leather banquettes; brass Art Deco sconces; a floor-to-ceiling expanse of Italian wines along one wall; a cherry-blossom arrangement that would shame a Christmas tree; otherwise, no dazzle and pleasantly little noise—orders are discreetly punched into a computer. Moments later, they emerge from a small printer on the kitchen counter where Pasternack works his way through a pile of striped bass while orchestrating the lunch flow. "Four times," he informs Pablo Martínez, at the garde-manger station— meaning that a party of four have placed their orders and are now ready for their *amuse-gueules,* a plate of grilled bruschetta topped with a mélange of cannelloni beans, smoked mackerel, olive oil, red onions, and parsley. As the first-course dishes leave the kitchen, he glances at a clock, scrawls the time on the printout, and clips it to a shelf at eye level. At the appropriate moment, he will cue his crew—Sarah Ochs, the sous-chef; Katie O'Donnell, the sauté cook; Mike Sneed, at the pasta station—to mobilize the entrées.

"Pablo, you got two asparagus, two caprese, and a mindora. You got a third caprese gonna go with the oysters and you got a fourth caprese gonna go with another asparagus. . . . Give me a chicken, got an octo, I got skate with a cod. I got a snapper with an octo, I got branzino. . . . We got two stripers, a cod, a snapper, an orata, and a fett"—fettuccine. "I got two times. . . . Two, two. Misto, order branzino, order snapper, a cod, make sure you got a branzino ahead of a cod, you got a cod, two stripers, snapper, and then an orata. . . . Double octo, and make 'em look soigné, Sarah. Put up a cod in a minute. You got another big branzino, you got a pimente. Mike, order two fetts. . . . All right, Pablo, you're gonna give me two asparagus, two caprese, and a spigola. Katie, you got asparagus and a caprese. Mike, you got the fett, it goes with the caprese. . . . Two two three three two. . . . Order three stripers and a porgy, another asparagus with arugula, another asparagus with a mista. . . . All right, Mike, spaghetti pimente. You got another spaghetti following the second branzino. You got a spaghetti with an orata. You got a spigola, snapper, skate, and an orata. . . ."

The temperature literally rises, but the atmosphere remains coolly businesslike. When Simon Dean, the Esca manager, wanders in holding an envelope and a magazine and says, "Dave, here's a piece of what looks like hate mail. Also, here's your copy of the latest issue of *Private Air Magazine: Life at the Speed of Luxury,*" Pasternack replies, "It's a little hard right now to be funny. I'd love to, but . . ." In fact, his mood is sanguine. A very nice piece of fish arrived that morning, a crimson shoulder cut from a seven-hundred-pound bluefin tuna—by way of Rod Mitchell, in Portland. "There's a lot of competition for these fish," he says. "I don't want to say I'm at the bottom of the pecking order. But I'm near the bottom. Plenty of people will pay a lot more than I will." At eighteen dollars a pound, the bluefin is too expensive to grill or sauté, so half of it will become crudo. The other half will go to Bistro du Vent, a calculatedly jointlike joint just around the corner, on Forty-second Street, that Pasternack and his Esca partners opened last January. There it will also be served raw, an appetizer à la steak tartare.

Four crudo plates are ready to be dispatched, but Pasternack first squirts a piece of bluefin with lemon juice, sprinkles it with pepper, sea salt, and olive oil, hands it to me, and declares, "This is the king of tuna, man. Think steak, filet mignon. This is what the Japanese'll pay exuberant prices for."

As it happens, he's just returned from Japan himself—his first visit, the highlight of which was a daily perambulation through Tsukiji, Tokyo's wholesale fish market ("like walking inside an aquarium"). He'd made the trip as the guest of Hiromi Go, an Esca regular.

"Hiromi's a very popular Japanese singer," he says. "He's like Elvis Presley over there. He's getting ready to record, like, his sixtieth album. He's been coming here for years and I'm always saying to him, 'When are you taking me to Tokyo?' So his wife set it up. I cooked two dinners, one for twelve people and one for forty. The second was in a Shinto shrine. I ate quite a few things I'd never had before."

Such as?

"Whale. It's really only fresh in Scandinavia, Russia, and Japan. Very interesting. A tuna-y texture and a liver-y finish. You know, in Japan they raise horses in the style of Kobe beef—massage it, give it *sake*, beer, different grains and grasses, play music for it. So I did a crudo dish that was horse, whale, and fatty tuna all on the same plate. They all looked alike. The whale could have been the tuna and the tuna could have been the horse."

A waiter comes in with the news that a customer has requested cocktail sauce to accompany what might best be described as an order of the original crudo—a half-dozen Peconic Bay oysters. Having just seen Pasternack gracing tidbits of abalone, weakfish, and opah with, respectively, gaila melon, crushed almonds, and *olio verde*, I expect him to take offense. Instead, he reaches into a knee-level cooler and removes a mixture of horseradish, fresh chiles, lemons, ketchup, capers, and olive oil. "It's their money," he says. "Give 'em what they want, they'll come back."

So that includes tartar sauce with the fritto misto?

"No. They ask for that, which I think happens maybe twice a year, we tell 'em we don't have it." He shrugs. "What're they gonna do? Hey, we don't have it, we don't have it."

I ONCE ASKED Joe Bastianich, who enjoys sport-fishing for tuna, about his experiences on the water with Pasternack, and he said, "Dave's fishing, that's a little too blue-collar for me." For his part, Pasternack, who seems constitutionally incapable of condescension, has said, "I don't understand freshwater fishing. That's too Zen for me, too proper. Saltwater fishing, you know, there's a lot more blood and guts." A few years ago, Pasternack was invited, along with some other New York chefs, to a culinary event in Jackson Hole, Wyoming. While there, he went fly-fishing on the Green River with Ed Artzt, a frequent Esca patron who was formerly the chief executive of Procter & Gamble. "It was my first time fly-fishing," Pasternack said. "I was good, I was a natural. I was the only guy who actually caught anything. I caught a cutthroat. After I took it off the hook, I went to open the cooler and everybody on the boat kind of looked at me like, What are you doing? I'm like, 'Dinner.' They go, 'No, everything here's catch-and-release.' I said, 'I spent the whole day to catch this one fish and we're gonna *throw it back*?' "

My recollection of my first fishing outing with Pasternack, though it took place fairly recently, is somewhat spotty. We were aboard a commercial boat called the Sorry Charlie, about three miles from Point Lookout, Long Island. As the tide was running out, a brisk wind was blowing in, which meant that conditions were, by my standards, insufficiently calm. I spent part of the morning in the cabin, seated atop a cooler, resting my head against a wall, wondering when the Dramamine was going to kick in, and smiling weakly when my shipmates periodically impugned my manhood. The captain, Mike Wasserman, struggled nobly to stay anchored over an old shipwreck that was a reliable gathering spot for black sea bass. He succeeded well enough for the group—five of us were fishing—to land about twenty-five keepers and store them in the live well. "The Rolls-Royce of fish," Pasternack, who caught the most, said. "Steamed, fried, poached, baked, sautéed, grilled—I'll take a black sea bass any day over a piece of tuna." In the afternoon, we moved close to the shore and, using clams for bait, hauled in dozens of stripers that had been trailing a clam dredger as it repeatedly plowed a half-mile stretch parallel to Rockaway Beach. At the end of the trip, Pasternack bought everything in the live well and the coolers, plus Wasserman's catch from the previous day: a hundred or so bass, and three conger eels that were headed for the *zuppa di pesce*.

The next time I went to sea was a sultry July day, when Pasternack was in quest of bluefish with his friend, piscatorial mentor, and supplier Artie Hoernig, the captain of Smokey III, a thirty-one-foot Down East-type cabin cruiser that he docks in Island Park. We met at 7 a.m. in the parking lot of Artie's South Shore Fish Market, where we were joined by Pete Hession, a retired U.P.S. driver. Hoernig, who is in his late fifties, has a mahogany tan, a neatly trimmed silver beard, bloodshot blue eyes, and an inexhaustible supply of fish stories. The date, he announced, happened to be the eighteenth anniversary of one of his most gratifying adventures, the landing of a seven-hundred-and-eighty-two-pound mako shark. That same year, Pasternack, then in his mid-twenties, caught a three-hundred-pound bull shark near Key West. He had the head mounted, and it hung in his bedroom until a couple of years ago, when his wife told him, "Either the garage or you give it away." It now occupies wall space at Artie's market, right next to the head of the mako.

Hoernig went inside and returned with the day's bait, twenty pounds of fresh and thirty pounds of frozen bunker, two flats of frozen spearing that would be used as chum, and ten pounds of frozen squid. A half hour later, this cargo got loaded onto the boat, along with three large coolers filled with crushed ice, and by nine o'clock we'd reached our destination, an area five miles offshore where Hoernig had planted about forty-five lobster pots.

The ocean surface was oddly placid. Hoernig: "It's like a fucking lake."

Hession: "I hope we see a breeze."

Pasternack: "The only breeze we're gonna see out here, Pete, is thunder-storms."

Using bait-casting reels with forty-pound-test wire leaders and heavy-test monofilament backing, we tossed treble hooks baited with thick chunks of bunker into water about sixty feet deep. From the get-go, the bluefish were excitable. Pasternack quickly landed a seven-pounder, I caught one, Paster-nack caught another. Then things got quiet for about fifteen minutes. "One, two, three, and that's it?" Hoernig said. "Probably a fucking mako's down there chasing these bastards."

When they resumed biting, Hoernig would say, "Davey's in!" or Hession would say, "Oh, Artie's in!" Then: "Pete's in!" Bluefish have notoriously sharp teeth and strong jaws, and the most prudent way to get one into a boat is with a gaff. As promised, there was ample gore—bluefish blood and bunker guts. At times, we had three fish on the line simultaneously. By eleven o'clock, we'd filled one cooler. A half hour later, Hoernig switched to an ultra-light spinning rod and tied on a bucktail jig baited with a piece of squid, rigged for what's referred to on the South Shore as "fluking." He soon landed a two-and-a-half-pounder, and Pasternack, in a competitive spirit, got busy fluking, too. Occasionally, someone would lower a white plastic bucket over the side and fill it with water for washing our bloody hands. As the midday sun poured down, Pasternack and Hoernig took to cupping handfuls and dousing their heads. "I'm getting fucking ready to jump in, man," Pasternack said. It was not yet one o'clock when the second cooler reached capacity—mostly blues, a few fluke, a sea bass. Time to go pull lobster pots.

Citing my journalistic priorities, I managed to steer clear of the heavy lifting. As Hoernig eased the boat alongside a buoy, Pasternack would use a gaff to grab the submerged rope, and Hession would wrap a couple of turns around a small electric winch attached to the starboard gunwale. Invariably, the ropes were coated with algae the consistency of sodden shredded wheat and the lobster traps were encrusted with tiny mussels the size of split peas. The first few pots contained little Jonah and calico crabs and conch, and por-gies flapping like birds, but were lobster-free. "No wonder your lobster's so expensive," Pasternack said.

"A labor of love," he said to me as he tossed clumps of algae overboard and prepared to dump putrescent bunker carcasses from the mesh bait bag inside a trap. Pasternack wore a plain white T-shirt, loose-fitting gray athletic shorts, white crew socks, calf-length white rubber boots, and an F.D.N.Y. Rescue cap. Varieties of fish flesh were pasted to his clothing, but he didn't appear to mind, unlike Hession, who concluded that the best way to clean the filth from his bluejeans was to tie them to a fishing line and drag them behind the boat. Which seemed like a clever idea until the line snapped, stranding him in his green plaid boxers. ("All I can say, Pete, is you're a victim of circumstance," Hoernig told him.)

Some squid eggs—transparent Gummi-worm-like masses—clung to one of the traps. I asked Pasternack whether he'd ever eaten them. He said that he hadn't, but that he'd tasted octopus eggs in Italy. Almost defensively, he added, "I ate bunker. I got Artie to eat it, too. Little ones. They fried 'em in his restaurant. We called 'em Hewlett Bay anchovies. The sardines of Long Island. It was good, right, Artie? People squirted lemon juice on 'em." He leaned over with the squid eggs, handed them to me, and said, "Here, put this in the cooler."

They hoisted twenty-two traps, good for twenty-one lobsters. As Pasternack relaunched traps by sliding them down a plank and off the rear of the boat, he whistled "I've Been Working on the Railroad."

"You like blue-fishing?" he asked me as we headed back.

Yes, I did.

He leaned against the gunwale. In the background: Atlantic Beach and the high-rises of the Rockaways. The sun was in his face, he was bloody and sweaty and due for a shave. Lunch had been a turkey-and-cheddar sub, and there were dabs of mayo at the corners of his mouth. "I told you, I don't always catch the biggest one, but I'm always catching 'em," he said. "Some guys are only about catching big fish. I've always been for quantity. I like to eat 'em. I'm a meat-and-potatoes guy."

I asked what he would do with the bluefish at Esca.

Palms up, he shook his head. "There's lots of good stuff to work with now," he said. "Lobster mushrooms. Great corn. Good tomatoes are starting to show up. This time of year it's easy to be a cook." Today, though, he'd been fishing and truly hadn't given it a thought. But tomorrow, back in the kitchen, he'd have an idea.

A Woman's Place Is Running the Kitchen
from *New York Times* (March 28, 2014)

When Barbara Lynch started working at Todd English's restaurant, Olives, in 1989, it was so popular that people would begin lining up outside in the afternoon. On weekends, as the restaurant endured three relentless "turns," with one table of diners replacing another, it seemed as if

English's reputation grew in proportion to how overwhelmed his kitchen felt. One evening, the chef was surveying his dining room—checking on tables, glad-handing guests—when a customer signaled for him to come over and inspect the *spaghetti alle vongole veraci*. Yes, the pasta was perfectly twirlable, and yes, the clams were open, but the dish was compromised by an unwelcome improvisation. English spotted it, snatched the bowl and darted into the kitchen, where the diminutive line cook with thick blue eyeliner and an AquaNet-affixed bouffant cowered behind her mise en place.

"Where is your earring?" English thundered. Before she could reply, Lynch recalls, he upended the dish—silky sauce, spaghetti and bivalves—onto Lynch. (English denies overturning the dish.)

At the time, she was one of the few women working behind the swinging doors of professional kitchens. And English's was a decidedly macho operation. Once, Lynch says, the chef beaned a slow-moving manager with a pound of butter. Another time, when he found Lynch crying in the walk-in refrigerator, he lifted her up and moved her back to her prep station. ("It was tough love," he says. "I only wanted good people to be better.") But he also gave her opportunities. When English opened his second restaurant, Figs, he tapped Lynch to create the signature handmade pizzas, pastas and antipasti. She says he came to appreciate her talent so much, in fact, that when she told him that she was going to become the head chef of a competing Italian restaurant, Rocco's, he flung a Coke bottle at her head. "I ran out the back door, and he ran out the front," Lynch recalls. "We ended up bumping into each other." It was the restaurant-equivalent of a shootout in a spaghetti western. "I was like: 'You [expletive, expletive.] You should be [expletive] proud of me, instead of [expletive] treating me like an [expletive].' " (English denies throwing a bottle.)

Lynch has been in charge of her own kitchen ever since. Today she owns a Boston-based hospitality group that has 260 employees and earns about $20 million annually. She oversees a catering company and a huddle of popular restaurants: No. 9 Park (a Brahmin Beacon Hill standard), Sportello (a date-night pasta place), Drink (a craft-cocktail bar), B&G Oysters (a seafood joint), the Butcher Shop (a meat counter and cafe), Menton (a fine-dining establishment) and Stir (an open demonstration kitchen where she offers classes). She has won three James Beard awards and is nominated this year for Outstanding Restaurateur. (If she wins, she'll be only the second woman to do so.) She is the sole female Relais & Châteaux grand chef in North America.

Lynch is one of the most accomplished chef-restaurateurs in America, but the fact that she remains largely a cipher outside Boston underscores a truth about the restaurant industry. Two decades after her brush with English, professional kitchens remain, as the San Francisco chef-owner Traci Des Jardins recently put it, one of "the last bastions of bad behavior"—and women don't thrive in them. Earlier this month, Bloomberg News reported that it was less likely for a woman to be hired as a head chef than as a C.E.O.

Food television may seem to offer inroads, but it also sets up additional obstacles. While male celebrity chefs come in many packages—from nerdy Alton Brown, to Falstaffian Mario Batali, to kindly Tom Colicchio—their female counterparts tend to embody a singular identity: a nice, cheerful cook making dinner for her family. But that caricature is markedly different from the tough, assertive women who actually run professional kitchens. With a few notable exceptions, like Cat Cora, female chefs on television showcase their skills in their own homes, or sets designed to look like them, reinforcing the notion that that's where women cook.

Lynch, by her own admission, was not made for TV. When she appeared on the finale of "Top Chef" in 2012, Grub Street asked, "Didn't she seem a little bit, well, scowly?" They noted that she looked as if "she'd rather be at the dentist's office," which she may well have. Television makes her anxious. "I'm still not that confident in myself," she says.

In an era when being a star chef offers endless spinoff vehicles—national tours, trademarked crockpots, 500-seat restaurants in Times Square—Lynch, who is 50, seems uniquely uninterested in extending her so-called brand. She has never had an eye to expand to other cities ("Boston has always been great with me") or sell cookware with her name on it ("I'm a chef, not a franchise"), and she is finished opening restaurants ("I got everything I wanted"). Now the only brand Lynch is interested in pushing is that of the female chef. "It's not about me anymore. It's about the next generation. We need more women in this business."

Lynch has taken a personal stance by providing mentorship to rising women. But what is needed, Lynch says, is a broader cultural shift. "It's important for women to get on television," she said at an industry panel this month. "Because that is the largest audience we have." It is a means to a necessary end, and she's all for it—just so long as she doesn't have to do it herself.

In 2012, Lynch pushed two young chefs from her restaurant group, Kristen Kish and Stephanie Cmar, to compete on "Top Chef." Their absence would gut Lynch's demonstration kitchen, but she shoved them out the door anyway, guaranteeing their jobs when they returned. They explained their friendship on the season premiere. "We bonded over the fact that we were getting boob sweat, because we were the only two girls on the line," Kish said of meeting Cmar, who showed off their matching spoon tattoos. By the end of the hour, Cmar was sent home; Kish was invited to stay.

"You think you can win 'Top Chef?' " Emeril Lagasse asked her.

"If I didn't, I wouldn't be here," Kish replied.

CULINARY SCHOOL TEACHES hard skills, but a chef's real training happens on the job. Lynch never went to culinary school, and she never had a professional mentor—"I learned how *not* to run a restaurant group from

Todd English," she said—and she still has some insecurities about being self-taught. "What am I doing here?" she asked recently, before speaking on a panel that included Kerry Healey, the first woman to be president of Babson College, and Carmen Ortiz, the first female U.S. attorney for the state of Massachusetts. "All Ph.D.'s? All college? I'm from a housing project. I didn't go to school. I'm afraid to talk, because I don't talk like that."

Lynch grew up in South Boston, one of seven children of a widowed mother. Knuckles Lynch, as she was called then, sold pot and was an amateur bookie ("I was an entrepreneur," she says). She has a way of making her upbringing sound serendipitous, even wholesome. She talks about running errands with her mother and buying freshly baked muffins; every Friday her family ate "the best tuna-fish salad," which her mother stretched with pickle juice. But Lynch's childhood was rough. She grew up next door to the mobster James (Whitey) Bulger, and she felt his squeeze on the neighborhood. "He was supposedly a nice guy, but the older I got, the more I realized he was getting everyone hooked on heroin. My sister was a heroin addict because of him," she says. The neighborhood field was nicknamed Needle Park.

By the time she was 15, she landed a waitressing gig, alongside her mother, at the tony St. Botolph Club. Later, she talked her way into a chef job on a Martha's Vineyard dinner cruise by saying that she'd cooked the fancy dishes she had really only served: sweetbreads under a glass cloche, Dover sole, Quahog chowder. Lynch spent the summer cooking lobster and filet mignon for 170 passengers. The night was over, she said, when the band started to play Neil Diamond's "America." ("When you heard the cymbals," she explained, "you had to get the dessert out, because we were docking in 10 minutes.") That job led to a prep-cook position at Harvest, a Cambridge stalwart, and then English hired her to work at a buzzy restaurant, Michela's. When he went out on his own to open Olives, she soon followed. But first she took a formative trip to Tuscany, where the neighboring *nonna*, Mita Antolini, showed her how to make traditional dishes: tomato sauce, Bolognese and gnocchi. Together, they roasted chestnuts, soaked them in *vin santo* and topped them with prosciutto and ate it all for lunch.

After working for English, Lynch eventually persuaded an executive from Stride Rite, the shoe company, to invest in her first restaurant. "I owed the I.R.S. $75,000. I lived with my mother. I drove an Isuzu Trooper without a license or insurance. Like, who the [expletive] is going to invest in me, right?" she said. But talent and tenacity made investors confident and she raised the money she needed. The restaurant, No. 9 Park, was an instant success.

IT'S TEMPTING TO FRAME Lynch's rise as a Horatio Alger story, but that doesn't do justice to her moxie. Since their inception about a quarter-century ago, only 12 percent of the winners of the James Beard award for Outstanding

Chef and 16 percent of Food & Wine's Best New Chefs have been women. Lynch has not won Outstanding Chef, but she received the Food & Wine prize in 1996. When she arrived in Aspen to collect her award, an airport driver held a sign with her name, next to another driver holding a sign that said, "Julia Child." "I made it!" she remembers thinking.

Recently Kish, who is 30, was similarly wowed while cooking next to Daniel Boulud at a fund-raiser for the Barbara Lynch Foundation. But it wasn't always obvious that she could have a career in the kitchen, either. She modeled throughout high school but disliked it. She was unhappy at college and left after her first year. Her mother suggested she try cooking. She attended Le Cordon Bleu, in Chicago, but found no mentors there. After graduation, she worked in kitchens where she was often the only woman, and the food she was making taught her little about her own style. A disastrous stint as the head chef of a restaurant where her paychecks bounced landed her out of work. Kish, who had done cocaine recreationally, began to rely on it and her use "got a little heavy for four months." Soon after, she gave it up and started fresh in Boston as a line cook. Eventually she found a job at Stir, where Kish learned quickly under Lynch's frank and fair direction. "If you ask most people, they're scared of her," Kish said of her boss. "Which is a good thing."

At Stir, Lynch guided Kish as Antolini had taught her, sometimes cooking side by side. When Kish noticed Lynch using a different technique from the one she had chosen—say, searing oiled scallops in a dry pan, rather than dropping dry scallops in an oiled pan—she'd ask why, and they'd discuss the benefits and drawbacks of each method. "She gave me the space to figure out exactly how I cook," Kish said, "and I would have never found it, because you work with so many chefs who are like: 'This is how you do it. Don't do it any other way.' She was there but not forceful." One day, Kish received a call from a harried Lynch, asking her to handle the menu for a special "Birds and Burgundy" class that night at Stir. When Lynch arrived later, Kish was in full swing; she'd prepped the meal, demonstrating her mastery of French cooking techniques, from consommé to *beurre blanc*. What Kish didn't know was that the demonstration kitchen, where she had to cook in front of people, under time pressure, while teaching, was the perfect preparation for competing on "Top Chef."

Kish had no interest in being on television, which she feared would play up her looks more than her skills. But Lynch insisted on it. "You have to do this," she said, after returning from her stint as a guest star the previous season. "You're young, beautiful and know how to cook. Now own it. The world is your oyster." She now says she would have dragged her to the set if she continued to refuse. "I knew she could win," Lynch said.

As Kish recalls it, Lynch's parting words were: "You're going to do great. Whatever happens, I'm proud of you." But it wasn't lost on Kish that she was representing her mentor; she competed with a note from Lynch in her back pocket. "I was like, 'I don't want to do badly, because I don't want to disappoint her.' I put a lot of pressure on myself," she said. She needn't have worried. On the season finale, Kish was declared the winner before she had the chance to serve dessert. (She was the second woman to win the title.) And when Kish returned to Boston, Lynch soon gave her another prize. She named her chef de cuisine at her Relais & Châteaux property, Menton, giving her free rein over the fine-dining tasting menu.

ONCE INSTALLED AT Menton, in June, Kish found herself stretched between her obligations as a head chef and her opportunities as a "Top Chef." Offers poured in; some she accepted (travel to London, Miami and the James Beard "Women in Whites" dinner in New York), others she rejected (a contract for hawking frozen food that would have paid more than her salary). Investors have pressed her to open her own restaurant; producers have tried to coax her back onto television. She is the rare female chef who has both the culinary chops and the telegenic appeal to suit the extraordinary demands of both professional settings. "There's this fine line that I'm continually struggling to ride," Kish says of deciding what's next. She's not averse to showcasing herself as a chef on television, but she also wants to follow the path of those chefs she admires—including Daniel Boulud, Eric Ripert, Gabrielle Hamilton and, above all, Barbara Lynch. And that means becoming her own boss.

In February, Kish told Lynch that she felt ready to go out on her own. Lynch didn't throw a Coke bottle at her. It seemed like the right decision. And earlier this month, during Kish's final shift, Lynch, who is separated from her husband, brought her girlfriend, Jacqueline Bernat, and her girlfriend's son to Menton for dinner. She invited a surprise guest to complete the table. "Oh, I know who that is," Kish said, and smiled when a server told her there was an unexpected fourth person. It was Jacqueline Westbrook. She and Kish have been together nearly a year, but they kept their relationship under wraps at first. Westbrook, who is the assistant to the Food & Wine editor in chief, Dana Cowin, recalls telling her boss, "So, you know my friend Kristen? Well, she's not just my friend."

For this V.I.P. table, Kish went off the menu, personalizing dishes and playing to her mentor's palate. "To remind her of Naples," Kish said, as she pushed an appetizer of seared scallops with brioche sauce out the door. "Chef Barbara whipped out her iPhone to take a picture," a server reported back, excitedly.

The sleeves of Kish's chef coat were rolled above her elbows as she deftly plated each dish, some requiring 28 placements: including six circles of leeks and three tiny purple mizuna leaves. She was far faster and more precise than her sous chef, but, she said graciously, "you wouldn't have noticed that if we hadn't been standing side by side."

As she expedited the restaurant's many orders, it was tough to keep pace with the rhythm of the meals, which could run up to nine courses, not including the cheese plate. At one point a cook they called Noodle prepared just seven wide ribbons of pasta for nine awaiting bowls, and the error so flustered him that he proceeded to make several more mistakes. He started mouthing off, and then he actually threw up his hands and spun in a circle. Kish, taking a broad stance, with her hands on her hips, turned to him and said, "Lose the [expletive] attitude, I swear to God." He did.

At the end of the night, the staff gathered for a meeting that was both exactly how you'd imagine a restaurant crew cuts back at midnight—noshing on piles of leftover bread and cheese, shotgunning cold cans of Miller High Life—and also like a corporate retreat. They stood in a circle and one by one encapsulated their evening's experience, after which Kish gave each of them a compliment. "You are wildly talented," she told a cook who had been plating the same smoked cobia appetizer for hours. Noodle squished a buttered croissant between two rolls to make a bread sandwich. When it was his turn, he said: "Chef, it's been a pleasure to work with you the past nine months. Sorry I've been so difficult. I'm working on it." And Kish replied: "Noodle, I've learned to love how much heart you put into it. I genuinely love you." The staff cheered. A kitchen can look like this too.

Carl von Clausewitz
(1780–1831)

CARL VON CLAUSEWITZ, a staff officer, administrator, teacher, and modernizer of the Prussian military, had his first personal experience of war in 1793, as a twelve-year-old lance corporal. His thought is distinguished by its flexibility, in contrast to the doctrinaire writings of many of his contemporaries, and his theories about war always contextualize it within social and political life. War, in his estimation, was inherently political, and it made no sense to consider it in a vacuum. As the historian Peter Paret notes, the treatise *On War*, despite being unfinished, is comprehensive, systematic, and stylistically precise. Clausewitz was interested, Paret reminds us, in "the concept of the role genius plays in war" as well as the inevitable uncertainty of the endeavor. The role of chance could never be eliminated in the conduct of war; one of the marks of the great military mind was therefore the recognition that its flux and fog could never be addressed by a rigid set of rules. Paret also notes Clausewitz's understanding of the role that humanistic education and the study of history might play in the theorizing of war. Largely complete in the form we know it in 1827, the work was published posthumously in 1832. It was neglected until later in the nineteenth century when Helmuth von Moltke (Moltke the

Elder) looked to it as a guide in his own efforts to modernize the German army. Moltke regarded it along with Homer and the Bible as an essential text. The chapter "On Military Genius," reproduced here, contains the argument that mastery in warfare is not simply a matter of the intellect but also one of character and temperament. (The following selection is translated by Michael Howard and Peter Paret.)

On Military Genius
from *On War* (1832)

Any complex activity, if it is to be carried on with any degree of virtuosity, calls for appropriate gifts of intellect and temperament. If they are outstanding and reveal themselves in exceptional achievements, their possessor is called a "genius."

We are aware that this word is used in many senses, differing both in degree and in kind. We also know that some of these meanings make it difficult to establish the essence of genius. But since we claim no special expertise in philosophy or grammar, we may be allowed to use the word in its ordinary meaning, in which "genius" refers to a very highly developed mental aptitude for a particular occupation.

Let us discuss this faculty, this distinction of mind for a moment, setting out its claims in greater detail, so as to gain a better understanding of the concept. But we cannot restrict our discussion to *genius* proper, as a superlative degree of talent, for this concept lacks measurable limits. What we must do is to survey all those gifts of mind and temperament that in combination bear on military activity. These, taken together, constitute *the essence of military genius.* We have said *in combination,* since it is precisely the essence of military genius that it does not consist in a single appropriate gift—courage, for example—while other qualities of mind or temperament are wanting or are not suited to war. Genius consists *in a harmonious combination of elements,* in which one or the other ability may predominate, but none may be in conflict with the rest.

If every soldier needed some degree of military genius our armies would be very weak, for the term refers to a special cast of mental or moral powers which can rarely occur in an army when a society has to employ its abilities in many different areas. The smaller the range of activities of a nation and the more the military factor dominates, the greater will be the incidence of military genius. This, however, is true only of its distribution, not of its quality. The latter depends on the *general intellectual development* of a given society. In any primitive, warlike race, the warrior spirit is far more common than among civilized peoples. It is possessed by almost every warrior: but in civilized societies only necessity will stimulate it in the people as a whole, since they lack the natural disposition for it. On the other hand, we will never find a savage who is a truly great commander, and very rarely one who would be considered a military genius, since this requires a degree of intellectual powers beyond anything that a primitive people can develop. Civilized societies, too, can obviously possess a war-like character to greater or lesser degree, and the more they develop it, the greater will be the number of men with military spirit in their armies. Possession of military genius coincides with the higher degrees of civilization: the most highly developed societies produce the most brilliant soldiers, as the Romans and the French have shown us. With them, as with every people renowned in war, the greatest names do not appear before a high level of civilization has been reached.

We can already guess how great a role intellectual powers play in the higher forms of military genius. Let us now examine the matter more closely.

War is the realm of danger; therefore *courage* is the soldier's first requirement.

Courage is of two kinds: courage in the face of personal danger, and courage to accept responsibility, either before the tribunal of some outside power or before the court of one's own conscience. Only the first kind will be discussed here.

Courage in face of personal danger is also of two kinds. It may be indifference to danger, which could be due to the individual's constitution, or to his holding life cheap, or to habit. In any case, it must be regarded as a permanent *condition*. Alternatively, courage may result from such positive motives as ambition, patriotism, or enthusiasm of any kind. In that case courage is a feeling, an emotion, not a permanent state.

These two kinds of courage act in different ways. The first is the more dependable; having become second nature, it will never fail. The other will often achieve more. There is more reliability in the first kind, more boldness in the second. The first leaves the mind calmer; the second tends to stimulate, but it can also blind. *The highest kind of courage is a compound of both.*

War is the realm of physical exertion and suffering. These will destroy us unless we can make ourselves indifferent to them, and for this birth or training must provide us with a certain strength of body and soul. If we do possess those qualities, then even if we have nothing but common sense to guide them we shall be well equipped for war: it is exactly these qualities that primitive and semicivilized peoples usually possess.

If we pursue the demands that war makes on those who practice it, we come to the region dominated by the *powers of intellect*. War is the realm of uncertainty; three quarters of the factors on which action in war is based are wrapped in a fog of greater or lesser uncertainty. A sensitive and discriminating judgment is called for; a skilled intelligence to scent out the truth.

Average intelligence may recognize the truth occasionally, and exceptional courage may now and then retrieve a blunder; but usually intellectual inadequacy will be shown up by indifferent achievement.

War is the realm of chance. No other human activity gives it greater scope: no other has such incessant and varied dealings with this intruder. Chance makes everything more uncertain and interferes with the whole course of events.

Since all information and assumptions are open to doubt, and with chance at work everywhere, the commander continually finds that things are not as he expected. This is bound to influence his plans, or at least the assumptions underlying them. If this influence is sufficiently powerful to cause a change in his plans, he must usually work out new ones; but for these the necessary information may not be immediately available. During an operation decisions have usually to be made at once: there may be no time to review the situation or even to think it through. Usually, of course, new information and reevaluation are not enough to make us give up our intentions: they only call them in question. We now know more, but this makes us more, not less uncertain. The latest reports do not arrive all at once: they merely trickle in. They continually impinge on our decisions, and our mind must be permanently armed, so to speak, to deal with them.

If the mind is to emerge unscathed from this relentless struggle with the unforeseen, two qualities are indispensable: *first, an intellect that, even in the darkest hour, retains some glimmerings of the inner light which leads to truth; and second, the courage to follow this faint light wherever it may lead.* The first of these qualities is described by the French term, *coup d'oeil*; the second is *determination.*

The aspect of war that has always attracted the greatest attention is the engagement. Because time and space are important elements of the engagement, and were particularly significant in the days when the cavalry attack was the decisive factor, the *idea of a rapid and accurate decision* was first based on an evaluation of time and space, and consequently received a name which refers to visual estimates only. Many theorists of war have employed the term in that limited sense. But soon it was also used of any sound decision taken in the midst of action—such as recognizing the right point to attack, etc. *Coup d'oeil* therefore refers not alone to the physical but, more commonly, to the inward eye. The expression, like the quality itself, has certainly always been more applicable to tactics, but it must also have its place in strategy, since here as well quick decisions are often needed. Stripped of metaphor and of the restrictions imposed on it by the phrase, the concept merely refers to the quick recognition of a truth that the mind would ordinarily miss or would perceive only after long study and reflection.

Determination in a single instance is an expression of courage; if it becomes characteristic, a mental habit. But here we are referring not to physical courage but to the courage to accept responsibility, courage in the face of a moral danger. This has often been called *courage d'esprit*, because it is created by the intellect. That, however, does not make it an act of the intellect: it is an act of temperament. Intelligence alone is not courage; we often see that the most intelligent people are irresolute. Since in the rush of events a man is governed by feelings rather than by thought, the intellect needs to arouse the quality of courage, which then supports and sustains it in action.

Looked at in this way, the role of determination is to limit the agonies of doubt and the perils of hesitation when the motives for action are inadequate. Colloquially, to be sure, the term "determination" also applies to a propensity for daring, pugnacity, boldness, or temerity. But when a man has adequate grounds for action—whether subjective or objective, valid or false—he cannot properly be called "determined." This would amount to putting oneself in his position and weighting the scale with a doubt that he never felt. In such a case it is only a question of strength or weakness. I am not such a pedant as to quarrel with common usage over a slight misuse of a word; the only purpose of these remarks is to preclude misunderstandings.

Determination, which dispells doubt, is a quality that can be aroused only by the intellect, and by a specific cast of mind at that. More is required to create determination than a mere conjunction of superior insight with the appropriate emotions. Some may bring the keenest brains to the most formidable problems, and may possess the courage to accept serious responsibilities; but when faced with a difficult situation they still find themselves unable to reach a decision. Their courage and their intellect work in separate compartments, not together; determination, therefore, does not result. It is engendered only by a *mental act*; the mind tells man that boldness is required, and thus gives direction to his will. This particular cast of mind, which employs the fear of *wavering* and *hesitating* to suppress all other fears, is the force that makes strong men determined. Men of low intelligence, therefore, cannot possess determination in the sense in which we use the word. They may act without hesitation in a crisis, but if they do, they act *without reflection*; and a man who acts without reflection cannot, of course, be torn by doubt. From time to time action of this type may even be appropriate; but, as I have said before, it is the *average result* that indicates the existence of military genius. The statement may surprise the reader who knows some determined cavalry officers who are little given to deep thought: but he must remember that we are talking about a special kind of intelligence, not about great powers of meditation.

In short, we believe that determination proceeds from a special type of mind, from a strong rather than a brilliant one. We can give further proof of this interpretation by pointing to the many examples of men who show great determination as junior officers, but lose it as they rise in rank. Conscious of the need to be decisive, they also recognize the risks entailed by a *wrong* decision; since they are unfamiliar with the problems now facing them, their mind loses its former incisiveness. The more used they had been to instant action, the more their timidity increases as they realize the dangers of the vacillation that ensnares them.

Having discussed *coup d'oeil* and determination it is natural to pass to a related subject: *presence of mind*. This must play a great role in war, the domain of the unexpected, since it is nothing but an increased capacity of dealing with the unexpected. We admire presence of mind in an apt repartee, as we admire quick thinking in the face of danger. Neither needs to be exceptional, so long as it meets the situation. A reaction following long and deep reflection may seem quite commonplace; as an immediate response, it may give keen pleasure. The expression "presence of mind" precisely conveys the speed and immediacy of the help provided by the intellect.

Whether this splendid quality is due to a special cast of mind or to steady nerves depends on the nature of the incident, but neither can ever be entirely lacking. A quick retort shows wit; resourcefulness in sudden danger calls, above all, for steady nerve.

Four elements make up the climate of war: danger, exertion, uncertainty, and chance. If we consider them together, it becomes evident how much fortitude of mind and character are needed to make progress in these impeding elements with safety and success. According to circumstance, reporters and historians of war use such terms as *energy, firmness, staunchness, emotional balance*, and *strength of character*. These products of a heroic nature could almost be treated as one and the same force—strength of will—which adjusts itself to circumstances: but though closely linked, they are not identical. A closer study of the interplay of psychological forces at work here may be worth while.

To begin with, clear thought demands that we keep one point in mind: of the weight, the burden, the resistance—call it what you like—that challenges the psychological strength of the soldier, only a small part is the *direct result of the enemy's activity, his resistance, or his operations.* The direct and primary impact of enemy activity falls, initially, on the soldier's person without affecting him in his capacity as commander. If, for example, the enemy resists four hours instead of two, the commander is in danger twice as long; but the higher an officer's rank, the less significant this factor becomes, and to the commander-in-chief it means nothing at all.

A second way in which the enemy's resistance *directly* affects the commander is the loss that is caused by prolonged resistance and the influence this exerts on his sense of responsibility. The deep anxiety which he must experience works on his strength of will and puts it to the test. Yet we believe that this is not by any means the heaviest burden he must bear, for he is answerable to himself alone. All other effects of enemy action, however, are felt by the men under his command, and *through them react on him*.

So long as a unit fights cheerfully, with spirit and elan, great strength of will is rarely needed; but once conditions become difficult, as they must when much is at stake, things no longer run like a well-oiled machine. The machine itself begins to resist, and the commander needs tremendous willpower to overcome this resistance. The machine's *resistance* need not consist of disobedience and argument, though this occurs often enough in individual soldiers. It is the impact of the ebbing of moral and physical strength, of the heart-rending spectacle of the dead and wounded, that the commander has to withstand—first in himself, and then in all those who, directly or indirectly, have entrusted him with their thoughts and feelings, hopes and fears. As each man's strength gives out, as it no longer responds to his will, the inertia of the whole gradually comes to rest on the commander's will alone. The ardor of his spirit must rekindle the flame of purpose in all others; his inward fire must revive their hope. Only to the extent that he can do this will he retain his hold on his men and keep control. Once that hold is lost, once his own courage can no longer revive the courage of his men, the mass will drag him down to the brutish world where danger is shirked and shame is unknown. Such are the burdens in battle that the commander's courage and strength of will must overcome if he hopes to achieve outstanding success. The burdens increase with the number of men in his command, and therefore the higher his position, the greater the strength of character he needs to bear the mounting load.

Energy in action varies in proportion to the strength of its motive, whether the motive be the result of intellectual conviction or of emotion. Great strength, however, is not easily produced where there is no emotion.

Of all the passions that inspire man in battle, none, we have to admit, is so powerful and so constant as the longing for honor and renown. The German language unjustly tarnishes this by associating it with two ignoble meanings in the terms "greed for honor" (*Ehrgeiz*) and "hankering after glory" (*Ruhmsucht*). The abuse of these noble ambitions has certainly inflicted the most disgusting outrages on the human race; nevertheless their origins entitle them to be ranked among the most elevated in human nature. In war they act as the essential breath of life that animates the inert mass. Other emotions may be more common and more venerated—patriotism, idealism, vengeance, enthusiasm of every kind—but they are no substitute for a thirst for fame and honor. They may, indeed, rouse the mass to action and inspire it, but they cannot give the commander the ambition to strive higher than the rest, as he must if he is to distinguish himself. They cannot give him, as can ambition, a personal, almost proprietary interest in every aspect of fighting, so that he turns each opportunity to best advantage—plowing with vigor, sowing with care, in the hope of reaping with abundance. It is primarily this spirit of endeavor on the part of commanders at all levels, this inventiveness, energy, and competitive enthusiasm, which vitalizes an army and makes it victorious. And so far as the commander-in-chief is concerned, we may well ask whether history has ever known a great general who was not ambitious; whether, indeed, such a figure is conceivable.

Staunchness indicates the will's resistance to a single blow; *endurance* refers to prolonged resistance.

Though the two terms are similar and are often used interchangeably, the difference between them is significant and unmistakable. Staunchness in face of a single blow may result from strong emotion, whereas intelligence helps sustain endurance. The longer an action lasts, the more deliberate endurance becomes, and this is one of its sources of strength.

We now turn to *strength of mind*, or of *character*, and must first ask what we mean by these terms.

Not, obviously, vehement display of feeling, or passionate temperament: that would strain the meaning of the phrase. We mean the ability to keep one's head at times of exceptional stress and violent emotion. Could strength of intellect alone account for such a faculty? We doubt it. Of course the opposite does not flow from the fact that some men of outstanding intellect do lose their self-control; it could be argued that a powerful rather than a capacious mind is what is needed. But it might be closer to the truth to assume that the faculty known as *self-control*—the gift of keeping calm even under the greatest stress—is rooted in temperament. It is itself an emotion which serves to balance the passionate feelings in strong characters without destroying them, and it is this balance alone that assures the dominance of the intellect. The counterweight we mean is simply the sense of human dignity, the noblest pride and deepest need of all: the urge *to act rationally at all times*. Therefore we would argue that a strong character is one *that will not be unbalanced by the most powerful emotions*.

If we consider how men differ in their emotional reactions, we first find a group with small capacity for being roused, usually known as "stolid" or "phlegmatic."

Second, there are men who are extremely active, but whose feelings never rise above a certain level, men whom we know to be sensitive but calm.

Third, there are men whose passions are easily inflamed, in whom excitement flares up suddenly but soon burns out, like gunpowder. And finally we come to those who do not react to minor matters, who will be moved only very gradually, not suddenly, but whose emotions attain great strength and durability. These are the men whose passions are strong, deep, and concealed.

These variants are probably related to the *physical forces* operating in the human being—they are part of that dual organism we call the nervous system, one side of which is physical, the other psychological. With our slight scientific knowledge we have no business to go farther into that obscure field; it is important nonetheless to note the ways in which these various psychological combinations can affect military activity, and to find out how far one can look for great strength of character among them.

Stolid men are hard to throw off balance, but total lack of vigor cannot really be interpreted as strength of character. It cannot be denied, however, that the imperturbability of such men gives them a certain narrow usefulness in war. They are seldom strongly motivated, lack initiative and consequently are not particularly active; on the other hand they seldom make a serious mistake.

The salient point about the second group is that trifles can suddenly stir them to act, whereas great issues are likely to overwhelm them. This kind of man will gladly help an individual in need, but the misfortune of an entire people will only sadden him; they will not stimulate him to action.

In war such men show no lack of energy or balance, but they are unlikely to achieve anything significant unless they possess a *very powerful intellect* to provide the needed stimulus. But it is rare to find this type of temperament combined with a strong and independent mind.

Inflammable emotions, feelings that are easily roused, are in general of little value in practical life, and therefore of little value in war. Their impulses are strong but brief. If the energy of such men is joined to courage and ambition they will often prove most useful at a modest level of command, simply because the action controlled by junior officers is of short duration. Often a single brave decision, a burst of emotional force, will be enough. A daring assault is the work of a few minutes, while a hard fought battle may last a day, and a campaign an entire year.

Their volatile emotions make it doubly hard for such men to preserve their balance; they often lose their heads, and nothing is worse on active service. All the same, it would be untrue to say that highly excitable minds could never be strong—that is, could never keep their balance even under the greatest strain. Why should they not have a sense of their own dignity, since as a rule they are among the finer natures? In fact, they usually have such a sense, but there is not time for it to take effect. Once the crisis is past, they tend to be ashamed of their behavior. If training, self-awareness, and experience sooner or later teaches them how to be on guard against themselves, then in times of great excitement an internal counterweight will assert itself so that they too can draw on great strength of character.

Lastly, we come to men who are difficult to move but have strong feelings— men who are to the previous type like heat to a shower of sparks. These are the men who are best able to summon the titanic strength it takes to clear away the enormous burdens that obstruct activity in war. Their emotions move as great masses do—slowly but irresistibly.

These men are not swept away by their emotions so often as is the third group, but experience shows that they too can lose their balance and be overcome by blind passion. This can happen whenever they lack the noble pride of self-control, or whenever it is inadequate. We find this condition mostly among great men in primitive societies, where passion tends to rule for lack of intellectual discipline. Yet even among educated peoples and civilized societies men are often swept away by passion, just as in the Middle Ages poachers chained to stags were carried off into the forest.

We repeat again: strength of character does not consist solely in having powerful feelings, but in maintaining one's balance in spite of them. Even with the violence of emotion, judgment and principle must still function like a ship's compass, which records the slightest variations however rough the sea.

We say a man has strength of character, or simply has character, if he sticks to his convictions, whether these derive from his own opinions or someone else's, whether they represent principles, attitudes, sudden insights, or any other mental force. Such *firmness* cannot show itself, of course, if a man keeps changing his mind. This need not be the consequence of external influence; the cause may be the workings of his own intelligence, but this would suggest a peculiarly insecure mind. Obviously a man whose opinions are constantly changing, even though this is in response to his own reflections, would not be called a *man of character.* The term is applied only to men whose views are *stable and constant.* This may be because they are well thought-out, clear, and scarcely open to revision; or, in the case of indolent men, because such people are not in the habit of mental effort and therefore have no reason for altering their views; and finally, because a firm decision, based on fundamental principle derived from reflection, is relatively immune to changes of opinion.

With its mass of vivid impressions and the doubts which characterize all information and opinion, there is no activity like war to rob men of confidence in themselves and in others, and to divert them from their original course of action.

In the dreadful presence of suffering and danger, emotion can easily overwhelm intellectual conviction, and in this psychological fog it is so hard to form clear and complete insights that changes of view become more understandable and excusable. Action can never be based on anything firmer than instinct, a sensing of the truth. Nowhere, in consequence, are differences of opinion so acute as in war, and fresh opinions never cease to batter at one's convictions. No degree of calm can provide enough protection: new impressions are too powerful, too vivid, and always assault the emotions as well as the intellect.

Only those general principles and attitudes that result from clear and deep understanding can provide a *comprehensive* guide to action. It is to these that opinions on specific problems should be anchored. The difficulty is to hold fast to these results of contemplation in the torrent of events and new opinions. Often there is a gap between principles and actual events that cannot always be bridged by a succession of logical deductions. Then a measure of self-confidence is needed, and a degree of skepticism is also salutary. Frequently nothing short of an imperative principle will suffice, which is not part of the immediate thought-process, but dominates it: that principle is in all doubtful cases *to stick to one's first opinion and to refuse to change unless forced to do so by a clear conviction.* A strong faith in the overriding truth of tested principles is needed; the *vividness* of transient impressions must not make us forget that such truth as they contain is of a lesser stamp. By giving precedence, in case of doubt, to our earlier convictions, by holding to them stubbornly, our actions acquire that quality of steadiness and consistency which is termed strength of character.

It is evident how greatly strength of character depends on balanced temperament; most men of emotional strength and stability are therefore men of powerful character as well.

Strength of character can degenerate into *obstinacy*. The line between them is often hard to draw in a specific case; but surely it is easy to distinguish them in theory.

Obstinacy *is not an intellectual defect*; it comes from reluctance to admit that one is wrong. To impute this to the mind would be illogical, for the mind is the seat of judgment. Obstinacy *is a fault of temperament*. Stubbornness and intolerance of contradiction result from a special kind of *egotism*, which elevates above everything else *the pleasure of its autonomous intellect, to which others must bow.* It might also be called vanity, if it were not something superior: vanity is content with the appearance alone; obstinacy demands the material reality.

We would therefore argue that strength of character turns to obstinacy as soon as a man resists another point of view not from superior insight or attachment to some higher principle, but because he *objects instinctively.* Admittedly, this definition may not be of much practical use; but it will nevertheless help us avoid the interpretation that obstinacy is simply a more intense form of strong character. There is a basic difference between the two. They are closely related, but one is so far from being *a higher degree* of the other that we can even find extremely obstinate men who are too dense to have much strength of character.

So far our survey of the attributes that a great commander needs in war has been concerned with qualities in which mind and temperament work together. Now we must address ourselves to a special feature of military activity—possibly the most striking even though it is not the most important—which is not related to temperament, and involves merely the intellect. I mean the relationship between warfare and terrain.

This relationship, to begin with, is *a permanent factor*—so much so that one cannot conceive of a regular army operating except in a definite space. Second, its importance is *decisive in the highest degree,* for it affects the operations of all forces, and at times entirely alters them. Third, its influence may be felt in the *very smallest feature of the ground*, but it can also dominate *enormous areas.*

In these ways the relationship between warfare and terrain determines the peculiar character of military action. If we consider other activities connected with the soil—gardening, for example, farming, building, hydraulic engineering, mining, game-keeping, or forestry—none extends to more than a very limited area, and a working knowledge of that area is soon acquired. But a commander must submit his work to a partner, space, which he can never completely reconnoiter, and which because of the constant movement and change to which he is subject he can never really come to know. To be sure, the enemy is generally no better off; but the handicap, though shared, is still a handicap, and the man with enough talent and experience to overcome it will have a real advantage. Moreover it is only in a general sense that the difficulty is the same for both sides; in any particular case the defender usually knows the area far better than his opponent.

This problem is unique. To master it a special gift is needed, which is given the too restricted name of *a sense of locality*. It is the faculty of *quickly and accurately grasping the topography of any area* which enables a man to find his way about at any time. Obviously this is an act of the imagination. Things are perceived, of course, partly by the naked eye and partly by the mind, which fills the gaps with guesswork based on learning and experience, and thus constructs a whole out of the fragments that the eye can see; but if the whole is to be vividly present to the mind, imprinted like a picture, like a map, upon the brain, without fading or blurring in detail, *it can only be achieved by the mental gift that we call imagination.* A poet or painter may be shocked to find that his Muse dominates these activities as well: to him it might seem odd to say that a young gamekeeper needs an unusually powerful imagination in order to be competent. If so, we gladly admit that this is to apply the concept narrowly and to a modest task. But however remote the connection, his skill must still derive from this natural gift, for if imagination is entirely lacking it would be difficult to combine details into a clear, coherent image. We also admit that a good memory can be a great help; but are we then to think of memory as a separate gift of the mind, or does imagination, after all, imprint those pictures in the memory more clearly? The question must be left unanswered, especially since it seems difficult even to conceive of these two forces as operating separately.

That practice and a trained mind have much to do with it is undeniable. Puységur, the celebrated quarter-master-general of Marshal Luxembourg, writes that at the beginning of his career he had little faith in his sense of locality; when he had to ride any distance at all to get the password, he invariably lost his way.

Scope for this talent naturally grows with increased authority. A hussar or scout leading a patrol must find his way easily among the roads and tracks. All he needs are a few landmarks and some modest powers of observation and imagination. A commander-in-chief, on the other hand, must aim at acquiring an overall knowledge of the configuration of a province, of an entire country. His mind must hold a vivid picture of the road-network, the river-lines and the mountain ranges, without ever losing a sense of his immediate surroundings. Of course he can draw general information from reports of all kinds, from maps, books, and memoirs. Details will be furnished by his staff. Nevertheless it is true that with a quick, unerring sense of locality his dispositions will be more rapid and assured; he will run less risk of a certain awkwardness in his concepts, and be less dependent on others.

We attribute this ability to the imagination; but that is about the only service that war can demand from this frivolous goddess, who in most military affairs is liable to do more harm than good.

With this, we believe, we have reached the end of our review of the intellectual and moral powers that human nature needs to draw upon in war. The vital contribution of intelligence is clear throughout. No wonder then, that war, though it may appear to be uncomplicated, cannot be waged with distinction except by men of outstanding intellect.

Once this view is adopted, there is no longer any need to think that it takes a great intellectual effort to outflank an enemy position (an obvious move, performed innumerable times) or to carry out a multitude of similar operations.

It is true that we normally regard the plain, efficient soldier as the very opposite of the contemplative scholar, or of the inventive intellectual with his dazzling range of knowledge. This antithesis is not entirely unrealistic; but it does not prove that courage alone will make an efficient soldier, or that having brains and using them is not a necessary part of being a good fighting man. Once again we must insist. no case is more common than that of the officer whose energy declines as he rises in rank and fills positions that are beyond his abilities. But we must also remind the reader that outstanding effort, the kind that gives men a distinguished name, is what we have in mind. Every level of command has its own intellectual standards, its own prerequisites for fame and honor.

A major gulf exists between a commander-in-chief—a general who leads the army as a whole or commands in a theater of operations— and the senior generals immediately subordinate to him. The reason is simple: the second level is subjected to much closer control and supervision, and thus gives far less scope for independent thought. People therefore often think outstanding intellectual ability is called for only at the top, and that for all other duties common intelligence will suffice. A general of lesser responsibility, an officer grown gray in the service, his mind well-blinkered by long years of routine, may often be considered to have developed a certain stodginess; his gallantry is respected, but his simplemindedness makes us smile. We do not intend to champion and promote these good men; it would contribute nothing to their efficiency, and little to their happiness. We only wish to show things as they are, so that the reader should not think that a brave but brainless fighter can do anything of outstanding significance in war.

Since in our view even junior positions of command require outstanding intellectual qualities for outstanding achievement, and since the standard rises with every step, it follows that we recognize the abilities that are needed if the second positions in an army are to be filled with distinction. Such officers may appear to be rather simple compared to the polymath scholar, the far-ranging business executive, the statesman; but we should not dismiss the value of their practical intelligence. It sometimes happens of course that someone who made his reputation in one rank carries it with him when he is promoted, without really deserving to. If not much is demanded of him, and he can avoid exposing his incompetence, it is difficult to decide what reputation he really deserves. Such cases often cause one to hold in low estimate soldiers who in less responsible positions might do excellent work.

Appropriate talent is needed at all levels if distinguished service is to be performed. But history and posterity reserve the name of "genius" for those who have excelled in the highest positions—as commanders-in-chief—since here the demands for intellectual and moral powers are vastly greater.

To bring a war, or one of its campaigns, to a successful close requires a thorough grasp of national policy. On that level strategy and policy coalesce: the commander-in-chief is simultaneously a statesman.

Charles XII of Sweden is not thought of as a great genius, for he could never subordinate his military gifts to superior insights and wisdom, and could never achieve a great goal with them. Nor do we think of Henry IV of France in this manner: he was killed before his skill in war could affect the relations between states. Death denied him the chance to prove his talents in this higher sphere, where noble feelings and a generous disposition, which effectively appeased internal dissension, would have had to face a more intractable opponent.

The great range of business that a supreme commander must swiftly absorb and accurately evaluate has been indicated in the first chapter. We argue that a commander-in-chief must also be a statesman, but he must not cease to be a general. On the one hand, he is aware of the entire political situation; on the other, he knows exactly how much he can achieve with the means at his disposal.

Circumstances vary so enormously in war, and are so indefinable, that a vast array of factors has to be appreciated—mostly in the light of probabilities alone. The man responsible for evaluating the whole must bring to his task the quality of intuition that perceives the truth at every point. Otherwise a chaos of opinions and considerations would arise, and fatally entangle judgment. Bonaparte rightly said in this connection that many of the decisions faced by the commander-in-chief resemble mathematical problems worthy of the gifts of a *Newton* or an *Euler*.

What this task requires in the way of higher intellectual gifts is a sense of unity and a power of judgment raised to a marvelous pitch of vision, which easily grasps and dismisses a thousand remote possibilities which an ordinary mind would labor to identify and wear itself out in so doing. Yet even that superb display of divination, the sovereign eye of genius itself, would still fall short of historical significance without the qualities of character and temperament we have described.

Truth in itself is rarely sufficient to make men act. Hence the step is always long from cognition to volition, from knowledge to ability. The most powerful springs of action in men lie in his emotions. He derives his most vigorous support, if we may use the term, from that blend of brains and temperament which we have learned to recognize in the qualities of determination, firmness, staunchness, and strength of character.

Naturally enough, if the commander's superior intellect and strength of character did not express themselves in the final success of his work, and were only taken on trust, they would rarely achieve historical importance.

What the layman gets to know of the course of military events is usually nondescript. One action resembles another, and from a mere recital of events it would be impossible to guess what obstacles were faced and overcome. Only now and then, in the memoirs of generals or of their confidants, or as the result of close historical study, are some of the countless threads of the tapestry revealed. Most of the arguments and clashes of opinion that precede a major operation are deliberately concealed because they touch political interests, or they are simply forgotten, being considered as scaffolding to be demolished when the building is complete.

Finally, and without wishing to risk a closer definition of the higher reaches of the spirit, let us assert that the human mind (in the normal meaning of the term) is far from uniform. If we then ask what sort of mind is likeliest to display the qualities of military genius, experience and observation will both tell us that it is the inquiring rather than the creative mind, the comprehensive rather than the specialized approach, the calm rather than the excitable head to which in war we would choose to entrust the fate of our brothers and children, and the safety and honor of our country.

Leo Tolstoy
(1828–1910)

WAR AND PEACE was written on Tolstoy's family estate at Yasnaya Polyana, a little over a hundred miles from Moscow; its composition took five years, from 1863 to 1868, and it was published in 1869. Tolstoy had grown up at Yasnaya Polyana. His life was one of privilege and some dissolution: he lost his ancestral house in a card game. The structure was carted away, but Tolstoy returned to the foundations and rebuilt the house after marrying in the early 1860s. By this time he had experienced guerrilla warfare while accompanying his brother's cavalry unit in Chechnya; as an artillery officer, he had also been a participant in the siege of Sevastopol. In the 1880s, Tolstoy underwent what is most often described as a spiritual crisis: renouncing the luxuries of his former life, as well as the copyright to his work, he lived the life of an ascetic prophet. His philosophy of Christian equality and pacifism attracted fervent acolytes; Russian writers in particular looked to him hopefully as a kind of sage. Jay Parini's novel *The Last Station*, which was made into a motion picture in 2009, dramatizes the eccentricities of Tolstoy's later life and his death at a railway station. Virginia Woolf called Tolstoy "the greatest of all novelists." "Even in a translation," she writes in her essay "The Russian Point of View," "we feel that we have been set on a mountain-top and had a telescope put into our hands. Everything is astonishingly clear and absolutely sharp." In *War and Peace* Tolstoy trains his telescope on the Napoleonic Wars. In the following excerpt, the Russian commander, Field Marshal Kutuzov, communes with one of the novel's central characters, Prince Andrei, a man who goes to war because he finds life at home not to his liking but who discovers in the process the emptiness of his heroic fantasies and a new kind of meaning and purpose in leading a regiment. Kutuzov, meanwhile, is one of the novel's great philosophers, and his watchwords "time and patience" encapsulate Tolstoy's own theory that history is not written by "great men," as so many nineteenth-century thinkers contended, but is instead the product of a complex chain of cause and effect—a process a leader can watch, perhaps sometimes gently guide, yet never control. Kutuzov's real power derives from his insight that he has almost none. (The following selections are translated by Constance Garnett.)

Time and Patience
from *War and Peace* (1869)

The adjutant came out to Prince Andrey in the porch, and invited him to lunch. Half an hour later Kutuzov sent for Prince Andrey. He was reclining in a low chair, still in the same unbuttoned military coat. He had a French novel in his hand, and at Prince Andrey's entrance laid a paper-knife in it and put it aside. It was *Les Chevaliers du Cygne*, a work by Madame de Genlis, as Prince Andrey saw by the cover.

"Well, sit down; sit down here. Let us have a little talk," said Kutuzov. "It's sad; very sad. But remember, my dear, think of me as a father, another father, to you . . . !"

Prince Andrey told Kutuzov all he knew about his father's end, and what he had seen at Bleak Hills.

"To think what we have been brought to!" Kutuzov cried suddenly, in a voice full of feeling, Prince Andrey's story evidently bringing vividly before him the position of Russia.

"Wait a bit; wait a bit!" he added, with a vindictive look in his face, and apparently unwilling to continue a conversation that stirred him too deeply, he said:

"I sent for you to keep you with me."

"I thank your highness!" answered Prince Andrey, "but I am afraid I am no more good for staff work," he said, with a smile, which Kutuzov noticed. He looked at him inquiringly. "And the great thing is," added Prince Andrey, "I am used to my regiment. I like the officers; and I think the men have come to like me. I should be sorry to leave the regiment. If I decline the honour of being in attendance on you, believe me . . ."

Kutuzov's podgy face beamed with a shrewd, good-natured, and yet subtly ironical expression. He cut Bolkonsky short.

"I'm sure you would have been of use to me. But you're right; you're right. It's not here that we want men. There are always a multitude of counsellors; but men are scarce. The regiments wouldn't be what they are if all the would-be counsellors would serve in them like you. I remember you at Austerlitz. I remember, I remember you with the flag!" said Kutuzov, and a flush of pleasure came into Prince Andrey's face at this reminiscence. Kutuzov held out his hand to him, offering him his cheek to kiss, and again Prince Andrey saw tears in the old man's eye. Though Prince Andrey knew Kutuzov's tears were apt to come easily, and that he was particularly affectionate and tender with him from the desire to show sympathy with his loss, yet he felt this reminder of Austerlitz agreeable and flattering.

"Go your own way, and God bless you in it. . . . I know your path is the path of honour!" He paused. "I missed you at Bucharest. I wanted some one to send . . ." And changing the subject, Kutuzov began talking of the Turkish war, and of the peace that had been concluded. "Yes, I have been roundly abused," he said, "both for the war and the peace . . . but it all happened in the nick of time." " 'Everything comes in time for him who knows how to wait,' " he said, quoting the French proverb. "And there were as many counsellors there as here, . . ." he went on, returning to the superfluity of advisers, a subject which evidently occupied his mind. "Ugh, counsellors and counsellors!" he said. "If we had listened to all of them, we should be in Turkey now. We should not have made peace, and the war would never have been over. Always in haste, and more haste, worse speed. Kamensky would have come to grief there, if he hadn't died. He went storming fortresses with thirty thousand men. It's easy enough to take fortresses, but it's hard to finish off a campaign successfully. Storms and attacks are not what's wanted, but *time* and *patience*. Kamensky sent his soldiers to attack Rustchuk, but I trusted to them alone— time and patience—and I took more fortresses than Kamensky, and made the

Turks eat horseflesh!" He shook his head. "And the French shall, too. Take my word for it," cried Kutuzov, growing warmer and slapping himself on the chest, "I'll make them eat horseflesh!" And again his eye was dim with tears.

"We shall have to give battle, though, shan't we?" said Prince Andrey.

"We must, if every one wants to; there is no help for it. . . . But, mark my words, my dear boy! The strongest of all warriors are these two—time and patience. They do it all, and our wise counsellors *n'entendent pas de cette oreille, voilà le mal*. Some say ay, and some say no. What's one to do?" he asked, evidently expecting a reply. "Come, what would you have me do?" he repeated, and his eyes twinkled with a profound, shrewd expression. "I'll tell you what to do," he said, since Prince Andrey still did not answer. "I'll tell you what to do, and what I do. *Dans le doute, mon cher*"—he paused—"*abstiens-toi*." He articulated deliberately the French saying.

"Well, good-bye, my dear. Remember, with all my heart, I feel for your sorrow, and that for you I'm not his highness, nor prince, nor commander-in-chief, but simply a father to you. If you want anything, come straight to me. Good-bye, my dear boy!" Again he embraced and kissed him.

And before Prince Andrey had closed the door, Kutuzov settled himself comfortably with a sigh, and renewed the unfinished novel of Madame Genlis, *Les Chevaliers du Cygne*.

How, and why it was, Prince Andrey could not explain, but after this interview with Kutuzov, he went back to his regiment feeling reassured as to the future course of the war, and as to the man to whom its guidance was intrusted. The more clearly he perceived the absence of everything personal in the old leader, who seemed to have nothing left of his own but habits of passions, and instead of an intellect grasping events and making plans, had only the capacity for the calm contemplation of the course of events, the more confident he felt that all would be as it should be. "He will put in nothing of himself. He will contrive nothing, will undertake nothing," thought Prince Andrey; "but he will hear everything, will think of everything, will put everything in its place, will not hinder anything that could be of use, and will not allow anything that could do harm. He knows that there is something stronger and more important than his will—that is the inevitable march of events, and he can see them, can grasp their significance, and, seeing their significance, can abstain from meddling, from following his own will, and aiming at something else. And the chief reason," thought Prince Andrey, "why one believes in him is that he's Russian, in spite of Madame Genlis's novel and the French proverbs, that his voice shook when he said, 'What we have been brought to!' and that he choked when he said 'he would make them eat horseflesh!' "

It was this feeling, more or less consciously shared by all, that determined the unanimous approval given to the appointment of Kutuzov to the chief command, in accordance with national sentiment, and in opposition to the intrigues at court.

.   .   .

"They ought to understand that we can but lose by taking the offensive. Time and patience, these are my champions!" thought Kutuzov. He knew the apple must not be picked while it was green. It will fall of itself when ripe, but if you pick it green, you spoil the apple and the tree and set your teeth on edge. Like an experienced hunter, he knew the beast was wounded, wounded as only the whole force of Russia could wound it; but whether to death or not, was a question not yet solved. Now from the sending of Lauriston and Bertemy, and from the reports brought by the irregulars, Kutuzov was almost sure that the wound was a deadly one. But more proof was wanted; he must wait.

"They want to run and look how they have wounded him. Wait a bit, you will see. Always manœuvres, attacks," he thought. "What for? Anything to distinguish themselves. As though there were any fun in fighting. They are like children from whom you can never get a sensible view of things because they all want to show how well they can fight. But that's not the point now. And what skilful manœuvres all these fellows propose! They think that when they have thought of two or three contingencies (he recalled the general plan from Petersburg) that they have thought of all of them. And there is no limit to them!"

The unanswered question, whether the wound dealt at Borodino were mortal or not, had been for a whole month hanging over Kutuzov's head. On one side, the French had taken possession of Moscow. On the other side, in all his being, Kutuzov felt beyond all doubt that the terrible blow for which, together with all the Russians, he had strained all his strength must have been mortal. But in any case proofs were wanted, and he had been waiting for them now a month, and as time went on he grew more impatient. As he lay on his bed through sleepless nights, he did the very thing these younger generals did, the very thing he found fault with in them. He imagined all possible contingencies, just like the younger generation, but with this difference that he based no conclusion on the suppositions, and that he saw these contingencies not as two or three, but as thousands. The more he pondered, the more of them he saw. He imagined all sorts of movements of Napoleon's army, acting as a whole or in part, on Petersburg, against him, to out-flank him (that was what he was most afraid of), and also the possibility that Napoleon would fight against him with his own weapon, that he would stay on in Moscow waiting for him to move. Kutuzov even imagined Napoleon's army marching back to Medyn and Yuhnov. But the one thing he could not foresee was what happened—the mad, convulsive stampede of Napoleon's army during the first eleven days of its march from Moscow—the stampede that made possible what Kutuzov did not yet dare to think about, the complete annihilation of the French. Dorohov's report of Broussier's division, the news brought by the irregulars of the miseries of Napoleon's army, rumours of preparations for leaving Moscow, all confirmed the supposition that the French army was beaten and preparing to take flight. But all this was merely supposition, that seemed of weight to the younger men, but not to Kutuzov. With his sixty years' experience he knew how much weight to attach to rumours; he knew how ready men are when they desire anything to manipulate all evidence so as to confirm what they desire; and he knew how readily in that case they let everything of an opposite significance pass unheeded. And the more Kutuzov desired this supposition to be correct, the less he permitted himself to believe it. This question absorbed all his spiritual energies. All the rest was for him the mere customary performance of the routine of life. Such a customary performance and observance of routine were his conversations with the staff-officers, his letters to Madame de Staël that he wrote from Tarutino, his French novels, distribution of rewards, correspondence with Petersburg, and so on. But the destruction of the French, which he alone foresaw, was the one absorbing desire of his heart.

.   .   .

In 1812 and 1813 Kutuzov was openly accused of blunders. The Tsar was dissatisfied with him. And in a recent history inspired by promptings from the highest quarters, Kutuzov is spoken of as a designing, intriguing schemer, who was panic-stricken at the name of Napoleon, and guilty through his blunders at Krasnoe and Berezina of robbing the Russian army of the glory of complete victory over the French. Such is the lot of men not recognised by Russian intelligence as "great men," *grands hommes*; such is the destiny of those rare and always solitary men who divining the will of Providence submit their personal will to it. The hatred and contempt of the crowd is the punishment of such men for their comprehension of higher laws.

Strange and terrible to say, Napoleon, the most insignificant tool of history, who never even in exile displayed one trait of human dignity, is the subject of the admiration and enthusiasm of the Russian historians; in their eyes he is a *grand homme*.

Kutuzov, the man who from the beginning to the end of his command in 1812, from Borodino to Vilna, was never in one word or deed false to himself, presents an example exceptional in history of self-sacrifice and recognition in the present of the relative value of events in the future. Kutuzov is conceived of by the historians as a nondescript, pitiful sort of creature, and whenever they speak of him in the year 1812, they seem a little ashamed of him.

And yet it is difficult to conceive of an historical character whose energy could be more invariably directed to the same unchanging aim. It is difficult to imagine an aim more noble and more in harmony with the will of a whole people. Still more difficult would it be to find an example in history where the aim of any historical personage has been so completely attained as the aim towards which all Kutuzov's efforts were devoted in 1812.

Kutuzov never talked of "forty centuries looking down from the Pyramids," of the sacrifices he was making for the fatherland, of what he meant to do or had done. He did not as a rule talk about himself, played no sort of part, always seemed the plainest and most ordinary man, and said the plainest and most ordinary things. He wrote letters to his daughters and to Madame de Staël, read novels, liked the company of pretty women, made jokes with the generals, the officers, and the soldiers, and never contradicted the people, who tried to prove anything to him. When Count Rastoptchin galloped up to him at Yautsky bridge, and reproached him personally with being responsible for the loss of Moscow, and said: "Didn't you promise not to abandon Moscow without a battle?" Kutuzov answered: "And I am not abandoning Moscow without a battle," although Moscow was in fact already abandoned. When Araktcheev came to him from the Tsar to say that Yermolov was to be appointed to the command of the artillery, Kutuzov said: "Yes, I was just saying so myself," though he had said just the opposite a moment before. What had he, the one man who grasped at the time all the vast issues of events, to do in the midst of that dull-witted crowd? What did he care whether Count Rastoptchin put down the disasters of the capital to him or to himself? Still less could he be concerned by the question which man was appointed to the command of the artillery.

This old man, who through experience of life had reached the conviction that the thoughts and words that serve as its expression are never the motive force of men, frequently uttered words, which were quite meaningless—the first words that occurred to his mind.

But heedless as he was of his words, he never once throughout all his career uttered a single word which was inconsistent with the sole aim for the attainment of which he was working all through the war. With obvious unwillingness, with bitter conviction that he would not be understood, he more than once, under the most different circumstances, gave expression to his real thought. His first differed from all about him after the battle of Borodino, which he alone persisted in calling a victory, and this view he continued to assert verbally and in reports and to his dying day. He alone said that *the loss of Moscow is not the loss of Russia*. In answer to the overtures for peace, his reply to Lauriston was: *There can be no peace, for such is the people's will*. He alone during the retreat of the French said that *all our manœuvres are unnecessary; that everything is being done of itself better than we could desire; that we must give the enemy a "golden bridge"; that the battles of Tarutino, of Vyazma, and of Krasnoe, were none of them necessary; that we must keep some men to reach the frontier with; that he wouldn't give one Russian for ten Frenchmen*. And he, this intriguing courtier, as we are told, who lied to Araktcheev to propitiate the Tsar, he alone dared to face the Tsar's displeasure by telling him at Vilna that *to carry the war beyond the frontier would be mischievous and useless*.

But words alone would be no proof that he grasped the significance of events at the time. His actions—all without the slightest deviation—were directed toward the one threefold aim: first, to concentrate all his forces to strike a blow at the French; secondly, to defeat them; and thirdly, to drive them out of Russia, alleviating as far as was possible the sufferings of the people and the soldiers in doing so.

He, the lingerer Kutuzov, whose motto was always "Time and Patience," the sworn opponent of precipitate action, he fought the battle of Borodino, and made all his preparations for it with unwonted solemnity. Before the battle of Austerlitz he foretold that it would be lost, but at Borodino, in spite of the conviction of the generals that the battle was a defeat, in spite of the fact, unprecedented in history, of his army being forced to retreat after the victory, he alone declared in opposition to all that it was a victory, and persisted in that opinion to his dying day. He was alone during the whole latter part of the campaign in insisting that there was no need of fighting now, that it was a mistake to cross the Russian frontier and to begin a new war. It is easy enough now that all the events with their consequences lie before us to grasp their significance, if only we refrain from attributing to the multitude the aims that only existed in the brains of some dozen or so of men.

But how came that old man, alone in opposition to the opinion of all, to gauge so truly the importance of events from the national standard, so that he never once was false to the best interests of his country?

The source of this extraordinary intuition into the significance of contemporary events lay in the purity and fervour of patriotic feeling in his heart.

It was their recognition of this feeling in him that led the people in such a strange manner to pick him out, an old man out of favour, as the chosen leader of the national war, against the will of the Tsar. And this feeling alone it was to which he owed his exalted position, and there he exerted all his powers as commander-in-chief not to kill and maim men, but to save them and have mercy on them.

This simple, modest, and therefore truly great figure, could not be cast into the false mould of the European hero, the supposed leader of men, that history has invented.

To the flunkey no man can be great, because the flunkey has his own flunkey conception of greatness.

A. J. Liebling
(1904–1963)

AS A LONGTIME correspondent for *The New Yorker*, A. J. "Joe" Liebling tackled subjects as diverse as food, boxing, Paris, and war. To all he brought the same insight and zest. As the present-day *New Yorker* editor David

Remnick writes in an introduction to his work, Liebling is "boundlessly curious, a listener, a boulevardier, a man of appetites and sympathy. He is erudite in an unsystematic, wised-up sort of way." Liebling grew up in New York City. He matriculated at Dartmouth College but was suspended and ultimately expelled for insufficient chapel attendance. Liebling returned to New York, where he worked as a journalist and attended the Pulitzer School of Journalism at Columbia. He gained experience as a police reporter on Manhattan's Lower East Side and as a copyreader for the *New York Times*. Liebling also studied at the Sorbonne and spent three years in France (1927–30). He returned to New York to work for various papers and was eventually hired by *The New Yorker* in 1935. In 1939 he began writing a "Letter from Paris" and continued to report on the war for the magazine. Coming home in 1942, after covering Allied operations in Africa, Liebling subsequently returned to England to cover the D-Day invasion: sailing on a landing craft across the Channel, he saw firsthand the carnage at the beaches. This portrait of Omar Bradley reveals the moment at which an unknown and somewhat unprepossessing general came into his own, galvanizing a demoralized division and remaining calm in a crisis. "Confusion" in war, Liebling writes, "though normal, is not inevitable."

Omar Bradley

from *Mollie and Other War Pieces* (1964)

The first meeting of General Omar Nelson Bradley with the international public, as represented by British and American newspaper and radio correspondents, occurred on the crest of a brush-covered hill at a place called Béja, in northern Tunisia, on April 22, 1943. The American phase of the Allied offensive against the Axis forces in Africa was about to begin. Bradley, who was fifty years old, held the temporary wartime rank of major general, and had no combat record in the First World War and no idiosyncrasies that could be expanded into a legend, had been named to succeed Lieutenant General George S. Patton as commander of the American II Corps, which was the whole American ground force engaged in the African fighting. Since even Patton, for all his pistol-slapping and advance publicity, had failed to make the II Corps work as an offensive unit, correspondents took his replacement by an unknown to mean that the Americans would have a minor role in the final battle against the Axis on the African continent. Press briefings at Patton's headquarters, conducted by an intelligence officer, had been like formal audiences, with all present required to buckle the chin straps of their tin hats, in token of instant readiness to face the moderately distant foe. Before the offensive began, the press-relations officer at Béja had announced with some little embarrassment (the P.R.O. had been commissioned straight out of the publicity department of a movie company, so he was naturally mindful of military dignity) that the new man had decided that he would brief the correspondents in person, and, as there were at least thirty of them and only one of him, he would come to the press camp for this purpose. The new man arrived in a jeep, carrying a map under his arm and attended by his aide, a captain of almost juvenile appearance, who carried an easel and a pointer. The General wore a tin hat—not buckled under the chin, probably because his reconnaissances sometimes took him into shelling and he didn't want his head jerked off. He also wore a canvas field jacket, G.I. pants, and canvas leggings, thus qualifying as the least dressed-up commander of an American army in the field since Zachary Taylor, who wore a straw hat. He had a long jaw and a high, notably convex forehead, and he was wearing spectacles. After the Green Hornet, with his ruddy, truculent face and his beefy, leather-sheathed calves, the new general, lanky and diffidently amiable, seemed a man of milk.

The aide set up the easel in press headquarters; then the General hung the map, took the pointer, and, in a high, not loud voice, as Missourian as the Truman voice that later became familiar to radio listeners, began to demonstrate how the II Corps intended to progress in an eleven-day drive to Mateur, the key to Bizerte, through enemy positions that had stopped the best troops of the British First Army for five months. Some people think a general should have a voice like a recorded bugle call played over a loudspeaker. But the Bradley delivery is really an asset—hesitant, slightly rustic, compelling the hearer to listen hard for the next phrase and at the same time convincing him of the General's candor. At Béja, he laid down his schedule with no more panache than a teacher outlining the curriculum for the new semester. The Americans, he said, had been moved from the south-central to the extreme northwest arc of the Allied semicircle facing the Axis redoubt—because, the correspondents had suspected up to this point, they were to make merely a holding attack, in country so rugged that they could switch quickly to the defensive if the Germans came at them. Meanwhile, the British First and Eighth Armies were to crash through at more promising points on the Axis perimeter. When a correspondent who had been with the British in this zone through the bitter months of frustration asked how the inexperienced 9th Division was going to get Green and Bald Hills, two notoriously nasty positions that had stopped the Guards, General Bradley said that that was up to General Manton Eddy, the division commander, but that he didn't expect any undue delay. All parts of the inquiring correspondent visible above his battle dress turned purple.

Only two American infantry divisions, the 1st and the 9th, appeared on the General's map. The absence of the corps's other infantry outfit, the 34th Division, was interpreted by some to mean that it was being held in defensive reserve and by others that it had been sent home as useless. Either supposition, if confirmed, would bear out the notion that the American attack was not too banefully intended. There was, however, a gap half as wide as a divisional front between the 9th and the 1st. "What are you going to have in there, sir?" a knowing fellow asked. The new general looked at him with a gratified, pedagogical smile, as at a pupil who had asked a bright question. "I'm going to patrol that with a troop of motorized cavalry," he said. (A couple of days later, when General Eddy expressed his own disquiet about the gap, Bradley told him reassuringly, "If they come through there, Bill Kean and I will go in with a couple of BARs." BARs are Browning automatic rifles. Kean, who later commanded the 25th Division in Korea, was then the II Corps's chief of staff.) The new general didn't have much more to say. It was a historic début, although nobody knew it at the time. Had any programs been printed, they would sell at a big premium today.

Bradley had been in Tunisia two months without a command when he took over the II Corps. General George Catlett Marshall, then Chief of Staff of the Army, had, General Marshall later said, sent Bradley there "to be Eisenhower's legs and wisdom." He spent most of his time at the front, returning to Algiers to tell the Commander-in-Chief what was going on. General Eisenhower was not only several hundred miles away; he was—nominally, at least—in command of the British First and Eighth Armies and the French XIX Corps, in addition to the Americans, and was also supreme political arbiter of North Africa, which left him only limited time for tactical details. This had been Bradley's first experience in a real war, and he had been looking at it closely—going up into forward observation posts, and talking to company and platoon leaders and to riflemen to check on what he had learned and taught in the previous thirty-two years. So he was bringing to his first recital what a music critic unafraid of clichés would call a ripened technique and a mature understanding of the content of the music. Into the gap in his offensive alignment, when the time came, he slipped the fresh 34th Division, and, pushing it forward in depth on a rather narrow front, he sent it against Hill 609, the highest eminence of the first range he had to fight across. The 1st had already reached the flanks of 609 and could put artillery fire on it to help the attackers. So employed, the 34th, which so far in this campaign had known only defeat and was considered a liability, took 609 and came out believing itself a division *d'élite*, which was most of what it needed to be one. This made the new general's military gifts manifest to his first audience, and they have never had cause to change their opinion of him. Many generals, in the course of history, have taken a hill at the cost of a division, and as many have lost a division without taking a hill. Bradley took a key hill and gained a division. His troops reached each of their objectives almost exactly in accordance with the schedule he had laid down. "There was one time when Matt Eddy was a few hours behind, up on the left flank," General Bradley said a couple of years later, during the campaign in western France, "but I told him to step on it."

Bradley explained that small bit of virtuosity seven years later, over a drink.

"All hills, with narrow draws between them—a country just laid out for defense," he said of northern Tunisia. "They'd get up in the hills, and when you went down in the draws to get around them, they'd put fire on you." He had thought he knew what to do about the hills, he said—go straight up them, as you would when hunting wild goats in the mountains of Hawaii. It had also occurred to him that the German 88, though its flat trajectory made it wonderful for shooting across valleys at vehicles in the open, would not be much good at firing over hills at close range to hit hidden soldiers on the reverse slopes. "I remember that gap between the Ninth and the First," he said. "What I was thinking was that if the suckers did come in over those hills, they wouldn't have any good road they could get far on, and we could round 'em up before they got far into our rear. It was about nine miles from where they were over to the Djebel Abiod road, and by the time they had climbed down there we could have armor to meet them."

The Chairman sipped at his drink and looked across at the staircase as if he could see the Djebel Abiod road, in the shadow of hills covered with purple wild flowers and separated by narrow black gorges in which dwarf cows found water. Then he smiled. "I wanted that gap for the Thirty-fourth," he said. "Alexander [General, now Viscount, Alexander, the field commander of the joint Allied forces in Africa] and Bedell Smith [Eisenhower's Chief of Staff] had wanted to send the Thirty-fourth home for retraining, they thought it was so bad. It had its tail down between its legs. I said, 'Leave it to me and I'll guarantee that it carries its first important objective, if I have to give it every gun in the Corps.' It's good for troops to feel they have an important objective. You may have to move them up and move them back once or twice when they're green, just to give them the habit of fighting, but if you do it too often they get the feeling they're being thrown away. That treatment had spoiled the Thirty-fourth. So I didn't want it in at the start, when they might think they were getting more of the same. Then I put them at 609. You remember it. It was almost a cliff. But the Thirty-fourth went up it. The suckers got down in the crevices when we put fire on it, and then after our fellows had passed over they came out and took them in the rear. But our fellows cleaned them up. After that, the Thirty-fourth had its tail over the dashboard. You couldn't hold it."

The Thirty-fourth was the division components of which had been so messed around with in the fighting between Sened and Maknassy, while other components had subsequently been set out on hills near Kasserine like goats set out to lure a tiger. Then, when the tiger, in the form of German armor, came, the American armored division that had been cast in the role of big-game hunter lost its nerve and let the Germans scoop up the infantry goats, along with about 100 of our tanks. The residue of the Thirty-fourth was left with a goat mentality, which it imparted to the replacements. Old Dr. Bradley's psychotherapy fixed it up. Confusion, though normal, is not inevitable.

The Taste of Banzo's Sword, from *Zen Flesh, Zen Bones*
(1957)

"THE TASTE OF Banzo's Sword" and two other vignettes reproduced in this anthology originally come from *101 Zen Stories* (1939), a collection of Chinese and Japanese Zen teachings from across the centuries. These stories, many of which were translated from the late thirteenth-century Japanese *Shaseki-shu*, or *Collection of Stone and Sand*, were subsequently assembled, together with anecdotes and koans from various sources in the influential compilation *Zen Flesh, Zen Bones*. Zen (or *Ch'an* in China) Buddhism is a meditative practice aimed at self-discovery. As Joel Kupperman explains in *Classic Asian Philosophy*, Zen stories of the kind collected in *Zen Flesh, Zen Bones* "dramatize (rather than explain) the philosophical element" of Zen; they are designed to offer a mode of living. Kupperman cautions against attempting to interpret Zen writing by searching for Western parallels: "Asian philosophy fitted to a Western template," he writes, "will emerge as a crude caricature." Paul Reps, one of the compilers of *Zen Flesh, Zen Bones*, writes, "Old Zen was so fresh it became treasured and remembered. Here are fragments of its skin, flesh, bones, but not its marrow—never found in words." In "The Taste of Banzo's Sword" we encounter the son of a famous swordsman who is deemed "too mediocre" to become a master. The master swordsman Banzo, however, finds a way to teach what the impatient father could not.

The Taste of Banzo's Sword

Matajuro Yagyu was the son of a famous swordsman. His father, believing that his son's work was too mediocre to anticipate mastership, disowned him.

So Matajuro went to Mount Futara and there found the famous swordsman Banzo. But Banzo confirmed the father's judgment. "You wish to learn swordsmanship under my guidance?" asked Banzo. "You cannot fulfill the requirements."

"But if I work hard, how many years will it take me to become a master?" persisted the youth.

"The rest of your life," replied Banzo.

"I cannot wait that long," explained Matajuro. "I am willing to pass through any hardship if only you will teach me. If I become your devoted servant, how long might it be?"

"Oh, maybe ten years," Banzo relented.

"My father is getting old, and soon I must take care of him," continued Matajuro. "If I work far more intensively, how long would it take me?"

"Oh, maybe thirty years," said Banzo.

"Why is that?" asked Matajuro. "First you say ten and now thirty years. I will undergo any hardship to master this art in the shortest time!"

"Well," said Banzo, "in that case you will have to remain with me for seventy years. A man in such a hurry as you are to get results seldom learns quickly."

"Very well," declared the youth, understanding at last that he was being rebuked for impatience, "I agree."

Matajuro was told never to speak of fencing and never to touch a sword. He cooked for his master, washed the dishes, made his bed, cleaned the yard, cared for the garden, all without a word of swordsmanship.

Three years passed. Still Matajuro labored on. Thinking of his future, he was sad. He had not even begun to learn the art to which he had devoted his life.

But one day Banzo crept up behind him and gave him a terrific blow with a wooden sword.

The following day, when Matajuro was cooking rice, Banzo again sprang upon him unexpectedly.

After that, day and night, Matajuro had to defend himself from unexpected thrusts. Not a moment passed in any day that he did not have to think of the taste of Banzo's sword.

He learned so rapidly he brought smiles to the face of his master. Matajuro became the greatest swordsman in the land.

Robert Frost
(1874–1963)

ONE OF THE most widely known and popular twentieth-century American poets, Robert Frost is often identified with New England, where he moved at the age of eleven, and where he returned after failing at farming in New Hampshire prompted a temporary move to England in the years before World War I. In England he made the acquaintance of several English poets, chief among them Edward Thomas, with whom he carried on a transatlantic correspondence until Thomas's death on the Western Front.

Birdsong was a preoccupation for both poets, and their correspondence contains frequent contrasts between the poet's artificial song and the bird's natural voice. Frost often took his subjects from scenes of rural life, and the unsentimental natural world forms the subject of his most powerful work. In "The Oven Bird," which follows the traditional fourteen-line form of the sonnet, Frost addresses the concept of mastery by finding in the bird a model of instinctive, unself-conscious indwelling. On its initial publication in the volume *Mountain Interval* (1920), the poem was the subject of some controversy after Frost rejected interpretations of it by certain critics.

The Oven Bird
from *Mountain Interval* (1920)

There is a singer everyone has heard,
Loud, a mid-summer and a mid-wood bird,
Who makes the solid tree trunks sound again.
He says that leaves are old and that for flowers
Mid-summer is to spring as one to ten.
He says the early petal-fall is past
When pear and cherry bloom went down in showers
On sunny days a moment overcast;
And comes that other fall we name the fall.
He says the highway dust is over all.
The bird would cease and be as other birds
But that he knows in singing not to sing.
The question that he frames in all but words
Is what to make of a diminished thing.

DISCUSSION QUESTIONS

1. *What do these readings suggest about how to build organizations and institutions from scratch? About how to resolve inherited problems?*

2. *What is the proper balance in a leader between technical mastery and the ability to recognize and foster the abilities of others?*

3. *What constitutes mastery in your organization?*

4. *Which is more common in the leaders of your organization or institution: academic or experiential knowledge? Which is valued more highly?*

5. *What kinds of professional and leadership education programs does your organization sponsor?*

ALBUM
Artists of Delay

If someone stops where they should not, they'll stop anywhere. If someone slights a person they should treat generously, they'll slight anyone. And if someone races ahead, they retreat in a hurry.

—MENCIUS, 13.44

In most public and corporate arenas a premium is placed on decisiveness. There are good reasons for this bias, moments of crisis in any career that require immediate action. Generals who refuse to advance, for example, have always maddened those who await the results of their campaigns: "And, once more let me tell you," Abraham Lincoln exhorted the dilatory General George B. McClellan in the spring of 1862, "it is indispensible to *you* that you strike a blow. *I* am powerless to help this. . . . I beg to assure you that I have never written you, or spoken to you, in greater kindness of feeling than now, nor with a fuller purpose to sustain you, so far as in my most anxious judgment, I consistently can. *But you must act.*" Even when there is sound policy behind their inaction, seemingly idle commanders provoke frustration. One of the selections that follow, for example, invites readers to consider the case of Fabius Maximus, who endured the incomprehension and disdain of his fellow Romans when he adopted the very un-Roman strategy of delay that ultimately defeated Hannibal.

Equally significant is the seductive romance that attaches to the split-second decision made under figurative or literal fire. Tangible action soothes while invisible contemplation provokes suspicion. One wants always to be seen to be doing something. Premature demands for "deliverables," "takeaways," and near-term profits short-circuit deliberative processes. Our culture has long been rich with maxims that endorse dispatch: *Make haste while the sun shines. Never put off until tomorrow what you can do today. A stitch in time saves nine.* And the prevailing prejudice in favor of defiant haste has only intensified in twenty-first-century life. Throughout the summer and autumn of 2009, to take one example, there was a sense of discomfort among many observers with the length of time it took President Barack Obama to complete a strategic assessment of U.S. involvement in Afghanistan. In announcing the administration's policy in a speech at West Point in December of that year, the president clearly felt the need to respond to critics with a justification of the deliberate pace of his decision making: "I insisted on a thorough review of our strategy. Now, let me be clear: There has never been an option before me that called for troop deployments before 2010, so there has been no delay or denial of resources necessary for the conduct of the war during this review period. Instead, the review has allowed me to ask the hard questions, and to explore all the different options, along with my national security team, our military and civilian leadership in Afghanistan, and our key partners. And given the stakes involved, I owed the American people—and our troops—no less."

Hesitation, especially in someone like a president, is often interpreted as weakness and indecision. Sometimes it is, but at other times delay is not a mark of irrational procrastination or lack of will. Yet the fear of seeming weak can prompt leaders to make quick work of decisions over which they ought to labor—and to be seen to labor. At times, paradoxically, fear induces compensatory fits of paralysis, in which what ought to be an easy decision turns agonizing. There is a difference not fully appreciated between the failure to take responsibility and the recognition that the time may not yet be ripe for decisive action. To suggest the value of delay is not to advocate leadership without principle or to encourage counterproductive habits of vacillation. But when discussion, debate, and reflection are construed as signs of cowardice rather than of a leader's capacity for measured judgment and a trust in that of the people with whom a leader has surrounded herself, the lineaments of a cultural pathology can be discerned.

There are times when the best, most prudent, if least romantic course consists not in doing but in waiting. Mastering the art of the wait entails knowing when to wait and for how long. It also presumes the cultivation of deep attention, a habit of mind explored elsewhere in this anthology. In this section, we encounter several masters of the wait. Elizabeth I is the centerpiece of this album. Her speeches to Parliament on marriage and the execution of her dangerous rival Mary Stuart reveal the queen at her cagey best. Elizabeth's delays, often coupled with prevarication and equivocation, were a necessary component to her survival in a ruthless world. The other texts here include the English poet John Milton's sonnet on his blindness, in which he meditates on the need for patience in the service of art, and excerpts from Plutarch's biography of Fabius Maximus as well as a few of his collected anecdotes about Augustus Caesar, which reveal nuances of the art of the wait. Finally, poems by Joseph Harrison and Yannis Ritsos offer a portrait of that great artist of delay: Penelope, the wife of the Greek hero Odysseus. For twenty years she waited for him while he first fought the Trojan War and then wandered the earth before returning to his home on the island of Ithaca.

RECOMMENDED READING AND VIEWING

Chrisoula Andreou and Mark D. White, editors, *The Thief of Time: Philosophical Essays of Procrastination* (2010)

Samuel Beckett, *Waiting for Godot* (1952)
Fail-Safe (1964), directed by Sidney Lumet
Malcolm Gladwell, *Blink: The Power of Thinking Without Thinking* (2005)
Homer, *Odyssey*, translated by Robert Fagles (eighth century BCE)

John Milton
(1608-1674)

WHEN MILTON EMBARKED on his poetic career, it was with the ambition
to produce England's great epic poem. He considered King Arthur a likely
subject but in the end chose "to justify the ways of God to men" in *Paradise
Lost*, a narrative poem about the fall, which imagines not only the psyches
of Adam and Eve but also those of Satan and God. It was the remarkable
acme of a career, beginning with pastoral poetry and culminating in epic,
modeled on those of his English predecessor Edmund Spenser and the
Roman poet Virgil, whose *Aeneid* is excerpted in "Studying the System."
Today it is Milton the poet we remember, yet it should not be forgotten that
he deployed his immense learning and intellectual energy in service of the
great political crisis of his day: the English Civil War. The same discipline
he devoted to the study of theology, literature, philosophy, history, politics,
and science, he also brought to the civil and religious contests of the 1630s
and 1640s. A staunch partisan of the Puritan cause, Milton penned numerous tracts and pamphlets articulating his positions on marriage and
divorce, the need for a free press, republican government, and the evils of
monarchy. He became Latin Secretary in the Commonwealth government
of Oliver Cromwell, and after the Restoration of Charles II, it was only
through the intercession of friends such as the poet Andrew Marvell that
Milton was not executed for his former allegiances and support of regicide.
In the 1650s, Milton suffered the death of two children and his wife, and he
began to go blind for unknown reasons. *Paradise Lost* was the product of
this period, as is this sonnet, which treats his physical transformation and
illustrates his faith in God's plan through allusions to the biblical parables
of the talents and the vineyard keeper.

When I Consider How My Light Is Spent (1673)

When I consider how my light is spent
   Ere half my days in this dark world and wide,
   And that one Talent which is death to hide

Lodged with me useless, though my soul more bent
To serve therewith my Maker, and present
My true account, lest He returning chide,
"Doth God exact day-labour, light denied?"
I fondly ask. But Patience, to prevent
That murmur, soon replies, "God doth not need
Either man's work or his own gifts. Who best
Bear his mild yoke, they serve him best. His state
Is kingly: thousands at his bidding speed,
And post o'er land and ocean without rest:
They also serve who only stand and wait."

Plutarch

(ca. 45–120)

PLUTARCH WAS BORN in the Boetian city of Chaeronea, in central Greece, which was at the time part of the Roman Empire. He himself records that he came to Athens to study philosophy, and he became a Platonist there. Staying long enough to acquire Athenian citizenship, Plutarch then moved to the city of Delphi, home to the oracle. In addition to his biographies of Greek and Roman leaders, Plutarch wrote prolifically in other genres. Collected since the medieval period under the title *Moralia*, these writings address not only ethical philosophy but also various aspects of society and culture as well as topics in theology, psychology, metaphysics, and aesthetics. The introduction to the Harvard Classics edition of Plutarch's *Lives* proposes, "The influence of these Lives it is almost impossible to exaggerate. All classes of people have taken delight in them, from kings to shepherds, and it is safe to say that the influence has always been wholesome. Not only do they supply a mass of information, vividly and picturesquely presented, regarding the leading personalities of some of the greatest periods of the world's history, but they offer in concrete and inspiring form the ideals of human character in the antique world incarnated in a series of great heroic figures." For centuries, Plutarch's *Lives* offered inspirational heroic examples considered worthy of emulation. That age stretched from the Renaissance through perhaps the early twentieth century, when the Harvard Classics series was published. Readers of Plutarch throughout history range from Montaigne and Henri IV of France to Jean-Jacques Rousseau, Benjamin Franklin, Thomas Jefferson, and Alexander Hamilton. In the first selection here Plutarch focuses on the Roman general Fabius Maximus. Fabius adopted a controversial approach to the threat presented by Hannibal, who had marched over the Alps with his elephants and was in the process of terrorizing Rome during what is known as the Second Punic War. Subsequently known as "Fabian Strategy," Fabius's method was to wait Hannibal out in a war of attrition rather than risk open battle with a tactical master, who would subsequently prove his dominance at the Battle of Cannae. In the second selection, from *Moralia*, Plutarch describes an antidote for a short temper from the life of Augustus Caesar. (The following selections come from the seventeenth-century Dryden translation.)

Fabius Maximus
from *Lives*

In this manner Fabius, having given the people better heart for the future, by making them believe that the gods took their side, for his own part placed his whole confidence in himself, believing that the gods bestowed victory and good fortune by the instrumentality of valour and of prudence; and thus prepared he set forth to oppose Hannibal, not with intention to fight him, but with the purpose of wearing out and wasting the vigour of his arms by lapse of time, of meeting his want of resources by superior means, by large numbers the smallness of his forces. With this design, he always encamped on the highest grounds, where the enemy's horse could have no access to him. Still he kept pace with them; when they marched he followed them; when they encamped he did the same, but at such a distance as not to be compelled to an engagement, and always keeping upon the hills, free from the insults of their horse; by which means he gave them no rest, but kept them in a continual alarm.

But this his dilatory way gave occasion in his own camp for suspicion of want of courage; and this opinion prevailed yet more in Hannibal's army. Hannibal was himself the only man who was not deceived, who discerned his skill and detected his tactics, and saw, unless he could by art or force bring him to battle, that the Carthaginians, unable to use the arms in which they were superior, and suffering the continual drain of lives and treasure in which they were inferior, would in the end come to nothing. He resolved, therefore, with all the arts and subtleties of war to break his measures, and to bring Fabius to an engagement, like a cunning wrestler, watching every opportunity to get good hold and close with his adversary. He at one time attacked, and sought to distract his attention, tried to draw him off in various directions, and endeavored in all ways to tempt him from his safe policy. All this artifice, though it had no effect upon the firm judgment and conviction of the dictator, yet upon the common soldier, and even upon the general of the horse himself, it had too great an operation: Minucius, unseasonably eager for action, bold and confident, humoured the soldiery, and himself contributed to fill them with wild eagerness and empty hopes, which they vented in reproaches upon Fabius, calling him Hannibal's pedagogue, since he did nothing else but follow him up and down and wait upon him. At the same time, they cried up Minucius for the only captain worthy to command the Romans; whose vanity and presumption rose so high in consequence, that he insolently jested at Fabius's encampment upon the mountains, saying that he seated them there as on a theatre, to behold the flames and desolation of their country. And he would sometimes ask the friends of the general, whether it were not his meaning, by thus leading them from mountain to mountain, to carry them at last (having no hopes on earth) up into heaven, or to hide them in the clouds from Hannibal's army? When his friends reported these things to the dictator, persuading him that, to avoid the general obloquy, he should engage the enemy, his answer was, "I should be more faint-hearted than they make me, if, through fear of idle reproaches, I should abandon my own convictions. It is no inglorious thing to have fear for the safety of our country, but to be turned from one's course by men's opinions, by blame, and by misrepresentation, shows a man unfit to hold an office such as this, which, by such conduct, he makes the slaves of those whose errors it is his business to control."

·   ·   ·

The enemies of Fabius thought they had sufficiently humiliated and subdued him by raising Minucius to be his equal in authority; but they mistook the temper of the man, who looked upon their folly as not his loss, but like Diogenes, who, being told that some persons derided him, made answer, "But I am not derided," meaning that only those were really insulted on whom such insults made an impression, so Fabius, with great tranquillity and unconcern, submitted to what happened, and contributed a proof to the argument of the philosophers that a just and good man is not capable of being dishonoured. His only vexation arose from his fear lest this ill counsel, by supplying opportunities to the diseased military ambition of his subordinate, should damage the public cause. Lest the rashness of Minucius should now at once run headlong into some disaster, he returned back with all privacy and speed to the army; where he found Minucius so elevated with his new dignity, that, a joint-authority not contenting him, he required by turns to have the command of the army every other day. This Fabius rejected, but was contented that the army should be divided; thinking each general singly would better command his part, than partially command the whole. The first and fourth legions he took for his own division, the second and third he delivered to Minucius; so also of the auxiliary forces each had an equal share.

Minucius, thus exalted, could not contain himself from boasting of his success in humiliating the high and powerful office of the dictatorship. Fabius quietly reminded him that it was, in all wisdom, Hannibal, and not Fabius, whom he had to combat; but if he must needs contend with his colleague, it had best be in diligence and care for the preservation of Rome; that it might not be said, a man so favoured by the people served them worse than he who had been ill-treated and disgraced by them.

The young general, despising these admonitions as the false humility of age, immediately removed with the body of his army, and encamped by himself. Hannibal, who was not ignorant of all these passages, lay watching his advantage from them. It happened that between his army and that of Minucius there was a certain eminence, which seemed a very advantageous and not difficult post to encamp upon; the level field around it appeared, from a distance, to be all smooth and even, though it had many inconsiderable ditches and dips in it, not discernible to the eye. Hannibal, had he pleased, could easily have possessed himself of this ground; but he had reserved it for a bait, or train, in proper season, to draw the Romans to an engagement. Now that Minucius and Fabius were divided, he thought the opportunity fair for his purpose; and, therefore, having in the night-time lodged a convenient number of his men in these ditches and hollow places, early in the morning he sent forth a small detachment, who, in the sight of Minucius, proceeded to possess themselves of the rising ground. According to his expectation, Minucius swallowed the bait, and first sent out his light troops, and after them some horse, to dislodge the enemy; and, at last, when he saw Hannibal in person advancing to the assistance of his men, marched down with his whole army drawn up. He engaged with the troops on the eminence, and sustained their missiles; the combat for some time was equal; but as soon as Hannibal perceived that the whole army was now sufficiently advanced within the toils he had set for them, so that their backs were open to his men whom he had posted in the hollows, he gave the signal; upon which they rushed forth from various quarters, and with loud cries furiously attacked Minucius in the rear. The surprise and the slaughter was great, and struck universal alarm and disorder through the whole army. Minucius himself lost all his confidence; he looked from officer to officer, and found all alike unprepared to face the danger, and yielding to a flight, which, however, could not end in safety. The Numidian horsemen were already in full victory riding about the plain, cutting down the fugitives.

Fabius was not ignorant of this danger of his countrymen; he foresaw what would happen from the rashness of Minucius, and the cunning of Hannibal; and, therefore, kept his men to their arms, in readiness to wait the event; nor would he trust to the reports of others, but he himself, in front of his camp, viewed all that passed. When, therefore, he saw the army of Minucius encompassed by the enemy, and that by their countenance and shifting their ground they appeared more disposed to flight than to resistance, with a great sigh, striking his hand upon his thigh, he said to those about him, "O Hercules! how much sooner than I expected, though later than he seemed to desire, hath Minucius destroyed himself!" He then commanded the ensigns to be led forward, and the army to follow, telling them, "We must make haste to rescue Minucius, who is a valiant man, and a lover of his country; and if he hath been too forward to engage the enemy, at another time we will tell him of it." Thus, at the head of his men, Fabius marched up to the enemy, and first cleared the plain of the Numidians; and next fell upon those who were charging the Romans in the rear, cutting down all that made opposition, and obliging the rest to save themselves by a hasty retreat, lest they should be environed as the Romans had been. Hannibal, seeing so sudden a change of affairs, and Fabius, beyond the force of his age, opening his way through the ranks up the hillside, that he might join Minucius, warily forbore, sounded a retreat, and drew off his men into their camp; while the Romans on their part were no less contented to retire in safety. It is reported that upon this occasion Hannibal said jestingly to his friends: "Did not I tell you, that this cloud which always hovered upon the mountains would, at some time or other, come down with a storm upon us?"

Fabius, after his men had picked up the spoils of the field, retired to his own camp, without saying any harsh or reproachful thing to his colleague; who, also, in his part, gathering his army together, spoke and said to them: "To conduct great matters and never commit a fault is above the force of human nature; but to learn and improve by the faults we have committed, is that which becomes a good and sensible man. Some reasons I may have to accuse fortune, but I have many more to thank her; for in a few hours she hath cured a long mistake, and taught me that I am not the man who should command others, but have need of another to command me; and that we are not to contend for victory over those to whom it is our advantage to yield. Therefore in everything else henceforth the dictator must be your commander; only in showing gratitude towards him I will still be your leader, and always be the first to obey his orders." Having said this, he commanded the Roman eagles to move forward, and all his men to follow him to the camp of Fabius. The soldiers, then, as he entered, stood amazed at the novelty of the sight, and were anxious and doubtful what the meaning might be. When he came near the dictator's tent, Fabius went forth to meet him, on which he at once laid his standards at his feet, calling him with a loud voice his father; while the soldiers with him saluted the soldiers here as their patrons, the term employed by freedmen to those who gave them their liberty. After silence was obtained, Minucius said, "You have this day, O dictator, obtained two victories; one by your valour and conduct over Hannibal, and another by your wisdom and goodness over your colleague; by one victory you preserved, and by the other instructed us; and when we were already suffering one shameful defeat from

Hannibal, by another welcome one from you we were restored to honour and safety. I can address you by no nobler name than that of a kind father, though a father's beneficence falls short of that I have received from you. Front a father I individually received the gift of life; to you I owe its preservation not for myself only, but for all these who are under me." After this, he threw himself into the arms of the dictator; and in the same manner the soldiers of each army embraced one another with gladness and tears of joy.

Not long after, Fabius laid down the dictatorship, and consuls were again created. Those who immediately succeeded observed the same method in managing the war, and avoided all occasions of fighting Hannibal in a pitched battle; they only succoured their allies, and preserved the towns from falling off to the enemy. But afterwards, when Terentius Varro, a man of obscure birth, but very popular and bold, had obtained the consulship, he soon made it appear that by his rashness and ignorance he would stake the whole commonwealth on the hazard. For it was his custom to declaim in all assemblies, that, as long as Rome employed generals like Fabius, there never would be an end of the war; vaunting that whenever he should get sight of the enemy, he would that same day free Italy from the strangers. With these promises he so prevailed, that he raised a greater army than had ever yet been sent out of Rome. There were enlisted eighty-eight thousand fighting men; but what gave confidence to the populace, only terrified the wise and experienced, and none more than Fabius; since if so great a body, and the flower of the Roman youth, should be cut off, they could not see any new resource for the safety of Rome. They addressed themselves, therefore, to the other consul, Aemilius Paulus, a man of great experience in war, but unpopular, and fearful also of the people, who once before upon some impeachment had condemned him; so that he needed encouragement to withstand his colleague's temerity. Fabius told him, if he would profitably serve his country, he must no less oppose Varro's ignorant eagerness than Hannibal's conscious readiness, since both alike conspired to decide the fate of Rome by a battle. "It is more reasonable," he said to him, "that you should believe me than Varro, in matters relating to Hannibal, when I tell you that if for this year you abstain from fighting with him, either his army will perish of itself, or else he will be glad to depart of his own will. This evidently appears, inasmuch as, notwithstanding his victories, none of the countries or towns of Italy come in to him, and his army is not now the third part of what it was at first." To this Paulus is said to have replied, "Did I only consider myself, I should rather choose to be exposed to the weapons of Hannibal than once more to the suffrages of my fellow-citizens, who are urgent for what you disapprove; yet since the cause of Rome is at stake, I will rather seek in my conduct to please and obey Fabius than all the world besides."

These good measures were defeated by the importunity of Varro; whom, when they were both come to the army, nothing would content but a separate command, that each consul should have his day; and when his turn came, he posted his army close to Hannibal, at a village called Cannae, by the river Aufidus. It was no sooner day, but he set up the scarlet coat flying over his tent, which was the signal of battle. This boldness of the consul, and the numerousness of his army, double theirs, startled the Carthaginians; but Hannibal commanded them to their arms, and with a small train rode out to take a full prospect of the enemy as they were now forming in their ranks, from a rising ground not far distant. One of his followers, called Gisco, a Carthaginian of equal rank with himself, told him that the numbers of the enemy were astonishing; to which Hannibal replied with a serious countenance, "There is one thing, Gisco, yet more astonishing, which you take no notice of;" and when Gisco inquired what, answered, that "in all those great numbers before us, there is not one man called Gisco." This unexpected jest of their general made all the company laugh, and as they came down from the hill they told it to those whom they met, which caused a general laughter amongst them all, from which they were hardly able to recover themselves. The army, seeing Hannibal's attendants come back from viewing the enemy in such a laughing condition, concluded that it must be profound contempt of the enemy, that made their general at this moment indulge in such hilarity.

According to his usual manner, Hannibal employed stratagems to advantage himself. In the first place, he so drew up his men that the wind was at their backs, which at that time blew with a perfect storm of violence, and, sweeping over the great plains of sand, carried before it a cloud of dust over the Carthaginian army into the faces of the Romans, which much disturbed them in the fight. In the next place, all his best men he put into his wings; and in the body which was somewhat more advanced than the wings, placed the worst and the weakest of his army. He commanded those in the wings, that, when the enemy had made a thorough charge upon that middle advance body, which he knew would recoil, as not being able to withstand their shock, and when the Romans in their pursuit should be far enough engaged within the two wings, they should, both on the right and the left, charge them in the flank, and endeavour to circumpass them. This appears to have been the chief cause of the Roman loss. Pressing upon Hannibal's front, which gave ground, they reduced the form of his army into a perfect half-moon, and gave ample opportunity to the captains of the chosen troops to charge them right and left on their flanks, and to cut off and destroy all who did not fall back before the Carthaginian wings united in their rear. To this general calamity, it is also said, that a strange mistake among the cavalry much contributed. For the horse of Aemilius receiving a hurt and throwing his master, those about him immediately alighted to aid the consul; and the Roman troops, seeing their commanders thus quitting their horses, took it for a sign that they should all dismount and charge the enemy on foot. At the sight of this, Hannibal was heard to say, "This pleases me better than if they had been delivered to me bound hand and foot." For the particulars of this engagement, we refer our reader to those authors who have written at large upon the subject.

The consul Varro, with a thin company, fled to Venusia; Aemilius Paulus, unable any longer to oppose the flight of his men, or the flight of his men, or the pursuit of the enemy, his body all covered with wounds, and his soul no less wounded with grief, sat himself down upon a stone, expecting the kindness of a despatching blow. His face was so disfigured, and all his person so stained with blood, that his very friends and domestics passing by knew him not. At last Cornelius Lentulus, a young man of patrician race, perceiving who he was, alighted from his horse, and, tendering it to him, desired him to get up and save a life so necessary to the safety of the commonwealth, which, at this time, would dearly want so great a captain. But nothing could prevail upon him to accept of the offer; he obliged young Lentulus, with tears in his eyes, to remount his horse; then standing up, he gave him his hand, and commanded him to tell Fabius Maximus that Aemilius Paulus had followed his directions to his very last, and had not in the least deviated from those measures which were agreed between them; but that it was his hard fate to be overpowered by Varro in the first place, and secondly by Hannibal. Having despatched Lentulus with this commission, he marked where the slaughter was greatest, and there threw himself upon the swords of the enemy. In this battle it is reported that fifty thousand Romans were slain, four thousand prisoners taken in the field, and ten thousand in the camp of both consuls.

The friends of Hannibal earnestly persuaded him to follow up his victory, and pursue the flying Romans into the very gates of Rome, assuring him that in five days' time he might sup in the Capitol; nor is it easy to imagine what consideration hindered him from it. It would seem rather that some supernatural or divine intervention caused the hesitation and timidity which he now displayed, and which made Barcas, a Carthaginian, tell him with indignation, "You know, Hannibal, how to gain a victory, but not how to use it." Yet it produced a marvelous revolution in his affairs; he, who hitherto had not one town, market, or seaport in his possession, who had nothing for the subsistence of his men but what he pillaged from day to day, who had no place of retreat or basis of operation, but was roving, as it were, with a huge troop of banditti, now became master of the best provinces and towns of Italy, and of Capua itself, next to Rome the most flourishing and opulent city, all which came over to him, and submitted to his authority.

It is the saying of Euripides, that "a man is in ill-case when he must try a friend," and so neither, it would seem, is a state in a good one, when it needs an able general. And so it was with the Romans; the counsel and actions of Fabius, which, before the battle, they had branded as cowardice and fear, now, in the other extreme, they accounted to have been more than human wisdom; as though nothing but a divine power of intellect could have seen so far, and foretold contrary to the judgment of all others, a result which, even now it had arrived, was hardly credible. In him, therefore, they placed their whole remaining hopes; his wisdom was the sacred altar and temple to which they fled for refuge, and his counsels, more than anything, preserved them from dispersing and deserting their city, as in the time when the Gauls took possession of Rome. He, whom they esteemed fearful and pusillanimous when they were, as they thought, in a prosperous condition, was now the only man, in this general and unbounded dejection and confusion, who showed no fear, but walked the streets with an assured and serene countenance, addressed his fellow-citizens, checked the women's lamentations, and the public gatherings of those who wanted thus to vent their sorrows. He caused the senate to meet, he heartened up the magistrates, and was himself as the soul and life of every office.

Two Sayings of Augustus Caesar
from *Moralia*

Athenodorus the philosopher, by reason of his old age, begged leave that he might retire from court, which Caesar granted; and as Athenodorus was taking his leave of him, Remember, said he, Caesar, whenever you are angry, to say or do nothing before you have repeated the four-and-twenty letters to yourself. Whereupon Caesar caught him by the hand and said, I have need of your presence still; and he kept him a year longer, saying, The reward of silence is a secure reward. He heard Alexander at the age of thirty two years had subdued the greatest part of the world and was at a loss what he should do with the rest of his time. But he wondered Alexander should not think it a lesser labor to gain a great empire than to set in order what he had gotten.

Elizabeth I
(1533–1603)

ELIZABETH TUDOR REIGNED from 1588 to 1603. Beset on all sides by Catholic adversaries, Protestant England survived through the latter half of the sixteenth century under the leadership of a monarch whom many regarded as a liability because of her sex. With a combination of immense learning, political savvy, and personal courage, the clever Elizabeth survived the reign of her Catholic half-sister Mary and succeeded to a lengthy rule, presiding over a period of great cultural and political achievement. In addition to recognizing and capitalizing on the talent she found among her advisers, the queen preserved power by refusing to marry, playing one suitor against the other, and managing a public relations campaign perhaps unequaled in the annals of history: the figure of Gloriana, the Virgin Queen, combined mythological trappings with very real power. One of Elizabeth's tactics, as the biographer Alison Weir explains in *The Life of Elizabeth I*, was delay. Elizabeth was, Weir writes, an occasionally "infuriating . . . mistress of the subtle art of procrastination . . . marvelously adept at delaying and dissembling." By deferring problems for which she could not find ready solutions, in the end Elizabeth usually crafted a prudent policy: "Whenever she could," Weir asserts, "she would play for time." In the following speeches (delivered in 1563 and 1586, the latter reproduced here in excerpt), Elizabeth responds to Parliament's insistence that she marry and, years later, resists others' calls for the execution of her enemy Mary Stuart, Queen of Scotland, whose death she did eventually and reluctantly order. The queen's brilliance and learning are always on display in her rhetoric. The allusion to Augustus Caesar refers to the anecdote from Plutarch collected in this album.

Replies to Parliamentary Petitions

ANSWER TO THE COMMONS' PETITION THAT SHE MARRY (JANUARY 28, 1563)

Williams, I have heard by you the common request of my Commons, which I may well term (me thinketh) the whole realm because they give, as I have heard, in all these matters of Parliament their common consent to such as be here assembled. The weight and greatness of this matter might cause in me, being a woman wanting both wit and memory, some fear to speak and bashfulness besides, a thing appropriate to my sex. But yet the princely seat and kingly throne wherein God (though unworthy) hath constituted me maketh these two causes to seem little in mine eyes, though grievous perhaps to your ears, and boldeneth me to say somewhat in this matter, which I mean only to touch but not presently to answer. For this so great a demand needeth both great and grave advice.

I read of a philosopher (whose deeds upon this occasion I remember better than his name) who always, when he was required to give answer in any hard question of school points, would rehearse over his alphabet before he would proceed to any further answer therein, not for that he could not presently have answered, but have his wits the riper and better sharpened to answer the matter withal. If he, a common man, but in matters of school took such delay the better to show his eloquent tale, great cause may justly move me in this so great a matter, touching the benefit of this realm and the safety of you all, to defer mine answer till some other time, wherein I assure you the consideration of my own safety (although I thank you for the great care that you seem to have thereof) shall be little in comparison of that great regard that I mean to have of the safety and surety of you all.

And though God of late seemed to touch me rather like one that He chastised than one that He punished, and though death possessed almost every joint of me, so as I wished then that the feeble thread of life, which lasted methought all too long, might by Clotho's hand have quietly been cut off; yet desired I not then life (as I have some witnesses here) so much for mine own safety as for yours. For I knew that in exchanging of this reign I should have enjoyed a better reign, where residence is perpetual.

There needs no boding of my bane. I know now as well as I did before that I am mortal. I know also that I must seek to discharge myself of that great burden that God hath laid upon me, for of them to whom much is committed, much is required. Think not that I, that in other matters have had convenient care of you all, will in this matter touching the safety of myself and you all be careless. For I know that this matter toucheth me much nearer than it doth you all, who, if the worst happen, can lose but your bodies. But if I take not that convenient care that it behooveth me to have therein, I hazard to lose both body and soul.

And though I am determined in this so great and weighty a matter to defer mine answer till some other time because I will not in so deep a matter wade with so shallow a wit, yet have I thought good to use these few words as well to show you that I am neither careless nor unmindful of your safety in this case (as I trust you likewise do not forget that by me you were delivered whilst you were hanging on the bough ready to fall into the mud, yea to be drowned in the dung), neither yet the promise which you have here made concerning your duties and due obedience (wherewith I assure you, I mean to charge you), as further to let you understand that I neither mislike any of your requests herein nor the great care that you seem to have of the surety and safety of your helps in this matter.

Lastly, because I will discharge some restless heads in whose brains the needless hammers beat with vain judgment that I should mislike this their petition, I say that of the matter and sum thereof I like and allow very well. As to the circumstances, if any be, I mean upon further advice further to answer. And so I assure you all that, though after my death you may have many stepdames, yet shall you never have any a more mother than I mean to be unto you all.

FROM QUEEN ELIZABETH'S SECOND REPLY TO THE
PARLIAMENTARY PETITIONS URGING THE EXECUTION OF MARY,
QUEEN OF SCOTS (NOVEMBER 24, 1586)

And now to say more unto you of myself, when I first came to the scepter and crown of this realm I did think more of God who gave it me than of the title. And therefore my first care was to set in order those things which did concern the Church of God and this religion in which I was born, in which I was bred, and in which I trust to die, not being ignorant how dangerous a thing it was to work in a kingdom a sudden alteration of religion, and that it was like to be a foundation and a ground for such great kings and princes as were mine enemies to build and work their devices upon, ill intended against me. But I committed my cause unto Him for whose sake I did it, knowing He could defend me, as I must confess He hath done unto this time, and doubt not but He will do unto the end. After that I did put myself to the school of experience, where I sought to learn what things were most fit for a king to have, and I found them to be four: namely, justice, temper, magnanimity, and judgment. Of the two last, I will say little, because I will not challenge nor arrogate to myself more than I know there is cause. Yet this may I say, and truly: that as Solomon, so I above all things have desired wisdom at the hands of God. And I thank Him He hath given me so much judgment and wit as that I perceive mine own imperfections many ways and mine ignorance in most things. As for magnanimity, I will pass it over. And for the course of justice, I protest that I never knew difference of persons—that I never set one before another but upon just cause, neither have preferred any to office or other place of ruling for the preferrer's sake, but that I knew or was made believe he was worthy and fit for it. Neither did I ever lend mine ear to any person contrary to order of law to pervert my verdict. And for temper, I have had always care to do as Augustus Caesar, who being moved to offense, before he attempted anything was willed to say over the alphabet. And I trust such hath been my actions and the carriage of myself as that my subjects have no cause in that respect to repent themself for their prince. And that I am staunch enough in mine actions I am sure there are sufficient witnesses here present.

Penelope, Two Views
Joseph Harrison and Yannis Ritsos
(b. 1957)   (1909–1990)

BORN IN RICHMOND, Virginia, Joseph Harrison studied at Yale University and Johns Hopkins University. He is the author of the poetry collections

Someone Else's Name and *Identity Theft*, and his work is frequently anthologized. Harrison is the winner of a 2005 Academy Award in Literature from the American Academy of Arts and Letters, and he was a John Simon Guggenheim Fellow in 2009. This poem, "The Cretonnes of Penelope" (1996), invites the reader to imagine the state of mind of one of literature's most celebrated models of patience: Penelope, the wife of Odysseus, the king of Ithaca, who waited twenty years for her husband to return from the Trojan War and from the enforced wanderings that followed the sack of Troy. Besieged by suitors who took advantage of Odysseus's absence to camp out in the hall, devour the food stores, and abuse the servants, Penelope made an agreement that she would marry one of the suitors once she had finished weaving the shroud she was making for her father-in-law. However, at night, in secret, Penelope would take out the stitching of the previous day, and thus she never made sufficient progress to finish the garment.

Yannis Ritsos offers another perspective on Penelope in his poem "Penelope's Despair" (1968), which is typical of his work in its use of mythological subjects. In his youth Ritsos endured his family's financial ruin, the illnesses of his parents and siblings, and his own bout with tuberculosis. As an adult, he suffered persecution and exile as a result of his support of the Greek Communist movement. Ritsos devoted his energies to deeply political writing, and his work was periodically banned in Greece. In addition to his career as a writer, Ritsos worked at various times as a law clerk, a librarian, an actor, and a dancer. During World War II, he was a member of the National Resistance Movement, a guerrilla organization. ("Penelope's Despair" is translated by Edmund Keeley.)

The Cretonnes of Penelope
(1996)

How stupid Penelope's suitors must have been,
Each morning as they elbowed for a place
Near her, and cocked their wits, eyeing each other,
Never to notice yesterday's tapestry
Had disappeared, like every day's before.

They kept maneuvering, and they kept score,
Each trying to get the better of this brother.
So each day's small creation went unseen
Unless some maid in waiting saw that face
Glancing from corners of the tapestry.

She wove a glimpse of him in every scene
She patterned on the vanishing tapestry.
Nor did it have to be obliquely traced
To fool the fools not looking any more,
Who couldn't tell one figure from another.

But if this game was all, she wanted more,
One friend (it wouldn't have to be a lover)
Who saw how the resourceful tapestry's
Long lesson in how never quite to mean
Inscribed the careful lines upon her face.

At night when she ripped up the tapestry
She felt she'd run a marathon in place.
Her sole delight was her most painful chore.
She knew she couldn't make it new again.
But when the sun came up she started over.

JOSEPH HARRISON

Penelope's Despair
(1968)

It wasn't that she didn't recognize him in the light from the hearth:
    it wasn't
the beggar's rags, the disguise—no. The signs were clear:
the scar on his knee, the pluck, the cunning in his eye. Frightened,
her back against the wall, she searched for an excuse,
a little time, so she wouldn't have to answer,
give herself away. Was it for him, then, that she'd used up
    twenty years,
twenty years of waiting and dreaming, for this miserable
blood-soaked, white-bearded man? She collapsed voiceless into a
    chair,
slowly studied the slaughtered suitors on the floor as though seeing
her own desires dead there. And she said "Welcome,"
hearing her voice sound foreign, distant. In the corner, her loom
covered the ceiling with a trellis of shadows; and all the birds she'd
    woven
with bright red thread in green foliage, now,
on this night of the return, suddenly turned ashen and black,
flying low on the flat sky of her final enduring.

YANNIS RITSOS

DISCUSSION QUESTIONS

1. *What are the various strategies of delay on display in these readings?*

2. *How does one tell the difference between justifiable hesitation and unwarranted procrastination?*

3. *How often has your desire to be perceived as a decisive leader hurried you into an impulsive, regrettable choice?*

CULTIVATING TRUST

He's here in double trust:
First, as I am his kinsman and his subject,
Strong both against the deed; then, as his host,
Who should against his murderer shut the door,
Not bear the knife myself.

—Macbeth contemplating the murder of Duncan
WILLIAM SHAKESPEARE,
Macbeth, act 1, scene 7

A shepherd who once pulled a thorn from a lion's paw is saved by the same lion after being unjustly thrown to the beasts at the public games. A lion refuses to make an alliance with an eagle unless the latter levels the playing field by surrendering its feathers. A bull invited to share in a lion's feast runs away when he sees the number of large pots and sharpened cleavers in his host's kitchen. An alliance between geese and swans runs aground when the swift swans abandon their slower partners to approaching hunters. The crows defeat the more powerful owls because their king heeds the right adviser.

Such acts of giving and betraying trust lie at the heart of many of the world's oldest stories. From Aesop to the *Pañcatantra* to the Brothers Grimm, numerous fables, parables, and tales from Eastern and Western traditions alike dwell on the necessity and hazard of surrendering trust.

Trust is often implicit and unconscious. Generally, we award it when we can discern both competence and a commitment ensured by goodwill. As the philosopher Annette Baier writes in "Trust and Antitrust," an essay originally published in 1986 in the journal *Ethics*, "Trust, the phenomenon we are so familiar with that we scarcely notice its presence and its variety, is shown by us and responded to by us not only with intimates but with strangers, and even with declared enemies." Melville's meditation on the monkey-rope in *Moby-Dick*, which can be found in "Studying the System," explores the predicament of being forced to repose an arbitrary trust in strangers.

That kind of trust is increasingly necessary in a global world of ephemeral and virtual connections, but of course trust is essential to the effective functioning of an entire spectrum of relationships, from the personal friendship to the doctor-patient relationship to the international coalition. As Baier suggests, trust simultaneously "leaves others an opportunity to harm one" and "shows one's confidence that they will not take it." It is only "once our vulnerability is brought home to us by actual wounds" that we retrospectively "come to realize what trust involves." Because we must depend on others for survival, however, we cannot afford to withhold trust entirely: it perforce structures friendships, communities, corporations, and countries.

Thus fundamental questions about whether we ought to extend trust—or are worthy of receiving it—animate daily encounters large and small. In contrast to contractual relationships, trust lacks a guarantee. If there is no opportunity for betrayal, philosophers insist, there is no room for trust. The eighteenth-century economist and moral philosopher Adam Smith linked the giving of trust and confidence with transparency in *The Theory of Moral Sentiments*:

> Frankness and openness conciliate confidence. We trust the man who seems willing to trust us. We see clearly, we think, the road by which he means to conduct us, and we abandon ourselves with pleasure to his guidance and direction. Reserve and concealment, on the contrary, call forth diffidence. We are afraid to follow the man who is going we do not know where. The great pleasure of conversation and society, besides, arises from a certain correspondence of sentiments and opinions, from a certain harmony of minds, which like so many musical instruments coincide and keep time with one another. But this most delightful harmony cannot be obtained unless there is a free communication of sentiments and opinions.

Trustworthiness—the meriting of the kind of trust Smith delineates—has long been considered a virtue. Measuring the trustworthiness of others involves a consideration, as Baier and others note, not only of their ability and good faith but also of their judgment and discretion regarding the scope of their trust.

As we imagine the workings of trust within organizations, we can see that autonomy and the production and circulation of knowledge are among the crucial benefits accruing to cultures of trust. The trust of others can foster the kind of self-trust that helps individuals reach their potential and flourish. "Self-trust," Ralph Waldo Emerson wrote, "is the first secret of success." Trust is potentially multidirectional and mutually reinforcing: it can flow up, down, and across organizations. In recent years, however, public trust has been strained by scandal and incompetence. The Pew Research Center reports, for example, that the American people's trust in government has declined from a high of 70 percent in 1958, during the Eisenhower administration, to a near-record low of 19 percent, during the government shutdown of 2013. In a Pew survey about attitudes toward federal agencies, the Centers for Disease Control and Prevention scored a 75 percent favorability rating while Congress ranked lowest at just 23 percent.

In a climate dominated by gross breaches of trust in the public and private sectors, leaders must figure out how to earn trust or repair the damage done by past betrayals—betrayals sometimes inherited from their predecessors. As the fable of the farmer and the snake intimates, however, healing such wounds proves extremely difficult: when a farmer, attempting to kill a snake that has fatally bitten his son, succeeds only in cutting off its tail, he is suddenly overtaken by remorse. Yet when the farmer tries to make peace with the snake, the latter replies that future amity is impossible because each will serve only to remind the other of an irrevocable wound.

The readings in this section explore psychological, social, and moral aspects of trust and confidence, and they emphasize the potential advantages of collaboration. In "The Monkey's Heroic Self-Sacrifice," we find the portrait of a leader who earns the trust of his followers by his willingness to make the ultimate sacrifice. A tale from *The Arabian Nights* offers an example of an enduring personal bond founded on competence and accordingly resistant to suspicion. Marcus Aurelius meditates on the necessity of trusting others: there is no shame, he argues, in interdependence, and there is always the possibility for maximizing the harmony of relationships. In Alvar Núñez Cabeza de Vaca's account of the Narváez Expedition, a stranded group of explorers must trust to the wisdom and ingenuity of the crowd. An interview with the master filmmaker Jean Renoir explores the fundamentally collaborative work of motion pictures, while General Martin Dempsey's elaboration of "mission command," a particular philosophy of military command and control, emphasizes the value of decentralization and collaboration in even the most rigidly hierarchical organizations. Finally, Malcolm Gladwell anatomizes the breach of trust that led to the Enron scandal.

RECOMMENDED READING AND VIEWING

Army of Shadows (1969), directed by Jean-Pierre Melville
Onora O'Neill, *A Question of Trust: The BBC Reith Lectures 2002*
Robert D. Putnam, *Bowling Alone: The Collapse and Revival of American Community* (2000)
Adam Smith, *The Wealth of Nations* (1776)
James Surowiecki, *The Wisdom of Crowds* (2004)

The Monkey's Heroic Self-Sacrifice, from *Jātaka Tales* (fourth century BCE)

THE *JĀTAKA TALES* are an important part of the traditions of Indian folk-lore and Buddhist scripture. Originally composed in Pali, a form of Sanskrit, the tales—more than five hundred in all—were collected over several centuries and are a product of collective authorship and the oral tradition. Each tale recounts a previous incarnation of the Buddha before he achieved enlightenment, and thus they are sometimes referred to as birth stories. Regarded as a book of wisdom, the *Jātaka Tales* appear throughout the popular culture of Southeast Asia in dramatic performances and in illustrations on temple walls. Often recommended as lessons for children, the tales also hold insights into adult behavior and the dynamics of community. They have the specific didactic purpose of explaining *karma*, or the consequences of one's actions for the next life. In the tale that follows, the Buddha, incarnated as a monkey, earns the trust of his troops and the respect of his enemies by sacrificing himself for the communal good. (The following selection is translated by H. T. Francis and E. J. Thomas.)

The Monkey's Heroic Self-Sacrifice

Once upon a time when Brahmadatta was reigning in Benares the Bodhisatta was born as a monkey. When he grew up and attained stature and stoutness, he was strong and vigorous, and lived in the Himalaya with a retinue of eighty thousand monkeys. Near the Ganges bank there was a mango tree (others say it was a banyan), with branches and forks, having a deep shade and thick leaves, like a mountain-top. Its sweet fruits, of divine fragrance and flavour, were as large as water pots: from one branch the fruits fell on the ground, from one into the Ganges water, from two into the main trunk of the tree. The Bodhisatta, while eating the fruit with a troop of monkeys, thought, "Someday danger will come upon us owing to the fruit of this tree falling on the water"; and so, not to leave one fruit on the branch which grew over the water, he made them eat or throw down the flowers at their season from the time they were of the size of a chick-pea. But notwithstanding, one ripe fruit, unseen by the eighty thousand monkeys, hidden by an ant's nest, fell into the river, and stuck in the net above the king of Benares, who was bathing for amusement with a net above him and another below. When the king had amused himself all day and was going away in the evening, the fishermen, who were drawing the net, saw the fruit and not knowing what it was, shewed it to the king. The king asked, "What is this fruit?" "We do not know, sire." "Who will know?" "The foresters, sire." He had the foresters called, and learning from them that it was a mango, he cut it with a knife, and first making the foresters eat of it, he ate of it himself and had some of it given to his seraglio and his ministers. The flavour of the ripe mango remained pervading the king's whole body. Possessed by desire of the flavour, he asked the foresters where that tree stood, and hearing that it was on a river bank in the Himalaya quarter, he had many rafts joined together and sailed upstream by the route shewn by the foresters. The exact account of days is not given. In due course they came to the place, and the foresters said to the king, "Sire, there is the tree." The king stopped the rafts and went on foot with a great retinue, and having a bed prepared at the foot of the tree, he lay down after eating the mango fruit and enjoying the various excellent flavours. At every side they set a guard and made a fire. When the men had fallen asleep, the Bodhisatta came at midnight with his retinue. Eighty thousand monkeys moving from branch to branch ate the mangoes. The king, waking and seeing the herd of monkeys, roused his men and calling his archers said, "Surround these monkeys that eat the mangoes so that they may not escape, and shoot them: to-morrow we will eat mangoes with monkey's flesh." The archers obeyed, saying, "Very well," and surrounding the tree stood with arrows ready. The monkey seeing them and fearing death, as they could not escape, came to the Bodhisatta and said, "Sire the archers stand round the tree, saying, 'We will shoot those vagrant monkeys': what are we to do?" and so stood shivering. The Bodhisatta said, "Do not fear, I will give you life"; and so comforting the herd of monkeys, he ascended a branch that rose up straight, went along another branch that stretched towards the Ganges, and springing from the end of it, he passed a hundred bow-lengths and lighted on a bush on the bank. Coming down, he marked the distance, saying, "That will be the distance I have come": and cutting a bamboo shoot at the root and stripping it, he said, "So much will be fastened to the tree, and so much will stay in the air," and so reckoned the two lengths, forgetting the part fastened on his own waist. Taking the shoot he fastened one end of it to the tree on the Ganges bank and the other to his own waist, and then cleared the space of a hundred bow-lengths with a speed of a cloud torn by the wind. From not reckoning the part fastened to his waist, he failed to reach the tree: so seizing a branch firmly with both hands he gave signal to the troop of monkeys, "Go quickly with good luck, treading on my back along the bamboo shoot." The eighty thousand monkeys escaped thus, after saluting the Bodhisatta and getting his leave. Devadatta was then a monkey and among that herd: he said, "This is a chance for me to see the last of my enemy," so climbing up a branch he made a spring and fell on the Bodhisatta's back. The Bodhisatta's heart broke and great pain came on him.

Devadatta having caused that maddening pain went away: and the Bodhi-satta was alone. The king being awake saw all that was done by the monkeys and the Bodhisatta: and he lay down thinking, "This animal, not reckon-ing his own life, has caused the safety of his troop." When day broke, being pleased with the Bodhisatta, he thought, "It is not right to destroy this king of the monkeys: I will bring him down by some means and take care of him": so turning the raft down the Ganges and building a platform there, he made the Bodhisatta come down gently, and had him clothed with a yellow robe on his back and washed in Ganges water, made him drink sugared water, and had his body cleansed and anointed with oil refined a thousand times; then he put an oiled skin on a bed and making him lie there, he set himself on a low seat, and spoke the first stanza:

You made yourself a bridge for them to pass in safety through:
What are you then to them, monkey, and what are they to you?

Hearing him, the Bodhisatta instructing the king spoke the other stanzas:

Victorious king, I guard the herd, I am their lord and chief,
When they were filled with fear of thee and stricken sore with grief.

I leapt a hundred times the length of bow outstretched that lies,
When I had bound a bamboo-shoot firmly around my thighs:

I reached the tree like thunder-cloud sped by the tempest's blast;
I lost my strength, but reached a bough: with hands I held it fast.

And as I hung extended there held fast by shoot and bough,
My monkeys passed across my back and are in safety now.

Therefore I fear no pain of death, bonds do not give me pain,
The happiness of those was won o'er whom I used to reign.

A parable for thee, O king, if thou the truth would'st read:
The happiness of kingdom and of army and of steed
And city must be dear to thee, if thou would'st rule indeed.

The Bodhisatta, thus instructing and teaching the king, died. The king, calling his ministers, gave orders that the monkey-king should have obse-quies like a king, and he sent to the seraglio, saying, "Come to the ceme-tery, as retinue for the monkey-king, with red garments, and dishevelled hair, and torches in your hands." The ministers made a funeral pile with a hundred waggon loads of timber. Having prepared the Bodhisatta's obse-quies in a royal manner, they took his skull, and came to the king. The king caused a shrine to be built at the Bodhisatta's burial-place, torches to be burnt there and offerings of incense and flowers to be made; he had the skull inlaid with gold, and put in front raised on a spear-point: honouring it with incense and flowers, he put it at the king's gate when he came to Benares, and having the whole city decked out he paid honour to it for seven days. Then taking it as a relic and raising a shrine, he honoured it with incense and garlands all his life; and established in the Bodhisatta's teaching he did alms and other good deeds, and ruling his kingdom righteously became destined for heaven.

The Tale of King Yunan and the Sage Duban, from *The Arabian Nights* (ca. 850)

THE EARLIEST SURVIVING fragment of *The Arabian Nights* dates from the ninth century, but its ultimate origins are unknown, as is its original language, which may have been Arabic, Persian, or Sanskrit. At the beginning of the eighteenth century, during the advent of European Orientalism, Antoine Galland published a French translation based on a fourteenth-century Syrian manuscript and supplemented by oral retellings. The first modern Arabic and English editions both date from the nineteenth century. As Daniel Heller-Roazen observes, the "simple and almost colloquial idiom" of the text marks it as highly unusual in the tradition of "Arabic belles lettres," which is distinguished by "eloquent diction and syntax." The individual tales of *The Arabian Nights* are contained within a frame story: Shahrayer, king of India and Indochina, having been tricked by an unfaithful wife, kills her and concludes, "Women are not to be trusted." The king thereafter weds a new woman every day and executes her after only one night. In a heroic attempt to save her people, Shahrazad weds the king and proceeds to outfox him through the art of storytelling. She is aided in this deadly game by her sister, who attends her in the royal bedroom and asks each night for "one of her lovely little stories" before she must bid her sister farewell forever. Shahrazad obliges by embarking on a riveting story that always remains unfinished at daybreak and must therefore resume the next night. Thus Shahrazad serially postpones her death. A superstition attaches to *The Arabian Nights*: to finish reading the tales is to die along with Shahrazad. The story reproduced here begins on the eleventh night. It is told in the voice of a fisherman, whose own story begins on the eighth night. The fisherman has imprisoned a demon in a jar, and the duplicitous demon's pleas to be released remind his captor of the story of King Yunan and the Sage Duban. It is a tale of court intrigue, evil counsel, and fortunate fidelity. (The following selection is translated by Husain Haddawy.)

The Tale of King Yunan and the Sage Duban

Demon, there was once a king called Yunan, who reigned in one of the cities of Persia, in the province of Zuman. This king was afflicted with leprosy, which had defied the physicians and the sages, who, for all the medicines they gave him to drink and all the ointments they applied, were unable to cure him. One day there came to the city of King Yunan a sage called Duban. This sage had read all sorts of books, Greek, Persian, Turkish, Arabic, Byzantine, Syriac, and Hebrew, had studied the sciences, and had learned their groundwork, as well as their principles and basic benefits. Thus he was versed in all the sciences, from philosophy to the lore of plants and herbs, the harmful as well as the beneficial. A few days after he arrived in the city of King Yunan, the sage heard about the king and his leprosy and the fact that the physicians and the sages were unable to cure him. On the following day, when God's morning dawned and His sun rose, the sage Duban put on his best clothes, went to King Yunan and, introducing himself, said, "Your Majesty, I have heard of that which has afflicted your body and heard that many physicians have treated you without finding a way to cure you. Your Majesty, I can treat you without giving you any medicine to drink or ointment to apply." When the king heard this, he said, "If you succeed, I will bestow on you riches that would be enough for you and your grandchildren. I will bestow favors on you, and I will make you my companion and friend." The king bestowed robes of honor on the sage, treated him kindly, and then asked him, "Can you really cure me from my leprosy without any medicine to drink or ointment to apply?" The sage replied, "Yes, I will cure you externally." The king was astonished, and he began to feel respect as well as great affection for the sage. He said, "Now, sage, do what you have promised." The sage replied, "I hear and obey. I will do it tomorrow morning, the Almighty God willing." Then the sage went to the city, rented a house, and there he distilled and extracted medicines and drugs. Then with his great knowledge and skill, he fashioned a mallet with a curved end, hollowed the mallet, as well as the handle, and filled the handle with his medicines and drugs. He likewise made a ball. When he had perfected and prepared everything, he went on the following day to King Yunan and kissed the ground before him.

But morning overtook Shahrazad, and she lapsed into silence. Then her sister Dinarzad said, "What a lovely story!" Shahrazad replied, "You have heard nothing yet. Tomorrow night I shall tell you something stranger and more amazing if the king spares me and lets me live!"

THE TWELFTH NIGHT

The following night Dinarzad said to her sister Shahrazad, "Please, sister, finish the rest of the story of the fisherman and the demon." Shahrazad replied, "With the greatest pleasure":

I heard, O King, that the fisherman said to the demon:

The sage Duban came to King Yunan and asked him to ride to the playground to play with the ball and mallet. The king rode out, attended by his chamberlains, princes, viziers, and lords and eminent men of the realm. When the king was seated, the sage Duban entered, offered him the mallet, and said, "O happy King, take this mallet, hold it in your hand, and as you race on the playground, hold the grip tightly in your fist, and hit the ball. Race until you perspire, and the medicine will ooze from the grip into your perspiring hand, spread to your wrist, and circulate through your entire body. After you perspire and the medicine spreads in your body, return to your royal palace, take a bath, and go to sleep. You will wake up cured, and that is all there is to it." King Yunan took the mallet from the sage Duban and mounted his horse. The attendants threw the ball before the king, who, holding the grip tightly in his fist, followed it and struggled excitedly to catch up with it and hit it. He kept galloping after the ball and hitting it until his palm and the rest of his body began to perspire, and the medicine began to ooze from the handle and flow through his entire body. When the sage Duban was certain that the medicine had oozed and spread through the king's body, he advised him to return to his palace and go immediately to the bath. The king went to the bath and washed himself thoroughly. Then he put on his clothes, left the bath, and returned to his palace.

As for the sage Duban, he spent the night at home, and early in the morning, he went to the palace and asked for permission to see the king. When he was allowed in, he entered and kissed the ground before the king; then, pointing toward him with his hand, he began to recite the following verses:

> The virtues you fostered are great;
> For who but you could sire them?
> Yours is the face whose radiant light
> Effaces the night dark and grim.
> Forever beams your radiant face;
> That of the world is still in gloom.
> You rained on us with ample grace,
> As the clouds rain on thirsty hills,
> Expending your munificence,
> Attaining your magnificence.

When the sage Duban finished reciting these verses, the king stood up and embraced him. Then he seated the sage beside him, and with attentiveness and smiles, engaged him in conversation. Then the king bestowed on the sage robes of honor, gave him gifts and endowments, and granted his wishes. For when the king had looked at himself the morning after the bath, he found that his body was clear of leprosy, as clear and pure as silver. He therefore felt exceedingly happy and in a very generous mood. Thus when he went in the morning to the reception hall and sat on his throne, attended by the Mamluks and chamberlains, in the company of the viziers and the lords of the realm, and the sage Duban presented himself, as we have mentioned, the king stood up, embraced him, and seated him beside him. He treated him attentively and drank and ate with him.

But morning overtook Shahrazad, and she lapsed into silence. Then her sister Dinarzad said, "Sister, what a lovely story!" Shahrazad replied, "The rest of the story is stranger and more amazing. If the king spares me and I am alive tomorrow night, I shall tell you something even more entertaining."

THE THIRTEENTH NIGHT

The following night Dinarzad said to her sister Shahrazad, "Sister, if you are not sleepy, tell us one of your lovely little tales to while away the night." Shahrazad replied, "With the greatest pleasure":

I heard, O happy King who is praiseworthy by the Grace of God, that King Yunan bestowed favors on the sage, gave him robes of honor, and granted his wishes. At the end of the day he gave the sage a thousand dinars and sent him home. The king, who was amazed at the skill of the sage Duban, said to himself, "This man has treated me externally, without giving me any draught to drink or ointment to apply. His is indeed a great wisdom for which he deserves to be honored and rewarded. He shall become my companion, confidant, and close friend." Then the king spent the night, happy at his recovery from his illness, at his good health, and at the soundness of his body. When morning came and it was light, the king went to the royal reception hall and sat on the throne, attended by his chief officers, while the princes, viziers, and lords of the realm sat to his right and left. Then the king called for the sage, and when the sage entered and kissed the ground before him, the king stood up to salute him, seated him beside him, and invited him to eat with him. The king treated him intimately, showed him favors, and bestowed on him robes of honor and many other gifts. Then he spent the whole day conversing with him, and at the end of the day he ordered that he be given a thousand dinars.

The sage went home and spent the night with his wife, feeling happy and thankful to God the Arbiter.

In the morning, the king went to the royal reception hall, and the princes and viziers came to stand in attendance. It happened that King Yunan had a vizier who was sinister, greedy, envious, and fretful, and when he saw that the sage had found favor with the king, who bestowed on him much money and many robes of honor, he feared that the king would dismiss him and appoint the sage in his place; therefore, he envied the sage and harbored ill will against him, for "nobody is free from envy." The envious vizier approached the king and, kissing the ground before him, said, "O excellent King and glorious Lord, it was by your kindness and with your blessing that I rose to prominence; therefore, if I fail to advise you on a grave matter, I am not my father's son. If the great King and noble Lord commands, I shall disclose the matter to him." The king was upset and asked, "Damn you, what advice have you got?" The vizier replied, "Your Majesty, 'He who considers not the end, fortune is not his friend.' I have seen your Majesty make a mistake, for you have bestowed favors on your enemy who has come to destroy your power and steal your wealth. Indeed, you have pampered him and shown him many favors, but I fear that he will do you harm." The king asked, "Whom do you accuse, whom do you have in mind, and at whom do you point the finger?" The vizier replied, "If you are asleep, wake up, for I point the finger at the sage Duban, who has come from Byzantium." The king replied, "Damn you, is he my enemy? To me he is the most faithful, the dearest, and the most favored of people, for this sage has treated me simply by making me hold something in my hand and has cured me from the disease that had defied the physicians and the sages and rendered them helpless. In all the world, east and west, near and far, there is no one like him, yet you accuse him of such a thing. From this day onward, I will give him every month a thousand dinars, in addition to his rations and regular salary. Even if I were to share my wealth and my kingdom with him, it would be less than he deserves. I think that you have said what you said because you envy him. This is very much like the situation in the story told by the vizier of King Sindbad when the king wanted to kill his own son."

But morning overtook Shahrazad, and she lapsed into silence. Then her sister Dinarzad said, "Sister, what a lovely story!" Shahrazad replied, "What is this compared with what I shall tell you tomorrow night! It will be stranger and more amazing."

THE FOURTEENTH NIGHT

The following night, when the king got into bed and Shahrazad got in with him, her sister Dinarzad said, "Please, sister, if you are not sleepy, tell us one of your lovely little tales to while away the night." Shahrazad replied, "Very well":

I heard, O happy King, that King Yunan's vizier asked, "King of the age, I beg your pardon, but what did King Sindbad's vizier tell the king when he wished to kill his own son?" King Yunan said to the vizier. "When King Sindbad, provoked by an envious man, wanted to kill his own son, his vizier said to him, 'Don't do what you will regret afterward.' "

Marcus Aurelius
(121–180)

THE ROMAN EMPEROR Marcus Aurelius is known chiefly for his *Meditations,* a key articulation of Stoic philosophy. In the original Greek, these observations bore the title "To Himself," which as the classicist Bernard Knox observes, properly describes this "book of self-exhortation; when Marcus writes 'you' he means himself. It is a remarkable document. The ruler of a world empire who had to deal not only with hard-fought campaigns on the threatened Balkan frontier but also with the ravages of a devastating plague here jots down his inmost thoughts as he steels himself for the daily struggle with the problems of a world in crisis." The selections below emphasize the virtues of truth, patience, and cooperation in everyday relations. (The following selection is translated by Jeremy Collier.)

Meditations

2.1

Remember to put yourself in mind every morning, that before night it will be your luck to meet with some busy-body, with some ungrateful, abusive fellow, with some knavish, envious, or unsociable churl or other. Now all this perverseness in them proceeds from their ignorance of good and evil; and since it has fallen to my share to understand the natural beauty of a good action, and the deformity of an ill one—since I am satisfied the person disobliging is of kin to me, and though we are not just of the same flesh and blood, yet our minds are nearly related, being both extracted from the Deity—I am likewise convinced that no man can do me a real injury, because no man can force me to misbehave myself, nor can I find it in my heart to hate or to be angry with one of my own nature and family. For we are all made for mutual assistance, as the feet, the hands, and the eyelids, as the rows of the upper and under teeth, from whence it follows that clashing and opposition is perfectly unnatural. Now such an unfriendly disposition is implied in resentment and aversion.

6.41

If you suppose anything which lies out of your command to be good or evil, your missing the one or falling into the other will unavoidably make you a malcontent against the gods, and cause you to hate those people whom you either know or suspect to be instrumental in your misfortune. To be plain, our being concerned for these objects often makes us very unreasonable and unjust. But if we confine the notion of good and evil to things in our power, then all the motives to complaint will drop off; then we shall neither remonstrate against Heaven, nor quarrel with any mortal living.

6.42

All people work in some measure towards the ends of Providence, some with knowledge and design, though others are not sensible of it. And thus, as I remember, Heraclitus observes, that those who are asleep may be said to help the world forward. In short, the grand design is carried on by different hands and different means. For even he that complaining makes head against his fate, and strives to pull the administration in pieces, even such a testy mortal as this contributes his share abundantly, for the universe had need even of such an one. Consider, then, how you are ranging yourself, and what workers you are joining. For He that governs the world will certainly make you good for something, and prove serviceable to his scheme, one way or other . . .

7.5

Is my intellect sufficient for this business or not? If it is, I will make use of my talent as given me by heaven for that purpose. If not, I will either let it alone, and resign it to a better capacity, unless that be contrary to my duty, or else I will do what I can. I will give my advice, and put the executing part into an abler hand, and thus the right moment and the general interest may be secured. For whatsoever I act, either by myself, or in conjunction with another, I am always to aim at the advantage of the community.

7.7

Never be ashamed of assistance. Like a soldier at the storming of a town, your business is to maintain your post, and execute your orders. Now suppose you happen to be lame at an assault, and cannot mount the breach upon your own feet, will you not suffer your comrade to help you?

7.22

It is the privilege of human nature to love those that disoblige us. To practise this, you must consider that the offending party is of kin to you, that ignorance is the cause of the misbehavior, and the fault is involuntary, that you will both of you quickly be in your graves; but especially consider that you have received no harm by the injury, for your mind is never the worse for it.

Alvar Núñez Cabeza de Vaca
(ca. 1490–ca. 1560)

ALVAR NÚÑEZ CABEZA de Vaca grew up during a period known as the Catholic *Reconquista* of Spain from the Islamic Moors who had long dominated the Iberian peninsula. King Ferdinand and Queen Isabella presided over a consolidation of power and an era of expansion—the age of Christopher Columbus and Amerigo Vespucci—but also the expulsion of the Jews and the launching of the infamous Inquisition. As a young man during this era, Cabeza de Vaca, serving in the army of the Holy Roman Emperor and as a steward for the dukes of Medina Sidonia, a position that likely involved him in military expeditions at home and abroad. In 1527, Cabeza de Vaca joined the expedition of Pánfilo de Narváez, the newly appointed Spanish governor of Florida. Things began to go awry when the fleet of five ships reached Cuba: losing two ships and many men in a hurricane, the survivors reached Florida to confront hostile inhabitants, unforgiving terrain, and dwindling supplies. Abandoning the remaining ships and marching inland, the expedition suffered further casualties until only Cabeza de Vaca and three others remained of an original complement of approximately six hundred men. This excerpt picks up the story on the inland march, when the members of the complement realize they will need to build more ships to escape the gulf. Cabeza de Vaca returned to Spain in 1537, after having trekked all the way across the continent to California and from there to Mexico City. (The following selection is translated by David Frye.)

How To Build a Ship,
from *Chronicle of the Narváez Expedition* (1542)

The following day we left Aute and walked all day long until we reached the place where I had been. It was an extremely difficult march, for neither did we have enough horses to carry the sick, nor did we know what relief we could give them, for they labored under illness every day, so that it was a matter of great pity and anguish to see the difficulties and hardships into which we were plunged. Once we arrived there, we saw how little relief we had for going farther: for we did not know where to go, nor could our men have gone forward even if we did, because most of them were sick—so sick that few would have been of any use whatever. Here I leave off telling this story at greater length, because each person can imagine what might happen in a land so strange and so bad, and so utterly lacking in any means of relief, whether for staying or for getting away.

But as the surest relief is always God our Lord, and in Him we never lost faith, something occurred that made things more intolerable than all this, for among the horsemen the majority began leaving in secret, hoping to find relief by themselves while forsaking the Governor and the sick, who were helpless and disabled. But since there were many hidalgos and men of good lineage among them, they did not allow this to happen without alerting the Governor and Your Majesty's officials. And as we decried their intentions, and we put before them the time at which they were forsaking their captain and the sick and disabled, and above all separating themselves from Your Majesty's service, they agreed that they would stay, and that what happened to one would happen to all, and none would forsake another.

The Governor, having seen this, summoned everyone jointly and severally, asking their opinions about this dismal land, that we might get away and seek some relief, for there was no relief in that land, as a third of the men were gravely ill and getting worse by the hour, so that we all felt sure we would end up like them, with death as our only prospect, which in such a place seemed even more serious to us. After looking at these and many other impediments and attempting to find relief in many ways, we settled on one means that was very difficult to put into practice, which was to build ships on which we could leave.

It seemed impossible to everyone, because we did not know how to build them, nor were there any tools, or iron, or a forge, or oakum, or pitch, or cordage, or lastly, any one of the many things that were needed; nor anyone who knew anything about it, to put some expertise into the task; and above all, there was nothing to eat while they were being built or anyone who could work in the fashion that we have described. Considering all this, we agreed to think it over at greater length, and our talk ceased for that day, and everyone went off, commending the matter to God our Lord, that He might lead it on the path that would best serve Him.

The next day God willed it that one of the men began saying that he would make some wooden tubes, and some deerskins could be used to make bellows. And since we were at a point when anything with some superficial appearance of relief seemed good to us, we told him to get to work. And we agreed to take our stirrups and spurs and crossbows, and anything else we had of iron, and use them to make nails and saws and axes and other tools, so great was our need for them. And to relieve our need for some provisions during the time this work was being done, we settled on making four raids into Aute, with all the horses and men that could go, and on killing a horse every day[1] and distributing it among those who were working on building the barks and those who were sick. The raids were carried out with such men and horses as were able, and from those raids they brought back as much as four hundred *hanegas*[2] of maize, though not without fights and skirmishes with the Indians. We had many palmettos gathered so that we could use their fiber and stems, twisting and preparing them to use in place of oakum for the barks[3] that they began to build, under the only carpenter we had in the company.

And we put so much diligence into it that, after beginning them on August 4, by September 20 there were five barks finished, each measuring twenty-two cubits,[4] caulked with palmetto oakum, and we tarred them with a sort of pitch that a Greek named Don Teodoro made from some pines. And using the same palmetto cloth, and the tails and manes of the horses, we made rope and cordage, and from our shirts we made sails. And from the junipers that grew there we made the oars that we thought necessary. And such was the land to which our sins had brought us that it was only with very great trouble that we could find stones to use for ballast and anchors in the barks; we had not seen any there at all. We also flayed the horses' legs whole and tanned the skin to make bags for carrying water.

During this time some were going around gathering shellfish in the nooks and inlets of the sea, at which the Indians fell upon them twice, killing ten of our men in plain view of the camp, without our being able to come to their aid; we found them shot through and through with arrows, for although several had good arms and armor, it was not enough to keep that from happening, since the Indians shot their arrows with all the skill and force that I mentioned above. And our pilots declared on oath that, from the bay we had named Bay of the Cross to this place, we had traveled two hundred and eighty leagues, more or less. In all this land we saw no mountains nor heard news of any at all. And before we embarked, not counting our men that the Indi-

---

1 *Cada tercer día*; a Spanish idiom meaning every other day, not "every third day" as the phrase is commonly understood in modern English. Comparing the number of days that the group remained near Aute (forty-eight) with the number of horses they had to start with (thirty-six, by the translator's count), it seems that they must have killed a horse *at least* every other day, not every third day.
2 One *hanega* or *fanega*, the most common Spanish grain measure, was roughly one hundred pounds of grain; 1.6 bushels; or (originally) one sack, or one fourth of a *carga* (load), the amount of grain a mule could carry.
3 *Barcas*; small, flat-bottomed boats.
4 *Codos*; one cubit is the length from the elbow to the tip of the outstretched hand; sometimes standardized as twenty-four *dedos* (sixteen or seventeen English inches), but Spain also had a "royal cubit" of twenty-seven *dedos* (eighteen or nineteen inches) and a nautical cubit of thirty-three *dedos* (a little under two feet). Depending on the *codo* used, the barks were thirty to forty-two feet long.

ans killed, more than forty men died from illness and hunger. By September 22, we had eaten up all the horses, and only one remained. And on that day we embarked in the following order: in the Governor's bark there went forty-nine men; in another one that he gave to the purser and the commissary went as many more; he gave the third one to Captain Alonso del Castillo and Andrés Dorantes, with forty-eight men; he gave another to two captains named Téllez and Peñalosa, with forty-seven men; he gave the other one to the inspector and to me, with forty-nine men. And after the supplies and clothing were put on board, the barks rose no more than one span above the waterline. Besides that, we were so crowded that we could not turn around. And the power of necessity is so great that it made us risk traveling like this and venturing out into such a troublesome sea, and without anyone among us having any knowledge of the art of seafaring.

George Stevens Jr.
(b. 1932)

THE OCCASION FOR this 1970 interview with the film director Jean Renoir (1894–1979) was a seminar at the American Film Institute (AFI). Under the auspices of the Harold Lloyd Master Seminars, AFI founder George Stevens Jr. has conducted interviews with filmmakers spanning Hollywood's Golden Age to the present day. Interviewees have ranged from Alfred Hitchcock, the so-called "master of suspense," to Meryl Streep, arguably the foremost film actor of our time. Collected in two volumes thus far, Stevens's conversations with directors, producers, screenwriters, and actors illuminate the collaborative alchemy of moviemaking. The interviewees offer insights into creative as well as financial aspects of making films (and the inevitable interrelation of the two), the often rigidly hierarchical organization of film sets, the sometimes difficult management of outsize egos and clashing personalities. Encompassing such masterpieces as the World War I drama *Grand Illusion* (1937) and the social satire *The Rules of the Game* (1939), Jean Renoir's career spanned several decades, including sojourns in Hollywood and India as well as his native France. Renoir's visual acuity was certainly sharpened by his father, the painter Auguste Renoir, and as the film historian David Thomson suggests, the director's "greatness lies in his repeated desire to take risks, to make new sorts of film, to be experimental." Renoir's style—his moving camera, deep-focus photography, and languorous takes—is of a piece with his generous spirit of trust and collaboration. His faith extends to actors as well as to the audience itself.

Interview with Jean Renoir
from *Conversations with the Great Moviemakers:*
Hollywood's Golden Age (2006)

April 14, 1970

The first question is simple: How do you start a film?

Well, I start with an idea when I can. That's not so easy. You know, I'm probably not the right person to ask such a question, because in the field of motion pictures I'm a director who has spent his life suggesting stories that nobody wanted. It's still going on. But I'm used to it and I'm not complaining, because the ideas which were forced on me were often better than my own ideas. A little mixture of what was brought to me and what I had in my imagination has provided a happy medium, which perhaps helped to make the picture a little more alive. Of course, even if you have to work on a story you don't like very much, you can always do a personal picture, one which will be the expression of your personality. The ideas inside you don't give up, and in the final result it's your picture and not someone else's. This is why I can't give you any recipe about how to start a picture.

Myself—excuse me if I talk about practical recollections—I was very much helped along in my career. I made about forty films, and an examination of my body of work shows that I owe my films to the most unexpected producers of the world. You know, I am not a man of general ideas, I am more an artist of the details. I pride myself on seeing that the details become the thing as a whole. I might start with this cup of coffee. Is this coffee? It's probably very good. Allow me to try. [*He drinks the coffee.*] No, your coffee is not excellent. But from such a cup of coffee you can start a story, a wonderful story.

Can you describe how this idea affects your general approach to the process of film-making?

For me, everything is one operation. It's like literature—you start a sentence and you don't finish it because you can't find the right word. Perhaps with film you find the right word in the cutting room. A picture is a whole. You cannot say, "This is the beginning, this is the middle and this is the end." No. I believe a picture is a state of mind. A picture, often when it is good, is the result of some inner belief which is so strong that you have to show what you want, in spite of a stupid story or difficulties about the commercial side of the film. Yes, it's a state of mind.

In my imagination I divide directors in two big categories: those who start from the camera, and those who don't. Some put the camera in a certain spot which is carefully chosen. It gives a beautiful background, and with props it gives them a certain idea which can symbolically help the telling of the story. Then they take the actors and put them in front of the lens. This means the role of the director is based on the service of the camera. Wonderful directors work that way, for example, René Clair. I will always remember one day I visited René on the set in the silent days. He was shooting a scene with an actor—not a great actor, but a good actor. In the script—I wanted to see a script, and they showed me the page that he was shooting—the jacket of the actor had to caress lightly an object on the table. René Clair shot the scene something like fifty times, and finally he got it and he was delighted. But I am the opposite: I like to start with the actors. I like to put them in a certain mood.

We directors are, simply, midwives. The actor has something inside himself, but very often he doesn't realize what he has in mind and his heart. I always try to start the work from the actor. You rehearse, and when you are happy about the rehearsal, you decide that you can give the rein to the cameraman. You ask the cameraman and soundman to come with you, and you decide what will be the angle of the shot. But this angle depends on the acting and not on the imagination of the director. That's more my method. Now, to talk about this in our profession is childish, because there is no method. You must change your method according to each different shot. The basis of my work is the actors, who make me adopt a different way of cutting the pictures. I always try not to cut the film during the shooting. This is why I use tracking shots and pans so often. It is for no other reason than I hate to cut the acting of someone during his inspiration.

A great director, perhaps the top director of his day, Jean-Luc Godard, is exactly the opposite of me. He starts with the camera. His frames are really a direct expression of his personality but without the in-between worries brought by actors. The actor has a headache and indigestion the day before. His wife left him, but he loves her. When you want to work with the actor, you have to absorb all those things. Now, myself—since I am not Goliath but perhaps a little David—I need all those things. I need the actor who comes to me and says, "Oh, I am so unhappy. I believe my mistress is cheating on me, I cannot stand it." Well, that's my job: to open the door to such confidence and to use that for the film. We directors are midwives using this method. Now, I say "method," but I don't believe in method. I believe that every director must have his *own* method. Does that answer your question?

It was a good start.

May I add a little comment to this question of the importance or the unimportance given to the actors? This is exactly the quarrel going on in every profession, between abstract act and nonabstract act. The director who is searching for an abstract emotion doesn't need forms or faces of actors. He can talk directly from his own chest to the heart of a spectator. Myself, I am more in favor of the other method, which we could compare to what is the figurative art in painting. That doesn't mean you cannot interweave all sorts of methods. I want to have an idea of the scene thanks to the rehearsal with the actors. When I have a clear idea of the scene, all of a sudden I realize everything I was doing was wrong, and I start again. Finally, when the scene shows something that seems to me sufficient, I bring the camera.

I'll tell you a little story. It was during the shooting of my picture *Grande illusion*. Perhaps some of you know the picture? You remember at the end Jean Gabin and Marcel Dalio are walking in the snow, and Dalio is wounded. He'd had a little accident and was limping. He couldn't go any further. Well, I had written two pages of beautiful literature to explain the situation. Gabin was, you know, like a poet, explaining about what's good, what's bad in nature. It was fantastic and I was proud of myself. But I was a little worried because the two actors didn't want to start the scene. They were finding reasons to do something else. Finally Gabin said to me, "Jean, we'd better tell you: your two pages of beautiful poetry are just trash." And it was true. Finally I had an idea, or perhaps it was Gabin. He was humming a tune I already used in the beginning of the picture "The Little Sailor." I took those very innocent words, and they became the center of the scene, which is, I think, very good.

But without the reluctance of Dalio, without my belief in the help the actors can give, I would have nothing. Nothing. Oh, I would have a perfectly drawn and conceived scene, but dull. Now, that explains, perhaps better than what I said before, my point of view with actors. In other words, you must not ask an actor to do what he cannot do. You know, there is an old slogan, very popular in our occidental civilization: you must look to an end higher than normal, and that way you will achieve something. Your aim must be very, very high. Myself, I am absolutely convinced that it is mere stupidity. The aim must be easy to reach, and by reaching it, you achieve more.

The trouble with us human beings is that we are often very stupid. Things are in front of us but we don't see them. An actress rehearses with a beautiful face full of emotion, but you don't see it. You're thinking of your camera angle. I'm not for that. I'm delighted to leave the occasion to chance and not rely on planning. I'm against planning. I'm in favor of the art and literature of the Middle Ages, up to the Renaissance. To me, the Renaissance is a barbarian order which replaced a great civilization. In the twelfth century—as it is in India and many parts of Asia today—you have a frame for everything, within which you are free to do what you want. I believe in this conception of art. The Renaissance brought about the cult of the individual, but I believe that the individual shows himself in an interesting way when he doesn't know that he shows himself. It must be in spite of himself. When you are in the studio and you stand beside the camera and yell, "I am going to express myself!" then you will express nothing. But if you are submerged in admiration for the gesture of an actor or, if it is a documentary picture, the beauty of the piece of nature you are confronted by, then you have a chance to reveal yourself behind those images more than if you choose to show yourself directly. Of course, this is my opinion, and I don't pretend that it is right. As I told you, every one of us must build up our own grammar, our own method, like the recipe in a cookbook.

I'd be interested in knowing when and how you rehearse with your actors. Since you clearly invite so much collaboration from them, do you rehearse just before you shoot or do you begin earlier?

Usually when you work on a picture, the schedule is too short. The money isn't there and you have to hurry. But if I had the time, I would work first in a rehearsal room with no props. This is a very old idea, the name of which is to work *à l'italien*, to rehearse the Italian way. This was very much in favor in the time of the commedia dell'arte in Italy. They brought this method to Paris and London. I tell you what it is—the most important characters and the directors sit down around a table and read the text, without any expression. They read the lines as they would the telephone directory, blah, blah, blah. Monotonous and flat. Let's say we have a little scene which represents a mother confronted suddenly with the death of her son. You are working on this scene and you ask the actress who plays the mother to help you find an expression. The actress might find four or five expressions she and other actors have used a million times before. But the text grows inside her, amongst the actors reciting it flat. The actor must have the feeling that she wrote the part, and you see a little sparkle. Oh, you cannot miss it—it is a baby. The midwife did her job! When you have this sparkle, you start rehearsals. Now, this method is never used because it takes too much time, and time is money in the picture business.

Any great theatrical or film movement must be paced for the slow digestion of situations. That was Stanislavsky's idea. If you want a completely sincere expression of an individual, then that's another question. The individuals who we want to give birth to are to be found partly in the work of the author, the surroundings, the direction and the actor. It's a mixture. Out of this mixture the problem is to have one human being who is real and alive.

Is this not also true when you are creating the story, this slow evolution from an idea?

Exactly, the same thing. After all, in any domain the problems are the same. Slow digestion.

You once said that the writer Marcel Pagnol had told you that ideas came on like an electric lightbulb. Is this true in your case?

Well, I would like this to be my case, as I told you. There are many lightbulbs in filmmaking and in book writing. For instance, one little lightbulb which is quite precious is the voice. One picture that I worked on *à l'italien* was *Boudu*. We didn't know exactly what to do with the Michel Simon character. He seems to be very simple, but he's not. One day Simon got up and started to walk and talk with the voice of Boudu. All of a sudden he said, "I am Boudu. Follow me."

Do you work with the crew—costumes, art direction, cinematographer—in the same way as you do with the actors?

You know, a picture is a little world. Something very important in life is balance. You must balance all the elements. What is very dangerous in pictures is that an actor becomes a star because of repetition of voice and the same gestures. The public becomes used to it, and though the poor soul makes millions, it's nothing to do with talent. To me it's something quite tragic to see a human being always repeating the same gestures that are not even real, not even the expression of reality.

From the start of your career you developed your ideas on camera movement. More and more you began to use tracking and staging in depth.

Well, the reason for my camera work was not to cut in the middle of the acting but to have the camera hanging on the actor, following the story. The camera is just a recording device and not a god. The camera is especially dangerous in this city, in Hollywood. It became so important that in the mind of many people it was the *only* thing that was important. Sometimes I will be on the set working with an actor and everything is wrong. The actor is not satisfied, I am not satisfied. The producer arrives and says, "Please, you are fussy, both of you, looking for the impossible. The shot is sufficient like that, and we must not waste time with such nonsensical tasks." But if the cameraman was looking to remove a little shadow at the tip of the nose of the star, he could take three days if he wanted.

When you shoot tracking shots, do you also attempt to shoot other material which will allow you to shorten the shot in editing if you need to? Or perhaps to change the rhythm?

No. It should be done, but I don't do it, and I'll tell you why. I believe it's a good thing to be committed—to play the game. You have the scene, you believe it's good, so you shoot it. When I can, I shoot my scenes only once. I like to be committed, to be a slave to my decision. If I know that I won't have those shots to cut, my main shot will be better. If I know I have those other shots, I say, "Oh, that's not very good, but we have the others." I don't like that attitude.

I do not have very good eyesight—I mean spiritual eyesight. I don't understand the problems of a shot before it is shot. When we are ready to shoot, when the lights are burning and the cameras are ready, all of a sudden I might think of something which was obvious that I hadn't seen before. The girl should not be wearing a hat, or instead of playing the scene standing and nervous, she should sit and stay still. This is why I cannot decide things in advance, whether the scene will be made up of many shots or with only one main shot. To be very frank, if we're talking of aesthetics, I don't like too many close shots. When I started in this business my first preoccupation was to find lenses which would allow the background to be clear, not out of focus.

I also hate to show people who seem to be just out of an icebox, sterilized. I like a little dirt from the outside to give some life to my shots. That's something else in preparation. I believe the ideal work is to prepare the shot, to be ready to shoot it, to be perfectly satisfied, then to understand the element you are missing, and to add this element. It is exactly like with old buildings. You buy an old farm in the Midwest. You want to fix it for living in. Probably you will get something much more alive than if you were to build a new house.

Story is often considered unnecessary in film today. I wonder if you could talk about that.

Well, as I said, it is the eternal quarrel between abstract art and figurative art. If the author feels he can express himself without the help of a subject, to build a bridge between his own inside and the spectator—good. My own preoccupation is slightly different. You know what my preoccupation is in pictures? It is that I would like the picture to give the feeling to the audience that it is unfinished. I believe that the work of art where the spectator does not collaborate is not a work of art. I like the people who look at the picture, perhaps, to build a different story on the side. Without the collaboration of the public we have nothing except dull art. The artists and the public must be in communion. We must arrive at such and such a point where the public is the maker and the artist becomes the spectator. But you'll notice I'm just dreaming aloud now.

Your films seem to proceed unsteadily, meandering without structure and with a life of their own. Yet when one sees a Renoir film, one says, "My God, look what he did." By the end, it appears to be a structured unit, a clean and clear statement about life.

Well, thank you very much. I believe that even in a nonreligious or nonpolitical story, even in a comedy, which is absolutely flat, or in a Western, if the author is possessed by certain convictions, those convictions will give a kind of meat to the work.

Do you feel it necessary in order for your films to work to get audience sympathy or involvement with the characters?

No, nothing is *necessary*. What you talk about can help, yes. And why not accept any help? Luckily we have it. I believe this question of communication depends on the film, on the author, the people. There is no rule. You talk about the sympathy of the public. Of course we all want it. You are in a preview, your picture is a little dull. The public doesn't follow you, and all of a sudden on the screen some actor cracks a joke which you wrote unwillingly. But you had to have something, you had to fill a space. You hear a little laughter among the audience and you feel like a million dollars. You would like to see who laughed and kiss him. Yes, we depend on the public. What is wrong is to believe the public is inevitably a crowd of ten million people. For some artists, the public is ten people, or one person. The size of the crowd isn't important. What is important is that you are in communication with somebody, with a spirit which is not your spirit but which can influence you for a short time. Now, I repeat—and excuse me if I repeat myself so often—those are my ideas. That doesn't mean they are good. Tomorrow I will perhaps have different ideas. I am not steady.

I would like to know what you look for in writing and directing a scene. You said you looked to see if it did something, but you didn't really explain what this thing is.

I will try to answer your question, which is a very difficult and interesting one. Excuse me if I go back to *Grande illusion*. When writing the screenplay I discovered that the film had another meaning. I discovered that the story was perhaps a little approach to a big problem, that of surrounding and of nations, which is the racist problem. It is also the problem of how people from different religions meet, how they cannot understand each other for some reason. To me the only important thing in the world is how to meet others, and *Grande illusion* was for me the chance to tell everything I had in my heart about such things. But when I wrote the screenplay I didn't know this; it was just an escape story. In certain scenes between Pierre Fresnay and

Erich von Stroheim we talk only of questions of surroundings and adaptations, questions of how to get along together. Though I don't ever forget that it was an escape story, the escape part was insignificant. It is by working on the picture that I was pulling out of myself certain ideas more important than I thought in the beginning.

When you have an additional idea—racism, how people meet, so forth—do you then work out how to write a scene based around these things?

Well, let's start with *Grande illusion* again. For instance, I have a scene between Dalio and Gabin. They are preparing a rope to escape. They talk, frankly, about racism. It might appear that it doesn't belong in the picture, but it does. It works. I had entire scenes which were shot only for this expression of origin, nation, race—for example, a scene where half a dozen French prisoners are preparing a show by sewing costumes. They are having a very serious conversation that has nothing to do with the scenery or costumes. It is a question of where you are going, where you come from. I could put fifty situations like this in my pictures.

In introducing ideas such as these into what is essentially an escape film, isn't it difficult to do so without stopping the flow of the picture or losing the interest of the audience?

It is terribly difficult. The problem is the change of style, though in *Grande illusion* it was easy. The setup was ideal for these kinds of discussions, and it was a very easy picture to shoot and write. *The Rules of the Game* was more difficult.

How did Grande illusion *come about?*

I was shooting *Toni* in the south of France. It was a film I made almost entirely on location. Nearby was a big military airfield. Everyone there could see I was shooting a picture—there were reflectors, cameras, trucks. The planes were above my head the whole day long, and I couldn't record any sound. I decided to pay a visit to the commanding officer of this base, and was confronted by a man with more medals than you could wear. He was a good friend of mine. In fact, during the First War he saved my life several times. He was a fighter in a squadron of fighting planes and I was a photographer. That's the way I became interested in movies—by taking photographs from above. Planes carrying cameras were not very fast and we thought that every time we were confronted by a German fighter, that was the end of us. Several times this man arrived with his little squad and *tak-tak-tak*—the Germans were happy to run away. At the time he was just a noncom, but he became a general. General Pensal was his name. He was shot down by the Germans seven times. He escaped seven times and he went back to his squadron seven times.

We were happy to meet up with each other again, and in the evening took the habit of having dinner together. He told me the story of how he escaped from German jails, and I thought it would make a good suspense story. I asked his permission to use a few of the stories he had told me, and then wrote a screenplay, convinced I had written a very banal escape story. I thought it was very commercial and that I would be able to find financing very easily. That's what I thought. For three years, my dear friends, I visited every office on the Champs-Elysées, in Rome and everywhere else. Everywhere I had the same answer: "No girls in your picture. We're not interested." Finally I met a man who was a—well, I don't want to insult people, but I don't know of any other word but *crook*. He was a brilliant, successful crook. That was his profession. He told me, "Jean, I believe in your picture." I said, "You are not in the film business, but people in the business don't believe in it." "That doesn't matter. How much do you want?" He gave me two million francs, and I shot the picture, and it was successful.

Could you elaborate on the problem of keeping the audience's attention alive, and yet introducing these ideas?

Well, I wrote a first draft of *The Rules of the Game* in which the individual was a little gray and out of focus. I had given too much importance to things like his rich life, his mistress, the château where he's living. I was hoping I could do something light, elegant and amusing with such a background. This happens to me all the time—for instance with *La Chienne*. The head of the studio, a very nice boy who wouldn't kill an elephant, gave me the money to shoot the film with the idea that it was going to be a hilarious farce. Of course I didn't contradict him, being sure that if he knew the truth, I would have to stop shooting. Once everything was shot, he realized I was shooting a somber drama and he told me, "At least I want to try to save the situation. You won't do the cutting." I said, "Okay, I won't do it." We started to fight, with our fists. I was stronger than he was. But the next day when I went to the studio, the policeman wouldn't let me in and said very politely, "Monsieur Renoir, it is forbidden." I was saved by a wonderful man who was making money for the studio—Mr. Monteaux, the president of the most important shoe company in France—and I was restored to my cutting room with only a few shots missing.

What is the origin of Octave, the character you yourself play in The Rules of the Game?

I thought certain situations needed a commentator and that I should add to my story a kind of master of ceremonies, like in a review on the stage. I found out that this master of ceremonies would say everything that I myself, the author, had in mind. I said, "Well, why not say it myself?" He is practically a tramp—the tramp in the tuxedo.

We'd like to know how you work with the art director on your films, how much control you exercise over the development of the sets?

May I say that I like to have control over every part of the picture—the art directors, the cameramen, the actors. I like to know intimately what they do, and to suggest and help them decide when there is a choice. But I don't believe in specialists. It can happen that an actor will tell me, "I don't like this part of the set." We have a discussion about it and change it if necessary. In other words, I don't like to make the important decisions alone. I like to feel that around my direction many of the problems are going on, and that I know them and am participating as much as the technicians or the actors are participating in my own worries.

Do you have any rules about casting?

That's where I like to have my friends help me, because I am very bad at casting. Sometimes to be bad helps me, in the way that I am attracted by a certain innocence. I am afraid of clichés and tricks. I am afraid of repeating situations we have already seen on the screen. People with not too much skill sometimes help me to keep a kind of—I use a very ambitious word, excuse me—to keep a kind of innocence.

What happens when you have a difficult actor and you have problems getting him to do what you want him to do? And what happens if you watch the footage and realize he is too hammy and overacting?

I never found an actor in complete opposition with me. Never. I have worked with people with the reputation to be impossible, and I've found them delightful. I believe that everything must come from inside the individual. Again, I use the comparison of the midwife. I don't like to tell the actor to scratch his nose. He must find for himself all those things. An actor must have the feeling that he wrote the part himself. He must reject what doesn't seem to come from him. Of course that brings discussions, but out of those discussions sometimes you find a very big improvement in the scene. I don't believe that an actor can overact. It seems to be a paradox. To me an actor is on the right track when his creation is a real human being. If he is on the wrong track, even if he hardly moves his lips, he is bad. In other words, it's not a question of being loud or exaggerating.

If you are involved in the picture, you cannot go back. What is shot is shot—you can never replace it. What you have to do is try to find a way to match your ideas and the exaggerations of this actor. If you have enough dialogue to allow an actor to play with his words to his discretion, unless he is a perfect idiot—and unless you are a perfect idiot, which may also happen—you always find a way, a kind of happy medium.

If you have a particular tone you're searching for and you want the actors to say a line in a particular way, how do you go about obtaining that?

By starting with no expression and repeating and repeating and repeating. You know, the results are fantastic. Sometimes I did it with actors who were unprepared for that, and they were amazed. It's beautiful the way it works.

Do you ever find yourself reading the line for them?

I hate this kind of work. Too many directors work like this. They tell the actor, "Sit down, my dear friends, and look at me. I am going to act a scene, and you are going to repeat what I just did." He acts a scene and he acts it badly, because if he is director instead of an actor, it's probably because he's a bad actor.

I have heard that sometimes you will give analogies to people to give them an idea of how to say a line.

No, I am very careful about that. I don't want an actor to imitate me. There is no reason why all of a sudden an actor should be Jean Renoir on the screen. After all, the purpose of art and moviemaking is to find yourself. If you are looking for a character who doesn't exist in life, an ideal character you build in your imagination, well, that's very wrong. If you can prove to the actor that it's false, the actor will be the first to look for something else, and perhaps find it.

I wonder how you feel about the French New Wave directors.

Well, it's difficult for me to judge them because, as we say in French, we are in the same boat. Judging them would be a bit like judging myself. I believe that in this world we proceed by little groups, and you must belong to a little group. That doesn't mean you lose your individuality—not at all. Belonging to a little group helps you to find it. I feel in the bottom of my heart that I am very close to this generation which came after me but who are very much looking for the same thing. We have different ideas on some points. For instance, Godard typically starts from the camera. I end with the camera. Truffaut is in between.

Truffaut seems the closest to you in style among the new directors.

Yes, definitely.

You speak of trying to avoid the staginess of the theater when making films, but in Golden Coach *there is a fascination with the stage and performing. I wonder if you could talk about the way theater relates to the way you view film.*

Well, I cannot answer your question directly because I shot *Golden Coach* probably ten years ago and I have forgotten what my state of mind was in this period. But I can relate your question to one that I am asking myself constantly. Perhaps it is the most important preoccupation regarding filmmaking I've had in my life. It is the question of the outside reality and the inside reality. For instance, you have an actor who is going to play the part of a sailor. Being very conscientious, he buys the real costume of a sailor. He will wear a cap which went through tempests and hurricanes of the sea. He will, perhaps, live in a boat not only to get used to the language of sailors but also to have the bronze skin of a man living constantly outside. He will act the part—and he will look exactly like a ham because he is not a good actor. That's one thing. Now, you suggest to Charlie Chaplin he should play the part of the sailor, and even with a cane and a derby and a tramp's suit he will be a sailor.

You have a reputation of having a hand of iron in a velvet glove. Is it true that on the set you never criticize or never allow yourself to become angry?

I am trying. I don't always succeed, but I try.

I read an article that said on every take—whether or not it seemed successful— you tell the actors that it was in fact good, but that you would rather try another interpretation. Is this a technique that you have used?

Often, yes. I hate to discourage people. The truth is, if you discourage an actor you may never find him again. You'll hide his personality behind a kind of mask of fear. An actor is an animal, extremely fragile. You get a little expression, it is not exactly what you wanted, but it's alive. It's something human. Don't kill it by pushing your own ideas into his imagination. No. Try softly and slowly to help him find what you believe is the truth, because in the picture the truth is the truth of the author. You said a hand of iron in a velvet glove? I am afraid very often I have a velvet hand in a glove of iron.

You spoke of getting the public to collaborate in your work. In writing the script, do you structure the story so that it encourages collaboration from the audience?

I believe it is good to work keeping in mind all aspects of the making of the picture. And since we cannot forget there is a public, and that we work for it, it's better to keep alive the idea of the public at all times during the organization of the picture.

In thinking of how the audience might respond, would you ever change a script in order to engage the audience in a certain way?

Well, of course you have to think of the public. Very often, to think of the public from the beginning leads you to using mechanical devices. My nephew is a cameraman and made a film about Picasso. In the film, Picasso says something repeatedly which to me is a big secret we should all share and use if we can. "Fill it." Those were his words. No empty space. You have a frame, the frame is a scene in a movie or is the frame of a painting. I agree with Picasso. You must fill this frame.

Martin E. Dempsey
(b. 1952)

GENERAL MARTIN E. Dempsey became the eighteenth chairman of the Joint Chiefs of Staff in 2011. As the highest-ranking military officer in the United States, the chairman serves as the principal military adviser to the president, the secretary of defense, and the National Security Council. Before assuming this post, Dempsey served as the army chief of staff. In addition to his considerable operational experience in Iraq, Dempsey was the acting commander of Central Command and led the army's Training and Doctrine Command, which is responsible for shaping the force by recruiting, training, and developing personnel as well as by building and integrating formations, capabilities, and matériel. Ever alert to changing landscapes and the necessary evolution of doctrine, Dempsey came to champion the doctrine of "mission command," a command-and-control (C2) principle according a great deal of trust to even junior members of the force and relying on their ability to interpret the commander's intent. Although the idea of mission command is especially popular among younger veterans of the twenty-first-century American wars in Iraq and Afghanistan, it can cause discomfort among those traditionalists who prefer a more hands-on style of leadership in a world where technology makes possible an unprecedented level of real-time direction. The concept in fact owes to a much older German tradition called *Auftragstaktik*, which was adopted by the Prussian army after Napoleon's victories at Jena and Auerstadt. It was described by retired Major General Werner Widder of the German army in a 2002 address to officers at the U.S. Command and General Staff College in Fort Leavenworth, Kansas, as a "command and control principle . . . based on mutual trust." Requiring "each soldier's unwavering commitment to perform his duty," it prizes "initiative and independent thought and action." Considered by its early Prussian opponents, the *Normaltaktikers*, as "a threat to military discipline, and thus by extension, to all things military," *Auftragstaktik* was predicated on the concept of the soldier as a free person who preserves in uniform both elemental human dignity and the basic liberties and responsibilities of a citizen. Dempsey outlines the tenets of the U.S. Armed Forces' version of mission command in this 2012 white paper.

Mission Command
(2012)

Mission command is the conduct of military operations through decentralized execution based upon mission-type orders. Successful mission command demands that subordinate leaders at all echelons exercise disciplined initiative and act aggressively and independently to accomplish the mission.
Joint Publication 3–0 "Joint Operations" 11 Aug 2011

INTRODUCTION

Our need to pursue, instill, and foster mission command is critical to our future success in defending the nation in an increasingly complex and uncertain operating environment. This paper offers ideas to inform the development of Joint Force 2020.

The basic principles of mission command—commander's intent, mission type orders and decentralized execution are not new concepts. They are a part of current joint and service doctrine.[1] But this is not enough; we will ask more of our leaders in the future. Conduct of mission command requires adaptable leaders at every echelon.

---

1 Variance in service doctrine (i.e.: "command by negation" or "centralized planning, decentralized execution") are simply phrasing choices that express the same idea.

1. THE FUTURE SECURITY ENVIRONMENT AND THE FUTURE FORCE

Joint Force 2020 will operate in a dynamic security environment that is different from today. The pace of change and the speed of operations will continue to accelerate. An increasingly competitive and interconnected world raises the potential for conflicts and crisis to escalate in multiple domains. Concurrently, the expansion and diversification of asymmetric threats will significantly challenge our ability to effectively execute military operations. The relevance of space and cyberspace to national security will grow exponentially in magnitude of importance. Our reliance on technological superiority is a potential vulnerability that our adversaries will seek to exploit, often in covert or indirect ways. We, as well as our Allies, confront this new security and operating environment in an era marked by fiscal constraint. This fiscal reality informs our difficult strategic choices and heightens our risks.

Joint Force 2020 must protect US national security interests against threats that routinely span regional boundaries and can rapidly assume global dimensions. The global application of integrated, discriminate military power in all domains calls for us to organize and conduct networked operations, where any force element can support or be supported by any other. US forces operating globally as a network will require unity of effort and prompt execution. Just as today, these attributes must accrue without over-centralization, as decentralized approaches will provide us competitive adaptability and tempo advantages.

Joint Force 2020's design is shaped by a decade of learned lessons in war. Our fight against a decentralized enemy has driven home the necessity to decentralize our capabilities and distribute our operations. Smaller units enabled to conduct decentralized operations at the tactical level with operational/ strategic implications will be increasingly the norm. Synchronization of time and tempo with expanded maneuver space (space and cyberspace) brings added complexity to synergizing and integrating actions and effects in both space and time. The reliance and synergy of disparate elements to achieve operational objectives is the genesis for a deeply interdependent Joint Force 2020; this drives the need to create jointness deeper and sooner in the force. Smaller, lighter forces operating in an environment of increased uncertainty, complexity and competitiveness will require freedom of action to develop the situation and rapidly exploit opportunities. Decentralization will occur beyond current comfort levels and habits of practice. Resident in the central figure of the commander, the ethos of mission command is a critical enabler of success.

2. MISSION COMMAND IS COMMANDER CENTRIC

The commander is the central figure in mission command. To the commander comes the mission for the unit; in the commander resides the authority and responsibility to act and to lead so that the mission may be accomplished. In mission command, the commander must blend the art of command and the science of control, as he, supported by the staff, integrates all joint warfighting functions.

In mission command, the commander must understand the problem, envision the end state, and visualize the nature and design of the operation. The commander must also describe time, space, resources and purpose, direct the joint warfighting functions and constantly assess the process. Critically he must understand the intent of the mission given him. In turn, he must clearly translate his intent to his subordinates. The missions given subordinates must be within their capabilities; the commander must understand what his subordinates can do, and trust—but not blindly—them to do it. In its highest state, shared context and understanding is implicit and intuitive between hierarchal and lateral echelons of command, enabling decentralized and distributed formations to perform as if they were centrally coordinated. When achieved, these practices result in decentralized formal decision-making throughout the force, leading implicitly to the opportunity to gain advantageous operational tempo over adversaries.

Tempo is our ability to operate at the speed of the problem. This is more than merely "being fast"—the tactical patience to allow a window of opportunity to open also contributes to tempo. To gain and maintain advantageous tempo, our leaders must be able to see, understand and rapidly exploit opportunities in both time and space, guided by their understanding of intent, their mission, environment and the capability of their force. Decisions are far less likely to be routinely relayed up the chain for institutional contemplation and wisdom. To do so is to surrender the initiative to the enemy. Joint Force 2020, with minimum communications, must act promptly and coherently in step to create the decisive amount of cumulative combat power at the right place and time.

Mental agility and superior speed in competitive cycles of decision-making are therefore attributes desired in the commanders of each echelon of the Joint Force 2020. Air Force officer and military strategist John Boyd famously captured the idea that decision-making occurs in recurring cycles of observe-orient-decide-act—the "OODA loop."[2] The key to victory in Colonel Boyd's thinking was the ability to create situations wherein one can make appropriate decisions more quickly than one's opponent. The practice of mission command in the Joint Force 2020 is in this spirit.

Mission command is not a mechanical process that the commander follows blindly. Instead, it is a continual cognitive effort to understand, to adapt, and to direct effectively the achievement of intent. Balancing the art

2 For a doctrinal discussion of the OODA loop, see MCDP 6 "Command and Control," Oct. 1996, pp. 63–65.

of command with the science of control, the commander positions himself as needed to best accomplish the mission. Mission command challenges commanders to cultivate a bias for action in their subordinates, develop mutual trust and understanding, and exercise moral nerve and restraint. Applicable across the range of military operations, it is executed by adaptive leaders and organizations capable of exercising initiative enabled by shared experiences, doctrine, education, and training.

3. KEY ATTRIBUTES FOR MISSION COMMAND

Several key attributes enable the practical application of mission command. These are understanding, intent, and trust. We will discuss each briefly in turn.

Understanding equips decision-makers at all levels with the insight and foresight required to make effective decisions, to manage the associated risks, and to consider second and subsequent order effects. This is the "inner eye"—the cognitive ability "at a glance" to see and understand a situation and thereby enable independent decision and correct action.[3] What changes for Joint Force 2020 is the increasing need for the commander to frequently frame and reframe[4] an environment of ill-structured problems to gain the context of operations by continuously challenging assumptions both before and during execution.

Importantly, in Joint Force 2020, leaders at every level must contribute to the common operating assessment of context, "co-creating it" as operations progress and situations change. Created knowledge at the point of action is critical to operational and tactical agility. Understanding in mission command must flow from both bottom-up and top-down. Shared context is a critical enabler of the next of the attributes relevant to mission command, that of intent.

Joint Doctrine defines "commander's intent" in part as "a clear and concise expression of the purpose of the operation and the desired military end state."[5] It then links intent explicitly to mission command. In mission command, *intent* fuses understanding, assigned mission, and direction to subordinates.

Joint Force 2020 will, by necessity, act by the guiding star of intent. Mission-type orders will be the norm. Commanders will be required to understand intent to the level of effect; that is, strategic to tactical and across

---

3 Carl von Clausewitz, *On War*, ed. and trans. Michael Howard and Peter Paret (Princeton, NJ: Princeton University Press, 1989). "When all is said and done, it really is the commander's *coup d'œil*, his ability to see things simply, to identify the whole business of war completely with himself, that is the essence of good generalship. Only if the mind works in this comprehensive fashion can it achieve the freedom it needs to dominate events and not be dominated by them" (p. 578).
4 Recent efforts regarding "Design" are aimed at providing the commander, supported by his staff, the cognitive tools to perform this vital task.
5 JP 3-0 "Joint Operations," 11 Aug. 2011. See Chapter II "the Art of Joint Command," pp. II-2 and II-8.

domains. They will be required to clearly translate their intent (and that of higher) to their subordinates and trust them to perform with responsible initiative in complex, fast-changing, chaotic circumstances.

Just as understanding informs commander's intent, *trust* informs the execution of that intent. Mission command for Joint Force 2020 requires trust at every echelon of the force. Building trust with subordinates and partners may be the most important action a commander will perform. Given our projected need for superior speed in competitive cycles of decision-making, it is clear that in Joint Force 2020, operations will move at the speed of trust.[6]

Coupled with shared understanding and intent, trust is the moral sinew that binds the distributed Joint Force 2020 together, enabling the many to act as one in the cross-domain application of the appropriate amount of cumulative combat power at the right place and time. Unless these attributes are made central to the basic character of the force, Joint Force 2020 will struggle to reach optimal performance levels. The task of imbuing mission command into training and leader development is an immediate challenge. The journey to 2020 is already underway.

4. INSTILLING MISSION COMMAND

Mission command must be institutionalized and operationalized into all aspects of the joint force—our doctrine, our education, our training, and our manpower and personnel processes. It must pervade the force and drive leader development, organizational design and inform material acquisitions. Service cultures are important in these efforts; the Joint Force derives strength from our distinct service cultures.

Joint and service doctrine, education and training are keys to achieving the habit of mission command; our doctrine must describe it, our schools must teach it, and we must train individually and collectively to it. The key attributes described in the previous section are the center of gravity in instilling mission command; if we do not successfully instill these traits in our people we will never instill them in our organization and practice.

Mission command is fundamentally a learned behavior to be imprinted into the DNA of the profession of arms. The education of our officer corps—joint and service—must begin at the start of service to instill the cognitive capability to understand, to receive and express intent, to take decisive initiative within intent, and to trust. We must place students into situations of uncertainty and

6 Dr. Stephen Covey, *The Speed of Trust* (New York, NY: Free Press, 2006). Dr. Covey has expressed the idea that trust is "the hidden variable" in the formula for organizational success. His phrase "the speed of trust" captures the idea that trust affects two outcomes in any organization: speed and cost. High trust engenders high speed and low cost ("the trust dividend"); the converse has the opposite outcome ("the trust tax").

complexity where creativity, adaptability, critical thinking and independent, rapid decision-making are essential elements. The moral courage or nerve to make decisions in these types of situations is to be actively rewarded.

Education in the key attributes of mission command must be progressively more challenging as officers progress in rank and experience. Education must develop the "inner eye" mentioned previously. Officers must be taught how to receive and give mission-type orders, and, critically, how to clearly express intent. Trust too is learned behavior to be developed during education; this goes to the need to balance the art of command with the science of control. As responsible exercise of mission command does not entail blind trust, education must give officers the ability to recognize the capability for mission command in subordinates and the skills to know when and how to adjust their level of supervision.

As education develops individual leaders, so does training prepare units for operational duty. Training for mission command is about building teams, both within the unit by the commander and externally to the unit by the commander with supported, supporting, and higher echelons of command. These teams must have implicit communication between them, guided and enabled by common understanding of intent, and accelerated by deep trust.

Like education, the truism "to train as you will fight" remains applicable to training. Training must replicate the distributed, chaotic, and uncertain nature of the expected operational environment. It must force commanders, supported by their staffs, to receive and clearly express intent. Training scenarios must require the commander to extend trust as they employ their force and constantly assess. Training for mission command requires it to be commander centric in ways that it is not often now; this will require an investment in those who can focus on the commander's development.

Training should place commanders in situations where fleeting opportunities present themselves, and those that see and act appropriately to those opportunities should be rewarded. Training must force commanders to become skilled at rapid decision making. Training is the optimum venue for a commander to learn how practically to delegate authority and accountability to subordinate and supporting commanders; this serves to build trust, teamwork, ease implicit and intuitive communications, and is vital for the development of the commanders of those echelons. Subordinate echelons must be allowed to own their own "white space" and thereby develop unit cohesion and exercise judgment and creativity in training.

Training is also the preferred venue to expose the commander to the things that get in the way of mission command. The first of these is the volume and the availability of information. Modern C2 systems transport and deliver information in quantities that can easily overwhelm the commander. Technology cannot replace the human ability to create and make intuitive judgment. Training should help the commander learn how to avoid information overload and "paralysis by analysis." Likewise, training should rehearse the commander in making rapid decisions without perfect or complete information. Training for mission command focuses the commander on gaining a comfort with uncertainty and chaos, and guided by intent, having the moral courage to decide quickly and act decisively.

Our training should also teach commanders what *not* to do. In a network-enabled force, the commander can easily penetrate to the lowest level of the command and take over the fight. This is dangerous for a number of reasons. No C2 technology has ever successfully eliminated the fog of war, but it can create the illusion of perfect clarity from a distance. This can lead to micromanagement, a debilitating inhibitor of trust in the lower echelons of the force. Training must reinforce in commanders that they demonstrate trust by exercising restraint in their close supervision of subordinates.

5. THE WAY AHEAD

The Services and the Joint Force share the responsibility in ensuring that mission command is a common attribute of our Profession of Arms. Our collective efforts must institutionalize mission command by adopting and formalizing the character traits that enable a bias for action and responsible initiative at all levels of the force. Our leader development efforts must create the climate for greater trust, and challenge leaders to the point of failure as a way to evaluate character, fortitude, and resiliency of personality in conditions of adversity. Critically, we must collectively promote a culture that values calculated risk as the means to generate opportunity.

Operational commanders have a vital role in effectively integrating mission command into operational art, planning, and execution. The operational commander as the practitioner of mission command is a powerful example. Beginning with a leadership climate that empowers subordinate leaders and lowers the decision-making threshold, commanders must fashion cohesive and reciprocal relationships of trust and mutual understanding among subordinates. They must ensure that continuous assessment flows from the forward edge of operations, before being distributed vertically and horizontally. Critically, commanders must set the example in regards to clear and timely vision, intent and guidance, enabling subordinates wide latitude in accomplishing mission objectives within the intent of seniors. How commanders shape behavior through reaction to failure is critical; mistakes of subordinates that nonetheless demonstrate responsible initiative guided by intent should be seen as building blocks in the development of mission command.

We will not embrace mission command from a simple combination of policy, doctrine, education, and training. These guide and shape, but they do not create belief and capability. *Understand* my *intent*: I challenge every leader in the Joint Force to be a living example of mission command. *You have my trust.*

Malcolm Gladwell
(b. 1963)

A FORMER SCIENCE and medicine writer for the *Washington Post*, a staff writer for *The New Yorker* since 1996, and the author of several bestselling books including *The Tipping Point*, *Blink*, and *Outliers*, Malcolm Gladwell translates sociological and psychological phenomena for a general audience. Reviewer Janet Maslin writes in the *New York Times* review of Gladwell's *David and Goliath: Underdogs, Misfits, and the Art of Battling Giants*, "The world becomes less complicated with a Malcolm Gladwell book in hand." Gladwell has been both praised and faulted for his ability to make complicated theories readily accessible, but he has an uncanny ability to identify trends of great interest and moment and to spark productive disagreement with his thought-provoking essays and books. In this 2007 piece, an examination of the Enron scandal, he tackles the distinction first articulated by the national-security analyst Gregory Treverton between mysteries and puzzles.

Open Secrets
from *The New Yorker* (January 8, 2007)

On the afternoon of October 23, 2006, Jeffrey Skilling sat at a table at the front of a federal courtroom in Houston, Texas. He was wearing a navy-blue suit and a tie. He was fifty-two years old, but looked older. Huddled around him were eight lawyers from his defense team. Outside, television-satellite trucks were parked up and down the block.

"We are here this afternoon," Judge Simeon Lake began, "for sentencing in United States of America versus Jeffrey K. Skilling, Criminal No. H-04-25." He addressed the defendant directly: "Mr. Skilling, you may now make a statement and present any information in mitigation."

Skilling stood up. Enron, the company he had built into an energy-trading leviathan, had collapsed into bankruptcy almost exactly five years before. In May, he had been convicted by a jury of fraud. Under a settlement agreement, almost everything he owned had been turned over to a fund to compensate former shareholders.

He spoke haltingly, stopping in mid-sentence. "In terms of remorse, Your Honor, I can't imagine more remorse," he said. He had "friends who have died, good men." He was innocent—"innocent of every one of these charges." He spoke for two or three minutes and sat down.

Judge Lake called on Anne Beliveaux, who worked as the senior administrative assistant in Enron's tax department for eighteen years. She was one of nine people who had asked to address the sentencing hearing.

"How would you like to be facing living off of sixteen hundred dollars a month, and that is what I'm facing," she said to Skilling. Her retirement savings had been wiped out by the Enron bankruptcy. "And, Mr. Skilling, that only is because of greed, nothing but greed. And you should be ashamed of yourself."

The next witness said that Skilling had destroyed a good company, the third witness that Enron had been undone by the misconduct of its management; another lashed out at Skilling directly. "Mr. Skilling has proven to be a liar, a thief, and a drunk," a woman named Dawn Powers Martin, a twenty-two-year veteran of Enron, told the court. "Mr. Skilling has cheated me and my daughter of our retirement dreams. Now it's his time to be robbed of his freedom to walk the earth as a free man." She turned to Skilling and said, "While you dine on Chateaubriand and champagne, my daughter and I clip grocery coupons and eat leftovers." And on and on it went.

The Judge asked Skilling to rise.

"The evidence established that the defendant repeatedly lied to investors, including Enron's own employees, about various aspects of Enron's business," the Judge said. He had no choice but to be harsh: Skilling would serve two hundred and ninety-two months in prison—twenty-four years. The man who headed a firm that *Fortune* ranked among the "most admired" in the world had received one of the heaviest sentences ever given to a white-collar criminal. He would leave prison an old man, if he left prison at all.

"I only have one request, Your Honor," Daniel Petrocelli, Skilling's lawyer, said. "If he received ten fewer months, which shouldn't make a difference in terms of the goals of sentencing, if you do the math and you subtract fifteen per cent for good time, he then qualifies under Bureau of Prisons policies to be able to serve his time at a lower facility. Just a ten-month reduction in sentence . . ."

It was a plea for leniency. Skilling wasn't a murderer or a rapist. He was a pillar of the Houston community, and a small adjustment in his sentence would keep him from spending the rest of his life among hardened criminals.

"No," Judge Lake said.

THE NATIONAL-SECURITY EXPERT Gregory Treverton has famously made a distinction between puzzles and mysteries. Osama bin Laden's whereabouts are a puzzle. We can't find him because we don't have enough information. The key to the puzzle will probably come from someone close to bin Laden, and until we can find that source bin Laden will remain at large.

The problem of what would happen in Iraq after the toppling of Saddam Hussein was, by contrast, a mystery. It wasn't a question that had a simple, factual answer. Mysteries require judgments and the assessment of uncertainty, and the hard part is not that we have too little information but that we have too much. The C.I.A. had a position on what a post-invasion Iraq would look like, and so did the Pentagon and the State Department and Colin Powell and Dick Cheney and any number of political scientists and journalists and think-tank fellows. For that matter, so did every cabdriver in Baghdad.

The distinction is not trivial. If you consider the motivation and methods behind the attacks of September 11th to be mainly a puzzle, for instance, then the logical response is to increase the collection of intelligence, recruit more spies, add to the volume of information we have about Al Qaeda. If you consider September 11th a mystery, though, you'd have to wonder whether adding to the volume of information will only make things worse. You'd want to improve the analysis within the intelligence community; you'd want more thoughtful and skeptical people with the skills to look more closely at what we already know about Al Qaeda. You'd want to send the counterterrorism team from the C.I.A. on a golfing trip twice a month with the counterterrorism teams from the F.B.I. and the N.S.A. and the Defense Department, so they could get to know one another and compare notes.

If things go wrong with a puzzle, identifying the culprit is easy: it's the person who withheld information. Mysteries, though, are a lot murkier: sometimes the information we've been given is inadequate, and sometimes we aren't very smart about making sense of what we've been given, and sometimes the question itself cannot be answered. Puzzles come to satisfying conclusions. Mysteries often don't.

If you sat through the trial of Jeffrey Skilling, you'd think that the Enron scandal was a puzzle. The company, the prosecution said, conducted shady side deals that no one quite understood. Senior executives withheld critical information from investors. Skilling, the architect of the firm's strategy, was a liar, a thief, and a drunk. *We were not told enough*—the classic puzzle premise—was the central assumption of the Enron prosecution.

"This is a simple case, ladies and gentlemen," the lead prosecutor for the Department of Justice said in his closing arguments to the jury:

> Because it's so simple, I'm probably going to end before my allotted time. It's black-and-white. Truth and lies. The shareholders, ladies and gentlemen, . . . buy a share of stock, and for that they're not entitled to much but they're entitled to the truth. They're entitled for the officers and employees

of the company to put their interests ahead of their own. They're entitled to be told what the financial condition of the company is.

They are entitled to honesty, ladies and gentlemen.

But the prosecutor was wrong. Enron wasn't really a puzzle. It was a mystery.

IN LATE JULY of 2000, Jonathan Weil, a reporter at the Dallas bureau of the *Wall Street Journal*, got a call from someone he knew in the investment-management business. Weil wrote the stock column, called "Heard in Texas," for the paper's regional edition, and he had been closely following the big energy firms based in Houston—Dynegy, El Paso, and Enron. His caller had a suggestion. "He said, 'You really ought to check out Enron and Dynegy and see where their earnings come from,' " Weil recalled. "So I did."

Weil was interested in Enron's use of what is called mark-to-market accounting, which is a technique used by companies that engage in complicated financial trading. Suppose, for instance, that you are an energy company and you enter into a hundred-million-dollar contract with the state of California to deliver a billion kilowatt hours of electricity in 2016. How much is that contract worth? You aren't going to get paid for another ten years, and you aren't going to know until then whether you'll show a profit on the deal or a loss. Nonetheless, that hundred-million-dollar promise clearly matters to your bottom line. If electricity steadily drops in price over the next several years, the contract is going to become a hugely valuable asset. But if electricity starts to get more expensive as 2016 approaches, you could be out tens of millions of dollars. With mark-to-market accounting, you estimate how much revenue the deal is going to bring in and put that number in your books at the moment you sign the contract. If, down the line, the estimate changes, you adjust the balance sheet accordingly.

When a company using mark-to-market accounting says it has made a profit of ten million dollars on revenues of a hundred million, then, it could mean one of two things. The company may actually have a hundred million dollars in its bank accounts, of which ten million will remain after it has paid its bills. Or it may be guessing that it will make ten million dollars on a deal where money may not actually change hands for years. Weil's source wanted him to see how much of the money Enron said it was making was "real."

Weil got copies of the firm's annual reports and quarterly filings and began comparing the income statements and the cash-flow statements. "It took me a while to figure out everything I needed to," Weil said. "It probably took a good month or so. There was a lot of noise in the financial statements, and to zero in on this particular issue you needed to cut through a lot of that." Weil spoke to Thomas Linsmeier, then an accounting professor at Michigan State, and they talked about how some finance companies in the nineteen-nineties had used mark-to-market accounting on subprime loans—that is, loans made to higher-credit-risk consumers—and when the economy declined and consumers defaulted or paid off their loans more quickly than expected, the lenders suddenly realized that their estimates of how much money they were going to make were far too generous. Weil spoke to someone at the Financial Accounting Standards Board, to an analyst at the Moody's investment-rating agency, and to a dozen or so others. Then he went back to Enron's financial statements. His conclusions were sobering. In the second quarter of 2000, $747 million of the money Enron said it had made was "unrealized"—that is, it was money that executives thought they were going to make at some point in the future. If you took that imaginary money away, Enron had shown a significant loss in the second quarter. This was one of the most admired companies in the United States, a firm that was then valued by the stock market as the seventh-largest corporation in the country, and there was practically no cash coming into its coffers.

Weil's story ran in the *Journal* on September 20, 2000. A few days later, it was read by a Wall Street financier named James Chanos. Chanos is a short-seller—an investor who tries to make money by betting that a company's stock will fall. "It pricked up my ears," Chanos said. "I read the 10-K and the 10-Q that first weekend," he went on, referring to the financial statements that public companies are required to file with federal regulators. "I went through it pretty quickly. I flagged right away the stuff that was questionable. I circled it. That was the first run-through. Then I flagged the pages and read the stuff I didn't understand, and reread it two or three times. I remember I spent a couple hours on it." Enron's profit margins and its return on equity were plunging, Chanos saw. Cash flow—the life blood of any business—had slowed to a trickle, and the company's rate of return was less than its cost of capital: it was as if you had borrowed money from the bank at nine-per-cent interest and invested it in a savings bond that paid you seven per-cent interest. "They were basically liquidating themselves," Chanos said.

In November of that year, Chanos began shorting Enron stock. Over the next few months, he spread the word that he thought the company was in trouble. He tipped off a reporter for *Fortune*, Bethany McLean. She read the same reports that Chanos and Weil had, and came to the same conclusion. Her story, under the headline "IS ENRON OVERPRICED?," ran in March of 2001. More and more journalists and analysts began taking a closer look at Enron, and the stock began to fall. In August, Skilling resigned. Enron's credit rating was downgraded. Banks became reluctant to lend Enron the money it needed to make its trades. By December, the company had filed for bankruptcy.

Enron's downfall has been documented so extensively that it is easy to overlook how peculiar it was. Compare Enron, for instance, with Watergate, the prototypical scandal of the nineteen-seventies. To expose the White House coverup, Bob Woodward and Carl Bernstein used a source—Deep Throat—who had access to many secrets, and whose identity had to be concealed. He warned Woodward and Bernstein that their phones might be tapped. When Woodward wanted to meet with Deep Throat, he would move a flower pot with a red flag in it to the back of his apartment balcony. That evening, he would leave by the back stairs, take multiple taxis to make sure he wasn't being followed, and meet his source in an underground parking garage at 2 A.M. Here, from *All the President's Men*, is Woodward's climactic encounter with Deep Throat:

> "Okay," he said softly. "This is very serious. You can safely say that fifty people worked for the White House and CRP to play games and spy and sabotage and gather intelligence. Some of it is beyond belief, kicking at the opposition in every imaginable way."
>
> Deep Throat nodded confirmation as Woodward ran down items on a list of tactics that he and Bernstein had heard were used against the political opposition: bugging, following people, false press leaks, fake letters, cancelling campaign rallies, investigating campaign workers' private lives, planting spies, stealing documents, planting provocateurs in political demonstrations.
>
> "It's all in the files," Deep Throat said. "Justice and the Bureau know about it, even though it wasn't followed up."
>
> Woodward was stunned. Fifty people directed by the White House and CRP to destroy the opposition, no holds barred?
>
> Deep Throat nodded.
>
> The White House had been willing to subvert—was that the right word?—the whole electoral process? Had actually gone ahead and tried to do it?
>
> Another nod. Deep Throat looked queasy.
>
> And hired fifty agents to do it?
>
> "You can safely say more than fifty," Deep Throat said. Then he turned, walked up the ramp and out. It was nearly 6:00 A.M.

Watergate was a classic puzzle: Woodward and Bernstein were searching for a buried secret, and Deep Throat was their guide.

Did Jonathan Weil have a Deep Throat? Not really. He had a friend in the investment-management business with some suspicions about energy-trading companies like Enron, but the friend wasn't an insider. Nor did Weil's source direct him to files detailing the clandestine activities of the company. He just told Weil to read a series of public documents that had been prepared and distributed by Enron itself. Woodward met with his secret source in an underground parking garage in the hours before dawn. Weil called up an accounting expert at Michigan State.

When Weil had finished his reporting, he called Enron for comment. "They had their chief accounting officer and six or seven people fly up to Dallas," Weil says. They met in a conference room at the *Journal*'s offices. The Enron officials acknowledged that the money they said they earned was virtually all money that they *hoped* to earn. Weil and the Enron officials then had a long conversation about how certain Enron was about its estimates of future earnings. "They were telling me how brilliant the people who put together their mathematical models were," Weil says. "These were M.I.T. Ph.D.s. I said, 'Were your mathematical models last year telling you that the California electricity markets would be going berserk this year? No? Why not?' They said, 'Well, this is one of those crazy events.' It was late September, 2000, so I said, 'Who do you think is going to win? Bush or Gore?' They said, 'We don't know.' I said, 'Don't you think it will make a difference to the market whether you have an environmentalist Democrat in the White House or a Texas oil man?" It was all very civil. "There was no dispute about the numbers," Weil went on. "There was only a difference in how you should interpret them."

Of all the moments in the Enron unravelling, this meeting is surely the strangest. The prosecutor in the Enron case told the jury to send Jeffrey Skilling to prison because Enron had hidden the truth: You're "entitled to be told what the financial condition of the company is," the prosecutor had said. But what truth was Enron hiding here? Everything Weil learned for his Enron exposé came from Enron, and when he wanted to confirm his numbers the company's executives got on a plane and sat down with him in a conference room in Dallas.

Nixon never went to see Woodward and Bernstein at the *Washington Post*. He hid in the White House.

THE SECOND, AND perhaps more consequential, problem with Enron's accounting was its heavy reliance on what are called special-purpose entities, or S.P.E.s.

An S.P.E. works something like this. Your company isn't doing well; sales are down and you are heavily in debt. If you go to a bank to borrow a hundred million dollars, it will probably charge you an extremely high interest rate, if it agrees to lend to you at all. But you've got a bundle of oil leases that over the next four or five years are almost certain to bring in a hundred million dollars. So you hand them over to a partnership—the S.P.E.—that you have set up with some outside investors. The bank then lends a hundred million dollars to the partnership, and the partnership gives the money to you. That bit of financial maneuvering makes a big difference. This kind of transaction did not (at the time) have to be reported in the company's balance sheet. So a company could raise capital without increasing its indebtedness. And because the bank is almost certain the leases will generate enough money to pay off the loan, it's willing to lend its money at a much lower interest rate. S.P.E.s have become commonplace in corporate America.

Enron introduced all kinds of twists into the S.P.E. game. It didn't always put blue-chip assets into the partnerships—like oil leases that would reliably generate income. It sometimes sold off less than sterling assets. Nor did it always sell those assets to outsiders, who presumably would raise questions about the value of what they were buying. Enron had its own executives manage these partnerships. And the company would make the deals work—that is, get the partnerships and the banks to play along—by guaranteeing that, if whatever they had to sell declined in value, Enron would make up the difference with its own stock. In other words, Enron didn't sell parts of itself to an outside entity; it effectively sold parts of itself to itself—a strategy that was not only legally questionable but extraordinarily risky. It was Enron's tangle of financial obligations to the S.P.E.s that ended up triggering the collapse.

When the prosecution in the Skilling case argued that the company had misled its investors, they were referring, in part, to these S.P.E.s. Enron's management, the argument went, had an obligation to reveal the extent to which it had staked its financial livelihood on these shadowy side deals. As the Powers Committee, a panel charged with investigating Enron's demise, noted, the company "failed to achieve a fundamental objective: they did not communicate the essence of the transactions in a sufficiently clear fashion to enable a reader of [Enron's] financial statements to understand what was going on." In short, we weren't told enough.

Here again, though, the lessons of the Enron case aren't nearly so straightforward. The public became aware of the nature of these S.P.E.s through the reporting of several of Weil's colleagues at the *Wall Street Journal*—principally John Emshwiller and Rebecca Smith—starting in the late summer of 2001. And how was Emshwiller tipped off to Enron's problems? The same way Jonathan Weil and Jim Chanos were: he read what Enron had reported in its own public filings. Here is the description of Emshwiller's epiphany, as described in Kurt Eichenwald's *Conspiracy of Fools*, the definitive history of the Enron debacle. (Note the verb "scrounged," which Eichenwald uses to describe how Emshwiller found the relevant Enron documents. What he means by that is "downloaded.")

> It was section eight, called "Related Party Transactions," that got John Emshwiller's juices flowing.

After being assigned to follow the Skilling resignation, Emshwiller had put in a request for an interview, then scrounged up a copy of Enron's most recent SEC filing in search of any nuggets.

What he found startled him. Words about some partnerships run by an unidentified "senior officer." Arcane stuff, maybe, but the numbers were huge. Enron reported more than $240 million in revenues in the first six months of the year from its dealings with them.

Enron's S.P.E.s were, by any measure, evidence of extraordinary recklessness and incompetence. But you can't blame Enron for covering up the existence of its side deals. It didn't; it disclosed them. The argument against the company, then, is more accurately that it didn't tell its investors *enough* about its S.P.E.s. But what is enough? Enron had some three thousand S.P.E.s, and the paperwork for each one probably ran in excess of a thousand pages. It scarcely would have helped investors if Enron had made all three million pages public. What about an edited version of each deal? Steven Schwarcz, a professor at Duke Law School, recently examined a random sample of twenty S.P.E. disclosure statements from various corporations—that is, summaries of the deals put together for interested parties—and found that on average they ran to forty single-spaced pages. So a summary of Enron's S.P.E.s would have come to a hundred and twenty thousand single-spaced pages. What about a summary of all those summaries? That's what the bankruptcy examiner in the Enron case put together, and it took up a thousand pages. Well, then, what about a summary of the summary of the summaries? That's what the Powers Committee put together. The committee looked only at the "substance of the most significant transactions," and its accounting still ran to two hundred numbingly complicated pages and, as Schwarcz points out, that was "with the benefit of hindsight and with the assistance of some of the finest legal talent in the nation."

A puzzle grows simpler with the addition of each new piece of information: if I tell you that Osama bin Laden is hiding in Peshawar, I make the problem of finding him an order of magnitude easier, and if I add that he's hiding in a neighborhood in the northwest corner of the city, the problem becomes simpler still. But here the rules seem different. According to the Powers report, many on Enron's board of directors failed to understand "the economic rationale, the consequences, and the risks" of their company's S.P.E. deals—and the directors sat in meetings where those deals were discussed in detail. In *Conspiracy of Fools*, Eichenwald convincingly argues that Andrew Fastow, Enron's chief financial officer, didn't understand the full economic implications of the deals, either, and he was the one who put them together.

"These were very, very sophisticated, complex transactions," says Anthony Catanach, who teaches accounting at the Villanova University School of

Business and has written extensively on the Enron case. Referring to Enron's accounting firm, he said, "I'm not even sure any of Arthur Andersen's field staff at Enron would have been able to understand them, even if it was all in front of them. This is senior-management-type stuff. I spent *two months* looking at the Powers report, just diagramming it. These deals were really convoluted."

Enron's S.P.E.s, it should be noted, would have been this hard to understand even if they were standard issue. S.P.E.s are by nature difficult. A company creates an S.P.E. because it wants to reassure banks about the risks of making a loan. To provide that reassurance, the company gives its lenders and partners very detailed information about a specific portion of its business. And the more certainty a company creates for the lender—the more guarantees and safeguards and explanations it writes into the deal—the less comprehensible the transaction becomes to outsiders. Schwarcz writes that Enron's disclosure was "necessarily imperfect." You can try to make financial transactions understandable by simplifying them, in which case you run the risk of smoothing over some of their potential risks, or you can try to disclose every potential pitfall, in which case you'll make the disclosure so unwieldy that no one will be able to understand it. To Schwarcz, all Enron proves is that in an age of increasing financial complexity the "disclosure paradigm"—the idea that the more a company tells us about its business, the better off we are—has become an anachronism.

DURING THE SUMMER of 1943, Nazi propaganda broadcasts boasted that the German military had developed a devastating "super weapon." Immediately, the Allied intelligence services went to work. Spies confirmed that the Germans had built a secret weapons factory. Aerial photographs taken over northern France showed a strange new concrete installation pointed in the direction of England. The Allies were worried. Bombing missions were sent to try to disrupt the mysterious operation, and plans were drawn up to deal with the prospect of devastating new attacks on English cities. Nobody was sure, though, whether the weapon was real. There seemed to be weapons factories there, but it wasn't evident what was happening inside them. And there was a launching pad in northern France, but it might have been just a decoy, designed to distract the Allies from bombing real targets. The German secret weapon was a puzzle, and the Allies didn't have enough information to solve it. There was another way to think about the problem, though, which ultimately proved far more useful: treat the German secret weapon as a mystery.

The mystery-solvers of the Second World War were small groups of analysts whose job was to listen to the overseas and domestic propaganda broadcasts of Japan and Germany. The British outfit had been around since shortly before the First World War and was run by the BBC. The American operation was known as the Screwball Division, the historian Stephen Mercado writes, and in the early nineteen-forties had been housed in a nondescript office building on K Street, in Washington. The analysts listened to the same speeches that anyone with a shortwave radio could listen to. They simply sat at their desks with headphones on, working their way through hours and hours of Nazi broadcasts. Then they tried to figure out how what the Nazis said publicly—about, for instance, the possibility of a renewed offensive against Russia—revealed what they felt about, say, invading Russia. One journalist at the time described the propaganda analysts as "the greatest collection of individualists, international rolling stones, and slightly batty geniuses ever gathered together in one organization." And they had very definite thoughts about the Nazis' secret weapon.

The German leadership, first of all, was boasting about the secret weapon in domestic broadcasts. That was important. Propaganda was supposed to boost morale. If the Nazi leadership said things that turned out to be misleading, its credibility would fall. When German U-boats started running into increasingly effective Allied resistance in the spring of 1943, for example, Joseph Goebbels, the Nazi minister of propaganda, tacitly acknowledged the bad news, switching his emphasis from trumpeting recent victories to predicting long-term success, and blaming the weather for hampering U-boat operations. Up to that point, Goebbels had never lied to his own people about that sort of news. So if he said that Germany had a devastating secret weapon it meant, in all likelihood, that Germany had a devastating secret weapon.

Starting from that premise, the analysts then mined the Nazis' public pronouncements for more insights. It was, they concluded, "beyond reasonable doubt" that as of November, 1943, the weapon existed, that it was of an entirely new type, that it could not be easily countered, that it would produce striking results, and that it would shock the civilian population upon whom it would be used. It was, furthermore, "highly probable" that the Germans were past the experimental stage as of May of 1943, and that something had happened in August of that year that significantly delayed deployment. The analysts based this inference, in part, on the fact that, in August, the Nazis abruptly stopped mentioning their secret weapon for ten days, and that when they started again their threats took on a new, less certain, tone. Finally, it could be tentatively estimated that the weapon would be ready between the middle of January and the middle of April, with a month's margin of error on either side. That inference, in part, came from Nazi propaganda in late 1943, which suddenly became more serious and specific in tone, and it seemed unlikely that Goebbels would raise hopes in this way if he couldn't deliver within a few months. The secret weapon was the Nazis' fabled V-1 rocket, and virtually every one of the propaganda analysts' predictions turned out to be true.

The political scientist Alexander George described the sequence of V-1 rocket inferences in his 1959 book *Propaganda Analysis*, and the striking thing about his account is how contemporary it seems. The spies were fighting a nineteenth-century war. The analysts belonged to our age, and the lesson of their triumph is that the complex, uncertain issues that the modern world throws at us require the mystery paradigm.

Diagnosing prostate cancer used to be a puzzle, for example: the doctor would do a rectal exam and feel for a lumpy tumor on the surface of the patient's prostate. These days, though, we don't wait for patients to develop the symptoms of prostate cancer. Doctors now regularly test middle-aged men for elevated levels of PSA, a substance associated with prostate changes, and, if the results look problematic, they use ultrasound imaging to take a picture of the prostate. Then they perform a biopsy, removing tiny slices of the gland and examining the extracted tissue under a microscope. Much of that flood of information, however, is inconclusive: elevated levels of PSA don't always mean that you have cancer, and normal levels of PSA don't always mean that you don't—and, in any case, there's debate about what constitutes a "normal" PSA level. Nor is the biopsy definitive: because what a pathologist is looking for is early evidence of cancer—and in many cases merely something that might one day turn into cancer—two equally skilled pathologists can easily look at the same sample and disagree about whether there is any cancer present. Even if they do agree, they may disagree about the benefits of treatment, given that most prostate cancers grow so slowly that they never cause problems. The urologist is now charged with the task of making sense of a maze of unreliable and conflicting claims. He is no longer confirming the presence of a malignancy. He's predicting it, and the certainties of his predecessors have been replaced with outcomes that can only be said to be "highly probable" or "tentatively estimated." What medical progress has meant for prostate cancer—and, as the physician H. Gilbert Welch argues in his book *Should I Be Tested for Cancer?*, for virtually every other cancer as well—is the transformation of diagnosis from a puzzle to a mystery.

That same transformation is happening in the intelligence world as well. During the Cold War, the broad context of our relationship with the Soviet bloc was stable and predictable. What we didn't know was details. As Gregory Treverton, who was a former vice-chair of the National Intelligence Council, writes in his book *Reshaping National Intelligence for an Age of Information*:

> Then the pressing questions that preoccupied intelligence were puzzles, ones that could, in principle, have been answered definitively if only the information had been available: How big was the Soviet economy? How many missiles did the Soviet Union have? Had it launched a "bolt from the blue" attack? These puzzles were intelligence's stock-in-trade during the Cold War.

With the collapse of the Eastern bloc, Treverton and others have argued that the situation facing the intelligence community has turned upside down. Now most of the world is open, not closed. Intelligence officers aren't dependent on scraps from spies. They are inundated with information. Solving puzzles remains critical: we still want to know precisely where Osama bin Laden is hiding, where North Korea's nuclear-weapons facilities are situated. But mysteries increasingly take center stage. The stable and predictable divisions of East and West have been shattered. Now the task of the intelligence analyst is to help policymakers navigate the disorder. Several years ago, Admiral Bobby R. Inman was asked by a congressional commission what changes he thought would strengthen America's intelligence system. Inman used to head the National Security Agency, the nation's premier puzzle-solving authority, and was once the deputy director of the C.I.A. He was the embodiment of the Cold War intelligence structure. His answer: revive the State Department, the one part of the U.S. foreign-policy establishment that isn't considered to be in the intelligence business at all. In a post–Cold War world of "openly available information," Inman said, "what you need are observers with language ability, with understanding of the religions, cultures of the countries they're observing." Inman thought we needed fewer spies and more slightly batty geniuses.

ENRON REVEALED THAT the financial community needs to make the same transition. "In order for an economy to have an adequate system of financial reporting, it is not enough that companies make disclosures of financial information," the Yale law professor Jonathan Macey wrote in a landmark law-review article that encouraged many to rethink the Enron case. "In addition, it is vital that there be a set of financial intermediaries, who are at least as competent and sophisticated at receiving, processing, and interpreting financial information . . . as the companies are at delivering it." Puzzles are "transmitter-dependent"; they turn on what we are told. Mysteries are "receiver dependent"; they turn on the skills of the listener, and Macey argues that, as Enron's business practices grew more complicated, it was Wall Street's responsibility to keep pace.

Victor Fleischer, who teaches at the University of Colorado Law School, points out that one of the critical clues about Enron's condition lay in the fact that it paid no income tax in four of its last five years. Enron's use of mark-to-market accounting and S.P.E.s was an accounting game that made the company look as though it were earning far more money than it was. But the I.R.S. doesn't accept mark-to-market accounting; you pay tax on income when you actually receive that income. And, from the I.R.S.'s perspective, all of Enron's fantastically complex maneuvering around its S.P.E.s was, as

Fleischer puts it, "a non-event": until the partnership actually sells the asset—and makes either a profit or a loss—an S.P.E. is just an accounting fiction. Enron wasn't paying any taxes because, in the eyes of the I.R.S., Enron wasn't making any money.

If you looked at Enron from the perspective of the tax code, that is, you would have seen a very different picture of the company than if you had looked through the more traditional lens of the accounting profession. But in order to do that you would have to be trained in the tax code and be familiar with its particular conventions and intricacies, and know what questions to ask. "The fact of the gap between [Enron's] accounting income and taxable income was easily observed," Fleischer notes, but not the source of the gap. "The tax code requires special training."

Woodward and Bernstein didn't have any special training. They were in their twenties at the time of Watergate. In *All the President's Men*, they even joke about their inexperience: Woodward's expertise was mainly in office politics; Bernstein was a college dropout. But it hardly mattered, because coverups, whistle-blowers, secret tapes, and exposés—the principal elements of the puzzle—all require the application of energy and persistence, which are the virtues of youth. Mysteries demand experience and insight. Woodward and Bernstein would never have broken the Enron story.

"There have been scandals in corporate history where people are really making stuff up, but this wasn't a criminal enterprise of that kind," Macey says. "Enron was vanishingly close, in my view, to having complied with the accounting rules. They were going over the edge, just a little bit. And this kind of financial fraud—where people are simply stretching the truth—falls into the area that analysts and short-sellers are supposed to ferret out. The truth wasn't hidden. But you'd have to look at their financial statements, and you would have to say to yourself, What's that about? It's almost as if they were saying, 'We're doing some really sleazy stuff in footnote 42, and if you want to know more about it ask us.' And that's the thing. Nobody did."

Alexander George, in his history of propaganda analysis, looked at hundreds of the inferences drawn by the American analysts about the Nazis, and concluded that an astonishing eighty-one per cent of them were accurate. George's account, however, spends almost as much time on the propaganda analysts' failures as on their successes. It was the British, for example, who did the best work on the V-1 rocket problem. They systematically tracked the "occurrence and volume" of Nazi reprisal threats, which is how they were able to pinpoint things like the setback suffered by the V-1 program in August of 1943 (it turned out that Allied bombs had caused serious damage) and the date of the Nazi V-1 rocket launch. K Street's analysis was lacklustre in comparison. George writes that the Americans "did not develop analytical techniques and hypotheses of sufficient refinement," relying instead on "impressionistic" analysis. George was himself one of the slightly batty geniuses of K Street, and, of course, he could easily have excused his former colleagues. They never left their desks, after all. All they had to deal with was propaganda, and their big source was Goebbels, who was a liar, a thief, and a drunk. But that is puzzle thinking. In the case of puzzles, we put the offending target, the C.E.O., in jail for twenty-four years and assume that our work is done. Mysteries require that we revisit our list of culprits and be willing to spread the blame a little more broadly. Because if you can't find the truth in a mystery—even a mystery shrouded in propaganda—it's not just the fault of the propagandist. It's your fault as well.

IN THE SPRING of 1998, Macey notes, a group of six students at Cornell University's business school decided to do their term project on Enron. "It was for an advanced financial-statement-analysis class taught by a guy at Cornell called Charles Lee, who is pretty famous in financial circles," one member of the group, Jay Krueger, recalls. In the first part of the semester, Lee had led his students through a series of intensive case studies, teaching them techniques and sophisticated tools to make sense of the vast amounts of information that companies disclose in their annual reports and S.E.C. filings. Then the students picked a company and went off on their own. "One of the second-years had a summer internship interview with Enron, and he was very interested in the energy sector," Krueger went on. "So he said, 'Let's do them.' It was about a six-week project, half a semester. Lots of group meetings. It was a ratio analysis, which is pretty standard business-school fare. You know, take fifty different financial ratios, then lay that on top of every piece of information you could find out about the company, the businesses, how their performance compared to other competitors."

The people in the group reviewed Enron's accounting practices as best they could. They analyzed each of Enron's businesses, in succession. They used statistical tools, designed to find telltale patterns in the company's financial performance—the Beneish model, the Lev and Thiagarajan indicators, the Edwards-Bell-Ohlsen analysis—and made their way through pages and pages of footnotes. "We really had a lot of questions about what was going on with their business model," Krueger said. The students' conclusions were straightforward. Enron was pursuing a far riskier strategy than its competitors. There were clear signs that "Enron may be manipulating its earnings." The stock was then at forty-eight dollars—at its peak, two years later, it was almost double that—but the students found it over-valued. The report was posted on the Web site of the Cornell University business school, where it has been, ever since, for anyone who cared to read twenty-three pages of analysis. The students' recommendation was on the first page, in boldfaced type: "Sell."

DISCUSSION QUESTIONS

1. *What are the various sources of trust and trustworthiness on display in these readings?*

2. *How are the grounds for trusting institutions different from those for trusting individuals?*

3. *How can leaders encourage trust and collaboration—and delegate decision-making—without surrendering authority and responsibility?*

4. *How does one repair damaged trust?*

5. *How can large, diffuse organizations and institutions forge trust in the absence of personal bonds between individuals separated by language, subculture, culture, or geographical distance?*

ALBUM
Con Artists

The cheaper the crook, the gaudier the patter.

—SAM SPADE to Wilmer Cook,
Dashiell Hammett, *The Maltese Falcon*

How much of the behavior we witness in the most successful leaders is just a kind of put-on—an act calculated to instill optimism in bleak times, to motivate others in the face of desperate odds, to win adherents to bold new schemes? We live in an age that claims to prize authenticity, even if it cannot quite define it, yet we are somehow primed to embrace the sham. Performance is not by definition unethical, of course; a facility for masking inner doubts, a Stoic calm, a hard-won *sprezzatura*, even a protean flexibility, might all in fact be compatible with moral leadership and sound organizations. The bluff is a time-honored tradition in business, poker, and war as well as a subject of academic study for social scientists interested in decision-making and strategic modeling. The economists Charles Cotton and Chang Liu, for example, have applied game theory to two of the celebrated military bluffs of Chinese history: the hundred horsemen and the empty city, both ruses whereby armies at a disadvantage outfoxed superior adversaries to win the day.

Yet how narrow the divide can seem between the gift of pretended confidence and the confidence trick: a general persuades his troops they are destined for victory by flipping a two-headed coin; a crow steals an easy meal by urging an eagle to drop a tortoise from a great height; a spy induces the inhabitants of a walled city to open its impregnable gates to a wooden horse; a little girl falls victim to the blandishments of a merciless wolf. Where is the line between ethical persuasion and a confidence game?

The figure of the trickster can be found in cultures across the globe: the coyote of Native American myth; France's Reynard the Fox; Eshu, the trickster god of Nigeria's Yoruba people; and the Egyptian trickster god Seth. What else is Shakespeare's Henry V but a confidence trickster, able to persuade his outnumbered English army to fight the formidable French while openly appraising their situation as that of "men wrecked upon a sand," likely to be swept away by "the next tide"? The trickster has had an exuberant American history. Showmen, hucksters, swindlers, frauds, and grifters have peddled everything from magic tricks and patent medicines to get-rich-quick schemes and old-time religion: P. T. Barnum, Sister Aimee, Charles Ponzi, Frank Abagnale, and Bernard Madoff.

The origins of the confidence, or con, man—a very particular type of thief—can be traced to a man named William Thompson, who operated in Manhattan in 1849. The *New-York Herald* reported his arrest in July of that year:

> For the last few months a man has been traveling about the city, known as the "Confidence Man," that is, he would go up to a perfect stranger in the street, and being a man of genteel appearance, would easily command an interview. Upon this interview he would say after some little conversation, "have you confidence in me to trust me with your watch until to-morrow;" the stranger at this novel request, supposing him to be some old acquaintance not at that moment recollected, allows him to take the watch, thus placing 'confidence' in the honesty of the stranger, who walks off laughing and the other supposing it to be a joke allows him so to do.

Amy Reading tells the story of Thompson (who was the original for the title character of Melville's *The Confidence-Man*) and other con artists in her book *The Mark Inside: A Perfect Swindle, a Cunning Revenge, and a Small History of the Big Con* (2012).

As the philosopher Annette Baier notes, "Exploitation and conspiracy, as much as justice and fellowship, thrive better in an atmosphere of trust. . . . Trust is always an invitation not only to confidence tricksters but also to terrorists, who discern its most easily destroyed and socially vital forms."

Like Macbeth finding in the witches the answer to his own unvoiced ambitions, the mark hears in the promises of the steerer and the inside man the fulfillment of his or her own desire to get rich quick. Using selective truths to smooth the way, the confidence artist preys on the craving of others to believe and to be "in the know." The chemistry teacher turned meth-making maestro Walter White, a popular-culture icon from the cable television series *Breaking Bad*, is a master of this tactic: he is capable of at once telling the most outlandish lies and invoking the absolute truth for perverse ends.

The selections included here offer a rogues' gallery ranging from the Japanese general Nobunaga ("In the Hands of Destiny") and the Greek admiral Lysander ("Patching Out the Lion's Skin") to the film director Cecil B. DeMille. Machiavelli explains the place of truth in the career of the prince, while the novel *Romance of the Three Kingdoms* shows us the role of duplicity in the success of a general. In "The Crane and the Crow" and C. K. Williams's poem "Hercules, Deianira, Nessus," we encounter ur-con artists from the ancient universes of fable and myth.

RECOMMENDED READING AND VIEWING

Sissela Bok, *Lying* (1978)
Geoffrey Chaucer, "The Pardoner's Tale," from *The Canterbury Tales* (1475)
House of Games (1987), directed by David Mamet
Thomas Hobbes, *Leviathan* (1651)
Herman Melville, *The Confidence-Man: His Masquerade* (1857)

The Crane and the Crow, from *Aesop's Fables*

PART OF THE fiber of the ancient Mediterranean world, *Aesop's Fables* is the product of a legendary fabulist whose own biography is itself largely the stuff of fiction. The historian Herodotus reports that Aesop was a slave in Samos, an island in the Aegean, and that he was killed at Delphi. From other sources we learn that Aesop was mute and hideously ugly but that the goddess Isis rewarded his fidelity with the ability to speak. Thus, the legend runs, Aesop earned his freedom but subsequently so outraged the citizens of Delphi that they executed him on a trumped-up charge of theft. Collections of the fables were produced throughout antiquity, retained their popularity after the fall of Rome, and enjoyed a resurgence in the late Middle Ages. William Caxton produced the first English translation in 1484. Only in the seventeenth century, notes the translator and editor Laura Gibbs, did the fables begin to be regarded as children's literature. Up to that point, their depictions of anthropomorphized animals were considered to have the power to illuminate the adult world. In the *Phaedo*, Plato reports that Socrates spent his last days in prison turning fables into verse: "How singular is the thing called pleasure," Socrates declares, here in Benjamin Jowett's translation: "and how curiously related to pain . . . I cannot help thinking that if Aesop had noticed them, he would have made a fable about God trying to reconcile their strife, and when he could not, he fastened their heads together." "The Crane and the Crow" does its work by expounding on the treachery of human beings from the perspective of two birds. (The following selection is translated by Laura Gibbs.)

The Crane and the Crow

A crane and a crow had made a mutual pledge of assistance, agreeing that the crane was to defend the crow from other birds, while the crow would use her powers of prophecy to warn the crane about future events. These two birds often went to the field of a certain man and ate the crops that he had sowed there, tearing them up by the roots. When the farmer saw what was happening to his field, he was upset, and said to his boy, "Give me a stone." The crow alerted the crane, and they prudently made their escape. On another occasion, the crow again heard the farmer asking for a stone and warned the crane so that the crane would not get hurt. After some thought, the man understood that the crow was able to predict what was happening. He said to the boy, "When I say, 'Give me some bread,' I want you to give me a stone." The farmer then went to the field and told the boy to give him some bread, so the boy gave him a stone. The farmer threw the stone at the crane and broke both his legs. The injured crane said to the crow, "What has become of your god-given prophecies? Why didn't you warn me that this was going to happen?" The crow then said to the crane, "In this case it is not my understanding that is at fault. The counsels of wicked people are always deceptive, since they say one thing and do another!"

For someone who seduces innocent people with his promises but later causes them nothing but trouble.

In the Hands of Destiny, from *Zen Flesh, Zen Bones*
(1957)

"IN THE HANDS OF DESTINY" and two other vignettes reproduced in this anthology come from *101 Zen Stories* (1939), a collection of Chinese and Japanese Zen teachings from across the centuries. These stories, many of which were translated from the late thirteenth-century Japanese *Shaseki-shu*, or *Collection of Stone and Sand*, were subsequently gathered together with anecdotes and koans assembled from various sources and periods in the influential compilation *Zen Flesh, Zen Bones*. Zen (*Ch'an* in China) Buddhism is a meditative practice aimed at self-discovery. As Joel Kupperman explains in *Classic Asian Philosophy*, the stories in *Zen Flesh, Zen Bones* "dramatize (rather than explain) the philosophical element" of Zen; they are designed to offer a mode of living. *Zen Flesh, Zen Bones* compiler Paul Reps calls attention to the potential importance of the collection: "The problem of our mind, relating conscious to preconscious awareness, takes us deep into everyday living. Dare we open our doors to the source of our being?" "In the Hands of Destiny" presents us with the warrior Nobunaga's method for motivating his outnumbered army.

In the Hands of Destiny

A great Japanese warrior named Nobunaga decided to attack the enemy although he had only one-tenth the number of men the opposition commanded. He knew that he would win, but his soldiers were in doubt.

On the way he stopped at a Shinto shrine and told his men: "After I visit the shrine I will toss a coin. If heads comes, we will win; if tails, we will lose. Destiny holds us in her hand."

Nobunaga entered the shrine and offered a silent prayer. He came forth and tossed a coin. Heads appeared. His soldiers were so eager to fight that they won their battle easily.

"No one can change the hand of destiny," his attendant told him after the battle.

"Indeed not," said Nobunaga, showing a coin which had been doubled, with heads facing either way.

Plutarch
(ca. 45–120)

PLUTARCH WAS BORN in the Boetian city of Chaeronea, in central Greece, which was at the time part of the Roman Empire. He himself tells us that he came to Athens to study philosophy, and there he became a Platonist. Plutarch then moved to the city of Delphi. For centuries, Plutarch's *Lives* offered inspirational heroic examples considered worthy of emulation. That age stretched from the Renaissance through perhaps the early twentieth century, and historical readers of Plutarch range from Montaigne to Ralph Waldo Emerson. Here Plutarch discusses a preference for dissembling and a concomitant disdain for oaths on the part of the Spartan admiral Lysander. (The following selection from *Lysander* comes from the seventeenth-century Dryden translation.)

Patching Out the Lion's Skin
from *Lysander*

But to those who loved honest and noble behavior in their commanders, Lysander, compared with Callicratidas, seemed cunning and subtle, managing most things in the war by deceit, extolling what was just when it was profitable, and when it was not, using that which was convenient, instead of that which was good; and not judging truth to be in nature better than falsehood, but setting a value upon both according to interest. He would laugh at those who thought Hercules's posterity ought not to use deceit in war: "For where the lion's skin will not reach, you must patch it out with the fox's." Such is the conduct recorded of him in the business about Miletus; for when his friends and connections, whom he had promised, raised to assist in suppressing popular government, and expelling their political opponents, had altered their minds, and were reconciled to their enemies, he pretended openly as if he was pleased with it, and was desirous to further the reconciliation, but privately he railed at and abused them, and provoked them to set upon the multitude. And as soon as ever he perceived a new attempt to be commencing, he at once came up and entered into the city, and the first of the conspirators he lit upon, he pretended to rebuke, and spoke roughly, as if he would punish them; but the others, meantime, he bade be courageous, and to fear nothing, now he was with them. And all this acting and dissembling was with the object that the most considerable men of the popular party might not fly away, but might stay in the city and be killed, which so fell out, for all who believed him were put to death.

There is a saying also, recorded by Androclides, which makes him guilty of great indifference to the obligations of an oath. His recommendation, according to this account, was to "cheat boys with dice, and men with oaths," an imitation of Polycrates of Samos, not very honorable to a lawful commander to take example, namely, from a tyrant; nor in character with Laconian usages, to treat gods as ill as enemies, or, indeed, even more injuriously; since he who overreaches by an oath admits that he fears his enemy, while he despises his God.

Niccolò Machiavelli
(1469–1527)

IN "THE QUESTION of Machiavelli," a 1971 essay in the *New York Review of Books*, the philosopher Isaiah Berlin wrote: "Few would deny that Machiavelli's writings, more particularly *The Prince*, have scandalized mankind more deeply and continuously than any other political treatise." Placed on the index of banned books in 1559 and variously interpreted ever since as everything from "a handbook for gangsters" (Bertrand Russell) to the apologia of an "anguished humanist," *The Prince* is truly frightening, according to Berlin, because it puts before its reader the prospect of "two incompatible moral worlds": "successful social existence" and "virtuous private life." In this chapter Machiavelli discusses the value of honesty to a prince. (The following selection is translated by Robert M. Adams.)

The Way Princes Should Keep Their Word
from *The Prince* (1532)

How praiseworthy it is for a prince to keep his word and live with integrity rather than by craftiness, everyone understands; yet we see from recent experience that those princes have accomplished most who paid little heed to keeping their promises, but who knew how to manipulate the minds of men craftily. In the end, they won out over those who tried to act honestly.

You should consider then, that there are two ways of fighting, one with laws and the other with force. The first is properly a human method, the second belongs to beasts. But as the first method does not always suffice, you sometimes have to turn to the second. Thus a prince must know how to make good use of both the beast and man. Ancient writers made subtle note of this fact when they wrote that Achilles and many other princes of antiquity were sent to be reared by Chiron the centaur, who trained them in his discipline. Having a teacher who is half man and half beast can only mean that a prince must know how to use both these two natures, and that one without the other has no lasting effect.

Since a prince must know how to use the character of beasts, he should pick for imitation the fox and the lion. As the lion cannot protect himself from traps, and the fox cannot defend himself from wolves, you have to be a fox in order to be wary of traps, and a lion to overawe the wolves. Those who try to live by the lion alone are badly mistaken. Thus a prudent prince cannot and should not keep his word when to do so would go against his interest, or when the reasons that made him pledge it no longer apply. Doubtless if all men were good, this rule would be bad; but since they are a sad lot, and keep no faith with you, you in your turn are under no obligation to keep it with them.

Besides, a prince will never lack for legitimate excuses to explain away his breaches of faith. Modern history will furnish innumerable examples of this behavior, showing how many treaties and promises have been made null and void by the faithlessness of princes, and how the man succeeded best who knew best how to play the fox. But it is necessary in playing this part that you conceal it carefully; you must be a great liar and hypocrite. Men are so simple of mind, and so much dominated by their immediate needs, that a deceitful man will always find plenty who are ready to be deceived. One of many recent examples calls for mention. Alexander VI never did anything else, never had another thought, except to deceive men, and he always found fresh material to work on. Never was there a man more convincing in his assertions, who sealed his promises with more solemn oaths, and who observed them less. Yet his deceptions were always successful, because he knew exactly how to manage this sort of business.

In actual fact, a prince may not have all the admirable qualities listed above, but it is very necessary that he should seem to have them. Indeed, I will venture to say that when you have them and exercise them all the time, they are harmful to you; when you just seem to have them, they are useful. It is good to appear merciful, truthful, humane, sincere, and religious; it is good to be so in reality. But you must keep your mind so disposed that, in case of need, you can turn to the exact contrary. This has to be understood: a prince, and especially a new prince, cannot possibly exercise all those virtues for which men are called "good." To preserve the state, he often has to do things against his word, against charity, against humanity, against religion. Thus he has to have a mind ready to shift as the winds of fortune and the varying circumstances of life may dictate. And as I said above, he should not depart from the good if he can hold to it, but he should be ready to enter on evil if he has to.

Hence a prince should take great care never to drop a word that does not seem imbued with the five good qualities noted above; to anyone who sees or hears him, he should appear all compassion, all honor, all humanity, all integrity, all religion. Nothing is more necessary than to seem to have this last virtue. Men in general judge more by the sense of sight than by the sense of touch, because everyone can see but only a few can test by feeling. Everyone sees what you seem to be, few know what you really are; and those few do not dare take a stand against the general opinion, supported by the majesty of the government. In the actions of all men, and especially of princes who are not subject to a court of appeal, we must always look to the end. Let a prince, therefore, win victories and uphold his state; his methods will always be considered worthy, and everyone will praise them, because the masses are always impressed by the superficial appearance of things, and by the outcome of an enterprise. And the world consists of nothing but the masses; the few have no influence when the many feel secure. A certain prince of our own time, whom it is just as well not to name, preaches nothing but peace and mutual trust, yet he is the determined enemy of both; and if on several different occasions he had observed either, he would have lost both his reputation and his throne.

The Justice of General Ts'ao,
from *Romance of the Three Kingdoms* (1522)

ROMANCE OF THE *Three Kingdoms* is generally regarded as China's oldest novel. Although it first appeared in print in 1522, attributed to one Lo Kuan-chung (ca. 1330–ca. 1400), there is considerable evidence that its composition dates to an earlier age. Chronicling the turbulent period following the end of the Han Dynasty (206 BCE–220 CE), when China disintegrated into three rival kingdoms, this tale of political chaos and civil war is preoccupied with questions of legitimacy and centralization: "Empires wax and wane," it begins, "states cleave asunder and coalesce." Into the vacuum of power created by the fall of the Han step several competitors, each of whom marshals support with a combination of force and cleverness. The rock musician Kaiser Kuo, who grew up, like many Chinese boys, on stories from *Romance of the Three Kingdoms*, commented to the *BBC News Magazine* in 2012: "The real story is about how to deploy people of talent. It's really all about management and when I read these stories today, I still find just tremendous relevance." The book dramatizes a contest of Confucian values against treachery and brutality, especially as embodied in the book's dynamic villain, Ts'ao Ts'ao (155–220 CE), whom the Chinese literature scholar Robert E. Hegel describes as a man of "cool calculations and pragmatic manipulations." A historical figure who was, among other things, a commentator on Sun Tzu's *The Art of War*, Ts'ao has become a byword for ruthlessness in the Chinese tradition. As the chapter excerpted here indicates, Ts'ao's cleverness is both linguistic and strategic in nature. He is an unsentimental master of public relations, anticipation, and advance planning. Sensitive to the weaknesses of others, he is quick to take advantage of trusting natures and capitalize on vulnerabilities. (The following selection is translated by C. H. Brewitt-Taylor.)

The Justice of General Ts'ao

Then came news that Sun Ts'e's fleet was near and would attack on the west. The other three land corps took each one face and the city was in a parlous state.

At this juncture Yuan Shu summoned his officers. Yang Ta-chiang explained the case. "Shouch'un has suffered from drought for several years and the people are on the verge of famine. Sending an army would add to the distress and anger the people, and victory would be uncertain. I advise not to send any more soldiers there, but to hold on till the besiegers are conquered by lack of supplies. Our noble chief, with his regiment of guards, will move over to the other side of the river, which is quite ready, and we shall also escape the enemy's ferocity."

So due arrangements being made to guard Shouch'un a general move was made to the other side of the Huai River. Not only the army went over but all the accumulated wealth of the Yuan family, gold and silver, jewels and precious stones, were moved.

Ts'ao Ts'ao's army of seventeen legions needed daily no inconsiderable quantity of food, and as the country around had been famine-stricken for several years nothing could be got there. So he tried to hasten the military operations and capture the city. On the other hand, the defenders knew the value of delay and simply held on. After a month's vigorous siege the fall of the city seemed as far off as it was at first and supplies were very short. Letters were sent to Sun Ts'e, who sent a hundred thousand measures of grain. When the usual distribution became impossible the Chief of the Commissariat, Jen Hsun, and the Controller of the Granaries, Wang Hou, presented a statement asking what was to be done.

"Serve out with a smaller measure," said Ts'ao. "That will save us for a time."

"But if the soldiers murmur, what then?"

"I shall have another device."

As ordered the controllers issued grain in a short measure. Ts'ao sent secretly to find out how the men took this and when he found that complaints were general and they were saying that he was fooling them, he sent a secret summons to the controller. When he came Ts'ao said, "I want to ask you to lend me something to pacify the soldiers with. You must not refuse."

"What does the Minister wish?"

"I want the loan of your head to expose to the soldiery."

"But I have done nothing wrong!" exclaimed the unhappy man.

"I know that, but if I do not put you to death there will be a mutiny. After you are gone your wife and children shall be my care. So you need not grieve on their account."

Wang Hou was about to remonstrate further but Ts'ao Ts'ao gave a signal, the executioners hustled him out and he was beheaded. His head was exposed on a tall pole and a notice said that in accordance with military law Wang Hou had been put to death for peculation and the use of a short measure in issuing grain.

This appeased the discontent. Next followed a general order threatening death to the various commanders if the city was not taken within three days. Ts'ao Ts'ao in person went up to the very walls to superintend the work of filling up the moat. The defenders kept up constant showers of stones and arrows. Two inferior officers, who left their stations in fear, were slain by Ts'ao

Ts'ao himself. Thereafter he went on foot to see that work went on continuously and no one dared be a laggard. Thus encouraged the army became invincible and no defence could withstand their onslaught. In a very short time the walls were scaled, the gates battered in and the besiegers were in possession. The officers of the garrison were captured alive and were executed in the market place. All the paraphernalia of imperial state were burned and the whole city wrecked.

When the question of crossing the river in pursuit of Yuan Shu came up Hsun Yu opposed it saying, "The country has suffered from short crops for years and we should be unable to get grain. An advance would weary the army, harm the people and possibly end in disaster. I advise a return to the capital to wait there till the spring wheat shall have been harvested and we have plenty of food."

Ts'ao Ts'ao hesitated and before he had made up his mind there came an urgent message saying Chang Hsiu, with the support of Liu Piao, was ravaging the country all round, that there was rebellion in Nanyang and Ts'ao Hung could not cope with it. He had been worsted already in several engagements and was in sore straits.

Ts'ao Ts'ao at once wrote to Sun Ts'e to command the river so as to prevent any move on the part of Liu Piao, while he prepared his army to go to deal with Chang Hsiu. Before marching he directed Liu Pei to camp at Hsiaop'ei, as he and Lu Pu, being as brothers, might help each other.

When Lu Pu had left for Hsuchou Ts'ao Ts'ao said secretly to Yuan-te, "I am leaving you at Hsiaop'ei as a pitfall for the tiger. You will only take advice from the two Ch'ens and there can be no mishap. You will find so-and-so your ally when needed."

So Ts'ao Ts'ao marched to Hsutu where he heard that Tuan Wei had slain Li Ts'ui and Wu Hsi had killed Kuo Ssu and they presented the heads of these two. Besides the whole clan of Li Ts'ui had been arrested and brought to the capital. They were all put to death at various gates and their heads exposed. People thought this very harsh dealing.

In the Emperor's palace a large number of officials were assembled at a peace banquet. The two successful leaders Tuan and Wu were rewarded with titles and sent to guard Ch'angan. They came to audience to express their gratitude and marched away.

Then Ts'ao Ts'ao sent in a memorial that Chang Hsiu was in rebellion and an army must be sent against him. The Emperor in person arranged the chariot and escorted his Minister out of the city when he went to take command of the expedition. It was the summer, the fourth month of the third year of the period Chien-An (199 A.D.). Hsun Yu was in chief military command in Hsutu.

The army marched away. In the course of the march they passed through a wheat district and the grain was ready for harvesting but the peasants had fled for fear and the corn was uncut. Ts'ao Ts'ao caused it to be made known all about that he was sent on the expedition by command of the Emperor to capture a rebel and save the people. He could not avoid moving in the harvest season but if any one trampled down the corn he should be put to death. Military law was so severe that the people need fear no damage. The people were very pleased and lined the road, wishing success to the expedition. When the soldiers passed wheat fields they dismounted and pushed aside the stalks so that none were trampled down.

One day, when Ts'ao Ts'ao was riding through the fields, a dove suddenly got up, startling the horse so that he swerved into the standing grain and a large patch was trampled down. Ts'ao at once called the Provost Marshal and bade him decree the sentence for the crime of trampling down corn.

"How can I deal with your crime?" asked the Provost Marshal.

"I made the rule and I have broken it. Can I otherwise satisfy public opinion?"

He laid hold of the sword by his side and made to take his own life. All hastened to prevent him and Kuo Chia said, "In ancient days, the days of the Spring and Autumn history, the laws were not applied to the persons of the most honourable. You are the supreme leader of a mighty army and must not wound yourself."

Ts'ao Ts'ao pondered for a long time. At last he said. "Since there exists the reason just quoted I may perhaps escape the death penalty."

Then with his sword he cut off his hair and threw it on the ground saying, "I cut off the hair as touching the head."

Then he sent a man to exhibit the hair throughout the whole army saying. "The Minister, having trodden down some corn, ought to have lost his head by the terms of the order, now here is his hair cut off as an attack on the head."

This deed was a stimulus to discipline all through the army so that not a man dared be disobedient. A poet wrote:—

> A myriad soldiers march along and all are brave and bold,
> And their myriad inclinations by one leader are controlled.
> That crafty leader shore his locks when forfeit was his head.
> O full of guile wert thou, Ts'ao Ts'ao, as every one has said.

Mervyn LeRoy
(1900–1987)

BORN IN SAN Francisco, a survivor of the 1908 earthquake, Mervyn LeRoy worked as a real-life newsboy until a customer offered him a job to play the part of a newsboy in a play. Thus began a show-business career: LeRoy did vaudeville until he moved to Hollywood in 1919, when he went to work in the wardrobe department at Warner Brothers. By 1927, he was directing his first film. In the years that followed LeRoy helmed several important social dramas, including *Little Caesar* (1931) and *I Am a Fugitive from a Chain Gang* (1932). He ranged widely over the course of his career at Warner Brothers and MGM from comedy to action and produced *The Wizard of Oz* (1939). This section of LeRoy's autobiography, *Mervyn LeRoy: Take One*, looks at his early days in film, when Cecil B. DeMille (1881–1959) was one of the industry's reigning kings. As a young man, DeMille was an actor and later the general manager of his mother's theater company until he formed a partnership with Jesse L. Lasky and Samuel Goldwyn in 1913. He went to Hollywood and directed *The Squaw Man* (1914), a pivotal feature that helped to make the motion picture a more substantial art form. DeMille was a consummate showman who brought high production values to his films, many of which featured plots based on the formula of sin redeemed. DeMille was the director-general of the Jesse L. Lasky Feature Play Company, later Paramount, where he worked for the rest of his career. He produced and directed some seventy films, including the 1923 epic *The Ten Commandments*, the filming of which LeRoy describes here. This episode suggests not only the strict hierarchy that shaped—and continues to shape—film sets but also the ways in which DeMille mastered every aspect of production, ensuring, by trickery if necessary, that the show would go on.

Cecil B. DeMille on the Set
from *Mervyn LeRoy: Take One* (1974)

looked around for something else to do. I was lucky. My friends, the actors at the boardinghouse, told me that Cecil B. DeMille was hiring actors by the hundreds for his coming epic, *The Ten Commandments*. Surely, Cecil would find a place for me in the huge cast, because he knew me. The next morning, I rushed over to the studio, presented myself to DeMille, and was immediately hired.

DeMille—Cecil, not William—had always seemed to like me. As the top director of that era, he had been the magnet that had drawn me to his set as often as I could go. I loved to watch him work. I remember one day his assistant director, Hezi Tate, had tried to throw me off the set. DeMille was way up on a boom camera; he saw what was going on and he called down, "Hey, Mervyn, where are you going?"

"I've been thrown off the set, Mr. DeMille," I called up.

DeMille yelled at Tate, "Hezi, you let Mervyn LeRoy stay on any set of mine as long as he wants to."

Tate was the man who once had replied to a DeMille bawling out by saying, "Yes, God, I'll do it your way."

So I was among friends when I hired on as one of the children of Israel for *The Ten Commandments*. I was excited. This would be a chance to watch DeMille, the greatest epic director of them all since D. W. Griffith, at close range. I'd be able to see an epic take shape from the inside. Everybody in Hollywood was excited about *The Ten Commandments*. The word was out that this was going to be the biggest, gaudiest, and most expensive motion picture yet made.

DeMille was a daring man, and he had a lot of guts. He had to have, when he took his idea to Adolph Zukor in New York. Zukor ran the studio, with Lasky's help, and he was a tough man with a dollar. Until that time, the costliest Hollywood movie had been *The Covered Wagon*, which director James Cruze had made for Lasky, for somewhere under eight hundred thousand dollars. DeMille went to New York and told Zukor he wanted to make a film about the flight of the Israelites from Egypt.

"How much?" That was Zukor's reaction. (DeMille wasn't surprised. Zukor's reaction was always "How much?")

DeMille didn't bat an eye. He just said, with a great display of outward calm, "One million dollars."

Zukor slid down in his chair and DeMille could only see the top of his head. He told me later that at that moment he remembered a classic story about Zukor and his short stature. Zukor was supposed to have been in his office when a society lady came in and said, "Sir, I am accustomed to having gentlemen rise to greet me." Zukor, in an offended tone, answered her: "But, madam, I have risen."

DeMille addressed what little he could see of the film magnate and told him all he was going to do for that million dollars. He explained the story and detailed the spectacle, scene by scene, and—after DeMille had spoken about how much money the picture could make—Zukor and Lasky finally agreed.

So we knew, in Hollywood, that this was going to be something special, the biggest thing the screen had yet seen. I looked forward with tremendous anticipation to being part of it. The experience would be of great help to me forty years later, when I made my own epic, *Quo Vadis*.

I was just one of a crowd—a crowd that would number, before we were finished, some 3,500 people. Almost all my friends were in the mob scene, too, so it was pleasant work.

DeMille had built a small city for his cast and crew in the desert northeast of Los Angeles. It had to be big, because, besides the 3,500 humans involved in the production, there were roughly 3,000 animals in it, too. There were tents for the actors and corrals for the animals. DeMille's own tent was, as befitted the leader of such a monumental expedition, larger and gaudier than all the rest. There were expensive imported (just for the occasion) Oriental rugs on the floor and he had gone out and purchased an antique four-poster bed, with the heads of snakes at the peak of each post, on which he would sleep at night.

No matter what is said about DeMille, there was one phase of movie-making at which he was a master. He knew how to organize a tremendous motion picture better than anyone else. That was the secret of his success with spectacles. Everything was planned and routinized, and the huge machine functioned like an army. It had to.

We were awakened at dawn—I seem to remember that it was 4:30 A.M., or some such dreadful hour—by a bugle blowing reveille. We lined up for breakfast at the mess tents. Then we were divided into groups, which were called by military names—platoons and companies—with assistant directors in charge. They had military titles, too. Lieutenants were in command of platoons, captains in command of companies. These officers gave us our instructions. They, in turn, had gotten their instructions from colonels and generals.

At the pinnacle of this mountain of military officialdom was the commanding general, DeMille himself. It was off limits for any but a select few to approach him directly. If there was any reason you had to consult the director, you had to do it through a strictly-by-channels chain. Among the actors, there were only a handful permitted the luxury of talking to the great man.

Theodore Roberts, the man who had given me my first acting job in San Francisco, was one. He was playing Moses. Others in that rarefied group were James Neill, who played Aaron, and a few others, such as Charles DeRoche, Estelle Taylor (later Mrs. Jack Dempsey), and Julia Faye. But even they found it difficult to get an audience with DeMille.

Once, I remember, Roberts and Neill wanted to see him, but were kept waiting by subordinates outside the command tent for almost an hour. Finally, Roberts grabbed DeMille's assistant director, Hezi Tate, and boomed: "Tell God that Moses and Aaron wish words with him."

The picture dragged on. We struggled through the sand in temperatures well over 100 degrees. I gobbled salt tablets and drank water, but I still lost weight. Yet every day was exhilarating, as I watched DeMille forge a film from that mass of humanity.

It was taking longer than he had anticipated, and that meant it was costing more money. The projected million-dollar budget looked less and less realistic. Zukor, the guardian of the buck, grew so worried he came out to the desert to see for himself what the problem was. He looked incongruous, that pale little man in his city suit out there with all of us tanned-to-a-crisp Israelites in our white robes.

I happened to be near them, when Zukor and DeMille got together. Their handshake was brief and perfunctory. They never were what you could call dear friends.

"Well, Cecil," Zukor said. "The money keeps piling up. What's the story?"

DeMille, hot and tired and nervous to begin with, blew up at that question, which came without the usual preliminaries of socially graceful conversation.

"What do you want me to do?" he bellowed. "Stop shooting now and release it as *The Five Commandments*?"

Zukor, of course, never intended that DeMille stop his filming. He just wanted him to hurry it up and get it done so the expenses would stop.

I learned much about the handling of crowds from my experience on *The Ten Commandments*. There wasn't much else for me to do but learn. My own role was merely that of an extra and, aside from keeping the sand out of my eyes and brushing the flies away from my face, I had no other major responsibilities. So I kept my eyes open and watched the Master, as we all called him, at work.

One of the key scenes in the picture was Moses' descent from Mount Sinai with the sacred tablet. We Israelites were clustered at the base of the mountain as Moses made his way down the slope. It was obviously a scene that was vital to the whole production and had to be just right. What DeMille wanted, he kept reminding us, were expressions of awe and reverence on our faces. We had been working in that heat for weeks and weeks, and it is hard for anybody to look reverential under those conditions. Actually, I guess we looked bored and uncomfortable, instead of awed and reverential. DeMille wasn't happy with what he saw.

He shot it once. Then he called a break, and we tried to find shade somewhere and sank down, exhausted. I saw DeMille talking to Tate, but didn't think much about it. The next thing I knew, the bell in the town church nearby was tolling. It was a new sound out there in the bleak desert and none of us knew what was happening. Then we heard the call for us to gather around DeMille.

He addressed us through his megaphone. His voice was breaking. He choked back sobs. And he told us how one of the members of the cast had died. He had just received the terrible news. The poor man, he said, had left a widow and eight children.

"Now, in his memory," he said, "I ask for two minutes of respectful silence."

We all stood there, silently, our faces mirroring the tragedy we had just heard. There were tears in many eyes. There were awed and reverential expressions on every face.

We had been had. While we stood there for that expression of respect for the departed, the cameras were grinding away. Nobody had died. It was just DeMille's way of getting what he wanted on film. That scene, of the Israelites at the foot of Mount Sinai waiting for Moses to descend, was hailed as one of the most magnificent and spiritual in the entire movie.

C. K. Williams
(b. 1936)

A NATIVE OF New Jersey, C. K. Williams attended Bucknell College and the
University of Pennsylvania. He teaches at Princeton. One of the most prominent U.S. poets writing today, Williams is the winner of several prizes,
including the National Book Critics Circle Award for *In Flesh and Blood*
(1987), the Pulitzer Prize for *Repair* (2000), and the National Book Award
for *The Singing* (2003). In addition to several books of poetry, he has published translations and prose criticism. Williams's signature is the long line,
which was popularized by Walt Whitman in the nineteenth century. Writing in the *New York Times*, Dan Chiasson argued that Williams "has been
misunderstood as an entirely 'social' poet, but his real subject is the mind
that attempts, never entirely successfully, to ward off the social world that
bombards it from every side." Chaisson continues, "His lines, longer than
those written by any other significant English-language poet, suggest a big,
Whitman-like appetite for worldly variety. This is not simply the case. Williams is a poet of imaginative composure amid real-world disarray. His fastidious, refined heart camps in the middle of the worldly misery that
minimizes its claims." In this version of the ancient story of Hercules,
Deianira, and the deadly shirt of Nessus, Williams explores the private
drama of a marriage set against the backdrop of the monstrous treacheries
of the mythological universe.

Hercules, Deianira, Nessus
from *The Vigil* (1997)

There was absolutely no reason after the centaur had pawed her and tried to
  mount her,
after Hercules waiting across the raging river for the creature to carry her to
  him
heard her cry out and launched an arrow soaked in the Hydra's incurable
  venom into the monster,
that Deianira should have believed him, Nessus, horrible thing, as he died,
  but she did.

We see the end of the story: Deianira anguished, aghast, suicide-sword in her
  hand;

Hercules's blood hissing and seething like water into which molten rods are
      plunged to anneal,
but how could a just-married girl hardly out of her father's house have
      envisioned all that,
and even conjecturing that Nessus was lying, plotting revenge, how could she
      have been sure?

We see the centaur as cunning, malignant, a hybrid from the savage time
      before ours
when emotion always was passion and passion was always unchecked by
      commandment or conscience;
she sees only a man-horse, mortally hurt, suddenly harmless, eyes suddenly
      soft as a foal's,
telling her, 'Don't be afraid, come closer, listen': offering homage, friendship, a
      favor.

In our age of scrutiny and dissection we know Deianira's mind better than
      she does herself:
we know the fortune of women as chattel and quarry, objects to be won then
      shunted aside;
we understand the cost of repression, the repercussions of unsatisfied rage
      and resentment,
but consciousness then was still new, Deianira inhabited hers like the light
      from a fire.

Or might she have glimpsed with that mantic prescience the gods hadn't
      taken away yet
her hero a lifetime later on the way home with another king's daughter,
      callow, but lovely,
lovely enough to erase from Hercules's scruples not only his vows but the
      simple convention
that tells you you don't bring a rival into your aging wife's weary, sorrowful
      bed?

. . . No, more likely the centaur's promise intrigued in itself: an infallible
      potion of love.
'Just gather the clots of blood from my wound: here, use my shirt, then hide it
      away.
Though so exalted, so regal a woman as you never would need it, it might still
      be of use:
whoever's shoulders it touches, no matter when, will helplessly, hopelessly
      love you forever.'

See Hercules now, in the shirt Deianira has sent him, approaching the fire of
an altar,
the garment suddenly clinging, the Hydra, his long-vanquished foe, alive in
its threads,
each thread a tentacle clutching at him, each chemical tentacle acid, adhering,
consuming,
charring before his horrified eyes skin from muscle, muscle from tendon,
tendon from bone.

Now Deianira, back then, the viscous gouts of Nessus's blood dyeing her
diffident hands:
if she could imagine us watching her there in her myth, how would she want
us to see her?
Surely as symbol, a petal of sympathy caught in the perilous rift between
culture and chaos,
not as the nightmare she is, a corpse with a slash of tardy self-knowledge deep
in its side.

What Hercules sees as he pounds up the bank isn't himself cremated alive on
his pyre,
shrieking as Jove his Olympian father extracts his immortal essence from its
agonized sheath:
he sees what's before him: the woman, his bride, kneeling to the dark, rushing
river,
obsessively scrubbing away, he must think, the nocuous, mingled reek of
horse, Hydra, human.

DISCUSSION QUESTIONS

1. *What is the relative worth of words and deeds in your organization?*

2. *Where is the line between the persuasion necessary to motivate others to
accomplish unpleasant, even dangerous, tasks, on one hand, and deception,
on the other?*

3. *In a world characterized by more than its share of duplicity, how can the
honest avoid becoming victims?*

NEGOTIATING WORLD
AND SELF

If you don't follow the same Way, don't make plans together.

—CONFUCIUS,
Analects, 15.40

The vales of literature are littered with the ruins of failed negotiations. Consider Shakespeare's *King Lear*, a text not infrequently cited in leadership contexts because it offers such a rich trove of bad examples. Perhaps Lear's greatest failing, and the fateful episode that sets up the ensuing tragedy, is his spectacularly inept decision to negotiate away his kingdom to his three daughters. The bargain he attempts to strike involves an exchange of real estate for filial devotion: whichever daughter professes the "most" love for her father will receive the "largest" share of territory. But Lear misreads all three of his daughters: Regan and Goneril provide inflationary accountings of a love they do not feel and thus win their shares, while the faithful Cordelia, refusing to barter with her love and rejecting the "glib and oily art" practiced by her sisters, says "Nothing." "Nothing," her father replies, "will come of nothing."

With Cordelia banished, Lear is left to the mercies of the treacherous Regan and Goneril, in whose households he is scheduled to stay by turns a month at a time. The scheme soon goes awry, and in a wrenching scene that reminds us of the opening negotiation, the two daughters collaborate in setting harder and harder conditions for their hospitality: they insist that Lear must reduce his retinue of a hundred knights to fifty, then twenty-five, then ten, then five, and finally not even one. "I gave you all," he replies in disbelief before his daughters bar their gates and leave him to the elements.

Several factors contribute to making Lear a poor negotiator. Placing his trust in the wrong people, he rejects the advice of wise counselors and fails to recognize Cordelia's silence for what it is: sincerity. Lacking self-knowledge, psychological insight, and emotional intelligence, he is blinded by his vanity and self-importance to the real sources of his power and authority and to the true natures of his eldest daughters. Finally, he knows only one mode: a royal one. He is "every inch a king," but as a king he is trained to resolve conflicts with exercises of power and entirely unpracticed in the ways of mediation and diplomacy.

Confucius advises us to make plans with only those who "follow the same Way," those who are, in other words, dedicated to the same principles. But effective negotiators do not always have this luxury. We would like to think that our negotiations are predicated on trust, but we often suspect our counterparts of self-interest at least and perhaps dark designs. Like former New Mexico governor Bill Richardson, we may even find ourselves sitting across the table from, in Richardson's terms, thugs, tyrants, schemers, and narcissists. Negotiators must often broker deals between sides that do not share common customs or assumptions. Richardson, for example, has attempted to resolve violent conflicts in places such as North Korea, Sudan, and Congo.

During the latter half of the twentieth century, negotiation and conflict resolution grew into busy fields of academic study. The publication of the enduring bestseller *Getting to Yes: Negotiating Agreement Without Giving In* introduced the theory of "principled negotiation" devised by Harvard law professors Roger Fisher and William Ury to an audience beyond academia. Fisher and Ury set forth four essential principles: separate the people from the problem; focus on interests, not positions; invent options for mutual gain; and insist on objective criteria. In recent years, the field of negotiation studies has boomed. Business magazines are full of "dos and don'ts" for prospective negotiators of all kinds, from the used car buyer to the mergers-and-acquisitions specialist. Drawing on law, economics, psychology, and sociology, projects such as Harvard's Program on Negotiation and Wharton's Executive Negotiation and Strategic Persuasion Workshops as well as various graduate programs in peace studies and conflict resolution take multidisciplinary approaches to the art and science of negotiation. Aspiring negotiators can even employ something called the Thomas-Kilmann Conflict Mode Instrument to assess whether they are competitors or collaborators. Competing gurus of negotiation often contradict one another, but certain recommendations emerge repeatedly. Many experts emphasize certain fundamental requirements: detailed research, self-awareness, emotional intelligence, cross-cultural sophistication, good listening skills, and flexibility. Others add performance and theatricality to this list of essentials.

In the selections that follow, authors ranging from an ancient Chinese mystic to a twenty-first-century novelist illuminate various aspects of negotiation. Montaigne engages in an exercise in self-awareness by comparing the civilized nations of Europe with the "cannibals" of the New World; in the process, he suggests the degree to which society has succeeded in concealing and distorting human motives. The fifteenth- and sixteenth-century courtiers Baldassare Castiglione and Francis Bacon offer insight into the arts of persuasion and the proper relationship between advisers and leaders. An episode from *Shahnameh*, the Persian Book of Kings, shows Alexander the Great being schooled in negotiation by the emperor of China. The nineteenth-century Lakota chief Red Cloud speaks eloquently on two occasions during a visit to New York City about conflict and amity, while Zadie Smith's speech, given almost 140 years later at the New York Public Library, chronicles the challenge of speaking in different voices and bridging two worlds. Elizabeth I reveals that sometimes the wisest course of action is refusing to negotiate at all, while Chuang Tzu suggests that another technique for mediating conflict is to transcend it altogether.

RECOMMENDED READING AND VIEWING

Argo (2012), directed by Ben Affleck
Euripides, *Antigone* (fifth century BCE)
Bill Richardson with Kevin Bleyer, *How to Sweet-Talk a Shark: Strategies and Stories from a Master Negotiator* (2013)
Rory Stewart, *The Places in Between* (2004)
Thucydides, "The Talks at Melos," from *The Peloponnesian War*, book 5

Michel de Montaigne
(1533–1592)

OFTEN CONSIDERED THE inventor of the modern essay, Michel de Montaigne was many things: scion of a noble family, public official, traveler, philosopher, counselor. He was also a man of freely avowed inconsistency: he valued books but prized experience; he enjoyed society but on his thirty-eighth birthday retreated permanently to a study on his estate, emerging only for his meals. Montaigne's father ensured that Latin was his son's first language: the boy spoke no French until the age of six. After studying law, Montaigne became counselor to the Parlement in Bordeaux and was twice the city's mayor. Siding with the Catholics in France's ferocious religious wars, Montaigne was nevertheless close to the Protestant champion Henri de Navarre. Montaigne took charge of the family estate and retired from public life in 1571, when he began to write the essays for which modernity prizes him. Translated into English in 1603 by John Florio, read by Shakespeare, Montaigne shares with the playwright a capacity for expressing movements of thought—for communicating interiority—by engaging in a conversation with the writers who formed him: Plutarch, Seneca, and Virgil above all. In her *New Yorker* essay "Me, Myself, and I," Jane Kramer captures Montaigne's achievement: "However you read them, Montaigne's books were utterly, if inexplicably, original. They were not confessional, like Augustine's, nor were they autobiographical. You could call them the autobiography of a mind." Montaigne wrote about many things—from cannibals to cowardice, from drunkenness to sex—yet he claimed always to be writing about himself. In this essay, alluded to in Claude Lévi-Strauss's "Men, Women, and Chiefs" ("Studying the System"), Montaigne uses the occasion of a visit of Tupinamba Indians from Brazil to France as a point of departure for a meditation on civilization and savagery and on the European's negotiation of his own savage self. (The following selection is translated by Donald Frame.)

Of Cannibals
from *Essays* (1580)

When King Pyrrhus passed over into Italy, after he had reconnoitered the formation of the army that the Romans were sending to meet him, he said: "I do not know what barbarians these are" (for so the Greeks called all foreign nations), "but the formation of this army that I see is not at all barbarous." The Greeks said as much of the army that Flaminius brought into their country, and so did Philip, seeing from a knoll the order and distribution of the Roman camp, in his kingdom, under Publius Sulpicius Galba. Thus we should beware of clinging to vulgar opinions, and judge things by reason's way, not by popular say.

I had with me for a long time a man who had lived for ten or twelve years in that other world which has been discovered in our century, in the place where Villegagnon landed, and which he called Antarctic France. This discovery of a boundless country seems worthy of consideration. I don't know if I can guarantee that some other such discovery will not be made in the future, so many personages greater than ourselves having been mistaken about this one. I am afraid we have eyes bigger than our stomachs, and more curiosity than capacity. We embrace everything, but we clasp only wind.

Plato brings in Solon, telling how he had learned from the priests of the city of Saïs in Egypt that in days of old, before the Flood, there was a great island named Atlantis, right at the mouth of the Strait of Gibraltar, which contained more land than Africa and Asia put together, and that the kings of that country, who not only possessed that island but had stretched out so far on the mainland that they held the breadth of Africa as far as Egypt, and the length of Europe as far as Tuscany, undertook to step over into Asia and subjugate all the nations that border on the Mediterranean, as far as the Black Sea; and for this purpose crossed the Spains, Gaul, Italy, as far as Greece, where the Athenians checked them; but that some time after, both the Athenians and themselves and their island were swallowed up by the Flood.

It is quite likely that that extreme devastation of waters made amazing changes in the habitations of the earth, as people maintain that the sea cut off Sicily from Italy—

> 'Tis said an earthquake once asunder tore
> These lands with dreadful havoc, which before
> Formed but one land, one coast
>
> VIRGIL

—Cyprus from Syria, the island of Euboea from the mainland of Boeotia; and elsewhere joined lands that were divided, filling the channels between them with sand and mud:

> A sterile marsh, long fit for rowing, now
> Feeds neighbor towns, and feels the heavy plow
>
> HORACE

But there is no great likelihood that that island was the new world which we have just discovered; for it almost touched Spain, and it would be an incredible result of a flood to have forced it away as far as it is, more than twelve hundred leagues; besides, the travels of the moderns have already almost revealed that it is not an island, but a mainland connected with the East Indies on one side, and elsewhere with the lands under the two poles; or, if it is separated from them, it is by so narrow a strait and interval that it does not deserve to be called an island on that account.

It seems that there are movements, some natural, others feverish, in these great bodies, just as in our own. When I consider the inroads that my river, the Dordogne, is making in my lifetime into the right bank in its descent, and that in twenty years it has gained so much ground and stolen away the foundations of several buildings, I clearly see that this is an extraordinary disturbance; for if it had always gone at this rate, or was to do so in the future, the face of the world would be turned topsy-turvy. But rivers are subject to changes: now they overflow in one direction, now in another, now they keep to their course. I am not speaking of the sudden inundations whose causes are manifest. In Médoc, along the seashore, my brother, the sieur d'Arsac, can see an estate of his buried under the sands that the sea spews forth; the tops of some buildings are still visible; his farms and domains have changed into very thin pasturage. The inhabitants say that for some time the sea has been pushing toward them so hard that they have lost four leagues of land. These sands are its harbingers; and we see great dunes of moving sand that march half a league ahead of it and keep conquering land.

The other testimony of antiquity with which some would connect this discovery is in Aristotle, at least if that little book *Of Unheard-of Wonders* is by him. He there relates that certain Carthaginians, after setting out upon the Atlantic Ocean from the Strait of Gibraltar and sailing a long time, at last discovered a great fertile island, all clothed in woods and watered by great deep rivers, far remote from any mainland; and that they, and others since, attracted by the goodness and fertility of the soil, went there with their wives and children, and began to settle there. The lords of Carthage, seeing that their country was gradually becoming depopulated, expressly forbade anyone to go there any more, on pain of death, and drove out these new inhabitants, fearing, it is said, that in course of time they might come to multiply so greatly as to supplant their former masters and ruin their state. This story of Aristotle does not fit our new lands any better than the other.

This man I had was a simple, crude fellow—a character fit to bear true witness; for clever people observe more things and more curiously, but they interpret them; and to lend weight and conviction to their interpretation, they cannot help altering history a little. They never show you things as they are, but bend and disguise them according to the way they have seen them; and to give credence to their judgment and attract you to it, they are prone to add something to their matter, to stretch it out and amplify it. We need a man either very honest, or so simple that he has not the stuff to build up false inventions and give them plausibility; and wedded to no theory. Such was my man; and besides this, he at various times brought sailors and merchants, whom he had known on that trip, to see me. So I content myself with his information, without inquiring what the cosmographers say about it.

We ought to have topographers who would give us an exact account of the places where they have been. But because they have over us the advantage of having seen Palestine, they want to enjoy the privilege of telling us news about all the rest of the world. I would like everyone to write what he knows, not only in this, but in all other subjects; for a man may have some special knowledge and experience of the nature of a river or a fountain, who in other matters knows only what everybody knows. However, to circulate this little scrap of knowledge, he will undertake to write the whole of physics. From this vice spring many great abuses.

Now, to return to my subject, I think there is nothing barbarous and savage in that nation, from what I have been told, except that each man calls barbarism whatever is not his own practice; for indeed it seems we have no other test of truth and reason than the example and pattern of the opinions and customs of the country we live in. *There* is always the perfect religion, the perfect government, the perfect and accomplished manners in all things. Those people are wild, just as we call wild the fruits that Nature has produced by herself and in her normal course; where really it is those that we have changed artificially and led astray from the common order, that we should rather call wild. The former retain alive and vigorous their genuine, their most useful and natural, virtues and properties, which we have debased in the latter in adapting them to gratify our corrupted taste. And yet for all that, the savor and delicacy of some uncultivated fruits of those countries is quite as excellent, even to our taste, as that of our own. It is not reasonable that art should win the place of honor over our great and powerful mother Nature. We have so overloaded the beauty and richness of her works by our inventions that we have quite smothered her. Yet wherever her purity shines forth, she wonderfully puts to shame our vain and frivolous attempts:

> Ivy comes readier without our care;
> In lonely caves the arbutus grows more fair;
> No art with artless bird song can compare
> PROPERTIUS

All our efforts cannot even succeed in reproducing the nest of the tiniest little bird, its contexture, its beauty and convenience; or even the web of the puny spider. All things, says Plato, are produced by nature, by fortune, or by art; the greatest and most beautiful by one or the other of the first two, the least and most imperfect by the last.

These nations, then, seem to me barbarous in this sense, that they have been fashioned very little by the human mind, and are still very close to their original naturalness. The laws of nature still rule them, very little corrupted by ours; and they are in such a state of purity that I am sometimes vexed that they were unknown earlier, in the days when there were men able to judge them better than we. I am sorry that Lycurgus and Plato did not know of them; for it seems to me that what we actually see in these nations surpasses not only all the pictures in which poets have idealized the golden age and all their inventions in imagining a happy state of man, but also the conceptions and the very desire of philosophy . They could not imagine a naturalness so pure and simple as we see by experience; nor could they believe that our society could be maintained with so little artifice and human solder. This is a nation, I should say to Plato, in which there is no sort of traffic, no knowledge of letters, no science of numbers, no name for a magistrate of for political superiority, no custom of servitude, no riches or poverty, no contacts, no successions, no partitions, no occupations but leisure ones, no care for any but common kinship, no clothes, no agriculture, no metal, no use of wine or wheat. The very words that signify lying, treachery, dissimulation, avarice, envy, belittling, pardon—unheard of. How far from this perfection would he find the republic that he imagined: *Men fresh sprung from the gods* [Seneca].

> These manners nature first ordained
> VIRGIL

For the rest, they live in a country with a very pleasant and temperate climate, so that according to my witnesses it is rare to see a sick man there; and they have assured me that they never saw one palsied, bleary-eyed, toothless, or bent with age. They are settled along the sea and shut in on the land side by great high mountains, with a stretch about a hundred leagues wide in between. They have a great abundance of fish and flesh which bear no resemblance to ours, and they eat them with no other artifice than cooking. The first man who rode a horse there, though he had had dealings with them on several other trips, so horrified them in this posture that they shot him dead with arrows before they could recognize him.

Their buildings are very long, with a capacity of two or three hundred souls; they are covered with the bark of great trees, the strips reaching to the ground at one end and supporting and leaning on one another at the top, in the manner of some of our barns, whose covering hangs down to the ground and acts as a side. They have wood so hard that they cut with it and make of it their swords and grills to cook their food. Their beds are of a cotton weave, hung from the roof like those in our ships, each man having his own; for the wives sleep apart from their husbands.

They get up with the sun, and eat immediately upon rising, to last them through the day, for they take no other meal than that one. Like some other Eastern peoples, of whom Suidas tells us, who drank apart from meals, they do not drink then; but they drink several times a day, and to capacity. Their drink is made of some root, and is of the color of our claret wines. They drink it only lukewarm. This beverage keeps only two or three days; it has a slightly sharp taste, is not at all heady, is good for the stomach, and has a laxative effect upon those who are not used to it; it is a very pleasant drink for anyone who is accustomed to it. In place of bread they use a certain white substance like preserved coriander. I have tried it; it tastes sweet and a little flat.

The whole day is spent in dancing. The younger men go to hunt animals with bows. Some of the women busy themselves meanwhile with warming their drink, which is their chief duty. Some one of the old men, in the morning before they begin to eat, preaches to the whole barnful in common, walking from one end to the other, and repeating one single sentence several times until he has completed the circuit (for the buildings are fully a hundred paces long). He recommends to them only two things: valor against the enemy and love for their wives. And they never fail to point out this obligation, as their refrain, that it is their wives who keep their drink warm and seasoned.

There may be seen in several places, including my own house, specimens of their beds, of their ropes, of their wooden swords and the bracelets with which they cover their wrists in combats, and of the big canes, open at one end, by whose sound they keep time in their dances. They are close shaven all over, and shave themselves much more cleanly than we, with nothing but a wooden or stone razor. They believe that souls are immortal, and that those who have deserved well of the gods are lodged in that part of heaven where the sun rises, and the damned in the west.

They have some sort of priests and prophets, but they rarely appear before the people, having their home in the mountains. On their arrival there is a great feast and solemn assembly of several villages—each barn, as I have described it, makes up a village, and they are about one French league from each other. The prophet speaks to them in public, exhorting them to virtue and their duty; but their whole ethical science contains only these two articles; resoluteness in war and affection for their wives. He prophesies to them things to come and the results they are to expect from their undertakings, and urges them to war or holds them back from it; but this is on the condition that when he fails to prophesy correctly, and if things turn out otherwise than he has predicted, he is cut into a thousand pieces if they catch him, and condemned as a false prophet. For this reason, the prophet who has once been mistaken is never seen again.

Divination is a gift of God; that is why its abuse should be punished as imposture. Among the Scythians, when the soothsayers failed to hit the mark, they were laid, chained hand and foot, on carts full of heather and drawn by oxen, on which they were burned. Those who handle matters subject to the control of human capacity are excusable if they do the best they can. But these others, who come and trick us with assurances of an extraordinary faculty that is beyond our ken, should they not be punished for making good their promise, and for the temerity of their imposture?

They have their wars with the nations beyond the mountains, further inland, to which they go quite naked, with no other arms than bows or wooden swords ending in a sharp point, in the manner of the tongues of our boar spears. It is astonishing what firmness they show in their combats, which never end but in slaughter and bloodshed; for as to routs and terror, they know nothing of either.

Each man brings back as his trophy the head of the enemy he has killed, and sets it up at the entrance to his dwelling. After they have treated their prisoners well for a long time with all the hospitality they can think of, each man who has a prisoner calls a great assembly of his acquaintances. He ties a rope to one of the prisoner's arms, by the end of which he holds him, a few steps away, for fear of being hurt, and gives his dearest friend the other arm to hold in the same way; and these two, in the presence of the whole assembly, kill him with their swords. This done, they roast him and eat him in common and send some pieces to their absent friends. This is not, as people think, for nourishment, as of old the Scythians used to do; it is to betoken an extreme revenge. And the proof of this came when they saw the Portuguese, who had joined forces with their adversaries, inflict a different kind of death on them when they took them prisoner, which was to bury them up to the waist, shoot the rest of their body full of arrows, and afterward hang them. They thought that these people from the other world, being men who had sown the knowledge of many vices among their neighbors and were much greater masters than themselves in every sort of wickedness, did not adopt this sort of vengeance without some reason, and that it must be more painful than their own; so they began to give up their old method and to follow this one.

I am not sorry that we notice the barbarous horror of such acts, but I am heartily sorry that, judging their faults rightly, we should be so blind to our own. I think there is more barbarity in eating a man alive than in eating him dead; and in tearing by tortures and the rack a body still full of feeling, in roasting a man bit by bit, in having him bitten and mangled by dogs and swine (as we have not only read but seen within fresh memory, not among ancient enemies, but among neighbors and fellow citizens, and what is worse, on the pretext of piety and religion), than in roasting and eating him after he is dead.

Indeed, Chrysippus and Zeno, heads of the Stoic sect, thought there was nothing wrong in using our carcasses for any purpose in case of need, and getting nourishment from them; just as our ancestors, when besieged by Caesar in the city of Alésia, resolved to relieve their famine by eating old men, women, and other people useless for fighting.

> The Gascons once, 'tis said, their life renewed
> By eating of such food.
>
> JUVENAL

And physicians do not fear to use human flesh in all sorts of ways for our health, applying it either inwardly or outwardly. But there never was any opinion so disordered as to excuse treachery, disloyalty, tyranny, and cruelty, which are our ordinary vices.

So we may well call these people barbarians, in respect to the rules of reason, but not in respect to ourselves, who surpass them in every kind of barbarity.

Their warfare is wholly noble and generous, and as excusable and beautiful as this human disease can be; its only basis among them is their rivalry in valor. They are not fighting for the conquest of new lands, for they still enjoy that natural abundance that provides them without toil and trouble with all necessary things in such profusion that they have no wish to enlarge their boundaries. They are still in that happy state of desiring only as much as their natural needs demand; anything beyond that is superfluous to them.

They generally call those of the same age, brothers; those who are younger, children; and the old men are fathers to all the others. These leave to their heirs in common the full possession of their property, without division or any other title at all than just the one that Nature gives to her creatures in bringing them into the world.

If their neighbors cross the mountains to attack them and win a victory, the gain of the victor is glory, and the advantage of having proved the master in valor and virtue; for apart from this they have no use for the goods of the vanquished, and they return to their own country, where they lack neither anything necessary nor that great thing, the knowledge of how to enjoy their condition happily and be content with it. These men of ours do the same in their turn. They demand of their prisoners no other ransom than that they confess and acknowledge their defeat. But there is not one in a whole century who does not choose to die rather than to relax a single bit, by word or look, from the grandeur of an invincible courage; not one who would not rather be killed and eaten than so much as ask not to be. They treat them very freely, so that life may be all the dearer to them, and usually entertain them with threats of their coming death, of the torments they will have to suffer, the preparations that are being made for that purpose, the cutting up of their limbs, and the feast that will be made at their expense. All this is done for the purpose of extorting from their lips some weak or base word, or making them want to flee, so as to gain the advantage of having terrified them and broken down their firmness. For indeed, if you take it the right way, it is in this point alone that true victory lies:

> It is no victory
> Unless the vanquished foe admits your mastery.
> CLAUDIAN

The Hungarians, very bellicose fighters, did not in olden times pursue their advantage beyond putting the enemy at their mercy. For having wrung a confession from him to this effect, they let him go unharmed and unransomed, except, at most, for exacting his promise never again to take up arms against them.

We win enough advantages over our enemies that are borrowed advantages, not really our own. It is the quality of a porter, not of valor, to have sturdier arms and legs; agility is a dead and corporeal quality; it is a stroke of luck to make our enemy stumble, or dazzle his eyes by the sunlight; it is a trick of art and technique, which may be found in a worthless coward, to be an able fencer. The worth and value of a man is in his heart and his will; there lies his real honor. Valor is the strength, not of legs and arms, but of heart and soul; it consists not in the worth of our horse or our weapons, but in our own. He who falls obstinate in his courage, *if he has fallen, he fights on his knees* [Seneca]. He who releases none of his assurance, no matter how great the danger of imminent death; who, giving up his soul, still looks firmly and scornfully at his enemy—he is beaten not by us, but by fortune; he is killed, not conquered.

The most valiant are sometimes the most unfortunate. Thus there are triumphant defeats that rival victories. Nor did those four sister victories, the fairest that the sun ever set eyes on—Salamis, Plataea, Mycale, and Sicily—ever date match all their combined glory against the glory of the annihilation of King Leonidas and his men at the pass of Thermopylae.

Who ever hastened with more glorious and ambitious desire to win a battle than Captain Ischolas to lose one? Who ever secured his safety more ingeniously and painstakingly than he did his destruction? He was charged to defend a certain pass in the Peloponnesus against the Arcadians. Finding himself wholly incapable of doing this, in view of the nature of the place and the inequality of the forces, he made up his mind that all who confronted the enemy would necessarily have to remain on the field. On the other hand, deeming it unworthy both of his own virtue and magnanimity and of the Lacedaemonian name to fail in his charge, he took a middle course between these two extremes, in this way. The youngest and fittest of his band he preserved for the defense and service of their country, and sent them home; and with those whose loss was less important, he determined to hold this pass, and by their death to make the enemy buy their entry as dearly as he could. And so it turned out. For he was presently surrounded on all sides by the Arcadians, and after slaughtering a large number of them, he and his men were all put to the sword. Is there a trophy dedicated to victors that would not be more due to these vanquished? The role of true victory is in fighting, not in coming off safely; and the honor of valor consists in combating, not in beating.

To return to our story. These prisoners are so far from giving in, in spite of all that is done to them, that on the contrary, during the two or three months that they are kept, they wear a gay expression; they urge their captors to hurry and put them to the test; they defy them, insult them, reproach them with their own cowardice and the number of battles they have lost to the prisoners' own people.

I have a song composed by a prisoner which contains this challenge, that they should all come boldly and gather to dine off him, for they will be eating at the same time their own fathers and grandfathers, who have served to feed and nourish his body. "These muscles," he says, "this flesh and these veins are your own, poor fools that you are. You do not recognize that the substance of your ancestors' limbs is still contained in them. Savor them well; you will find in them the taste of your own flesh." An idea that certainly does not smack of barbarity. Those that paint these people dying, and who show the execution, portray the prisoner spitting in the face of his slayers and scowling at them. Indeed, to the last gasp they never stop braving and defying their enemies by word and look. Truly here are real savages by our standards; for either they must be thoroughly so, or we must be; there is an amazing distance between their character and ours.

The men there have several wives, and the higher their reputation for valor the more wives they have. It is a remarkably beautiful thing about their marriages that the same jealousy our wives have to keep us from the affection and kindness of other women, theirs have to win this for them. Being more concerned for their husbands' honor than for anything else, they strive and scheme to have as many companions as they can, since that is a sign of their husbands' valor.

Our wives will cry "Miracle!" but it is no miracle. It is a properly matrimonial virtue, but one of the highest order. In the Bible, Leah, Rachel, Sarah, and Jacob's wives gave their beautiful handmaids to their husbands; and Livia seconded the appetites of Augustus, to her own disadvantage; and Stratonice, the wife of King Deiotarus, not only lent her husband for his use a very beautiful young chambermaid in her service, but carefully brought up her children, and backed them up to succeed to their father's estates.

And lest it be thought that all this is done through a simple and servile bondage to usage and through the pressure of the authority of their ancient customs, without reasoning or judgement, and because their minds are so stupid that they cannot take any other course, I must cite some examples of their capacity. Besides the warlike song I have just quoted, I have another, a love song, which begins in this vein: "Adder, stay; stay, adder, that from the pattern of your coloring my sister may draw the fashion and the workmanship of a rich girdle that I may give to my love; so may your beauty and your pattern be forever preferred to all other serpents." This first couplet is the refrain of the song. Now I am familiar enough with poetry to be a judge of this: not only is there nothing barbarous in this fancy, but it is altogether Anacreontic. Their language, moreover, is a soft language, with an agreeable sound, somewhat like Greek in its ending.

Three of these men, ignorant of the price they will pay some day, in loss of repose and happiness, for gaining knowledge of the corruptions of this side of the ocean; ignorant also of the fact that of this intercourse will come their ruin (which I suppose is already well advanced: poor wretches, to let themselves be tricked by the desire for new things, and to have left the serenity of their own sky to come and see ours!)—three of these men were at Rouen, at the time the late King Charles IX was there. The king talked to them for a long time; they were shown our ways, our splendor, the aspect of a fine city. After that, someone asked their opinion, and wanted to know what they had found most amazing. They mentioned three things, of which I have forgotten the third, and I am very sorry for it; but I still remember two of them. They said that in the first place they thought it very strange that so many grown men, bearded, strong, and armed, who were around the king (it is likely that they were talking about the Swiss of his guard) should submit to obey a child, and that one of them was not chosen to command instead. Second (they have a way in their language of speaking of men as halves of one another), they had noticed that there were among us men full and gorged with all sorts of good things, and that their other halves were beggars at their doors, emaciated with hunger and poverty; and they thought it strange that these needy halves could endure such an injustice, and did not take the others by the throat, or set fire to their houses.

I had a very long talk with one of them; but I had an interpreter who followed my meaning so badly, and who was so hindered by his stupidity in taking in my ideas, that I could get hardly any satisfaction from the man. When I asked him what profit he gained from his superior position among his people (for he was a captain, and our sailors called him king), he told me that it was to march foremost in war. How many men followed him? He pointed to a piece of ground, to signify as many as such a space could hold; it might have been four or five thousand men. Did all his authority expire with the war? He said that this much remained, that when he visited the villages dependent on him, they made paths for him through the underbrush by which he might pass quite comfortably.

All this is not bad—but what's the use? They don't wear breeches.

Baldassare Castiglione
(1478–1529)

BORN IN ITALY, near Mantua, Baldassare Castiglione was a courtier and diplomat best remembered for his book *Il cortegiano* (*The Courtier*), a dialogue fashioned after classical models, published a year before his death in 1528. Of noble birth and armed with a humanist education in Milan, Castiglione attended the dukes of Urbino and Mantua and later served as papal nuncio to the court of Charles V of Spain, where he died of a fever. Also referred to as a conduct book, a popular genre in Castiglione's day, *Il cortegiano* offered a range of advice for aspiring courtiers. Presenting an ideal of the courtier—a mirror for imitation—Castiglione's dialogues are set in the court of Urbino while the participants are actual historical figures. Perhaps the concept most readily associated with the book is that of *sprezzatura*: the accomplishment of duties with apparent ease. Its spirit might be translated for modern audiences as "Never let them see you sweat." The dialogues are divided into four books: the first introduces the concepts *sprezzatura* and *gracia* (grace); the second discusses the arts of conversation and humor; the third discourses on love; and the fourth elaborates on the proper relationship between a courtier and his prince. The following passage comes from the last book, and it reveals an ideal world in which the graciousness of the courtier might help to remind the prince of his better nature and to save him from the grosser corruptions of power. *Il cortegiano* was first translated into English in 1561, by Sir Thomas Hoby; it had a great influence on Sir Philip Sidney and other Elizabethan courtiers. (The translation reproduced here is that of Charles S. Singleton.)

Speaking the Truth
from *The Courtier* (1528)

"Therefore, I think that the aim of the perfect Courtier, which we have not spoken of up to now, is so to win for himself, by means of the accomplishments ascribed to him by these gentlemen, the favor and mind of the prince whom he serves that he may be able to tell him, and always will tell him, the truth about everything he needs to know, without fear or risk of displeasing him; and that when he sees the mind of his prince inclined to a wrong action, he may dare to oppose him and in a gentle manner avail himself of the favor acquired by his good accomplishments, so as to dissuade him of every evil intent and bring him to the path of virtue. And thus, having in himself the goodness which these gentlemen attributed to him, together with readiness of wit, charm, prudence, knowledge of letters and of many other things—the Courtier will in every instance be able adroitly to show the prince how much honor and profit will come to him and to his from justice, liberality, magnanimity, gentleness, and the other virtues that befit a good prince; and, on the other hand, how much infamy and harm result from the vices opposed to these virtues. Hence, I think that even as music, festivals, games, and the other pleasant accomplishments are, as it were, the flower; so to bring or help one's prince toward what is right and to frighten him away from what is wrong are the true fruit of Courtiership. And because the real merit of good deeds consists chiefly in two things, one of which is to choose a truly good end to aim at, and the other is to know how to find means timely and fitting to attain that good end—it is certain that a man aims at the best end when he sees to it that his prince is deceived by no one, listens to no flatterers or slanderers or liars, and distinguishes good from evil, loving the one and hating the other.

"I think too that the accomplishments attributed to the Courtier by these gentlemen may be a good means of attaining that end—and this because, among the many faults that we see in many of our princes nowadays, the greatest are ignorance and self-conceit. And the root of these two evils is none other than falsehood: which vice is deservedly odious to God and to men, and more harmful to princes than any other; because they have the greatest lack of what they would most need to have in abundance—I mean, someone to tell them the truth and make them mindful of what is right: because their enemies are not moved by love to perform these offices, but are well pleased to have them live wickedly and never correct themselves; and, on the other hand, their enemies do not dare to speak ill of them in public for fear of being punished. Then among their friends there are few who have free access to them, and those few are wary of reprehending them for their faults as freely as they would private persons, and, in order to win grace and favor, often think of nothing save how to suggest things that can delight and please their fancy, although these things be evil and dishonorable; thus, from friends these men become flatterers, and, to gain profit from their close association, always speak and act in order to please, and for the most part make their way by dint of lies that beget ignorance in the prince's mind, not only of outward things but of himself; and this may be said to be the greatest and most monstrous falsehood of all, for an ignorant mind deceives itself and inwardly lies to itself.

"From this it results that, besides never hearing the truth about anything at all, princes are made drunk by the great license that rule gives; and by a profusion of delights are submerged in pleasures, and deceive themselves so and have their minds so corrupted—seeing themselves always obeyed and almost adored with so much reverence and praise, without ever the least contradiction, let alone censure—that from this ignorance they pass to an extreme self-conceit, so that then they become intolerant of any advice or opinion from others. And since they think that to know how to rule is a very easy thing, and that to succeed therein they need no other art or discipline save sheer force, they give their mind and all their thoughts to maintaining the power they have, deeming true happiness to lie in being able to do what one wishes. Therefore some princes hate reason or justice, thinking it would be a kind of bridle and a way of reducing them to servitude, and of lessening the pleasure and satisfaction they have in ruling if they chose to follow it, and that their rule would be neither perfect nor complete if they were obliged to obey duty and honor, because they think that one who obeys is not a true ruler.

"Therefore, following these principles and allowing themselves to be transported by self-conceit, they become arrogant, and with imperious countenance and stern manner, with pompous dress, gold, and gems, and by letting themselves be seen almost never in public, they think to gain authority among men and to be held almost as gods. And to my mind these princes are like the colossi that were made last year at Rome on the day of the festival in Piazza d'Agone, which outwardly had the appearance of great men and horses in a triumph, and which within were full of tow and rags. But princes of this kind are much worse in that these colossi were held upright by their own great weight, whereas these princes, since they are ill-balanced within and are heedlessly placed on uneven bases, fall to their ruin by reason of their own weight, and pass from one error to a great many: for their ignorance, together with the false belief that they cannot make a mistake and that the power they have comes from their own wisdom, brings them to seize states boldly, by fair means or foul, whenever the possibility presents itself.

"But if they would take it upon themselves to know and do what they ought, they would then strive not to rule as they now strive to rule, because they would see how monstrous and pernicious a thing it is when subjects, who have to be governed, are wiser than the princes who have to govern. Take note that ignorance of music, of dancing, of horsemanship, does no harm to anyone; nevertheless, one who is not a musician is ashamed and dares not sing in the presence of others, or dance if he does not know how, or ride if he does not sit his horse well. But from not knowing how to govern peoples there come so many woes, deaths, destructions, burnings, ruins, that it may be said to be the deadliest plague that exists on earth. And yet some princes who are so very ignorant of government are not ashamed to attempt to govern, I will not say in the presence of four or six men, but before the whole world, for they hold such a high rank that all eyes gaze upon them and hence not only their great but their least defects are always seen. Thus, it is recorded that Cimon was blamed for loving wine, Scipio for loving sleep, Lucullus for loving feasts. But would to God that the princes of our day might accompany their sins with as many virtues as did those ancients; who, even though they erred in some things, yet did not flee from the promptings and teachings of anyone who seemed to them able to correct those errors; nay, they made every effort to order their lives on the model of excellent men: as Epaminondas on that of Lysias the Pythagorean, Agesilaus on that of Xenophon, Scipio on that of Panaetius, and countless others. But if some of our princes should happen upon a strict philosopher, or anyone at all who might try openly and artlessly to reveal to them the harsh face of true virtue, and teach them what good conduct is and what a good prince's life ought to be, I am certain they would abhor him as they would an asp, or indeed would deride him as a thing most vile.

"I say, then, that, since the princes of today are so corrupted by evil customs and by ignorance and a false esteem of themselves, and since it is so difficult to show them the truth and lead them to virtue, and since men seek to gain their favor by means of lies and flatteries and such vicious ways— the Courtier, through those fair qualities that Count Ludovico and messer Federico have given him, can easily, and must, seek to gain the good will and captivate the mind of his prince that he may have free and sure access to speak to him of anything whatever without giving annoyance. And if he is such as he has been said to be, he will have little trouble in succeeding in this, and will thus be able always adroitly to tell him the truth about all things; and also, little by little, to inform his prince's mind with goodness, and teach him continence, fortitude, justice, and temperance, bringing him to taste how much sweetness lies hidden beneath the slight bitterness that is at first tasted by anyone who struggles against his vices; which are always noxious and offensive and attended by infamy and blame, just as the virtues are beneficial, smiling, and full of praise. And he will be able to incite his prince to these by the example of the famous captains and other excellent men to whom the ancients were wont to make statues of bronze, of marble, and sometimes of gold, and to erect these in public places, both to honor these men and to encourage others, so that through worthy emulation they may be led to strive to attain that glory too.

"In this way the Courtier will be able to lead his prince by the austere path of virtue, adorning it with shady fronds and strewing it with pretty flowers to lessen the tedium of the toilsome journey for one whose strength is slight; and now with music, now with arms and horses, now with verses, now with discourse of love, and with all those means whereof these gentlemen have spoken, to keep his mind continually occupied in worthy pleasures, yet always impressing upon him also some virtuous habit along with these enticements, as I have said, beguiling him with salutary deception; like shrewd doctors who often spread the edge of the cup with some sweet cordial when they wish to give a bitter-tasting medicine to sick and over-delicate children.

"Thus, by using the veil of pleasure to such an end, the Courtier will reach his aim in every time and place and activity, and for this will deserve much greater praise and reward than for any other good work that he could do in the world. For there is no good more universally beneficial than a good prince, nor any evil more universally pernicious than a bad prince: likewise, there is no punishment atrocious and cruel enough for those wicked courtiers who direct gentle and charming manners and good qualities of character to an evil end, namely to their own profit, and who thereby seek their prince's favor in order to corrupt him, turn him from the path of virtue, and bring him to vice; for such as these may be said to contaminate with a deadly poison, not a single cup from which one man alone must drink, but the public fountain that is used by all the people."

Abolqasem Ferdowsi
(940–1020)

SHAHNAMEH, OR THE Persian Epic of Kings, is the masterpiece of Abolqasem Ferdowsi, a poet born near Tus, in Khorasan, in what is today northeastern Iran. The city of Tus is now home to Ferdowsi's mausoleum, built in 1934. *Shahnameh* was written at the behest of the princes of Khorasan, who were instrumental in reviving Persian culture in the wake of the seventh-century Arab Conquest, which toppled the Sasanian Empire. Ferdowsi lived through another conquest, that of the Ghaznavid Turks, but his epic attests to the enduring cultural legacy of Persia, serial incursions notwithstanding. Azar Nafisi writes that living in a land of conquest, Persians locate in their poets the "true guardians of their true home." Ferdowsi's poem chronicles heroes and kings. The episode presented here centers on the career of Alexander the Great, called Sekandar by Ferdowsi. Sekandar's presence in Persian literature reveals the vast extent of his conquest and degree of his influence. This excerpt depicts an imaginary encounter between Sekandar and the emperor of China. In fact, Alexander's eastward march stopped in India. (The following selection is translated by Dick Davis.)

Sekandar Visits the Emperor of China
from *Shahnameh*

Now Sekandar led his army toward China. For forty days they traveled, until they reached the sea. There the army made camp and the king pitched his brocade pavilion. He summoned a scribe to write a letter to the Chinese emperor from Sekandar, the seizer of cities. The message was filled with promises and threats, and when it was completed Sekandar himself went as the envoy, taking with him an intelligent companion who was one with him in heart and speech and who could advise him as to what to do and what not to do. He entrusted his troops to the army's commander and chose five Greeks as his escort.

When news reached the Chinese emperor that an envoy was approaching his country, he sent troops out to meet him. Sekandar reached the court and the emperor came forward in welcome, but his heart was filled with suspicious thoughts. Sekandar ran forward and made his obeisance to him, and then was seated in the palace for a long while. The emperor questioned him and made much of him and assigned him noble sleeping quarters. As the sun rose over the mountains, dying their summits gold, the envoy was summoned to court. Sekandar spoke at length, saying what was appropriate, and then handed over the letter. It was addressed from the king of Greece, possessor of the world, lord of every country, on whom other kings call down God's blessings. It continued, "My orders for China are that she remain prosperous, and that she should not prepare for war against me; it was war against me that destroyed Foor, and Dara, who was the lord of the world, and Faryan the Arab, and other sovereigns. From the east to the west no one ignores my commands, the heavens themselves do not know the number of my troops, and Venus and the sun could not count them. If you disobey any command of mine you will bring distress on yourself and your country. When you read my letter, bring me tribute; do not trouble yourself about this, or look for evil allies to make war on me. If you come you will see me in the midst of my troops, and when I see that you are honest and mean well I shall confirm you in the possession of your crown and throne, and no misfortune will come to you. If, however, you are reluctant to come before your king, send me things that are peculiar to China—your country's gold work, horses, swords, seal rings, clothes, cloth, ivory thrones, fine brocade, necklaces, crowns—that is, if you have no wish to be harmed by me. Send my soldiers back to me, and rest assured that your wealth, throne, and crown are safe."

When the emperor of China saw what was in the letter, he started up in fury, but then chose silence as a better course. He laughed and said to the envoy, "May your king be a partner to the heavens! Tell me what you know about him. Tell me about his conversation, his height and appearance, and what kind of a man he is." The envoy said, "Great lord of China, you should understand that there is no one else in the world like Sekandar. In his manliness, policy, good fortune, and wisdom he surpasses all that anyone could imagine. He is as tall as a cypress tree, has an elephant's strength, and is as generous as the waters of the Nile; his tongue can be as cutting as a sword, but he can charm an eagle down from the clouds." When he heard all this, the emperor changed his mind. He ordered that wine and a banquet be laid out in the palace gardens. He drank till evening brought darkness to the world, and the company became tipsy. Then he said to the envoy, "May your king be Jupiter's partner. At first light I'll compose an answer to his letter, and what I write will make the day seem splendid to your eyes." Sekandar was half drunk, and he staggered from the garden to his quarters with an orange in his hand.

When the sun rose in Leo and the heavens dispelled the darkness, Sekandar went to the emperor, and all suspicious thoughts were far from his heart. The emperor asked him, "How did you spend the night? When you left you were quite overcome with wine." Then he summoned a scribe, who brought paper, musk, and ambergris, and dictated a letter. He began with praise of God, the lord of chivalry, justice, and ability, of cultivated behavior, abstinence, and piety, and called down his blessings on the Greek king. Then he continued, "Your eloquent envoy has arrived, bringing the king's letter. I have read through the royal words and discussed its contents with my nobles. As for your claims concerning the wars against Dara, Faryan, and Foor, in which you were victorious, so that you became a shepherd whose flock consists of kings, you should not consider what comes about through the will of the Lord of the Sun and Moon as the result of your own valor and the might of your army. When a great man's days are numbered, what difference does it make whether he dies in battle or at a banquet? If they died in battle with you this is because their fate was fixed for that day, and fate is not to be hurried or delayed. You should not pride yourself so much on your victories over them, because even if you are made of iron there is no doubt that you too will die. Where now are Feraydun, Zahhak, and Jamshid, who came like the wind and left like a breath? I am not afraid of you and I will not make war against you, neither shall I puff myself up with pride as you are doing. It is not my habit to shed blood, and besides it would be unworthy of my faith for me to do evil in this way. You summon me, but to no purpose; I serve God, not kings. I send with this more riches than you have dreamed of, so that there shall be no doubting my munificence."

These words were an arrow in Sekandar's vital organs, and he blushed with shame. In his heart he said, "Never again shall I go somewhere disguised as my own envoy." He returned to his quarters and prepared to leave the Chinese court.

The proud emperor opened his treasuries' doors, since he was not a man who found generosity difficult. First he ordered that fifty crowns and ten ivory thrones encrusted with jewels be brought; then a thousand camel loads of gold and silver goods, and a thousand more of Chinese brocades and silks, of camphor, musk, perfumes, and ambergris. He had little regard for wealth, and it eased his heart to be bountiful in this way. He had ten thousand each of the pelts of gray squirrel, ermine, and sable brought, and as many carpets and crystal goblets, and his wise treasurer saw to their being loaded on pack animals. Then he added three hundred silver saddles and fifty golden ones, together with three hundred red-haired camels loaded with Chinese rarities. He chose as envoy an eloquent and dignified Chinese sage and told him to take his message to the Greek king with all goodwill and splendor, and to say that Sekandar would be warmly welcomed at the Chinese court for as long as he wished to stay there.

The envoy traveled with Sekandar, unaware that he was the Greek king. But when Sekandar's regent came forward and the king told him of his adventures, and the army congratulated him on his safe return and bowed to the ground before him, the envoy realized that he was indeed the Greek king and dismounted in consternation. Sekandar said to him, "There is no need for apologies, but do not tell your emperor of this!" They rested for a night, and the next morning Sekandar sat on the royal throne. He gave gifts to the envoy and said to him, "Go to your emperor and tell him that I say 'You have found honor and respect with me. If you wish to stay where you are, all China is yours, and if you wish to go elsewhere, that too is open to you. I shall rest here for a while, because such a large army as mine cannot be mobilized quickly.'" The envoy returned like the wind, and gave Sekandar's message to the emperor.

Red Cloud
(1820–1909)

THE OGLALA SIOUX chief Red Cloud, born on the Great Plains of Nebraska, learned warfare during raids against the neighboring Pawnee and Crow tribes. Red Cloud's conflict with white settlers began when gold was discovered in Montana and the U.S. Army began to build the Bozeman Trail, a road from Fort Laramie, Wyoming, to the gold fields of Montana. Red Cloud led a war against the army in 1865, and two years later, work on the Bozeman Trail was stopped. In 1868, Red Cloud negotiated a settlement in which the Sioux were given land in South Dakota, while the chief himself moved to a reservation in Nebraska. He visited President Ulysses S. Grant in Washington and delivered the following speeches in New York City before returning to the West. In the years to come, even as hostilities intensified in the 1870s and 1880s, Red Cloud continued to negotiate peacefully with the government, against the wishes of other Indian leaders, including his own son. As the American Indian Relief Council biography of Red Cloud notes, the chief's diplomacy earned him enemies on both sides: "He was accused by some younger Oglala of selling out, while government officials accused him of secretly aiding the Sioux and Cheyenne bands that defeated General George Custer at Little Bighorn." Delivered in June 1870, Red Cloud's speeches at the St. Nicholas Hotel to New York's Indian Peace Commissioners and to the public at Cooper Union demonstrate not only his eloquence but also the tragedy of his position as a negotiator in a conflict wholly uneven, the resolution of which seemed but a matter of time and attrition. (Both addresses are reproduced here as they were recorded in the *New York Times*.)

Speech at St. Nicholas Hotel
from *New York Times* (June 16, 1870)

My friend: The Great Spirit placed me and my people on this land poor and naked. When the white men came we gave them lands, and did not wish to hurt them. But the white man drove us back and took our lands.

Then the Great Father made us many promises, but they are not kept. He promised to give us large presents, and when they came to us they were small; they seemed to be lost on the way. I came from my people to lay their affairs before the Great Father and I tell him just what I mean and what my people wish, and I gain nothing. I asked him for seventeen horses for my young men to ride from the border to our camps, and he does not give them. I wish no stock and no presents. The Great Spirit placed me here poor and naked. I appear so before you, and I do not feel sorry for that. I am not mad—I am in good humor—but I have received no satisfaction. I am disappointed. I cannot change my claims. I am not Spotted Tail. What I say I stick to. My people understand what I come here for, and I should lose my power if I did not stick to one course. You (to Gen. Smith) are my friend. You always talk straight and I am not blaming you.

Gen. Smith then endeavored to explain that the Great Father and his assistants were not in office when the treaty of 1868 was made, and were bound by its provisions, but would try to change the law, and if the Indians would remain peaceable, in time they might accomplish all they desired. The presents he spoke of were for him personally, and would not be reckoned on the account of the nation. Moreover, he thought he could get for him the horses he desired, but would not positively promise them. Here Mr. Cooper interposed and told Gen. Smith that if the Government would not furnish the horses, he would.

Red Cloud replied that he came here to see his friends, and he found them good men. He was not mad, but had a good heart, and wished to keep peace. It was well for white men to say, "Do not kill our men," but they kill the Indians first, and there was a brave warrior by his side whose son and brother had been killed, and who himself had been shot twice by soldiers. If the present and the horses were offered to him together, and freely, he would take them. He wished to be friendly.

Gen. Smith then explained to him the wish of his visitors. They would take him about the City and its grounds during the day, and to the theater in the evening, and to-morrow (today) they wished him to meet the people and talk to them. Then they would start for home and go directly through. To this he assented, and this ended the formal interview.

Speech at Cooper Union
from *New York Times* (June 17, 1870)

My Brothers and my Friends who are before me today: God Almighty has made us all, and He is here to hear what I have to say to you today. The Great Spirit made us both. He gave us lands and He gave you lands.

You came here and we received you as brothers. When the Almighty made you, He made you all white and clothed you. When He made us He made us with red skins and poor. When you first came we were very many and you were few. Now you are many and we are few. You do not know who appears before you to speak. He is a representative of the original American race, the first people of this continent. We are good, and not bad. The reports which you get about us are all on one side. You hear of us only as murderers and thieves. We are not so. If we had more lands to give to you we would give them, but we have no more. We are driven into a very little island, and we want you, our dear friends, to help us with the Government of the United States. The Great Spirit made us poor and ignorant. He made you rich and wise and skillful in things which we knew nothing about. The good Father made you to eat tame game and us to eat wild game. Ask any one who has gone through to California. They will tell you we have treated them well. You have children. We, too, have children, and we wish to bring them up well. We ask you to help us do it. At the mouth of Horse Creek, in 1852, the Great Father made a treaty with us. We agreed to let him pass through our territory unharmed for fifty-five years. We kept our word. We committed no murders, no depredations, until the troops came there. When the troops were sent there trouble and disturbance arose. Since that time there have been various goods sent from time to time to us, but only once did they reach us, and soon the Great Father took away the only good man he had sent us, Col. Fitzpatrick. The Great Father said we must go to farming, and some of our men went to farming near Fort Laramie, and were treated very badly indeed. We came to Washington to see our Great Father that peace might be continued. The Great Father that made us both wishes peace to be kept; we want to keep peace. Will you help us? In 1868 men came out and brought papers. We could not read them, and they did not tell us truly what was in them. We thought the treaty was to remove the forts, and that we should then cease from fighting. But they wanted to send us traders on the Missouri. We did not want to go on the Missouri, but wanted traders where we were. When I reached Washington the Great Father explained to me what the treaty was, and showed me that the interpreters had deceived me. All I want is right and justice. I have tried to get from the Great Father what is right and just. I have not altogether succeeded. I want you to help me to get what is right and just. I represent the whole Sioux nation, and they will be bound by what I say. I am no Spotted Tail, to say one thing one day and be bought for a pin the next. Look at me. I am poor and naked, but I am the Chief of the nation. We do not want riches, but we want to train our children right. Riches would do us no good. We could not take them with us to the other world. We do not want riches, we want peace and love.

The riches that we have in this world, Secretary Cox said truly, we cannot take with us to the next world. Then I wish to know why Commissioners are sent out to us who do nothing but rob us and get the riches of this world away from us? I was brought up among the traders, and those who came out there in the early times treated me well and I had a good time with them. They taught us to wear clothes and to use tobacco and ammunition. But, by and by, the Great Father sent out a different kind of men; men who cheated and drank whisky; men who were so bad that the Great Father could not keep them at home and so sent them out there. I have sent a great many words to the Great Father but they never reached him. They were drowned on the way, and I was afraid the words I spoke lately to the Great Father would not reach you, so I came to speak to you myself; and now I am going away to my home. I want to have men sent out to my people whom we know and can trust. I am glad I have come here. You belong in the East and I belong in the West, and I am glad I have come here and that we could understand one another. I am very much obliged to you for listening to me. I go home this afternoon. I hope you will think of what I have said to you. I bid you all an affectionate farewell.

Zadie Smith
(b. 1975)

ZADIE SMITH IS one of the most exciting young Anglophone novelists of the twenty-first century. Born in London, she graduated from Cambridge University in 1997, and her first novel *White Teeth* was published three years later. It garnered several prizes, including the Whitbread First Novel Award, the Orange Prize for Fiction, and both the Best First Book and overall Commonwealth Writers Prizes. Smith's other novels include *The Autograph Man* (2002), *On Beauty* (2005), and *NW* (2012), which was one of the *New York Times'* 10 Best Books of 2012. Smith also writes short stories and nonfiction, including the incisive collection *Changing My Mind: Occasional Essays* (2009). "Speaking in Tongues" debuted as a 2008 lecture at the New York Public Library, and it was first published in the *New York Review of Books*. Smith speaks of her personal negotiation of two tongues, two races, and two identities as well as that of Barack Obama.

Speaking in Tongues

from *New York Review of Books* (February 26, 2009)

1.

Hello. This voice I speak with these days, this English voice with its rounded vowels and consonants in more or less the right place—this is not the voice of my childhood. I picked it up in college, along with the unabridged *Clarissa* and a taste for port. Maybe this fact is only what it seems to be—a case of bald social climbing—but at the time I genuinely thought *this* was the voice of lettered people, and that if I didn't have the voice of lettered people I would never truly be lettered. A braver person, perhaps, would have stood firm, teaching her peers a useful lesson by example: not all lettered people need be of the same class, nor speak identically. I went the other way. Partly out of cowardice and a constitutional eagerness to please, but also because I didn't quite see it as a straight swap, of this voice for that.

My own childhood had been the story of this and that combined, of the synthesis of disparate things. It never occurred to me that I was leaving the London district of Willesden for Cambridge. I thought I was *adding* Cambridge to Willesden, this new way of talking to that old way. Adding a new kind of knowledge to a different kind I already had. And for a while, that's how it was: at home, during the holidays, I spoke with my old voice, and in the old voice seemed to feel and speak things that I couldn't express in college, and vice versa. I felt a sort of wonder at the flexibility of the thing. Like being alive twice.

But flexibility is something that requires work if it is to be maintained. Recently my double voice has deserted me for a single one, reflecting the smaller world into which my work has led me. Willesden was a big, colorful, working-class sea; Cambridge was a smaller, posher pond, and almost univocal; the literary world is a puddle. This voice I picked up along the way is no longer an exotic garment I put on like a college gown whenever I choose—now it is my only voice, whether I want it or not. I regret it; I should have kept both voices alive in my mouth. They were both a part of me. But how the culture warns against it! As George Bernard Shaw delicately put it in his preface to the play *Pygmalion*, "many thousands of [British] men and women . . . have sloughed off their native dialects and acquired a new tongue."

Few, though, will admit to it. Voice adaptation is still the original British sin. Monitoring and exposing such citizens is a national pastime, as popular as sex scandals and libel cases. If you lean toward the Atlantic with your high-rising terminals you're a sell-out; if you pronounce borrowed European words in their original style—even if you try something as innocent as *par-*

migiano for "parmesan"—you're a fraud. If you go (metaphorically speaking) down the British class scale, you've gone from Cockney to "mockney," and can expect a public tar and feathering; to go the other way is to perform an unforgivable act of class betrayal. Voices are meant to be unchanging and singular. There's no quicker way to insult an ex-pat Scotsman in London than to tell him he's lost his accent. We feel that our voices are who we are, and that to have more than one, or to use different versions of a voice for different occasions, represents, at best, a Janus-faced duplicity, and at worst, the loss of our very souls.

Whoever changes their voice takes on, in Britain, a queerly tragic dimension. They have betrayed that puzzling dictum "To thine own self be true," so often quoted approvingly as if it represented the wisdom of Shakespeare rather than the hot air of Polonius. *"What's to become of me? What's to become of me?"* wails Eliza Doolittle, realizing her middling dilemma. With a voice too posh for the flower girls and yet too redolent of the gutter for the ladies in Mrs. Higgins's drawing room.

But Eliza—patron saint of the tragically double-voiced—is worthy of closer inspection. The first thing to note is that both Eliza and *Pygmalion* are entirely didactic, as Shaw meant them to be. "I delight," he wrote,

> in throwing [*Pygmalion*] at the heads of the wiseacres who repeat the parrot cry that art should never be didactic. It goes to prove my contention that art should never be anything else.

He was determined to tell the unambiguous tale of a girl who changes her voice and loses her self. And so she arrives like this:

> Don't you be so saucy. You ain't heard what I come for yet. Did you tell him I come in a taxi? . . . Oh, we are proud! He ain't above giving lessons, not him: I heard him say so. Well, I ain't come here to ask for any compliment; and if my moneys not good enough I can go elsewhere. . . . Now you know, don't you? I'm come to have lessons, I am. And to pay for em too: make no mistake. . . . I want to be a lady in a flower shop stead of selling at the corner of Tottenham Court Road. But they wont take me unless I can talk more genteel.

And she leaves like this:

> I can't. I could have done it once; but now I can't go back to it. Last night, when I was wandering about, a girl spoke to me; and I tried to get back into the old way with her; but it was no use. You told me, you know, that when a child is brought to a foreign country, it picks up the language in a

few weeks, and forgets its own. Well, I am a child in your country. I have forgotten my own language, and can speak nothing but yours.

By the end of his experiment, Professor Higgins has made his Eliza an awkward, in-between thing, neither flower girl nor lady, with one voice lost and another gained, at the steep price of everything she was, and everything she knows. Almost as afterthought, he sends Eliza's father, Alfred Doolittle, to his doom, too, securing a three-thousand-a-year living for the man on the condition that Doolittle lecture for the Wannafeller Moral Reform World League up to six times a year. This burden brings the philosophical dustman into the close, unwanted embrace of what he disdainfully calls "middle class morality." By the time the curtain goes down, both Doolittles find themselves stuck in the middle, which is, to Shaw, a comi-tragic place to be, with the emphasis on the tragic. What are they fit for? What will become of them?

How persistent this horror of the middling spot is, this dread of the interim place! It extends through the specter of the tragic mulatto, to the plight of the transsexual, to our present anxiety—disguised as genteel concern—for the contemporary immigrant, tragically split, we are sure, between worlds, ideas, cultures, voices—whatever will become of them? Something's got to give—one voice must be sacrificed for the other. What is double must be made singular.

But this, the apparent didactic moral of Eliza's story, is undercut by the fact of the play itself, which is an orchestra of many voices, simultaneously and perfectly rendered, with no shade of color or tone sacrificed. Higgins's Harley Street high-handedness is the equal of Mrs. Pierce's lower-middle-class gentility, Pickering's kindhearted aristocratic imprecision every bit as convincing as Arthur Doolittle's Nietzschean Cockney-by-way-of-Wales. Shaw had a wonderful ear, able to reproduce almost as many quirks of the English language as Shakespeare's. Shaw was in possession of a gift he wouldn't, or couldn't, give Eliza: he spoke in tongues.

It gives me a strange sensation to turn from Shaw's melancholy Pygmalion story to another, infinitely more hopeful version, written by the new president of the United States of America. Of course, his ear isn't half bad either. In *Dreams from My Father*, the new president displays an enviable facility for dialogue, and puts it to good use, animating a cast every bit as various as the one James Baldwin—an obvious influence—conjured for his own many-voiced novel *Another Country*. Obama can do young Jewish male, black old lady from the South Side, white woman from Kansas, Kenyan elders, white Harvard nerds, black Columbia nerds, activist women, churchmen, security guards, bank tellers, and even a British man called Mr. Wilkerson, who on a starry night on safari says credibly British things like: "I believe that's the Milky Way." This new president doesn't just speak *for* his people. He can *speak* them. It is a disorienting talent in a president; we're so unused to it. I have to pinch myself to remember who wrote the following well-observed scene, seemingly plucked from a comic novel:

> "Man, I'm not going to any more of these bullshit Punahou parties."
>
> "Yeah, that's what you said the last time. . . ."
>
> "I mean it this time. . . . These girls are A-1, USDA-certified racists. All of 'em. White girls. Asian girls—shoot, these Asians worse than the whites. Think we got a disease or something."
>
> "Maybe they're looking at that big butt of yours. Man, I thought you were in training."
>
> "Get your hands out of my fries. You ain't my bitch, nigger . . . buy your own damn fries. Now what was I talking about?"
>
> "Just 'cause a girl don't go out with you doesn't make her a racist."

This is the voice of Obama at seventeen, as remembered by Obama. He's still recognizably Obama; he already seeks to unpack and complicate apparently obvious things ("Just 'cause a girl don't go out with you doesn't make her a racist"); he's already gently cynical about the impassioned dogma of other people ("Yeah, that's what you said the last time"). And he has a sense of humor ("Maybe they're looking at that big butt of yours"). Only the voice is different: he has made almost as large a leap as Eliza Doolittle. The conclusions Obama draws from his own Pygmalion experience, however, are subtler than Shaw's. The tale he tells is not the old tragedy of gaining a new, false voice at the expense of a true one. The tale he tells is all about addition. His is the story of a genuinely many-voiced man. If it has a moral it is that each man must be true to his selves, plural.

For Obama, having more than one voice in your ear is not a burden, or not solely a burden—it is also a gift. And the gift is of an interesting kind, not well served by that dull publishing-house title *Dreams from My Father: A Story of Race and Inheritance* with its suggestion of a simple linear inheritance, of paternal dreams and aspirations passed down to a son, and fulfilled. *Dreams from My Father* would have been a fine title for John McCain's book *Faith of My Fathers*, which concerns exactly this kind of linear masculine inheritance, in his case from soldier to soldier. For Obama's book, though, it's wrong, lopsided. He corrects its misperception early on, in the first chapter, while discussing the failure of his parents' relationship, characterized by their only son as the end of a dream. "Even as that spell was broken," he writes, "and the worlds that they thought they'd left behind reclaimed each of them, I *occupied the place* where their dreams had been."

To *occupy* a dream, to exist in a dreamed space (conjured by both father and mother), is surely a quite different thing from simply *inheriting* a dream. It's more interesting. What did Pauline Kael call Cary Grant? "*The Man from Dream City.*" When Bristolian Archibald Leach became suave Cary Grant, the transformation happened in his voice, which he subjected to a strange, indefinable manipulation, resulting in that heavenly sui generis accent, neither west country nor posh, American nor English. It came from nowhere, *he* came from nowhere. Grant seemed the product of a collective dream, dreamed up by moviegoers in hard times, as it sometimes feels voters have dreamed up Obama in hard times. Both men have a strange reflective quality, typical of the self-created man—we see in them whatever we want to see. "*Everyone wants to be Cary Grant,*" said Cary Grant. "*Even I want to be Cary Grant.*" It's not hard to imagine Obama having that same thought, backstage at Grant Park, hearing his own name chanted by the hopeful multitude. *Everyone wants to be Barack Obama. Even I want to be Barack Obama.*

2.

But I haven't described Dream City. I'll try to. It is a place of many voices, where the unified singular self is an illusion. Naturally, Obama was born there. So was I. When your personal multiplicity is printed on your face, in an almost too obviously thematic manner, in your DNA, in your hair and in the neither this nor that beige of your skin—well, anyone can see you come from Dream City. In Dream City everything is doubled, everything is various. You have no choice but to cross borders and speak in tongues. That's how you get from your mother to your father, from talking to one set of folks who think you're not black enough to another who figure you insufficiently white. It's the kind of town where the wise man says "I" cautiously, because "I" feels like too straight and singular a phoneme to represent the true multiplicity of his experience. Instead, citizens of Dream City prefer to use the collective pronoun "we."

Throughout his campaign Obama was careful always to say we. He was noticeably wary of "I." By speaking so, he wasn't simply avoiding a singularity he didn't feel, he was also drawing us in with him. He had the audacity to suggest that, even if you can't see it stamped on their faces, most people come from Dream City, too. Most of us have complicated back stories, messy histories, multiple narratives.

It was a high-wire strategy, for Obama, this invocation of our collective human messiness. His enemies latched on to its imprecision, emphasizing the exotic, un-American nature of Dream City, this ill-defined place where you could be from Hawaii and Kenya, Kansas and Indonesia all at the same time, where you could jive talk like a street hustler and orate like a senator.

What kind of a crazy place is that? But they underestimated how many people come from Dream City, how many Americans, in their daily lives, conjure contrasting voices and seek a synthesis between disparate things. Turns out, Dream City wasn't so strange to them.

Or did they never actually see it? We now know that Obama spoke of *Main Street* in Iowa and of *sweet potato pie* in Northwest Philly, and it could be argued that he succeeded because he so rarely misspoke, carefully tailoring his intonations to suit the sensibility of his listeners. Sometimes he did this within one speech, within one line: "We worship an *awesome* God in the blue states, and we don't like federal agents poking around our libraries in the red states." *Awesome God* comes to you straight from the pews of a Georgia church; *poking around* feels more at home at a kitchen table in South Bend, Indiana. The balance was perfect, cunningly counterpoised and never accidental. It's only now that it's over that we see him let his guard down a little, on *60 Minutes*, say, dropping in that culturally, casually black construction "Hey, I'm not stupid, *man*, that's why I'm president," something it's hard to imagine him doing even three weeks earlier. To a certain kind of mind, it must have looked like the mask had slipped for a moment.

Which brings us to the single-voiced Obamanation crowd. They rage on in the blogs and on the radio, waiting obsessively for the mask to slip. They have a great fear of what they see as Obama's doubling ways. "He says one thing but he means another"—this is the essence of the fear campaign. He says he's a capitalist, but he'll spread your wealth. He says he's a Christian, but really he's going to empower the Muslims. And so on and so forth. These are fears that have their roots in an anxiety about voice. *Who is he?* people kept asking. *I mean, who is this guy, really?* He says *sweet potato pie* in Philly and *Main Street* in Iowa! When he talks to us, he sure *sounds* like us—but behind our backs he says we're clinging to our religion, to our guns. And when Jesse Jackson heard that Obama had lectured a black church congregation about the epidemic of absent black fathers, he experienced this, too, as a tonal betrayal; Obama was "talking down to black people." In both cases, there was the sense of a double-dealer, of someone who tailors his speech to fit the audience, who is not *of* the people (because he is able to look at them objectively) but always above them.

The Jackson gaffe, with its Oedipal violence ("I want to cut his nuts out"), is especially poignant because it goes to the heart of a generational conflict in the black community, concerning what we will say in public and what we say in private. For it has been a point of honor, among the civil rights generation, that any criticism or negative analysis of our community, expressed, as they often are by white politicians, without context, without real empathy or understanding, should not be repeated by a black politician when the white community is listening, even if (*especially* if) the criticism happens to be true (more than half of all black American children live in single-parent households). Our business is our business. Keep it in the family; don't wash your dirty linen in public; stay unified. (Of course, with his overheard gaffe, Jackson unwittingly broke his own rule.)

Until Obama, black politicians had always adhered to these unwritten rules. In this way, they defended themselves against those two bogeymen of black political life: the Uncle Tom and the House Nigger. The black politician who played up to, or even simply echoed, white fears, desires, and hopes for the black community was in danger of earning these epithets—even Martin Luther King was not free from such suspicions. Then came Obama, and the new world he had supposedly ushered in, the postracial world, in which what mattered most was not blind racial allegiance but factual truth. It was felt that Jesse Jackson was sadly out of step with this new postracial world: even his own son felt moved to publicly repudiate his "ugly rhetoric." But Jackson's anger was not incomprehensible nor his distrust unreasonable. Jackson lived through a bitter struggle, and bitter struggles deform their participants in subtle, complicated ways. The idea that one should speak one's cultural allegiance first and the truth second (and that this is a sign of authenticity) is precisely such a deformation.

Right up to the wire, Obama made many black men and women of Jackson's generation suspicious. How can the man who passes between culturally black and white voices with such flexibility, with such ease, be an honest man? How *will* the man from Dream City keep it real? Why won't he speak with a clear and unified voice? These were genuine questions for people born in real cities at a time when those cities were implacably divided, when the black movement had to yell with a clear and unified voice, or risk not being heard at all. And then he won. Watching Jesse Jackson in tears in Grant Park, pressed up against the varicolored American public, it seemed like he, at least, had received the answer he needed: only a many-voiced man could have spoken to that many people.

A clear and unified voice. In that context, this business of being biracial, of being half black and half white, is awkward. In his memoir, Obama takes care to ridicule a certain black girl called Joyce—a composite figure from his college days who happens also to be part Italian and part French and part Native American and is inordinately fond of mentioning these facts, and who likes to say:

> I'm not black . . . I'm *multiracial*. . . . Why should I have to choose between them? . . . It's not white people who are making me choose. . . . No—it's *black people* who always have to make everything racial. *They're* the ones making me choose. *They're* the ones who are telling me I can't be who I am. . . .

He has her voice down pat and so condemns her out of her own mouth. For she's the third bogeyman of black life, the tragic mulatto, who secretly wishes she "passed," always keen to let you know about her white heritage. It's the fear of being mistaken for Joyce that has always ensured that I ignore the box marked "biracial" and tick the box marked "black" on any questionnaire I fill out, and call myself unequivocally a black writer and roll my eyes at anyone who insists that Obama is not the first black president but the first biracial one. But I also know in my heart that it's an equivocation; I know that Obama has a double consciousness, is black and, at the same time, white, as I am, unless we are suggesting that one side of a person's genetics and cultural heritage cancels out or trumps the other.

But to mention the double is to suggest shame at the singular. Joyce insists on her varied heritage because she fears and is ashamed of the singular black. I suppose it's possible that subconsciously I am also a tragic mulatto, torn between pride and shame. In my conscious life, though, I cannot honestly say I feel proud to be white and ashamed to be black or proud to be black and ashamed to be white. I find it impossible to experience either pride or shame over accidents of genetics in which I had no active part. I understand how those words got into the racial discourse, but I can't sign up to them. I'm not proud to be female either. I am not even proud to be human—I only love to be so. As I love to be female and I love to be black, and I love that I had a white father.

It's telling that Joyce is one of the few voices in *Dreams from My Father* that is truly left out in the cold, outside of the expansive sympathy of Obama's narrative. She is an entirely didactic being, a demon Obama has to raise up, if only for a page, so everyone can watch him slay her. I know the feeling. When I was in college I felt I'd rather run away with the Black Panthers than be associated with the Joyces I occasionally met. It's the Joyces of this world who "talk down to black folks." And so to avoid being Joyce, or being seen to be Joyce, you unify, you speak with one voice.

And the concept of a unified black voice is a potent one. It has filtered down, these past forty years, into the black community at all levels, settling itself in that impossible injunction "keep it real," the original intention of which was unification. We were going to unify the concept of Blackness in order to strengthen it. Instead we confined and restricted it. To me, the instruction "keep it real" is a sort of prison cell, two feet by five. The fact is, it's too narrow. I just can't live comfortably in there. *"Keep it real"* replaced the blessed and solid genetic fact of Blackness with a flimsy imperative. It made Blackness a quality each individual black person was constantly in danger of losing. And almost anything could trigger the loss of one's Blackness: attending certain universities, an impressive variety of jobs, a fondness for opera, a white girlfriend, an interest in golf. And of course, any change in the voice. There was a popular school of thought that maintained the voice was at the very heart of the thing; fail to keep it real there and you'd never see your Blackness again.

How absurd that all seems now. And not because we live in a postracial world—we don't—but because the reality of race has diversified. Black reality has diversified. It's black people who talk like me, and black people who talk like L'il Wayne. It's black conservatives and black liberals, black sportsmen and black lawyers, black computer technicians and black ballet dancers and black truck drivers and black presidents. We're all black, and we all love to be black, and we all sing from our own hymn sheet. We're all surely black people, but we may be finally approaching a point of human history where you can't talk up or down to us anymore, but only *to us*. *He's talking down to white people*—how curious it sounds the other way round! In order to say such a thing one would have to think collectively of white people, as a people of one mind who speak with one voice—a thought experiment in which we have no practice. But it's worth trying. It's only when you play the record backward that you hear the secret message.

3.

For reasons that are obscure to me, those qualities we cherish in our artists we condemn in our politicians. In our artists we look for the many-colored voice, the multiple sensibility. The apogee of this is, of course, Shakespeare: even more than for his wordplay we cherish him for his lack of allegiance. *Our* Shakespeare sees always both sides of a thing, he is black and white, male and female—he is everyman. The giant lacunae in his biography are merely a convenience; if any new facts of religious or political affiliation were ever to arise we would dismiss them in our hearts anyway. Was he, for example, a man of Rome or not? He has appeared, to generations of readers, not of one religion but of both, in truth, beyond both. Born into the middle of Britain's fierce Catholic–Protestant culture war, how could the bloody absurdity of those years not impress upon him a strong sense of cultural contingency?

It was a war of ideas that began for Will—as it began for Barack—in the dreams of his father. For we know that John Shakespeare, a civic officer in Protestant times, oversaw the repainting of medieval frescoes and the destruction of the rood loft and altar in Stratford's own fine Guild Chapel, but we also know that in the rafters of the Shakespeare home John hid a secret Catholic "Spiritual Testament," a signed profession of allegiance to the old faith. A strange experience, to watch one's own father thus divided, professing one thing in public while practicing another in private. John Shakespeare was a kind of equivocator: it's what you do when you're in a corner, when you can't be a Catholic and a loyal Englishman at the same time. When you can't be both black and white. Sometimes in a country ripped apart by dogma, those who wish to keep their heads—in both senses—must learn to split themselves in two.

And this we *still* know, here, at a four-hundred-year distance. No one can hope to be president of these United States without professing a committed and straightforward belief in two things: the existence of God and the principle of American exceptionalism. But how many of them equivocated, and who, in their shoes, would not equivocate, too?

Fortunately, Shakespeare was an artist and so had an outlet his father didn't have—the many-voiced theater. Shakespeare's art, the very medium of it, allowed him to do what civic officers and politicians can't seem to: speak simultaneous truths. (Is it not, for example, experientially true that one can both believe and *not* believe in God?) In his plays he is woman, man, black, white, believer, heretic, Catholic, Protestant, Jew, Muslim. He grew up in an atmosphere of equivocation, but he lived in freedom. And he offers us freedom: to pin him down to a single identity would be an obvious diminishment, both for Shakespeare and for us. Generations of critics have insisted on this irreducible multiplicity, though they have each expressed it different ways, through the glass of their times. Here is Keats's famous attempt, in 1817, to give this quality a name:

> At once it struck me, what quality went to form a Man of Achievement especially in Literature and which Shakespeare possessed so enormously —I mean *Negative Capability*, that is when man is capable of being in uncertainties, Mysteries, doubts, without any irritable reaching after fact and reason.

And here is Stephen Greenblatt doing the same, in 2004:

> There are many forms of heroism in Shakespeare, but ideological heroism—the fierce, self-immolating embrace of an idea or institution—is not one of them.

For Keats, Shakespeare's many voices are quasi-mystical as suited the Romantic thrust of Keats's age. For Greenblatt, Shakespeare's negative capability is sociopolitical at root. Will had seen too many wild-eyed martyrs, too many executed terrorists, too many wars on the Catholic terror. He had watched men rage absurdly at rood screens and write treatises in praise of tables. He had seen men disemboweled while still alive, their entrails burned before their eyes, and all for the preference of a Latin Mass over a common prayer or vice versa. He understood what fierce, singular certainty creates and what it destroys. In response, he made himself a diffuse, uncertain thing, a mass of contradictory, irresolvable voices that speak truth plurally. Through the glass of 2009, "negative capability" looks like the perfect antidote to "ideological heroism."

From our politicians, though, we still look for ideological heroism, despite everything. We consider pragmatists to be weak. We call men of balance naive fools. In England, we once had an insulting name for such people:

trimmers. In the mid-1600s, a trimmer was any politician who attempted to straddle the reviled middle ground between Cavalier and Roundhead, Parliament and the Crown; to call a man a trimmer was to accuse him of being insufficiently committed to an ideology. But in telling us of these times, the nineteenth-century English historian Thomas Macaulay draws our attention to Halifax, great statesman of the Privy Council, set up to mediate between Parliament and Crown as London burned. Halifax proudly called himself a trimmer, assuming it, Macaulay explains, as

> a title of honour, and vindicat[ing], with great vivacity, the dignity of the appellation. Everything good, he said, trims between extremes. The temperate zone trims between the climate in which men are roasted and the climate in which they are frozen. The English Church trims between the Anabaptist madness and the Papist lethargy. The English constitution trims between the Turkish despotism and Polish anarchy. Virtue is nothing but a just temper between propensities any one of which, if indulged to excess, becomes vice.

Which all sounds eminently reasonable and Aristotelian. And Macaulay's description of Halifax's character is equally attractive:

> His intellect was fertile, subtle, and capacious. His polished, luminous, and animated eloquence . . . was the delight of the House of Lords. . . . His political tracts well deserve to be studied for their literary merit.

In fact, Halifax is familiar—he sounds like the man from Dream City. This makes Macaulay's caveat the more striking:

> Yet he was less successful in politics than many who enjoyed smaller advantages. Indeed, those intellectual *peculiarities which make his writings valuable* frequently impeded him in the contests of active life. For he always saw passing events, not in the point of view in which they commonly appear to one who bears a part in them, but in the point of view in which, after the lapse of many years, they appear to the philosophic historian.

To me, this is a doleful conclusion. It is exactly men with such intellectual peculiarities that I have always hoped to see in politics. But maybe Macaulay is correct: maybe the Halifaxes of this world make, in the end, better writers than politicians. A lot rests on how this president turns out—but that's a debate for the future. Here I want instead to hazard a little theory, concerning the evolution of a certain type of voice, typified by Halifax, by Shakespeare, and very possibly the president. For the voice of what Macaulay called "the philosophic historian" is, to my mind, a valuable and particular one, and I think someone should make a proper study of it. It's a voice that develops in a man over time; my little theory sketches four developmental stages.

The first stage in the evolution is contingent and cannot be contrived. In this first stage, the voice, by no fault of its own, finds itself trapped between two poles, two competing belief systems. And so this first stage necessitates the second: the voice learns to be flexible between these two fixed points, even to the point of equivocation. Then the third stage: this native flexibility leads to a sense of being able to "see a thing from both sides." And then the final stage, which I think of as the mark of a certain kind of genius: the voice relinquishes ownership of itself, develops a creative sense of disassociation in which the claims that are particular to it seem no stronger than anyone else's. There it is, my little theory—I'd rather call it a story. It is a story about a wonderful voice, occasionally used by citizens, rarely by men of power. Amidst the din of the 2008 culture wars it proved especially hard to hear.

In this lecture I have been seeking to tentatively suggest that the voice that speaks with such freedom, thus unburdened by dogma and personal bias, thus flooded with empathy, might make a good president. It's only now that I realize that in all this utilitarianism I've left joyfulness out of the account, and thus neglected a key constituency of my own people, the poets! Being many-voiced may be a complicated gift for a president, but in poets it is a pure delight in need of neither defense nor explanation. Plato banished them from his uptight and annoying republic so long ago that they have lost all their anxiety. They are fancy-free.

"I am a Hittite in love with a horse," writes Frank O'Hara.

> I don't know what blood's
> in me I feel like an African prince I am a girl walking downstairs
> in a red pleated dress with heels I am a champion taking a fall
> I am a jockey with a sprained ass-hole I am the light mist
> in which a face appears
> and it is another face of blonde I am a baboon eating a banana
> I am a dictator looking at his wife I am a doctor eating a child
> and the child's mother smiling I am a Chinaman climbing a mountain
> I am a child smelling his father's underwear I am an Indian
> sleeping on a scalp
> and my pony is stamping in
> the birches,
> and I've just caught sight of the
> Niña, the Pinta and the Santa
> Maria.
> What land is this, so free?

Frank O'Hara's republic is of the imagination, of course. It is the only land of perfect freedom. Presidents, as a breed, tend to dismiss this land, thinking it has nothing to teach them. If this new president turns out to be different, then writers will count their blessings, but with or without a president on board, writers should always count their blessings. A line of O'Hara's reminds us of this. It's carved on his gravestone. It reads: "Grace to be born and live as variously as possible."

But to live variously cannot simply be a gift, endowed by an accident of birth; it has to be a continual effort, continually renewed. I felt this with force the night of the election. I was at a lovely New York party, full of lovely people, almost all of whom were white, liberal, highly educated, and celebrating with one happy voice as the states turned blue. Just as they called Iowa my phone rang and a strident German voice said: "Zadie! Come to Harlem! It's vild here. I'm in za middle of a crazy reggae bar—it's so vonderful! Vy not come now!"

I mention he was German only so we don't run away with the idea that flexibility comes only to the beige, or gay, or otherwise marginalized. Flexibility is a choice, always open to all of us. (He was a writer, however. Make of that what you will.)

But wait: all the way uptown? A crazy reggae bar? For a minute I hesitated, because I was at a lovely party having a lovely time. Or was that it? There was something else. In truth I thought: but I'll be ludicrous, in my silly dress, with this silly posh English voice, in a crowded bar of black New Yorkers celebrating. It's amazing how many of our cross-cultural and cross-class encounters are limited not by hate or pride or shame, but by another equally insidious, less-discussed, emotion: embarrassment. A few minutes later, I was in a taxi and heading uptown with my Northern Irish husband and our half-Indian, half English friend, but that initial hesitation was ominous; the first step on a typical British journey. A hesitation in the face of difference, which leads to caution before difference and ends in fear of it. Before long, the only voice you recognize, the only life you can empathize with, is your own. You will think that a novelist's screwy leap of logic. Well, it's my novelist credo and I believe it. I believe that flexibility of voice leads to a flexibility in all things. My audacious hope in Obama is based, I'm afraid, on precisely such flimsy premises.

It's my audacious hope that a man born and raised between opposing dogmas, between cultures, between voices, could not help but be aware of the extreme contingency of culture. I further audaciously hope that such a man will not mistake the happy accident of his own cultural sensibilities for a set of natural laws, suitable for general application. I even hope that he will find himself in agreement with George Bernard Shaw when he declared, "Patriotism is, fundamentally, a conviction that a particular country is the best in the world because you were born in it." But that may be an audacious hope too far. We'll see if Obama's lifelong vocal flexibility will enable him to say proudly with one voice "I love my country" while saying with another voice

"It is a country, like other countries." I hope so. He seems just the man to demonstrate that between those two voices there exists no contradiction and no equivocation but rather a proper and decent human harmony.

Francis Bacon
(1561–1626)

IN "OF NEGOCIATING" Francis Bacon tailors his advice to a range of possible scenarios and urges the need for a suite of diverse approaches. Composed centuries before the advent of electronic modes of communication, Bacon's thoughts on suiting the medium to the message and on the general advantage of the spoken word over the letter, together with his analysis of the role of body language, remain especially useful for those potential negotiators so habituated to virtual interfaces that face-to-face communication puts them at an immediate disadvantage. Modeled in part on those of Montaigne, Bacon's *Essays*, published in 1597, were quite popular in the seventeenth century and today remain intelligent guides to practical problems such as that of negotiation.

Of Negociating
from *Essays Civil and Moral* (1597)

IT is generally better to deal by speech than by letter; and by the mediation of a third than by a man's self. Letters are good, when a man would draw an answer by letter back again; or when it may serve for a man's justification afterwards to produce his own letter; or where it may be danger to be interrupted, or heard by pieces. To deal in person is good, when a man's face breedeth regard, as commonly with inferiors; or in tender cases, where a man's eye upon the countenance of him with whom he speaketh may give him a direction how far to go; and generally, where a man will reserve to himself liberty, either to disavow or to expound. In choice of instruments, it is better to choose men of a plainer sort, that are like to do that that is committed to them, and to report back again faithfully the success, than those that are cunning to contrive out of other men's business somewhat to grace themselves, and will help the matter in report for satisfaction sake. Use also such persons as affect the business wherein they are employed; for that quickeneth much; and such as are fit for the matter; as bold men for expostulation, fair-spoken men for persuasion, crafty men for inquiry and observation, froward and absurd men for business that doth not well bear out itself. Use also such as have been lucky, and prevailed before in things wherein you have employed them; for that breeds confidence, and they will strive to maintain their prescription. It is better to sound a person with whom one deals afar off, than to fall upon the point at first; except you mean to surprise him by some short question. It is better dealing with men in appetite, than with those that are where they would be. If a man deal with another upon conditions, the start or first performance is all; which a man cannot reasonably demand, except either the nature of the thing be such, which must go before; or else a man can persuade the other party that he shall still need him in some other thing; or else that he be counted the honester man. All practice is to discover, or to work. Men discover themselves in trust, in passion, at unawares, and of necessity, when they would have somewhat done and cannot find an apt pretext. If you would work any man, you must either know his nature and fashions, and so lead him; or his ends, and so persuade him; or his weakness and disadvantages, and so awe him; or those that have interest in him, and so govern him. In dealing with cunning persons, we must ever consider their ends, to interpret their speeches; and it is good to say little to them, and that which they least look for. In all negociations of difficulty, a man may not look to sow and reap at once; but must prepare business, and so ripen it by degrees.

Elizabeth I
(1533–1603)

IN THIS 1597 dressing-down of an ambassador who presumed too much, Elizabeth reveals that there are moments when a refusal to negotiate is in fact the smartest play. The queen's secretary of state and privy councillor, Robert Cecil, delighted by Elizabeth's wit, described her rebuke in a letter to the royal favorite, Robert Devereux, Earl of Essex, as "one of the best answers *extempore* in Latin that ever I heard, being much moved to be so challenged in public, especially so much against her expectation." Elizabeth reigned in England from 1588 to 1603. Beset on all sides by Catholic adversaries, Protestant England survived through the latter half of the sixteenth century under the leadership of a monarch whom many regarded as a liability because of her sex. With a combination of immense learning, political savvy, and personal courage, the clever Elizabeth survived multiple assassination attempts and the more ordinary physical dangers of the sixteenth-century world. During her lengthy rule she presided over a period of great cultural and political achievement perhaps best embodied in the plays of William Shakespeare. (The following selection comes from a seventeenth-century translation.)

Queen Elizabeth's Latin Rebuke to the Polish Ambassador, Paul de Jaline, July 25, 1597

O how have I been deceived! I expected an embassage, but you have brought to me a complaint; I was certified by letters that you were an ambassador, but I have found you an herald. Never in my lifetime have I heard such an oration. I marvel much at so great and insolent a boldness in open Presence; neither do I believe if your king were present that he himself would deliver such speeches. But if you have been commanded to use suchlike speeches (whereof I greatly doubt) it is here unto to be attributed: that seeing your king is a young man and newly chosen, not so fully by right of blood as by right of election, that he doth not so perfectly know the course of managing affairs of this nature with other princes as his elders have observed with us, or perhaps others will observe which shall succeed him in his place hereafter.

And as concerning yourself, you seem to have read many books, but the books of princes you have not so much as touched, but show yourself utterly ignorant what is convenient between kings. And where you make mention so often of the law of nature and the laws of nations, know you that this is the law of nature and of nations: that when hostility interposeth herself between princes, it is lawful for either party to cease on either's provisions for war, from whence soever derived, and to foresee that they be not converted to their own hurts. This, I say, is the law of nature and of nations.

And where you recite the new affinity with the House of Austria, what account soever you make thereof, you are not ignorant that some one of that House would have had the kingdom of Polonia from your king. For other matters, for which time and place serve not, seeing they are many and must be considered by themselves, this you shall expect: to be certified of them by some of our councillors that shall be appointed to those matters. In the meantime, fare you well and repose yourself.

Chuang Tzu
(ca. 365–ca. 290 BCE)

IN CONTRAST TO Lao Tzu, the perhaps apocryphal author of the *Tao Te Ching*, there almost certainly was a historical personage named Chuang Tzu; nevertheless, the details of his life remain hazy. As his translator David Hinton notes, most of what we know about Chuang Tzu comes from his own writings. Chaung Tzu's oeuvre comprises *The Inner Chapters*, *The*

Outer Chapters, and *Miscellaneous Chapters*. Scholars generally regard only the first as the work of Chuang Tzu; the other portions seem to be fragments written by different hands and organized by subsequent editors. Chuang Tzu lived in what is known as the Warring States period, one of the most turbulent epochs in Chinese history and one of the most productive eras of Chinese philosophy. Launched by the philosophy of Confucius, a "Hundred Schools of Thought" sprang up in response to the violent chaos. The contributors to this growing body of wisdom were itinerant scholars who, disciples in tow, offered counsel to governors throughout the country. Chuang Tzu, was "the odd man out" among his contemporaries, according to Hinton, because he was less interested in social philosophy than in poetry and the "spiritual ecology" associated with Taoism. Burton Watson describes Chuang Tzu's thought as characterized by a "skepticism and mystical detachment" born of political oppression and contrasting sharply with Confucian optimism, which focused on "concrete social, political, and ethical reforms." "Essentially," Watson writes in his introduction to Chuang Tzu's *Basic Writings*, "all of the philosophers of ancient China addressed themselves to the same problem: how is man to live in a world dominated by chaos, suffering, and absurdity?" According to Watson, Chuang Tzu offered a "radically different" answer: "free yourself from the world" and its imprisoning conventions and values. In this selection from *The Inner Chapters*, Chuang Tzu approaches the problem of conflict resolution with characteristically mystical guidance: transcend it. (The following selection is translated by David Hinton.)

Suppose You and I Have an Argument

from *The Inner Chapters*

Suppose you and I have an argument. Suppose you win and I lose. Does that mean you're really right and I'm wrong? Suppose I win and you lose. Does that mean I'm really right and you're wrong? Is one of us right and the other wrong? Are we both right and both wrong? If we can't figure it out ourselves, others must be totally in the dark, so who could we get to settle it? We could get someone who agrees with you, but if they agree with you how could they decide who's right and wrong? We could get someone who agrees with me, but if they agree with me how could they decide? We could get someone who disagrees with both of us, but if they disagree with both of us how could they decide? We could get someone who agrees with both of us, but if they agree with both of us how could they decide? Not I nor you nor anyone else can know who is right and who wrong. So what do we do? Wait for someone else to come along who can decide?

What is meant by *an accord reaching to the very limits of heaven?* I'd say: Right isn't merely right; so isn't merely so. If right is truly right, then not-right is so far from being right that there's no argument. And if so is truly so, not-so is so far from being so that there's no argument. When voices in transformation wait for each other to decide, it's like waiting for nothing. *An accord reaching to the very limits of heaven:* because it's endless, we live clear through all the years. Forget the years, forget Duty: move in the boundless, and the boundless becomes your home.

DISCUSSION QUESTIONS

1. *What are the most and least effective methods of negotiation demonstrated in these readings?*

2. *What are the most useful strategies for negotiation across cultures?*

3. *Under what circumstances is negotiation inappropriate?*

4. *How much of a leader's time ought to be consumed with internal and external negotiations?*

5. *What are the structures for negotiation in your organization or institution?*

TAKING RESPONSIBILITY

[Y]ou were right, and I was wrong.

—ABRAHAM LINCOLN,
letter to Ulysses S. Grant (July 13, 1863)

In the culture of impatience and demagoguery to which we are presently consigned, there is apparently nothing so worthy of celebration as having the courage of one's convictions; nothing—no cruelty, betrayal, or vice— more damaging to a political career than the disgrace of having changed one's mind. Having the courage of one's convictions in periods of adversity may be a stance of great responsibility, but it can also become a most dangerous virtue, shared by martyrs and fanatics alike: a virtue to which even those with bankrupt aims might default. Thomas Becket had that kind of courage in fatal measure; so, to the misfortune of the men he commanded, did George Armstrong Custer.

It takes a rather different kind of courage to admit to not yet knowing one's mind, to having altered an opinion in the light of new evidence or a reinterpretation of the old, to having made an error in judgment. Taking responsibility for missteps, mistakes, and misjudgments—to say nothing of the grosser ethical lapses that have dominated the late twentieth- and early twenty-first-century financial and political arenas—especially in an age enamored of decisiveness, is a difficult act.

This is precisely the sort of courage Abraham Lincoln displayed in a letter to Ulysses S. Grant not long after the surrender of Vicksburg in the summer of 1863; the full letter appears elsewhere in this anthology in "Abraham Lincoln: Artist of Judgment." After rehearsing his initial doubts about Grant's operational decisions leading up to the Union victory, Lincoln concluded, "I now wish to make the personal acknowledgment that you were right, and I was wrong." The elegance of Lincoln's confession owes to its being wholly unforced. His misgivings might well have remained the president's own secret without harming his relationship with Grant. Nor does Lincoln seem concerned that his admission of a mistake will in any way interfere with civilian authority over the military in future. It takes a particular—and not the most common—kind of self-confidence to behave in such a way. It is difficult to imagine Donald Rumsfeld, for example, crafting such a message to former Army Chief of Staff Eric Shinseki, the Cassandra whose prediction about the troop numbers needed for the invasion of Iraq was publicly dismissed by then Secretary of Defense Rumsfeld and his deputy Paul Wolfowitz.

In any high-pressure environment, especially in the arenas of foreign policy and national security, one sees the infectious, almost irresistible, ease with which self-confidence circulates, readying people for tasks they may not wish to perform and for missions that may cost them everything. Such confidence is an invaluable commodity in this world, but, like ambition, it has a double edge. No leader wants to look uncertain, but bluster too easily passes for justified confidence while only the most secure can muster the courage to admit their lack of sureness when required. It is no easy thing to cultivate and preserve the quality of mind on display in Lincoln's letter to Grant within such environments, but owning mistakes and taking responsibility for risky courses of action are essential capacities in any leader.

One of the most gracious, least dogmatic formulation of this state of mind appears in Montaigne: "As for our pupil's talk, let his virtue and his sense of right and wrong shine through it and have no guide but reason," he writes in "On Educating Children," here translated by M. A. Screech. "Make him understand that confessing an error which he discovers in his own argument even when he alone has noticed it is an act of justice and integrity, which are the main qualities he pursues; stubbornness and rancour are vulgar qualities, visible in common souls whereas to think again, to change one's mind and to give up a bad case in the heat of the argument are rare qualities showing strength and wisdom."

Montaigne's philosophy was refined by war as well as peace, in the public arena as well as the private retreat, through wide reading as well as practical experience. He is a staunch ally on a campaign to promote the value of changing one's mind among those whose task it will be to command confidence, calm fears, perhaps even to demand that others follow them to unhappy places at the peril of their own lives: to those who therefore can least afford to be accused of the vanity of absolute certainty or convicted of lacking the courage to think again.

The following readings explore different aspects of individual and communal responsibility. In Hector, the champion of Troy, we find a man willing to accept responsibility for his city even if it means sacrificing his family. Marcus Aurelius and Mencius meditate on the discipline a leader needs in order to fulfill responsibilities to the people, while Matthew's version of some of Jesus's parables highlights the idea of storytelling itself as part of a leader's duty. In two scenes from *Henry V* and *Julius Caesar*, Shakespeare dramatizes leaders wrestling with ethical questions and conflicting loyalties, while Melville presents us with a brave man facing a dilemma in the figure of Starbuck, first mate of the *Pequod* in *Moby-Dick*. Through the voice of the private detective Sam Spade, the novelist Dashiell Hammett offers an informal, idiosyncratic code of ethics. Finally, Rachel Carson challenges readers by insisting that responsibility for the environment belongs not only to leaders but to all members of society.

RECOMMENDED READING AND VIEWING

Herbert Bix, *Hirohito and the Making of Modern Japan* (2000)
Dexter Filkins, "The Fall of the Warrior King," *New York Times Magazine* (October 23, 2005)
The Fog of War: Eleven Lessons from the Life of Robert S. McNamara (2003), directed by Errol Morris
Paul Fussell, "Thank God for the Atom Bomb," *New Republic* (August 1981)
Upton Sinclair, *The Jungle* (1906)

Homer
(eighth century BCE)

ABOUT HOMER THERE is at once everything and almost nothing to say. To this single poet we attribute the great epics of ancient Greek culture, the *Iliad* and the *Odyssey*, both of which began life as oral poetry. Tradition has it that Homer came from Ionia, but nothing is known for certain. The *Iliad* chronicles the Greek war against Troy, spurred initially by the Trojan prince Paris's theft of Helen from her husband Menelaus, the king of Sparta. Yet by the time the poem begins, *in medias res*, the Greeks have lost whatever solidarity initially bound together their coalition. Much of the poem involves persuading the aggrieved Achilles to return to the fight. On the Trojan side, all look to Hector, the great champion. Unlike Achilles, Hector is not a machine of war; rather, as this passage from the end of the poem's sixth book suggests, he is a soldier expertly trained to battle who never loses sight of the private sacrifices his public commitment entails. In taking leave of his wife and child, Hector offers a rationale for his conduct and a full acknowledgment of the probable personal cost of defending his city. (The following selection is translated by Robert Fagles.)

Hector Returns to Troy
from *Iliad*

                              A flash of his helmet
and off he strode and quickly reached his sturdy,
well-built house. But white-armed Andromache—
Hector could not find her in the halls.
She and the boy and a servant finely gowned
were standing watch on the tower, sobbing, grieving.
When Hector saw no sign of his loyal wife inside
he went to the doorway, stopped and asked the servants,
"Come, please, tell me the truth now, women.
Where's Andromache gone? To my sisters' house?   10
To my brothers' wives with their long flowing robes?
Or Athena's shrine where the noble Trojan women
gather to win the great grim goddess over?"

    A busy, willing servant answered quickly,
"Hector, seeing you want to know the truth,
she hasn't gone to your sisters, brothers' wives
or Athena's shrine where the noble Trojan women
gather to win the great grim goddess over.
Up to the huge gate-tower of Troy she's gone
because she heard our men are so hard-pressed,   20
the Achaean fighters coming on in so much force.
She sped to the wall in panic, like a madwoman—
the nurse went with her, carrying your child."

    At that, Hector spun and rushed from his house,
back by the same way down the wide, well-paved streets
throughout the city until he reached the Scaean Gates,
the last point he would pass to gain the field of battle.
There his warm, generous wife came running up to meet him,
Andromache the daughter of gallant-hearted Eetion
who had lived below Mount Placos rich with timber,   30
in Thebe below the peaks, and ruled Cilicia's people.
His daughter had married Hector helmed in bronze.
She joined him now, and following in her steps
a servant holding the boy against her breast,
in the first flush of life, only a baby,
Hector's son, the darling of his eyes
and radiant as a star . . .

Hector would always call the boy Scamandrius,
townsmen called him Astyanax, Lord of the City,
since Hector was the lone defense of Troy.   40
The great man of war breaking into a broad smile,
his gaze fixed on his son, in silence. Andromache,
pressing close beside him and weeping freely now,
clung to his hand, urged him, called him: "Reckless one,
my Hector—your own fiery courage will destroy you!
Have you no pity for *him,* our helpless son? Or me,
and the destiny that weighs me down, your widow,
now so soon? Yes, soon they will kill you off,
all the Achaean forces massed for assault, and then,
bereft of you, better for me to sink beneath the earth.   50
What other warmth, what comfort's left for me,
once you have met your doom? Nothing but torment!
I have lost my father. Mother's gone as well.
Father . . . the brilliant Achilles laid him low
when he stormed Cilicia's city filled with people,
Thebe with her towering gates. He killed Eetion,
not that he stripped his gear—he'd some respect at least—
for he burned his corpse in all his blazoned bronze,
then heaped a grave-mound high above the ashes
and nymphs of the mountain planted elms around it,   60
daughters of Zeus whose shield is storm and thunder.
And the seven brothers I had within our halls . . .
all in the same day went down to the House of Death,
the great godlike runner Achilles butchered them all,
tending their shambling oxen, shining flocks.
                                        And mother,
who ruled under the timberline of woody Placos once—
he no sooner haled her here with his other plunder
than he took a priceless ransom, set her free
and home she went to her father's royal halls
where Artemis, showering arrows, shot her down.   70
You, Hector—you are my father now, my noble mother,
a brother too, and you are my husband, young and warm
        and strong!
Pity me, please! Take your stand on the rampart here,
before you orphan your son and make your wife a widow.
Draw your armies up where the wild fig tree stands,
there, where the city lies most open to assault,
the walls lower, easily overrun. Three times
they have tried that point, hoping to storm Troy,

their best fighters led by the Great and Little Ajax,
famous Idomeneus, Atreus' sons, valiant Diomedes.   80
Perhaps a skilled prophet revealed the spot—
or their own fury whips them on to attack."

    And tall Hector nodded, his helmet flashing:
"All this weighs on my mind too, dear woman.
But I would die of shame to face the men of Troy
and the Trojan women trailing their long robes
if I would shrink from battle now, a coward.
Nor does the spirit urge me on that way.
I've learned it all too well. To stand up bravely,
always to fight in the front ranks of Trojan soldiers,   90
winning my father great glory, glory for myself.
For in my heart and soul I also know this well:
the day will come when sacred Troy must die,
Priam must die and all his people with him,
Priam who hurls the strong ash spear . . .
                                Even so,
it is less the pain of the Trojans still to come
that weighs me down, not even of Hecuba herself
or King Priam, or the thought that my own brothers
in all their numbers, all their gallant courage,
may tumble in the dust, crushed by enemies—   100
That is nothing, nothing beside your agony
when some brazen Argive hales you off in tears,
wrenching away your day of light and freedom!
Then far off in the land of Argos you must live,
laboring at a loom, at another woman's beck and call,
fetching water at some spring, Messeis or Hyperia,
resisting it all the way—
the rough yoke of necessity at your neck.
And a man may say, who sees you streaming tears,
'There is the wife of Hector, the bravest fighter   110
they could field, those stallion-breaking Trojans,
long ago when the men fought for Troy.' So he will say
and the fresh grief will swell your heart once more,
widowed, robbed of the one man strong enough
to fight off your day of slavery.
                      No, no,
let the earth come piling over my dead body
before I hear your cries, I hear you dragged away!"

In the same breath, shining Hector reached down
for his son—but the boy recoiled,
cringing against his nurse's full breast,   120
screaming out at the sight of his own father,
terrified by the flashing bronze, the horsehair crest,
the great ridge of the helmet nodding, bristling terror—
so it struck his eyes. And his loving father laughed,
his mother laughed as well, and glorious Hector,
quickly lifting the helmet from his head,
set it down on the ground, fiery in the sunlight,
and raising his son he kissed him, tossed him in his arms,
lifting a prayer to Zeus and the other deathless gods:
"Zeus, all you immortals! Grant this boy, my son   130
may be like me, first in glory among the Trojans,
strong and brave like me, and rule all Troy in power
and one day let them say, 'He is a better man than his father!'—
when he comes home from battle bearing the bloody gear
of the mortal enemy he has killed in war—
a joy to his mother's heart."
                              So Hector prayed
and placed his son in the arms of his loving wife.
Andromache pressed the child to her scented breast,
smiling through her tears. Her husband noticed,
and filled with pity now, Hector stroked her gently,   140
trying to reassure her, repeating her name: "Andromache,
dear one, why so desperate? Why so much grief for me?
No man will hurl me down to Death, against my fate.
And fate? No one alive has ever escaped it,
neither brave man nor coward, I tell you—
it's born with us the day that we are born.
So please go home and tend to your own tasks,
the distaff and the loom, and keep the women
working hard as well. As for the fighting,
men will see to that, all who were born in Troy   150
but I most of all."
                     Hector aflash in arms
took up his horsehair-crested helmet once again.
And his loving wife went home, turning, glancing
back again and again and weeping live warm tears.
She quickly reached the sturdy house of Hector,
man-killing Hector,
and found her women gathered there inside

and stirred them all to a high pitch of mourning.
So in his house they raised the dirges for the dead,
for Hector still alive, his people were so convinced   160
that never again would he come home from battle,
never escape the Argives' rage and bloody hands.

Marcus Aurelius
(121–180)

ADMIRED BY EDWARD GIBBON, the eighteenth-century author of *Decline and Fall of the Roman Empire*, Marcus Aurelius, the Roman emperor and Stoic philosopher, was also a great favorite among the Victorians, including Walter Pater and Matthew Arnold. Arnold thought Marcus Aurelius's name should be as familiar to readers as that of Socrates because of the wisdom imparted by the *Meditations*, especially on the subject of "the ground-motives of human action." In the following selections (translated by Jeremy Collier), Marcus meditates on the incomparable guides of justice, honesty, self-control, and courage.

Meditations

3.6

If, in the whole compass of human life, you find anything preferable to justice and truth; to temperance and fortitude; to a mind self-satisfied with its own rational conduct, and entirely resigned to fate—if, I say, you know anything better than this, turn to it with your whole soul, and enjoy it, accounting it the best. But if there is nothing more valuable than the divinity implanted within you, and this is master of its appetites, examines all impressions, and has detached itself from the senses, as Socrates used to say, and shows itself submissive to the government of the gods, and helpful and benevolent to mankind—if all things are trifles compared with this, give way to nothing else. For if you are once inclined to any such thing, it will no longer be in your power to give your undivided preference to what is your own peculiar good, for it is not lawful that anything of another kind of nature, as either popular applause, or power, or riches, or pleasures, should be suffered to contest with what is rationally and politically good. All these things, if but for a while they begin to please, presently prevail, and pervert a man's mind. Let your choice therefore run all one way, and be bold and resolute for that which is best. Now what is profitable is best. If that means profitable to man as he is a rational being, stand to it; but if it means profitable to him as a mere animal, reject it, and keep your judgment without arrogance. Only take care to make inquiry secure.

3.7

Think nothing for your interest which makes you break your word, quit your modesty, hate, suspect, or curse any person, or inclines you to any practice which will not bear the light and look the world in the face. For he that values his mind and the worship of his divinity before all other things, need act no tragic part, laments under no misfortune, and wants neither solitude nor company; and, which is still more, he will neither fly from life nor pursue it, but is perfectly indifferent about the length or shortness of the time in which his soul shall be encompassed by his body. And if he were to expire this moment, he is as ready for it as for any other action that may be performed with modesty and decency. For all his life long, this is his only care—that his mind may always be occupied as befits a rational and social creature.

Mencius
(fourth century BCE)

REGARDED IN CHINA as the second sage after Confucius, Mencius, a latinization of Meng Tzu (Master Meng), was also, in the words of his translator David Hinton, "the great thinker of the heart." Mencius supplies, Hinton explains, what is largely missing from Confucius's emphasis on society's adherence to ritual: compassion, moral sympathy, acknowledgment of the "inner self," and advocacy for the role of the individual in shaping the state. Distinguished by his compassion, Mencius, like Confucius, Chuang Tzu, and others, responded to the chaos of the age. Born near the home of Confucius and taught by a disciple of Confucius's grandson Master Szu, Mencius was an itinerant sage. "Sharing," as Hinton explains, "with most other philosophers of the time a faith in the political mission of the intellectual, he traveled with his disciples to the various states advising their rulers, hoping his ideas would be adopted and so lead to a more humane society." Believing in the profound goodness of the people and partaking of the Taoist emphasis on humanity's connection to the cosmos, Mencius was largely neglected for over a millennium until the rise of Neo-Confucianism in the eleventh century. Both selections here focus on the ruler's responsibilities to the people.

from *Mencius*

THE GOVERNOR OF P'ING LU

Mencius went to P'ing Lu and said to the governor there: "If you had a spearman who abandoned his post three times in a single day, would you discharge him or not?"

"I wouldn't wait for three times," replied Governor K'ung Chü-hsin.

"But you have abandoned your own post many times," countered Mencius. "In years of calamity and failed harvests, how many thousands of your people suffered—young and old alike abandoned to gutters and ditches, the strong scattered to every corner of the land?"

"But there was nothing I could do."

"Suppose someone entrusted their cattle and sheep to your care. Surely you would try to find grass and hay for them. And if you couldn't find any, would you return them to their owner or just stand by and watch them die?"

"So, I myself am to blame."

Some time later, Mencius went to see the emperor and said: "I know five provincial governors in your country. The only one who understands how he himself is to blame is K'ung Chü-hsin. Shall I tell you what happened?"

"I myself am to blame," replied the emperor.

TYRANT CHIEH

Mencius said: "In serving their sovereign, people these days all say: *I'm expanding his territory and filling his treasury.* But what the world now calls a distinguished minister, the ancients called a plunderer of the people. To enrich a sovereign when he doesn't make the Way his purpose and Humanity his resolve—that is to enrich another tyrant Chieh.

"They say: *I'm forming alliances and winning wars for him.* But what the world now calls a distinguished minister, the ancients called a plunderer of the people. To strengthen a sovereign for war when he doesn't make the Way his purpose and Humanity his resolve—that is to empower another tyrant Chieh.

"When you abide by the Way of our times, leaving the practices of this world unchanged, then even if you're given all beneath Heaven, you won't keep it for a single morning."

The Gospel According to St. Matthew
(first century CE)

HERE IS MATTHEW's narrative of Jesus's teaching. First Jesus offers his reasons for using parables; next he uses the parables of the sower and the talents to articulate an ethics of personal responsibility—both his own responsibility as a leader for reaching the people through storytelling and also the individual's responsibility in the absence of a leader. The translation from the Greek is the King James Version, commissioned by James I of England and first published in 1611. The translators aimed at as literal a translation as possible, and as the editor Austin Busch notes, the King James Version "often does a better job of capturing the strangeness of the New Testament's Greek than do modern versions."

Parable of the Sower and Parable of the Talents
from Matthew, The New Testament, King James Version

13 The same day went Jesus out of the house, and sat by the sea side. [2]And great multitudes were gathered together unto him, so that he went into a ship, and sat; and the whole multitude stood on the shore. [3]And he spake many things unto them in parables, saying, Behold, a sower went forth to sow; [4]and when he sowed, some seeds fell by the way side, and the fowls came and devoured them up: [5]some fell upon stony places, where they had not much earth: and forthwith they sprung up, because they had no deepness of earth: [6]and when the sun was up, they were scorched; and because they had no root, they withered away. [7]And some fell among thorns; and the thorns sprung up, and choked them: [8]but other fell into good ground, and brought forth fruit, some an hundredfold, some sixtyfold, some thirtyfold. [9]Who hath ears to hear, let him hear.

[10]And the disciples came, and said unto him, Why speakest thou unto them in parables? [11]He answered and said unto them, Because it is given unto you to know the mysteries of the kingdom of heaven, but to them it is not given. [12]For whosoever hath, to him shall be given, and he shall have more abundance: but whosoever hath not, from him shall be taken away even that he hath. [13]Therefore speak I to them in parables: because they seeing see not; and hearing they hear not, neither do they understand. [14]And in them is fulfilled the prophecy of Esaias, which saith, By hearing ye shall hear, and shall not understand; and seeing ye shall see, and shall not perceive:

¹⁵for this people's heart is waxed gross, and their ears are dull of hearing, and their eyes they have closed; lest at any time they should see with their eyes, and hear with their ears, and should understand with their heart, and should be converted, and I should heal them. ¹⁶But blessed are your eyes, for they see: and your ears, for they hear. ¹⁷For verily I say unto you, That many prophets and righteous men have desired to see those things which ye see, and have not seen them; and to hear those things which ye hear, and have not heard them.

¹⁸Hear ye therefore the parable of the sower. ¹⁹When any one heareth the word of the kingdom, and understandeth it not, then cometh the wicked one, and catcheth away that which was sown in his heart. This is he which received seed by the way side. ²⁰But he that received the seed into stony places, the same is he that heareth the word, and anon with joy receiveth it; ²¹yet hath he not root in himself, but dureth for a while: for when tribulation or persecution ariseth because of the word, by and by he is offended. ²²He also that received seed among the thorns is he that heareth the word; and the care of this world, and the deceitfulness of riches, choke the word, and he becometh unfruitful. ²³But he that received seed into the good ground is he that heareth the word, and understandeth it; which also beareth fruit, and bringeth forth, some an hundredfold, some sixty, some thirty.

25:14
For the kingdom of heaven is as a man travelling into a far country, who called his own servants, and delivered unto them his goods. ¹⁵And unto one he gave five talents, to another two, and to another one; to every man according to his several ability; and straightway took his journey. ¹⁶Then he that had received the five talents went and traded with the same, and made them other five talents. ¹⁷And likewise he that had received two, he also gained other two. ¹⁸But he that had received one went and digged in the earth, and hid his lord's money. ¹⁹After a long time the lord of those servants cometh, and reckoneth with them. ²⁰And so he that had received five talents came and brought other five talents, saying, Lord, thou deliveredst unto me five talents: behold, I have gained beside them five talents more. ²¹His lord said unto him, Well done, thou good and faithful servant: thou hast been faithful over a few things, I will make thee ruler over many things: enter thou into the joy of thy lord. ²²He also that had received two talents came and said, Lord, thou deliveredst unto me two talents: behold, I have gained two other talents beside them. ²³His lord said unto him, Well done, good and faithful servant; thou hast been faithful over a few things, I will make thee ruler over many things: enter thou into the joy of thy lord. ²⁴Then he which had received the one talent came and said, Lord, I knew thee that thou art an hard man, reaping where thou hast not

sown, and gathering where thou hast not strawed: [25]and I was afraid, and went and hid thy talent in the earth: lo, there thou hast that is thine. [26]His lord answered and said unto him, Thou wicked and slothful servant, thou knewest that I reap where I sowed not, and gather where I have not strawed: [27]thou oughtest therefore to have put my money to the exchangers, and then at my coming I should have received mine own with usury. [28]Take therefore the talent from him, and give it unto him which hath ten talents. [29]For unto every one that hath shall be given, and he shall have abundance: but from him that hath not shall be taken away even that which he hath. [30]And cast ye the unprofitable servant into outer darkness: there shall be weeping and gnashing of teeth.

William Shakespeare
(1564–1616)

NO SMALL AMOUNT of energy has been devoted to proving that someone other than William Shakespeare wrote the plays traditionally attached to his name, but the so-called mystery that enshrouds the author's life is belied by the facts we know, including the documentation of his birth and death, his family's residence at Stratford-on-Avon, his probable grammar school education, his marriage, his career as an actor and playwright in London, and his petitions to courts of law. None of this would be of much interest, of course, were it not for the sharp insights into human character that his body of work offers. Along with his French contemporary Michel de Montaigne, Shakespeare is perhaps his age's premier observer of human nature. One does not read Shakespeare for his plots, which are often cobbled together from a variety of sources; instead, it is for his dramatizations of the mind's inner workings and the relationship between individual psychologies and social forces that we look to his work. The following excerpts from *Henry V* and *Julius Caesar* consider the question of responsibility. In the first, Henry V, disguised as a knight, has a conversation with a few of the soldiers in his army that touches on questions of justice and personal responsibility. The second selection opens a window into the mind of Brutus, the most principled and ambivalent of Caesar's assassins. Brutus attempts to balance what he owes to his friend with what the health of the state demands.

A Little Touch of Harry in the Night

from *Henry V,* act 4, scene 1

COURT Brother John Bates, is not that the morning which breaks yonder?

BATES I think it be. But we have no great cause to desire the approach of day.

WILLIAMS We see yonder the beginning of the day, but I think we shall never see the end of it.—Who goes there?   5

KING A friend.

WILLIAMS Under what captain serve you?

KING Under Sir Thomas Erpingham.

WILLIAMS A good old commander and a most kind gentleman. I pray you, what thinks he of our estate?   10

KING Even as men wrecked upon a sand, that look to be washed off the next tide.

BATES He hath not told his thought to the King?

KING No, nor it is not meet he should. For though I speak it to you, I think the King is but a man, as I am. The violet smells to him as it 15 doth to me; the element shows to him as it doth to me. All his senses have but human conditions. His ceremonies laid by, in his nakedness he appears but a man. And though his affections are higher mounted than ours, yet when they stoop, they stoop with the like wing. There-fore, when he sees reason of fears as we do, his fears, out of doubt, be of 20 the same relish as ours are. Yet, in reason, no man should possess him with any appearance of fear, lest he by showing it should dishearten his army.

BATES He may show what outward courage he will, but I believe, as cold a night as 'tis, he could wish himself in Thames up to the neck. And so I 25 would he were, and I by him, at all adventures, so we were quit here.

KING By my troth, I will speak my conscience of the King. I think he would not wish himself anywhere but where he is.

10. **estate:** situation.
16. **the element shows:** the sky appears.
17. **conditions:** limitations.
18. **affections:** desires.
19. **stoop:** Plummet down (term from falconry).
20. **of fears:** to fear.
21. **relish:** taste; kind.
21–22. **possess him with:** induce him to experience.
26. **at all adventures:** whatever might happen; **quit:** away from.
27. **troth:** oath.

BATES Then I would he were here alone. So should he be sure to be
ransomed, and a many poor men's lives saved.   30

KING I dare say you love him not so ill to wish him here alone, howsoever
you speak this to feel other men's minds. Methinks I could not die anywhere so contented as in the King's company, his cause being just and
his quarrel honorable.

WILLIAMS That's more than we know.   35

BATES Ay, or more than we should seek after. For we know enough if we
know we are the King's subjects. If his cause be wrong, our obedience
to the King wipes the crime of it out of us.

WILLIAMS But if the cause be not good, the King himself hath a heavy
reckoning to make when all those legs and arms and heads chopped off 40
in a battle shall join together at the latter day and cry all, "We died at
such a place"—some swearing, some crying for a surgeon, some upon
their wives left poor behind them, some upon the debts they owe, some
upon their children rawly left. I am afeard there are few die well that
die in a battle, for how can they charitably dispose of anything when 45
blood is their argument? Now, if these men do not die well, it will be
a black matter for the King that led them to it—who to disobey were
against all proportion of subjection.

KING So, if a son that is by his father sent about merchandise do sinfully
miscarry upon the sea, the imputation of his wickedness, by your rule, 50
should be imposed upon his father that sent him. Or if a servant, under
his master's command transporting a sum of money, be assailed by
robbers and die in many irreconciled iniquities, you may call the business
of the master the author of the servant's damnation. But this is not so.
The King is not bound to answer the particular endings of his soldiers, 55
the father of his son, nor the master of his servant, for they purpose not
their death when they purpose their services. Besides, there is no king,
be his cause never so spotless, if it come to the arbitrement of swords,
can try it out with all unspotted soldiers. Some, peradventure, have
on them the guilt of premeditated and contrived murder; some, of 60
beguiling virgins with the broken seals of perjury; some, making the

32. **feel:** test.
41. **latter day:** Last Judgment, when human beings are to be resurrected in the body.
44. **rawly:** abruptly/poorly.
46. **argument:** business.
47. **who:** whom.
48. **against . . . subjection:** to defy all proper relationships of authority and subordination.
50. **imputation of:** blame for.
53. **irreconciled iniquities:** unatoned sin.
58. **arbitrement:** settlement.
59. **unspotted:** unblemished; **peradventure:** perhaps.

wars their bulwark, that have before gored the gentle bosom of peace with pillage and robbery. Now, if these men have defeated the law and outrun native punishment, though they can outstrip men, they have no wings to fly from God. War is his beadle. War is his vengeance. So 65 that here men are punished for before-breach of the King's laws in now the King's quarrel. Where they feared the death, they have borne life away; and where they would be safe, they perish. Then if they die unprovided, no more is the King guilty of their damnation than he was before guilty of those impieties for the which they are now visited. 70 Every subject's duty is the King's, but every subject's soul is his own. Therefore should every soldier in the wars do as every sick man in his bed: wash every mote out of his conscience. And dying so, death is to him advantage; or not dying, the time was blessedly lost wherein such preparation was gained. And in him that escapes, it were not sin 75 to think that, making God so free an offer, he let him outlive that day to see his greatness and to teach others how they should prepare.

WILLIAMS 'Tis certain, every man that dies ill, the ill upon his own head. The King is not to answer it.

BATES I do not desire he should answer for me, and yet I determine to 80 fight lustily for him.

KING I myself heard the King say he would not be ransomed.

WILLIAMS Ay, he said so to make us fight cheerfully. But when our throats are cut he may be ransomed and we never the wiser.

KING If I live to see it, I will never trust his word after. 85

WILLIAMS You pay him then! That's a perilous shot out of an eldergun, that a poor and a private displeasure can do against a monarch. You may as well go about to turn the sun to ice with fanning in his face with a peacock's feather! You'll never trust his word after! Come, 'tis a foolish saying. 90

KING Your reproof is something too round; I should be angry with you if the time were convenient.

WILLIAMS Let it be a quarrel between us, if you live.

---

62. **bulwark:** defense (against the law).
64. **native:** at home.
65. **beadle:** police officer.
66. **before-breach:** earlier breaking.
69. **unprovided:** unprepared.
70. **visited:** punished.
73. **mote:** speck.
74. **advantage:** profit.
76. **he:** God.
78. **ill:** in sin.
86. **an eldergun:** a popgun.
91. **round:** blunt.

KING I embrace it.

WILLIAMS How shall I know thee again?   95

KING Give me any gage of thine and I will wear it in my bonnet. Then if
  ever thou dar'st acknowledge it, I will make it my quarrel.

WILLIAMS Here's my glove. Give me another of thine.

KING There.

  [*They exchange gloves.*]

WILLIAMS This will I also wear in my cap. If ever thou come to me and 100
  say after tomorrow, "This is my glove," by this hand I will take thee a
  box on the ear.

KING If ever I live to see it, I will challenge it.

WILLIAMS Thou dar'st as well be hanged.

KING Well, I will do it, though I take thee in the King's company.   105

WILLIAMS Keep thy word. Fare thee well.

BATES Be friends, you English fools, be friends! We have French quarrels
  enough, if you could tell how to reckon.

KING Indeed, the French may lay twenty French crowns to one they will 110
  beat us, for they bear them on their shoulders. But it is no English treason to cut French crowns, and tomorrow the King himself will be a
  clipper.

  Exeunt Soldiers.

Upon the King! "Let us our lives, our souls,
Our debts, our careful wives,
Our children, and our sins, lay on the King!"   115
We must bear all. O hard condition,
Twin-born with greatness, subject to the breath
Of every fool whose sense no more can feel
But his own wringing. What infinite heartsease
Must kings neglect that private men enjoy!   120
And what have kings that privates have not too,
Save ceremony, save general ceremony?
And what art thou, thou idol ceremony?
What kind of god art thou, that suffer'st more
Of mortal griefs than do thy worshippers?   125

---

96. **gage:** token.

108. **reckon:** count.

109. **crowns:** coins; heads.

111. **crowns:** "Clipping," or shaving, precious metal off coins was punishable as treason.

119. **wringing:** pain.

What are thy rents? What are thy comings-in?
O ceremony, show me but thy worth.
What is thy soul of adoration?
Art thou aught else but place, degree, and form.
Creating awe and fear in other men,   130
Wherein thou art less happy, being feared,
Than they in fearing?
What drink'st thou oft, instead of homage sweet,
But poisoned flattery? O be sick, great greatness,
And bid thy ceremony give thee cure!   135
Think'st thou the fiery fever will go out
With titles blown from adulation?
Will it give place to flexure and low bending?
Canst thou, when thou command'st the begger's knee,
Command the health of it? No, thou proud dream   140
That play'st so subtly with a king's repose.
I am a king that find thee, and I know
'Tis not the balm, the scepter, and the ball,
The sword, the mace, the crown imperial,
The intertissued robe of gold and pearl,   145
The farced title running fore the king,
The throne he sits on, nor the tide of pomp
That beats upon the high shore of this world—
No, not all these, thrice-gorgeous ceremony,
Not all these, laid in bed majestical,   150
Can sleep so soundly as the wretched slave
Who, with a body filled and vacant mind,
Gets him to rest, crammed with distressful bread;
Never sees horrid night, the child of hell,
But like a lackey, from the rise to set,   155
Sweats in the eye of Phoebus, and all night
Sleeps in Elysium; next day after dawn
Doth rise and help Hyperion to his horse,

126. **rents:** revenues; **comings-in:** income.
128. **What is thy soul of adoration?:** What is the secret of the adoration you inspire?
129. **aught:** anything.
138. **flexure:** bowing.
142. **find:** expose.
143. **ball:** orb (royal accessory).
146. **farced:** stuffed.
155. **lackey:** servant.
156. **Phoebus:** the sun.
157. **Elysium:** classical paradise.
158. **Hyperion:** the sun's charioteer.

And follows so the ever-running year
With profitable labor to his grave.   160
And but for ceremony such a wretch,
Winding up days with toil and nights with sleep.
Had the forehand and vantage of a king.
The slave, a member of the country's peace,
Enjoys it, but in gross brain little wots   165
What watch the king keeps to maintain the peace,
Whose hours the peasant best advantages.

The Deliberation of Brutus
Julius Caesar, act 2, scene 1

ROME. BRUTUS' HOUSE.

Enter BRUTUS *in his orchard.*

BRUTUS What, Lucius, ho!
 I cannot by the progress of the stars
 Give guess how near to day. Lucius, I say!
 I would it were my fault to sleep so soundly,
 When, Lucius, when? Awake, I say! What, Lucius!   5

 Enter LUCIUS,

LUCIUS Called you, my lord?
BRUTUS Get me a taper in my study, Lucius,
 When it is lighted, come and call me here.
LUCIUS I will, my lord.   *Exit.*
BRUTUS It must be by his death. And for my part   10
 I know no personal cause to spurn at him
 But for the general. He would be crowned:
 How that might change his nature, there's the question.
 It is the bright day that brings forth the adder

163. **forehand:** advantage.
165. **wots:** thinks.
167. **best advantages:** most profits from.

10. **his:** i.e., Caesar's
11. **spurn:** kick.
12. **general:** the public (good).

And that craves wary walking. Crown him that,   15
And then I grant we put a sting in him
That at his will he may do danger with.
Th'abuse of greatness is when it disjoins
Remorse from power. And to speak truth of Caesar,
I have not known when his affections swayed   20
More than his reason. But 'tis a common proof
That lowliness is young ambition's ladder,
Whereto the climber-upward turns his face;
But when he once attains the upmost round
He then unto the ladder turns his back,   25
Looks in the clouds, scorning the base degrees
By which he did ascend. So Caesar may.
Then lest he may, prevent. And since the quarrel
Will bear no color for the thing he is,
Fashion it thus: that what he is, augmented,   30
Would run to these and these extremities.
And therefore think him as a serpent's egg,
Which, hatched, would as his kind grow mischievous,
And kill him in the shell.

>   *Enter* LUCIUS.

LUCIUS   The taper burneth in your closet, sir.   35
Searching the window for a flint, I found
This paper, thus sealed up, and I am sure
It did not lie there when I went to bed.

>   *Gives him the letter.*

BRUTUS   Get you to bed again; it is not day.
Is not tomorrow, boy, the Ides of March?   40
LUCIUS   I know not, sir.
BRUTUS   Look in the calendar and bring me word.
LUCIUS   I will, sir.

15. **craves:** calls for.
19. **Remorse:** scruples, conscience.
20. **affections swayed:** emotions influenced, ruled (held sway).
21. **proof:** experience.
22. **lowliness:** humility.
24. **upmost round:** top rung of a ladder.
26. **base degree:** i.e., lower rung.
28-29: **since . . . is:** because the argument cannot be grounded in his present conduct.
30. **Fashion:** describe.
33. **kind:** nature; **mischievous:** harmful.
35. **closet:** private room.

BRUTUS The exhalations whizzing in the air
    Give so much light that I may read by them.   45

     [He] *opens the letter and reads.*

    Brutus, thou sleep'st. Awake, and see thy self!
    Shall Rome, etc. Speak, strike, redress!"
    "Brutus, thou sleep'st. Awake!"
    Such instigations have been often dropped
    Where I have took them up.   50
    "Shall Rome, etc." Thus must I piece it out:
    Shall Rome stand under one man's awe? What, Rome?
    My ancestors did from the streets of Rome
    The Tarquin drive when he was called a king.
    "Speak, strike, redress!" Am I entreated   55
    To speak and strike? O Rome, I make thee promise,
    If the redress will follow, thou receivest
    Thy full petition at the hand of Brutus.

     Enter LUCIUS

LUCIUS Sir, March is wasted fifteen days.

     Knock within.

BRUTUS 'Tis good. Go to the gate, somebody knocks.   60

                                     [*Exit* LUCIUS.]

    Since Cassius first did whet me against Caesar
    I have not slept.
    Between the acting of a dreadful thing
    And the first motion, all the interim is
    Like a phantasma or a hideous dream.   65
    The genius and the mortal instruments
    Are then in council, and the state of man,
    Like to a little kingdom, suffers then
    The nature of an insurrection.

---

44. **exhalations:** meteors.
54. **Tarquin:** Tarquinius Superbus, in legend the last king of Rome.
58. **full petition:** i.e., all that has been asked (by the citizens).
61. **whet:** incite.
64. **motion:** impulse.
66. **genius:** inward spirit; **instruments:** bodily parts.

Enter LUCIUS

LUCIUS Sir, 'tis your brother Cassius at the door,   70
    Who doth desire to see you.
BRUTUS   Is he alone?
LUCIUS No, sir, there are moe with him.
BRUTUS   Do you know them?
LUCIUS No, sir, their hats are plucked about their ears
    And half their faces buried in their cloaks,   75
    That by no means I may discover them
    By any mark of favor.
BRUTUS   Let 'em enter.

                                [*Exit* LUCIUS.]

    They are the faction. O conspiracy,
    Sham'st thou to show thy dang'rous brow by night,
    When evils are most free? O then by day
    Where wilt thou find a cavern dark enough   80
    To mask thy monstrous visage? Seek none, conspiracy:
    Hide it in smiles and affability;
    For if thou path, thy native semblance on,
    Not Erebus itself were dim enough
    To hide thee from prevention.   85

      Enter the conspirators, CASSIUS, CASCA, DECIUS, CINNA,
      METELLUS, *and* TREBONIUS

CASSIUS I think we are too bold upon your rest.
    Good morrow, Brutus. Do we trouble you?
BRUTUS I have been up this hour, awake all night.
    Know I these men that come along with you?
CASSIUS Yes, every man of them; and no man here   90
    But honors you, and every one doth wish
    You had but that opinion of yourself
    Which every noble Roman bears of you.
    This is Trebonius.

70. **brother:** i.e., brother-in-law.
72. **moe:** more.
73. **plucked about:** i.e., pulled (down) around.
75. **discover:** identify.
76. **mark of favor:** distinguishing physical feature.
83. **path . . . on:** i.e., if you pursue your course without a disguise.
84. **Erebus:** a god symbolizing the dark underworld.
85. **prevention:** being forestalled, hindered.
86. **bold upon:** bold (intruding) upon.

BRUTUS   He is welcome hither.

CASSIUS This, Decius Brutus.

BRUTUS   He is welcome too.   95

CASSIUS This, Casca; this, Cinna; and this, Metellus Cimber.

BRUTUS They are all welcome.
    What watchful cares do interpose themselves
    Betwixt your eyes and night?

CASSIUS Shall I entreat a word?   100

    They whisper.

DECIUS Here lies the east. Doth not the day break here?

CASCA No.

CINNA O, pardon, sir, it doth, and yon grey lines
    That fret the clouds are messengers of day.

CASCA You shall confess that you are both deceived.   105
    Here, as I point my sword, the sun arises,
    Which is a great way growing on the south,
    Weighing the youthful season of the year.
    Some two months hence, up higher toward the north
    He first presents his fire, and the high east   110
    Stands, as the Capitol, directly here.

BRUTUS   [*Coming forward with* CASSIUS.]
    Give me your hands all over one by one.

CASSIUS And let us swear our resolution.

BRUTUS No, not an oath! If not the face of men,
    The sufferance of our souls, the time's abuse—   115
    If these be motives weak, break off betimes,
    And every man hence to his idle bed;
    So let high-sighted tyranny range on,
    Till each man drop by lottery. But if these
    (As I am sure they do) bear fire enough   120
    To kindle cowards and to steel with valor

98. **watchful cares:** cares that keep you awake.
104. **fret:** interlace with.
107. **growing on:** advancing on.
108. **weighing:** considering.
110. **high:** due.
112. **all over:** all of you.
114. **face:** (grim) expressions.
115. **sufferance:** suffering.
116. **betimes:** immediately, at once.
117. **idle:** unused.
118. **high-sighted:** arrogant.
119. **drop by lottery:** die by chance (i.e., at the tyrant's whim); **these:** i.e., these motives.

The melting spirits of women, then, countrymen,
What need we any spur but our own cause
To prick us to redress? What other bond
Than secret Romans that have spoke the word   125
And will not palter? And what other oath
Than honesty to honesty engaged
That this shall be or we will fall for it?
Swear priests and cowards and men cautelous,
Old feeble carrions, and such suffering souls   130
That welcome wrongs; unto bad causes swear
Such creatures as men doubt. But do not stain
The even virtue of our enterprise,
Nor th'insuppressive mettle of our spirits,
To think that or our cause or our performance   135
Did need an oath, when every drop of blood
That every Roman bears, and nobly bears,
Is guilty of a several bastardy
If he do break the smallest particle
Of any promise that hath passed from him.   140
CASSIUS But what of Cicero? Shall we sound him?
      I think he will stand very strong with us.
CASCA Let us not leave him out.
CINNA   No, by no means.
METELLUS O, let us have him, for his silver hairs
      Will purchase us a good opinion   145
      And buy men's voices to commend our deeds.
      It shall be said his judgment ruled our hands;
      Our youths and wildness shall no whit appear,
      But all be buried in his gravity.
BRUTUS O, name him not, let us not break with him,   150
      For he will never follow anything
      That other men begin.
CASSIUS   Then, leave him out.

125. **Than:** than that of.
126. **palter:** waver.
129. **Swear:** i.e., let swear; **cautelous:** cautious, wary.
130. **carrions:** carcasses, corpselike men.
132. **doubt:** suspect.
133. **even:** just.
134. **insuppressive:** irrepressible.
135. **or our cause:** either our cause.
138. **several:** separate.
141. **sound him:** sound him out.
150. **break with him:** disclose to him (the plans).

CASCA Indeed he is not fit.

DECIUS Shall no man else be touched but only Caesar?

CASSIUS Decius, well urged. I think it is not meet   155
    Mark Antony, so well beloved of Caesar,
    Should outlive Caesar. We shall find of him
    A shrewd contriver. And, you know, his means,
    If he improve them, may well stretch so far
    As to annoy us all, which to prevent,   160
    Let Antony and Caesar fall together.

BRUTUS Our course will seem too bloody, Caius Cassius,
    To cut the head off and then hack the limbs—
    Like wrath in death and envy afterwards—
    For Antony is but a limb of Caesar.   165
    Let's be sacrificers, but not butchers, Caius.
    We all stand up against the spirit of Caesar,
    And in the spirit of men there is no blood.
    O, that we then could come by Caesar's spirit
    And not dismember Caesar! But, alas,   170
    Caesar must bleed for it. And, gentle friends,
    Let's kill him boldly, but not wrathfully;
    Let's carve him as a dish fit for the gods,
    Not hew him as a carcass fit for hounds.
    And let our hearts, as subtle masters do,   175
    Stir up their servants to an act of rage
    And after seem to chide 'em. This shall make
    Our purpose necessary, and not envious,
    Which so appearing to the common eyes,
    We shall be called purgers, not murderers.   180
    And for Mark Antony, think not of him,
    For he can do no more than Caesar's arm
    When Caesar's head is off.

CASSIUS   Yet I fear him,
    For in the engrafted love he bears to Caesar—

155. **meet:** proper, fitting.
158. **shrewd:** malicious.
159. **improve:** make the most of.
160. **annoy:** harm.
164. **envy:** malice.
169. **come by:** obtain.
174. **hew:** chop up.
175. **subtle:** cunning, crafty.
176. **servants:** passions.
178. **envious:** malicious.
184. **engrafted:** deep-rooted.

BRUTUS Alas, good Cassius, do not think of him.   185
    If he love Caesar, all that he can do
    Is to himself—take thought and die for Caesar;
    And that were much he should, for he is given
    To sports, to wildness, and much company.
TREBONIUS There is no fear in him. Let him not die,   190
    For he will live and laugh at this hereafter.

        Clock strikes.

BRUTUS Peace, count the clock.
CASSIUS   The clock hath stricken three.
TREBONIUS 'Tis time to part.
CASSIUS   But it is doubtful yet
    Whether Caesar will come forth today or no,
    For he is superstitious grown of late,   195
    Quite from the main opinion he held once
    Of fantasy, of dreams, and ceremonies.
    It may be these apparent prodigies,
    The unaccustomed terror of this night,
    And the persuasion of his augerers   200
    May hold him from the Capitol today.
DECIUS Never fear that. If he be so resolved
    I can o'ersway him, for he loves to hear
    That unicorns may be betrayed with trees,
    And bears with glasses, elephants with holes,   205
    Lions with toils, and men with flatterers.
    But when I tell him he hates flatterers
    He says he does, being then most flattered.
    Let me work:
    For I can give his humor the true bent,   210
    And I will bring him to the Capitol.
CASSIUS Nay, we will all of us be there to fetch him.

187. **take thought:** become melancholy.
188. **that . . . should:** that is more than he is likely to perform.
190. **no fear:** nothing to fear.
196. **Quite from:** . . . contrary to.
197. **ceremonies:** omens.
199. **unaccustomed:** unusual.
200. **augerers:** Roman priests.
204. **betrayed with trees:** fooled into impaling themselves on trees.
205. **glasses:** mirrors; **holes:** pitfalls.
206. **toils:** nets.
210. **humor:** disposition; **bent:** direction.

BRUTUS By the eighth hour, is that the uttermost?
CINNA Be that the uttermost, and fail not then.
METELLUS Caius Ligarius doth bear Caesar hard,   215
    Who rated him for speaking well of Pompey.
    I wonder none of you have thought of him.
BRUTUS Now, good Metellus, go along by him.
    He loves me well, and I have given him reasons.
    Send him hither and I'll fashion him.   220
CASSIUS The morning comes upon's. We'll leave you, Brutus,
    And, friends, disperse yourselves, but all remember
    What you have said and show yourselves true Romans.
BRUTUS Good gentlemen, look fresh and merrily.
    Let not our looks put on our purposes,   225
    But bear it as our Roman actors do,
    With untired spirits and formal constancy.
    And so good morrow to you every one.

Exeunt [all but] BRUTUS.

    Boy! Lucius! Fast asleep? It is no matter.
    Enjoy the honey-heavy dew of slumber.   230
    Thou hast no figures nor no fantasies
    Which busy care draws in the brains of men,
    Therefore thou sleep'st so sound.

Enter PORTIA.

PORTIA   Brutus, my lord.
BRUTUS Portia! What mean you? Wherefore rise you now?
    It is not for your health thus to commit   235
    Your weak condition to the raw cold morning.
PORTIA Nor for yours neither. Y'have ungently, Brutus,
    Stole from my bed; and yesternight at supper
    You suddenly arose and walked about,
    Musing and sighing, with your arms across,   240
    And when I asked you what the matter was,
    You stared upon me with ungentle looks.

213. **uttermost:** latest.
215. **hard:** ill will, a grudge.
216. **rated:** berated.
218. **by:** to.
220. **fashion:** transform; i.e., convince.
225. **put on:** show, reveal.
227. **formal constancy:** outward resolution.
231. **figures:** imaginings.
237. **ungently:** unkindly.
240. **across:** crossed, folded (indicating melancholy).

Purged you further, then you scratched your head
And too impatiently stamped with your foot.
Yet I insisted, yet you answered not,   245
But with an angry wafture of your hand
Gave sign for me to leave you. So I did,
Fearing to strengthen that impatience
Which seemed too much enkindled, and withal
Hoping it was but an effect of humor,   250
Which sometime hath his hour with every man.
It will not let you eat, nor talk, nor sleep;
And could it work so much upon your shape
As it hath much prevailed on your condition,
I should not know you, Brutus. Dear my lord,   255
Make me acquainted with your cause of grief.
BRUTUS   I am not well in health, and that is all.
PORTIA   Brutus is wise, and were he not in health
He would embrace the means to come by it.
BRUTUS   Why, so I do. Good Portia, go to bed.   260
PORTIA   Is Brutus sick? And is it physical
To walk unbraced and suck up the humors
Of the dank morning? What, is Brutus sick?
And will he steal out of his wholesome bed
To dare the vile contagion of the night,   265
And tempt the rheumy and unpurgèd air
To add unto this sickness? No, my Brutus,
You have some sick offence within your mind,
Which by the right and virtue of my place
I ought to know of. [*Kneels.*] And upon my knees   270
I charm you, by my once commended beauty,
By all your vows of love, and that great vow
Which did incorporate and make us one,
That you unfold to me, your self, your half,
Why you are heavy, and what men tonight   275

246. **wafture:** wave.
251. **his:** i.e., its.
254. **condition:** disposition.
261. **physical:** good for one's health.
262. **unbracèd:** with an unlaced doublet; **humors:** vapors.
266. **rheumy:** moist.
268 **sick offence:** harmful disorder.
269. **virtue:** power (as prerogative).
271. **charm:** conjure, entreat.
275. **heavy:** heavyhearted, sad.

Have had resort to you; for here have been
Some six or seven who did hide their faces
Even from darkness.
BRUTUS   Kneel not, gentle Portia.
PORTIA   I should not need if you were gentle Brutus.
   Within the bond of marriage, tell me, Brutus,   280
   Is it excepted I should know no secrets
   That appertain to you? Am I your self
   But, as it were, in sort or limitation,
   To keep with you at meals, comfort your bed,
   And talk to you sometimes? Dwell I but in the suburbs   285
   Of your good pleasure? If it be no more
   Portia is Brutus' harlot, not his wife.
BRUTUS   You are my true and honorable wife,
   As dear to me as are the ruddy drops
   That visit my sad heart.   290
PORTIA   If this were true, then should I know this secret.
   I grant I am a woman, but withal
   A woman that Lord Brutus took to wife.
   I grant I am a woman, but withal
   A woman well reputed, Cato's daughter.   295
   Think you I am no stronger than my sex,
   Being so fathered and so husbanded?
   Tell me your counsels; I will not disclose 'em.
   I have made strong proof of my constancy,
   Giving myself a voluntary wound   300
   Here, in the thigh. Can I bear that with patience
   And not my husband's secrets?
BRUTUS   O ye gods,
   Render me worthy of this noble wife!

   Knock.

   Hark, hark, one knocks. Portia, go in a while,
   And by and by thy bosom shall partake   305
   The secrets of my heart.
   All my engagements I will construe to thee.

---

285. **suburbs:** outlying areas, fringes.
292. **withal:** still, even yet.
295. **Cato's daughter:** Marcus Porcius Cato was known for his moral rectitude.
298. **counsels:** secrets.
307. **engagements:** formal agreements.

All the charactery of my sad brows.
Leave me with haste.

Exit PORTIA.

Lucius, who's that knocks?

Enter LUCIUS *and* LIGARIUS.

LUCIUS Here is a sick man that would speak with you.   310
BRUTUS Caius Ligarius, that Metellus spake of.
Boy, stand aside.

[*Exit* LUCIUS.]

Caius Ligarius, how?
LIGARIUS Vouchsafe good morrow from a feeble tongue.
BRUTUS O, what a time have you chose out, brave Caius,
To wear a kerchief. Would you were not sick!   315
LIGARIUS I am not sick if Brutus have in hand
Any exploit worthy the name of honor.
BRUTUS Such an exploit have I in hand, Ligarius,
Had you a healthful ear to hear of it.
LIGARIUS By all the gods that Romans bow before,   320
I here discard my sickness!

[*He pulls off his kerchief.*]

Soul of Rome,
Brave son, derived from honorable loins,
Thou, like an exorcist, hast conjured up
My mortified spirit. Now bid me run
And I will strive with things impossible,   325
Yea, get the better of them. What's to do?
A piece of work that will make sick men whole.
LIGARIUS But are not some whole that we must make sick?
BRUTUS That must we also. What it is, my Caius,
I shall unfold to thee as we are going   330
To whom it must be done.
LIGARIUS   Set on your foot,

308. **charactery:** handwriting, i.e., the meaning behind his serious expression.
312. **how:** an exclamation of surprise.
313. **Vouchsafe:** receive graciously.
315. **kerchief:** a headscarf worn by the sick.
324. **mortified:** deadened.
327. **whole:** healthy.
331. **Set on your foot:** proceed.

And with a heart new-fired I follow you
To do I know not what; but it sufficeth
That Brutus leads me on.

    Thunder.

BRUTUS   Follow me then.

                                       Exeunt.

Herman Melville
(1819–1891)

THE TWO PASSAGES excerpted here come from *Moby-Dick*. In them Melville describes the personality and behavior of Starbuck, the first mate of the *Pequod*, a nineteenth-century whaling ship out of Nantucket. Starbuck is known from the outset for his prudence and his belief that "the most reliable and useful courage was that which arises from the fair estimation of the encountered peril." There is nothing rash or reckless in Starbuck's character; he is a responsible steward of men and matériel. However, when Captain Ahab threatens to risk everything in his monomaniacal pursuit of the white whale, Starbuck must decide whether to take the bold and irreversible step of mutinying against his tyrannical commander.

A Valor-Ruined Man
from *Moby-Dick* (1851)

The chief mate of the Pequod was Starbuck, a native of Nantucket, and a Quaker by descent. He was a long, earnest man, and though born on an icy coast, seemed well adapted to endure hot latitudes, his flesh being hard as twice-baked biscuit. Transported to the Indies, his live blood would not spoil like bottled ale. He must have been born in some time of general drought and famine, or upon one of those fast days for which his state is famous. Only some thirty arid summers had he seen; those summers had dried up all his physical superfluousness. But this, his thinness, so to speak, seemed no more the token of wasting anxieties and cares, than it seemed the indication of any bodily blight. It was merely the condensation of the man. He was by no means ill-looking; quite the contrary. His pure tight skin was an excellent fit; and closely wrapped up in it, and embalmed with inner health and strength, like a revivified Egyptian, this Starbuck seemed prepared to endure for long ages to come, and to endure always, as now; for be it Polar snow or torrid sun, like a patent chronometer, his interior vitality was warranted to do well in all climates. Looking into his eyes, you seemed to see there the yet lingering images of those thousand-fold perils he had calmly confronted through life. A staid, steadfast man, whose life for the most part was a telling pantomime of action, and not a tame chapter of sounds. Yet, for all his hardy sobriety and fortitude, there were certain qualities in him which at times affected, and in some cases seemed well nigh to overbalance all the rest. Uncommonly conscientious for a seaman, and endued with a deep natural reverence, the wild watery loneliness of his life did therefore strongly incline him to superstition; but to that sort of superstition, which in some organizations seems rather to spring, somehow, from intelligence than from ignorance. Outward portents and inward presentiments were his. And if at times these things bent the welded iron of his soul, much more did his far-away domestic memories of his young Cape wife and child, tend to bend him still more from the original ruggedness of his nature, and open him still further to those latent influences which, in some honest-hearted men, restrain the gush of dare-devil daring, so often evinced by others in the more perilous vicissitudes of the fishery. "I will have no man in my boat," said Starbuck, "who is not afraid of a whale." By this, he seemed to mean, not only that the most reliable and useful courage was that which arises from the fair estimation of the encountered peril, but that an utterly fearless man is a far more dangerous comrade than a coward.

"Aye, aye," said Stubb, the second mate, "Starbuck, there, is as careful a man as you'll find anywhere in this fishery." But we shall ere long see what that word "careful" precisely means when used by a man like Stubb, or almost any other whale hunter.

Starbuck was no crusader after perils; in him courage was not a sentiment; but a thing simply useful to him, and always at hand upon all mortally practical occasions. Besides, he thought, perhaps, that in this business of whaling, courage was one of the great staple outfits of the ship, like her beef and her bread, and not to be foolishly wasted. Wherefore he had no fancy for lowering for whales after sun-down; nor for persisting in fighting a fish that too much persisted in fighting him. For, thought Starbuck, I am here in this critical ocean to kill whales for my living, and not to be killed by them for theirs; and that hundreds of men had been so killed Starbuck well knew. What doom was his own father's? Where, in the bottomless deeps, could he find the torn limbs of his brother?

With memories like these in him, and, moreover, given to a certain superstitiousness, as has been said; the courage of this Starbuck which could, nevertheless, still flourish, must indeed have been extreme. But it was not in reasonable nature that a man so organized, and with such terrible experiences and remembrances as he had; it was not in nature that these things should fail in latently engendering an element in him, which, under suitable circumstances, would break out from its confinement, and burn all his courage up. And brave as he might be, it was that sort of bravery chiefly, visible in some intrepid men, which, while generally abiding firm in the conflict with seas, or winds, or whales, or any of the ordinary irrational horrors of the world, yet cannot withstand those more terrific, because more spiritual terrors, which sometimes menace you from the concentrating brow of an enraged and mighty man.

But were the coming narrative to reveal, in any instance, the complete abasement of poor Starbuck's fortitude, scarce might I have the heart to write it; for it is a thing most sorrowful, nay shocking, to expose the fall of valor in the soul. Men may seem detestable as joint stock-companies and nations; knaves, fools, and murderers there may be; men may have mean and meagre faces; but, man, in the ideal, is so noble and so sparkling, such a grand and glowing creature, that over any ignominious blemish in him all his fellows should run to throw their costliest robes. That immaculate manliness we feel within ourselves, so far within us, that it remains intact though all the outer character seem gone; bleeds with keenest anguish at the undraped spectacle of a valor-ruined man. Nor can piety itself, at such a shameful sight, completely stifle her upbraidings against the permitting stars. But this august dignity I treat of, is not the dignity of kings and robes, but that abounding dignity which has no robed investiture. Thou shalt see it shining in the arm that wields a pick or drives a spike; that democratic dignity which, on all hands, radiates without end from God; Himself! The great God absolute! The centre and circumference of all democracy! His omnipresence, our divine equality!

If, then, to meanest mariners, and renegades and castaways, I shall hereafter ascribe high qualities, though dark; weave round them tragic graces; if even the most mournful, perchance the most abased, among them all, shall at times lift himself to the exalted mounts; if I shall touch that workman's arm with some ethereal light; if I shall spread a rainbow over his disastrous set of sun; then against all mortal critics bear me out in it, thou just Spirit of Equality, which hast spread one royal mantle of humanity over all my kind! Bear me out in it, thou great democratic God! who didst not refuse to the swart convict, Bunyan, the pale, poetic pearl; Thou who didst clothe with doubly hammered leaves of finest gold, the stumped and paupered arm of old Cervantes; Thou who didst pick up Andrew Jackson from the pebbles; who didst hurl him upon a war horse; who didst thunder him higher than a throne! Thou who, in all Thy mighty, earthly marchings, ever cullest Thy selectest champions from the kingly commons; bear me out in it, O God!

.   •   •   •

During the most violent shocks of the Typhoon, the man at the Pequod's jaw-bone tiller had several times been reelingly hurled to the deck by its spasmodic motions, even though preventer tackles had been attached to it—for they were slack—because some play to the tiller was indispensable.

In a severe gale like this, while the ship is but a tossed shuttlecock to the blast, it is by no means uncommon to see the needles in the compasses, at intervals, go round and round. It was thus with the Pequod's; at almost every shock the helmsman had not failed to notice the whirling velocity with which they revolved upon the cards; it is a sight that hardly anyone can behold without some sort of unwonted emotion.

Some hours after midnight, the Typhoon abated so much, that through the strenuous exertions of Starbuck and Stubb—one engaged forward and the other aft—the shivered remnants of the jib and fore and main-top-sails were cut adrift from the spars, and went eddying away to leeward, like the feathers of an albatross, which sometimes are cast to the winds when that storm-tossed bird is on the wing.

The three corresponding new sails were now bent and reefed, and a storm-trysail was set further aft; so that the ship soon went through the water with some precision again; and the course—for the present, East-south-east—which he was to steer, if practicable, was once more given to the helmsman. For during the violence of the gale, he had only steered according to its vicissitudes. But as he was now bringing the ship as near her course as possible, watching the compass meanwhile, lo! a good sign! the wind seemed coming round astern; aye, the foul breeze became fair!

Instantly the yards were squared, to the lively song of "*Ho! the fair wind! oh-he-yo cheerly, men!*" the crew singing for joy, that so promising an event should so soon have falsified the evil portents preceding it.

In compliance with the standing order of his commander—to report immediately, and at any one of the twenty-four hours, any decided change in the affairs of the deck,—Starbuck had no sooner trimmed the yards to the breeze—however reluctantly and gloomily,—than he mechanically went below to apprise Captain Ahab of the circumstance.

Ere knocking at his state-room, he involuntarily paused before it a moment. The cabin lamp—taking long swings this way and that—was burning fitfully, and casting fitful shadows upon the old man's bolted door,—a thin one, with fixed blinds inserted, in place of upper panels. The isolated subterraneousness of the cabin made a certain humming silence to reign there, though it was hooped round by all the roar of the elements. The loaded muskets in the rack were shiningly revealed, as they stood upright against the forward bulkhead. Starbuck was an honest, upright man; but out of Starbuck's heart, at that instant when he saw the muskets, there strangely evolved an evil thought; but so blent with its neutral or good accompaniments that for the instant he hardly knew it for itself.

"He would have shot me once," he murmured, "yes, there's the very musket that he pointed at me;—that one with the studded stock; let me touch it—lift it. Strange, that I, who have handled so many deadly lances, strange, that I should shake so now. Loaded? I must see. Aye, aye; and powder in the pan;—that's not good. Best spill it?—wait. I'll cure myself of this. I'll hold the musket boldly while I think.—I come to report a fair wind to him. But how fair? Fair for death and doom,—*that's* fair for Moby Dick. It's a fair wind that's only fair for that accursed fish.—The very tube he pointed at me!—the very one; *this* one—I hold it here; he would have killed me with the very thing I handle now.—Aye and he would fain kill all his crew. Does he not say he will not strike his spars to any gale? Has he not dashed his heavenly quadrant? and in these same perilous seas, gropes he not his way by mere dead reckoning of the error-abounding log? and in this very Typhoon, did he not swear that he would have no lightning-rods? But shall this crazed old man be tamely suffered to drag a whole ship's company down to doom with him?—Yes, it would make him the wilful murderer of thirty men and more, if this ship come to any deadly harm; and come to deadly harm, my soul swears this ship will, if Ahab have his way. If, then, he were this instant put aside, that crime would not be his. Ha! is he muttering in his sleep? Yes, just there,—in there, he's sleeping. Sleeping? aye, but still alive, and soon awake again. I can't withstand thee, then, old man. Not reasoning; not remonstrance; not entreaty wilt thou hearken to; all this thou scornest. Flat obedience to thy own flat commands, this is all thou breathest. Aye, and say'st the men have vow'd thy vow; say'st all of us are Ahabs. Great God forbid!—But is there no other way? no lawful way?—Make him a prisoner to be taken home? What! hope to wrest this old man's living power from his own living hands? Only a fool would try it. Say he were pinioned even; knotted all over with ropes and hawsers; chained down to ring-bolts on this cabin floor; he would be more hideous than a caged tiger, then. I could not endure the sight; could not possibly fly his howlings; all comfort, sleep itself, inestimable reason would leave me on the long intolerable voyage. What, then, remains? The land is hundreds of leagues away, and locked Japan the nearest. I stand alone here upon an open sea, with two oceans and a whole continent between me and law.—Aye, aye, 'tis so.—Is heaven a murderer when its lightning strikes a would-be murderer in his bed, tindering sheets and skin together?—And would I be a murderer, then, if"——and slowly, stealthily, and half sideways looking, he placed the loaded musket's end against the door.

"On this level, Ahab's hammock swings within; his head this way. A touch, and Starbuck may survive to hug his wife and child again.—Oh Mary!

Mary!—boy! boy! boy!—But if I wake thee not to death, old man, who can tell to what unsounded deeps Starbuck's body this day week may sink, with all the crew! Great God, where art thou? Shall I? shall I?——The wind has gone down and shifted, sir; the fore and main topsails are reefed and set; she heads her course."

"Stern all! Oh Moby Dick, I clutch thy heart at last!"

Such were the sounds that now came hurtling from out the old man's tormented sleep, as if Starbuck's voice had caused the long dumb dream to speak.

The yet levelled musket shook like a drunkard's arm against the panel; Starbuck seemed wrestling with an angel; but turning from the door, he placed the death-tube in its rack, and left the place.

"He's too sound asleep, Mr. Stubb; go thou down, and wake him, and tell him. I must see to the deck here. Thou know'st what to say."

Dashiell Hammett
(1894–1961)

BORN IN MARYLAND, Dashiell Hammett left school in his early teens and began a series of jobs that exposed him to a wide variety of people and environments: freight clerk, stevedore, messenger, railroad laborer, Pinkerton detective. Hammett went on to pioneer a new style of American writing. His lean "hard-boiled" prose, featuring unsentimental, fast-paced dialogue that translated wonderfully to the movie screen, influenced writers for generations. Before turning to novels, Hammett wrote for "pulp" magazines such as *Black Mask*. His first novel, *Red Harvest* (1928), featured the Continental Op, a narrator he had cultivated in his earlier stories. In *The Maltese Falcon* (1930) he introduced the character of the private detective Sam Spade. In the following excerpt from the end of the novel, Spade tries to tell his client Brigid O'Shaugnessy, whom he loves but cannot trust, why he must turn her in for the murder of his partner, Miles Archer. In the process he articulates a kind of private detective's code of conduct. Hammett's own life was distinguished by its principled political commitments. Despite the spots on his lungs from the tuberculosis he had contracted during World War I, when the United States entered World War II, Hammett somehow persuaded the recruiters to accept him into the army again in his forties, even consenting to the condition of having all his teeth pulled. For three years, he edited an army newspaper in the Aleutians. After the war, targeted for his involvement with leftist political movements, including membership in the Communist Party and presidency of the Civil Rights Congress, Hammett refused to cooperate with the House Committee on Un-American Activities and was blacklisted along with other members of the so-called Hollywood Ten. He served five months in prison for contempt of court rather than naming names.

If They Hang You

from *The Maltese Falcon* (1930)

Spade said: "Miles hadn't many brains, but, Christ! he had too many years' experience as a detective to be caught like that by the man he was shadowing. Up a blind alley with his gun tucked away on his hip and his overcoat buttoned? Not a chance. He was as dumb as any man ought to be, but he wasn't quite that dumb. The only two ways out of the alley could be watched from the edge of Bush Street over the tunnel. You'd told us Thursby was a bad actor. He couldn't have tricked Miles into the alley like that, and he couldn't have driven him in. He was dumb, but not dumb enough for that."

He ran his tongue over the inside of his lips and smiled affectionately at the girl. He said: "But he'd've gone up there with you, angel, if he was sure nobody else was up there. You were his client, so he would have had no reason for not dropping the shadow on your say-so, and if you caught up with him and asked him to go up there he'd've gone. He was just dumb enough for that. He'd've looked you up and down and licked his lips and gone grinning from ear to ear—and then you could've stood as close to him as you liked in the dark and put a hole through him with the gun you had got from Thursby that evening."

Brigid O'Shaughnessy shrank back from him until the edge of the table stopped her. She looked at him with terrified eyes and cried: "Don't—don't talk to me like that, Sam! You know I didn't! You know—"

"Stop it." He looked at the watch on his wrist. "The police will be blowing in any minute now and we're sitting on dynamite. Talk!"

She put the back of a hand on her forehead. "Oh, why do you accuse me of such a terrible—?"

"Will you stop it?" he demanded in a low impatient voice. "This isn't the spot for the schoolgirl-act. Listen to me. The pair of us are sitting under the gallows." He took hold of her wrists and made her stand up straight in front of him. "Talk!"

"I—I—How did you know he—he licked his lips and looked—?"

Spade laughed harshly. "I knew Miles. But never mind that. Why did you shoot him?"

She twisted her wrists out of Spade's fingers and put her hands up around the back of his neck, pulling his head down until his mouth all but touched hers. Her body was flat against his from knees to chest. He put his arms around her, holding her tight to him. Her dark-lashed lids were half down over velvet eyes. Her voice was hushed, throbbing: "I didn't mean to, at first. I didn't, really. I meant what I told you, but when I saw Floyd couldn't be frightened I—"

Spade slapped her shoulder. He said: "That's a lie. You asked Miles and me to handle it ourselves. You wanted to be sure the shadower was somebody you knew and who knew you, so they'd go with you. You got the gun from Thursby that day—that night. You had already rented the apartment at the Coronet. You had trunks there and none at the hotel and when I looked the apartment over I found a rent-receipt dated five or six days before the time you told me you rented it."

She swallowed with difficulty and her voice was humble. "Yes, that's a lie, Sam. I did intend to if Floyd— I—I can't look at you and tell you this, Sam." She pulled his head farther down until her cheek was against his cheek, her mouth by his ear, and whispered: "I knew Floyd wouldn't be easily frightened, but I thought that if he knew somebody was shadowing him either he'd— Oh, I can't say it, Sam!" She clung to him, sobbing.

Spade said: "You thought Floyd would tackle him and one or the other of them would go down. If Thursby was the one then you were rid of him. If Miles was, then you could see that Floyd was caught and you'd be rid of him. That it?"

"S-something like that."

"And when you found that Thursby didn't mean to tackle him you borrowed the gun and did it yourself. Right?"

"Yes—though not exactly."

"But exact enough. And you had that plan up your sleeve from the first. You thought Floyd would be nailed for the killing."

"I—I thought they'd hold him at least until after Captain Jacobi had arrived with the falcon and—"

"And you didn't know then that Gutman was here hunting for you. You didn't suspect that or you wouldn't have shaken your gunman. You knew Gutman was here as soon as you heard Thursby had been shot. Then you knew you needed another protector, so you came back to me. Right?"

"Yes, but—oh, sweetheart!—it wasn't only that. I would have come back to you sooner or later. From the first instant I saw you I knew—"

Spade said tenderly: "You angel! Well, if you get a good break you'll be out of San Quentin in twenty years and you can come back to me then."

She took her cheek away from his, drawing her head far back to stare up without comprehension at him.

He was pale. He said tenderly: "I hope to Christ they don't hang you, precious, by that sweet neck." He slid his hands up to caress her throat.

In an instant she was out of his arms, back against the table, crouching, both hands spread over her throat. Her face was wild-eyed, haggard. Her dry

mouth opened and closed. She said in a small parched voice: "You're not—"
She could get no other words out.

Spade's face was yellow-white now. His mouth smiled and there were
smile-wrinkles around his glittering eyes. His voice was soft, gentle. He said:
"I'm going to send you over. The chances are you'll get off with life. That
means you'll be out again in twenty years. You're an angel. I'll wait for you."
He cleared his throat. "If they hang you I'll always remember you."

She dropped her hands and stood erect. Her face became smooth and
untroubled except for the faintest of dubious glints in her eyes. She smiled
back at him, gently. "Don't, Sam, don't say that even in fun. Oh, you frightened me for a moment! I really thought you— You know you do such wild
and unpredictable things that—" She broke off. She thrust her face forward
and stared deep into his eyes. Her cheeks and the flesh around her mouth
shivered and fear came back into her eyes. "What—? Sam!" She put her hand
to her throat again and lost her erectness.

Spade laughed. His yellow-white face was damp with sweat and though he
held his smile he could not hold softness in his voice. He croaked: "Don't be
silly. You're taking the fall. One of us has got to take it, after the talking those
birds will do. They'd hang me sure. You're likely to get a better break. Well?"

"But—but, Sam, you can't! Not after what we've been to each other. You
can't—"

"Like hell I can't."

She took a long trembling breath. "You've been playing with me? Only
pretending you cared—to trap me like this? You didn't—care at all? You
didn't—don't—I-love me?"

"I think I do," Spade said. "What of it?" The muscles holding his smile in
place stood out like wales. "I'm not Thursby. I'm not Jacobi. I won't play the
sap for you."

"That is not just," she cried. Tears came to her eyes. "It's unfair. It's contemptible of you. You know it was not that. You can't say that."

"Like hell I can't," Spade said. "You came into my bed to stop me asking
questions. You led me out yesterday for Gutman with that phoney call for
help. Last night you came here with them and waited outside for me and came
in with me. You were in my arms when the trap was sprung—I couldn't have
gone for a gun if I'd had one on me and couldn't have made a fight of it if I
had wanted to. And if they didn't take you away with them it was only because
Gutman's got too much sense to trust you except for short stretches when he
has to and because he thought I'd play the sap for you and—not wanting to
hurt you—wouldn't be able to hurt him."

Brigid O'Shaughnessy blinked her tears away. She took a step towards him
and stood looking him in the eyes, straight and proud. "You called me a liar,"
she said. "Now you are lying. You're lying if you say you don't know down in
your heart that, in spite of anything I've done, I love you."

Spade made a short abrupt bow. His eyes were becoming bloodshot, but there was no other change in his damp and yellowish fixedly smiling face. "Maybe I do," he said. "What of it? I should trust you? You who arranged that nice little trick for—for my predecessor, Thursby? You who knocked off Miles, a man you had nothing against, in cold blood, just like swatting a fly, for the sake of double-crossing Thursby? You who double-crossed Gutman, Cairo, Thursby—one, two, three? You who've never played square with me for half an hour at a stretch since I've known you? I should trust you? No, no, darling. I wouldn't do it even if I could. Why should I?"

Her eyes were steady under his and her hushed voice was steady when she replied: "Why should you? If you've been playing with me, if you do not love me, there is no answer to that. If you did, no answer would be needed."

Blood streaked Spade's eyeballs now and his long-held smile had become a frightful grimace. He cleared his throat huskily and said: "Making speeches is no damned good now." He put a hand on her shoulder. The hand shook and jerked. "I don't care who loves who I'm not going to play the sap for you. I won't walk in Thursby's and Christ knows who else's footsteps. You killed Miles and you're going over for it. I could have helped you by letting the others go and standing off the police the best way I could. It's too late for that now. I can't help you now. And I wouldn't if I could."

She put a hand on his hand on her shoulder. "Don't help me then," she whispered, "but don't hurt me. Let me go away now."

"No," he said. "I'm sunk if I haven't got you to hand over to the police when they come. That's the only thing that can keep me from going down with the others."

"You won't do that for me?"

"I won't play the sap for you."

"Don't say that, please." She took his hand from her shoulder and held it to her face. "Why must you do this to me, Sam? Surely Mr. Archer wasn't as much to you as—"

"Miles," Spade said hoarsely, "was a son of a bitch. I found that out the first week we were in business together and I meant to kick him out as soon as the year was up. You didn't do me a damned bit of harm by killing him."

"Then what?"

Spade pulled his hand out of hers. He no longer either smiled or grimaced. His wet yellow face was set hard and deeply lined. His eyes burned madly. He said: "Listen. This isn't a damned bit of good. You'll never understand me, but I'll try once more and then we'll give it up. Listen. When a man's partner is killed he's supposed to do something about it. It doesn't make any difference what you thought of him. He was your partner and you're supposed to do something about it. Then it happens we were in the detective business. Well, when one of your organization gets killed it's bad business to let the killer get away with it. It's bad all around—bad for that one organization, bad for every detective everywhere. Third, I'm a detective and expecting me to run criminals down and then let them go free is like asking a dog to catch a rabbit and let it go. It can be done, all right, and sometimes it is done, but it's not the natural thing. The only way I could have let you go was by letting Gutman and Cairo and the kid go. That's—"

"You're not serious," she said. "You don't expect me to think that these things you're saying are sufficient reason for sending me to the—"

"Wait till I'm through and then you can talk. Fourth, no matter what I wanted to do now it would be absolutely impossible for me to let you go without having myself dragged to the gallows with the others. Next, I've no reason in God's world to think I can trust you and if I did this and got away with it you'd have something on me that you could use whenever you happened to want to. That's five of them. The sixth would be that, since I've also got something on you, I couldn't be sure you wouldn't decide to shoot a hole in *me* some day. Seventh, I don't even like the idea of thinking that there might be one chance in a hundred that you'd played me for a sucker. And eighth—but that's enough. All those on one side. Maybe some of them are unimportant. I won't argue about that. But look at the number of them. Now on the other side we've got what? All we've got is the fact that maybe you love me and maybe I love you."

"You know," she whispered, "whether you do or not."

"I don't. It's easy enough to be nuts about you." He looked hungrily from her hair to her feet and up to her eyes again. "But I don't know what that amounts to. Does anybody ever? But suppose I do? What of it? Maybe next month I won't. I've been through it before—when it lasted that long. Then what? Then I'll think I played the sap. And if I did it and got sent over then I'd be sure I was the sap. Well, if I send you over I'll be sorry as hell   I'll have some rotten nights—but that'll pass. Listen." He took her by the shoulders and bent her back, leaning over her. "If that doesn't mean anything to you forget it and we'll make it this: I won't because all of me wants to—wants to say to hell with the consequences and do it—and because—God damn you— you've counted on that with me the same as you counted on that with the others." He took his hands from her shoulders and let them fall to his sides.

She put her hands up to his cheeks and drew his face down again. "Look at me," she said, "and tell me the truth. Would you have done this to me if the falcon had been real and you had been paid your money?"

"What difference does that make now? Don't be too sure I'm as crooked as I'm supposed to be. That kind of reputation might be good business— bringing in high-priced jobs and making it easier to deal with the enemy."

She looked at him, saying nothing.

He moved his shoulders a little and said: "Well, a lot of money would have been at least one more item on the other side of the scales."

She put her face up to his face. Her mouth was slightly open with lips a little thrust out. She whispered: "If you loved me you'd need nothing more on that side."

Spade set the edges of his teeth together and said through them: "I won't play the sap for you."

She put her mouth to his, slowly, her arms around him, and came into his arms. She was in his arms when the door-bell rang.

SPADE, LEFT ARM around Brigid O'Shaughnessy, opened the corridor-door. Lieutenant Dundy, Detective-sergeant Tom Polhaus, and two other detectives were there.

Spade said: "Hello, Tom. Get them?"

Polhaus said: "Got them."

"Swell. Come in. Here's another one for you." Spade pressed the girl forward. "She killed Miles."

Rachel Carson
(1907–1964)

PUBLISHED TWO YEARS before its author's death from cancer, *Silent Spring* (1962) caused an immediate sensation with its exposure of the pervasive use of toxic pesticides, the long-term effects of which were not fully known. The book subsequently became a cornerstone of the environmental movement. Trained as a marine biologist, Carson worked for the U.S. Fish and Wildlife Service. *Silent Spring* was not her first bestseller: she had achieved that with *The Sea Around Us* (1951), which won a National Book Award and earned its author an international reputation. Her learning, observational powers, and literary skills were also on display in two other books, the earlier *Under the Sea Wind* (1941) and *The Edge of the Sea* (1955). *Silent Spring*, long sections of which were initially published in serial form in *The New Yorker*, awakened the concern of the government and the public as well as the ire of the chemical industry. Carson appeared before Congress to testify about the dangers of the indiscriminate use of pesticides, while the Monsanto Company mounted a campaign called "The Desolate Year," which offered an apocalyptic portrait of a world ravaged by insects. As her *New York Times* obituary noted, Carson was "no armchair naturalist." She was constantly at work outdoors, and her experiences included a trip on a fishing trawler to the Georges Banks. Carson's biographer Linda Lear asserts that *Silent Spring* "contained the kernel of social revolution." The biologist Edward O. Wilson ranks it with Harriet Beecher Stowe's *Uncle Tom's Cabin* and John Muir's *Our National Parks* as a book that changed the course of history by forcing the public to reevaluate its attitudes, priorities, and institutions. Carson was a quiet thought-leader whose book urges us to take responsibility for the environment and to recognize our "obligation to endure."

Silent Spring
(1962)

The history of life on earth has been a history of interaction between living things and their surroundings. To a large extent, the physical form and the habits of the earth's vegetation and its animal life have been molded by the environment. Considering the whole span of earthly time, the opposite effect, in which life actually modifies its surroundings, has been relatively slight. Only within the moment of time represented by the present century has one species—man—acquired significant power to alter the nature of his world.

During the past quarter century this power has not only increased to one of disturbing magnitude but it has changed in character. The most alarming of all man's assaults upon the environment is the contamination of air, earth, rivers, and sea with dangerous and even lethal materials. This pollution is for the most part irrecoverable; the chain of evil it initiates not only in the world that must support life but in living tissues is for the most part irreversible. In this now universal contamination of the environment, chemicals are the sinister and little-recognized partners of radiation in changing the very nature of the world—the very nature of its life. Strontium 90, released through nuclear explosions into the air, comes to earth in rain or drifts down as fall out, lodges in soil, enters into the grass or corn or wheat grown there, and in time takes up its abode in the bones of a human being, there to remain until his death. Similarly, chemicals sprayed on croplands or forests or gardens lie long in soil, entering into living organisms, passing from one to another in a chain of poisoning and death. Or they pass mysteriously by underground streams until they emerge and, through the alchemy of air and sunlight, combine into new forms that kill vegetation, sicken cattle, and work unknown harm on those who drink from once pure wells. As Albert Schweitzer has said, "Man can hardly even recognize the devils of his own creation."

It took hundreds of millions of years to produce the life that now inhabits the earth—eons of time in which that developing and evolving and diversifying life reached a state of adjustment and balance with its surroundings. The environment, rigorously shaping and directing the life it supported, contained elements that were hostile as well as supporting. Certain rocks gave out dangerous radiation; even within the light of the sun, from which all life draws its energy, there were short-wave radiations with power to injure. Given time—

time not in years but in millennia—life adjusts, and a balance has been reached. For time is the essential ingredient; but in the modern world there is no time.

The rapidity of change and the speed with which new situations are created follow the impetuous and heedless pace of man rather than the deliberate pace of nature. Radiation is no longer merely the background radiation of rocks, the bombardment of cosmic rays, the ultraviolet of the sun that have existed before there was any life on earth; radiation is now the unnatural creation of man's tampering with the atom. The chemicals to which life is asked to make its adjustment are no longer merely the calcium and silica and copper and all the rest of the minerals washed out of the rocks and carried in rivers to the sea; they are the synthetic creations of man's inventive mind, brewed in his laboratories, and having no counterparts in nature.

To adjust to these chemicals would require time on the scale that is nature's; it would require not merely the years of a man's life but the life of generations. And even this, were it by some miracle possible, would be futile, for the new chemicals come from our laboratories in an endless stream; almost five hundred annually find their way into actual use in the United States alone. The figure is staggering and its implications are not easily grasped—500 new chemicals to which the bodies of men and animals are required somehow to adapt each year, chemicals totally outside the limits of biologic experience.

Among them are many that are used in man's war against nature. Since the mid-1940's over 200 basic chemicals have been created for use in killing insects, weeds, rodents, and other organisms described in the modern vernacular as "pests"; and they are sold under several thousand different brand names.

These sprays, dusts, and aerosols are now applied almost universally to farms, gardens, forests, and homes—nonselective chemicals that have the power to kill every insect, the "good" and the "bad," to still the song of birds and the leaping of fish in the streams, to coat the leaves with a deadly film, and to linger on in soil—all this though the intended target may be only a few weeds or insects. Can anyone believe it is possible to lay down such a barrage of poisons on the surface of the earth without making it unfit for all life? They should not be called "insecticides," but "biocides."

The whole process of spraying seems caught up in an endless spiral. Since DDT was released for civilian use, a process of escalation has been going on in which ever more toxic materials must be found. This has happened because insects, in a triumphant vindication of Darwin's principle of the survival of the fittest, have evolved super races immune to the particular insecticide used, hence a deadlier one has always to be developed—and then a deadlier one than that. It has happened also because, for reasons to be described later, destructive insects often undergo a "flareback," or resurgence, after spraying, in numbers greater than before. Thus the chemical war is never won, and all life is caught in its violent crossfire.

Along with the possibility of the extinction of mankind by nuclear war, the central problem of our age has therefore become the contamination of man's total environment with such substances of incredible potential for harm—substances that accumulate in the tissues of plants and animals and even penetrate the germ cells to shatter or alter the very material of heredity upon which the shape of the future depends.

Some would-be architects of our future look toward a time when it will be possible to alter the human germ plasm by design. But we may easily be doing so now by inadvertence, for many chemicals, like radiation, bring about gene mutations. It is ironic to think that man might determine his own future by something so seemingly trivial as the choice of an insect spray.

All this has been risked—for what? Future historians may well be amazed by our distorted sense of proportion. How could intelligent beings seek to control a few unwanted species by a method that contaminated the entire environment and brought the threat of disease and death even to their own kind? Yet this is precisely what we have done. We have done it, moreover, for reasons that collapse the moment we examine them. We are told that the enormous and expanding use of pesticides is necessary to maintain farm production. Yet is our real problem not one of *overproduction?* Our farms, despite measures to remove acreages from production and to pay farmers *not* to produce, have yielded such a staggering excess of crops that the American taxpayer in 1962 is paying out more than one billion dollars a year as the total carrying cost of the surplus-food storage program. And is the situation helped when one branch of the Agriculture Department tries to reduce production while another states, as it did in 1958, "It is believed generally that reduction of crop acreages under provisions of the Soil Bank will stimulate interest in use of chemicals to obtain maximum production on the land retained in crops."

All this is not to say there is no insect problem and no need of control. I am saying, rather, that control must be geared to realities, not to mythical situations, and that the methods employed must be such that they do not destroy us along with the insects.

THE PROBLEM WHOSE attempted solution has brought such a train of disaster in its wake is an accompaniment of our modern way of life. Long before the age of man, insects inhabited the earth—a group of extraordinarily varied and adaptable beings. Over the course of time since man's advent, a small percentage of the more than half a million species of insects have come into conflict with human welfare in two principal ways: as competitors for the food supply and as carriers of human disease.

Disease-carrying insects become important where human beings are crowded together, especially under conditions where sanitation is poor, as in time of natural disaster or war or in situations of extreme poverty and deprivation. Then control of some sort becomes necessary. It is a sobering fact, however, as we shall presently see, that the method of massive chemical control has had only limited success, and also threatens to worsen the very conditions it is intended to curb.

Under primitive agricultural conditions the farmer had few insect problems. These arose with the intensification of agriculture—the devotion of immense acreages to a single crop. Such a system set the stage for explosive increases in specific insect populations. Single-crop farming does not take advantage of the principles by which nature works; it is agriculture as an engineer might conceive it to be. Nature has introduced great variety into the landscape, but man has displayed a passion for simplifying it. Thus he undoes the built-in checks and balances by which nature holds the species within bounds. One important natural check is a limit on the amount of suitable habitat for each species. Obviously then, an insect that lives on wheat can build up its population to much higher levels on a farm devoted to wheat than on one in which wheat is intermingled with other crops to which the insect is not adapted.

The same thing happens in other situations. A generation or more ago, the towns of large areas of the United States lined their streets with the noble elm tree. Now the beauty they hopefully created is threatened with complete destruction as disease sweeps through the elms, carried by a beetle that would have only limited chance to build up large populations and to spread from tree to tree if the elms were only occasional trees in a richly diversified planting.

Another factor in the modern insect problem is one that must be viewed against a background of geologic and human history: the spreading of thousands of different kinds of organisms from their native homes to invade new territories. This worldwide migration has been studied and graphically described by the British ecologist Charles Elton in his recent book *The Ecology of Invasions*. During the Cretaceous Period, some hundred million years ago, flooding seas cut many land bridges between continents and living things found themselves confined in what Elton calls "colossal separate nature reserves." There, isolated from others of their kind, they developed many new species. When some of the land masses were joined again, about 15 million years ago, these species began to move out into new territories—a movement that is not only still in progress but is now receiving considerable assistance from man.

The importation of plants is the primary agent in the modern spread of species, for animals have almost invariably gone along with the plants, quarantine being a comparatively recent and not completely effective innovation. The United States Office of Plant Introduction alone has introduced almost 200,000 species and varieties of plants from all over the world. Nearly half of the 180 or so major insect enemies of plants in the United States are accidental imports from abroad, and most of them have come as hitchhikers on plants.

In new territory, out of reach of the restraining hand of the natural enemies that kept down its numbers in its native land, an invading plant or animal is able to become enormously abundant. Thus it is no accident that our most troublesome insects are introduced species.

These invasions, both the naturally occurring and those dependent on human assistance, are likely to continue indefinitely. Quarantine and massive chemical campaigns are only extremely expensive ways of buying time. We are faced, according to Dr. Elton, "with a life-and-death need not just to find new technological means of suppressing this plant or that animal"; instead we need the basic knowledge of animal populations and their relations to their surroundings that will "promote an even balance and damp down the explosive power of outbreaks and new invasions."

Much of the necessary knowledge is now available but we do not use it. We train ecologists in our universities and even employ them in our governmental agencies but we seldom take their advice. We allow the chemical death rain to fall as though there were no alternative, whereas in fact there are many, and our ingenuity could soon discover many more if given opportunity.

Have we fallen into a mesmerized state that makes us accept as inevitable that which is inferior or detrimental, as though having lost the will or the vision to demand that which is good? Such thinking, in the words of the ecologist Paul Shepard, "idealizes life with only its head out of water, inches above the limits of toleration of the corruption of its own environment . . . Why should we tolerate a diet of weak poisons, a home in insipid surroundings, a circle of acquaintances who are not quite our enemies, the noise of motors with just enough relief to prevent insanity? Who would want to live in a world which is just not quite fatal?"

Yet such a world is pressed upon us. The crusade to create a chemically sterile, insect-free world seems to have engendered a fanatic zeal on the part of many specialists and most of the so-called control agencies. On every hand there is evidence that those engaged in spraying operations exercise a ruthless power. "The regulatory entomologists . . . function as prosecutor, judge and jury, tax assessor and collector and sheriff to enforce their own orders," said Connecticut entomologist Neely Turner. The most flagrant abuses go unchecked in both state and federal agencies.

It is not my contention that chemical insecticides must never be used. I do contend that we have put poisonous and biologically potent chemicals indiscriminately into the hands of persons largely or wholly ignorant of their potentials for harm. We have subjected enormous numbers of people to contact with these poisons, without their consent and often without their knowledge. If the Bill of Rights contains no guarantee that a citizen shall be secure against lethal poisons distributed either by private individuals or by public officials, it is surely only because our forefathers, despite their considerable wisdom and foresight, could conceive of no such problem.

I contend, furthermore, that we have allowed these chemicals to be used with little or no advance investigation of their effect on soil, water, wildlife, and man himself. Future generations are unlikely to condone our lack of prudent concern for the integrity of the natural world that supports all life.

There is still very limited awareness of the nature of the threat. This is an era of specialists, each of whom sees his own problem and is unaware of or intolerant of the larger frame into which it fits. It is also an era dominated by industry, in which the right to make a dollar at whatever cost is seldom challenged. When the public protests, confronted with some obvious evidence of damaging results of pesticide applications, it is fed little tranquilizing pills of half truth. We urgently need an end to these false assurances, to the sugar coating of unpalatable facts. It is the public that is being asked to assume the risks that the insect controllers calculate. The public must decide whether it wishes to continue on the present road, and it can do so only when in full possession of the facts. In the words of Jean Rostand, "The obligation to endure gives us the right to know."

.   .   .

We stand now where two roads diverge. But unlike the roads in Robert Frost's familiar poem, they are not equally fair. The road we have long been traveling is deceptively easy, a smooth superhighway on which we progress with great speed, but at its end lies disaster. The other fork of the road—the one "less traveled by"—offers our last, our only chance to reach a destination that assures the preservation of our earth.

The choice, after all, is ours to make. If, having endured much, we have at last asserted our "right to know," and if, knowing, we have concluded that we are being asked to take senseless and frightening risks, then we should no longer accept the counsel of those who tell us that we must fill our world with poisonous chemicals; we should look about and see what other course is open to us.

A truly extraordinary variety of alternatives to the chemical control of insects is available. Some are already in use and have achieved brilliant success. Others are in the stage of laboratory testing. Still others are little more than ideas in the minds of imaginative scientists, waiting for the opportunity to put them to the test. All have this in common: they are *biological* solutions, based on understanding of the living organisms they seek to control, and of the whole fabric of life to which these organisms belong. Specialists representing various areas of the vast field of biology are contributing—entomologists, pathologists, geneticists, physiologists, biochemists, ecologists—all pouring their knowledge and their creative inspirations into the formation of a new science of biotic controls.

"Any science may be likened to a river," says a Johns Hopkins biologist, Professor Carl P. Swanson. "It has its obscure and unpretentious beginning; its quiet stretches as well as its rapids; its periods of drought as well as of fullness. It gathers momentum with the work of many investigators and as it is fed by other streams of thought; it is deepened and broadened by the concepts and generalizations that are gradually evolved."

So it is with the science of biological control in its modern sense.

. . .

The current vogue for poisons has failed utterly to take into account these most fundamental considerations. As crude a weapon as the cave man's club, the chemical barrage has been hurled against the fabric of life—a fabric on the one hand delicate and destructible, on the other miraculously tough and resilient, and capable of striking back in unexpected ways. These extraordinary capacities of life have been ignored by the practitioners of chemical control who have brought to their task no "high-minded orientation," no humility before the vast forces with which they tamper.

The "control of nature" is a phrase conceived in arrogance, born of the Neanderthal age of biology and philosophy, when it was supposed that nature exists for the convenience of man. The concepts and practices of applied entomology for the most part date from that Stone Age of science. It is our alarming misfortune that so primitive a science has armed itself with the most modern and terrible weapons, and that in turning them against the insects it has also turned them against the earth.

DISCUSSION QUESTIONS

1. *How does one reconcile personal with larger institutional or organizational loyalties?*

2. *Justice, honesty, self-control, and courage are Marcus Aurelius's guides. What are yours?*

3. *What are some effective techniques for owning errors?*

4. *How far do our responsibilities extend to future generations?*

5. *Henry V and Williams, a private soldier in his army, have a spirited debate about obedience and individual responsibility: Who is more persuasive?*

ALBUM
Artists of Persuasion

I am no orator, as Brutus is;

. . .

. . . I only speak right on . . .

—MARK ANTONY
William Shakespeare,
Julius Caesar, act 3, scene 2

I n confessing himself "no orator" to the plebeians of Rome, who are in a state
of considerable unrest after the murder of Julius Caesar, Shakespeare's Mark
Antony resorts to one of the rhetorician's favorite tricks: the aw-shucks insistence that he or she lacks a way with words. That other masterful Shakespear-
ean orator, Henry V, employs this tactic, too, ingeniously protesting to the
French princess he would marry that he is unable to court her with "cunning"
or "eloquence"; rather, he can speak only "downright oaths" and "plain soldier."
In both instances, of course, we encounter speakers who feign inarticulateness.
Henry and Antony demonstrate superior oratorical skills: capable of inspiring
others to sacrifice themselves in a seemingly hopeless gamble, in Henry's case,
and, in Antony's, of swaying public opinion with stunning swiftness.

The real-life Antony was also the vilified object of one of antiquity's
great oratorical triumphs: Cicero's *Philippics*, a ferocious polemic modeled
on the Greek Demosthenes's attacks on the king of Macedonia. The effect of
these speeches on Antony is revealed in Plutarch's account of the murder of
Cicero by Antony's lieutenant Herennius: "Herennius cut off his head, and,
by Antony's command, his hands also, by which his Philippics were written.
. . . Antony . . . commanded his head and hands to be fastened up over the
rostra, where the orators spoke; a sight which the Roman people shuddered to
behold, and they believed they saw there, not the face of Cicero, but the image
of Antony's own soul."

Who knew better than Antony the potential force of eloquence? His own funeral oration for Caesar, so richly dramatized in Shakespeare's verse, had such a profound effect on his auditors that, according to Plutarch, he incited the Romans to riot: "perceiving the people to be infinitely affected with what he had said, he began to mingle with his praises language of commiseration, and horror at what had happened, and, as he was ending his speech, he took the under-clothes of the dead, and held them up, showing them stains of blood and the holes of the many stabs, calling those who had done this act villains and bloody murderers. All which excited the people to such indignation, that they would not defer the funeral, but, making a pile of tables and forms in the very market-place, set fire to it; and every one, taking a brand, ran to the conspirators' houses, to attack them." Antony's melodramatic hijacking of the plebeians' grief and anger is a prime example of the appeal to pathos in public speaking that Aristotle warned can "pervert" auditors by distracting them from the facts. Aristotle regarded the appeal to logos (or logic) as the nobler art of persuasion.

Antiquity is rich in rhetorical theory: the rhetorical handbook, Thomas Habinek suggests in *Ancient Rhetoric and Oratory*, "is quite possibly the single best-attested genre of writing from the ancient world." In addition to Aristotle's *Rhetoric*, prospective orators have turned for centuries both to the example and to the theoretical writings of Cicero as well as to the rhetoric teacher Quintilian's twelve-volume treatise *The Orator's Education*. From Aristotle and other theorists, we inherit not only the classification of appeals to pathos, logos, and ethos (the credibility of the speaker) but also the idea of the five canons of rhetoric (invention, arrangement, style, memory, and delivery), and a wealth of terminology and techniques.

These theories were extremely popular throughout the Renaissance: Antony and Shakespeare's other great rhetoricians—Henry V, Richard III, Portia—are the creations of a culture of the word. Elizabethan England was a place where verbal facility was highly prized. Shakespeare lived in an age as strongly committed to the word as our own is devoted to the image. As the editors of *The Norton Anthology of English Literature* propose, "Renaissance literature is the product of a rhetorical culture, a culture steeped in the arts of persuasion and trained to process complex verbal signals. (The contemporary equivalent would be the ease with which we deal with complex visual signals, effortlessly processing such devices as fade-out, montage, crosscutting, and morphing.)"

In the twentieth and twenty-first centuries, a general facility with the visual image—chiefly embodied in a global infatuation with the medium of film—has been accompanied, especially in the United States, with a growing mistrust of linguistic agility. Zadie Smith alludes to a particular manifestation of this phenomenon in "Speaking in Tongues" ("Negotiating Self and World").

In *Fast-Talking Dames*, a book of film criticism, Maria DiBattista suggests the degree to which the verbal deftness that characterized, for example, the screwball comedies of the 1930s and 1940s, has come to be regarded with suspicion in American popular culture, eclipsed by a different kind of accomplishment. "Verbal minimalism, impatient with moral ambiguity and its complex syntax, remains the linguistic fashion of the times. . . . The marquee value of fast talk is lamentably undervalued at a time when laconic manhood is still rated high as a masculine ideal." DiBattista traces this idea through the cinematic genre of the Western, which "identified the laconic, even the inarticulate, as the very sign of the manly. That iconic Western figure John Wayne perfected the image of the 'quiet man' who conserves his strength for things too important to put into words."

How has the tendency to regard rhetoric with suspicion affected the way leaders speak? How have social media and other forms of digital and virtual communication altered the ways in which we deliver and receive language? The speeches that follow, dating from the Renaissance to World War II, offer various examples of leaders speaking during times of crisis.

RECOMMENDED READING

Cicero, *The Philippics* (44–43 BCE)
Han Fei Tzu, "The Difficulties of Persuasion," from *Basic Writings*, translated
    by Burton Watson (third century BCE)
Sinclair Lewis, *Elmer Gantry* (1927)
William Safire, *Lend Me Your Ears: Great Speeches in History* (1992)
William Shakespeare, *Richard III*

Virginia Woolf
(1882–1941)

THE DAUGHTER OF the prominent critic, scholar, athlete, and larger-than-life Victorian personality Leslie Stephen, Virginia Woolf grew up in a complicated house vibrant with culture, literature, and art. Woolf would later become part of an intellectual community called the Bloomsbury Group, named for the London neighborhood in which its members lived; it included other luminaries such as Lytton Strachey, John Maynard Keynes, and E. M. Forster. In addition to writing novels and literary and cultural criticism, Woolf, together with her husband Leonard, founded the Hogarth Press, which published the poetry of T. S. Eliot and the writings of Sigmund Freud. Bouts of depression marked Woolf's adult life; her particular dread of war, forged during World War I, resurfaced with the advent of World War II and contributed to her suicide in 1941. Woolf's chief aim in her fiction was to craft a new mode of representing consciousness, and through her pioneering modernist style she rendered a vivid internal world of thought and feeling. The brilliance of her revolutionary fiction, including the novels *Mrs. Dalloway* and *To the Lighthouse*, was matched by her non-fiction prose: *A Room of One's Own*, the lucid criticism published as *The Common Reader*, and essays such as those collected in *The Death of the Moth* (1942). Woolf was also an accomplished diarist. The essay "Professions for Women," first published in *The Death of the Moth*, was originally delivered as a speech to the London/National Society for Women's Service on January 21, 1931. Woolf, anatomizing the obstacles facing women who hoped to pursue the profession of writing, attempted to persuade her auditors to free themselves from the overbearing weight of historical phantoms.

Professions for Women
(1931)

When your secretary invited me to come here, she told me that your Society is concerned with the employment of women and she suggested that I might tell you something about my own professional experiences. It is true I am a woman; it is true I am employed; but what professional experiences have I had? It is difficult to say. My profession is literature; and in that profession there are fewer experiences for women than in any other, with the exception of the stage—fewer, I mean, that are peculiar to women. For the road was cut many years ago—by Fanny Burney, by Aphra Behn, by Harriet Martineau, by Jane Austen, by George Eliot many famous women, and many more unknown and forgotten, have been before me, making the path smooth, and regulating my steps. Thus, when I came to write, there were very few material obstacles in my way. Writing was a reputable and harmless occupation. The family peace was not broken by the scratching of a pen. No demand was made upon the family purse. For ten and sixpence one can buy paper enough to write all the plays of Shakespeare—if one has a mind that way. Pianos and models, Paris, Vienna and Berlin, masters and mistresses, are not needed by a writer. The cheapness of writing paper is, of course, the reason why women have succeeded as writers before they have succeeded in the other professions.

But to tell you my story—it is a simple one. You have only got to figure to yourselves a girl in a bedroom with a pen in her hand. She had only to move that pen from left to right—from ten o'clock to one. Then it occurred to her to do what is simple and cheap enough after all—to slip a few of those pages into an envelope, fix a penny stamp in the corner, and drop the envelope into the red box at the corner. It was thus that I became a journalist; and my effort was rewarded on the first day of the following month—a very glorious day it was for me—by a letter from an editor containing a cheque for one pound ten shillings and sixpence. But to show you how little I deserve to be called a professional woman, how little I know of the struggles and difficulties of such lives, I have to admit that instead of spending that sum upon bread and butter, rent, shoes and stockings, or butcher's bills, I went out and bought a cat—a beautiful cat, a Persian cat, which very soon involved me in bitter disputes with my neighbours.

What could be easier than to write articles and to buy Persian cats with the profits? But wait a moment. Articles have to be about something. Mine, I seem to remember, was about a novel by a famous man. And while I was writing this review, I discovered that if I were going to review books I should need to do battle with a certain phantom. And the phantom was a woman, and when I came to know her better I called her after the heroine of a famous poem, The Angel in the House. It was she who used to come between me and my paper when I was writing reviews. It was she who bothered me and wasted my time and so tormented me that at last I killed her. You who come of a younger and happier generation may not have heard of her—you may not know what I mean by the Angel in the House. I will describe her as shortly as I can. She was intensely sympathetic. She was immensely charming. She was utterly unselfish. She excelled in the difficult arts of family life. She sacrificed herself daily. If there was chicken, she took the leg; if there was a draught she sat in it—in short she was so constituted that she never had a mind or a wish of her own, but preferred to sympathize always with the minds and wishes of others. Above all—I need not say it—she was pure. Her purity was supposed to be her chief beauty—her blushes, her great grace. In those days—the last of Queen Victoria—every house had its Angel. And when I came to write I encountered her with the very first words. The shadow of her wings fell on my page; I heard the rustling of her skirts in the room. Directly, that is to say, I took my pen in my hand to review that novel by a famous man, she slipped behind me and whispered: "My dear, you are a young woman. You are writing about a book that has been written by a man. Be sympathetic; be tender; flatter; deceive; use all the arts and wiles of our sex. Never let anybody guess that you have a mind of your own. Above all, be pure." And she made as if to guide my pen. I now record the one act for which I take some credit to myself, though the credit rightly belongs to some excellent ancestors of mine who left me a certain sum of money—shall we say five hundred pounds a year?—so that it was not necessary for me to depend solely on charm for my living. I turned upon her and caught her by the throat. I did my best to kill her. My excuse, if I were to be had up in a court of law, would be that I acted in self-defence. Had I not killed her she would have killed me. She would have plucked the heart out of my writing. For, as I found, directly I put pen to paper, you cannot review even a novel without having a mind of your own, without expressing what you think to be the truth about human relations, morality, sex. And all these questions, according to the Angel of the House, cannot be dealt with freely and openly by women; they must charm, they must conciliate, they must—to put it bluntly—tell lies if they are to succeed. Thus, whenever I felt the shadow of her wing or the radiance of her halo upon my page, I took up the inkpot and flung it at her. She died hard. Her fictitious nature was of great assistance to her. It is far harder to kill a phantom than a reality. She was always creeping back when I thought I had despatched her. Though I flatter myself that I killed her in the end, the struggle was severe; it took much time that had better have been spent upon learning Greek grammar; or in roaming the world in search of adventures. But it was a real experience; it was an experience that was found to befall all women writers at that time. Killing the Angel in the House was part of the occupation of a woman writer.

But to continue my story. The Angel was dead; what then remained? You may say that what remained was a simple and common object—a young woman in a bedroom with an inkpot. In other words, now that she had rid herself of falsehood, that young woman had only to be herself. Ah, but what is "herself"? I mean, what is a woman? I assure you, I do not know. I do not believe that you know. I do not believe that anybody can know until she has expressed herself in all the arts and professions open to human skill. That indeed is one of the reasons why I have come here out of respect for you, who are in process of showing us by your experiments what a woman is, who are in process of providing us, by your failures and successes, with that extremely important piece of information.

But to continue the story of my professional experiences. I made one pound ten and six by my first review; and I bought a Persian cat with the proceeds. Then I grew ambitious. A Persian cat is all very well, I said; but a Persian cat is not enough. I must have a motor car. And it was thus that I became a novelist—for it is a very strange thing that people will give you a motor car if you will tell them a story. It is a still stranger thing that there is nothing so delightful in the world as telling stories. It is far pleasanter than writing reviews of famous novels. And yet, if I am to obey your secretary and tell you my professional experiences as a novelist, I must tell you about a very strange experience that befell me as a novelist. And to understand it you must try first to imagine a novelist's state of mind. I hope I am not giving away professional secrets if I say that a novelist's chief desire is to be as unconscious as possible. He has to induce in himself a state of perpetual lethargy. He wants life to proceed with the utmost quiet and regularity. He wants to see the same faces, to read the same books, to do the same things day after day, month after month, while he is writing, so that nothing may break the illusion in which he is living—so that nothing may disturb or disquiet the mysterious nosings about, feelings round, darts, dashes and sudden discoveries of that very shy and illusive spirit, the imagination. I suspect that this state is the same both for men and women. Be that as it may, I want you to imagine me writing a novel in a state of trance. I want you to figure to yourselves a girl sitting with a pen in her hand, which for minutes, and indeed for hours, she never dips into the inkpot. The image that comes to my mind when I think of this girl is the image of a fisherman lying sunk in dreams on the verge of a deep lake with a rod held out over the water. She was letting her imagination sweep unchecked round every rock and cranny of the world that lies submerged in the depths of our unconscious being. Now came the experience, the experience that I believe to be far commoner with women writers than with men. The line raced through the girl's fingers. Her imagination had rushed away. It had sought the pools, the depths, the dark places where the largest fish slumber. And then there was a smash. There was an explosion. There was foam and confusion. The imagination had dashed itself against something hard. The girl was roused from her dream. She was indeed in a state of the most acute and difficult distress. To speak without figure she had thought of something, something about the body, about the passions which it was unfitting for her as a woman to say. Men, her reason told her, would be shocked. The consciousness of what men will say of a woman who speaks the truth about her passions had roused her from her artist's state of unconsciousness. She could write no more. The trance was over. Her imagination could work no longer. This I believe to be a very common experience with women writers—they are impeded by the extreme conventionality of the other sex. For though men sensibly allow themselves great freedom in these respects, I doubt that they realize or can control the extreme severity with which they condemn such freedom in women.

These then were two very genuine experiences of my own. These were two of the adventures of my professional life. The first—killing the Angel in the House—I think I solved. She died. But the second, telling the truth about my own experiences as a body, I do not think I solved. I doubt that any woman has solved it yet. The obstacles against her are still immensely powerful—and yet they are very difficult to define. Outwardly, what is simpler than to write books? Outwardly, what obstacles are there for a woman rather than for a man? Inwardly, I think, the case is very different; she has still many ghosts to fight, many prejudices to overcome. Indeed it will be a long time still, I think, before a woman can sit down to write a book without finding a phantom to be slain, a rock to be dashed against. And if this is so in literature, the freest of all professions for women, how is it in the new professions which you are now for the first time entering?

Those are the questions that I should like, had I time, to ask you. And indeed, if I have laid stress upon these professional experiences of mine, it is because I believe that they are, though in different forms, yours also. Even when the path is nominally open—when there is nothing to prevent a woman from being a doctor, a lawyer, a civil servant—there are many phantoms and obstacles, as I believe, looming in her way. To discuss and define them is I think of great value and importance; for thus only can the labour be shared, the difficulties be solved. But besides this, it is necessary also to discuss the ends and the aims for which we are fighting, for which we are doing battle with these formidable obstacles. Those aims cannot be taken for granted; they must be perpetually questioned and examined. The whole position, as I see it—here in this hall surrounded by women practising for the first time in history I know not how many different professions—is one of extraordinary interest and importance. You have won rooms of your own in the house hitherto exclusively owned by men. You are able, though not without great labour and effort, to pay the rent. You are earning your five hundred pounds a year. But this freedom is only a beginning; the room is your own, but it is still bare. It has to be furnished; it has to be decorated; it has to be shared. How are you going to furnish it, how are you going to decorate it? With whom are you going to share it, and upon what terms? These, I think are questions of the utmost importance and interest. For the first time in history you are able to ask them; for the first time you are able to decide for yourselves what the answers should be. Willingly would I stay and discuss those questions and answers—but not tonight. My time is up; and I must cease.

Franklin D. Roosevelt and Winston Churchill
(1882–1945)   (1874–1965)

ALLIES WHO ALSO cultivated a strong personal friendship sustained by an extensive correspondence and transatlantic visits, Franklin D. Roosevelt and Winston Churchill gave voice to some of the twentieth century's most powerful expressions of freedom and some of history's most enduring political sentiments. Their skills, rhetorical and political, were devoted largely to crisis: Roosevelt's first terms as president of the United States were dominated by the Great Depression; he subsequently supported Great Britain's fight against Fascism—a battle long waged by Churchill in speeches and writing—through the lend-lease program. After the attack on Pearl Harbor on December 7, 1941, Roosevelt led the United States into World War II. As the historian Doris Kearns Goodwin notes in *No Ordinary Time*, by the time they met, the two men had long admired each other from afar: "Churchill had applauded Roosevelt's 'valiant effort' to end the depression, while

Roosevelt had listened with increasing respect to Churchill's lonely warnings against the menace of Adolf Hitler." One of those "lonely warnings," issued by radio broadcast "to the people of the United States" in 1938, a few years before Churchill became prime minister, is reproduced here in "The Defence of Freedom and Peace." Of Roosevelt, Churchill once declared: "He is the truest friend; he has the farthest vision; he is the greatest man I have ever known." That vision is on display in both of the speeches included here: the first of the series of radio addresses that came to be known as "fireside chats," in which the president spoke directly to the American people, and an address to Congress on the subject of the "four freedoms." Roosevelt's masterful rhetoric is today graphically displayed on the walls of the Franklin Delano Roosevelt Memorial in Washington, D.C. The latter speech is also the inspiration for the Four Freedoms Park, located at the southern tip of New York City's Roosevelt Island.

Franklin D. Roosevelt
First Fireside Chat on Banking
(March 12, 1933)

My friends, I want to talk for a few minutes with the people of the United States about banking—to talk with the comparatively few who understand the mechanics of banking, but more particularly with the overwhelming majority who use banks for the making of deposits and the drawing of checks. I want to tell you what has been done in the last few days, and why it was done, and what the next steps are going to be. I recognize that the many proclamations from the state capitals and from Washington, the legislation, the Treasury regulations and so forth, couched for the most part in banking and legal terms, ought to be explained for the benefit of the average citizen. I owe this in particular because of the fortitude and good temper with which everybody has accepted the inconvenience and hardships of the banking holiday. And I know that when you understand what we in Washington have been about I shall continue to have your cooperation as fully as I have had your sympathy and help during the past week.

First of all, let me state the simple fact that when you deposit money in a bank the bank does not put the money into a safe deposit vault. It invests your money in many different forms of credit—in bonds, in commercial paper, in mortgages, and in many other kinds of loans. In other words, the bank puts your money to work to keep the wheels of industry and of agriculture turning round. A comparatively small part of the money that you put into the bank is kept in currency—an amount which in normal times is wholly sufficient to cover the cash needs of the average citizen. In other words, the total amount of all the currency in the country is only a comparatively small proportion of the total deposits in all of the banks of the country.

What, then, happened during the last few days of February and the first few days of March? Because of undermined confidence on the part of the public, there was a general rush by a large portion of our population to turn bank deposits into currency or gold—a rush so great that the soundest banks couldn't get enough currency to meet the demand. The reason for this was that on the spur of the moment it was, of course, impossible to sell perfectly sound assets of a bank and convert them into cash except at panic prices far below their real value.

By the afternoon of March 3, a week ago last Friday, scarcely a bank in the country was open to do business. Proclamations closing them in whole or in part had been issued by the governors in almost all of the states.

It was then that I issued the proclamation providing for the national bank holiday, and this was the first step in the government's reconstruction of our financial and economic fabric.

The second step, last Thursday, was the legislation promptly and patriotically passed by the Congress confirming my proclamation and broadening my powers so that it became possible in view of the requirement of time to extend the holiday and lift the ban of that holiday gradually in the days to come. This law also gave authority to develop a program of rehabilitation of our banking facilities, and I want to tell our citizens in every part of the nation that the national Congress—Republicans and Democrats alike—showed by this action a devotion to public welfare and a realization of the emergency and the necessity for speed that it is difficult to match in all our history.

The third stage has been the series of regulations permitting the banks to continue their functions to take care of the distribution of food and household necessities and the payment of payrolls.

This bank holiday, while resulting in many cases in great inconvenience, is affording us the opportunity to supply the currency necessary to meet the situation. Remember that no sound bank is a dollar worse off than it was when it closed its doors last week. Neither is any bank which may turn out not to be in a position for immediate opening. The new law allows the twelve federal reserve banks to issue additional currency on good assets and thus banks that reopen will be able to meet every legitimate call. The new currency is being sent out by the Bureau of Engraving and Printing in large volume to every part of the country. It is sound currency because it is backed by actual, good assets.

Another question you will ask is this: why are all the banks not to be reopened at the same time? The answer is simple, and I know you will understand it. Your government does not intend that the history of the past few years shall be repeated. We do not want and will not have another epidemic of bank failures.

As a result, we start tomorrow, Monday, with the opening of banks in the twelve federal reserve bank cities—those banks which on first examination by the Treasury have already been found to be all right. That will be followed on Tuesday by the resumption of all other functions by banks already found to be sound in cities where there are recognized clearing houses. That means about 250 cities of the United States. In other words, we are moving as fast as the mechanics of the situation will allow us.

On Wednesday and succeeding days banks in smaller places all through the country will resume business, subject, of course, to the government's physical ability to complete its survey. It is necessary that the reopening of banks be extended over a period in order to permit the banks to make applications for the necessary loans, to obtain currency needed to meet their requirements, and to enable the government to make commonsense checkups.

Please let me make it clear to you that if your bank does not open the first day, you are by no means justified in believing that it will not open. A bank that opens on one of the subsequent days is in exactly the same status as the bank that opens tomorrow.

I know that many people are worrying about state banks that are not members of the Federal Reserve System. There is no occasion for that worry. These banks can and will receive assistance from member banks and from the Reconstruction Finance Corporation and of course they are under the immediate control of the state banking authorities. These state banks are following the same course as the national banks except that they get their licenses to resume business from the state authorities, and these authorities have been asked by the secretary of the treasury to permit their good banks to open up on the same schedule as the national banks. And so I am confident that the state banking departments will be as careful as the national government in the policy relating to the opening of banks and will follow the same broad theory.

It is possible that when the banks resume a very few people who have not recovered from their fear may again begin withdrawals. Let me make it clear to you that the banks will take care of all needs except of course the hysterical demands of hoarders—and it is my belief that hoarding during the past week has become an exceedingly unfashionable pastime in every part of our nation. It needs no prophet to tell you that when the people find that they can get their money—that they can get it when they want it for all legitimate purposes—the phantom of fear will soon be laid. People will again be glad to have their money where it will be safely taken care of and where they can use it conveniently at any time. I can assure you, my friends, that it is safer to keep your money in a reopened bank than it is to keep it under the mattress.

The success of our whole national program depends, of course, upon the cooperation of the public—on its intelligent support and its use of a reliable system.

Remember that the essential accomplishment of the new legislation is that it makes it possible for banks more readily to convert their assets into cash than was the case before. More liberal provision has been made for banks to borrow on these assets at the reserve banks and more liberal provision has also been made for issuing currency on the security of these good assets. This currency is not fiat currency. It is issued only on adequate security, and every good bank has an abundance of such security.

One more point before I close. There will be, of course, some banks unable to reopen without being reorganized. The new law allows the government to assist in making these reorganizations quickly and effectively and even allows the government to subscribe to at least a part of any new capital that may be required.

I hope you can see, my friends, from this essential recital of what your government is doing that there is nothing complex, nothing radical, in the process.

We had a bad banking situation. Some of our bankers had shown themselves either incompetent or dishonest in their handling of the people's funds. They had used the money entrusted to them in speculations and unwise loans. This was, of course, not true in the vast majority of our banks, but it was true in enough of them to shock the people of the United States for a time into a sense of insecurity and to put them into a frame of mind where they did not differentiate, but seemed to assume that the acts of a comparative few had tainted them all. And so it became the government's job to straighten out this situation and to do it as quickly as possible. And the job is being performed.

I do not promise you that every bank will be reopened or that individual losses will not be suffered, but there will be no losses that possibly could be avoided; and there would have been more and greater losses had we continued to drift. I can even promise you salvation for some at least of the sorely pressed banks. We shall be engaged not merely in reopening sound banks but in the creation of more sound banks through reorganization.

It has been wonderful to me to catch the note of confidence from all over the country. I can never be sufficiently grateful to the people for the loyal support that they have given me in their acceptance of the judgment that has dictated our course, even though all our processes may not have seemed clear to them.

After all, there is an element in the readjustment of our financial system more important than currency, more important than gold, and that is the confidence of the people themselves. Confidence and courage are the essentials of success in carrying out our plan. You people must have faith; you must not be stampeded by rumors or guesses. Let us unite in banishing fear. We have provided the machinery to restore our financial system; and it is up to you to support and make it work.

It is your problem, my friends, your problem no less than it is mine. Together we cannot fail.

Franklin D. Roosevelt
The Four Freedoms (January 6, 1941)

In the future days, which we seek to make secure, we look forward to a world founded upon four essential human freedoms.

The first is freedom of speech and expression—everywhere in the world.

The second is freedom of every person to worship God in his own way—everywhere in the world.

The third is freedom from want—which, translated into world terms, means economic understandings which will secure to every nation a healthy peacetime life for its inhabitants—everywhere in the world.

The fourth is freedom from fear—which, translated into world terms, means a world-wide reduction of armaments to such a point and in such a thorough fashion that no nation will be in a position to commit an act of physical aggression against any neighbor—anywhere in the world.

That is no vision of a distant millennium. It is a definite basis for a kind of world attainable in our own time and generation. That kind of world is the very antithesis of the so-called new order of tyranny which the dictators seek to create with the crash of a bomb.

To that new order we oppose the greater conception—the moral order. A good society is able to face schemes of world domination and foreign revolutions alike without fear.

Since the beginning of our American history, we have been engaged in change—in a perpetual peaceful revolution—a revolution which goes on steadily, quietly adjusting itself to changing conditions—without the concentration camp or the quick-lime in the ditch. The world order which we seek is the cooperation of free countries, working together in a friendly, civilized society.

This nation has placed its destiny in the hands and heads and hearts of its millions of free men and women; and its faith in freedom under the guidance of God. Freedom means the supremacy of human rights everywhere. Our support goes to those who struggle to gain those rights or keep them. Our strength is our unity of purpose.

To that high concept there can be no end save victory.

Winston Churchill
The Defence of Freedom and Peace (October 16, 1938)

I avail myself with relief of the opportunity of speaking to the people of the United States. I do not know how long such liberties will be allowed. The stations of uncensored expression are closing down; the lights are going out; but there is still time for those to whom freedom and parliamentary government mean something, to consult together. Let me, then, speak in truth and earnestness while time remains.

The American people have, it seems to me, formed a true judgment upon the disaster which has befallen Europe. They realise, perhaps more clearly than the French and British publics have yet done, the far-reaching consequences of the abandonment and ruin of the Czechoslovak Republic. I hold to the conviction I expressed some months ago, that if in April, May or June, Great Britain, France, and Russia had jointly declared that they would act together upon Nazi Germany if Herr Hitler committed an act of unprovoked aggression against this small State, and if they had told Poland, Yugoslavia, and Rumania what they meant to do in good time, and invited them to join the combination of peace-defending Powers, I hold that the German Dictator would have been confronted with such a formidable array that he would have been deterred from his purpose. This would also have been an opportunity for all the peace-loving and moderate forces in Germany, together with the chiefs of the German Army, to make a great effort to re-establish something like sane and civilised conditions in their own country. If the risks of war which were run by France and Britain at the last moment had been boldly faced in good time, and plain declarations made, and meant, how different would our prospects be today!

But all these backward speculations belong to history. It is no good using hard words among friends about the past, and reproaching one another for what cannot be recalled. It is the future, not the past, that demands our earnest and anxious thought. We must recognize that the Parliamentary democracies and liberal, peaceful forces have everywhere sustained a defeat which leaves them weaker, morally and physically, to cope with dangers which have vastly grown. But the cause of freedom has in it a recuperative power and virtue which can draw from misfortune new hope and new strength. If ever there was a time when men and women who cherish the ideals of the founders of the British and American Constitutions should take earnest counsel with one another, that time is now.

All the world wishes for peace and security. Have we gained it by the sacrifice of the Czechoslovak Republic? Here was the model democratic State of Central Europe, a country where minorities were treated better than anywhere else. It has been deserted, destroyed and devoured. It is now being digested. The question which is of interest to a lot of ordinary people, common people, is whether this destruction of the Czechoslovak Republic will bring upon the world a blessing or a curse.

We must all hope it will bring a blessing; that after we have averted our gaze for a while from the process of subjugation and liquidation, everyone will breathe more freely; that a load will be taken off our chests; we shall be able to say to ourselves: "Well, that's out of the way, anyhow. Now let's get on with our regular daily life." But are these hopes well founded or are we merely making the best of what we had not the force and virtue to stop? That is the question that the English-speaking peoples in all their lands must ask themselves today. Is this the end, or is there more to come?

There is another question which arises out of this. Can peace, goodwill, and confidence be built upon submission to wrong-doing backed by force?

One may put this question in the largest form. Has any benefit or progress ever been achieved by the human race by submission to organised and calculated violence? As we look back over the long story of the nations we must see that, on the contrary, their glory has been founded upon the spirit of resistance to tyranny and injustice, especially when these evils seemed to be backed by heavier force. Since the dawn of the Christian era a certain way of life has slowly been shaping itself among the Western peoples, and certain standards of conduct and government have come to be esteemed. After many miseries and prolonged confusion, there arose into the broad light of day the conception of the right of the individual; his right to be consulted in the government of his country; his right to invoke the law even against the State itself. Independent Courts of Justice were created to affirm and inforce this hard-won custom. Thus was assured throughout the English-speaking world, and in France by the stern lessons of the Revolution, what Kipling called, "Leave to live by no man's leave underneath the law." Now in this resides all that makes existence precious to man, and all that confers honour and health upon the State.

We are confronted with another theme. It is not a new theme; it leaps out upon us from the Dark Ages—racial persecution, religious intolerance, deprivation of free speech, the conception of the citizen as a mere soulless fraction of the State. To this has been added the cult of war. Children are to be taught in their earliest schooling the delights and profits of conquest and aggression. A whole mighty community has been drawn painfully, by severe privations, into a warlike frame. They are held in this condition, which they relish no more than we do, by a party organisation, several millions strong, who derive all kinds of profits, good and bad, from the upkeep of the regime. Like the Communists, the Nazis tolerate no opinion but their own. Like the Communists, they feed on hatred. Like the Communists, they must seek, from time to time, and always at shorter intervals, a new target, a new prize, a new victim. The Dictator, in all his pride, is held in the grip of his Party machine. He can go forward; he cannot go back. He must blood his hounds and show them sport, or else, like Actaeon of old, be devoured by them. All-strong without, he is all-weak within. As Byron wrote a hundred years ago: "These Pagod things of Sabre sway, with fronts of brass and feet of clay."

No one must, however, underrate the power and efficiency of a totalitarian state. Where the whole population of a great country, amiable, good-hearted, peace-loving people are gripped by the neck and by the hair by a Communist or a Nazi tyranny—for they are the same things spelt in different ways—the rulers for the time being can exercise a power for the purposes of war and external domination before which the ordinary free parliamentary societies are at a grievous practical disadvantage. We have to recognise this. And then, on top of all, comes this wonderful mastery of the air which our century has discovered, but of which, alas, mankind has so far shown itself unworthy. Here is this air power with its claim to torture and terrorise the women and children, the civil population of neighbouring countries.

This combination of medieval passion, a party caucus, the weapons of modern science, and the blackmailing power of air-bombing, is the most monstrous menace to peace, order and fertile progress that has appeared in the world since the Mongol invasions of the thirteenth century.

The culminating question to which I have been leading is whether the world as we have known it—the great and hopeful world of before the war, the world of increasing hope and enjoyment for the common man, the world of honoured tradition and expanding science—should meet this menace by submission or by resistance. Let us see, then, whether the means of resistance remain to us today. We have sustained an immense disaster; the renown of France is dimmed. In spite of her brave, efficient army, her influence is profoundly diminished. No one has a right to say that Britain, for all her blundering, has broken her word—indeed, when it was too late, she was better than her word. Nevertheless, Europe lies at this moment abashed and distracted before the triumphant assertions of dictatorial power. In the Spanish Peninsula, a purely Spanish quarrel has been carried by the intervention, or shall I say the "non-intervention" (to quote the current Jargon) of Dictators into the region of a world cause.

But it is not only in Europe that these oppressions prevail. China is being torn to pieces by a military clique in Japan; the poor, tormented Chinese people there are making a brave and stubborn defence. The ancient empire of Ethiopia has been overrun. The Ethiopians were taught to look to the sanctity of public law, to the tribunal of many nations gathered in majestic union. But all failed; they were deceived, and now they are winning back their right to live by beginning again from the bottom a struggle on primordial lines. Even in South America, the Nazi regime begins to undermine the fabric of Brazilian society.

Far away, happily protected by the Atlantic and Pacific Oceans, you, the people of the United States, to whom I now have the chance to speak, are the spectators, and I may add the increasingly involved spectators of these tragedies and crimes. We are left in no doubt where American conviction and sympathies lie; but will you wait until British freedom and independence have succumbed, and then take up the cause when it is three-quarters ruined, yourselves alone? I hear that they are saying in the United States that because England and France have failed to do their duty therefore the American people can wash their hands of the whole business. This may be the passing mood of many people, but there is no sense in it. If things have got much worse, all the more must we try to cope with them.

For, after all, survey the remaining forces of civilisation; they are overwhelming. If only they were united in a common conception of right and duty, there would be no war. On the contrary, the German people, industrious, faithful, valiant, but alas! lacking in the proper spirit of civic independence, liberated from their present nightmare, would take their honoured place in the vanguard of human society. Alexander the Great remarked that the people of Asia were slaves because they had not learned to pronounce the word "No." Let that not be the epitaph of the English-speaking peoples or of Parliamentary democracy, or of France, or of the many surviving liberal States of Europe.

There, in one single word, is the resolve which the forces of freedom and progress, of tolerance and good will, should take. It is not in the power of one nation, however formidably armed, still less is it in the power of a small group of men, violent, ruthless men, who have always to cast their eyes back over their shoulders, to cramp and fetter the forward march of human destiny. The preponderant world forces are upon our side; they have but to be combined to be obeyed. We must arm. Britain must arm. America must arm. If, through an earnest desire for peace, we have placed ourselves at a disadvantage, we must make up for it by redoubled exertions, and, if necessary, by fortitude in suffering.

We shall, no doubt, arm. Britain, casting away the habits of centuries, will decree national service upon her citizens. The British people will stand erect, and will face whatever may be coming.

But arms—instrumentalities, as President Wilson called them—are not sufficient by themselves. We must add to them the power of ideas. People say we ought not to allow ourselves to be drawn into a theoretical antagonism between Nazidom and democracy; but the antagonism is here now. It is this very conflict of spiritual and moral ideas which gives the free countries a great part of their strength. You see these dictators on their pedestals, surrounded by the bayonets of their soldiers and the truncheons of their police. On all sides they are guarded by masses of armed men, cannons, aeroplanes, fortifications, and the like—they boast and vaunt themselves before the world, yet in their hearts there is unspoken fear. They are afraid of words and thoughts; words spoken abroad, thoughts stirring at home—all the more powerful because forbidden—terrify them. A little mouse of thought appears in the room, and even the mightiest potentates are thrown into panic. They make frantic efforts to bar our thoughts and words; they are afraid of the workings of the human mind. Cannons, airplanes, they can manufacture in large quantities; but how are they to quell the natural promptings of human nature, which after all these centuries of trial and progress has inherited a whole armoury of potent and indestructible knowledge?

Dictatorship—the fetish worship of one man—is a passing phase. A state of society where men may not speak their minds, where children denounce their parents to the police, where a business man or small shopkeeper ruins his competitor by telling tales about his private opinions; such a state of society cannot long endure if brought into contact with the healthy outside world. The light of civilised progress with its tolerances and co-operation, with its dignities and joys, has often in the past been blotted out. But I hold the belief that we have now at last got far enough ahead of barbarism to control it, and to avert it, if only we realise what is afoot and make up our minds in time. We shall do it in the end. But how much harder our toil for every day's delay!

Is this a call to war? Does anyone pretend that preparation for resistance to aggression is unleashing war? I declare it to be the sole guarantee of peace. We need the swift gathering of forces to confront not only military but moral aggression; the resolute and sober acceptance of their duty by the English-speaking peoples and by all the nations, great and small, who wish to walk with them. Their faithful and zealous comradeship would almost between night and morning clear the path of progress and banish from all our lives the fear which already darkens the sunlight to hundreds of millions of men.

Shakespeare Rallies the Troops

THESE THREE SPEECHES reveal a fascinating transmigration of ideas from fiction to reality. Henry V's speech at Agincourt—which continues to animate, either through direct quotation or through a borrowing of ideas, the speeches of some military officers today—explicitly informed the orations of the World War II generals Bernard Montgomery (1887–1976) and George Patton (1885–1945). The offer to provide a passport home to any soldier wishing to go—a motif found in Shakespeare's speech, which Henry delivers before the battle to a sick and outnumbered English army preparing to confront the formidable French—reappears in Montgomery's address, given soon after the British general had taken command of troops in North Africa whose morale had been destroyed by a series of defeats at the hands of the German general Erwin Rommel. Patton makes use of a different element in Henry V's speech: the appeal to shame and honor. Both Montgomery and Patton knew their Shakespeare well and were able to turn their reading to practical advantage.

Henry V at Agincourt

from *Henry V,* act 4, scene 3

If we are marked to die, we are enough
To do our country loss, and if to live,
The fewer men, the greater share of honor.
God's will, I pray thee wish not one man more.
By Jove, I am not covetous for gold,   5
Nor care I who doth feed upon my cost;
It ernes me not if men my garments wear;
Such outward things dwell not in my desires.
But if it be a sin to covet honor
I am the most offending soul alive.   10
No, faith, my coz, wish not a man from England.
God's peace, I would not lose so great an honor
As one man more methinks would share from me,
For the best hope I have. Oh, do not wish one more!
Rather proclaim it, Westmorland, through my host   15
That he which hath no stomach to this fight,
Let him depart; his passport shall be made
And crowns for convoy put into his purse.
We would not die in that man's company
That fears his fellowship to die with us.   20

2. **To do our country loss:** For our country to lose.
7. **ernes:** grieves.
11. **coz:** kinsmen.
13. **share:** deprive.
15. **host:** army.
16. **stomach:** appetite; courage.
18. **crowns for convoy:** money for transport.
20. **fellowship:** duty as our companion.

This day is called the feast of Crispian.
He that outlives this day and comes safe home
Will stand a-tiptoe when this day is named
And rouse him at the name of Crispian.
He that shall see this day and live old age   25
Will yearly on the vigil feast his neighbors
And say, "Tomorrow is Saint Crispian."
Then will he strip his sleeve and show his scars
And say, "These wounds I had on Crispin's day."
Old men forget; yet all shall be forgot   30
But he'll remember, with advantages,
What feats he did that day. Then shall our names,
Familiar in his mouth as household words—
Harry the King, Bedford and Exeter,
Warwick and Talbot, Salisbury and Gloucester—   35
Be in their flowing cups freshly remembered.
This story shall the good man teach his son,
And Crispin Crispian shall ne'er go by
From this day to the ending of the world
But we in it shall be remembered,   40
We few, we happy few, we band of brothers—
For he today that sheds his blood with me
Shall be my brother. Be he ne'er so vile,
This day shall gentle his condition.
And gentlemen in England now abed   45
Shall think themselves accursed they were not here.
And hold their manhoods cheap whiles any speaks
That fought with us upon Saint Crispin's day.

Bernard Montgomery, We Will Stand and Fight Here
(1942)

I want first of all to introduce myself to you. You do not know me. I do not
know you. But we have got to work together; therefore we must understand
each other, and we must have confidence each in the other. I have only been

---

21. **feast of Crispian:** October 25, dedicated to the martyred brothers Crispin and Crispianos (or
Crispinian).
26. **vigil:** eve of the saint's day.
31. **advantages:** embellishments
43. **vile:** lowborn
44. **gentle his condition:** Shall raise him to gentlemanly rank.

here a few hours. But from what I have seen and heard since I arrived I am prepared to say, here and now, that I have confidence in you. We will then work together as a team; and together we will gain the confidence of this great army and go forward to final victory in Africa.

I believe that one of the first duties of a commander is to create what I call "atmosphere," and in that atmosphere his staff, subordinate commanders, and troops will live and work and fight.

I do not like the general atmosphere I find here. It is an atmosphere of doubt, of looking back to select the next place to which to withdraw, of loss of confidence in our ability to defeat Rommel, of desperate defense measures by reserves in preparing positions in Cairo and the Delta.

All that must cease.

Let us have a new atmosphere.

The defense of Egypt lies here at Alamein and on the Ruweisat Ridge. What is the use of digging trenches in the Delta? It is quite useless; if we lose this position we lose Egypt; all the fighting troops now in the Delta must come here at once, and will. *Here* we will stand and fight; there will be no further withdrawal. I have ordered that all plans and instructions dealing with further withdrawal are to be burned, and at once. We will stand and fight *here*.

If we can't stay here alive, then let us stay here dead.

I want to impress on everyone that the bad times are over. Fresh divisions from the UK are now arriving in Egypt, together with ample reinforcements for our present divisions. We have three hundred to four hundred new Sherman tanks coming and these are actually being unloaded at Suez *now*. Our mandate from the prime minister is to destroy the Axis forces in North Africa; I have seen it, written on half a sheet of notepaper. And it will be done. If anyone here thinks it can't be done, let him go at once; I don't want any doubters in this party. It can be done, and it will be done: beyond any possibility of doubt.

Now I understand that Rommel is expected to attack at any moment. Excellent. Let him attack.

I would sooner it didn't come for a week, just give me time to sort things out. If we have two weeks to prepare we will be sitting pretty; Rommel can attack as soon as he likes after that, and I hope he does.

Meanwhile, we ourselves will start to plan a great offensive; it will be the beginning of a campaign which will hit Rommel and his army for six right out of Africa.

But first we must create a reserve corps, mobile and strong in armor, which we will train *out of the line*. Rommel has always had such a force in his Africa Corps, which is never used to hold the line but which is always in reserve, available for striking blows. Therein has been his great strength. We will create such a corps ourselves, a British Panzer Corps; it will consist of two armored divisions and one motorized division; I gave orders yesterday for it to begin to form, back in the Delta.

I have no intention of launching our great attack until we are completely ready; there will be pressure from many quarters to attack soon; *I will not attack until we are ready*, and you can rest assured on that point.

Meanwhile, if Rommel attacks while we are preparing, let him do so with pleasure; we will merely continue with our own preparations and *we* will attack when *we* are ready, and not before.

I want to tell you that I always work on the Chief of Staff system. I have nominated Brigadier de Guingand as Chief of Staff Eighth Army. I will issue orders through him. Whatever he says will be taken as coming from me and will be acted on *at once*. I understand there has been a great deal of "belly-aching" out here. By bellyaching I mean inventing poor reasons for *not* doing what one has been told to do.

All this is to stop at once.

I will tolerate no bellyaching.

If anyone objects to doing what he is told, then he can get out of it: and at once. I want that made very clear right down through the Eighth Army.

I have little more to say just at present. And some of you may think it is quite enough and may wonder if I am mad.

I assure you I am quite sane.

I understand there are people who often think I am slightly mad; so often that I now regard it as rather a compliment.

All I have to say to that is that if I am slightly mad, there are a large number of people I could name who are raving lunatics!

What I have done is to get over to you the "atmosphere" in which we will now work and fight, you must see that that atmosphere permeates right through the Eighth Army to the most junior private soldier. All the soldiers must know what is wanted; when they see it coming to pass there will be a surge of confidence throughout the army.

I ask you to give me your confidence and to have faith that what I have said will come to pass.

There is much work to be done.

The orders I have given about no further withdrawal will mean a complete change in the layout of our dispositions; also, we must begin to prepare for our great offensive.

The first thing to do is to move our HQ to a decent place where we can live in reasonable comfort and where the army staff can all be together and side by side with the HQ of the Desert Air Force. This is a frightful place here, depressing, unhealthy, and a rendezvous for every fly in Africa; we shall do no good work here. Let us get over there by the sea where it is fresh and healthy.

If officers are to do good work they must have decent messes, and be comfortable. So off we go on the new line.

The Chief of Staff will be issuing orders on many points very shortly, and I am always available to be consulted by the senior officers of the staff. The great point to remember is that we are going to finish with this chap Rommel once and for all. It will be quite easy. There is no doubt about it.

He is definitely a nuisance. Therefore we will hit him a crack and finish with him.

George Patton, Speech to the Third Army
(1944)

Be seated.

Men, this stuff that some sources sling around about America wanting to stay out of this war, not wanting to fight, is a crock of bullshit. Americans love to fight, traditionally. All real Americans love the sting and clash of battle. Americans love a winner. Americans will not tolerate a loser. Americans despise cowards. Americans play to win. That's why Americans have never lost nor will ever lose a war.

You are not all going to die. Only 2 percent of you right here today would be killed in a major battle. Death must not be feared. Death, in time, comes to all of us. And every man is scared in his first battle. If he says he's not, he's a goddam liar. Some men are cowards but they fight the same as the brave men or they get the hell slammed out of them watching men fight who are just as scared as they are. Remember that the enemy is just as frightened as you are, and probably more so. They are not supermen.

The real hero is the man who fights even though he's scared. Some men get over their fright in a minute under fire, others take an hour, for some it takes days, but a real man will never let his fear of death overpower his honor, his sense of duty to his country and to his manhood.

All through your army careers, you men have bitched about what you call "chickenshit drilling." That, like everything else in this army, has a definite purpose. That purpose is alertness. Alertness must be bred into every soldier. A man must be alert at all times if he expects to stay alive. If you're not alert, sometime, a German son-of-a-bitch is going to sneak up behind you and beat you to death with a sockful of shit! There are four hundred neatly marked graves somewhere in Sicily, all because one man went to sleep on the job. But they are German graves, because we caught the bastard asleep.

An army is a team. It lives, sleeps, eats, and fights as a team. This individual hero stuff is a lot of horseshit. The bilious bastards who write that kind of stuff for the *Saturday Evening Post* don't know any more about real fighting under fire than they know about fucking! We have the finest food, the finest equipment, the best spirit, and the best men in the world. Why, by God, I actually pity those poor sons-of-bitches we're going up against.

My men don't surrender, and I don't want to hear of any soldier under my command being captured unless he has been hit. Even if you are hit, you can still fight back. The kind of man that I want in my command is just like the lieutenant in Libya, who, with a Luger against his chest, jerked off his helmet, swept the gun aside with one hand, and busted the hell out of the Kraut with his helmet. Then he jumped on the gun and went out and killed another German before they knew what the hell was coming off. And, all of that time, this man had a bullet through a lung. There was a real man!

Every single man in this army has a job to do and he must do it. Every man is a vital link in the great chain. What if every truck driver suddenly decided that he didn't like the whine of those shells overhead, turned yellow, and jumped headlong into a ditch? The cowardly bastard could say, "Hell, they won't miss me, just one man in thousands." But, what if every man thought that way? Where in the hell would we be now? What would our country, our loved ones, our homes, even the world, be like? No, goddamnit, Americans don't think like that. Every man does his job, serves the whole. Ordnance men are needed to supply the guns and machinery of war to keep us rolling. Quartermasters are needed to bring up food and clothes because where we are going there isn't a hell of a lot to steal. Every last man on KP has a job to do, even the one who heats our water to keep us from getting the "GI Shits." Each man must not think only of himself, but also of his buddy fighting beside him.

One of the bravest men that I ever saw was a fellow on top of a telegraph pole in the midst of a furious firefight in Tunisia. I stopped and asked what the hell he was doing up there at a time like that. He answered, "Fixing the wire, Sir." I asked, "Isn't that a little unhealthy right about now?" He answered, "Yes, Sir, but the goddamned wire has to be fixed." I asked, "Don't those planes strafing the road bother you?" And he answered, "No, Sir, but you sure as hell do!"

Now, there was a real man. A real soldier. There was a man who devoted all he had to his duty, no matter how seemingly insignificant his duty might appear at the time, no matter how great the odds. And you should have seen those trucks on the road to Tunisia. Those drivers were magnificent. All day and all night they rolled over those son-of-a-bitching roads, never stopping, never faltering from their course, with shells bursting all around them all of the time. We got through on good old American guts. Many of those men drove for over forty consecutive hours. These men weren't combat men, but they were soldiers with a job to do. They did it, and in one hell of a way they did it. They were part of a team. Without team effort, without them, the fight would have been lost. All of the links in the chain pulled together and the chain became unbreakable.

Remember, men, you men don't know I'm here. No mention of that fact is to be made in any letters. The world is not supposed to know what the hell happened to me. I'm not supposed to be commanding this army. I'm not even supposed to be here in England. Let the first bastards to find out be the goddamn Germans. We want to get the hell over there. The quicker we clean up this mess, the quicker we can take a little jaunt against the purple-pissing Japs and clean out their nest, too. Before the goddamn marines get all of the credit.

Sure, we want to go home. We want this war to be over with. The quickest way to get it over with is to go get the bastards who started it. The quicker they are whipped, the quicker we can go home. The shortest way home is through Berlin and Tokyo. And when we get to Berlin, I am personally going to shoot that paper-hanging son-of-a-bitch Hitler. Just like I'd shoot a snake!

When a man is lying in a shell hole, if he just stays there all day, a German will get to him eventually. The hell with that idea. The hell with taking it. My men don't dig foxholes. I don't want them to. Foxholes only slow up an offensive. Keep moving. And don't give the enemy time to dig one either. We'll win this war, but we'll win it only by fighting and by showing the Germans that we've got more guts than they have; or ever will have.

War is a bloody, killing business. You've got to spill their blood, or they will spill yours. Rip them up the belly. Shoot them in the guts. When shells are hitting all around you and you wipe the dirt off your face and realize that instead of dirt it's the blood and guts of what once was your best friend beside you, you'll know what to do!

I don't want to get any messages saying, "I am holding my position." We are not holding a goddamned thing. Let the Germans do that. We are advancing constantly and we are not interested in holding on to anything, except the enemy's balls. We are going to twist his balls and kick the living shit out of him all of the time. Our basic plan of operation is to advance and to keep advancing regardless of whether we have to go over, under, or through the enemy.

From time to time there will be some complaints that we are pushing our people too hard. I don't give a good goddamn about such complaints. I believe in the old and sound rule that an ounce of sweat will save a gallon of blood. The harder we push, the more Germans we will kill. The more Germans we kill, the fewer of our men will be killed. Pushing means fewer casualties. I want you all to remember that.

There is one great thing that you men will all be able to say after this war is over and you are home once again. You may be thankful that twenty years from now, when you are sitting by the fireplace with your grandson on your knee and he asks you what you did in the great World War II, you won't have to shift him to the other knee, cough, and say, "Well, your grand-daddy shoveled shit in Louisiana." No, sir, you can look him straight in the eye and say, "Son, your granddaddy rode with the Great Third Army and a son-of-a-goddamned-bitch named Georgie Patton!"

That is all.

DISCUSSION QUESTIONS

1. *Patton's vocabulary is often earthy and crude. What is the place of colloquial—even profane—language in motivating others?*

2. *Not everyone is comfortable with public speaking. What helpful principles can you take away from these speeches?*

3. *What are some fundamental differences between spoken and written forms of persuasion? Which situations call for which types of approach?*

LEARNING FROM FAILURE

[I]t is possible to fail in many ways . . .

—ARISTOTLE,
Nicomachean Ethics, 2.6

To Aristotle's observation about the ubiquity and diversity of failure, we might add the following precept: It is *desirable* to fail in many ways. Indeed, those who study the habits of mind of successful entrepreneurs argue that failure is a necessary part of the processes of invention, innovation, and creativity. Saras D. Sarasvathy, a professor at the University of Virginia's Darden School of Business and the originator of the concept of "effectual entrepreneurship," asserts in *Effectuation: Elements of Entrepreneurial Enterprise* that successful entrepreneurs "do not seek to avoid failure; they seek to make success happen. This entails a recognition that failing is an integral part of venturing well." These entrepreneurs exhibit a "willingness to fail" and learn "to outlive failures by keeping them small and killing them young."

Leaders who believe they can legislate against failure tend to create climates in which entrepreneurial spirit is muzzled and individuals are so risk-averse that they may behave in ways—ignoring warning signs, concealing minor flaws or errors, refusing to adjust and adapt—that paradoxically court the kinds of catastrophic failures systems may not be able to survive. Organizations committed to "zero defects"—in other words, to the fantasy of total control—also militate against precisely the kinds of small-scale failures that may lead to new discoveries and learning opportunities. Lean enterprise models, by contrast, drawing on Japanese manufacturing principles, presume a scenario of continuous improvement predicated on experimentation, learning, and responsiveness to change.

Fear of failure paralyzes the public sector as well. Teams such as New Urban

Mechanics are working to change that by getting "government used to the idea of failing," as team member Nigel Jacobs noted. In a March 2013 article on the MIT Center for Civic Media website, Rodrigo Davies touted recent successes of New Urban Mechanics in the city of Boston. Applying the "lean startup" methodology developed by Silicon Valley's Eric Ries to municipal government, Davies explains, the Mechanics host new projects and thus encourage experimentation and risk-taking within organizations by supporting the rapid fielding and evaluation of new initiatives. In welcoming a team to Philadelphia, Mayor Michael A. Nutter celebrated the fact that "New Urban Mechanics will have the flexibility to experiment, the ability to re-invent public-private partnerships and the strategic vision to create real change for Philadelphia."

New Urban Mechanics describes its approach as follows:

> While the language may sound new, the principles of New Urban Mechanics—collaborating with constituents, focusing on the basics of government, and pushing for bolder ideas—are not. . . .
>
> The Mechanics focus on a broad range of areas from increasing civic participation, to improving City streets, to boosting educational outcomes. The specific projects are diverse as well—from better-designed trash cans to high-tech apps for smart phones.
>
> Across all these projects, the office strives to engage constituents and institutions in developing and piloting projects that will reshape City government and improve the services we provide.

As Davies reported, the organization has also partnered with the Emerson College Engagement Game Lab on a platform now called "Community PlanIt," which uses video game technology to address community planning issues.

Despite a desire to improve and innovate, the individual's aversion to failure is often so strong that organizations must work to establish environments more hospitable to experimentation. One way to do this is to encourage play, not as frivolous luxury or childish indulgence, but as a necessary component to unlocking creativity and innovation. New York City's Institute of Play, for example, advocates games as essential learning mechanisms in a world where the definition "of knowing has shifted from being able to recall and repeat information to being able to find it, evaluate it and use it compellingly at the right time and in the right context." The importance of play in the context of leading change and fostering adaptability is that it authorizes failure: "There are other attributes of games that facilitate learning. One of these is the state of being known as play. Much of the activity of play consists in failing to reach the goal established by a game's rules. And yet players rarely experience this failure as an obstacle to trying again and again, as they work toward mastery. There is something in play that gives players permission to take risks considered outlandish or impossible in 'real life.' There is something in play that activates the tenacity and persistence required for effective learning."

The following selections offer examples of those who play well and those who do not; of those who fail and grow and those who habitually, even compulsively, repeat their mistakes. The stories of Ulysses S. Grant, the emperor Babur, and the mythical poet Orpheus, for each of whom failure leads to self-examination and increased self-awareness, contrast sharply with the tragedy of the stubborn ancient king Croesus. Meanwhile, the careers of Alexander the Great and the Arctic explorer Vilhjalmur Stefansson present examples of complex and ambiguous careers punctuated by spectacular triumphs and failures.

RECOMMENDED READING

George Eliot, *Middlemarch: A Study of Provincial Life* (1874)
Greg Grandin, *Fordlandia: The Rise and Fall of Henry Ford's Forgotten Jungle City* (2009)
Thomas Hardy, *The Mayor of Casterbridge: The Life and Death of a Man of Character* (1886)
Robert Falcon Scott, *Journals: Captain Scott's Last Expedition* (2006)
Ernest Shackleton, *South: The* Endurance *Expedition* (1919)

Anne Fadiman
(b. 1953)

A WRITER WHO specializes in the genre of the essay and a former editor of *The American Scholar*, one of the nation's most distinguished quarterlies, Anne Fadiman is the author of the essay collections *Ex Libris: Confessions of a Common Reader* and *At Large and At Small: Familiar Essays*. Her work has appeared in *The New Yorker*, *Harper's Magazine*, and the *New York Times*. Fadiman's book *The Spirit Catches You and You Fall Down* is an account of a Hmong family living with an epileptic daughter in California. This exploration of treating illness across a cultural divide won the 1997 National Book Critics Circle Award. Fadiman has also won National Magazine Awards and the 2012 Richard H. Brodhead Prize for Teaching Excellence at Yale University, where she was named the inaugural Francis Writer in Residence in 2005. "The Arctic Hedonist" (2004) charts Fadiman's long-time infatuation with the eccentric Arctic explorer Vilhjalmur Stefansson, who despite being "one of the greatest solo operators in history" was also, according to Fadiman, "a terrible leader."

The Arctic Hedonist

from *The American Scholar* (2004)

My father was an insomniac. He used to while away the small hours of the night with mental games, of which his favorite was called I Shook Hands with Shakespeare. He had shaken hands with the actress Cornelia Otis Skinner, who had in turn presumably shaken hands with her father, Otis Skinner. *He* had shaken hands with Edwin Booth . . . and so on, down through Junius Brutus Booth, Edmund Kean, David Garrick, Thomas Betterton, Sir William D'Avenant, and Richard Burbage. Finally, as dawn crept through the blinds, William Shakespeare extended his hand. (My father admitted a shaky manual link between Kean, who was born in 1787, and Garrick, who died in 1779.)

I myself have shaken hands with the arctic explorer Vilhjalmur Stefansson. Our degrees of separation number only two. Aware of my febrile interest in the history of polar exploration, my father once mentioned that, many years earlier, he had been introduced to Stefansson.

"*Stefansson?*" I panted. "What was he like?"

"The only thing I recall," said my father, "is his unfortunate smell."

I didn't hold this against Stefansson; it was part and parcel of being an explorer. (One of his expeditionary companions once noted that "he considers any attention to cleanliness, hygiene and camp sanitation as 'military fads.'") In any case, through Stefansson (or, in some cases, through people *he* met), I have also clasped hands with Robert E. Peary, Matthew Henson, Fridtjof Nansen, Roald Amundsen, Robert Falcon Scott, and Ernest Shackleton— the men who dominated the great period of Arctic and Antarctic exploration between 1880 and the First World War.

I have spent many nights establishing these bonds (*Let's see . . . Stefansson must have met Amundsen in 1906, when they were both at Herschel Island; Amundsen visited Nansen in Norway in 1900—or was it 1899?*), and, like my father, discovered that the handshaking game is far better at keeping one awake all night than at putting one to sleep.

The closest hand was the best; it still felt warm. For more than twenty years, I have therefore considered Vilhjalmur Stefansson "my explorer." During the course of three expeditions between 1906 and 1918, my explorer was the first white man to visit the Copper Inuit of Victoria Island; traveled twenty thousand miles by dogsled; discovered the world's last major landmasses, a series of islands in the Canadian archipelago; and set what a colleague called "the world's record for continuous Polar service" (five and a half years, an interval Stefansson considered nothing to boast about, since many of his Inuit friends had lived in the Arctic without apparent difficulty for more than eight decades).

What most endeared Stefansson to me was his conviction that the far north was not meant to be endured; it was meant to be enjoyed. If you knew what you were doing, you could have a "bully time" up there. His favorite temperature was -40°. (Temperatures below -50° were manageable but not quite so bully, since they required you to breathe through your mouth. "Your nose," he observed, "is less likely to freeze when there is cold air merely outside of it instead of both inside and out.") When he was above 66° north latitude, he insisted that his spirits were jollier, his appetite keener, and his wavy brown hair thicker. His most famous book, a 784-page account of his third expedition, was called *The Friendly Arctic*.

THE FRIENDLY ARCTIC? In 1921, when it was published, Macmillan might as well have brought out a book called *The Friendly Pit Viper*. The previous century had seen a series of arctic catastrophes, from Sir John Franklin's 1845 expedition in search of the Northwest Passage (130 dead of scurvy, starvation, and lead poisoning), to George Washington De Long's 1879 attempt to reach the North Pole from Siberia (20 dead of exposure, starvation, and drowning), to Adolphus Greely's 1881 expedition to Ellesmere Island (19 dead of exposure, starvation, and drowning). It was true that in 1909 Robert Peary claimed to have reached the North Pole, but he would have had a more comfortable journey had he not lost eight of his toes to frostbite on an earlier expedition.

The Friendly Arctic was an in-your-face title, and that's why Stefansson chose it. After all, he wrote, everyone knows what the Arctic is like:

> The land up there is all covered with eternal ice; there is everlasting winter with intense cold; and the corollary of the everlastingness of the winter is the absence of summer and the lack of vegetation. The country, whether land or sea, is a lifeless waste of eternal silence. The stars look down with a cruel glitter, and the depressing effect of the winter darkness upon the spirit of man is heavy beyond words. On the fringes of this desolation live the Eskimos, the filthiest and most benighted people on earth, pushed there by more powerful nations farther south, and eking out a miserable existence amidst hardship.

Wrong, wrong, wrong, wrong. Eternally icy? Montana, Stefansson explained, in the tone a parent might use to drum something obvious into an unusually dim-witted child, is far colder; arctic summers are hot; there are 762 species of arctic flowering plants. Silent? In the summer, the tundra resounds with the squawks of ducks, the cackles of geese, the cries of plovers, the screams of loons, and the howls of wolves (which, when heard on starlit nights, constitute "the most romantic sort of music"). Once the ice starts to freeze against the coast, there is a high-pitched screeching as one cake slides over the other, like the thousand-times magnified creaking of a rusty hinge. There is the crashing when cakes as big as a church wall, after being tilted on edge, finally pass beyond their equilibrium and topple down upon the ice; and when extensive floes, perhaps six or more feet in thickness, gradually bend under the resistless pressure of the pack until they buckle up and snap, there is a groaning as of supergiants in torment and a booming which at a distance of a mile or two sounds like a cannonade.

Depressing? According to Stefansson, "an Eskimo laughs as much in a month as the average white man does in a year." A benighted people? The Inuit are honest, considerate, courteous, hospitable, fun-loving, self-sufficient, and morally superior to any but the "rarest and best of our race."

In other words, the Arctic was not (as Peary had described it, using the sort of language to which readers had become accustomed) "a trackless, colorless, inhospitable desert"; it was a high-latitude Arcadia. Precipitation was light; gale-force winds were rare; water was abundant, even at sea, since salt leaches out of ice floes within a few seasons, rendering them deliciously fresh. Illness was infrequent; tuberculosis was seldom transmitted during the winter because "the spit is likely to freeze when it is voided." And the region flowed, if not with milk and honey, then with caribou, polar bear, walrus, and seals, all there for the taking (even if shooting seals beneath the polar ice "resembles hunting as we commonly think of it less than it does prospecting"). Why burden your sledges with heavy provisions, thereby limiting an expedition's duration and range, when, if you merely did what the Inuit had been doing for centuries, you could live off the land? "Do not let worry over to-morrow's breakfast interfere with your appetite at dinner," Stefansson liked to tell his men. "The friendly Arctic will provide."

If the Arctic was so friendly, it followed that you didn't need to be a masochist in order to explore it. Stefansson had nothing but contempt for "heroes who conquered the Frozen North," since he considered the Frozen North a myth and the metaphor of battle entirely wrongheaded (friends don't fight). He believed that this sort of bunkum had been invented to satisfy readers who, from the vantage of their overstuffed armchairs, found narratives of ease and pleasure less thrilling than hyperbolic accounts of "suffering, heroic perseverance against formidable odds, and tragedy either actual or narrowly averted." Stefansson's stance—partly a pose, but only partly—was that being an arctic explorer was no harder than any other job. He wrote to a friend that the prospect of returning to the far north was as pleasant as, and not much different from, the prospect of spending a winter in Heidelberg. Finding your way to a remote Inuit camp was "no more wonderful than knowing that a fifteen-minute walk will take you to the Flatiron Building from the Washington Arch." Why pretend you were bristling with machismo when living in the Arctic was a piece of cake?

I RECOGNIZED THE Stefansson shtick just last week when I was reading a German fairy tale to my seven-year-old son. Its plot revolved around a king who assigns progressively more impossible tasks to a cocksure young man— stealing a dragon's flying horse, stealing the dragon's coverlet, and finally stealing the dragon himself. The penalty for failure is death by dismemberment. Every time the king ups the ante, our hero says, "Is that all? That is easily done." In fairy tales, such characters are never punished for their bravado; they always perform their assigned tasks without breaking a sweat and end up marrying the king's daughter. In this case, the young man not only follows the prescribed formula for success but has the pleasure of seeing the dragon eat the king for dinner.

The voice of that young man is the same voice Tom Wolfe had so much fun with in *The Right Stuff,* that of the airline pilot who, as his plane seems about to crash, drawls into the intercom:

> "Now, folks, uh . . . this is the captain . . . ummmm . . . We've got a little ol' red light up here on the control panel that's tryin' to tell us that the *landin'* gears're not . . . uh . . . *lock*in' into position when we lower 'em . . . Now . . . *I* don't believe that little ol' red light knows what it's *talk*in' about—I believe it's that little ol' red *light* that iddn' workin' right" . . . faint chuckle, long pause, as if to say, *I'm not even sure all this is really worth going into— still, it may amuse you . . .." But* . . . I guess to play it by the rules, we oughta *hum*or that little ol' light . . ."

You know this pilot will never have an elevated pulse, never admit there's an emergency, and never crash the plane.

I first encountered this attitude of studied insouciance thirty years ago, when I took a wilderness course at the National Outdoor Leadership School in Wyoming, during an era of outdoorsmanship considerably more primitive than the present one. Our catchphrase was "No prob." Five weeks without tents or stoves? No prob. We slept under tarps suspended from trees and lit fires twice a day, forearming ourselves for rainy days by squirreling little bundles of dry sticks in our pockets—our six-foot-four-inch leader tenderly called them "twiggies," to underline how very cozy and unintimidating the whole venture was—just as Stefansson squirreled handfuls of dry *Cassiope tetragona* (arctic heather) in *his* pockets. No fancy freeze-dried food? No prob. We baked bread, pizzas, even birthday cakes by heaping hot coals on our frying pan lids, and cleaned the burnt pans with swags of limber pine, which we called Wind River Brillo. No food at all during the five-day "survival expedition" at the end of the course? No prob. We fished for trout and foraged for grouse whortleberries. Those five days were the hungriest of my life, but I wouldn't have dreamed of admitting it. (Stefansson: "Any traveler who complains about going three or four days without food will get scant sympathy from me.") That dragon was *easy* to steal.

A few years later, when I became an instructor at NOLS, the ratio of bluster to genuine *joie de vivre* declined precipitously. We pooh-poohed Outward Bound, our competitor in the wilderness-skills field, as unnecessarily anhedonic. OB promised to build character by asking its disciples to face fear and hardship; NOLS asked, as Stefansson had, "What hardship?" One winter we took out a group of mountaineering students for a couple of weeks to climb Wind River Peak on skis. It was ten below zero, but we built both a small igloo and a gigantic snow cave, in whose toasty precincts we threw off most of our clothes and stretched as luxuriously as cats next to a radiator. At night, when we schussed the snowfields above Deep Creek Lakes, the hoarfrost reflected the full moon, and it was almost as bright as day.

This was small stuff, and very long ago. But, years later, it was enough to make me understand what Stefansson meant when he described hunting caribou on Banks Island on a cold, clear day: "In his exuberance of good health it is difficult for the arctic hunter to feel anything but pleasure in almost any kind of weather or almost any circumstance. I suppose what I am trying to explain is about what the Biblical writer had in mind when he spoke of a strong man rejoicing to run a race."

STEFANSSON HAD JUST the sort of upbringing you'd expect: pioneer-style, in a one-room cabin in the Dakota Territory, with scant food but plenty of Norse sagas recited in the evening by his Icelandic parents, who had emigrated first to Manitoba and then to the United States. When he was eighteen, he set himself up as a winter grazier, caring for the livestock of local farmers. The great blizzard of 1897 hit during his first season, and all his assistants quit, unwilling to work on skis or shovel their way into barns buried in snowdrifts. No prob. Stefansson carried on alone and, of course (because the young man in the fairy tale never labors in vain), didn't lose a single head of cattle.

At the University of North Dakota, Stefansson was thrown out of his boardinghouse for espousing Darwinism and then expelled from college for spotty attendance and "a spirit of insubordination." (His fellow students staged a mock funeral; his hearse was a wheelbarrow, his widow a black-clad classmate whose tears were facilitated by an onion wrapped in a handkerchief.) No prob. After finishing up at the University of Iowa and attending graduate school at Harvard, where he switched his field from divinity to anthropology, he was offered the post of ethnologist on the 1906 Anglo-American Polar Expedition to northwest Canada. He and his expedition never ended up intersecting, since he traveled overland to the Mackenzie Delta—solo, of course—and the ship that carried his colleagues failed to penetrate the ice beyond Point Barrow, two hundred miles to the west. No prob. He spent the winter living with the Inuit, collecting ethnographic artifacts, learning Inuktitut, and formulating his belief that the only way to get along in the Arctic was to dress and hunt and eat like a local. "I was gradually being broken in to native ways," he wrote.

> By the middle of October, I had thrown away my nearly outworn woollen suit and was fur clad from head to heel, an Eskimo to the skin. I never regretted the lack of a single item of such arctic clothing as money can buy in America or Europe.... A reasonably healthy body is all the equipment a white man needs for a comfortable winter among the arctic Eskimos.

Two more expeditions followed, one primarily ethnographic, the other geographic and scientific. By the end of his tenth arctic winter, Stefansson was the uncontested master of what he called "polarcraft," a body of knowledge he later codified in a volume called the *Arctic Manual*. Although it was commissioned by the U.S. Army as a survival guide for Air Corps fliers who made emergency landings in the far north, its author couldn't resist transforming it into a how-to book on what *he* liked to do—live off the land, with minimal provisions, for years at a time. (For instance, a downed flier would be unlikely to make use of his suggestion that the best caribou-skin clothes are made by Inuit seamstresses with whom one has been acquainted for several seasons.)

The *Arctic Manual* is my favorite Stefansson book. The chances that I will ever need to apply its lessons may be slim. But just as devotees of Martha Stewart feel more secure knowing they could make a wedding centerpiece from belt buckles and gumdrops, even if they never actually *have* to, so I derive a certain degree of comfort from reading and rereading Stefansson's arctic tips. It reassures me to know that pussy willow fuzz can be used for the wick of a seal-oil lamp. That two lemon-sized chunks of iron pyrite, struck together, will start a fire faster than matches. That it is possible to cook with the hair and wool of a musk ox or grizzly bear, one hide being sufficient for two or three eight-quart pots. That if you are not ashore during the spring thaw, you should select a thick floe on which to spend the summer, and resume your travel in the fall. That a dead seal can be easily dragged, but a polar bear tends to flip upside down. That you should not rub decayed caribou brains on your clothes, since the hides will stiffen. That one advantage of skin boats is that they can be boiled and eaten. That the best way to approach a seal you wish to shoot is to look like a seal yourself: wear dark clothing, wriggle along the ice, and occasionally flex your legs from the knees as if scratching lice with your hind flippers.

It is important to understand that these pieces of advice are offered in a spirit not of grit-teethed stoicism—*I may be facing death, but, by God, at least I know enough not to rub decayed caribou brains on my clothes*—but of casual bonhomie, as if the author and the reader were in perfect agreement that this stuff is *fun*. Stefansson wasn't a survivor; he was a voluptuary. Why would anyone wish to wear wool when "nothing feels so good against the skin—not even silk—as underwear of the skin of a young caribou"? Why live in a house when an igloo, lit with a single candle, resembles "a hemisphere of diamonds"? Why employ Inuit or Indians to do one's hunting when one could have the thrill of doing it oneself? "I would as soon think of engaging a valet to play my golf," he observed, "or of going to the theatre by proxy."

Stefansson admitted that his hunting had not always been fruitful. In lean times he had eaten snowshoe lashings, sealskins intended for boot soles, and the remains of a bowhead whale that had been beached for four years. (It tasted like felt.) But when the Arctic chose to show its friendly aspect, its cuisine practically made him swoon. Frozen raw polar bear meat had the consistency of raw oysters; half-frozen, it was more like ice cream. The soft, sweet ends of mammal, bird, and fish bones were scrumptious. Seal-blood soup, an especial favorite, warranted a recipe that might have intrigued Brillat-Savarin:

> When the meat has been sufficiently cooked it is removed from the pot which is still hanging over the fire. Blood is then poured slowly into the boiling broth with brisk stirring the while. In winter small chunks of frozen blood dropped in one after the other take the place of the liquid blood poured in summer. . . . The consistency of the prepared dish should be about that of "English pea soup."

The pinnacle of northern fare was caribou flesh: in ascending order of "gustatory delight," the brisket, ribs, and vertebrate; the tongue; the head, especially the fat behind the eyes; the little lump of fat near the patella of the hind leg; and the marrow of the bones near the hoof, which was generally rolled into little balls and eaten raw. Stefansson maintained that a high-fat, all-meat diet not only pleased the palate but also cured depression, prevented scurvy, reduced tooth decay, and relieved constipation. (When he was in his late forties and living in New York City, he undertook to prove his nutritional theories by spending a year, under the supervision of Bellevue Hospital, on an exclusively carnivorous diet. Not only did he remain healthy, but he was proud to report that X-rays revealed an "unusual . . . absence of gas from the intestinal tract during the meat-eating period.")

Given the abundance of northern pleasures, it is not surprising that Stefansson envisioned a time when the Arctic would be viewed not as the end of the earth but as a vital crossroads. Musk oxen and reindeer would be domesticated for world consumption, "not for the exclusive delectation of wolves, wolverines, foxes and ravens." The skies would be filled with airplanes traveling the shortest routes between New York, London, Moscow, and Peking; the seas would be filled with submarines. In his book *The Northward Course of Empire*, he reproduced a graph conceived by an American sociologist named S. Columb Gil-Fillan. The horizontal axis was chronological, from 3400 B.C. to 2200 A.D.: the vertical axis was meteorological. The great world centers were arrayed along this graph, with Upper Egypt (mean annual temperature 77°) succeeded by Athens (63°), Rome (59°), Constantinople (57°), London (50°), and Moscow (39°), among others. The implication was clear: in a few hundred years the Arctic would be the nexus of civilization.

MY STEFANSSON SHELF grew over the years, augmented by birthday contributions from my husband. The books, all out of print, were beautiful old volumes with tissue-thin maps tucked in pockets at the back. They were all *by* Stefansson. It was only when I started work on this essay that I bought a half-dozen books *about* Stefansson. And that is where the probs began.

I learned that not everyone liked my explorer as much as I did. After Stefansson visited Australia on a lecture tour in 1925, a *Sydney Bulletin* reporter observed delicately that "our late visitor . . . is a many sided man. I would call him nothing less than an Hexagon, and he may even be an irregular crystal." Controversial during his lifetime (his peers thought him a publicity hound, his bosses thought him a troublesome maverick), Stefansson has attracted a new round of criticism in recent years—the same period of polar revisionism during which Peary was accused of fraud and Scott was exposed as a dangerous bumbler. The two most serious charges are that Stefansson abandoned his Inuit family and that he was responsible for the deaths of eleven men on his third expedition.

For two decades I had read Stefansson's laconic references to Fannie Pannigabluk, the widowed seamstress who accompanied him and his friend Natkusiak on much of his second expedition. It had never occurred to me that she was Stefansson's mistress; after all, he noted several times that every expedition required an Inuit seamstress to make and repair caribou-hide and sealskin clothing. Gísli Pálsson, an Icelandic anthropologist who has interviewed four of Stefansson's Inuit grandchildren, writes, "Pannigabluk was presented as primarily a domestic worker, with no formal recognition of her role as either spouse, partner, or key informant." Stefansson never publicly acknowledged either the relationship or the son it produced; nor, apparently, did he provide financial support. It is true that Robert Peary and Matthew

Henson also had sons by Inuit women, and that both of them jettisoned their families in similar fashion. Peary went a step further and published a nude photograph of his mistress. But *Stefansson*? The man who wrote of the Inuit, "I cannot see how anyone who knows them can wish more for anything than that he was rich and could repay their kindness fully"?

The accusations that swirl around Stefansson's third expedition allege an even more serious abandonment. In July of 1913, the HMCS *Karluk* steamed out of Port Clarence, Alaska, en route to the Beaufort Sea, with Stefansson and half the members of the Canadian Arctic Expedition on board. (The rest were on two other ships, bound for scientific work in the Northwest Territories.) By mid-August, the *Karluk* was icebound. In mid-September, Stefansson, accompanied by three staff members and two Inuit, left the ship on a ten-day trip, ostensibly to provide fresh caribou for his men. Two days later, the sixty-mile-an-hour winds of the season's first blizzard dislodged the *Karluk*'s ice floe, and the ship drifted hundreds of miles to the west, far out of Stefansson's reach. The *Karluk* was eventually crushed in the ice, and most of its men made their way to Wrangel Island, north of Siberia. They suffered severe hardships there—starvation, snow blindness, frostbite, gangrene, and, in one case, the amputation of a toe with the tin shears used to make cooking pots from empty gasoline containers. Eleven died. Many years later, one of the survivors wrote: "Not all the horrors of the Western Front, not the rubble of Arras, nor the hell of Ypres, nor all the mud of Flanders leading to Passchendaele, could blot out the memories of that year in the Arctic."

It is indisputable that Stefansson left the ship; the question is whether he intended to return. In *The Ice Master: The Doomed 1913 Voyage of the* Karluk, Jennifer Niven argues that he did not: caribou were scarce in the area; he left his best hunters on board the *Karluk*; and—the most damning evidence—the ship's meteorologist believed that Stefansson, who had been observed reading the diaries from De Long's catastrophic 1879 expedition two days before he departed, left the ship "for fear of losing his life."

The Canadian historian Richard J. Diubaldo disagrees, in his scrupulously fair-minded biography *Stefansson and the Canadian Arctic*, he argues that "there is strong evidence to suggest that he wished he had never left." I share his view. If Stefansson had no intention of returning, why did he leave his chronometer and thirteen hundred dollars on board? Why did he leave detailed instructions on the flags and beacons that were to guide his return over the ice? Why didn't he take the best sledges? After the blizzard, why did he hasten west along the coast to Cape Smythe, if not to overtake the *Karluk*?

I think Stefansson took off for a week because he couldn't bear to be on board a ship that wasn't moving, couldn't bear to sit around playing bridge or listening to his men give concerts on the mandolin and harmonica. Stasis was poison to him. But whether or not he abandoned ship, I am now convinced that he is responsible for the deaths of his men. He assembled the expedition hastily, recruiting an inexperienced crew that included a drug addict who carried his hypodermic needles around in a pocket-sized case. He insisted on using a ship that had been declared unsound by his captain. And though he was one of the greatest solo operators in history, he was a terrible leader. He had no idea how to organize large groups of men or large amounts of cargo, and he had so little regard for his staff and crew that, instead of welcoming them as soon as he arrived at the naval yard from which the *Karluk* would soon embark, he kept them waiting while he held a five-hour press conference.

Worst of all was his cavalier attitude toward the men he lost. His journal entry from August 11, 1915, when he heard the news, disposes of their fate in two sentences and then goes on to discuss possible ship charters. He blamed his men for being less competent than he would have been in their situation—in effect, for being so foolish as to succumb to the myth of the Frozen North. Did he fail to realize that *The Friendly Arctic* might not be the most tasteful title for a book about a botched venture on which eleven people died?

THE FRONTISPIECE OF *The Friendly Arctic* is a black-and-white photograph of Stefansson dragging a seal across the ice. He is wearing mukluks and a caribou-skin parka. Under his right arm he carries a rifle; under his left, a harpoon. His head is bare, and he is alone.

He selected the picture while he was living at the Harvard Club in New York City, beginning a feverish career of lecturing and writing that made him, in the words of one biographer. "the equivalent of a senior officer who has become too valuable to go out on combat patrols, and must sit at his headquarters surrounded by his staff." He shelved his plans to camp on an ice floe with one or two companions, moving with the polar drift for a couple of years. Instead, from his desk, he organized abortive schemes to colonize Wrangel Island and breed reindeer on Baffin Island. He lived for forty-four years after he returned from his third expedition, and—because of illness, because his reputation in Canada declined, because he had kicked himself permanently upstairs—he never traveled in the Arctic again.

It is not as great a tragedy as the abandonment of one's family, not as great as the loss of eleven lives, but it is nonetheless a tragedy that when *The Friendly Arctic* appeared, the Macmillan Company could not include the same note it had inserted before the title page of *My Life with the Eskimo* in 1913:

NOTE TO THE FIRST EDITION

The publishers regret that owing to Mr. Stefansson's departure on his new expedition to the far North he was unable to read the final proofs of this volume.

Herodotus
(ca. 484–ca. 425–414 BCE)

CICERO DUBBED HERODOTUS "the father of history." While historians today no longer take the liberties their father took with facts, Herodotus's sense of narrative—his shaping of events to tell a particular kind of story—still distinguishes the practice of history. Herodotus was, as Bernard Knox observes, "the first writer we know of to recreate, on an epic scale, the remote and immediate past of his contemporary world." Herodotus was born in Halicarnassus, in modern Turkey, which was at the time dominated by the Persian Empire. When Herodotus was still a child, a Greek coalition defeated the Persian Xerxes at Thermopylae and in the sea battle of Salamis (480 BCE). In the years that followed, Athens and Sparta grew in power until their rivalry broke out in the Peloponnesian Wars, which continued throughout Herodotus's adult life. Drawing on oral sources and folk wisdom, Herodotus's work is an amalgam of history, geography, and ethnography. Traveling extensively throughout Asia Minor and Greece, he ranged as far as Babylon, Egypt, Tyre, and the Black Sea. This excerpt from *The Histories* centers on Croesus (ca. 560–546 BCE), the ruler of Lydia, who was vanquished by the Persian Cyrus. The Polish journalist Ryszard Kapuscinski, who followed the historian's path, suggests in *Travels with Herodotus* that Croesus's fate illustrates the "second law" of Herodotus: "*Human happiness never remains long in the same place.*" Herodotus narrates Croesus's dispute with the Athenian sage Solon, the king's repeated misreadings of oracles, his resultant personal and political losses, and an exchange with Cyrus. (The following selections are translated by Walter Blanco.)

The Story of Croesus
from *The Histories*

After Croesus added these conquered people to the Lydian empire, all the sages living in Greece at that time began to visit Sardis at the height of its wealth. Each came for his own reasons, especially Solon the Athenian, who had written laws for the Athenians at their command, and had then gone abroad for ten years. He sailed away on the pretext of seeing the world, but it was really so that he could not be compelled to repeal any of the laws he had laid down. That was something the Athenians were not able to do on their own, because they were bound by solemn oaths to obey for ten years whatever laws Solon had made for them.

So for these reasons—as well as to see the world—Solon left home to visit Amasis in Egypt and especially Croesus in Sardis. When he arrived, he was feasted in the palace by Croesus. Three or four days later, at Croesus' command, servants took Solon on a tour of the treasury and showed him how great and prosperous everything was. In due time, after Solon had observed and considered everything, Croesus asked, "Many stories have come to us, my Athenian guest, about your wisdom and your travels—how you have roamed around and seen so much of the world in your quest for knowledge. Well, this urge has come over me to ask you whether you have so far seen anybody you consider to be more fortunate than all other men."

He asked this expecting that the most fortunate of men would turn out to be himself. Solon did not use any delicate flattery, but told him the straight truth: "Tellus the Athenian, O King."

Croesus was amazed at what he said, and asked severely, "What makes you think that Tellus was so fortunate!"

Solon said, "In the first place, Tellus came from a thriving city and had honest, handsome sons. Also, he saw them all have children, all of whom survived. In the second place, he had a prosperous life, by our standards, and the end of that life was glorious. He came to the rescue during a battle between the Athenians and their neighbors in Eleusis and died nobly after breaking the enemy's ranks. The Athenians honored him highly and buried him at the public expense right where he fell."

Solon had piqued Croesus with all that he had said about Tellus' good fortune, but Croesus, fully believing that he would at least come in second, asked who the next most fortunate might be.

Instead, Solon said, "Cleobis and Biton. They were Argives who made a good living and in addition to that had great physical strength. They were both prizewinning athletes, and this is the story most often told about them. The Argives were celebrating the feast of Hera, and it was absolutely necessary for their mother to be brought to the temple in her oxcart. But the oxen did not arrive from the field in time. Seeing that they were running out of time, the young men slipped in under the yoke themselves and dragged the wagon along with their mother riding in it. They arrived at the temple after covering over five and a half miles. Their action was seen by the entire congregation, and it was followed by the finest end a life can have. In it, god showed plainly through Cleobis and Biton that it is better for a man to die than to live.

"The Argive men gathered around congratulating the young men on their strength, while the women congratulated their mother. What sons she had! The mother was overjoyed both with the deed and with the praise. She stood before the statue of Hera and prayed that the goddess would give to her sons, Cleobis and Biton, who had honored her so highly, the very best thing that it was possible for a human being to have. After this prayer, while everyone was sacrificing and feasting, the young men lay down to sleep in that very same temple and never rose up again, transfixed in death. The Argives made the kind of statues of them that are made only for the very greatest men and dedicated them in Delphi."

Solon, then, gave the second prize for happiness to these two, and Croesus angrily said, "So then, my Athenian guest, as far as you are concerned, our prosperity amounts to nothing, and you do not even consider us on a par with private citizens!"

Solon said, "When you ask me about human affairs, you ask someone who knows how jealous and provocative god is. In the fullness of time, a man must see many things he doesn't want to see, and endure many things he doesn't want to endure. I'll set the limit of a person's life at seventy years. In those seventy years there are twenty-five thousand two hundred days, not counting any months thrown in. But if you make every other year longer by a month so that the seasons come around to the right place, then besides the seventy years there are thirty-five months, or one thousand and fifty days. All in all, then, these seventy years add up to twenty-six thousand two hundred and fifty days, and from one day to the next absolutely nothing happens the same way twice. Thus, my dear Croesus, humans are the creatures of pure chance.

"Now, you seem to me to be very rich and to be the monarch of many people, but I couldn't say anything about this question you keep asking me until I find out that you have ended your life well, because the rich man isn't any better off than the man who has enough for his everyday needs unless his luck stays with him and he keeps on having the best of everything until he dies happily. Many people who are super rich are unlucky, you know, while many lucky people are just moderately well-off. Now, the very rich but unlucky man has only two advantages over the lucky man, while the lucky man has many advantages over the unlucky rich man. First, the rich man is better able to gratify his desires, and second, he is able to afford the trouble they bring. The lucky man, on the other hand, is better off than the unlucky rich man in these ways: while he is not as able to afford desire and trouble, his good luck keeps these things away from him. He suffers no bodily harm, he doesn't get sick, he experiences no misfortunes, he has good children, and he is handsome. If, in addition to all this, he dies happily, then he is the one you are looking for—the man who deserves to be called happy. Until he dies, though, you must hold off and not call him happy—just lucky.

"Of course, it is impossible for a mere mortal to combine all these things, just as no country is completely sufficient unto itself. It will have this, but it will lack that. The one that has the most—that one is the best. Thus, no one person is self-sufficient: he will have one thing, but he will be lacking in another. To me, whoever has the most of these things, and keeps on having them, and then happily ends his life, he is the one, Your Highness, who rightly carries the title you seek. You have to see how everything turns out, for god gives a glimpse of happiness to many people, and then tears them up by the very roots."

Solon did not at all please Croesus with what he said, and Croesus dismissed him without ceremony, thinking that someone who set aside the present good and urged you to look at how things turned out was a complete ignoramus.

After Solon left, though, Croesus got his great comeuppance from god, I suppose because he thought that he was the happiest man in the world. As soon as he fell asleep that night, a dream came to him which showed him the truth about the disaster that would happen to his son. Croesus had two sons. One was a cripple—a deaf mute—and the other was by far the most outstanding young man of his generation. His name was Atys. Now, the dream showed Croesus that he would lose Atys through a wound from an iron spearhead. When he woke up, he gave this dreadful dream a great deal of thought. First, he chose a wife for his son. Also, Atys had been accustomed to command Lydian military forces, but Croesus no longer sent him anywhere on business of that kind. He took spears and javelins and all such weapons of war out of the men's living quarters and heaped them up in the women's bedrooms, lest one of them fall from a wall onto his son.

While Croesus was busy with the arrangements for his son's wedding, a man in the grip of a great misfortune came to Sardis, a man with blood on his hands. He was of Phrygian descent and belonged to the royal family. He came to Croesus' home and begged to be cleansed of his guilt according to the customs of the country; and Croesus purged his guilt away. The Lydian rite of purification is very similar to the Greek. After Croesus performed the customary ritual, he asked him who he was and where he came from, saying, "Who are you, stranger, and what part of Phrygia have you come from to be a suppliant at my hearth? What man or woman did you kill?"

He answered, "I am the son of Gordias, the son of Midas, Your Highness, and my name is Adrastus. I accidentally killed my own brother, and I am here because I was driven away and completely disinherited by my father."

Croesus replied: "You are descended from friends, and you have come among friends. Remain with us, where you shall want for nothing. You will gain all the more if you bear this misfortune as lightly as possible."

And so Adrastus lived with Croesus.

At the same time, a monster of a boar appeared on Mount Olympus, in Mysias. He kept coming down from the mountain and destroying the fields and crops of the Mysians. The Mysians often went after him, but they could never do him any harm—he harmed them instead. Finally, some Mysian messengers went to Croesus and said, "A monster boar has appeared on our land, Your Majesty, and destroys our crops. We have tried our hardest to catch him, but we can't. We beg you to send your son with some dogs and some handpicked young men back with us so that we can drive this animal from our land."

That is what they asked for, but Croesus remembered the message of the dream and said this to them: "Forget about my son—I couldn't send him with you. He is newly married, and that's what's on his mind now. I will, though, send the picked men and my whole pack of hunting dogs, and I'll order everyone who goes with you to do his utmost to rid your land of this beast."

That was his answer, and the Mysians were satisfied with it, but Croesus' son went up to him after hearing their request. Because Croesus was refusing to send him with them, the young man said, "The finest and noblest thing I once had was my reputation for hunting and fighting. But now you keep me away from both of them, though you don't see any cowardice or lack of enthusiasm in me. What kind of face am I supposed to wear when I go in and out of the marketplace? How do you suppose I look to my fellow citizens—to my bride! What kind of man will she think she's living with? Now, you must either let me go out after this animal or give me a good reason why what you have done is better for me."

Croesus said, "Son, I'm not doing this because I see any cowardice or other fault in you. A dream vision hovered over me in my sleep and said that you would have a short life because you would be killed by an iron spearpoint. It was because of this vision that I hurried up your marriage and will not send you out on this mission. I'm protecting you so that maybe I can steal you away from death while I live. You are my only son—I don't count that cripple as mine."

The young man answered, "I excuse you for protecting me after seeing such a vision. But you didn't understand it—the dream's meaning escaped you, and it's right that I should explain it to you. Now, you say that the dream told you that I would die because of an iron spearpoint. But what kind of hands does a boar have, and what kind of iron spearpoint are you so afraid of? If the dream had said that I would be killed by a tusk or by something else that belongs to this animal, then you would have to do what you are doing. But it was by a spear! So since this is not a battle against men, let me go."

Croesus answered, "Somehow, son, you've gotten the best of me with your interpretation of this dream, and since I've lost, I'll change my mind and let you go on the hunt."

After saying this, though, Croesus sent for Adrastus the Phrygian, and when he arrived, Croesus told him, "Adrastus, when you were struck down by your terrible misfortune—for which I do not blame you—I purged your guilt, welcomed you into my home, and took care of all your expenses. Now you owe me a favor in return for the favor I did for you. I want you to be my son's bodyguard while he goes out on this hunt in case any highwaymen show up and try to do you any harm on the road. Besides, you ought to go where you, too, can shine by your deeds. That is your birthright, and, anyway, you have the strength for it."

Adrastus answered, "Ordinarily I would not go on this mission. It's not fitting for me, after my terrible experience, to go among successful men my own age. I don't want to—and there are many reasons why I'd keep myself away from it. But now, since you insist, and since I must please you (for I do have an obligation to return your favors), I am ready to do this, and you can expect that your son, whom you order me to guard, will return none the worse for my protection."

After he gave Croesus this answer, the party set out, provided with picked men and dogs. When they arrived at Mount Olympus, they started hunting for the beast, and when they found it, they stood around it in a circle and hurled their spears at it. At that moment the stranger, the one who had been purged of his homicide, the man called Adrastus, hurled his spear at the boar but missed it and hit the son of Croesus instead. Atys, struck with the point of the spear, fulfilled the prophecy of the dream.

Someone started running to Croesus to report the news. When he arrived in Sardis, this messenger told Croesus about the fight with the animal and the fate of his son. Croesus was utterly bewildered by his son's death and was especially outraged that the man who had killed him was the man he had purged of a homicide. He became so furious over the calamity that he bitterly invoked Zeus as "the Purifier," and called on him to witness what he had suffered from the stranger. Croesus also invoked the very same god under the epithets of "the God of Hospitality," and "the God of Friendship"—the God of Hospitality because he had unknowingly welcomed the stranger who was to be the killer of his son into his home and fed him, and the God of Friendship because he had sent that man as a protector and found him to be an enemy.

Later, the Lydians appeared bearing the corpse, with the killer following behind it. Then Adrastus stood in front of the body and with outstretched hands tried to surrender himself to Croesus, demanding to have his throat cut over the corpse. He talked about his first misfortune, and how on top of that he had destroyed the man who had cleansed him, and how he was not fit to live. Even though he was in his own private grief, Croesus pitied Adrastus when he heard these words and said, "I have all the justice I want from you, stranger, since you have pronounced a sentence of death on yourself. Besides, you are not the cause of my troubles; you just unwillingly brought them about. It was some god, who long ago foretold what the future would be."

Croesus gave his son a fitting burial. Then, after people had left, when all was quiet around the tomb, Adrastus, the son of Gordias, the son of Midas, he who was the killer of his own brother and, in a way, the killer of the man who had purged his guilt, believing himself to be the unluckiest man he had ever known, cut his own throat over the grave.

For two years, Croesus sat idle, in deep mourning over the loss of his son. Then, when the empire of Astyages, the son of Cyaxares, was destroyed by Cyrus, the son of Cambyses, the growing strength of the Persians put an end to Croesus' grief, and he began to ponder whether he could seize that growing Persian power before it became too great. As soon as he had formed this intention, he tested the oracles in Greece and the one in Libya. He sent messengers off in different directions—some to Delphi, some to Abae, in Phocis, some to Dodona. Some were sent to Amphiaraus and to Trophonius, and some to Branchidae in Milesia. Those were the Greek oracles to which Croesus sent off messengers for consultation, while he dispatched others to consult the oracle of Ammon in Libya. He sent them to test what the oracles knew, so that if he found that they gave true opinions he could send to them a second time to ask whether he should try to make war on Persia.

He sent the Lydians to test the oracles after giving them the following command: beginning with the day they set out from Sardis, they should count the remaining days until they came to the hundredth day. Then they should consult the oracle, asking what Croesus, the son of Alyattes and king of the Lydians, happened to be doing. They should write down whatever prophecies each of the oracles gave and then bring them back to him. Now, no one can say what the other oracles prophesied, but at Delphi, as soon as the Lydians entered the temple to consult the god and ask the question they had been ordered to ask, the Pythian priestess, speaking in hexameters, said:

> And I know the number of the sands and the dimensions of the sea,
> And I understand the mute, and hear those who do not speak.
> Into my brain comes the smell of the strong-shelled tortoise
> Seething in bronze with the flesh of lambs,
> Bronze spread beneath it and covered with bronze above.

The Lydians wrote down the prophecy of the priestess and set off for Sardis. When all the others who had been sent abroad were present with their prophecies, Croesus unfolded each of the writing tablets and read over its contents. None of them pleased him, but when he heard the one from Delphi, he immediately accepted it and said a prayer, in the belief that the only real oracle was the one in Delphi, because it had figured out what he had been doing. You see, after he had sent his messengers to consult the oracles, he came up with the following idea while waiting for the appointed day—it was something no one should be able to figure out or guess. He himself had chopped up a turtle and a lamb and then boiled them together in a bronze pot topped with a bronze lid.

·　·　·

Croesus commanded those who were going to deliver the gifts to the shrines to ask the oracles whether he should make war on Persia and whether he should conclude a friendly alliance with any other army. When they came to the oracles to which they had been sent, the Lydians dedicated the offerings and consulted the oracles, saying, "Croesus, king of the Lydians and of other peoples, in the belief that you are mankind's only true oracles, has given you gifts to match the discoveries you made and now asks you whether he should make war on Persia and whether he should conclude an alliance with any other army."

That is what they asked, and the oracles were of one mind: they prophesied to Croesus that if he made war on Persia, he would destroy a great empire. They also advised him to find out who the most powerful Greeks were and to befriend them.

When the answers were brought back to Croesus, he was overjoyed with the oracles and expected to destroy Cyrus' empire quickly. After finding out its population, he sent again to Pythia with gifts for the Delphians: two staters of gold for each man. In return, the Delphians gave Croesus and the Lydians rights of first consultation without a fee, front-row seats at Pythian games and festivals, and the right, in perpetuity, for any Lydian who so desired to become a citizen of Delphi.

Having regaled the Delphians with these gifts, Croesus consulted the oracle for a third time, for after he had gotten the truth from the oracle, he used it to the full. He asked whether his monarchy would last for a long time. And the Pythian priestess said this:

> But when a mule becomes king of the Medes,
> Do not stay then, tender-footed Lydian,
> But flee to the many-pebbled banks of the Hermus
> And do not be ashamed to be a coward.

When they returned with these verses, Croesus was more pleased with them than with anything else because he believed that a mule would never rule over the Medes instead of a man and that therefore neither he nor any of his descendants would ever cease to reign.

·   ·   ·

"Master," said Croesus [to Cyrus, the Persian king, by whom he had been defeated], "you will make me most happy if you let me send these fetters to the god of the Greeks, the one I honored above all other gods, and to ask him whether it is his custom to deceive those who serve him well." Cyrus asked him what complaint he had against the god in making this request. Croesus went back to the beginning and told him about his intentions, about the oracles' answers, and especially his offerings, and about how, encouraged by the prophecy, he had made war on Persia. After relating all this, he ended up by again asking to be allowed to blame the god for the whole thing. Cyrus laughed and said, "You will get this from me, Croesus, and anything else you want whenever you want it."

When Croesus heard this, he sent some Lydians to Delphi with instructions to lay the fetters at the threshold of the temple and to ask whether the god was not ashamed to have egged Croesus on with prophecies to make war on Persia when that meant that the power of Croesus would be destroyed—from which, they were to say as they showed the fetters, the god got firstfruits such as these. They should ask this, as well as whether it was customary for Greek gods to be so ungrateful.

It is said that the Lydians arrived and gave their messages and that the Pythian priestess told them this: "Even a god cannot avoid what has been foreordained. Croesus makes up for the crime of his ancestor five generations ago, that bodyguard of the Heraclids who truckled to a woman's guile, killed his master, and took a title that did not belong to him. Loxian Apollo would have liked the suffering of Sardis to happen in the time of Croesus' sons, and not in the time of Croesus, but he could not get around the Fates. Yet he granted as many favors as they allowed. He put off the fall of Sardis by three years—so let Croesus know that his capture came three years later than the appointed time. In addition to this, Loxias helped him when he was being burned alive. And, as far as the actual prophecy is concerned, Croesus complains about it unfairly, for Loxias prophesied to him that if he made war on Persia he would destroy a great empire. Now, if he was going to plan well, he ought to have sent someone to ask in response to this whether the god meant Cyrus' empire or his own. But he did not understand what was said and he did not ask any further questions, so he has no one to blame but himself. As to the last thing he consulted the oracle about, Loxias said what he said about the mule, and Croesus did not understand that, either. Cyrus was really the mule because he was born to two people who were not of the same race, and his mother was superior to his father. She was a Mede and the daughter of Astyages, king of the Medes, while his father was a Persian—their subject—who lived with his own queen though he was beneath her in every way."

That was the answer the Pythian priestess gave to the Lydians, who brought it back to Sardis and repeated it to Croesus. He heard it, and acknowledged that the fault was his and not the god's.

Plutarch
(ca. 45–120)

PERHAPS THE MOST widely read of Plutarch's biographies of Greek and Roman statesmen and soldiers is that of Alexander the Great, an enigmatic figure whose march across the world continues to command our curiosity across the millennia. The intrepid twentieth-century British traveler Freya Stark once decided to follow his march through Turkey. We know Alexander primarily as a figure of conquest and war, but Stark's *In Alexander's Path: A Travel Memoir* makes the case that Alexander's was less the sensibility of the conqueror than that of the traveler. In reimagining Alexander as motivated less by territorial ambition than by a "passion for exploration," Stark highlights the figure of Alexander as adventurer and dreamer rather than destroyer: he weeps on the banks of the Beas River in the Punjab, where his soldiers mutinied, "not for the unfinished conquest . . . but for the unsolved problem" of surveying and mapping the outer reaches of the known world, "with which his mind was busy when he died." Animated by "the explorer's readiness for the unknown," Alexander's "path" in Stark's account is in the end an empire of the imagination: he conquered the world, but long after that conquest had dissolved he has continued "to hold its imagination as long as histories are written." Stark insists: "No empire before or since has been so persuasive, nor has any conversion except a religious one been so complete and widespread as was his hellenizing of the Asiatic world." Plutarch's biography, capturing Alexander's creative and destructive visions, presents a portrait of contradictions: his intellect and learning; his appreciation for wisdom in its poetic and philosophical forms; his impetuosity and unceasing restlessness; and his driving ambition to outshine the accomplishments of the mythical Achilles, the great warrior of Homer's *Iliad*. (The following excerpt comes from the seventeenth-century Dryden translation.)

Alexander
from *Lives*

Doubtless also it was to Aristotle that he owed the inclination he had, not to the theory only, but likewise to the practice of the art of medicine. For when any of his friends were sick, he would often prescribe them their course of diet, and medicines proper to their disease, as we may find in his epistles. He was naturally a great lover of all kinds of learning and reading; and Onesicritus informs us that he constantly laid Homer's Iliads, according to the copy corrected by Aristotle, called the casket copy, with his dagger under his pillow, declaring that he esteemed it a perfect portable treasure of all military virtue and knowledge. When he was in the upper Asia, being destitute of other books, he ordered Harpalus [his treasurer] to send him some; who furnished him with Philistus' History, a great many of the plays of Euripides, Sophocles, and Æschylus, and some dithyrambic odes, composed by Telestes and Philoxenus.

.   .   .

Soon after, the Grecians [Alexander's destruction of Thebes], being assembled at the Isthmus, declared their resolution of joining with Alexander in the war against the Persians, and proclaimed him their general. While he stayed here, many public ministers and philosophers came from all parts to visit him and congratulated him on his election, but contrary to his expectation, Diogenes of Sinope, who then was living at Corinth, thought so little of him, that instead of coming to compliment him, he never so much as stirred out of the suburb called the Cranium, where Alexander found him lying along in the sun. When he saw so much company near him, he raised himself a little, and vouchsafed to look upon Alexander; and when he kindly asked him whether he wanted anything, "Yes," said he, "I would have you stand from between me and the sun." Alexander was so struck at this answer, and surprised at the greatness of the man, who had taken so little notice of him, that as he went away he told his followers, who were laughing at the moroseness of the philosopher, that if he were not Alexander, he would choose to be Diogenes.

Then he went to Delphi, to consult Apollo concerning the success of the war he had undertaken, and happening to come on one of the forbidden days, when it was esteemed improper to give any answer from the oracle, he sent messengers to desire the priestess to do her office; and when she refused, on the plea of a law to the contrary, he went up himself, and began to draw her by force into the temple, until tired and overcome with his importunity, "My son," said she, "thou art invincible." Alexander taking hold of what she spoke, declared he had received such an answer as he wished for, and that it was needless to consult the god any further. Among other prodigies that attended the departure of his army, the image of Orpheus at Libethra, made of cypress-wood, was seen to sweat in great abundance, to the discouragement of many. But Aristander told him that, far from presaging any ill to him, it signified he should perform acts so important and glorious as would make the poets and musicians of future ages labour and sweat to describe and celebrate them.

His army, by their computation who make the smallest amount, consisted of thirty thousand foot and four thousand horse; and those who make the most of it, speak but of forty-three thousand foot and three thousand horse.

Aristobulus says, he had not a fund of above seventy talents for their pay, nor had he more than thirty days' provision, if we may believe Duris; Onesicritus tells us he was two hundred talents in debt. However narrow and disproportionable the beginnings of so vast an undertaking might seem to be, yet he would not embark his army until he had informed himself particularly what means his friends had to enable them to follow him, and supplied what they wanted, by giving good farms to some, a village to one, and the revenue of some hamlet or harbour-town to another. So that at last he had portioned out or engaged almost all the royal property; which giving Perdiccas an occasion to ask him what he would leave himself, he replied, his hopes. "Your soldiers," replied Perdiccas, "will be your partners in those," and refused to accept of the estate he had assigned him. Some others of his friends did the like, but to those who willingly received or desired assistance of him, he liberally granted it, as far as his patrimony in Macedonia would reach, the most part of which was spent in these donations.

With such vigorous resolutions, and his mind thus dispersed, he passed the Hellespont, and at Troy sacrificed to Minerva, and honoured the memory of the heroes who were buried there, with solemn libations; especially Achilles, whose gravestone he anointed, and with his friends, as the ancient custom is, ran naked about his sepulchre, and crowned it with garlands, declaring how happy he esteemed him, in having while he lived so faithful a friend, and when he was dead, so famous a poet to proclaim his actions. While he was viewing the rest of the antiquities and curiosities of the place, being told he might see Paris's harp, if he pleased, he said he thought it not worth looking on, but he should be glad to see that of Achilles, to which he used to sing the glories and great actions of brave men.

·   ·   ·

Among the treasures and other booty that was taken from Darius [after Alexander defeated the Persian army], there was a very precious casket, which being brought to Alexander for a great rarity, he asked those about him what they thought fittest to be laid up in it; and when they had delivered their various opinions, he told them he should keep Homer's Iliad in it. This is attested by many credible authors, and if what those of Alexandria tell us, relying upon the authority of Heraclides, be true, Homer was neither an idle nor an unprofitable companion to him in his expedition. For when he was master of Egypt, designing to settle a colony of Grecians there, he resolved to build a large and populous city, and give it his own name. In order to which, after he had measured and staked out the ground with the advice of the best architects, he chanced one night in his sleep to see a wonderful vision; a grey-headed old man, of a venerable aspect, appeared to stand by him, and pronounce these verses:—

"An island lies, where loud the billows roar,
Pharos they call it, on the Egyptian shore."

Alexander upon this immediately rose up and went to Pharos, which, at that time, was an island lying a little above the Canobic mouth of the river Nile, though it has now been joined to the mainland by a mole. As soon as he saw the commodious situation of the place, it being a long neck of land, stretching like an isthmus between large lagoons and shallow waters on one side and the sea on the other, the latter at the end of it making a spacious harbour, he said, Homer, besides his other excellences, was a very good architect, and ordered the plan of a city to be drawn out answerable to the place. To do which, for want of chalk, the soil being black, they laid out their lines with flour, taking in a pretty large compass of ground in a semi-circular figure, and drawing into the inside of the circumference equal straight lines from each end, thus giving it something of the form of a cloak or cape; while he was pleasing himself with his design, on a sudden an infinite number of great birds of several kinds, rising like a black cloud out of the river and lake, devoured every morsel of the flour that had been used in setting out the lines; at which omen even Alexander himself was troubled, till the augurs restored his confidence again by telling him it was a sign the city he was about to build would not only abound in all things within itself, but also be the nurse and feeder of many nations.

.   .   .

But when he perceived his favourites grow so luxurious and extravagant in their way of living and expenses that Hagnon, the Teian, wore silver nails in his shoes, that Leonnatus employed several camels only to bring him powder out of Egypt to use when he wrestled, and that Philotas had hunting nets a hundred furlongs in length, that more used precious ointment than plain oil when they went to bathe, and that they carried about servants every where with them to rub them and wait upon them in their chambers, he reproved them in gentle and reasonable terms, telling them he wondered that they who had been engaged in so many single battles did not know by experience, that those who labour sleep more sweetly and soundly than those who are laboured for, and could fail to see by comparing the Persians' manner of living with their own that it was the most abject and slavish condition to be voluptuous, but the most noble and royal to undergo pain and labour. He argued with them further, how it was possible for any one who pretended to be a soldier, either to look well after his horse, or to keep his armour bright and in good order, who thought it much to let his hands be serviceable to what was nearest to him, his own body, "Are you still to learn," said he, "that the end and perfection of our victories is to avoid the vices and infirmities of those whom we subdue?" And to strengthen his precepts by example, he applied himself now more vigorously then ever to hunting and warlike expeditions, embracing all opportunities of hardship and danger, insomuch that a Lacedæmonian, who was there on an embassy to him, and chanced to be by when he encountered with and mastered a huge lion, told him he had fought gallantly with the beast, which of the two should be king. Craterus caused a representation to be made of this adventure, consisting of the lion and the dogs, of the king engaged with the lion, and himself coming in to his assistance, all expressed in figures of brass, some of which were by Lysippus, and the rest by Leochares; and had it dedicated in the temple of Apollo at Delphi. Alexander exposed his person to danger in this manner, with the object both of inuring himself and inciting others to the performance of brave and virtuous actions.

But his followers, who were grown rich, and consequently proud, longed to indulge themselves in pleasure and idleness, and were weary of marches and expeditions, and at last went on so far as to censure and speak ill of him. All which at first he bore very patiently, saying it became a king well to do good to others, and be evil spoken of. Meantime, on the smallest occasions that called for a show of kindness to his friends, there was every indication on his part of tenderness and respect. Hearing Peucestes was bitten by a bear, he wrote to him that he took it unkindly he should send others notice of it and not make him acquainted with it; "But now," said he, "since it is so, let me know how you do, and whether any of your companions forsook you when you were in danger, that I may punish them." He sent Hephæstion, who was absent about some business, word how, while they were fighting for their diversion with an ichneumon, Craterus was by chance run through both thighs with Perdiccas's javelin. And upon Peucestes's recovery from a fit of sickness, he sent a letter of thanks to his physician Alexippus. When Craterus was ill, he saw a vision in his sleep, after which he offered sacrifices for his health, and bade him do so likewise. He wrote also to Pausanias, the physician, who was about to purge Craterus with hellebore, partly out of an anxious concern for him, and partly to give him a caution how he used that medicine. He was so tender of his friends' reputation that he imprisoned Ephialtes and Cissus, who brought him the first news of Harpalus's flight and withdrawal from his service, as if they had falsely accused him. When he sent the old and infirm soldiers home, Eurylochus, a citizen of Ægæ, got his name enrolled among the sick, though he ailed nothing, which being discovered, he confessed he was in love with a young woman named Telesippa, and wanted to go along with her to the sea-side. Alexander inquired to whom the woman belonged, and being told she was a free courtesan, "I will assist you," said he to Eurylochus, "in your amour if your mistress be to be gained either by presents or persuasions; but we must use no other means, because she is free-born."

It is surprising to consider upon what slight occasions he would write letters to serve his friends. As when he wrote one in which he gave order to search for a youth that belonged to Seleucus, who was run away into Cilicia; and in another thanked and commanded Peucestes for apprehending Nicon, a servant of Craterus; and in one to Megabyzus, concerning a slave that had taken sanctuary in a temple, gave directions that he should not meddle with him while he was there, but if he could entice him out by fair means, then he gave him leave to seize him. It is reported of him that when he first sat in judgment upon capital causes he would lay his hand upon one of his ears while the accuser spoke, to keep it free and unprejudiced in behalf of the party accused. But afterwards such a multitude of accusations were brought before him, and so many proved true, that he lost his tenderness of heart, and gave credit to those also that were false; and especially when anybody spoke ill of him, he would be transported out of his reason, and show himself cruel and inexorable, valuing his glory and reputation beyond his life or kingdom.

He now, as we said, set forth to seek Darius, expecting he should be put to the hazard of another battle, but heard he was taken and secured by Bessus, upon which news he sent home the Thessalians, and gave them a largess of two thousand talents over and above the pay that was due to them. This long and painful pursuit of Darius—for in eleven days he marched thirty-three hundred furlongs—harassed his soldiers so that most of them were ready to give it up, chiefly for want of water. While they were in this distress, it happened that some Macedonians who had fetched water in skins upon their mules from a river they had found out came about noon to the place where Alexander was, and seeing him almost choked with thirst, presently filled an helmet and offered it to him. He asked them to whom they were carrying the water; they told him to their children, adding, that if his life were but saved, it was no matter for them, they should be able well enough to repair that loss, though they all perished. Then he took the helmet into his hands, and looking round about, when he saw all those who were near him stretching their heads out and looking earnestly after the drink, he returned it again with thanks without tasting a drop of it. "For," said he, "if I alone drink, the rest will be out of heart." The soldiers no sooner took notice of his temperance and magnanimity upon this occasion, but they one and all cried out to him to lead them forward boldly, and began whipping on their horses. For whilst they had such a king they said they defied both weariness and thirst, and looked upon themselves to be little less than immortal. But though they were all equally cheerful and willing, yet not above threescore horse were able, it is said, to keep up, and to fall in with Alexander upon the enemy's camp, where they rode over abundance of gold and silver that lay scattered about, and passing by a great many chariots full of women that wandered here and there for want of drivers, they endeavored to overtake the first of those that fled, in hopes to meet with Darius among them. And at last, after much trouble, they found him lying in a chariot, wounded all over with darts, just at the point of death. However, he desired they would give him some drink, and when he had drunk a little cold water, he told Polystratus, who gave it him, that it had become the last extremity of his ill fortune to receive benefits and not be able to return them. "But Alexander," said he, "whose kindness to my mother, my wife, and my children I hope the gods will recompense, will doubtless thank you for your humanity to me. Tell him, therefore, in token of my acknowledgment, I give him this right hand," with which words he took hold of Polystratus's hand and died. When Alexander came up to them, he showed manifest tokens of sorrow, and taking off his own cloak, threw it upon the body to cover it. And some time afterwards, when Bessus was taken, he ordered him to be torn to pieces in this manner. They fastened him to a couple of trees which were bound down so as to meet, and then being let loose, with a great force returned to their places, each of them carrying that part of the body along with it that was tied to it. Darius's body was laid in state, and sent to his mother with pomp suitable to his quality. His brother Exathres, Alexander received into the number of his intimate friends.

· · ·

From hence he marched into Parthia, where not having much to do, he first put on the barbaric dress, perhaps with the view of making the work of civilising them the easier, as nothing gains more upon men than a conformity to their fashions and customs. Or it may have been as a first trial, whether the Macedonians might be brought to *adore* as the Persians did their kings, by accustoming them by little and little to bear with alteration of his rule and course of life in other things. However, he followed not the Median fashion, which was altogether foreign and uncouth, and adopted neither the trousers nor the sleeved vest, nor the tiara for the head, but taking a middle way between the Persian mode and the Macedonian, so contrived his habit that it was not so flaunting as the one, and yet more pompous and magnificent than the other. At first he wore this habit only when he conversed with the barbarians, or within doors, among his intimate friends and companions, but afterwards he appeared in it abroad, when he rode out, and at public audiences, a sight which the Macedonians beheld with grief; but they so respected his other virtues and good qualities that they felt it reasonable in some things to gratify his fancies and his passion of glory, in pursuit of which he hazarded himself so far, that, besides his other adventures, he had but lately been wounded in the leg by an arrow, which had so shattered the shank-bone that splinters were taken out. And on another occasion he received a violent blow with a stone upon the nape of the neck, which dimmed his sight for a good while afterwards. And yet all this could not hinder him from exposing himself freely to any dangers, insomuch that he passed the river Orexartes, which he took to be the Tanais, and putting the Scythians to flight, followed them above a hundred furlongs, though suffering all the time from a diarrhœa.

Here many affirm that the Amazon came to give him a visit. So Clitarchus, Polyclitus, Onesicritus, Antigenes, and Ister tell us. But Aristobulus and Chares who held the office of reporter of requests, Ptolemy and Anticlides, Philon the Theban, Philip of Theangela, Hecatæus the Eretrian, Philip the Chalcidian, and Duris the Samian, say it is wholly a fiction. And truly Alexander himself seems to confirm the latter statement, for in a letter in which he gives Antipater an account of all that happened, he tells him that the King of Scythia offered him his daughter in marriage, but makes no mention at all of the Amazon. And many years after, when Onesicritus read this story in his fourth book to Lysimachus, who then reigned, the king laughed quietly and asked, "Where could I have been at that time?"

But it signifies little to Alexander whether this be credited or no. Certain it is, that apprehending the Macedonians would be weary of pursuing the war, he left the greater part of them in their quarters; and having with him in Hyrcania the choice of his men only, amounting to twenty thousand foot and three thousand horse, he spoke to them in this effect: That hitherto the barbarians had seen them no otherwise than as it were in a dream, and if they should think of returning when they had only alarmed Asia, and not conquered it, their enemies would set upon them as upon so many women. However he told them he would keep none of them with him against their will, they might go if they pleased; he should merely enter his protest, that when on his way to make the Macedonians the masters of the world, he was left alone with a few friends and volunteers. This is almost word for word, as he wrote in a letter to Antipater, where he adds, that when he had thus spoken to them, they all cried out, they would go along with him whithersoever it was his pleasure to lead them. After succeeding with these, it was no hard matter for him to bring over the multitude, which easily followed the example of their betters. Now, also, he more and more accommodated himself in his way of living to that of the natives, and tried to bring them also as near as he could to the Macedonian customs, wisely considering that whilst he was engaged in an expedition which would carry him far from thence, it would be wiser to depend upon the good-will which might arise from intermixture and association as a means of maintaining tranquillity, than upon force and compulsion. In order to this, he chose out thirty thousand boys, whom he put under masters to teach them the Greek tongue, and to train them up to arms in the Macedonian discipline. As for his marriage with Roxana, whose youthfulness and beauty had charmed him at a drinking entertainment, where he first happened to see her taking part in a dance, it was indeed a love affair, yet it seemed at the same time to be conducive to the object he had in hand. For it gratified the conquered people to see him choose a wife from among themselves, and it made them feel the most lively affection for him, to find that in the only passion which he, the most temperate of men, was overcome by, he yet forbore till he could obtain her in a lawful and honourable way.

Noticing also that among his chief friends and favourites, Hephæstion most approved all that he did, and complied with and imitated him in his change of habits, while Craterus continued strict in the observation of the customs and fashions of his own country, he made it his practice to employ the first in all transactions with the Persians, and the latter when he had to do with the Greeks or Macedonians. And in general he showed more affection for Hephæstion, and more respect for Craterus; Hephæstion, as he used to say, being Alexander's, and Craterus the king's friend. And so these two friends always bore in secret a grudge to each other, and at times quarrelled openly, so much so that once in India they drew upon one another, and were proceeding in good earnest, with their friends on each side to second them, when Alexander rode up and publicly reproved Hephæstion, calling him fool and madman, not to be sensible that without his favour he was nothing. He rebuked Craterus also in private, severely, and then causing them both to come into his presence, he reconciled them, at the same time swearing by Ammon and the rest of the gods, that he loved them two above all other men, but if ever he perceived them fall out again he would be sure to put both of them to death, or at least the aggressor. After which they neither ever did or said anything, so much as in jest, to offend one another.

· · ·

The king had a present of Grecian fruit brought him from the sea-coast, which was so fresh and beautiful that he was surprised at it, and called Clitus to him to see it, and to give him a share of it. Clitus was then sacrificing, but he immediately left off and came, followed by three sheep, on whom the drink-offering had been already poured preparatory to sacrificing them. Alexander, being informed of this, told his diviners, Aristander and Cleomantis the Lacedæmonian, and asked them what it meant; on whose assuring him it was an ill omen, he commanded them in all haste to offer sacrifices for Clitus's safety, forasmuch as three days before he himself had seen a strange vision in his sleep, of Clitus all in mourning, sitting by Parmenio's sons who were dead. Clitus, however, stayed not to finish his devotions, but came straight to supper with the king, who had sacrificed to Castor and Pollux. And when they had drunk pretty hard, some of the company fell a-singing the verses of one Pranichus, or as others say of Pierion, which were made upon those captains who had been lately worsted by the barbarians, on purpose to disgrace and turn them to ridicule. This gave offence to the older men who were there, and they upbraided both the author and the singer of the verses, though Alexander and the younger men about him were much amused to hear them, and encouraged them to go on, till at last Clitus, who had drunk too much, and was besides of a forward and willful temper, was so nettled that he could hold no longer, saying it was not well done to expose the Macedonians before the barbarians and their enemies, since though it was their unhappiness to be overcome, yet they were much better men than those who laughed at them. And when Alexander remarked, that Clitus was pleading his own cause, giving cowardice the name of misfortune, Clitus started up: "This cowardice, as you are pleased to term it," said he to him, "saved the life of a son of the gods, when in flight from Sptihridates's sword; it is by the expense of Macedonian blood, and by these wounds, that you are now raised to such a height as to be able to disown your father Philip, and call yourself the son of Ammon." "Thou base fellow," said Alexander, who was now thoroughly exasperated, "dost thou think to utter these things everywhere of me, and stir up the Macedonians to sedition, and not be punished for it?" "We are sufficiently punished already," answered Clitus, "if this be the recompense of our toils, and we must esteem theirs a happy lot who have not lived to see their countrymen scourged with Median rods and forced to sue to the Persians to have access to their king." While he talked thus at random, and those near Alexander got up from their seats and began to revile him in turn, the elder men did what they could to compose the disorder. Alexander, in the meantime turning about to Xenodochus, the Pardian, and Artemius, the Colophonian, asked him if they were not of opinion that the Greeks, in comparison with the Macedonians, behaved themselves like so many demigods among wild beasts. But Clitus for all this would not give over, desiring Alexander to speak out if he had anything more to say, or else why did he invite men who were freeborn and accustomed to speak their minds openly without restraint to sup with him. He had better live and converse with barbarians and slaves who would not scruple to bow the knee to his Persian girdle and his white tunic. Which words so provoked Alexander that, not able to suppress his anger any longer, he threw one of the apples that lay upon the table at him, and hit him, and then looked about for his sword. But Aristophanes, one of his life-guard, had hid that out of the way, and others came about him and besought him, but in vain; for, breaking from them, he called out aloud to his guards in the Macedonian language, which was a certain sign of some great disturbance in him, and commanded a trumpeter to sound, giving him a blow with his clenched fist for not instantly obeying him; though afterwards the same man was commended for disobeying an order which would have put the whole army into tumult and confusion. Clitus still refusing to yield, was with much trouble forced by his friends out of the room. But he came in again immediately at another door, very irreverently and confidently singing the verses out of Euripides's Andromache—

"In Greece, alas! how ill things ordered are!"

Upon this, at last, Alexander, snatching a spear from one of the soldiers, met Clitus as he was coming forward and was putting by the curtain that hung before the door, and ran him through the body. He fell at once with a cry and a groan. Upon which the king's anger immediately vanishing, he came perfectly to himself, and when he saw his friends about him all in a profound silence, he pulled the spear out of the dead body, and would have thrust it into his own throat, if the guards had not held his hands, and by main force carried him away into his chamber, where all that night and the next day he wept bitterly, till being quite spent with lamenting and exclaiming, he lay as it were speechless, only fetching deep sighs. His friends apprehending some harm from his silence, broke into the room, but he took no notice of what any of them said, till Aristander putting him in mind of the vision he had seen concerning Clitus, and the prodigy that followed, as if all had come to pass by an unavoidable fatality, he then seemed to moderate his grief. They now brought Callisthenes, the philosopher, who was the near friend of Aristotle, and Anaxarchus of Abdera, to him. Callisthenes used moral language, and gentle and soothing means, hoping to find access for words of reason, and get a hold upon the passion. But Anaxarchus, who had always taken a course of his own in philosophy, and had a name for despising and slighting his contemporaries, as soon as he came in, cried aloud, "Is this the Alexander whom the whole world looks to, lying here weeping like a slave, for fear of the censure and reproach of men, to whom he himself ought to be a law and measure of equity, if he would use the right his conquests have given him as supreme lord and governor of all, and not be the victim of a vain and idle opinion? Do not you know," said he, "that Jupiter is represented to have Justice and Law on each hand of him, to signify that all the actions of a conqueror are lawful and just?" With these and the like speeches, Anaxarchus indeed allayed the king's grief, but withal corrupted his character, rendering him more audacious and lawless then he had been. Nor did he fail these means to insinuate himself into his favour, and to make Callisthenes's company, which at all times, because of his austerity, was not very acceptable, more uneasy and disagreeable to him.

.   .   .

The extent of King Taxiles's dominions in India was thought to be as large as Egypt, abounding in good pastures, and producing beautiful fruits. The king himself had the reputation of a wise man, and at his first interview with Alexander he spoke to him in these terms: "To what purpose," said he, "should we make war upon one another, if the design of your coming into these parts be not to rob us of our water or our necessary food, which are the only things that wise men are indispensably obliged to fight for? As for other riches and possessions, as they are accounted in the eye of the world, if I am better provided of them than you, I am ready to let you share with me; but if fortune has been more liberal to you than me, I have no objection to be obliged to you," This discourse pleased Alexander so much that, embracing him, "Do you think," said he to him, "your kind words and courteous behaviour will bring you off in this interview without a contest? No, you shall not escape so. I shall contend and do battle with you so far, that how obliging soever you are, you shall not have the better of me." Then receiving some presents from him, he returned him others of greater value, and to complete his bounty gave him in money ready coined one thousand talents; at which his old friends were much displeased, but it gained him the hearts of many of the barbarians. But the best soldiers of the Indians now entering into the pay of several of the cities, undertook to defend them, and did it so bravely, that they put Alexander to a great deal of trouble, till at last, after capitulation, upon the surrender of the place, he fell upon them as they were marching away, and put them all to the sword. This one breach of his word remains as a blemish upon his achievements in war, which he otherwise had performed throughout with that justice and honour that became a king. Nor was he less incommoded by the Indian philosophers, who inveighed against those princes who joined the party, and solicited the free nations to oppose him. He took several of these also and caused them to be hanged.

.   .   .

When he came into Persia, he distributed money among the women, as their own kings had been wont to do, who as often as they came thither gave every one of them a piece of gold; on account of which custom, some of them, it is said, had come but seldom, and Ochus was so sordidly covetous that, to avoid this expense, he never visited his native country once in all his reign. Then finding Cyrus's sepulchre opened and rifled, he put Polymachus, who did it, to death, though he was a man of some distinction, a born Macedonian of Pella. And after he had read the inscription, he caused it to be cut again below the old one in Greek characters; the words being these: "O man, whosoever thou art, and from whencesoever thou comest (for I know thou wilt come), I am Cyrus, the founder of the Persian empire; do not grudge me this little earth which covers my body." The reading of this sensibly touched Alexander, filling him with the thought of the uncertainty and mutability of human affairs.

Babur
(1483–1530)

ZAHIRUDDIN MUHAMMAD BABUR was born a Timurid prince in Fergana, present-day Uzbekistan, north of the Hindu Kush. Descended from the Turkic Amir Temür (known as Tamerlane in the West), Babur pursued the family business of conquest. He began at home and in modern Tajikistan, where the absence of a principle of fixed succession gave rise to incessantly warring factions. Despite his remarkable abilities as a commander, however, Babur ultimately lost Fergana to a more powerful prince and so moved south through Afghanistan to conquer Kabul. From there, operating in the same region in which Alexander the Great had before him, he looked to Pakistan and India, eventually forging the Mughal Empire, which stretched from Kandahar to Bengal and was ultimately secured by his grandson Akbar. Babur's autobiography, the *Baburnama*, was written in the Timurid language of Chaghatay Turkish and translated into Persian during the reign of Akbar. As the book's recent English translator Wheeler M. Thackston notes, the *Baburnama* is "the first—and until relatively recently times, the only—true autobiography in Islamic literature." The events recounted here, from "Kabul," the book's second part, took place in 1504 (Babur uses the Hegira date 910). Babur's physical and intellectual accomplishments were many. On display here are not only his remarkable endurance but also his keen eye for sociological and geographical detail. The selection culminates in a miserable winter journey from Herat to Kabul.

The Trek to Kabul
from *Baburnama*

Oranges, citrons, and rice are abundant, and heady wines are brought from Kafiristan. The people there tell strange stories that seem impossible but are heard over and over. For example: The lower part of the Kunar and Nur Gul district is called Lamata Kandi; below it belongs to Dara-i-Nur and Atar. Throughout the mountains above Lamata Kandi—in Kunar, Nur Gul, Bajaur, Swat, and those regions—it is well known that when a woman dies they put her on a cot and lift it at the four corners. If she has not done an evil deed, she causes the men who are carrying her to shake involuntarily in so violent a manner that if they try to stop themselves from shaking, the corpse falls from the cot. If she has done an evil deed, she causes no movement. Not only has this been heard from these people, but the mountain people from Bajaur and Swat are also unanimous in relating the tale. Haydar Ali, the sultan of Bajaur, kept an iron control over Bajaur. When his mother died, he did not weep, he did not mourn, and he did not put on black, but he said, "Go put her on the cot. If there is no movement I'll burn her." They put her on the cot and the desired motion caused by the corpse occurred. Only when he heard this did he put on black and begin to mourn.

·   ·   ·

Ghorband. Another is the district of Ghorband. It is probably called Ghorband because one goes to Ghor through a pass there, and in that region a pass is called *band*. The Hazaras have occupied the entrances to the valleys. A few villages have meager sources of revenue. They say that silver and lapis lazuli mines can be found in the Ghorband mountains.

Altogether there are some twelve or thirteen villages in the mountains, with Mata, Kaja, and Parwan at the top and Dur Nama at the bottom. They produce fruit, and in these parts the wines of Khwaja Khawand Sa'id are the strongest of all. Since the villages are isolated on mountain skirts and summits, the people are not accustomed to paying taxes, although they do give some tribute.

In the foothills below the villages, between the mountain and the Baran River, are two tracts of flatland, one called Kurra Taziyan and the other Dasht-i-Shaykh. In the summer the *chikin tala* grass is very good. Aymaqs and Turks come here in the summer.

Tulips of many varieties cover the foothills. Once, when I had them counted, there turned out to be thirty-two or thirty-three unique varieties. One sort, which gives off a bit of the scent of red roses, for which reason it is called a *gulboy* tulip, is found in Dasht-i-Shaykh and nowhere else. In these same foothills, below Parwan, in a patch of ground at the mouth of the Ghorband defile, the centifoil tulip grows. Between these two flatlands is a smallish mountain on which is a spot of sand extending all the way down the mountain called Khwaja Reg-i-Rawan. They say that in the summer the sound of drums comes from the sand.

·   ·   ·

Marching out of Kohat, we headed up the Hangu road in the direction of Bangash. Between Kohat and Hangu is a valley with a road running through it and mountains on either side. While we were marching through the valley, the Afghans from Kohat and vicinity massed on both sides of the valley, shouting and creating confusion. Malik Bu-Sa'id Kamari, who knew all of Afghanistan well and was our guide on this campaign, said, "Up ahead, on the right side of the road, is a patch of isolated mountain. If these Afghans cross from this mountain to that one, we can circle around and take them." Thank God, the Afghans moved exactly as Malik Bu-Sa'id Kamari had wished. A troop of warriors was sent immediately to take the narrows between the two peaks. The rest of the army was ordered to come in from all directions and give the Afghans their due. When the assault was made from all sides, the Afghans were not able to put up a fight. In a flash a hundred, 150 embattled Afghans were seized. Some were captured alive, but mostly only heads were brought. If Afghans are unable to fight they come before their enemies with grass in their teeth, as if to say, "I am your cow." We witnessed that custom there: the defeated Afghans held grass in their teeth. Those who were brought in alive were ordered beheaded, after which a tower of skulls was erected in the camp.

The next morning we marched out of there and dismounted in Hangu. The Afghans in that region had turned an isolated mountain into a *sangar*, a word we had heard when we came to Kabul that refers to a fortified mountain. As soon as the army reached it, they smashed the fortifications and cut off the heads of a hundred or so rebellious Afghans, which they brought back to Hangu. Another tower of skulls was erected.

After marching from Hangu we stopped for a night, then camped below Bangash in a place called Thal. Here too the army made raids on the Afghans in the area. One of the raiding parties returned from a sangar rather lightly laden.

When we marched from Thal toward Bannu, without a road to follow, we spent one night along the way before heading down a steep descent and through a long, narrow defile. The soldiers, camels, and horses had had a rough time. We had to leave behind most of the cattle taken as booty. The frequented road lay a league or two to our right; the one we were on was not for horses. It was said to be called Gosfand Lyar because occasionally shepherds and herdsmen brought their flocks and herds down this pass through the defile. (*Lyar* means road in the Afghan language.) Our guide was Malik Bu-Sa'id Kamari. Most of the soldiers blamed him for the difficulty we faced.

Immediately after the Bangash and Naghar mountains, Bannu lies on an open plain as flat as a board. The Bangash river runs through Bannu and provides irrigation. To the north are the mountains of Bangash and Naghar. To the south are Chaupara and the Indus River. To the east is Dinkot, and to the west Dasht, which is also called Bazar and Tank. The Afghan tribes Kurani, Givi, Sur, Isa Khel, and Niazi cultivate this province.

As soon as we stopped in Bannu, we received word that the tribes of the plain had made a sangar in the mountains to the north. The army was dispatched under the command of Jahangir Mirza. Apparently it was the Givis' sangar. In no time at all it was taken, a massacre ensued, and many heads were cut off and brought back. Many fine textiles fell into the soldiers' hands. A tower of skulls was erected. After the sangar was taken, Shadi Khan, one of the Givi chiefs, came with grass between his teeth to pay homage. We pardoned the captives.

When we had raided Kohat, we had decided to raid the Afghans in the vicinity of Bangash and Bannu and then return by the Naghar or Barmal roads. After raiding Bannu, those who knew the lay of the land said that Dasht was nearby and the people were numerous. Furthermore, the road was good and led to Barmal.

.   .   .

BABUR LEAVES HERAT FOR KABUL

On the pretext of finding winter quarters, we left Herat on the seventh of Sha'ban [December 23, 1506]. We marched, stopping a day or two at a time in the Badghis region, so that those who had gone to their estates to collect revenue and on business could join us. We halted and delayed so much that two or three days out of Langar-i-Mir Ghiyas we saw the Ramadan moon. Some of the warriors who had gone to their estates rejoined us; others came to Kabul twenty days to a month later than we, while still others stayed and joined the mirzas' service.

.   .   .

Leaving Langar-i-Mir Ghiyas, we skirted the villages of Gharjistan and came to Chaghcharan. There was snow all the way from Langar to Gharjistan. The farther we went the deeper it was. Chaghcharan belonged to Zu'n-Nun Beg and was under the charge of his servant Mirak Jan Apardi. We purchased all of Zu'n-Nun Beg's grain. Two or three marches out of Chaghcharan the snow was so deep it came above the horses' stirrups and in most places the horses' hooves did not reach the ground. Still it kept on snowing.

Out of Cheraghdan the road was completely obscured. In the Langar-i-Mir Ghiyas region we deliberated over which road we should take to Kabul. I and most of the others were of the opinion that since it was winter, the mountain road would be fraught with danger. The Kandahan road, although slightly longer, would be safer. Qasim Beg said that the latter road was too long and we should go by the former. In so saying he made a great mistake, but by that road we went.

Our guide was a Pashai named Sultan. Whether he was too old or faint-hearted, or whether because of the depth of the snow, in any case he lost the road and could not guide us. Since it was at Qasim Beg's insistence that we had come by this road, and it reflected upon his honor, he and his sons trampled down the snow, found the road again, and went on ahead. One day the snow was so deep and the road so obscured that no matter what we did we could not go on. There was nothing for us to do but turn back and camp in a place with firewood. I appointed seventy or eighty warriors to retrace our steps to find and bring to guide us any Hazaras who were wintering in the valley. We did not move from this camp for three or four days until those who had gone out returned. When they did return, they did not bring with them anyone who could show us the way. Trusting in God, we sent Sultan Pashai ahead and set out back down the very road where we had gotten lost. During those few days we endured much hardship and misery, more than I had experienced in my whole life. At that time I composed this line:

> Is there any cruelty or misery the spheres can inflict I have not suffered?
> Is there any pain or torment my wounded heart has not suffered?

For nearly a week we proceeded, unable to cover more than a league or a league-and-a-half a day. I became a snow trampler with ten or fifteen of my ichkis, Qasim Beg, his sons Tengriberdi and Qambar-Ali, and another two or three of their servants. We progressed on foot. One person would advance for eight to ten yards, trampling down the snow. Every time we put our foot down we would sink in to the waist or chest and pack down the snow. After going however many paces, the lead man would stop, exhausted. Then another would move to the front. Together these ten, fifteen, or twenty people could pack down enough snow for an unmounted horse to be led through. Sinking down to the stirrups or girth strap, the horse could be pulled forward for ten or fifteen paces before it gave out. It was drawn aside and another unmounted horse could be led forward. In this manner we ten to twenty persons trampled down the snow, and our horses were dragged through. Then all the rest of those who enjoyed the titles of fearless warriors and begs entered the prepared, packed-down road without dismounting and proceeded with their heads hung low. It was no time to compel or insist. Anyone with stamina and fortitude will join in such a labor without waiting for an invitation. By compressing the snow and creating a road, we made it in three or four days from that horrible place to a cave known as Khawal Qutï, below what is called the Zirrin Pass.

That day there was an amazing snowstorm. It was so terrible we all thought we were going to die. The people there call the caves and hollows in the mountains *khawals*. As we arrived the storm was unbelievably fierce. We dismounted right in front of the khawal. The snow was so deep that the horses had difficulty coming across a road that had been trampled and packed down.

The days were at their shortest, and it was still light when the first people reached the cave. By the prayer and nighttime they were still coming. Thereafter they dismounted where they stood. Many spent the night on horseback.

The cave seemed to be rather small. I took a shovel and cleared away enough snow at the mouth of the cave to make myself a place to sit. I dug down chest deep, and still I did not reach the ground, but it was a bit of shelter from the wind. There I sat down. Several people asked me to come inside, but I refused. I figured that to leave my people out in the snow and the storm, with me comfortable in a warm place, or to abandon all the people to hardship and misery, with me here asleep without a care, was neither manly nor comradely. Whatever hardship and difficulty there was, I would suffer it too. Whatever the people could endure, I could too. There is a Persian proverb: "Death with friends is a feast." In the midst of such a storm there I sat in a dug-out hole. By the time of the night prayer the snowstorm was still raging so much that I sat all huddled up. Four spans of snow were on my back and covering my head and ears. My ears got frostbite. At the night prayer those who had made a thorough inspection of the cave called out, "The cave is really big. There's enough room for everybody." When I heard this, I shook the snow off myself and, calling the warriors who were nearby to come in, went into the cave. There was enough room for forty or fifty people comfortably. Everyone brought out their provisions, hardtack, parched grain, and whatever they had. In the midst of such cold and such a storm, what a marvelously warm, safe, and secure place we had!

At dawn the storm stopped. We set out early and, by trampling down the snow again, made it to the top of the pass. The road itself seemed to take a turn and go higher up to the Zirrin Pass. We did not follow it higher but went right down the valley bottom. It was late in the day before we reached the other side of the pass. We spent the night at the mouth of the valley: it was bitterly cold, and spent in utter misery and hardship. Many people got frostbitten: Käpä's feet, Sevindük the Turcoman's hands, and Akhi's feet. Early the next day we proceeded straight down the valley. Although we could see this was not the road, we put our trust in God and marched through the valley bottom. In places with treacherous slopes and precipices we had to dismount. It was evening when we emerged through the mouth of the valley. Not even the oldest men with the longest memory could remember this pass having been crossed with the snow so deep; it was not even known whether it had ever occurred to anyone to attempt a crossing at this time of year. Although for a few days we had experienced a great deal of difficulty, in the end it was due to the depth of the snow that we were able to get ourselves to our destination. If it had not been so deep, how could those trackless slopes and falls have been crossed? Had it not been so deep, the horses and beasts of burden would all have been stuck on the first slope.

Whatever happens, good or bad, when you look closely, you'll find that it is all for the best.

Night had fallen by the time we reached Yakawlang. The Yakawlang people had heard of our arrival and we were greeted with warm houses, fat sheep, hay and fodder for the horses, abundant water, and plenty of kindling and dung for fires. To be delivered from such cold and snow and to find such a village and warm houses, to be saved from hardship and misery and to discover bread and fat sheep—this is a comfort that only those who have endured hardships can know, a relief that only those who have undergone travails can comprehend. Easy of mind and heart we stayed in Yakawlang for one day. From there we proceeded one stage. The next day was the Ramadan feast. Passing through Bamian and crossing the Shibartu Pass, we stopped before reaching Jangalak.

Ulysses S. Grant
(1822–1885)

A MISTAKE IN the registers at West Point turned Hiram Ulysses Grant into Ulysses S. Grant, and it stuck. Grant's reputation has undergone serial revision since his death in 1885: a global celebrity after he led the Union Army to victory in the American Civil War, Grant subsequently became to his detractors a bumbler, a drunk, and a dupe. As his contemporary Henry Adams, no great fan, observed, "When in action he was superb and safe to follow; only when torpid was he dangerous." After service in the Mexican War, Grant's deep unhappiness in a remote post in California away from his family led to his resignation from the army in 1854. It was the crisis of the Civil War that roused Grant's extraordinary powers of concentration and determination, and he rose rapidly from a colonelcy in the militia to a regular army commission and command of the Union Army, which he led to victory: he accepted Robert E. Lee's surrender at Appomattox Courthouse, Virginia, in 1865. Grant was carried on the tide of popularity to the presidency in 1868. Despite an indifferent two terms marred by scandal and the incompetence of various members of his administration, Grant subsequently cemented his popularity on a world tour before drifting from one bad business investment to the next. In 1884, having just gone bankrupt after being swindled by his banking partner and received a diagnosis of terminal throat cancer, he retreated to a cottage near Saratoga, New York, to write his memoirs. He was encouraged in this enterprise by Samuel Clemens (Mark Twain), whose publishing house of C. L. Webster & Company agreed to sell the memoirs through subscription. Grant finished the memoirs about a week before he died: the $500,000 the book earned saved his family. *Personal Memoirs* is ranked as one of the finest examples of the genre of the military memoir. Grant's clarity, forthrightness, and plain style have attracted fans as diverse as Gertrude Stein, Matthew Arnold, and Gore Vidal. The memoirs follow Grant from Ohio and West Point through the Mexican War, which he thought "one of the most unjust ever waged by a stronger against a weaker nation," and the Civil War, which he judged a war of principle, all the while deploring its cost in blood. The first passage excerpted here offers a parallel portrait of two of Grant's commanders in Mexico: Winfield Scott and, Grant's model, Zachary Taylor. The next episode, often held up as evidence that Grant was not afraid of Robert E. Lee, charts with characteristic honesty his transition from a combatant responsible only for himself to a commander on whom the lives of others depended. The final vignette involves drilling troops.

A Valuable Lesson

from *Personal Memoirs of Ulysses S. Grant* (1885–1886)

As I looked down that long line of about three thousand armed men, advancing toward a larger force also armed, I thought what a fearful responsibility General Taylor must feel, commanding such a host and so far away from friends.

.   .   .

General Taylor was not an officer to trouble the administration much with his demands, but was inclined to do the best he could with the means given him. He felt his responsibility as going no further. If he had thought that he was sent to perform an impossibility with the means given him, he would probably have informed the authorities of his opinion and left them to determine what should be done. If the judgment was against him he would have gone on and done the best he could with the means at hand, without parading his grievance before the public. No soldier could face either danger or responsibility more calmly than he. These are qualities more rarely found than genius or physical courage.

General Taylor never made any great show or parade, either of uniform or retinue. In dress he was possibly too plain, rarely wearing anything in the field to indicate his rank, or even that he was an officer; but he was known to every soldier in his army, and was respected by all.

. . .

I had now been in battle with two leading commanders conducting armies in a foreign land. The contrast between the two was very marked. General Taylor never wore uniform, but dressed himself entirely for comfort. He moved about the field in which he was operating to see the situation through his own eyes. Often he would be without staff-officers, and when he was accompanied by them there was no prescribed order in which they followed. He was very much given to sitting his horse sideways,—with both feet on one side,—particularly on the battle-field. General Scott was the reverse in all these particulars. He always wore all the uniform prescribed or allowed by law when he inspected his lines. Word would be sent to all division and brigade commanders in advance, notifying them of the hour when the commanding general might be expected. This was done so that all the army might be under arms to salute their chief as he passed. On these occasions he wore his dress-uniform, cocked hat, aiguillettes, saber, and spurs. His staff proper, besides all officers constructively on his staff,—engineers, inspectors, quartermasters, etc., that could be spared,—followed, also in uniform and in prescribed order. Orders were prepared with great care, and evidently with the view that they should be a history of what followed.

In their modes of expressing thought these two generals contrasted quite as strongly as in their other characteristics. General Scott was precise in language; cultivated a style peculiarly his own; was proud of his rhetoric; not averse to speaking of himself,—often in the third person,—and he could bestow praise upon the person he was talking about without the least embarrassment. Taylor was not a conversationalist, but on paper he could put his meaning so plainly that there could be no mistaking it. He knew how to express what he wanted to say in the fewest well-chosen words, but would not sacrifice meaning to the construction of high-sounding sentences. But with their opposite characteristics both were great and successful soldiers; both were true, patriotic, and upright in all their dealings. Both were pleasant to serve under—Taylor was pleasant to serve with. Scott saw more through the eyes of his staff-officers than through his own; his plans were deliberately prepared, and fully expressed in orders. Taylor saw for himself, and gave orders to meet the emergency without reference to how they would read in history.

. . .

My sensations as we approached what I supposed might be "a field of battle" were anything but agreeable. I had been in all the engagements in Mexico that it was possible for one person to be in, but not in command. If some one else had been colonel and I had been lieutenant-colonel I do not think

I would have felt any trepidation. Before we were prepared to cross the Mississippi River at Quincy my anxiety was relieved, for the men of the besieged regiment came straggling into town. I am inclined to think both sides got frightened and ran away.

I took my regiment to Palmyra and remained there for a few days, until relieved by the Nineteenth Illinois Infantry. From Palmyra I proceeded to Salt River, the railroad-bridge over which had been destroyed by the enemy. Colonel John M. Palmer at that time commanded the Fourteenth Illinois, which was acting as a guard to workmen who were engaged in rebuilding this bridge. Palmer was my senior and commanded the two regiments as long as we remained together. The bridge was finished in about two weeks, and I received orders to move against Colonel Thomas Harris, who was said to be encamped at the little town of Florida, some twenty-five miles south of where we then were.

At the time of which I now write we had no transportation, and the country about Salt River was sparsely settled, so that it took some days to collect teams and drivers enough to move the camp and garrison equipage of a regiment nearly a thousand strong, together with a week's supply of provisions and some ammunition. While preparations for the move were going on I felt quite comfortable; but when we got on the road and found every house deserted I was anything but easy. In the twenty-five miles we had to march we did not see a person, old or young, male or female, except two horsemen who were on a road that crossed ours. As soon as they saw us they decamped as fast as their horses could carry them. I kept my men in the ranks and forbade their entering any of the deserted houses or taking anything from them. We halted at night on the road and proceeded the next morning at an early hour. Harris had been encamped in a creek-bottom for the sake of being near water. The hills on either side of the creek extend to a considerable height   possibly more than a hundred feet. As we approached the brow of the hill from which it was expected we could see Harris's camp, and possibly find his men ready formed to meet us, my heart kept getting higher and higher, until it felt to me as though it was in my throat. I would have given anything then to have been back in Illinois, but I had not the moral courage to halt and consider what to do; I kept right on. When we reached a point from which the valley below was in full view I halted. The place where Harris had been encamped a few days before was still there, and the marks of a recent encampment were plainly visible, but the troops were gone. My heart resumed its place. It occurred to me at once that Harris had been as much afraid of me as I had been of him. This was a view of the question I had never taken before, but it was one I never forgot afterward. From that event to the close of the war I never experienced trepidation upon confronting an enemy, though I always felt more or less anxiety. I never forgot that he had as much reason to fear my forces as I had his. The lesson was valuable.

.   .   .

Up to this time my regiment had not been carried in the school of the soldier beyond the company drill, except that it had received some training on the march from Springfield to the Illinois River. There was now a good opportunity of exercising it in the battalion drill. While I was at West Point the tactics used in the army had been Scott's, and the musket the flint-lock. I had never looked at a copy of tactics from the time of my graduation. My standing in that branch of studies had been near the foot of the class. In the Mexican war, in the summer of 1846, I had been appointed regimental quartermaster and commissary, and had not been at a battalion drill since. The arms had been changed since then and Hardee's tactics had been adopted. I got a copy of tactics and studied one lesson, intending to confine the exercise of the first day to the commands I had thus learned. By pursuing this course from day to day I thought I would soon get through the volume.

We were encamped just outside of town on the common, among scattering suburban houses with inclosed gardens; and when I got my regiment in line and rode to the front I soon saw that if I attempted to follow the lesson I had studied I would have to clear away some of the houses and garden fences to make room. I perceived at once, however, that Hardee's tactics—a mere translation from the French, with Hardee's name attached—was nothing more than common sense and the progress of the age applied to Scott's system. The commands were abbreviated and the movement expedited. Under the old tactics almost every change in the order of march was preceded by a "halt"; then came the change, and then the "forward march." With the new tactics all these changes could be made while in motion. I found no trouble in giving commands that would take my regiment where I wanted it to go and carry it around all obstacles. I do not believe that the officers of the regiment ever discovered that I had never studied the tactics that I used.

Czeslaw Milosz
(1911–2004)

BORN IN LITHUANIA, then part of Russia, Milosz returned with his family to their native Poland after World War I. Having published his first poetry between the wars, Milosz worked for the underground press during the Nazi occupation of his country. After World War II he served as Poland's cultural attaché in Paris, but he defected in 1951 to escape the repressive policies of his country's Communist government. In the 1960s, Milosz moved to a post at the University of California at Berkeley, where he was a professor of Slavic Languages and Literatures, and he became a United States citizen in 1970. In addition to the Prix Littéraire Européen and other honors, Milosz won the Nobel Prize for Literature in 1980, an achievement that prompted Polish authorities to lift the official condemnation of his work, which had nevertheless survived in popular underground editions. He died in Kraków. Milosz wrote numerous books of poetry and prose. His anti-Communist work *The Captive Mind* powerfully exposed the inhumanity of totalitarianism. The poem "Orpheus and Eurydice" (2004) is a modern retelling of an ancient myth. Orpheus, the father of lyric poetry, ventures to the underworld to win back his wife, killed by a snake on their wedding day. Violating the condition set by Persephone, the queen of the underworld, that he not look back until reaching daylight, Orpheus loses Eurydice a second time and finds himself free to return to poetry. (The translation from the Polish is by Milosz and Robert Hass.)

Orpheus and Eurydice
(2004)

Standing on flagstones of the sidewalk at the entrance to Hades
Orpheus hunched in a gust of wind
That tore at his coat, rolled past in waves of fog,
Tossed the leaves of trees. The headlights of cars
Flared and dimmed in each succeeding wave.

He stopped at the glass-panelled door, uncertain
Whether he was strong enough for that ultimate trial.

He remembered her words: "You are a good man."
He did not quite believe it. Lyric poets
Usually have—as he knew—cold hearts.
It is like a medical condition. Perfection in art
Is given in exchange for such an affliction.

Only her love warmed him, humanized him.
When he was with her, he thought differently about himself.
He could not fail her now, when she was dead.

He pushed open the door and found himself walking in a labyrinth,
Corridors, elevators. The livid light was not light but the dark of the earth.

Electronic dogs passed him noiselessly.
He descended many floors, a hundred, three hundred, down.

He was cold, aware that he was Nowhere.
Under thousands of frozen centuries,
On an ashy trace where generations had moldered,
In a kingdom that seemed to have no bottom and no end.

Thronging shadows surrounded him.
He recognized some of the faces.
He felt the rhythm of his blood.
He felt strongly his life with its guilt
And he was afraid to meet those to whom he had done harm.
But they had lost the ability to remember
And gave him only a glance, indifferent to all that.

For his defense he had a nine-stringed lyre.
He carried in it the music of the earth, against the abyss
That buries all of sound in silence.
He submitted to the music, yielded
To the dictation of a song, listening with rapt attention,
Became, like his lyre, its instrument.

Thus he arrived at the palace of the rulers of that land.
Persephone, in her garden of withered pear and apple trees,
Black, with naked branches and verrucose twigs,
Listened from the funereal amethyst of her throne.

He sang the brightness of mornings and green rivers,
He sang of smoking water in the rose-colored daybreaks,
Of colors: cinnabar, carmine, burnt sienna, blue,
Of the delight of swimming in the sea under marble cliffs,
Of feasting on a terrace above the tumult of a fishing port,
Of the tastes of wine, olive oil, almonds, mustard, salt,
Of the flight of the swallow, the falcon,
Of a dignified flock of pelicans above a bay,
Of the scent of an armful of lilacs in summer rain,
Of his having composed his words always against death
And of having made no rhyme in praise of nothingness.

I don't know—said the goddess—whether you loved her or not.
Yet you have come here to rescue her.

She will be returned to you. But there are conditions:
You are not permitted to speak to her, or on the journey back
To turn your head, even once, to assure yourself that she is behind you.

And so Hermes brought forth Eurydice.
Her face no longer hers, utterly gray,
Her eyelids lowered, beneath the shade of her lashes.
She stepped rigidly, directed by the hand
Of her guide. Orpheus wanted so much
To call her name, to wake her from that sleep.
But he refrained, for he had accepted the conditions.

And so they set out. He first, and then, not right away,
The slap of the god's sandals and the light patter
Of her feet fettered by her robe, as if by a shroud.
A steep climbing path phosphorized
Out of darkness like the walls of a tunnel.
He would stop and listen. But then
They stopped, too, and the echo faded.
And when he began to walk the double tapping commenced again.
Sometimes it seemed closer, sometimes more distant.
Under his faith a doubt sprang up
And entwined him like cold bindweed.
Unable to weep, he wept at the loss
Of the human hope for the resurrection of the dead,
Because he was, now, like every other mortal.
His lyre was silent, yet he dreamed, defenseless.
He knew he must have faith and he could not have faith.
And so he would persist for a very long time,
Counting his steps in a half-wakeful torpor.

Day was breaking. Shapes of rock loomed up
Under the luminous eye of the exit from the underground.
It happened as he expected. He turned his head
And behind him on the path was no one.

Sun. And sky. And in the sky white clouds.
Only now everything cried to him: Eurydice!
How will I live without you, my consoling one!
But there was a fragrant scent of herbs, the low humming of bees,
And he fell asleep with his cheek on the sun-warmed earth.

DISCUSSION QUESTIONS

1. *How do various systems of promotion and compensation encourage or discourage risk-taking and constructive failure?*

2. *What do the examples here tell us about when to follow the rules and when to improvise?*

3. *Is failure simply an inevitable outcome of which we make the best—a convenient virtue? Or is it an intrinsically good thing?*

4. *How can individuals and organizations learn to profit from failures?*

5. *Is there an ethics of failure?*

RESISTING THE SYSTEM

Go down, Moses,
Way down in Egyptland,
Tell old Pharaoh
To let my people go.

—SPIRITUAL, TRADITIONAL

It may well be one of the most maddening refrains in all of literature: "I would prefer not to." So replies a copyist in a Wall Street law firm to his employer's request that he proofread a document in Herman Melville's story "Bartleby, the Scrivener," first published in *Putnam's Magazine* in 1853. The lawyer who narrates the story is thunderstruck. "At first Bartleby did an extraordinary quantity of writing," he explains, not "cheerfully" perhaps, but "silently, palely, mechanically." On the third day, however, the lawyer's "natural expectancy of instant compliance" is frustrated by the unexpected resistance of his new scrivener: "Bartleby in a singularly mild, firm voice, replied, 'I would prefer not to.' "

Soon this is Bartleby's only response to any request, yet because it is accompanied not by "anger, impatience or impertinence," but only with his accustomed calm, the lawyer does not fire him. Something about Bartleby's manner restrains his employer even as it infuriates him: "Nothing so aggravates an earnest person," he declares, "as a passive resistance." Even after Bartleby, who has taken up residence in the lawyer's office, ceases to do any work at all, it takes a long time for his employer to fire him. Eventually removed and incarcerated as a vagrant, Bartleby ultimately starves to death because he prefers not to eat.

Melville's parable of passive resistance echoes Henry David Thoreau's "Resistance to Civil Government," published a few years earlier in 1849. There Thoreau documents his reasons for choosing to spend a night in the Concord jail rather than pay his poll tax because of his opposition to the Mexican War and slavery. He argues that most citizens serve the state "not as men mainly, but as machines . . . A very few, as heroes, patriots, martyrs, reformers in the great sense, and *men*, serve the State with their consciences also, and so necessarily resist it for the most part; and they are commonly treated by it as enemies." The time had come, Thoreau insisted, "for honest men to rebel and revolutionize."

Persuaded of Thoreau's potential yet disappointed by his lack of ambition, Ralph Waldo Emerson complained about his friend: "Instead of engineering for all America, he was the captain of a huckleberry party." Thoreau may have fallen short while he lived, but the delayed impact of his doctrine of civil disobedience was far-reaching and profound. In the twentieth century it informed Mohandas Gandhi's leadership of Indian resistance to British rule as well as Martin Luther King Jr.'s "nonviolent campaign" for civil rights: "We know through painful experience," King wrote in "Letter from Birmingham Jail," "that freedom is never voluntarily given by the oppressor; it must be demanded by the oppressed." King outlines there the deeper history of the civil disobedience in which he was engaged: back through the Boston Tea Party to the early Christian martyrs, Socrates, and those who rebelled against the laws of Nebuchadnezzar in the Old Testament.

The readings that follow offer various historical examples of resistance—nonviolent but also violent—in an attempt to ascertain the conditions under which certain individuals have discovered the courage to resist oppression. They also examine some of the attributes required to lead resistance in the face of overwhelming obstacles and to sustain original principles even in vertiginous circumstances. The selections begin with excerpts from Exodus that document Moses's transformation from reluctant rebel to iron-willed leader. They move to Barbara W. Tuchman's account of the fourteenth-century Peasants' Revolt in England and its defeat. Mary Wollstonecraft and Frederick Douglass identify ways in which tyrannical systems deform individuals; both writers call attention to the fact that the ability to resist is predicated on the awakening of self-awareness. Three addresses to courts of law, the first by the American Socialist Eugene V. Debs, the second by Gandhi, and the third by Nelson Mandela, offer portraits in words of three men willing to go to jail—even to die—to resist the injustices they perceived in their respective societies.

Finally, the collection of poems and songs included in this section shows us the power of art as an expression of political and social resistance. In a 2013 op-ed in the *New York Times* on the subject of the rise of anti-Semitism in Hungary, the journalist Marianne Szegedy-Maszak called attention to the Budapest Festival Orchestra's performance of *Red Heifer*, an opera written by the orchestra's conductor, Ivan Fischer, about a nineteenth-century blood libel in which a group of Jews were falsely accused of murdering a young girl. Fischer is one of several Hungarian artists to speak out against the repressive rise of the country's radical right-wing parties. "It [the opera] is a true story, one that uses the distant past to illuminate a dark time in the present," writes Szegedy-Maszak. "Of course it is unlikely to change any minds. But the simple fact of it is an affirmation of the power of art to accomplish what decent politicians cannot."

RECOMMENDED READING AND VIEWING

Brute Force (1947), directed by Jules Dassin
Ralph Ellison, *Invisible Man* (1952)
Maxine Hong Kingston, *The Woman Warrior: Memoirs of a Girlhood Among Ghosts* (1975)
Thomas Paine, *Rights of Man* (1791)
Kazik (Simha Rotem), *Memoirs of a Warsaw Ghetto Fighter*, translated by Barbara Harshav (2001)

The Book of Exodus

HERE IS THE Old Testament's great story of resistance: the uprising of Moses and the children of Israel against the Egyptian Pharaoh. The translation provided is the King James Version (KJV). Commissioned by James I of England and first published in 1611, the KJV did not achieve widespread popularity until the early eighteenth century. The translators aimed at as literal a translation as possible, and as the editor Herbert Marks notes, the KJV has the added advantage of being "undertaken at a privileged moment in the history of written English, when the linguistic energy of the sixteenth century was balanced by a new firmness of prose syntax." "Literalism and eloquence conspire," writes Marks, "in what, for most readers today, is perhaps the defining quality of the KJV: a certain elevated strangeness." In this excerpt from the Book of Exodus, that strangeness is apt for the account of God's calling of Moses to lead the rebellion against Pharaoh. The chapters chronicle not only the initial summons but also the reluctance and trepidation of Moses to undertake such a monumental mission. In the next several chapters, omitted here, Moses makes several unsuccessful demands to Pharaoh to let his people go. Meanwhile, Pharaoh's increasingly repressive measures cause the Israelites, suffering from "anguish of spirit" and "cruel bondage" (6.9), to grow increasingly reluctant to follow Moses. The narrative resumes after the visitation of the plagues and the parting of the Red Sea, with the difficult aftermath of deliverance, when Moses must meet the challenges of leading a people whose overwhelming relief at being released from bondage has made them susceptible to distraction and corruption.

Moses

from Exodus, The Old Testament, King James Version

3 Now Moses kept the flock of Jethro his father in law, the priest of Midian: and he led the flock to the backside of the desert, and came to the mountain of God, even to Horeb. ²And the angel of the LORD appeared unto him in a flame of fire out of the midst of a bush: and he looked, and, behold, the bush burned with fire, and the bush was not consumed. ³And Moses said, I will now turn aside, and see this great sight, why the bush is not burnt. ⁴And when the LORD saw that he turned aside to see, God called unto him out of the midst of the bush, and said, Moses, Moses. ⁵And he said, Here am I. And he said, Draw not nigh hither: put off thy shoes from off thy feet, for the place whereon thou standest is holy ground. ⁶Moreover he said, I am the God of thy father, the God of Abraham, the God of Isaac, and the God of Jacob. And Moses hid his face; for he was afraid to look upon God.

⁷And the LORD said, I have surely seen the affliction of my people which are in Egypt, and have heard their cry by reason of their taskmasters; for I know their sorrows; ⁸and I am come down to deliver them out of the hand of the Egyptians, and to bring them up out of that land unto a good land and a large, unto a land flowing with milk and honey; unto the place of the Canaanites, and the Hittites, and the Amorites, and the Perizzites, and the Hivites, and the Jebusites. ⁹Now therefore, behold, the cry of the children of Israel is come unto me: and I have also seen the oppression wherewith the Egyptians oppress them. ¹⁰Come now therefore, and I will send thee unto Pharaoh, that thou mayest bring forth my people the children of Israel out of Egypt? ¹¹And Moses said unto God, Who am I, that should go unto Pharaoh, and that I should bring forth the children of Israel out of Egypt? ¹²And he said, Certainly I will be with thee; and this shall be a token unto thee, that I have sent thee: When thou hast brought forth the people out of Egypt, ye shall serve God upon this mountain.

¹³And Moses said unto God, Behold, when I come unto the children of Israel, and shall say unto them, The God of your fathers hath sent me unto you; and they shall say to me, What is his name? what shall I say unto them? ¹⁴And God said unto Moses, I AM THAT I AM: And he said, Thus shalt thou say unto the children of Israel, I am hath sent me unto you. ¹⁵And God said moreover unto Moses, Thus shalt thou say unto the children of Israel, The LORD God of your fathers, the God of Abraham, the God of Isaac, and the God of Jacob, hath sent me unto you: this is my name for ever, and this is my memorial unto all generations. ¹⁶Go, and gather the elders of Israel together, and say

unto them, The LORD God of your fathers, the God of Abraham, of Isaac, and of Jacob, appeared unto me, saying, I have surely visited you, and seen that which is done to you in Egypt: ¹⁷and I have said, I will bring you up out of the affliction of Egypt unto the land of the Canaanites, and the Hittites, and Amorites, and the Perizzites, and the Hivites, and the Jebusites, unto a land flowing with milk and honey. ¹⁸And they shall hearken to thy voice: and thou shalt come, thou and the elders of Israel, unto the king of Egypt, and ye shall say unto him, The LORD God of the Hebrews hath met with us: and now let us go, we beseech thee, three days' journey into the wilderness, that we may sacrifice to the LORD our God. ¹⁹And I am sure that the king of Egypt will not let you go, no, not by a mighty hand. ²⁰And I will stretch out my hand, and smite Egypt with all my wonders which I will do in the midst thereof: and after that he will let you go. ²¹And I will give this people favour in the sight of the Egyptians: and it shall come to pass, that, when ye go, ye shall not go empty: ²²but every woman shall borrow of her neighbour, and of her that sojourneth in her house, jewels of silver, and jewels of gold, and raiment: and ye shall put them upon your sons, and upon your daughters; and ye shall spoil the Egyptians.

4 And Moses answered and said, But, behold, they will not believe me, nor hearken unto my voice: for they will say, The Lord hath not appeared unto thee. ²And the LORD said unto him, What is that in thine hand? And he said, a rod. ³And he said, Cast it on the ground. And he cast it on the ground, and it became a serpent; and Moses fled from before it. ⁴And the Lord said unto Moses, Put forth thine hand, and take it by the tail. And he put forth his hand, and caught it, and it became a rod in his hand: ⁵that they may believe that the LORD God of their fathers, the God of Abraham, the God of Isaac, and the God of Jacob, hath appeared unto thee. ⁶And the LORD said furthermore unto him, Put now thine hand into thy bosom. And he put his hand into his bosom: and when he took it out, behold, his hand was leprous as snow. ⁷And he said, Put thine hand into thy bosom again. And he put his hand into his bosom again; and plucked it out of his bosom, and, behold, it was turned again as his other flesh. ⁸And it shall come to pass, if they will not believe thee, neither hearken to the voice of the first sign, that they will believe the voice of the latter sign. ⁹And it shall come to pass, if they will not believe also these two signs, neither hearken unto thy voice, that thou shalt take of the water of the river, and pour it upon the dry land: and the water which thou takest out of the river shall become blood upon the dry land.

¹⁰And Moses said unto the LORD, O my Lord, I am not eloquent, neither heretofore, nor since thou hast spoken unto thy servant: but I am slow of speech, and of a slow tongue. ¹¹And the LORD said unto him, Who hath made man's mouth? or who maketh the dumb, or deaf, or the seeing, or the blind? have not I the LORD? ¹²Now therefore go, and I will be with thy mouth, and teach thee what thou shalt say. ¹³And he said, O my Lord, send, I pray thee, by the hand of him

whom thou wilt send. ¹⁴And the anger of the LORD was kindled against Moses, and he said, Is not Aaron the Levite thy brother? I know that he can speak well. And also, behold, he cometh forth to meet thee: and when he seeth thee, he will be glad in his heart. ¹⁵And thou shalt speak unto him, and put words in his mouth: and I will be with thy mouth, and with his mouth, and will teach you what ye shall do. ¹⁶And he shall be thy spokesman unto the people: and he shall be, even he shall be to thee instead of a mouth, and thou shalt be to him instead of God. ¹⁷And thou shalt take this rod in thine hand, wherewith thou shalt do signs. ¹⁸And Moses went and returned to Jethro his father in law, and said unto him, Let me go, I pray thee, and return unto my brethren which are in Egypt, and see whether they be yet alive. And Jethro said to Moses, Go in peace.

32 And when the people saw that Moses delayed to come down out of the mount, the people gathered themselves together unto Aaron, and said unto him, Up, make us gods, which shall go before us; for as for this Moses, the man that brought us up out of the land of Egypt, we wot not what is become of him. ²And Aaron said unto them, Break off the golden earrings, which are in the ears of your wives, of your sons, and of your daughters, and bring them unto me. ³And all the people brake off the golden earrings which were in their ears, and brought them unto Aaron. ⁴And he received them at their hand, and fashioned it with a graving tool, after he had made it a molten calf: and they said, These be thy gods, O Israel, which brought thee up out of the land of Egypt. ⁵And when Aaron saw it, he built an altar before it; and Aaron made proclamation, and said, To morrow is a feast to the LORD. ⁶And they rose up early on the morrow, and offered burnt offerings, and brought peace offerings; and the people sat down to eat and to drink, and rose up to play.

⁷And the LORD said unto Moses, Go, get thee down; for thy people, which thou broughtest out of the land of Egypt, have corrupted themselves: ⁸they have turned aside quickly out of the way which I commanded them: they have made them a molten calf, and have worshipped it, and have sacrificed thereunto, and said, These be thy gods, O Israel, which have brought thee up out of the land of Egypt. ⁹And the LORD said unto Moses, I have seen this people, and, behold, it is a stiffnecked people: ¹⁰now therefore let me alone, that my wrath may wax hot against them, and that I may consume them: and I will make of thee a great nation. ¹¹And Moses besought the LORD his God, and said, LORD, why doth thy wrath wax hot against thy people, which thou hast brought forth out of the land of Egypt with great power, and with a mighty hand? ¹²Wherefore should the Egyptians speak, and say, For mischief did he bring them out, to slay them in the mountains, and to consume them from the face of the earth? Turn from thy fierce wrath, and repent of this evil against thy people. ¹³Remember Abraham, Isaac, and Israel, thy servants, to whom thou swarest by thine own self, and saidist unto them, I will multi-

ply your seed as the stars of heaven, and all this land that I have spoken of will I give unto your seed, and they shall inherit it for ever. ¹⁴And the LORD repented of the evil which he thought to do unto his people.

¹⁵And Moses turned, and went down from the mount, and the two tables of the testimony were in his hand: the tables were written on both their sides; on the one side and on the other were they written. ¹⁶And the tables were the work of God, and the writing was the writing of God, graven upon the tables. ¹⁷And when Joshua heard the noise of the people as they shouted, he said unto Moses, There is a noise of war in the camp. ¹⁸And he said, It is not the voice of them that shout for mastery, neither is it the voice of them that cry for being overcome: but the noise of them that sing do I hear. ¹⁹And it came to pass, as soon as he came nigh unto the camp, that he saw the calf, and the dancing: and Moses' anger waxed hot, and he cast the tables out of his hands, and brake them beneath the mount. ²⁰And he took the calf which they had made, and burnt it in the fire, and ground it to powder, and strawed it upon the water, and made the children of Israel drink of it.

²¹And Moses said unto Aaron, What did this people unto thee, that thou hast brought so great a sin upon them? ²²And Aaron said, Let not the anger of my lord wax hot: thou knowest the people, that they are set on mischief. ²³For they said unto me, Make us gods, which shall go before us: for as for this Moses, the man that brought us up out of the land of Egypt, we wot not what is become of him. ²⁴And I said unto them, Whosoever hath any gold, let them break it off. So they gave it me: then I cast it into the fire, and there came out this calf.

²⁵And when Moses saw that the people were naked; (for Aaron had made them naked unto their shame among their enemies:) ²⁶then Moses stood in the gate of the camp, and said, Who is on the LORD's side? let him come unto me. And all the sons of Levi gathered themselves together unto him. ²⁷And he said unto them, Thus saith the LORD God of Israel, Put every man his sword by his side, and go in and out from gate to gate throughout the camp, and slay every man his brother, and every man his companion, and every man his neighbour. ²⁸And the children of Levi did according to the word of Moses: and there fell of the people that day about three thousand men. ²⁹For Moses had said, Consecrate yourselves to day to the LORD, even every man upon his son, and upon his brother; that he may bestow upon you a blessing this day.

³⁰And it came to pass on the morrow, that Moses said unto the people, Ye have sinned a great sin: and now I will go up unto the LORD; peradventure I shall make an atonement for your sin. ³¹And Moses returned unto the LORD, and said, Oh, this people have sinned a great sin, and have made them gods of gold. ³²Yet now, if thou wilt forgive their sin—; and if not, blot me, I pray thee, out of thy book which thou hast written. ³³And the LORD said unto Moses, Whosoever hath sinned against me, him will I blot out of my book. ³⁴Therefore now go, lead the people unto the place of which I have spoken unto thee:

behold, mine Angel shall go before thee: nevertheless in the day when I visit I will visit their sin upon them.

³⁵And the LORD plagued the people, because they made the calf, which Aaron made.

33 And the LORD said unto Moses, Depart, and go up hence, thou and the people which thou hast brought up out of the land of Egypt, unto the land which I sware unto Abraham, to Isaac, and to Jacob, saying, Unto thy seed will I give it: ²and I will send an angel before thee; and I will drive out the Canaanite, the Amorite, and the Hittite, and the Perizzite, the Hivite, and the Jebusite: ³unto a land flowing with milk and honey: for I will not go up in the midst of thee; for thou art a stiffnecked people: lest I consume thee in the way. ⁴And when the people heard these evil tidings, they mourned: and no man did put on him his ornaments. ⁵For the LORD had said unto Moses, Say unto the children of Israel, Ye are a stiffnecked people: I will come up into the midst of thee in a moment, and consume thee: therefore now put off thy ornaments from thee, that I may know what to do unto thee. ⁶And the children of Israel stripped themselves of their ornaments by the mount Horeb.

⁷And Moses took the tabernacle, and pitched it without the camp, afar off from the camp, and called it the Tabernacle of the congregation. And it came to pass, that every one which sought the LORD went out unto the tabernacle of the congregation, which was without the camp. ⁸And it came to pass, when Moses went out unto the tabernacle, that all the people rose up, and stood every man at his tent door, and looked after Moses, until he was gone into the tabernacle. ⁹And it came to pass, as Moses entered into the tabernacle, the cloudy pillar descended, and stood at the door of the tabernacle, and the LORD talked with Moses. ¹⁰And all the people saw the cloudy pillar stand at the tabernacle door: and all the people rose up and worshipped, every man in his tent door. ¹¹And the LORD spake unto Moses face to face, as a man speaketh unto his friend. And he turned again into the camp: but his servant Joshua, the son of Nun, a young man, departed not out of the tabernacle.

¹²And Moses said unto the LORD, See, thou sayest unto me, Bring up this people: and thou hast not let me know whom thou wilt send with me. Yet thou hast said, I know thee by name, and thou hast also found grace in my sight. ¹³Now therefore, I pray thee, if I have found grace in thy sight, shew me now thy way, that I may know thee, that I may find grace in thy sight: and consider that this nation is thy people. ¹⁴And he said, My presence shall go with thee, and I will give thee rest. ¹⁵And he said unto him, If thy presence go not with me, carry us not up hence. ¹⁶For wherein shall it be known here that I and thy people have found grace in thy sight? is it not in that thou goest with us? so shall we be separated, I and thy people, from all the people that are upon the face of the earth. ¹⁷And the LORD said unto Moses, I will do this thing also

that thou hast spoken: for thou hast found grace in my sight, and I know thee by name.

[18]And he said, I beseech thee, shew me thy glory. [19]And he said, I will make all my goodness pass before thee, and I will proclaim the name of the LORD before thee; and will be gracious to whom I will be gracious, and will shew mercy on whom I will shew mercy. [20]And he said, Thou canst not see my face: for there shall no man see me, and live. [21]And the LORD said, Behold, there is a place by me, and thou shalt stand upon a rock: [22]and it shall come to pass, while my glory passeth by, that I will put thee in a clift of the rock, and will cover thee with my hand while I pass by: [23]and I will take away mine hand, and thou shalt see my back parts: but my face shall not be seen.

34 And the LORD said unto Moses, Hew thee two tables of stone like unto the first: and I will write upon these tables the words that were in the first tables, which thou brakest. [2]And be ready in the morning, and come up in the morning unto mount Sinai, and present thyself there to me in the top of the mount. [3]And no man shall come up with thee, neither let any man be seen throughout all the mount; neither let the flocks nor herds feed before that mount. [4]And he hewed two tables of stone like unto the first; and Moses rose up early in the morning, and went up unto mount Sinai, as the LORD had commanded him, and took in his hand the two tables of stone. [5]And the LORD descended in the cloud, and stood with him there, and proclaimed the name of the LORD. [6]And the LORD passed by before him, and proclaimed, The LORD, The LORD God, merciful and gracious, longsuffering, and abundant in goodness and truth, [7]keeping mercy for thousands, forgiving iniquity and transgression and sin, and that will by no means clear the guilty; visiting the iniquity of the fathers upon the children and upon the children's children, unto the third and to the fourth generation. [8]And Moses made haste, and bowed his head toward the earth, and worshipped. [9]And he said, If now I have found grace in thy sight, O Lord, let my Lord, I pray thee go among us; for it is a stiffnecked people; and pardon our iniquity and our sin, and take us for thine inheritance.

[10]And he said, Behold, I make a covenant: before all thy people I will do marvels, such as have not been done in all the earth, nor in any nation: and all the people among which thou art shall see the work of the LORD: for it is a terrible thing that I will do with thee.

[11]Observe thou that which I command thee this day: behold, I drive out before thee the Amorite, and the Canaanite, and the Hittite, and the Perizzite, and the Hivite, and the Jebusite. [12]Take heed to thyself, lest thou make a covenant with the inhabitants of the land whither thou goest, lest it be for a snare in the midst of thee: [13]but ye shall destroy their altars, break their images, and cut down their groves: [14]for thou shalt worship no other god: for the LORD,

whose name is Jealous, is a jealous God: [15]lest thou make a covenant with the inhabitants of the land, and they go a whoring after their gods, and do sacrifice unto their gods, and one call thee, and thou eat of his sacrifice; [16]and thou take of their daughters unto thy sons, and their daughters go a whoring after their gods, and make thy sons go a whoring after their gods.

[17]Thou shalt make thee no molten gods.

[18]The feast of unleavened bread shalt thou keep. Seven days thou shalt eat unleavened bread, as I commanded thee, in the time of the month Abib: for in the month Abib thou camest out from Egypt.

[19]All that openeth the matrix is mine; and every firstling among thy cattle, whether ox or sheep, that is male. [20]But the firstling of an ass thou shalt redeem with a lamb: and if thou redeem him not, then shalt thou break his neck. All the firstborn of thy sons thou shalt redeem. And none shall appear before me empty.

[21]Six days thou shalt work, but on the seventh day thou shalt rest: in earing time and in harvest thou shalt rest.

[22]And thou shalt observe the feast of weeks, of the firstfruits of wheat harvest, and the feast of ingathering at the year's end. [23]Thrice in the year shall all your men children appear before the Lord God, the God of Israel. [24]For I will cast out the nations before thee, and enlarge thy borders: neither shall any man desire thy land, when thou shalt go up to appear before the Lord thy God thrice in the year.

[25]Thou shalt not offer the blood of my sacrifice with leaven; neither shall the sacrifice of the feast of the passover be left unto the morning.

[26]The first of the firstfruits of thy land thou shalt bring unto the house of the Lord thy God.

Thou shalt not seethe a kid in his mother's milk.

[27]And the Lord said unto Moses, Write thou these words: for after the tenor of these words I have made a covenant with thee and with Israel. [28]And he was there with the Lord forty days and forty nights; he did neither eat bread, nor drink water. And he wrote upon the tables the words of the covenant, the ten commandments.

[29]And it came to pass, when Moses came down from mount Sinai with the two tables of testimony in Moses' hand, when he came down from the mount, that Moses wist not that the skin of his face shone while he talked with him. [30]And when Aaron and all the children of Israel saw Moses, behold, the skin of his face shone; and they were afraid to come nigh him. [31]And Moses called unto them; and Aaron and all the rulers of the congregation returned unto him: and Moses talked with them. [32]And afterward all the children of Israel came nigh: and he gave them in commandment all that the Lord had spoken with him in mount Sinai. [33]And till Moses had done speaking with them, he put a vail on his face. [34]But when Moses went in before the Lord to speak with

him, he took the vail off, until he came out. And he came out, and spake unto the children of Israel that which he was commanded. [35]And the children of Israel saw the face of Moses, that the skin of Moses' face shone: and Moses put the vail upon his face again, until he went in to speak with him.

Barbara W. Tuchman
(1912–1989)

A PROLIFIC HISTORIAN, the winner of two Pulitzer Prizes, Barbara Tuchman offered readers vivid accounts of various figures and events in history, including the years leading up to World War I in *The Guns of August*, the career of General Joseph W. Stilwell in *Stilwell and the American Experience in China, 1911–45*, and the achievements and upheavals of the fourteenth century in *A Distant Mirror*, the book from which this selection comes. Without formal academic training as a historian, Tuchman thought deeply about the profession. Insight into her thinking on this subject can be found in *Practicing History* (1981), a collection of historiographical writings. Leery of "philosophies" because they tempted the historian "to manipulate his facts in the interest of his system," she nevertheless developed "a sense of history as accidental and perhaps cyclical, of human conduct as a steady stream running through endless fields of changing circumstances." Tuchman believed "a proper understanding of cause and effect . . . must be written in terms of what was known and believed at the time, not from the perspective of hindsight." In this excerpt Tuchman narrates the story of a violent revolt of English peasants in 1381, inspired by "a developing sense of freedom" and ultimately "defeated more by fraud than by force."

The Peasants' Revolt
from *A Distant Mirror* (1978)

While France smoldered, true revolt erupted in June 1381 in England, not of the urban class but of the peasants. In a country whose economy was largely rural, they were the working class that mattered. The third poll tax in four years, to include everyone over the age of fifteen, was the precipitant. Voted in November 1380 by a subservient Parliament to finance Lancaster's ambitions in Spain, the collection brought in only two thirds of the expected sum, not least because tax commissioners were easily bribed to overlook families or falsify their numbers. A second round of collecting became necessary, which could have been foreseen as an invitation to trouble if the lords and prelates and royal uncles of Richard's government had paid attention to the constant complaints of rural insubordination. They did not, and brought upon themselves the most fearful challenge of the century.

At the end of May, villages in Essex on the east coast just above London refused payment; the resistance spread with some evidence of planning, and burst into violence in Kent, the adjoining county south of the Thames. Peasants mingled with yeomen from the French wars armed themselves with rusty swords, scythes, axes, and longbows blackened by age, and triumphantly stormed a castle where a runaway villein had been imprisoned. Electing Wat Tyler, an eloquent demagogue and veteran of the wars, as their commander-in-chief, they seized Canterbury, forced the mayor to swear fealty to "King Richard and the Commons," and liberated from the Archbishop's prison the ideologue of the movement, John Ball. He was a vagrant priest, scholar, and zealot who had been wandering the country for twenty years, frequently hauled in by the authorities for prophesying against Church and state and preaching radical doctrines of equality.

Although the poll tax was the igniting spark, the fundamental grievance was the bonds of villeinage and the lack of legal and political rights. Villeins could not plead in court against their lord, no one spoke for them in Parliament, they were bound by duties of servitude which they had no way to break except by forcibly obtaining a change of the rules. That was the object of the insurrection, and of the march on the capital that began from Canterbury.

As the Kentishmen swept forward to London, covering the seventy miles in two days, the Essex rebels marched southward to meet them. Abbeys and monasteries on the way were a special object of animosity because they were the last to allow commutation of servile labor. In the towns, artisans and small tradesmen, sharing the quarrel of the little against the great, gave aid and food to the peasants. As the sound of the rising spread to other counties, riots and outbreaks widened.

The "mad multitude" on its march from Kent and Essex opened prisons, sacked manors, and burned records. Some personally hated landlords and officials were murdered and their heads carried around on poles. Others, in fear of death, fled to hide in the same woods where villein outlaws frequently hid from them. Certain lords were forced by the rebels to accompany them "whether they would or not," either to supply needed elements of command or the appearance of participation by the gentry.

At the same time, peasant spokesmen swore to kill "all lawyers and servants of the King they could find." Short of the King, their imagined champion, all officialdom was their foe—sheriffs, foresters, tax-collectors, judges, abbots, lords, bishops, and dukes—but most especially men of the law because the law was the villeins' prison. Not accidentally, the Chief Justice of England,

Sir John Cavendish, was among their first victims, along with many clerks and jurors. Every attorney's house on the line of march reportedly was destroyed.

If the Jacquerie 23 years earlier had been an explosion without a program, the Peasants' Revolt arose out of a developing idea of freedom. Though theoretically free, villeins wanted abolition of the old bonds, the right to commute services to rent, a riddance of all the restrictions heaped up by the Statute of Laborers over the past thirty years in the effort to clamp labor in place. They had listened to Lollard priests, and to secular preachers moved by the evils of the time, and to John Ball's theories of leveling. "Matters cannot go well in England," was his theme, "until all things shall be held in common; when there shall be neither vassals nor lords, when the lords shall be no more masters than ourselves. . . . Are we not all descended from the same parents, Adam and Eve?"

Wyclif's spirit, which had dared deny the most pervasive authority of the time, was abroad. What had happened in the last thirty years, as a result of plague, war, oppression, and incompetence, was a weakened acceptance of the system, a mistrust of government and governors, lay and ecclesiastical, an awakening sense that authority could be challenged—that change was in fact possible. Moral authority can be no stronger than its acknowledgment. When officials were venal—as even the poor could see they were in the bribing of tax commissioners—and warriors a curse and the Church oppressive, the push for change gained strength.

It was encouraged by the preachers' castigation of the powerful. "The tournaments of the rich," they said, "are the torments of the poor." They regularly denounced "evil princes," "false executors who increase the sorrows of widows," "wicked ecclesiastics who show the worst example to the people," and, above all, nobles who empty the purses of the poor by their extravagance, and disdain them for "lowness of blod or foulenesse of body," for deformed shape of body or limb, for dullness of wit and uncunning of craft, and deign not to speak to them, and who are themselves stuffed with pride—of ancestry, fortune, gentility, possessions, power, comeliness, strength, children, treasure—"prowde in lokynge, prowde in spekyng, . . . prowde in goinge, standynge and sytting." All would be drawn by fiends to Hell on the Day of Judgment.

On that day of wrath, said the Dominican John Bromyard in terms that spoke directly to the peasant, the rich would have hung around their necks the oxen and sheep and beasts of the field that they had seized without paying for. The "righteous poor," promised a Franciscan friar, "will stand up against the cruel rich at the Day of Judgment and will accuse them of their works and severity on earth. 'Ha, ha!' will say the others, horribly frightened, 'These are the folk formerly in contempt. See how they are honored—they are among the sons of God! What are riches and pomp to us now who are abased?'"

If the meek were indeed the sons of God (even if they too were scolded by the preachers for greed, cheating, and irreverence), why should they wait for their rights until the Day of Judgment? If all men had a common origin in Adam and Eve, how should some be held in hereditary servitude? If all were equalized by death, as the medieval idea constantly emphasized, was it not possible that inequalities on earth were contrary to the will of God?

AT ITS CLIMAX on the outskirts of London, the Peasants' Revolt came to the edge of overpowering the government. No measures had been taken against the oncoming horde, partly from contempt for all Wills and Cobbs and Jacks and black-nailed louts, partly from mediocre leadership and lack of ready resources. Lancaster was away on the Scottish border, Buckingham was in Wales, and the only organized armed forces were already embarking at Plymouth for Spain under the command of the third brother, Edmund of Cambridge. Except for 500 or 600 men-at-arms in the King's retinue, the crown controlled no police or militia; London's citizens were unreliable because many were in sympathy and some in active connivance with the rebels.

Twenty thousand peasants were camped outside the walls demanding parley with the King. While they promised him safety, they shouted for the heads of Archbishop Sudbury and Sir Robert Hailes, the Chancellor and Treasurer, whom they held responsible for the poll tax, and for the head, too, of the arch "traitor," John of Gaunt, symbol of misgovernment and a failing war. John Ball harangued them with a fierce call to cast off the yoke they had borne for so long, to exterminate all great lords, judges, and lawyers and gain for all men equal freedom, rank, and power.

In agitated council, the government could find no course but to negotiate. Richard II, a slight fair boy of fourteen, accompanied by his knights, rode out to meet the insurgents and hear their demands: abolition of the poll tax and of all bonds of servile status, commutation at a rate of four pence an acre, free use of forests, abolition of the game laws—all these to be confirmed in charters sealed by the King. Everything the rebels asked was conceded in the hope of getting them to disperse and go home.

Meanwhile, partisans had opened the city's gates and bridges to a group led by Wat Tyler, who gained possession of the Tower of London and murdered Archbishop Sudbury and Sir Robert Hailes. Balked of Gaunt, they flung themselves upon his palace of the Savoy and tore it apart in an orgy of burning and smashing. At Wat Tyler's order, it was to be not looted but destroyed. Barrels of gunpowder found in storage were thrown on the flames, tapestries ripped, precious jewels pounded to bits with ax heads. The Temple, center of the law with all its deeds and records, was similarly destroyed. Killing followed; Lombards and Flemings (hated simply as foreigners), magnates, officials, and designated "traitors" (such as the rich merchant Sir Richard Lyons, who had been impeached by the Good Parliament and restored by Lancaster) were hunted down and slain.

In the hectic sequence of events, only Richard moved in a magic circle of reverence for the King's person. Perched on a tall war-horse before the peasants, a charming boy robed in purple embroidered with the royal leopards, wearing a crown and carrying a gold rod, gracious and smiling and gaining confidence from his sway over the mob, he granted charters written out and distributed by thirty clerks on the spot. On this basis, many groups of peasants departed, believing in the King as their protector.

While in London, Sir Robert Knollys, the Master of War, was urgently assembling an armed force, Wat Tyler, inflamed by blood and conquest, was exhorting his followers toward a massacre of the ruling class and a takeover of London. He was no longer to be satisfied by the promised charters, which he suspected were hollow, and he knew he would never be included in any pardon. He could only go forward toward a seizure of power. According to Walsingham, he boasted that "in four days' time all the laws of England would be issuing from his mouth."

He returned to the camp at Smithfield for another meeting with the King, where he put forth a new set of demands so extreme as to suggest that their purpose was to provoke rejection and provide a pretext for seizing Richard in person: all inequalities of rank and status were to be abolished, all men to be equal below the King, the Church to be disendowed and its estates divided among the commons, England to have but one bishop and the rest of the hierarchy to be eliminated. The King promised everything consistent with the "regality of his crown." Accounts of the next moments are so variously colored by the passions of the time that the scene remains forever obscure. Apparently Tyler picked a quarrel with a squire of the King's retinue, drew a dagger, and in a flash was himself struck down by the short sword of William Walworth, Mayor of London.

All was confusion and frenzy. The peasants drew their bows; some arrows flew. Richard, with extraordinary nerve, ordering no one to follow, rode forward alone, saying to the rebels, "Sirs, what is it you require? I am your captain. I am your King. Quiet yourselves." While he parleyed, Knollys' force, hastily summoned, rode up and surrounded the camp in mailed might with visors down and weapons gleaming. Dismayed and leaderless, the peasants were cowed; Wat Tyler's head displayed on a lance completed their collapse, like that of the Jacques at the death of Guillaume Cale.

Ordered to lay down their arms and assured of pardons to encourage dispersal, they trailed homeward. Leaders, including John Ball, were hanged and the rising elsewhere in England was suppressed—with sufficient brutality, if not the wild massacre that had taken place in France after the Jacquerie. Except for scattered retribution, the English revolt, too, was over within a month, defeated more by fraud than by force. The pardons issued in the King's name were revoked without compunction, and the charters canceled by a landowners' Parliament on the grounds that they had been issued under duress. To a deputation from Essex who came to remind the King of his promise to end villeinage, Richard replied, "Villeins ye are, and villeins ye shall remain."

The assumptions of autocrats are often behind the times. Economic forces were already propelling the decline of villeinage, and commutation continued, despite the crushing of the revolt, until the unfree peasant gradually disappeared. Whether the revolt hastened or delayed the process is obscure, but the immediate outcome encouraged complacency in the ruling class, beginning with the King. Perhaps intoxicated by success, Richard developed all the instincts of absolutism except the toughness to quell his opponents, and was to end as the victim of one of them. The military saw no need for improvement; the Church was stiffened against reform. Alarmed by the Lollards' leveling doctrines, the privileged class turned against them. In Gower's "Corruptions of the Age," the poet denounced them as breeders of division between church and state sent into the world by Satan. Lollardy went underground, long postponing the Protestant separation.

In these "days of wrath and anguish, days of calamity and misery," the laboring men's revolt seemed to many but one more tribulation signifying, like the Black Death, the anger of God. An anonymous poet, associating the rising of the peasants with an earthquake that occurred in 1382 and with the "pestilens," concluded that these three things

> Beeth tokenes of grete vengaunce and wrake
> That schulde falle for synnes sake.

Even the French raids on the English coast could be taken, as the monk Walsingham suggested, as the Lord "calling men to repentance by means of such terrors." Seen in these terms, revolt conveyed no political significance. "Man cannot change," a Florentine diarist wrote at this time, "that which God, for our sins, has willed."

Mary Wollstonecraft
(1759–1797)

ONE OF THE most incisive thinkers of the late eighteenth-century age of revolution, Mary Wollstonecraft wrote in several genres including the philosophical treatise, the novel, and the travel journal. Her work touched on a variety of subjects ranging from education to politics. *A Vindication of the Rights of Men*, which Wollstonecraft published in 1790, was arguably the most astute of the many responses penned in the 1790s to Edmund Burke's *Reflections on the Revolution in France*. Wollstonecraft's thinking about the situation of women in *A Vindication of the Rights of Woman* is likewise distinguished by its powerful recognition of the ways in which tyrannical systems corrupt those who endure them over time. In this regard, her insights share something fundamental with those of George Orwell in "Shooting an Elephant" ("Studying the System"). Throughout her career, in an age devoted to "reason" and scientific schemes for political improvement, Wollstonecraft attempted to theorize the essential role of sentiment in social and political relations. It was not perhaps until the twentieth century that her writing received the attention it deserved. The piece excerpted here discusses ways in which women have been subjugated throughout history and the ways in which they have subjugated themselves.

The Tyranny of the System
from *A Vindication of the Rights of Woman* (1792)

In the present state of society it appears necessary to go back to first principles in search of the most simple truths, and to dispute with some prevailing prejudice every inch of ground. To clear my way I must be allowed to ask some plain questions, and the answers will probably appear as unequivocal as the axioms on which reasoning is built; though, when entangled with various motives of action, they are formally contradicted, either by the words or conduct of men.

In what does man's pre-eminence over the brute creation consist? The answer is as clear as that a half is less than the whole; in Reason.

What acquirement exalts one being above another? Virtue; we spontaneously reply.

For what purpose were the passions implanted? That man by struggling with them might attain a degree of knowledge denied to the brutes; whispers Experience.

Consequently the perfection of our nature and capability of happiness, must be estimated by the degree of reason, virtue, and knowledge, that distinguish the individual, and direct the laws which bind society: and that from the exercise of reason, knowledge and virtue naturally flow, is equally undeniable, if mankind be viewed collectively.

The rights and duties of man thus simplified, it seems almost impertinent to attempt to illustrate truths that appear so incontrovertible; yet such deeply rooted prejudices have clouded reason, and such spurious qualities have assumed the name of virtues, that it is necessary to pursue the course of reason as it has been perplexed and involved in error, by various adventitious circumstances, comparing the simple axiom with casual deviations.

Men, in general, seem to employ their reason to justify prejudices, which they have imbibed, they can scarcely trace how, rather than to root them out. The mind must be strong that resolutely forms its own principles; for a kind of intellectual cowardice prevails which makes many men shrink from the task, or only do it by halves. Yet the imperfect conclusions thus drawn, are frequently very plausible, because they are built on partial experience, on just, though narrow, views.

Going back to first principles, vice skulks, with all its native deformity, from close investigation; but a set of shallow reasoners are always exclaiming that these arguments prove too much, and that a measure rotten at the core may be expedient. Thus expediency is continually contrasted with simple principles, till truth is lost in a mist of words, virtue, in forms, and knowledge rendered a sounding nothing, by the specious prejudices that assume its name.

That the society is formed in the wisest manner, whose constitution is founded on the nature of man, strikes, in the abstract, every thinking being so forcibly, that it looks like presumption to endeavour to bring forward proofs; though proof must be brought, or the strong hold of prescription will never be forced by reason; yet to urge prescription as an argument to justify the depriving men (or women) of their natural rights, is one of the absurd sophisms which daily insult common sense.

·　　·　　·

In the infancy of society, when men were just emerging out of barbarism, chiefs and priests, touching the most powerful springs of savage conduct, hope and fear, must have had unbounded sway. An aristocracy, of course, is naturally the first form of government. But, clashing interests soon losing their equipoise, a monarchy and hierarchy break out of the confusion of ambitious struggles, and the foundation of both is secured by feudal tenures. This appears to be the origin of monarchical and priestly power, and the dawn of civilization. But such combustible materials cannot long be pent up; and, getting vent in foreign wars and intestine insurrections, the people acquire some power in tumult, which obliges their rulers to gloss over their oppression with a shew of right. Thus, as wars, agriculture, commerce, and literature, expand the mind, despots are compelled to make covert corruption hold fast the power which was formerly snatched by open force. And this baneful lurking gangrene is most quickly spread by luxury and superstition, the sure dregs of ambition. The indolent puppet of a court first becomes a luxurious monster, or fastidious sensualist, and then makes the contagion which his unnatural state spread, the instrument of tyranny.

It is the pestiferous purple which renders the progress of civilization a curse, and warps the understanding, till men of sensibility doubt whether the expansion of intellect produces a greater portion of happiness or misery. But the nature of the poison points out the antidote; and had Rousseau mounted one step higher in his investigation, or could his eye have pierced through the foggy atmosphere, which he almost disdained to breathe, his active mind would have darted forward to contemplate the perfection of man in the establishment of true civilization, instead of taking his ferocious flight back to the night of sensual ignorance.

. . .

I may be accused of arrogance; still I must declare what I firmly believe, that all the writers who have written on the subject of female education and manners from Rousseau to Dr. Gregory, have contributed to render women more artificial, weak characters, than they would otherwise have been; and, consequently, more useless members of society. I might have expressed this conviction in a lower key, but I am afraid it would have been the whine of affectation, and not the faithful expression of my feelings, of the clear result, which experience and reflection have led me to draw. When I come to that division of the subject, I shall advert to the passages that I more particularly disapprove of, in the works of the authors I have just alluded to; but it is first necessary to observe, that my objection extends to the whole purport of those books, which tend, in my opinion, to degrade one half of the human species, and render women pleasing at the expense of every solid virtue.

. . .

Many are the causes that, in the present corrupt state of society, contribute to enslave women by cramping their understandings and sharpening their senses. One, perhaps, that silently does more mischief than all the rest, is their disregard of order.

To do every thing in an orderly manner, is a most important precept, which women, who, generally speaking, receive only a disorderly kind of education, seldom attend to with that degree of exactness that men, who from their infancy are broken into method, observe. This negligent kind of guess-work, for what other epithet can be used to point out the random exertions of a sort of instinctive common sense, never brought to the test of reason? prevents their generalizing matters of fact—so they do to-day, what they did yesterday, merely because they did it yesterday.

This contempt of the understanding in early life has more baneful consequences than is commonly supposed; for the little knowledge which women of strong minds attain, is, from various circumstances, of a more desultory kind than the knowledge of men, and it is acquired more by sheer observations on real life, than from comparing what has been individually observed with the results of experience generalized by speculation. Led by their dependent situation and domestic employments more into society, what they learn is rather by snatches; and as learning is with them, in general, only a secondary thing, they do not pursue any one branch with that persevering ardour necessary to give vigour to the faculties, and clearness to the judgment. In the present state of society, a little learning is required to support the character of a gentleman; and boys are obliged to submit to a few years of discipline. But in the education of women, the cultivation of the understanding is always subordinate to the acquirement of some corporeal accomplishment; even while enervated by confinement and false notions of modesty, the body is prevented from attaining that grace and beauty which relaxed half-formed limbs never exhibit. Besides, in youth their faculties are not brought forward by emulation; and having no serious scientific study, if they have natural sagacity it is turned too soon on life and manners. They dwell on effects, and modifications, without tracing them back to causes; and complicated rules to adjust behaviour are a weak substitute for simple principles.

As a proof that education gives this appearance of weakness to females, we may instance the example of military men, who are, like them, sent into the world before their minds have been stored with knowledge or fortified by principles. The consequences are similar; soldiers acquire a little superficial knowledge, snatched from the muddy current of conversation, and, from continually mixing with society, they gain, what is termed a knowledge of the world; and this acquaintance with manners and customs has frequently been confounded with a knowledge of the human heart. But can the crude fruit of casual observation, never brought to the test of judgment, formed by comparing speculation and experience, deserve such a distinction? Soldiers, as well as women, practice the minor virtues with punctilious politeness. Where is then the sexual difference, when the education has been the same? All the difference that I can discern, arises from the superior advantage of liberty, which enables the former to see more of life.

It is wandering from my present subject, perhaps, to make a political remark; but, as it was produced naturally by the train of my reflections, I shall not pass it silently over.

Standing armies can never consist of resolute, robust men; they may be well disciplined machines, but they will seldom contain men under the influence of strong passions, or with very vigorous faculties. And as for any depth of understanding, I will venture to affirm, that it is as rarely to be found in the army as amongst women; and the cause, I maintain, is the same. It may be further observed, that officers are also particularly attentive to their persons, fond of dancing, crowded rooms, adventures, and ridicule.[1] Like the *fair* sex, the business of their lives is gallantry.—They were taught to please, and they only live to please. Yet they do not lose their rank in the distinction of sexes, for they are still reckoned superior to women, though in what their superiority consists, beyond what I have just mentioned, it is difficult to discover.

The great misfortune is this, that they both acquire manners before morals, and a knowledge of life before they have, from reflection, any acquaintance with the grand ideal outline of human nature. The consequence is natural; satisfied with common nature, they become a prey to prejudices, and taking all their opinions on credit, they blindly submit to authority. So that, if they have any sense, it is a kind of instinctive glance, that catches proportions, and decides with respect to manners; but fails when arguments are to be pursued below the surface, or opinions analyzed.

May not the same remark be applied to women? Nay, the argument may be carried still further, for they are both thrown out of a useful station by the unnatural distinctions established in civilized life. Riches and hereditary honours have made cyphers of women to give consequence to the numerical figure; and idleness has produced a mixture of gallantry and despotism into society, which leads the very men who are the slaves of their mistresses to tyrannize over their sisters, wives, and daughters. This is only keeping them in rank and file, it is true. Strengthen the female mind by enlarging it, and there will be an end to blind obedience; but, as blind obedience is ever sought for by power, tyrants and sensualists are in the right when they endeavour to keep women in the dark, because the former only want slaves, and the latter a play-thing. The sensualist, indeed, has been the most dangerous of tyrants, and women have been duped by their lovers, as princes by their ministers, whilst dreaming that they reigned over them.

Frederick Douglass
(1818–1895)

BORN A SLAVE in Maryland, Frederick Douglass escaped to the north in 1838, and settled in New Bedford, Massachusetts, under an assumed name in order to avoid recapture. Douglass was a deeply eloquent international

---

1. Why should women be censured with petulant acrimony, because they seem to have a passion for a scarlet coat? Has not education placed them more on a level with soldiers than any other class of men? [Wollstonecraft's note]

spokesman for abolition, and he chronicled his own harrowing bondage and subsequent freedom in several autobiographies. The first of those works, *Narrative of the Life of Frederick Douglass, an American Slave, Written by Himself*, was published by the Anti-Slavery Office in Boston, in 1845. In his 2012 novel *Transatlantic* Colum McCann offers a richly imagined account of Douglass's lecture tour to Ireland following the book's publication in support of the abolitionist cause. In his autobiography Douglass details his experiences in rural Maryland and in Baltimore, where he was sent to learn the ship-caulking trade and where he learned to read, an activity prohibited by law in the slaveholding states. At first he was encouraged in this enterprise by Mrs. Auld, the wife of his new owner, but once the fact that Douglass was learning his letters was revealed to Mr. Auld, he had to continue in secret. Douglass here reveals the importance of reading, in particular his encounter with an anti-slavery debate in *The Columbian Orator*, to his awakening sense of himself as a slave. Originally published in 1797, this collection of sermons, speeches, and miscellaneous extracts edited by Caleb Bingham, was used as a primer in American schools in the early decades of the nineteenth century. In it Douglass discovered for the first time words for his own anguish.

Taking the Ell
from *Narrative of the Life of Frederick Douglass* (1845)

I lived in Master Hugh's family about seven years. During this time, I succeeded in learning to read and write. In accomplishing this, I was compelled to resort to various stratagems. I had no regular teacher. My mistress, who had kindly commenced to instruct me, had, in compliance with the advice and direction of her husband, not only ceased to instruct, but had set her face against my being instructed by any one else. It is due, however, to my mistress to say of her, that she did not adopt this course of treatment immediately. She at first lacked the depravity indispensable to shutting me up in mental darkness. It was at least necessary for her to have some training in the exercise of irresponsible power, to make her equal to the task of treating me as though I were a brute.

My mistress was, as I have said, a kind and tender-hearted woman; and in the simplicity of her soul she commenced, when I first went to live with her, to treat me as she supposed one human being ought to treat another. In entering upon the duties of a slaveholder, she did not seem to perceive that I sustained to her the relation of a mere chattel, and that for her to treat me as a human being was not only wrong, but dangerously so. Slavery proved as injurious to her as it did to me. When I went there, she was a pious, warm, and tender-hearted woman. There was no sorrow or suffering for which she had not a tear. She had bread for the hungry, clothes for the naked, and comfort for every mourner that came within her reach. Slavery soon proved its ability to divest her of these heavenly qualities. Under its influence, the tender heart became stone, and the lamblike disposition gave way to one of tiger-like fierceness. The first step in her downward course was in her ceasing to instruct me. She now commenced to practice her husband's precepts. She finally became even more violent in her opposition than her husband himself. She was not satisfied with simply doing as well as he had commanded; she seemed anxious to do better. Nothing seemed to make her more angry than to see me with a newspaper. She seemed to think that here lay the danger. I have had her rush at me with a face made all up of fury, and snatch from me a newspaper, in a manner that fully revealed her apprehension. She was an apt woman; and a little experience soon demonstrated, to her satisfaction, that education and slavery were incompatible with each other.

From this time I was most narrowly watched. If I was in a separate room any considerable length of time, I was sure to be suspected of having a book, and was at once called to give an account of myself. All this, however, was too late. The first step had been taken. Mistress, in teaching me the alphabet, had given me the *inch*, and no precaution could prevent me from taking the *ell*.

The plan which I adopted, and the one by which I was most successful, was that of making friends of all the little white boys whom I met in the street. As many of these as I could, I converted into teachers. With their kindly aid, obtained at different times and in different places, I finally succeeded in learning to read. When I was sent of errands, I always took my book with me, and by going one part of my errand quickly, I found time to get a lesson before my return. I used also to carry bread with me, enough of which was always in the house, and to which I was always welcome; for I was much better off in this regard than many of the poor white children in our neighborhood. This bread I used to bestow upon the hungry little urchins, who, in return, would give me that more valuable bread of knowledge. I am strongly tempted to give the names of two or three of those little boys, as a testimonial of the gratitude and affection I bear them; but prudence forbids;—not that it would injure me, but it might embarrass them; for it is almost an unpardonable offence to teach slaves to read in this Christian country. It is enough to say of the dear little fellows, that they lived on Philpot Street, very near Durgin and Bailey's shipyard. I used to talk this matter of slavery over with them. I would sometimes say to them, I wished I could be as free as they would be when they got to be men. "You will be free as soon as you are twenty-one, *but I am a slave for life!* Have not I as good a right to be free as you have?" These words used to trouble them; they would express for me the liveliest sympathy, and console me with the hope that something would occur by which I might be free.

I was now about twelve years old, and the thought of being *a slave for life* began to bear heavily upon my heart. Just about this time, I got hold of a book entitled "The Columbian Orator." Every opportunity I got, I used to read this book. Among much of other interesting matter, I found in it a dialogue between a master and his slave. The slave was represented as having run away from his master three times. The dialogue represented the conversation which took place between them, when the slave was retaken the third time. In this dialogue, the whole argument in behalf of slavery was brought forward by the master, all of which was disposed of by the slave. The slave was made to say some very smart as well as impressive things in reply to his master— things which had the desired though unexpected effect; for the conversation resulted in the voluntary emancipation of the slave on the part of the master.

In the same book, I met with one of Sheridan's mighty speeches on and in behalf of Catholic emancipation. These were choice documents to me. I read them over and over again with unabated interest. They gave tongue to interesting thoughts of my own soul, which had frequently flashed through my mind, and died away for want of utterance. The moral which I gained from the dialogue was the power of truth over the conscience of even a slaveholder. What I got from Sheridan was a bold denunciation of slavery, and a powerful vindication of human rights. The reading of these documents enabled me to utter my thoughts, and to meet the arguments brought forward to sustain slavery; but while they relieved me of one difficulty, they brought on another even more painful than the one of which I was relieved. The more I read, the more I was led to abhor and detest my enslavers. I could regard them in no other light than a band of successful robbers, who had left their homes, and gone to Africa, and stolen us from our homes, and in a strange land reduced us to slavery. I loathed them as being the meanest as well as the most wicked of men. As I read and contemplated the subject, behold! that very discontentment which Master Hugh had predicted would follow my learning to read had already come, to torment and sting my soul to unutterable anguish. As I writhed under it, I would at times feel that learning to read had been a curse rather than a blessing. It had given me a view of my wretched condition, without the remedy. It opened my eyes to the horrible pit, but to no ladder upon which to get out. In moments of agony, I envied my fellow-slaves for their stupidity. I have often wished myself a beast. I preferred the condition of the meanest reptile to my own. Any thing, no matter what, to get rid of thinking! It was this everlasting thinking of my condition that tormented me. There was no getting rid of it. It was pressed upon me by every object within sight or hearing, animate or inanimate. The silver trump of freedom had roused my soul to eternal wakefulness. Freedom now appeared, to disappear no more forever. It was heard in every sound, and seen in every thing. It was ever present to torment me with a sense of my wretched condition. I saw nothing without seeing it, I heard nothing without hearing it, and felt nothing without feeling it. It looked from every star, it smiled in every calm, breathed in every wind, and moved in every storm.

I often found myself regretting my own existence, and wishing myself dead; and but for the hope of being free, I have no doubt but that I should have killed myself, or done something for which I should have been killed. While in this state of mind, I was eager to hear any one speak of slavery. I was a ready listener. Every little while, I could hear something about the abolitionists. It was some time before I found what the word meant. It was always used in such connections as to make it an interesting word to me. If a slave ran away and succeeded in getting clear, or if a slave killed his master, set fire to a barn, or did any thing very wrong in the mind of a slaveholder, it was spoken of as the fruit of *abolition*. Hearing the word in this connection very often, I set about learning what it meant. The dictionary afforded me little or no help. I found it was "the act of abolishing;" but then I did not know what was to be abolished. Here I was perplexed. I did not dare to ask any one about its meaning, for I was satisfied that it was something they wanted me to know very little about. After a patient waiting, I got one of our city papers, containing an account of the number of petitions from the north, praying for the abolition of slavery in the District of Columbia, and of the slave trade between the States. From this time I understood the words *abolition* and *abolitionist*, and always drew near when that word was spoken, expecting to hear something of importance to myself and fellow-slaves. The light broke in upon me by degrees. I went one day down on the wharf of Mr. Waters; and seeing two Irishmen unloading a scow of stone, I went, unasked, and helped them. When we had finished, one of them came to me and asked me if I were a slave. I told him I was. He asked, "Are ye a slave for life?" I told him that I was. The good Irishman seemed to be deeply affected by the statement. He said to the other that it was a pity so fine a little fellow as myself should be a slave for life. He said it was a shame to hold me. They both advised me to run away to the north; that I should find friends there, and that I should be free. I pretended not to be interested in what they said, and treated them as if I did not understand them; for I feared they might be treacherous. White men have been known to encourage slaves to escape, and then, to get the reward, catch them and return them to their masters. I was afraid that these seemingly good men might use me so; but I nevertheless remembered their advice, and from that time I resolved to run away. I looked forward to a time at which it would be safe for me to escape. I was too young to think of doing so immediately; besides, I wished to learn how to write, as I might have occasion to write my own pass. I consoled myself with the hope that I should one day find a good chance. Meanwhile, I would learn to write.

The idea as to how I might learn to write was suggested to me by being in Durgin and Bailey's ship-yard, and frequently seeing the ship carpenters, after hewing, and getting a piece of timber ready for use, write on the timber the name of that part of the ship for which it was intended. When a piece of timber was intended for the larboard side, it would be marked thus—"L." When a piece was for the starboard side, it would be marked thus—"S." A piece for the larboard side forward, would be marked thus—"L. F." When a piece was for starboard side forward, it would be marked thus—"S. F." For larboard aft, it would be marked thus—"L. A." For starboard aft, it would be marked thus—"S. A." I soon learned the names of these letters, and for what they were intended when placed upon a piece of timber in the ship-yard. I immediately commenced copying them, and in a short time was able to make the four letters named. After that, when I met with any boy who I knew could write, I would tell him I could write as well as he. The next word would be, "I don't believe you. Let me see you try it." I would then make the letters which I had been so fortunate as to learn, and ask him to beat that. In this way I got a good many lessons in writing, which it is quite possible I should never have gotten in any other way. During this time, my copy-book was the board fence, brick wall, and pavement; my pen and ink was a lump of chalk. With these, I learned mainly how to write. I then commenced and continued copying the Italics in Webster's Spelling Book, until I could make them all without looking on the book. By this time, my little Master Thomas had gone to school, and learned how to write, and had written over a number of copy-books. These had been brought home, and shown to some of our near neighbors, and then laid aside. My mistress used to go to class meeting at the Wilk Street meetinghouse every Monday afternoon, and leave me to take care of the house. When left thus, I used to spend the time in writing in the spaces left in Master Thomas's copy-book, copying what he had written. I continued to do this until I could write a hand very similar to that of Master Thomas. Thus, after a long, tedious effort for years, I finally succeeded in learning how to write.

·   ·   ·

I lived with Mr. Covey one year. During the first six months, of that year, scarce a week passed without his whipping me. I was seldom free from a sore back. My awkwardness was almost always his excuse for whipping me. We were worked fully up to the point of endurance. Long before day we were up, our horses fed, and by the first approach of day we were off to the field with our hoes and ploughing teams. Mr. Covey gave us enough to eat, but scarce time to eat it. We were often less than five minutes taking our meals. We were often in the field from the first approach of day till its last lingering ray had left us; and at saving-fodder time, midnight often caught us in the field binding blades.

Covey would be out with us. The way he used to stand it, was this. He would spend the most of his afternoons in bed. He would then come out fresh in the evening, ready to urge us on with his words, example, and frequently with the whip. Mr. Covey was one of the few slaveholders who could and did work with his hands. He was a hard-working man. He knew by himself just what a man or a boy could do. There was no deceiving him. His work went on in his absence almost as well as in his presence; and he had the faculty of making us feel that he was ever present with us. This he did by surprising us. He seldom approached the spot where we were at work openly, if he could do it secretly. He always aimed at taking us by surprise. Such was his cunning, that we used to call him, among ourselves, "the snake." When we were at work in the cornfield, he would sometimes crawl on his hands and knees to avoid detection, and all at once he would rise nearly in our midst, and scream out, "Ha, ha! Come, come! Dash on, dash on!" This being his mode of attack, it was never safe to stop a single minute. His comings were like a thief in the night. He appeared to us as being ever at hand. He was under every tree, behind every stump, in every bush, and at every window, on the plantation. He would sometimes mount his horse, as if bound to St. Michael's, a distance of seven miles, and in half an hour afterwards you would see him coiled up in the corner of the wood-fence, watching every motion of the slaves. He would, for this purpose, leave his horse tied up in the woods. Again, he would sometimes walk up to us, and give us orders as though he was upon the point of starting on a long journey, turn his back upon us, and make as though he was going to the house to get ready; and, before he would get half way thither, he would turn short and crawl into a fence-corner, or behind some tree, and there watch us till the going down of the sun.

Mr. Covey's *forte* consisted in his power to deceive. His life was devoted to planning and perpetrating the grossest deceptions. Every thing he possessed in the shape of learning or religion, he made conform to his disposition to deceive. He seemed to think himself equal to deceiving the Almighty. He would make a short prayer in the morning, and a long prayer at night; and, strange as it may seem, few men would at times appear more devotional than he. The exercises of his family devotions were always commenced with singing; and, as he was a very poor singer himself, the duty of raising the hymn generally came upon me. He would read his hymn, and nod at me to commence. I would at times do so; at others, I would not. My non-compliance would almost always produce much confusion. To show himself independent of me, he would start and stagger through with his hymn in the most discordant manner. In this state of mind, he prayed with more than ordinary spirit. Poor man! such was his disposition, and success at deceiving, I do verily believe that he sometimes deceived himself into the solemn belief, that he was a sincere worshipper of the most high God; and this, too, at a time when he may be said to have been guilty of compelling his woman slave to commit the sin of adultery. The facts in the case are these: Mr. Covey was a poor man; he was just commencing in life; he was only able to buy one slave; and, shocking as is the fact, he bought her, as he said, for *a breeder*. This woman was named Caroline. Mr. Covey bought her from Mr. Thomas Lowe, about six miles from St. Michael's. She was a large, able-bodied woman, about twenty years old. She had already given birth to one child, which proved her to be just what he wanted. After buying her, he hired a married man of Mr. Samuel Harrison, to live with him one year; and him he used to fasten up with her every night! The result was, that, at the end of the year, the miserable woman gave birth to twins. At this result Mr. Covey seemed to be highly pleased, both with the man and the wretched woman. Such was his joy, and that of his wife, that nothing they could do for Caroline during her confinement was too good, or too hard, to be done. The children were regarded as being quite an addition to his wealth.

If at any one time of my life more than another, I was made to drink the bitterest dregs of slavery, that time was during the first six months of my stay with Mr. Covey. We were worked in all weathers. It was never too hot or too cold; it could never rain, blow, hail, or snow, too hard for us to work in the field. Work, work, work, was scarcely more the order of the day than of the night. The longest days were too short for him, and the shortest nights too long for him. I was somewhat unmanageable when I first went there, but a few months of this discipline tamed me. Mr. Covey succeeded in breaking me. I was broken in body, soul, and spirit. My natural elasticity was crushed, my intellect languished, the disposition to read departed, the cheerful spark that lingered about my eye died; the dark night of slavery closed in upon me; and behold a man transformed into a brute!

Sunday was my only leisure time. I spent this in a sort of beast-like stupor, between sleep and wake, under some large tree. At times I would rise up, a flash of energetic freedom would dart through my soul, accompanied with a faint beam of hope, that flickered for a moment, and then vanished. I sank down again, mourning over my wretched condition. I was sometimes prompted to take my life, and that of Covey, but was prevented by a combination of hope and fear. My sufferings on this plantation seem now like a dream rather than a stern reality.

Our house stood within a few rods of the Chesapeake Bay, whose broad bosom was ever white with sails from every quarter of the habitable globe. Those beautiful vessels, robed in purest white, so delightful to the eye of freemen, were to me so many shrouded ghosts, to terrify and torment me with thoughts of my wretched condition. I have often, in the deep stillness of a summer's Sabbath, stood all alone upon the lofty banks of that noble bay, and traced, with saddened heart and tearful eye, the countless number of sails moving off to the mighty ocean. The sight of these always affected me powerfully. My thoughts would compel utterance; and there, with no audience but the Almighty, I would pour out my soul's complaint, in my rude way, with an apostrophe to the moving multitude of ships:—

"You are loosed from your moorings, and are free; I am fast in my chains, and am a slave! You move merrily before the gentle gale, and I sadly before the bloody whip! You are freedom's swift-winged angels, that fly round the world; I am confined in bands of iron! O that I were free! O, that I were on one of your gallant decks, and under your protecting wing! Alas! betwixt me and you, the turbid waters roll. Go on, go on. O that I could also go! Could I but swim! If I could fly! O, why was I born a man, of whom to make a brute! The glad ship is gone; she hides in the dim distance. I am left in the hottest hell of unending slavery. O God, save me! God, deliver me! Let me be free! Is there any God? Why am I a slave? I will run away. I will not stand it. Get caught, or get clear, I'll try it. I had as well die with ague as the fever. I have only one life to lose. I had as well be killed running as die standing. Only think of it; one hundred miles straight north, and I am free! Try it? Yes! God helping me, I will. It cannot be that I shall live and die a slave. I will take to the water. This very bay shall yet bear me into freedom. The steamboats steered in a north-east course from North Point. I will do the same; and when I get to the head of the bay, I will turn my canoe adrift, and walk straight through Delaware into Pennsylvania. When I get there, I shall not be required to have a pass; I can travel without being disturbed. Let but the first opportunity offer, and, come what will, I am off. Meanwhile, I will try to bear up under the yoke. I am not the only slave in the world. Why should I fret? I can bear as much as any of them. Besides, I am but a boy, and all boys are bound to some one. It may be that my misery in slavery will only increase my happiness when I get free. There is a better day coming."

Thus I used to think, and thus I used to speak to myself; goaded almost to madness at one moment, and at the next reconciling myself to my wretched lot.

I have already intimated that my condition was much worse, during the first six months of my stay at Mr. Covey's, than in the last six. The circumstances leading to the change in Mr. Covey's course toward me form an epoch in my humble history. You have seen how a man was made a slave; you shall see how a slave was made a man. On one of the hottest days of the month of August, 1833, Bill Smith, William Hughes, a slave named Eli, and myself, were engaged in fanning wheat. Hughes was clearing the fanned wheat from before the fan. Eli was turning, Smith was feeding, and I was carrying wheat to the fan. The work was simple, requiring strength rather than intellect; yet, to one entirely unused to such work, it came very hard. About three o'clock of that day, I broke down; my strength failed me; I was seized with a violent aching of the head, attended with extreme dizziness; I trembled in every limb. Finding what was coming, I nerved myself up, feeling it would never do to stop work. I stood as long as I could stagger to the hopper with grain. When I could stand no longer, I fell, and felt as if held down by an immense weight. The fan of course stopped; every one had his own work to do; and no one could do the work of the other, and have his own go on at the same time.

Mr. Covey was at the house, about one hundred yards from the treading-yard where we were fanning. On hearing the fan stop, he left immediately, and came to the spot where we were. He hastily inquired what the matter was. Bill answered that I was sick, and there was no one to bring wheat to the fan. I had by this time crawled away under the side of the post and rail-fence by which the yard was enclosed, hoping to find relief by getting out of the sun. He then asked where I was. He was told by one of the hands. He came to the spot, and, after looking at me awhile, asked me what was the matter. I told him as well as I could, for I scarce had strength to speak. He then gave me a savage kick in the side, and told me to get up. I tried to do so, but fell back in the attempt. He gave me another kick, and again told me to rise. I again tried, and succeeded in gaining my feet; but, stooping to get the tub with which I was feeding the fan, I again staggered and fell. While down in this situation, Mr. Covey took up the hickory slat with which Hughes had been striking off the half-bushel measure, and with it gave me a heavy blow upon the head, making a large wound, and the blood ran freely; and with this again told me to get up. I made no effort to comply, having now made up my mind to let him do his worst. In a short time after receiving this blow, my head grew better. Mr. Covey had now left me to my fate. At this moment I resolved, for the first time, to go to my master, enter a complaint, and ask his protection. In order to do this, I must that afternoon walk seven miles; and this, under the circumstances, was truly a severe undertaking. I was exceedingly feeble; made so as much by the kicks and blows which I received, as by the severe fit of sickness to which I had been subjected. I, however, watched my chance, while Covey was looking in an opposite direction, and started for St. Michael's. I succeeded in getting a considerable distance on my way to the woods, when Covey discovered me, and called after me to come back, threatening what he would do if I did not come. I disregarded both his calls and his threats, and made my way to the woods as fast as my feeble state would allow; and thinking I might be overhauled by him if I kept the road, I walked through the woods, keeping far enough from the road to avoid detection, and near enough to prevent losing my way. I had not gone far before my little strength again failed me. I could go no farther. I fell down, and lay for a considerable time. The blood was yet oozing from the wound on my head. For a time I thought I should bleed to death; and think now that I should have done so, but that the blood so matted my hair as to stop the wound. After lying there about three quarters of an hour, I nerved myself up again, and started on my way, through bogs and briers, barefooted and bareheaded, tearing my feet sometimes at nearly every step; and after a journey of about seven miles, occupying some five hours to perform it, I arrived at master's store. I then presented an appearance enough to affect any but a heart of iron. From the crown of my head to my feet, I was covered with blood. My hair was all clotted with dust and blood; my shirt was stiff with blood. I suppose I looked like a man who had escaped a den of wild beasts, and barely escaped them. In this state I appeared before my master, humbly entreating him to interpose his authority for my protection. I told him all the circumstances as well as I could, and it seemed, as I spoke, at times to affect him. He would then walk the floor, and seek to justify Covey by saying he expected I deserved it. He asked me what I wanted. I told him, to let me get a new home; that as sure as I lived with Mr. Covey again, I should live with but to die with him; that Covey would surely kill me; he was in a fair way for it. Master Thomas ridiculed the idea that there was any danger of Mr. Covey's killing me, and said that he knew Mr. Covey; that he was a good man, and that he could not think of taking me from him; that, should he do so, he would lose the whole year's wages; that I belonged to Mr. Covey for one year, and that I must go back to him, come what might; and that I must not trouble him with any more stories, or that he would himself *get hold of me*. After threatening me thus, he gave me a very large dose of salts, telling me that I might remain in St. Michael's that night, (it being quite late,) but that I must be off back to Mr. Covey's early in the morning; and that if I did not, he would *get hold of me*, which meant that he would whip me. I remained all night, and, according to his orders, I started off to Covey's in the morning, (Saturday morning,) wearied in body and broken in spirit. I got no supper that night, or breakfast that morning. I reached Covey's about nine o'clock; and just as I was getting over the fence that divided Mrs. Kemp's fields from ours, out ran Covey with his cowskin, to give me another whipping. Before he could reach me, I succeeded in getting to the cornfield; and as the corn was very high, it afforded me the means of hiding. He seemed very angry, and searched for me a long time. My behavior was altogether unaccountable. He finally gave up the chase, thinking, I suppose, that I must come home for something to eat; he would give himself no further trouble in looking for me. I spent that day mostly in the woods, having the alternative before me,—to go home and be whipped to death, or stay in the woods and be starved to death. That night, I fell in with Sandy Jenkins, a slave with whom I was somewhat acquainted. Sandy had a free wife who lived about four miles from Mr. Covey's; and it being Saturday, he was on his way to see her. I told him my circumstances, and he very kindly invited me to go home with him. I went home with him, and talked this whole matter over, and got his advice as to what course it was best for me to pursue. I found Sandy an old adviser. He told me, with great solemnity, I must go back to Covey; but that before I went, I must go with him into another part of the woods, where there was a certain *root*, which, if I would take some of it with me, carrying it *always on my right side*, would render it impossible for Mr. Covey, or any other white man, to whip me. He said he had carried it for years; and since he had done so, he had never received a blow, and never expected to while he carried it. I at first rejected the idea, that the simple carrying of a root in my pocket would have any such effect as he had said, and was not disposed to take it; but Sandy impressed the necessity with much earnestness, telling me it could do no harm, if it did no good. To please him, I at length took the root, and, according to his direction, carried it upon my right side. This was Sunday morning. I immediately started for home; and upon entering the yard gate, out came Mr. Covey on his way to meeting. He spoke to me very kindly, bade me drive the pigs from a lot near by, and passed on towards the church. Now, this singular conduct of Mr. Covey really made me begin to think that there was something in the *root* which Sandy had given me; and had it been on any other day than Sunday, I could have attributed the conduct to no other cause than the influence of that root; and as it was, I was half inclined to think the *root* to be something more than I at first had taken it to be. All went well till Monday morning. On this morning, the virtue of the *root* was fully tested. Long before daylight, I was called to go and rub, curry, and feed, the horses. I obeyed, and was glad to obey. But whilst thus engaged, whilst in the act of throwing down some blades from the loft, Mr. Covey entered the stable with a long rope; and just as I was half out of the loft, he caught hold of my legs, and was about tying me. As soon as I found what he was up to, I gave a sudden spring, and as I did so, he holding to my legs, I was brought sprawling on the stable floor. Mr. Covey seemed now to think he had me, and could do what he pleased; but at this moment—from whence came the spirit I don't know—I resolved to fight; and, suiting my action to the resolution, I seized Covey hard by the throat; and as I did so, I rose. He held on to me, and I to him. My resistance was so entirely unexpected that Covey seemed taken all aback. He trembled like a leaf. This gave me assurance, and I held him uneasy, causing the blood to run where I touched him with the ends of my fingers. Mr. Covey soon called out to Hughes for help. Hughes came, and, while Covey held me, attempted to tie my right hand. While he was in the act of doing so, I watched my chance, and gave him a heavy kick close under the ribs. This kick fairly sickened Hughes, so that he left me in the hands of Mr. Covey. This kick had the effect of not only weakening Hughes, but Covey also. When he saw Hughes bending over with pain, his courage quailed. He asked me if I meant to persist in my resistance. I told him I did, come what might; that he had used me like a brute for six months, and that I was determined to be used so no longer. With that, he strove to drag me to a stick that was lying just out of the stable door. He meant to knock me down. But just as he was leaning over to get the stick, I seized him with both hands by his collar, and brought him by a sudden snatch to the ground. By this time, Bill came. Covey called upon him for assistance. Bill wanted to know what he could do. Covey said, "Take hold of him, take hold of him!" Bill said his master hired him out to work, and not to help to whip me; so he left Covey and myself to fight our own battle out. We were at it for nearly two hours. Covey at length let me go, puffing and blowing at a great rate, saying that if I had not resisted, he would not have whipped me half so much. The truth was, that he had not whipped me at all. I considered him as getting entirely the worst end of the bargain; for he had drawn no blood from me, but I had from him. The whole six months afterwards, that I spent with Mr. Covey, he never laid the weight of his finger upon me in anger. He would occasionally say, he didn't want to get hold of me again. "No," thought I, "you need not; for you will come off worse than you did before."

'This battle with Mr. Covey was the turning-point in my career as a slave. It rekindled the few expiring embers of freedom, and revived within me a sense of my own manhood. It recalled the departed self-confidence, and inspired me again with a determination to be free. The gratification afforded by the triumph was a full compensation for whatever else might follow, even death itself. He only can understand the deep satisfaction which I experienced, who has himself repelled by force the bloody arm of slavery. I felt as I never felt before. It was a glorious resurrection, from the tomb of slavery, to the heaven of freedom. My long-crushed spirit rose, cowardice departed, bold defiance took its place; and I now resolved that, however long I might remain a slave in form, the day had passed forever when I could be a slave in fact. I did not hesitate to let it be known of me, that the white man who expected to succeed in whipping, must also succeed in killing me.

Eugene V. Debs
(1855–1926)

BORN IN TERRE Haute, Indiana, Eugene Debs, the son of poor immigrants, left high school to work for the railroads scraping paint from locomotives; later he became a fireman. Debs's introduction to labor movements began when he joined the Brotherhood of Locomotive Firemen. In 1893, he became president of the American Railway Union. He would found the Industrial Workers of the World in 1905. The labor movements of the late nineteenth and early twentieth centuries demanded living wages, safety regulations, and eight-hour workdays. Debs led the American Railway Union during the 1894 Pullman strike. After a clash with federal troops brought in as strikebreakers, he was put in jail for six months for contempt of court, despite being defended by Clarence Darrow. It was at this time that Debs began to espouse European socialism; he never joined the Communist Party because of his distrust of the Soviet Union's repressive policies. In 1900, Debs ran the first of several unsuccessful presidential campaigns on the Socialist ticket. He came closest in 1912, winning 6 percent of the vote against Woodrow Wilson, William Howard Taft, and Theodore Roosevelt. In 1916, Debs won a seat in the Indiana State Congress. After making an anti-war speech in 1918, he was jailed under the Espionage Act. Sentenced to ten years in a federal penitentiary, Debs was released in 1921 by then president Warren Harding. This address to the court occurred during the 1918 trial; in it Debs articulates the indignation over injustice and inequity that fueled his activist career.

Statement to the Court (1918)

Your honor, years ago I recognized my kinship with all living beings, and I made up my mind that I was not one bit better than the meanest of earth. I said then, and I say now, that while there is a lower class, I am in it, while there is a criminal element I am of it, and while there is a soul in prison, I am not free.

I listened to all that was said in this court in support and justification of this prosecution, but my mind remains unchanged. I look upon the Espionage law as a despotic enactment in flagrant conflict with democratic principles and with the spirit of free institutions.

I have no fault to find with this court or with the trial. Everything in connection with this case has been conducted upon a dignified plane, and in a respectful and decent spirit. . . .

Your honor, I have stated in this court that I am opposed to the social system in which we live; that I believe in a fundamental change—but if possible by peaceable and orderly means.

Let me call your attention to the fact this morning that in the present system 5 per cent of our people own and control two-thirds of our wealth; 65 per cent of our people, embracing the working class who produce all wealth, have but 5 per cent to show for it.

Standing here this morning, I recall my boyhood. At fourteen I went to work in a railroad shop; at sixteen I was firing a freight engine on a railroad.

I remember all the hardships and privations of that earlier day, and from that time until now my heart has been with the working class. I could have been in Congress long ago. I have preferred to go to prison.

In the struggle—the fierce and unceasing struggle—between the toilers and producers and their exploiters, I have tried as best I might to serve those among whom I was born, and whose lot I expect to share to the end of my days.

I am thinking this morning of the men in the mills and factories; of the men in the mines and on the railroads. I am thinking of the women who for a paltry wage are compelled to work out their barren lives; of the little children who in this system are robbed of their childhood and in their tender years are seized in the remorseless grasp of Mammon and forced into the industrial dungeons, there to feed the monster machines while they themselves are being starved and stunted, body and soul. I see them dwarfed and diseased and their little lives broken and blasted because in this high noon of our twentieth century Christian civilization money is still so much more important than the flesh and blood of childhood. In very truth gold is god today and rules with pitiless sway in the affairs of men.

In this country—the most favored beneath the bending skies—we have vast areas of the richest and most fertile soil, material resources in inexhaustible abundance, the most marvellous productive machinery on earth, and millions of eager workers ready to apply their labor to that machinery to produce in abundance for every man, woman and child—and if there are still vast numbers of our people who are the victims of poverty and whose lives are an unceasing struggle all the way from youth to old age, until at last death comes to their rescue and stills their aching hearts and lulls these hapless victims to dreamless sleep, it is not the fault of the Almighty; it cannot be charged to nature, but it is due entirely to the outgrown social system in which we live that ought to be abolished not only in the interest of the toiling masses but in the higher interest of all humanity.

I am thinking of the children of poverty, the little girls in the textile mills of the East and in the cotton factories of the South, at work in a vitiated atmosphere, when they ought to be at play or at school, who, when they do grow up, if they live long enough, and approach the marriage state, will be unfit for it. Their nerves are worn out, their tissue is exhausted, their vitality is spent. They have been fed to industry. Their lives have been coined into gold. Their offspring are born weak and tired. That is why there are so many so-called failures in our modern life.

Your honor, the 5 per cent of our people that I have made reference to constitute the plutocratic element that absolutely rules our country. They privately own and control our common necessities. They wear no crowns; they wield no scepters; they sit upon no thrones; and yet they are our economic masters and political rulers.

I believe, your honor, in common with all Socialists, that this nation ought to own and control its own industries. I believe, as all Socialists do, that all things that are jointly needed and used ought to be jointly owned—that industry, the basis of our social life, instead of being the private property of the few and operated for their enrichment, ought to be the common property of all, democratically administered in the interest of all.

John D. Rockefeller has today an income of sixty million dollars a year, five million dollar a month, two hundred thousand dollars a day. He does not produce a penny of it. I make no attack on Mr. Rockefeller personally. I do not in the least dislike him. If he were in need and it were in my power to help him, I should serve him as gladly as I would any other human being. I have no quarrel with Mr. Rockefeller personally, nor with any other capitalist. I am simply opposing a social order in which it is possible for one man who does absolutely nothing that is useful, to amass a fortune of hundreds of millions of dollars, while millions of men and women who work all the days of their lives secure barely enough for a wretched existence.

This order of things cannot always endure. I have registered my protest against it. I recognize the feebleness of my effort, but, fortunately, I am not alone. There are multiplied thousands of others who, like myself, have come to realize that before we may truly enjoy the blessings of civilized life, we must reorganize society upon a mutual and co-operative basis; and to this end we have organized a great economic and political movement that spreads over the face of all the earth.

There are today upwards of sixty millions of Socialists, loyal, devoted, adherents to this cause, regardless of nationality, race, creed, color or sex. They are all making common cause. They are spreading with tireless energy the propaganda of the new social order. They are waiting, watching and work-ing hopefully through all the hours of the day and the night. They are still in a minority. But they have learned how to be patient and to bide their time. They feel—they know, indeed,—that the time is coming, in spite of all opposi-tion, all persecution, when this emancipating gospel will spread among all the peoples, and when this minority will become the triumphant majority and, sweeping into power, inaugurate the greatest social and economic change in history.

In that day we shall have the universal commonwealth—the harmonious co-operation of every nation with every other nation on earth.

. . .

Your honor, I ask no mercy and I plead for no immunity. I realize that finally the right must prevail. I never so clearly comprehended as now the great struggle between the powers of greed and exploitation on the one hand and upon the other the rising hosts of industrial freedom and social justice.

I can see the dawn of the better day for humanity. The people are awakening. In due time they will and must come to their own.

Mohandas Gandhi
(1869–1948)

THE LEADER OF the nationalist movement that eventually ended centuries of the British Raj in India, Gandhi, who came to be known as "Mahatma," or "great soul," advocated non-violent protest as a means of achieving political and social reforms. Gandhi's philosophical commitments were an amalgam of Hindu and Christian principles, together with the pacifism of Leo Tolstoy and the civil disobedience advocated by Henry David Thoreau. Gandhi called his doctrine *satyagraha*, "devotion to truth." Trained as a barrister in England, Gandhi first engaged in political activism in South Africa, where he spent two decades and was jailed repeatedly for his protest against the mistreatment of Indian immigrants. Finally, in 1914, having won concessions from the South African government, Gandhi went home to India, where his movement gained a vast following. Gandhi mobilized protests against the Rowlatt Acts, under the auspices of which the British interned Indians suspected of sedition. Through a platform of "peaceful non-cooperation," Indians, under Gandhi's leadership, boycotted British goods and staged various demonstrations. In 1922, Gandhi was arrested for articles written in response to the repressive acts. He was sentenced to six years, of which he served two. This is the speech he delivered at his trial. In the years that followed, Gandhi resigned from the Indian National Congress in protest over its political methods. When Britain finally granted Indian independence in 1947 and decreed the partition of the country into the two separate states of India and Pakistan, Gandhi fasted in hopes of ending the civil violence between Hindus and Muslims that swept across India. He was assassinated in 1948 by a Hindu fanatic.

Nonviolence Is the First Article of My Faith (1922)

I wanted to avoid violence, I want to avoid violence. Nonviolence is the first article of my faith. It is also the last article of my creed. But I had to make my choice. I had either to submit to a system which I considered had done an irreparable harm to my country, or incur the risk of the mad fury of my people bursting forth, when they understood the truth from my lips. I know that my people have sometimes gone mad. I am deeply sorry for it, and I am therefore here to submit not to a light penalty but to the highest penalty. I do not ask for mercy. I do not plead any extenuating act. I am here, therefore, to invite and cheerfully submit to the highest penalty that can be inflicted upon me for what in law is a deliberate crime and what appears to me to be the highest duty of a citizen. The only course open to you, the judge, is, as I am just going to say in my statement, either to resign your post or inflict on me the severest penalty, if you believe that the system and law you are assisting to administer are good for the people. I do not expect that kind of conversation, but by the time I have finished with my statement, you will perhaps have a glimpse of what is raging within my breast to run this maddest risk which a sane man can run.

I owe it perhaps to the Indian public and to the public in England to placate which this prosecution is mainly taken up that I should explain why from a staunch loyalist and cooperator I have become an uncompromising disaffectionist and non-cooperator. To the court too I should say why I plead guilty to the charge of promoting disaffection toward the government established by law in India.

My public life began in 1893 in South Africa in troubled weather. My first contact with British authority in that country was not of a happy character. I discovered that as a man and as an Indian I had no rights. More correctly, I discovered that I had no rights as a man because I was an Indian.

But I was baffled. I thought that this treatment of Indians was an excrescence upon a system that was intrinsically and mainly good. I gave the government my voluntary and hearty cooperation, criticizing it freely where I felt it was faulty but never wishing its destruction.

Consequently, when the existence of the empire was threatened in 1899 by the Boer challenge, I offered my services to it, raised a volunteer ambulance corps, and served at several actions that took place for the relief of Ladysmith. Similarly in 1906, at the time of the Zulu revolt, I raised a stretcher–bearer party and served till the end of the "rebellion." On both these occasions I received medals and was even mentioned in dispatches. For my work in South Africa I was given by Lord Hardinge a Kaiser-i-Hind Gold Medal. When the war broke out in 1914 between England and Germany, I raised a volunteer ambulance corps in London consisting of the then resident Indians in London, chiefly students. Its work was acknowledged by the authorities to be valuable. Lastly, in India, when a special appeal was made at the War Conference in Delhi in 1918 by Lord Chelmsford for recruits, I struggled at the cost of my health to raise a corps in Kheda, and the response was being made when the hostilities ceased and orders were received that no more recruits were wanted. In all these efforts at service I was actuated by the belief that it was possible by such services to gain a status of full equality in the empire for my countrymen.

The first shock came in the shape of the Rowlatt Act, a law designed to rob the people of all real freedom. I felt called upon to lead an intensive agitation against it. Then followed the Punjab horrors beginning with the massacre at Jallianwala Bagh and culminating in crawling orders, public floggings, and other indescribable humiliations. I discovered too that the plighted word of the prime minister to the Mussulmans of India regarding the integrity of Turkey and the holy places of Islam was not likely to be fulfilled. But in spite of the forebodings and the grave warnings of friends, at the Amritsar Congress in 1919, I fought for cooperation and working with the Montagu-Chelmsford reforms, hoping that the prime minister would redeem his promise to the Indian Mussulmans, that the Punjab wound would be healed, and that the reforms, inadequate and unsatisfactory though they were, marked a new era of hope in the life of India.

But all that hope was shattered. The Khilafat promise was not to be redeemed. The Punjab crime was whitewashed, and most culprits went not only unpunished but remained in service and in some cases continued to draw pensions from the Indian revenue, and in some cases were even rewarded. I saw too that not only did the reforms not mark a change of heart, but they were only a method of further draining India of her wealth and of prolonging her servitude.

I came reluctantly to the conclusion that the British connection had made India more helpless than she ever was before, politically and economically. A disarmed India has no power of resistance against any aggressor if she wanted to engage in an armed conflict with him. So much is this the case that some of our best men consider that India must take generations before she can achieve the dominion status. She has become so poor that she has little power of resisting famines. Before the British advent, India spun and wove in her millions of cottages just the supplement she needed for adding to her meager agricultural resources. This cottage industry, so vital for India's existence, has been ruined by incredibly heartless and inhuman processes as described by English witnesses. Little do town dwellers know how the semi-starved masses of India are slowly sinking to lifelessness. Little do they know that their miserable comfort represents the brokerage they get for the work they do for the foreign exploiter, that the profits and the brokerage are sucked from the masses. Little do they realize that the government established by law in British India is carried on for this exploitation of the masses. No sophistry, no jugglery in figures can explain away the evidence that the skeletons in many villages present to the naked eye. I have no doubt whatsoever that both England and the town dwellers of India will have to answer, if there is a God above, for this crime against humanity which is perhaps unequaled in history. The law itself in this country has been used to serve the foreign exploiter. My unbiased examination of the Punjab Martial Law cases has led me to believe that at least 95 percent of convictions were wholly bad. My experience of political cases in India leads me to the conclusion that in nine out of every ten the condemned men were totally innocent. Their crime consisted in the love of their country. In ninety-nine cases out of a hundred justice has been denied to Indians as against Europeans in the courts of India. This is not an exaggerated picture. It is the experience of almost every Indian who has had anything to do with such cases. In my opinion, the administration of the law is thus prostituted consciously or unconsciously for the benefit of the exploiter.

The greater misfortune is that Englishmen and their Indian associates in the administration of the country do not know that they are engaged in the crime I have attempted to describe. I am satisfied that many Englishmen and Indian officials honestly believe that they are administering one of the best systems devised in the world and that India is making steady though slow progress. They do not know that a subtle but effective system of terrorism and an organized display of force, on the one hand, and the deprivation of all powers of retaliation or self-defense, on the other, have emasculated the people and induced in them the habit of simulation. This awful habit has added to the ignorance and the self-deception of the administrators. Section 124-A, under which I am happily charged, is perhaps the prince among the political sections of the Indian Penal Code designed to suppress the liberty of the citizen. Affection cannot be manufactured or regulated by law. If one has an affection for a person or system, one should be free to give the fullest expression to his disaffection, so long as he does not contemplate, promote, or incite to violence. But the section under which Mr. Banker [a colleague in nonviolence] and I are charged is one under which mere promotion of disaffection is a crime. I have studied some of the cases tried under it, and I know that some of the most loved of India's patriots have been convicted under it. I consider it a privilege, therefore, to be charged under that section. I have endeavored to give in their briefest outline the reasons for my disaffection. I have no personal ill will against any single administrator; much less can I have any disaffection toward the king's person. But I hold it to be a virtue to be disaffected toward a government which in its totality has done more harm to India than any previous system. India is less manly under the British rule than she ever was before. Holding such a belief, I consider it to be a sin to have affection for the system. And it has been a precious privilege for me to be able to write what I have in the various articles, tendered in evidence against me.

In fact, I believe that I have rendered a service to India and England by showing in non-cooperation the way out of the unnatural state in which both are living. In my humble opinion, non-cooperation with evil is as much a duty as is cooperation with good. But in the past, non-cooperation has been deliberately expressed in violence to the evildoer. I am endeavoring to show to my countrymen that violent non-cooperation only multiplies evil and that as evil can only be sustained by violence, withdrawal of support of evil requires complete abstention from violence. Nonviolence implies voluntary submission to the penalty for non-cooperation with evil. I am here, therefore, to invite and submit cheerfully to the highest penalty that can be inflicted upon me for what in law is a deliberate crime and what appears to me to be the highest duty of a citizen. The only course open to you, the judge, is either to resign your post, and thus dissociate yourself from evil if you feel that the law you are called upon to administer is an evil and that in reality I am innocent, or to inflict on me the severest penalty if you believe that the system and the law you are assisting to administer are good for the people of this country and that my activity is therefore injurious to the public weal.

Nelson Mandela
(1918–2013)

A KING'S WARD, a lawyer, a guerrilla, a prisoner, and a president—Nelson Mandela led a life of serial transformation on his way to becoming one of the most dynamic leaders of the twentieth century. No one did more to help avert the mass violence so many predicted would accompany the end of South African apartheid (the Afrikaans word for "apartness"), the system of racial segregation that dominated the country for decades. Born the son of a Thembu chief in a village in the southern region of Transkei—the Thembu form a part of the Xhosa nation—Mandela went, after his father's death, to live in the home of the foremost Thembu chief, where he had the opportunity to watch the drama of tribal councils and where he acquired what some have called "his regal self-confidence" and the sense that "he was the equal of any man," according to Bill Keller, who wrote Mandela's obituary in the *New York Times*. After college in the 1940s, Mandela became involved in the African National Congress (ANC), one of the major groups fighting to end apartheid. At first Mandela had faith in nonviolent means of protest; by the early 1960s, however, no longer believing in the effectiveness of nonviolence, he took command of the ANC's liberation army, Umkhonto we Sizwe (Spear of the Nation). Inspired by the writings of Che Guevara, Mandela led his force in various acts of sabotage, including blowing up power stations and planting land mines. Having gone underground for several years, after a 1961 acquittal on treason charges, Mandela was captured and accused of capital crimes of sabotage and attempting the violent overthrow of the government. The Rivonia Trial (1963–64), named for the location of the farmhouse where Mandela and his fellow conspirators had their secret headquarters, ended in a conviction and life sentences for Mandela and several other defendants. The monumental speech Mandela gave at the trial, formally addressed to the judge ("My Lord"), was in reality an announcement to the world of Mandela's principles and his willingness to die for them. Keller calls the end, which is excerpted here, "a coda of his convictions that would endure as an oratorical highlight in South African history." Mandela spent twenty-seven years in prison, where he eventually became the face of the anti-apartheid movement worldwide. In jail on Robben Island, working in limestone quarries and enduring the various hardships of imprisonment, Mandela learned the skills of negotiation and reconciliation that would become the hallmarks of his statesmanship. In a 2007 interview for what would become Mandela's obituary, Keller asked his subject, "After such barbarous torment, how do you keep hatred in check?" Mandela's answer, Keller reports, "was almost dismissive," and he paraphrases it as follows: "Hating clouds the mind. It gets in the way of strategy. Leaders cannot afford to hate." "In a post-heroic age," Philip Gourevitch eulogized the South African leader in *The New Yorker* (December 16, 2013), "Mandela attained the stature of a classical hero—at once a righteously angry warrior and a wise and just peacemaker, an emblem of reconciliation."

I Am Prepared to Die
from *Nelson Mandela's statement from the dock at the opening of the defence case in the Rivonia Trial* (1963)

Our fight is against real and not imaginary hardships or, to use the language of the State Prosecutor, 'so-called hardships'. Basically, My Lord, we fight against two features which are the hallmarks of African life in South Africa and which are entrenched by legislation which we seek to have repealed. These features are poverty and lack of human dignity, and we do not need communists or so-called 'agitators' to teach us about these things.

·   ·   ·

The lack of human dignity experienced by Africans is the direct result of the policy of white supremacy. White supremacy implies black inferiority. Legislation designed to preserve white supremacy entrenches this notion. Menial tasks in South Africa are invariably performed by Africans. When anything has to be carried or cleaned the white man will look around for an African to do it for him, whether the African is employed by him or not. Because of this sort of attitude, whites tend to regard Africans as a separate breed. They do not look upon them as people with families of their own; they do not realise that we have emotions—that we fall in love like white people do; that we want to be with our wives and children like white people want to be with theirs; that we want to earn money, enough money to support our families properly, to feed and clothe them and send them to school. And what 'house-boy' or 'garden-boy' or labourer can ever hope to do this?

Pass laws, which to the Africans are among the most hated bits of legislation in South Africa, render any African liable to police surveillance at any time. I doubt whether there is a single African male in South Africa who has not at some stage had a brush with the police over his pass. Hundreds and thousands of Africans are thrown into jail each year under pass laws. Even worse than this is the fact that pass laws keep husband and wife apart and lead to the breakdown of family life.

Poverty and the breakdown of family life have secondary effects. Children wander about the streets of the townships because they have no schools to go to, or no money to enable them to go to school, or no parents at home to see that they go to school, because both parents, if there be two, have to work to keep the family alive. This leads to a breakdown in moral standards, to an alarming rise in illegitimacy, and to growing violence which erupts not only politically, but everywhere. Life in the townships is dangerous. There is not a day that goes by without somebody being stabbed or assaulted. And violence is carried out of the townships into the white living areas. People are afraid to walk alone in the streets after dark. Housebreakings and robberies are increasing, despite the fact that the death sentence can now be imposed for such offences. Death sentences cannot cure the festering sore.

The only cure is to alter the conditions under which Africans are forced to live and to meet their legitimate grievances. Africans want to be paid a living wage. Africans want to perform work which they are capable of doing, and not work which the Government declares them to be capable of. We want to be allowed to live where we obtain work, and not be endorsed out of an area because we were not born there. We want to be allowed and not to be obliged to live in rented houses which we can never call our own. We want to be part of the general population, and not confined to living in our ghettoes. African men want to have their wives and children to live with them where they work, and not to be forced into an unnatural existence in men's hostels. Our women want to be with their men folk and not to be left permanently widowed in the reserves. We want to be allowed out after eleven o'clock at night and not to be confined to our rooms like little children. We want to be allowed to travel in our own country and to seek work where we want to, where we want to and not where the Labour Bureau tells us to. We want a just share in the whole of South Africa; we want security and a stake in society.

Above all, My Lord, we want equal political rights, because without them our disabilities will be permanent. I know this sounds revolutionary to the whites in this country, because the majority of voters will be Africans. This makes the white man fear democracy.

But this fear cannot be allowed to stand in the way of the only solution which will guarantee racial harmony and freedom for all. It is not true that the enfranchisement of all will result in racial domination. Political division, based on colour, is entirely artificial and, when it disappears, so will the domination of one colour group by another. The ANC has spent half a century fighting against racialism. When it triumphs as it certainly must, it will not change that policy.

This then is what the ANC is fighting. Our struggle is a truly national one. It is a struggle of the African people, inspired by our own suffering and our own experience. It is a struggle for the right to live. [*Someone coughs.*]

During my lifetime I have dedicated my life to this struggle of the African people. I have fought against white domination, and I have fought against black domination. I have cherished the ideal of a democratic and free society in which all persons will live together in harmony and with equal opportunities. It is an ideal for which I hope to live for and to see realised. But, My Lord, if it needs be, it is an ideal for which I am prepared to die.

Songs of Resistance

THE FOLLOWING COLLECTION of lyrics, ranging from the spiritual to ballads and blues, illuminates the role of music in giving voice to resistance. The first several selections emerge directly from the American folk tradition, to which both African and European modes contributed but which evolved in particular ways in the light of American economic, social, and political realities. The first song, "Been in the Storm So Long," is an African-American spiritual dating from the antebellum period. Like "We Shall Overcome" and "Go Tell It on the Mountain," this spiritual became an important anthem of the civil rights movement in the 1960s. Repurposed for the political moment, these songs were performed at rallies by freedom singers such as Bernice Johnson Reagon, who explained the importance of music to the movement as follows: "All the established academic categories in which I had been educated fell apart during this period, revealing culture to be not luxury, not leisure, not entertainment, but the lifeblood of a community."

The next several selections are ballads, the first three from the African-American tradition. "Sinking of the *Titanic*," which like many ballads exists in widely differing versions, tells the story of a black crewmember who tries in vain to warn the arrogant captain of the impending disaster and who survives the wreck while the rich "white folks" go to their watery deaths. "De Ballit of de Boll Weevil" narrates a very different kind of disaster: the spread of the destructive boll weevil north from Mexico to the cotton crops of Texas and beyond. In his endless search for "a home," the boll weevil doubles for the migrant African-American picker traveling from one cotton field to the next in search of work. "John Henry" tells the story of one of the most famous American folk heroes, a steel driver who wins a race with a steam drill to dig a tunnel on the Chesapeake and Ohio Railroad yet kills himself in the process. Colson Whitehead's 2001 novel *John Henry Days* gave new life to this epic African-American folk hero.

Like blights, floods, droughts, and other natural disasters, the railroad is a central theme of American folk music not only because, like the building of the levees along the banks of the Mississippi River, it offered needed but often brutal work, but also because, as the *Chicago Tribune* columnist Vernon Jarrett explains, it became a symbol of "mobility" for African-Americans hoping to move north during the Great Migration. "John Henry," "Railroad Bill," "Casey Jones," and many other popular folk songs all emerge from the experience of building and riding the railroads. Jarrett, who grew up in Tennessee, recalled to the oral historian Studs Terkel, that everyone would go down to the depot on Saturday afternoons to watch the trains: "We were always aware there was another place outside of this. Somewhere. That you *could* go somewhere." Music, as Jarrett explained, became a primary avenue of expression for this dream of mobility.

One of the characteristics of folk music is that it evolves as it migrates with its singers. The ballad is never fixed, as the great collectors John and Alan Lomax suggest in their introduction to *American Ballads and Folk Songs*: its fluidity gives it life. "The Cryderville Jail," which the Lomaxes include in their chapter on "White Desperadoes," provides an ideal example of this phenomenon. Extant in many versions, the song proved easily adaptable to the miseries of any local jail from West Virginia to Texas.

The next two selections, Woody Guthrie's "Do Re Mi" and W. C. Handy's "St. Louis Blues," are both self-conscious adaptations of folk forms. Guthrie's "Dust Bowl Ballad" anatomizes the plight of those migrant farm workers, the "Okies," who finally reached the promised land of California during the Depression only to find themselves unwelcome. This is the story of John Steinbeck's *The Grapes of Wrath*, and Steinbeck noted that the music he heard in the migrant camps expressed a "fierceness and the will to fight" against hardship. "You can burn books," he wrote in a foreword to a collection of Guthrie's songs: "you can guard against handbills and pamphlets, but you cannot prevent singing."

In *The Land Where the Blues Began* Alan Lomax, whose field recordings offer a rich treasury of the form, traces the roots of this "moody song style" of the Mississippi Delta to the economic deprivation and oppressive violence of the postbellum South. In this form of musical expression Lomax locates a "nourishing river of black cultural practice," asserting "an independent and irrepressible culture" in the face of Jim Crow. W. C. Handy was one of the first professional popularizers of the blues, and his compositions brought a regional music to a national audience of black and white listeners. "St. Louis Blues," one of Handy's best-known songs, is perhaps most readily associated with Bessie Smith, who recorded it in 1925 with Louis Armstrong. Few artists were more important to the history and evolution of the form than Smith, called the Empress of the Blues, who pioneered blues recordings in the 1920s. The songs she performed were frank and unapologetic: their themes ranged from sexual jealousy and violence ("Black Mountain Blues" and "Gimme a Pigfoot") to natural disaster ("Backwater Blues"). As the historian David Suisman notes in the journal *Souls*, blues songs such as "St. Louis Blues," which treat themes of "love and sex," also conveyed "a broad array of concerns about personal and social freedom."

The blues tradition—its formal structure as well as its customary themes—has proved receptive to the resistant voices of other minorities and marginalized groups. For example, the poet Marilyn Chin adapts the blues form to an investigation of aspects of the Asian-American experience in "Blues on Yellow." The AAB lyric pattern of the traditional blues structures Chin's poem as well. Born in Hong Kong, Chin, who is a novelist, teacher, and translator, as well as a prize-winning poet, grew up in Oregon. Her work is never shy about the costs of cultural assimilation. This poem comes from the volume *Rhapsody in Plain Yellow* (2002), which combines a wealth of Eastern and Western musical sources to create a polyphonous collection of poems. In a 2002 review for the *Los Angeles Times*, Carol Muske-Dukes wrote, "Like a whirling acrobat-musician from the Peking Opera—sounding brass gongs and blue ululations of joy and melancholy—Marilyn Chin lands blazing before us with 'Rhapsody in Plain Yellow.' It's difficult to describe a book this ambitious in style and syncopation."

Been in the Storm So Long

I've been in the storm so long,
You know I've been in the storm so long,
Oh Lord, give me more time to pray,
I've been in the storm so long.

I am a motherless child,
Singin' I am a motherless child,
Singin' Oh Lord, give me more time to pray,
I've been in the storm so long.

This is a needy time,
This is a needy time,
Singin' Oh Lord, give me more time to pray,
I've been in the storm so long.

Lord, I need you now,
Lord, I need you now,
Singin' Oh Lord, give me more time to pray,
I've been in the storm so long.

My neighbors need you now,
My neighbors need you now,
Singin' Oh Lord, give me more time to pray,
I've been in the storm so long.

My children need you now,
My children need you now,
Singin' Oh Lord, give me more time to pray,
I've been in the storm so long.

Just look what a shape I'm in,
Just look what a shape I'm in,
Cryin' Oh Lord, give me more time to pray,
I've been in the storm so long.

Sinking of the *Titanic*

It was 1912 when the awful news got around
That the great *Titanic* was sinking down.
Shine came running up on deck, told the Captain, "Please,
The water in the boiler room is up to my knees."

Captain said, "Take your black self on back down there!
I got a hundred-fifty pumps to keep the boiler room clear."
Shine went back in the hole, started shovelling coal,
Singing, "Lord, have mercy, Lord, on my soul!"

Just then half the ocean jumped across the boiler room deck.
Shine yelled to the Captain, "The water's 'round my neck!"
Captain said, "Go back! Neither fear nor doubt!
I got a hundred more pumps to keep the water out."

"Your words sound happy and your words sound true,
But this is one time, Cap, your words won't do.
I don't like chicken and I don't like ham—
And I don't believe your pumps is worth a damn!"

De Ballit of de Boll Weevil

Oh, have you heard de lates',
De lates' of de songs?
It's about dem little Boll Weevils,
Dey's picked up bofe feet an' gone
A-lookin' for a home.

De Boll Weevil is a little bug
F'um Mexico, dey say,
He come to try dis Texas soil
En thought he better stay,
A-lookin' for a home,
Jes a-lookin' for a home.

De nigger say to de Boll Weevil
"Whut makes yo' head so red?"
"I's been wanderin' de whole worl' ovah
Till it's a wonder I ain't dead,
A-lookin' for a home,
Jes a-lookin' for a home."

First time I saw Mr. Boll Weevil,
He wuz on de western plain;
Next time I saw him,
He wuz ridin' on a Memphis train,
A-lookin' for a home,
Jes a-lookin' for a home.

De nex' time I saw him,
He was runnin' a spinnin' wheel;
De nex' time I saw him,

He was ridin' in an automobile,
A-lookin' for a home,
Jes a-lookin' for a home.

De fus' time I saw de Boll Weevil
He wuz settin' on de square
De nex' time I saw de Boll Weevil
He had all his family dere—
Dey's a-lookin' for a home,
Jes a-lookin' for a home.

Then the Farmer got angry,
Sent him up in a balloon;
"Good-by, Mr. Farmer;
I'll see you again next June.
A-lookin' for a home,
Jes a-lookin' for a home."

De Farmer took de Boll Weevil
An' buried him in hot san';
De Boll Weevil say to de Farmer
"I'll stan' it like a man,
Fur it is my home,
It is my home."

Den de Farmer took de Boll Weevil
An' lef' him on de ice;
Says de Boll Weevil to de Farmer,
"Dis is mighty cool an' nice.
Oh, it is my home,
It is my home."

Mr. Farmer took little Weevil
And put him in Paris Green;
"Thank you, Mr. Farmer;
It's the best I ever seen.
It is my home,
It's jes my home."

Den de Farmer say to de Merchant:
"We's in an awful fix;
De Boll Weevil's et all de cotton up
An' lef' us only sticks.

We's got no home,
Oh, we's got no home."

Den de Merchant say to de Farmer,
"Whut do you tink o' dat?
Ef you kin kill de Boll Weevil
I'll give you a bran-new Stetson hat,
A Stetson hat,
Oh, a Stetson hat."

Oh, de Farmer say to de Merchant,
"I ain't made but only one bale,
An' befo' I bring yo' dat one
I'll fight an' go to jail,
I'll have a home,
I'll have a home."

De Sharpshooter say to de Boll Weevil,
"What you doin' in dis square?"
An' the Boll Weevil say to de Sharpshooter,
"Ise makin' my home in here,
Here in dis square,
Here in dis square."

Oh, de Boll Weevil say to de Dutchman,
"Jes' poison me ef yo' dare,
An' when yo' come to make yo' crop
I'll punch out every square,
When de sun gits hot,
When de sun gits hot."

De Boll Weevil say to de Farmer,
"You better lemme alone,
I've et up all yo' cotton
An' now I'll begin on de co'n,
I'll have a home,
I'll have a home."

Boll Weevil say to de Doctor,
"Better po' out all yo' pills,
When I git through wid de Farmer,
He cain't pay no doctor's bills.

He'll have no home,
He'll have no home."

Boll Weevil say to de Preacher,
"You better close yo' chu'ch do',
When I git through wid de Farmer,
He cain't pay de Preacher no mo',
Won't have no home,
Won't have no home."

De Merchant got half de cotton,
De Boll Weevil got de res';
Didn't leave de nigger's wife
But one cold cotton dress.
And it's full of holes,
Oh, it's full of holes.

Rubber-tired buggy,
Decorated hack,
Took dem Boll Weevils to de graveyard,
An' ain't goin' bring 'em back.
Dey gone at las',
Oh, dey gone at las'.

Ef anybody axes you
Who wuz it writ dis song,
Tell 'em 'twuz a dark-skinned nigger
Wid a pair o' blue duskins on,
A-lookin' for a home,
Jes a-lookin' for a home.

John Henry

When John Henry was a little fellow,
  You could hold him in the palm of your hand,
He said to his pa, "When I grow up
  I'm gonna be a steel-driving man.
    Gonna be a steel-driving man."

When John Henry was a little baby,
  Setting on his mammy's knee,

He said "The Big Bend Tunnel on the C. & O. Road
  Is gonna be the death of me,
    Gonna be the death of me."

One day his captain told him,
  How he had bet a man
That John Henry would beat his steam-drill down,
  Cause John Henry was the best in the land,
    John Henry was the best in the land.

John Henry kissed his hammer,
  White man turned on steam,
Shaker held John Henry's trusty steel,
  Was the biggest race the world had ever seen,
    Lord, biggest race the world ever seen.

John Henry on the right side
  The steam drill on the left,
"Before I'll let your steam drill beat me down,
  I'll hammer my fool self to death,
    Hammer my fool self to death."

John Henry walked in the tunnel,
  His captain by his side,
The mountain so tall, John Henry so small,
  He laid down his hammer and he cried,
    Laid down his hammer and he cried.

Captain heard a mighty rumbling,
  Said "The mountain must be caving in,"
John Henry said to the captain,
  "It's my hammer swinging in de wind,
    My hammer swinging in de wind."

John Henry said to his shaker,
  "Shaker, you'd better pray;
For if ever I miss this piece of steel,
  Tomorrow'll be your burial day,
    Tomorrow'll be your burial day."

John Henry said to his shaker,
  "Lordy, shake it while I sing,

I'm pulling my hammer from my shoulders down,
  Great Gawdamighty, how she ring,
    Great Gawdamighty, how she ring!"

John Henry said to his captain,
  "Before I ever leave town,
Gimme one mo' drink of dat tom-cat gin,
  And I'll hammer dat steam driver down,
    I'll hammer dat steam driver down."

John Henry said to his captain,
  "Before I ever leave town,
Gimme a twelve-pound hammer wid a whale-bone handle,
  And I'll hammer dat steam driver down,
    I'll hammer dat steam drill on down."

John Henry said to his captain,
  "A man ain't nothin but a man,
But before I'll let dat steam drill beat me down,
  I'll die wid my hammer in my hand,
    Die wid my hammer in my hand,"

The man that invented the steam drill
  He thought he was mighty fine,
John Henry drove down fourteen feet,
  While the steam drill only made nine,
    Steam drill only made nine.

"Oh, lookaway over yonder, captain,
  You can't see like me,"
He gave a long and loud and lonesome cry,
  "Lawd, a hammer be the death of me,
    A hammer be the death of me!"

John Henry had a little woman,
  Her name was Polly Ann,
John Henry took sick, she took his hammer,
  She hammered like a natural man,
    Lawd, she hammered like a natural man.

John Henry hammering on the mountain
  As the whistle blew for half-past two,

The last words his captain heard him say,
  "I've done hammered my insides in two,
    Lawd, I've hammered my insides in two."

The hammer that John Henry swung
  It weighed over twelve pound,
He broke a rib in his left hand side
  And his intrels fell on the ground,
    And his intrels fell on the ground.

John Henry, O, John Henry,
  His blood is running red,
Fell right down with his hammer to the ground,
  Said, "I beat him to the bottom but I'm dead,
    Lawd, beat him to the bottom but I'm dead."

When John Henry was laying there dying,
  The people all by his side,
The very last words they heard him say,
  "Give me a cool drink of water 'fore I die,
    Cool drink of water 'fore I die."

John Henry had a little woman,
  The dress she wore was red,
She went down the track, and she never looked back,
  Going where her man fell dead,
    Going where her man fell dead.

John Henry had a little woman,
  The dress she wore was blue,
De very last words she said to him,
  "John Henry, I'll be true to you,
    John Henry, I'll be true to you."

"Who's gonna shoes yo' little feet,
  Who's gonna glove yo' hand,
Who's gonna kiss yo' pretty, pretty cheek,
  Now you done lost yo man?
    Now you done lost yo' man?"

"My mammy's gonna shoes my little feet,
  Pappy gonna glove my hand,
My sister's gonna kiss my pretty, pretty cheek,

Now I done lost my man,
  Now I done lost my man."

They carried him down by the river,
  And buried him in the sand,
And everybody that passed that way,
  Said, "There lies that steel-driving man,
    There lies a steel-driving man."

They took John Henry to the river,
  And buried him in the sand,
And every locomotive come a-roaring by,
  Says "There lies that steel-drivin' man,
    Lawd, there lies a *steel*-drivin' man."

Some say he came from Georgia,
  And some from Alabam,
But it's wrote on the rock at the Big Bend Tunnel,
  That he was an East Virginia man,
    Lord, Lord, an East Virginia man.

The Cryderville Jail

Old Dad Morton has got us in jail,
'Tis hard!
Old Dad Morton has got us in jail,
Both father and mother refused bail,
'Tis hard!
With the doors all locked and barred,
With a big long chain bound down to the floor,
Damn their fool souls, how could they do more?
'Tis hard times in the Cryderville jail,
'Tis hard times, I say [*or* poor boys].

There's a big bull ring in the middle of the floor,
And a damned old jailer to open the door.

Your pockets he'll pick, your clothes he will sell,
You hands he will handcuff, Goddam him to Hell!

It's both of my feet bound in the cell,
My hands tied behind, Goddam him to Hell!

And here's to the cook, I wish he was dead,
It's old boiled beef and old corn bread.

The chuck they give us is beef and corn bread,
As old as Hell and as heavy as lead.

We pop it down in us within our cells,
Just like the pop from Heaven to Hell.

The coffee is rough, and the yard is full of hogs,
And we are guarded by two bulldogs.

No longer than yesterday I heard the jailer say,
He was feeding the prisoners at two dollars a day.

The times was so hard at such a poor pay,
He couldn't feed 'em grub but two times a day.

Our bed is made of old rotten rugs.
When we lay down, we are all covered with bugs.

And the bugs they swear if we don't give bail,
We are bound to get busy in the Tucson jail.

The nits and the lice, climb in the jist,
One fell down and hollered, "Jesus Christ!"

I said, "Mister Jailer, please lend me your knife,
For the lice and the bedbugs have threatened my life."

Old Judge Simpkins will read us the law,
The damndest fool judge you ever saw.

And here's to the lawyer, he'll come to your cell,
"Give me five dollars and I'll clear you in spite of Hell."

But your money they will get before they will rest;
Then say, "Plead guilty, for I think it is best."

There sits the jury, a devil of a crew,
They will look the poor prisoner through and through.

Your privileges they will take, your clothes they will sell,
Get drunk on the money, Goddam 'em to Hell.

And here's to the sheriff, I like to forgot,
He's the biggest old rascal we have in the lot.

And now I have come to the end of my song;
I'll leave it to the boys as I go along.

As to gamblin' and stealin', I never shall fail,
And I don't give a damn for lyin' in jail.

They'll send us away for a year or two,
For makin' a barrel of mountain dew.

Do Re Mi

Lots of folks back East, they say, leavin' home every day,
Beatin' the hot old dusty way to the California line.
'Cross the desert sands they roll, gettin' out of that old dust bowl,
They think they're goin' to a sugar bowl, but here is what they find
Now, the police at the port of entry say,
"You're number fourteen thousand for today."

Oh, if you ain't got the do re mi, folks, if you ain't got the do re mi,
Why, you better go back to beautiful Texas, Oklahoma, Kansas,
    Georgia, Tennessee.
California is a garden of Eden, a paradise to live in or see;
But believe it or not, you won't find it so hot
If you ain't got the do re mi

If you want to buy you a home or a farm, that can't do nobody harm,
Or take your vacation by the mountains or sea.
Don't swap your old cow for a car, you'd better stay right where
    you are,
You'd better take this little tip from me.
'Cause I look through the want ads every day
But the headlines on the papers always say:

If you ain't got the do re mi, boys, if you ain't got the do re mi,
Why, you better go back to beautiful Texas, Oklahoma, Kansas,
    Georgia, Tennessee.

California is a garden of Eden, a paradise to live in or see;
But believe it or not, you won't find it so hot
If you ain't got the do re mi.

WOODY GUTHRIE

St. Louis Blues

I hate to see de evenin' sun go down
I hate to see de evenin' sun go down
Cause mah baby, he done lef' dis town

Feelin' tomorrow lak I feel today
Feelin' tomorrow lak I feel today
I'll pack mah trunk, an' make mah getaway

St. Louis woman wid her diamon' rings
Pulls dat man aroun' by her apron strings
'Twant for powder an' for store-bought hair
De man I love would not gone nowhere

Got de St. Louis blues, jes as blue as I can be
Dat man got a heart lak a rock cast in de sea
Or else he wouldn't have gone so far from me

Been to de gypsy to get mah fortune tol'
To de gypsy, done got mah fortune tol'
Cause I'm most wild 'bout mah jelly roll

Gypsy done tol' me, "Don't you wear no black"
Yes, she done tol' me, "Don't you wear no black.
Go to St. Louis, you can win him back"

Help me to Cairo; make St. Louis by mahself
Git to Cairo, find mah ol' frien', Jeff
Gwine to pin mahself close to his side
If I flag his train, I sho can ride

I loves dat man lak a schoolboy loves his pie
Lak a Kentucky Colonel loves his mint an' rye
I'll love mah baby till de day I die

You ought to see dat stovepipe brown o' mine
Lak he owns de Dimon' Joseph line
He'd make a cross-eyed 'oman go stone blind

Blacker than midnight, teeth lak flags of truce
Blackest man in de whole St. Louis
Blacker de berry, sweeter is de juice. . . .

A black headed gal make a freight train jump de track
Said, a black headed gal make a freight train jump de track
But a long tall gal makes a preacher "Ball de Jack"

Lawd, a blond headed woman makes a good man leave the town
I said, blond headed woman makes a good man leave the town
But a red headed woman make a boy slap his papa down. . . .

                              W. C. HANDY

Blues on Yellow

The canary died in the gold mine, her dreams got lost in the sieve.
The canary died in the gold mine, her dreams got lost in the sieve.
Her husband the crow killed under the railroad, the spokes hath shorn
        his wings.

Something's cookin' in Chin's kitchen, ten thousand yellow-bellied
        sapsuckers baked in a pie.
Something's cookin' in Chin's kitchen, ten thousand yellow bellied
        sapsuckers baked in a pie.
Something's cookin' in Chin's kitchen, die die yellow bird, die die.

O crack an egg on the griddle, yellow will ooze into white.
O crack an egg on the griddle, yellow will ooze into white.
Run, run, sweet little Puritan, yellow will ooze into white.

If you cut my yellow wrists, I'll teach my yellow toes to write.
If you cut my yellow wrists, I'll teach my yellow toes to write.
If you cut my yellow fists, I'll teach my yellow feet to fight.

Do not be afraid to perish, my mother, Buddha's compassion is nigh.
Do not be afraid to perish, my mother, our boat will sail tonight.

Your babies will reach the promised land, the stars will be their guide.

I am so mellow yellow, mellow yellow, Buddha sings in my veins.
I am so mellow yellow, mellow yellow, Buddha sings in my veins.
O take me to the land of the unreborn, there's no life on earth without
    pain.

MARILYN CHIN

Poetry of Exile

TURNED BY CIRCUMSTANCE into poets of exile, Osip Mandelstam (1891–1938) and Heberto Padilla (1932–2000) used verse as a vehicle for political resistance. Mandelstam, an initial supporter of the Russian Revolution, broke with Bolshevism after the judicial murder of his friend and fellow poet Nikolay Gumilev, husband of the poet Anna Akhmatova, in 1921. In 1934, Mandelstam himself was charged with counterrevolutionary activity and sentenced to the Gulag, where he died four years later. The novelist José Manuel Prieto, writing in the *New York Review of Books*, called Mandelstam's epigram on Stalin (1933), which provoked his arrest, "perhaps the twentieth century's most important political poem, written by one of its greatest poets against the man who may well be said to have been the cruelest of its tyrants."

Mandelstam fought the tyranny of Stalin, while Heberto Padilla resisted that of Fidel Castro. Like Mandelstam, Padilla, too, was an initial supporter of the revolutionary regime. But he was jailed in 1971, on charges of plotting "against the powers of the state," and later exiled from his native Cuba. In the words of Roberto González Echevarría, professor of Spanish and comparative literature at Yale University, Padilla "will be forever known as the first poet to have the stature and courage to object to the repression of Fidel Castro's regime." "A Prayer for the End of the Century" (1982) challenges all those cynical witnesses to the cataclysms of the twentieth century to take responsibility for the future. ("Poem No. 286 [On Stalin]" is translated by Burton Raffel and Alla Burago; "A Prayer for the End of the Century" is translated by Alastair Reid and Andrew Hurley.)

Poem No. 286 (On Stalin)
(1933)

We live, not feeling the ground under our feet,
no one hears us more than a dozen steps away,

And when there's enough for half a small chat—
ah, we remember the Kremlin mountaineer:

Thick fingers, fat like worms, greasy,
words solid as iron weights,

Huge cockroach whiskers laughing,
boot-tops beaming.

And all around him a rabble of thin-necked captains:
he toys with the sweat of half-men.

Some whistle, some meow, some snivel,
he's the only one looking, jabbing,

He forges decrees like horseshoes—decrees and decrees:
This one gets it in the balls, that one in the forehead, him right between
    the eyes.

Whenever he's got a victim, he glows like a broadchested
Georgian munching a raspberry.

OSIP MANDELSTAM

A Prayer for the End of the Century
(1982)

We who have always looked with tolerant irony
    on the mottled objects of the end of the century:
                     the vast structures
    and men stiff in dark clothes
We for whom the end of the century was at most
    an engraving and a prayer in French
We who thought that after a hundred years there would be only

a black bird lifting a grandmother's bonnet
We who have seen the collapse of
                                    parliaments
and the patched backside of liberalism
We who learned to distrust illustrious myths
and who see as totally impossible
(uninhabitable)
halls with candelabra
tapestries
and Louis XV chairs
We children and grandchildren of melancholy terrorists
and superstitious scientists
We who know that the error exists today
that someone will have to condemn tomorrow
We who are living the last years of this century
wander about unable to improvise
                                    movements
not already planned in advance
we gesture in a space more straitening
than the lines of an etching;
we put on formal clothes again,
as though we were attending another parliament,
while the candelabra sputter at the cornice
and the black birds
tear at the bonnet of that hoarse-voiced girl.

HEBERTO PADILLA

DISCUSSION QUESTIONS

1. *How do these stories of resistance compare to Starbuck's story in "Taking Responsibility"?*

2. *What ethical questions must be satisfied before one makes a commitment to resist?*

3. *We usually associate resistance with political action, but what is the role of poetry, song, and art in resistance?*

4. *How does one maintain whatever is gained in a successful resistance over time, once the fervor of rebellion has passed?*

5. *What do Wollstonecraft and Douglass suggest might be some of the preconditions for individual resistance?*

ALBUM
Abraham Lincoln, Artist of Judgment

Life is short, the art long, opportunity fleeting; experiment
hazardous, judgment difficult. The physician must not only be
prepared to do what is right himself, but also to make the patient,
the attendants, and externals cooperate.

—HIPPOCRATES, *Aphorisms*, 1.1

"I have no more time for Mr. Capen," Abraham Lincoln (1809–1865) wrote on April 26, 1863, in a rare display of annoyance, after being importuned once too often by a quack meteorologist whose forecast for sun had just been contradicted by ten hours of rain. Yet it took a great deal to wear down Lincoln's patience. He had secretaries, of course, but the personal energy he devoted to individual requests, petitions, and complaints would be deemed beneath the importance of most modern leaders. As his biographer David Herbert Donald notes, "Lincoln worked harder than almost any other American President." The Lincoln White House was a chaotic environment; the president's early attempts "to be orderly and businesslike" were superseded by what Donald calls a "systematic lack of system" that nevertheless "seemed to work."

Lincoln had long been a hard worker. Elected president in 1860, he had come a very long way from his hardscrabble origins. Born in Kentucky, Lincoln grew up in backwoods settlements there and in Indiana before moving to Illinois in 1830. He went to school only sporadically in his early years, but he was a determined reader who pored over the family Bible and also borrowed whatever books he could, continuing his education well into his twenties. Among the books he read in these formative years were *Aesop's Fables*, Daniel Defoe's *Robinson Crusoe*, William Grimshaw's *History of the United States*, and, later, Samuel Kirkham's *English Grammar*, the poetry of Robert Burns, and Shakespeare.

Lincoln held a series of jobs—river boatman, farmhand, keeper of a general store, and surveyor—before he began to read law and consider a political career. He was elected to the state legislature and then, in 1846, to the United States Congress. He lost a race for the Senate to Stephen A. Douglas in 1859, but the positions he outlined during the campaign, in debate with Douglas and in the "House Divided" speech of 1858, garnered national attention, and he launched a successful bid for the presidency the following year. The Civil War dominated his presidency, and Lincoln was only a few months into his second term when he was shot at Ford's Theatre by John Wilkes Booth on April 14, 1865.

Today even the most diligent public figures are protected from the Mr. Capens of the world. They are moved from one event to the next by schedulers, aides, and personal security detachments. They travel by cavalcade and personal plane, for if they traveled like the rest of us, they would, like the rest of us, never get anywhere on time. Yet they always appear to be running late and to have no time. At appropriate moments someone whispers in their ear that the car is waiting or knocks on the door to inform them the meeting must end. This is the insulation that comes with the job.

There was far less of it in 1863, the pivotal year in the Civil War. In January the president issued the Emancipation Proclamation. During the next several months, he oversaw two campaigns: Ulysses S. Grant's Vicksburg Campaign in the West and the fitful, largely ineffectual movements first of Ambrose Burnside and then of Joseph Hooker in the East. By July 4 Vicksburg had fallen and Gettysburg had been won. In November Lincoln would deliver the Gettysburg Address, which the historian Garry Wills has called "the words that remade America."

The toll the presidency took on Lincoln, vividly measured in contemporary photographs, is such a commonplace I need not dwell on it here. What is worth examining is the proximity of the man not only to the extraordinary demands of the country's highest public office but also to the defiantly ordinary stuff of life, from the citizens lining the corridors of the White House—a phenomenon Steven Spielberg's 2012 film *Lincoln* documents so effectively—to the correspondence streaming in. Lincoln's disregard for his personal safety gave his bodyguards fits.

Examining a week or even a day in Lincoln's epistolary life reveals how little of the ordinary the president seems to have been spared during this momentous period. Lincoln operated always on many different levels simultaneously, managing panoramic strategic initiatives even as he addressed the everyday concerns of private citizens. Over the course of his days, he endorsed job applicants for even minor political offices; arranged for the mustering out of drummer boys; reviewed the petitions of paymasters accused of theft; pardoned soldiers for various offenses; facilitated a mother's search for her wounded son; recommended candidates for admission to West Point; addressed a Mrs. Green's complaint that her husband had not been promoted in timely fashion; communicated to his wife the death of their son Tad's pet goat; and on a daily basis scolded, cajoled, inspired, and nursed the wounded egos of the fractious, jealous generals on whom the Union's hopes depended.

When we think of Lincoln's political vision and rhetorical capacity, perhaps we imagine that he preserved them despite all the distractions. Yet what if it was his very proximity to the mundane that made those triumphs of intellect possible? Policy makers and political visionaries rarely have such constant exposure to the motivations of real people, such intimacy with their pettiness as well as their extraordinary capacity for endurance.

To see the juxtaposition of large and small in Lincoln's daily life is to consider whether an understanding of the momentous, global, and strategic is truly possible without the shaping force of the quotidian. Perhaps we have moved beyond the point where the individuals chosen to solve our problems can dwell in the real. Yet being steeped in the real helped to hone Lincoln's judgment of people and ideas. The letters that follow illustrate Lincoln's sharp sense of each recipient's psychology and the particular emotional register in which he needed to couch his appeals. Stern one moment, avuncular the next, the letters somehow manage to balance reprimand with encouragement, praise with caution. The section culminates in the Second Inaugural Address, a masterpiece of rhetoric that promises reconciliation and unity without ever surrendering the threat of just retribution.

RECOMMENDED READING AND VIEWING

David Herbert Donald, *Lincoln* (1996)

Doris Kearns Goodwin, *Team of Rivals: The Political Genius of Abraham Lincoln* (2005)

Lincoln (2012), directed by Steven Spielberg

James M. McPherson, *Tried by War: Abraham Lincoln as Commander in Chief* (2008)

Garry Wills, *Lincoln at Gettysburg: The Words That Remade America* (1992)

Letter to David Hunter

New Jersey native David Hunter (1802–1886) graduated from West Point in 1822. He was court-martialed just a few years after graduation because he killed three men in duels. After President John Quincy Adams reinstated him, Hunter served for another decade before resigning. He rejoined the army during the Mexican War and went on to serve in various Union Army commands during the Civil War. As commander of the Department of the South in 1862, Hunter was one of several Union generals who independently abolished slavery in their areas of control (and had their decrees rescinded by the president) before Lincoln issued the Emancipation Proclamation. The letter printed here comes from an earlier period in Hunter's Civil War career, after he had been transferred to the Department of Kansas, which he regarded as a demotion from his previous assignment as the commander of the Western Department. Lincoln here responds to Hunter's complaint that he had been exiled to a sideshow of the war.

To David Hunter

Executive Mansion, Washington,
Major General Hunter. Dec. 31, 1861.

Dear Sir: Yours of the 23rd. is received; and I am constrained to say it is difficult to answer so ugly a letter in good temper. I am, as you intimate, losing much of the great confidence I placed in you, not from any act or omission of yours touching the public service, up to the time you were sent to Leavenworth, but from the flood of grumbling despatches and letters I have seen from you since. I knew you were being ordered to Leavenworth at the time it was done; and I aver that with as tender a regard for your honor and your sensibilities as I had for my own, it never occurred to me that you were being "humiliated, insulted and disgraced"; nor have I, up to this day, heard an intimation that you have been wronged, coming from any one but yourself. No one has blamed you for the retrograde movement from Springfield, nor for the information you gave Gen. Cameron; and this you could readily understand, if it were not for your unwarranted assumption that the ordering you to Leavenworth must necessarily have been done as a *punishment* for some *fault*. I thought then, and think yet, the position assigned to you is as respo[n]sible, and as honorable, as that assigned to Buell. I know that Gen. McClellan expected more important results from it. My impression is that at the time you were assigned to the new Western Department, it had not been determined to re-place Gen. Sherman in Kentucky; but of this I am not certain, because the idea that a command in Kentucky was very desireable, and one in the farther West, very undesireable, had never occurred to me. You constantly speak of being placed in command of only 3000. Now tell me, is not this mere impatience? Have you not known all the while that you are to command four or five times that many?

I have been, and am sincerely your friend; and if, as such, I dare to make a suggestion, I would say you are adopting the best possible way to ruin yourself. "Act well your part, there all the honor lies." He who does *something* at the head of one Regiment, will eclipse him who does *nothing* at the head of a hundred. Your friend as ever, A. LINCOLN

ANNOTATION

Major General Hunter's endorsement on the envelope containing Lincoln's letter is as follows: "The President in reply to my 'ugly letter.'—This letter was kept on his table for more than a month, and then sent by a private conveyance, with directions to hand it to me only when I was in a good humor!!!!.—" Hunter's letter of December 23, 1861, is in part as follows: "I am very deeply mortified, humiliated, insulted and disgraced. . . . I am sent here [Fort Leavenworth] into banishment, with not three thousand effective men under my command, while one of the Brigadiers, General Buell, is in command of near one hundred thousand men in Kentucky. The only sin I have committed is my carrying out your views in relation to the retrograde movement from Springfield. . . . So it appears that I have been deprived of a command, suitable to my rank, for presuming to answer . . . official questions put to me by the Secretary of War . . . for in no other way was I connected with the Fremont troubles. . . ."

Letters to George B. McClellan

George B. McClellan (1826–1885) was one of the most controversial Union generals. Known as "Young Napoleon," he had observed European warfare at the siege of Sevastopol. McClellan graduated from West Point in 1846 and served with the engineers. He performed ably in the Mexican War and then resigned to work for the railroads. During the Civil War, he rose to prominence after the North's devastating defeat at First Bull Run, when he resurrected the Army of the Potomac and devised the Peninsula Campaign against Richmond. Once in command, however, McClellan was distinguished by a defiant lack of aggression. Lee exploited his fundamental conservatism, and the siege of Richmond proved a failure. McClellan's reputation was again restored after Second Bull Run, but his delay in pursuing Lee's army after the bloody battle of Antietam allowed the enemy to escape and sealed his fate as a Union commander. McClellan ran for president in 1864 and later served as governor of New Jersey. The first of the three letters reproduced here were written during the Peninsula Campaign, while the latter two were sent just before Lincoln relieved McClellan and gave his command to Ambrose Burnside on November 5, 1862.

To George B. McClellan

Major General McClellan. Washington,
My dear Sir. April 9. 1862

Your despatches complaining that you are not properly sustained, while they do not offend me, do pain me very much.

Blencker's Division was withdrawn from you before you left here; and you knew the pressure under which I did it, and, as I thought, acquiesced in it—certainly not without reluctance.

After you left, I ascertained that less than twenty thousand unorganized men, without a single field battery, were all you designed to be left for the defence of Washington, and Manassas Junction; and part of this even, was to go to Gen. Hooker's old position. Gen. Banks' corps, once designed for Manassas Junction, was diverted, and tied up on the line of Winchester and Strausburg, and could not leave it without again exposing the upper Potomac, and the Baltimore and Ohio Railroad. This presented, (or would present, when McDowell and Sumner should be gone) a great temptation to the enemy to turn back from the Rappahanock, and sack Washington. My explicit order that Washington should, by the judgment of *all* the commanders of Army corps, be left entirely secure, had been neglected. It was precisely this that drove me to detain McDowell.

I do not forget that I was satisfied with your arrangement to leave Banks at Mannassas Junction; but when that arrangement was broken up, and *nothing* was substituted for it, of course I was not satisfied. I was constrained to substitute something for it myself. And now allow me to ask "Do you really think I should permit the line from Richmond, *via* Mannassas Junction, to this city to be entirely open, except what resistance could be presented by less than twenty thousand unorganized troops?" This is a question which the country will not allow me to evade.

There is a curious mystery about the *number* of the troops now with you. When I telegraphed you on the 6th. saying you had over a hundred thousand with you, I had just obtained from the Secretary of War, a statement, taken as he said, from your own returns, making 108,000 then with you, and *en route* to you. You now say you will have but 85,000, when all *en route* to you shall have reached you. How can the discrepancy of 23,000 be accounted for?

As to Gen. Wool's command, I understand it is doing for you precisely what a like number of your own would have to do, if that command was away.

I suppose the whole force which has gone forward for you, is with you by this time; and if so, I think it is the precise time for you to strike a blow. By delay the enemy will relatively gain upon you—that is, he will gain faster, by *fortifications* and *re-inforcements*, than you can by re-inforcements alone.

And, once more let me tell you, it is indispensable to *you* that you strike a blow. *I* am powerless to help this. You will do me the justice to remember I always insisted, that going down the Bay in search of a field, instead of fighting at or near Mannassas, was only shifting, and not surmounting, a difficulty— that we would find the same enemy, and the same, or equal, intrenchments, at either place. The country will not fail to note—is now noting—that the present hesitation to move upon an intrenched enemy, is but the story of Manassas repeated.

I beg to assure you that I have never written you, or spoken to you, in greater kindness of feeling than now, nor with a fuller purpose to sustain you, so far as in my most anxious judgment, I consistently can. *But you must act.* Yours very truly

A. LINCOLN

To George B. McClellan

Washington City, D.C.
Majr. Genl. McClellan Oct. 24 [25]. 1862

I have just read your despatch about sore tongued and fatiegued horses. Will you pardon me for asking what the horses of your army have done since the battle of Antietam that fatigue anything? A. LINCOLN

ANNOTATION

> Lincoln obviously misdated this telegram, since McClellan's dispatch to Halleck transmitting a report of Colonel Robert Williams of the First Massachusetts Cavalry was not received at the War Department until 12 M., October 25. Williams reported as follows:

> "I have in camp 267 horses . . . of these, 128 are positively and absolutely unable to leave the camp, from the following causes, viz, sore-tongue, grease, and consequent lameness, and sore backs. . . . The horses, which are still sound, are absolutely broken down from fatigue and want of flesh. . . ."

McClellan replied to Lincoln at 6 P.M. October 25, as follows:

> "In reply to your telegram of this date, I have the honor to state, from the time this army left Washington, on the 7th of September, my cavalry has been constantly employed in making reconnaissances, scouting, and picketing. Since the battle of Antietam, six regiments have made a trip of 200 miles, marching 55 miles in one day, while endeavoring the reach Stuart's cavalry.

> "General Pleasonton, in his official report, states that he, with the remainder of our available cavalry, while on Stuart's track, marched 78 miles in twenty-four hours.

> "Besides these two remarkable expeditions, our cavalry has been engaged in picketing and scouting 150 miles of river front ever since the battle of Antietam, and has made repeated reconnaissances since that time, engaging the enemy on every occasion, and, indeed, it has performed harder service since the battle than before. I beg that you will also

consider that this same cavalry was brought from the Peninsula, where it encountered most laborious service, and was, at the commencement of this campaign, in low condition, and from that time to the present has had no time to recruit.

"If any instance can be found where overworked cavalry has performed more labor than mine since the battle of Antietam, I am not conscious of it."

To George B. McClellan

Executive Mansion, Washington,
Majr. Gen. McClellan. Oct. 27. 1862

Yours of yesterday received. Most certainly I intend no injustice to any; and if I have done any, I deeply regret it. To be told after more than five weeks total inaction of the Army, and during which period we had sent to that Army every fresh horse we possibly could, amounting in the whole to 7918 that the cavalry horses were too much fatiegued to move, presented a very cheerless, almost hopeless, prospect for the future; and it may have forced something of impatience into my despatches. If not recruited, and rested then, when could they ever be? I suppose the river is rising, and I am glad to believe you are crossing. A. LINCOLN

Letter to Joseph Hooker

Joseph Hooker (1814–1879) was a Massachusetts native who saw service in the Second Seminole War after his graduation from West Point in 1837. Known for losing the Battle of Chancellorsville, Hooker served ably in division- and corps-level commands but proved to be a failure as commander of the Army of the Potomac, a responsibility given to him after Ambrose Burnside was routed at the Battle of Fredericksburg. Relieved after Chancellorsville, Hooker went on to serve effectively in charge of smaller organizations under Meade, under Grant at Chattanooga, and under Sherman at the Battle of Atlanta and on the March to the Sea. This letter was written soon after Lincoln had given Hooker the Army of the Potomac. Never short on fighting spirit, Hooker also evidently spent considerable time intriguing against other generals such as Burnside. Lincoln here reprimands him for his past conduct yet wishes him success in future.

To Joseph Hooker

Major General Hooker: Executive Mansion,
General. Washington, January 26, 1863.

I have placed you at the head of the Army of the Potomac. Of course I have done this upon what appear to me to be sufficient reasons. And yet I think it best for you to know that there are some things in regard to which, I am not quite satisfied with you. I believe you to be a brave and a skilful soldier, which, of course, I like. I also believe you do not mix politics with your profession, in which you are right. You have confidence in yourself, which is a valuable, if not an indispensable quality. You are ambitious, which, within reasonable bounds, does good rather than harm. But I think that during Gen. Burnside's command of the Army, you have taken counsel of your ambition, and thwarted him as much as you could, in which you did a great wrong to the country, and to a most meritorious and honorable brother officer. I have heard, in such way as to believe it, of your recently saying that both the Army and the Government needed a Dictator. Of course it was not *for* this, but in spite of it, that I have given you the command. Only those generals who gain successes, can set up dictators. What I now ask of you is military success, and I will risk the dictatorship. The government will support you to the utmost of its ability, which is neither more nor less than it has done and will do for all commanders. I much fear that the spirit which you have aided to infuse into the Army, of criticising their Commander, and withholding confidence from him, will now turn upon you. I shall assist you as far as I can, to put it down. Neither you, nor Napoleon, if he were alive again, could get any good out of an army, while such a spirit prevails in it.

And now, beware of rashness. Beware of rashness, but with energy, and sleepless vigilance, go forward, and give us victories.

Yours very truly A. LINCOLN

ANNOTATION

Hooker was called to the White House for an interview, and this letter presumably was handed to him at that time. It remained unknown until after Hooker's death in 1879, and the circumstances of the interview, as well as Hooker's reception of the president's views, have not been adequately recorded. All accounts known to the editors reveal an abundance of conjecture and rationalized recollection after the fact.

Letter to John M. Schofield

John M. Schofield (1831–1906) was, among other things, the author of a definition of discipline still memorized by West Point cadets today. It was part of a speech against hazing that he delivered in 1879, while serving as the superintendent of the Military Academy: "The discipline which makes the soldiers of a free country reliable in battle is not to be gained by harsh or tyrannical treatment," Schofield insisted.

> On the contrary, such treatment is far more likely to destroy than to make an army. It is possible to impart instruction and to give commands in such a manner and such a tone of voice to inspire in the soldier no feeling but an intense desire to obey, while the opposite manner and tone of voice cannot fail to excite strong resentment and a desire to disobey. The one mode or the other of dealing with subordinates springs from a corresponding spirit in the breast of the commander. He who feels the respect which is due to others cannot fail to inspire in them regard for himself, while he who feels, and hence manifests, disrespect toward others, especially his inferiors, cannot fail to inspire hatred against himself.

Schofield was regarded by some as too conciliatory to the South during the postwar Reconstruction. In 1863, while commanding the Department of Missouri, Schofield had to manage the guerrilla warfare along the Kansas-Missouri border. In this letter Lincoln gives him advice on how to handle the factions that dominated his department.

To John M. Schofield

Executive Mansion,
Gen. J. M. Schofield Washington, May 27. 1863.

My dear Sir: Having relieved Gen. Curtis and assigned you to the command of the Department of the Missouri—I think it may be of some advantage for me to state to you why I did it. I did not relieve Gen. Curtis because of any full conviction that he had done wrong by commission or omission. I did it because of a conviction in my mind that the Union men of Missouri, constituting, when united, a vast majority of the whole people, have entered into a pestilent factional quarrel among themselves, Gen. Curtis, perhaps not of choice, being the head of one faction, and Gov. Gamble that of the other. After months of labor to reconcile the difficulty, it seemed to grow worse and worse until I felt it my duty to break it up some how; and as I could not remove Gov. Gamble, I had to remove Gen. Curtis. Now that you are in the position, I wish you to undo nothing merely because Gen. Curtis or Gov. Gamble did it; but to exercise your own judgment, and do *right* for the public interest. Let your military measures be strong enough to repel the invader and keep the peace, and not so strong as to unnecessarily harass and persecute the people. It is a difficult *role*, and so much greater will be the honor if you perform it well. If both factions, or neither, shall abuse you, you will probably be about right. Beware of being assailed by one, and praised by the other. Yours truly

A. LINCOLN

ANNOTATION

The envelope in which the draft was filed bears Lincoln's endorsement "To Gen Schofield—May 27. 1863. & to Gen Curtis June 8. 1863." Schofield replied on June 1, "I have the honor to acknowledge the receipt of your letter . . . explaining the reasons which induced you to make a change in the command of this department, and your wish as to the principle which shall guide me. . . . I shall not fail to carry out your wishes to the fullest extent in my power, and shall be thankful for such instructions and advice as you may at any time be pleased to give me. The most serious difficulty I shall have to overcome will arise from the differences to which you allude between the factions into which the Union people are unfortunately divided. It shall be my highest aim, while keeping aloof from either faction, to reconcile their differences so far as my influence should extend, or at least to so conduct my administration as to give neither any just cause of complaint. . . ."

Letters to Ulysses S. Grant

Ulysses S. Grant's biography is given in "Learning from Failure." In Grant Lincoln finally found the general he was searching for, and the two men had a fine working relationship characterized by mutual respect and a shared commitment to ending the war as quickly as possible. The series of letters presented here reveal several facets of Lincoln's relationship with the man into whose hands he placed the fate of the Union Army in 1864. The first commends Grant's ultimately successful siege of Vicksburg, which surrendered on July 4, 1863. The second reveals Lincoln's trust in his commander, while the third encourages the general's aggressive spirit. In the final letter Lincoln asks Grant for a personal favor.

To Ulysses S. Grant

Major General Grant Executive Mansion,
My dear General Washington, July 13, 1863.

I do not remember that you and I ever met personally. I write this now as a grateful acknowledgment for the almost inestimable service you have done the country. I wish to say a word further. When you first reached the vicinity of Vicksburg, I thought you should do, what you finally did—march the troops across the neck, run the batteries with the transports, and thus go below; and I never had any faith, except a general hope that you knew better than I, that the Yazoo Pass expedition, and the like, could succeed. When you got below, and took Port-Gibson, Grand Gulf, and vicinity, I thought you should go down the river and join Gen. Banks; and when you turned Northward East of the Big Black, I feared it was a mistake. I now wish to make the personal acknowledgment that you were right, and I was wrong. Yours very truly

A. LINCOLN

ANNOTATION

General Grant did not acknowledge receipt of this letter until August 23 when he replied to Lincoln's letter of August 9.

To Ulysses S. Grant

Executive Mansion Washington,
Lieutenant General Grant. April 30, 1864

Not expecting to see you again before the Spring campaign opens, I wish to express, in this way, my entire satisfaction with what you have done up to this time, so far as I understand it. The particulars of your plans I neither know, or seek to know. You are vigilant and self-reliant; and, pleased with this, I wish not to obtrude any constraints or restraints upon you. While I am very anxious that any great disaster, or the capture of our men in great numbers, shall be avoided, I know these points are less likely to escape your attention than they would be mine. If there is anything wanting which is within my power to give, do not fail to let me know it.

And now with a brave Army, and a just cause, may God sustain you.

Yours very truly A. LINCOLN

General Grant replied on May 1:

> "Your very kind letter of yesterday is just received. The confidence you express for the future, and satisfaction with the past, in my military administration is acknowledged with pride. It will be my earnest endeavor that you, and the country, shall not be disappointed.
>
> From my first entrance into the volunteer service of the country, to the present day, I have never had cause of complaint, have never expressed or implied a complaint, against the Administration, or the Sec. of War, for throwing any embarrassment in the way of my vigorously prosecuting what appeared to me my duty. Indeed since the promotion which placed me in command of all the Armies, and in view of the great responsibility, and importance of success, I have been astonished at the readiness with which every thing asked for has been yielded without even an explanation being asked. Should my success be less than I desire, and expect, the least I can say is, the fault is not with you."

To Ulysses S. Grant

"*Cypher*"
Lieut. Gen. Grant Executive Mansion,
City Point, Va. Washington, August 17, 1864.

I have seen your dispatch expressing your unwillingness to break your hold where you are. Neither am I willing. Hold on with a bull-dog gripe, and chew & choke, as much as possible.

A. LINCOLN

On August 15 Grant telegraphed Halleck: "If there is any danger of an uprising in the North to resist the draft or for any other purpose our loyal Governor's ought to organize the militia at once to resist it. If we are to draw troops from the field to keep the loyal States in harness it will prove difficult to suppress the rebellion in the disloyal States. My withdrawal now from the James River would insure the defeat of Sherman. Twenty thousand men sent to him at this time would destroy the greater part of Hood's army, and leave us men wherever required. General Heintzelman can get from the Governors of Ohio, Indiana, and Illinois a militia organization that will deter the discontented from committing any over act. I hope the President will call on Governors of States to organize thoroughly to preserve the peace until after the election. . . ."

To Ulysses S. Grant

Executive Mansion, Washington,
Lieut. General Grant: Jan. 19, 1865.

Please read and answer this letter as though I was not President, but only a friend. My son, now in his twenty second year, having graduated at Harvard, wishes to see something of the war before it ends. I do not wish to put him in the ranks, nor yet to give him a commission, to which those who have already served long, are better entitled, and better qualified to hold. Could he, without embarrassment to you, or detriment to the service, go into your Military family with some nominal rank, I, and not the public, furnishing his necessary means? If no, say so without the least hesitation, because I am as anxious, and as deeply interested, that you shall not be encumbered as you can be yourself. Yours truly

A. LINCOLN

ANNOTATION

On January 21 Grant replied from Annapolis Junction, Maryland: "Your favor of this date in relation to your son serving in some Military capacity is received. I will be most happy to have him in my Military family in the manner you propose. The nominal rank given him is immaterial but I would suggest that of Capt. as I have three staff officers now, of conciderable service, in no higher grade. Indeed I have one officer with only the rank of Lieut. who has been in the service from the beginning of the war. This however will make no difference and I would still say give the rank of Capt. Please excuse my writing on a half sheet. I had no resource but to take the blank half of your letter."

Robert T. Lincoln was appointed captain and assistant adjutant general of Volunteers, February 11, 1865, and resigned June 10, 1865.

Correspondence with the War Department

These three pieces of correspondence are representative of Lincoln's almost daily attention to the smallest details of war while he simultaneously managed larger strategic considerations. Henry Andrews was a deserter sentenced to be shot. Edwin M. Stanton was Lincoln's secretary of war.

Endorsement Concerning Henry Andrews

[January 7, 1864]

The case of Andrews is really a very bad one, as appears by the record already before me. Yet before receiving this I had ordered his punishment commuted to imprisonment for during the war at hard labor, and had so telegraphed. I did this, not on any merit in the case, but because I am trying to evade the butchering business lately. A. LINCOLN.

To Edwin M. Stanton

March 10, 1864

The widow of Commander Ward of the Navy, killed at Mathia's Point early in the war appeals to me to discharge her son, who has enlisted in the New York 6th. . . . For the memory of his father [killed in action on June 27, 1861] and that his mother is an indigent widdow, let him be discharged.

To Edwin M. Stanton

Hon. Sec. of War Executive Mansion,
My dear Sir Washington, March 15. 1864.

Please see the gallant Drummer-boy, Robert H. Hendershot, whose history is briefly written on the fine drum presented him which he now carries. He must have a chance, and if you can find any situation suitable to him, I shall be obliged. Yours truly

A. LINCOLN

ANNOTATION

Robert H. Hendershot of the Eighth Michigan Volunteers, born in December, 1850, was barely twelve years old when he distinguished himself at the Battle of Fredericksburg on December 13, 1862. He was discharged for disability at Falmouth, Virginia, December 27, 1862, and accounts of his exploits in the Battle of Murfreesboro, are unreliable. Following his discharge, he became something of a celebrity and an attraction at Barnum's Museum. His drum, referred to by Lincoln, was the present of the Tribune Association of New York. There is no record of his appointment by Stanton, but he was eventually employed as messenger in the office of U.S. Treasurer Francis E. Spinner who recommended that he be appointed to West Point on January 1, 1865. According to William S. Dodge, *Rob-*

ert Henry Hendershot; or, The Brave Drummer Boy of the Rappahannock (Chicago, 1867), his appointment was the last one Lincoln made for West Point, but no record has been found of his entrance.

Second Inaugural Address

Thousands of words have been written about this magnificent and magnificently brief address. Perhaps Garry Wills says it best in the epilogue to *Lincoln at Gettysburg*, where he writes of the "counterrhetoric of joint responsibility for the historical sin of slavery that gives Lincoln's last great statement on the war its tortured radiance." Wills continues, "It was inappropriate, at Gettysburg, to talk about the *sins* of the men to whom he was paying tribute. He talked of rebirth from blood, there, but not of washing away the crimes of the past, as he does in the Second Inaugural Address. In this last speech, war is made to pay history's dues in a prophet's ledger, whose scales balance precisely the blood drawn by the lash and by the bayonet." Few American political speeches come even close to its concentrated force.

Second Inaugural Address
March 4, 1865

[Fellow Countrymen:]

At this second appearing to take the oath of the presidential office, there is less occasion for an extended address than there was at the first. Then a statement, somewhat in detail, of a course to be pursued, seemed fitting and proper. Now, at the expiration of four years, during which public declarations have been constantly called forth on every point and phase of the great contest which still absorbs the attention, and engrosses the enerergies [*sic*] of the nation, little that is new could be presented. The progress of our arms, upon which all else chiefly depends, is as well known to the public as to myself; and it is, I trust, reasonably satisfactory and encouraging to all. With high hope for the future, no prediction in regard to it is ventured.

On the occasion corresponding to this four years ago, all thoughts were anxiously directed to an impending civil-war. All dreaded it—all sought to avert it. While the inaugural address was being delivered from this place, devoted altogether to *saving* the Union without war, insurgent agents were in the city seeking to *destroy* it without war—seeking to dissol[v]e the Union, and divide effects, by negotiation. Both parties deprecated war; but one of them would *make* war rather than let the nation survive; and the other would *accept* war rather than let it perish. And the war came.

One eighth of the whole population were colored slaves, not distributed generally over the Union, but localized in the Southern part of it. These slaves constituted a peculiar and powerful interest. All knew that this interest was, somehow, the cause of the war. To strengthen, perpetuate, and extend this interest was the object for which the insurgents would rend the Union, even by war; while the government claimed no right to do more than to restrict the territorial enlargement of it. Neither party expected for the war, the magnitude, or the duration, which it has already attained. Neither anticipated that the *cause* of the conflict might cease with, or even before, the conflict itself should cease. Each looked for an easier triumph, and a result less fundamental and astounding. Both read the same Bible, and pray to the same God; and each invokes His aid against the other. It may seem strange that any men should dare to ask a just God's assistance in wringing their bread from the sweat of other men's faces; but let us judge not that we be not judged. The prayers of both could not be answered; that of neither has been answered fully. The Almighty has His own purposes. "Woe unto the world because of offences! for it must needs be that offences come; but woe to that man by whom the offence cometh!" If we shall suppose that American Slavery is one of those offences which, in the providence of God, must needs come, but which, having continued through His appointed time, He now wills to remove, and that He gives to both North and South, this terrible war, as the woe due to those by whom the offence came, shall we discern therein any departure from those divine attributes which the believers in a Living God always ascribe to Him? Fondly do we hope—fervently do we pray—that this mighty scourge of war may speedily pass away. Yet, if God wills that it continue, until all the wealth piled by the bond-man's two hundred and fifty years of unrequited toil shall be sunk, and until every drop of blood drawn with the lash, shall be paid by another drawn with the sword, as was said three thousand years ago, so still it must be said "the judgments of the Lord, are true and righteous altogether."

With malice toward none; with charity for all; with firmness in the right, as God gives us to see the right, let us strive on to finish the work we are in; to bind up the nation's wounds; to care for him who shall have borne the battle, and for his widow, and his orphan—to do all which may achieve and cherish a just, and a lasting peace, among ourselves, and with all nations.

DISCUSSION QUESTIONS

1. *Are Lincoln's leadership and management strategies possible in today's world?*

2. *How does Lincoln adapt his tone and approach to each recipient and situation?*

3. *What are the most effective aspects of Lincoln's rhetoric?*

DISCIPLINING DESIRE

In the nighttime of all beings,
the self-controlled man is awake;
that time when beings are awake
is nighttime for the seeing sage.

—*Bhagavad Gita*

Macbeth is, in several senses, the great tragedy of the night: the nocturnal setting of so much of the play's action is matched by the darkness of deep desire and the concealed terrors of conscience. In an introduction to the play the critic Frank Kermode proposes that nowhere "does Shakespeare show a nation so cruelly occupied by the powers of darkness; and *Macbeth* is, for all its brevity, his most intensive study of evil at work in the individual and in the world at large."

Greatness in Shakespeare's protagonists is never unalloyed; it is blended always with larger or lesser shares of ambivalence, pettiness, weakness, and cruelty. In the case of the character of Macbeth, undeniable virtue is inconveniently yoked to an ambition of such capacity and unrelenting momentum that even Macbeth himself cannot in the end fully comprehend, but only acquiesce in, it: "I am in blood / Stepped in so far that, should I wade no more, / Returning were as tedious as go o'er."

Macbeth's is a complicated, nuanced evil: in the witches' prophecy that he will one day become king he finds an external manifestation of his own ambitions for power and position, yet he never surrenders his understanding of what is right, even as he is swiftly propelled toward bloody acts. Unlike Shakespeare's less sympathetic and complex villains, Richard III perhaps chief among them, but also Iago (*Othello*) and Edmund (*King Lear*), Macbeth and Lady Macbeth, as the critic A. C. Bradley notes, "remain to the end tragic, even grand." They are not, Bradley suggests, "vulgar souls." Rather, they are fired by one and the same passion of ambition; and to a considerable extent they are alike. The disposition of each is high, proud, and commanding. They are born to rule, if not to reign. They are peremptory or contemptuous to their inferiors. They are not children of light, like Brutus and Hamlet; they are of the world. We observe in them no love of country, and no interest in the welfare of anyone outside their family. Their habitual thoughts and aims are, and, we imagine, long have been, all of station and power. And though in both there is something, and in one [Macbeth] much, of what is higher—honour, conscience, humanity—they do not live consciously in the light of these things or speak their language.

The language of this play is itself distinctive. Macbeth is the leanest of Shakespeare's late tragedies. Brief and brutal though his universe may be, however, Macbeth himself speaks a rich and sometimes even leisurely poetry full of sophisticated imagery, beautiful turns of phrase, and elegiac expression. The actor Derek Jacobi explains the great difficulty he had in assimilating Macbeth's divergent personality when he arrived at Macbeth's great soliloquy on crime, consequence, and ambition in act 1, scene 7:

> The soliloquy is full of extraordinary images—"pity, like a naked new born babe," and so on—all occurring to him on the instant. He is a highly intelligent, imaginative, articulate man, quite unlike the brutal, non-thinking slasher of the battlefield, the tried, and honed, killing machine. Here we are in contact with that other side of him, the great contrast with his life as a soldier; in his own head he lives in an astonishing imaginative world which he is able to express sensationally and beautifully. His head is full of the mixture of good and evil. At this moment the evil side of him, which we all possess, is getting the upper hand and in order to balance it he brings up the best, the purest, the most innocent of images, of angels, and new-born babies, and the sky. They are all pure, unsullied, wonderful images; goodness pours out of them; they're shining. And on the other side are the dark, blood-driven, evil, dank thoughts.

Our first impression notwithstanding, Macbeth is never unthinking: he broods to the end on the vicissitudes of his career, the costs of his decisions, and the impotence of his ambition. Yet he never quite renounces his crimes even as he acknowledges their enormity. He never slackens his destructive pace even as the passion behind his ambition abates before the growing murkiness of its ultimate object, which seems to be some abstract notion of power embodied in the throne of Scotland.

Having established ambition as Macbeth's motive force, Shakespeare nevertheless leaves us wondering what the source and aim of his perpetual restlessness—what the nineteenth-century critic William Hazlitt described as the characteristic "anxiety and the agitation of his mind"—really is. Macbeth's career illustrates the principle that ambition, like courage, is morally neutral yet sometimes contingent on unscrupulous behavior. Lady Macbeth complains that her husband is "not without ambition, but without / The illness should attend it." As philosophers from Plutarch to Bacon have argued, the desire for fame and excellence is the necessary motor of public life, but when thwarted by custom or circumstance, ambitious desire quickly becomes a destructive force. The effects of that force are all too palpable in the wasted kingdom of Scotland with which Shakespeare leaves us in this tragedy.

Although *Macbeth* was performed as early as 1606, the first authoritative text of the play is that of the First Folio, the edition assembled by John Heminge and Henry Condell, fellow actors in Shakespeare's theater company, the King's Men. It is usually assumed that this version, printed in 1623, was based on the promptbook used during performances. Without the First Folio, we would have fewer than half of the plays attributed to Shakespeare, who was careless to a degree that surprises many modern readers about preserving his writing for the stage.

FURTHER READING AND VIEWING

Francis Bacon, "Of Ambition," from *Essays* (1625)
Double Indemnity (1944), directed by Billy Wilder
The Godfather (1972), directed by Francis Ford Coppola
My Dearest Friend: Letters of Abigail and John Adams (2007), edited by Margaret A. Hogan and C. James Taylor
Throne of Blood (1957), directed by Akira Kurosawa

Macbeth
Character List

KING Duncan of Scotland
MALCOLM, his son, later Prince of Cumberland
DONALDBAIN, another son
CAPTAIN in King Duncan's army

MACBETH, Thane of Glamis, later Thane of Cawdor, later King of Scotland
THREE MURDERERS, attending Macbeth
A PORTER at Macbeth's Castle
SEYTON, a servant of Macbeth
LADY MACBETH, Macbeth's wife, later Queen of Scotland
GENTLEWOMAN, servant of Lady Macbeth
Scottish DOCTOR, attending Lady Macbeth

SIX WITCHES, including the three weïrd sisters
HECATE, leader of the witches
THREE APPARITIONS: an armed head, a bloody child, a child crowned
A show of eight KINGS

BANQUO, a thane of Scotland, later appearing as a GHOST
FLEANCE, his son

MACDUFF, Thane of Fife
WIFE of Macduff
SON, child of Macduff and Wife

LENNOX
ROSS
MENTEITII } Scottish thanes
ANGUS
CAITHNESS

English DOCTOR
OLD MAN
SIWARD, English Earl of Northumberland
YOUNG SIWARD, his son
MESSENGER
LORD
SERVANT
SOLDIER

Lords, Soldiers, Servants, Drummers, a Sewer

1.1

Thunder and lightning. Enter three WITCHES.

FIRST WITCH When shall we three meet again?
    In thunder, lightning, or in rain?
SECOND WITCH When the hurly-burly's done,
    When the battle's lost and won.
THIRD WITCH That will be ere the set of sun.   5
FIRST WITCH Where the place?
SECOND WITCH Upon the heath.
THIRD WITCH There to meet with Macbeth.
FIRST WITCH I come, Grimalkin!
ALL Paddock calls anon!   10
    Fair is foul, and foul is fair,
    Hover through the fog and filthy air.

Exeunt.

1.2

Alarum within. Enter KING [*Duncan*], MALCOLM, DONALDBAIN.
LENNOX, *with Attendants, meeting a bleeding* CAPTAIN.

KING What bloody man is that? He can report,
    As seemeth by his plight, of the revolt
    The newest state.
MALCOLM   This is the sergeant
    Who like a good and hardy soldier fought
    'Gainst my captivity. —Hail, brave friend!   5
    Say to the King the knowledge of the broil
    As thou didst leave it.

1.1. **Location: outdoors.**
3. **hurly-burly:** commotion.
7. **heath:** open, uncultivated ground with low shrubs.
9. **Grimalkin:** gray cat, the name of the witch's familiar (attendant spirit).
10. **SP** ALL: Editors have unnecessarily made this line start a dialogue between the Second Witch and Third Witch; **Paddock:** toad, another familiar; **anon:** at once.
1.2. **Location: a military camp.**
0.1. **SD** *Alarum:* a call to arms by a trumpet or other instrument; *within:* behind the back wall of the stage.
3. **sergeant:** a military officer; the rank is probably "captain," as indicated by the stage direction and speech prefixes.
6. **broil:** battle.

CAPTAIN   Doubtful it stood,
     As two spent swimmers that do cling together
     And choke their art. The merciless Macdonald—
     Worthy to be a rebel, for to that   10
     The multiplying villainies of nature
     Do swarm upon him—from the Western Isles
     Of kerns and galloglasses is supplied;
     And Fortune, on his damnèd quarry smiling,
     Showed like a rebel's whore. But all's too weak,   15
     For brave Macbeth—well he deserves that name—
     Disdaining Fortune with his brandished steel,
     Which smoked with bloody execution,
     Like valor's minion carved out his passage
     Till he faced the slave,   20
     Which ne'er shook hands nor bade farewell to him,
     Till he unseamed him from the nave to th' chops,
     And fixed his head upon our battlements.
KING   O valiant cousin, worthy gentleman!
CAPTAIN   As whence the sun 'gins his reflection,   25
     Shipwrecking storms and direful thunders,
     So from that spring whence comfort seemed to come,
     Discomfort swells. Mark, King of Scotland, mark:
     No sooner justice had, with valor armed,
     Compelled these skipping kerns to trust their heels,   30
     But the Norwegian lord, surveying vantage,

---

8. **spent:** exhausted.
9. **choke their art:** make impossible the art of swimming.
10. **that:** that end.
11. **villainies of nature:** (1) evil aspects of his nature; (2) villainous rebels.
12. **Western Isles:** the Hebrides and, perhaps, Ireland.
13. **kerns:** light-armed Irish foot soldiers; **galloglasses:** soldiers on horse with axes.
14–15. **Fortune . . . whore:** Fortune, seeming to favor its intended victim Macdonald (**quarry**), appeared to be his consort. (Fortune was proverbially a strumpet and unfaithful, so the metaphor is ominous for Macdonald.)
19. **minion:** darling.
20. **slave:** Macdonald.
21. **Which:** who.
22. Till he split him open from the navel to the jaws.
24. **cousin:** a general term of affection, here indicating a specific familial relation; see 1.7.13.
25. **whence:** from the place where; **'gins his reflection:** begins its turning back across the sky.
26. If the verb **come** (27) is understood at the end of the line, there is no need to add "break" or some such word, as editors often do. The movement of the sun after the spring equinox was thought to cause storms.
27. **spring:** (1) season of spring; (2) source.
30. **skipping . . . heels:** flighty foot-soldiers to retreat.
31. **surveying vantage:** seeing an advantage.

With furbished arms and new supplies of men
Began a fresh assault.

KING Dismayed not this our captains, Macbeth and Banquo?

CAPTAIN Yes, as sparrows eagles or the hare the lion.   35
If I say sooth, I must report they were
As cannons overcharged with double cracks;
So they doubly redoubled strokes upon the foe.
Except they meant to bathe in reeking wounds,
Or memorize another Golgotha,   40
I cannot tell—
But I am faint. My gashes cry for help.

KING So well thy words become thee as thy wounds;
They smack of honor both. —Go get him surgeons.

　　　　　　　　　　　　　[*Exit* CAPTAIN, *attended.*]

　　　　Enter ROSS *and* ANGUS.

Who comes here?

MALCOLM   The worthy Thane of Ross.   45

LENNOX What a haste looks through his eyes!
So should he look that seems to speak things strange.

ROSS God save the King!

KING Whence cam'st thou, worthy thane?

ROSS From Fife, great King,   50
Where the Norwegian banners flout the sky
And fan our people cold.
Norway himself, with terrible numbers,
Assisted by that most disloyal traitor,
The Thane of Cawdor, began a dismal conflict.   55
Till that Bellona's bridegroom, lapped in proof,
Confronted him with self-comparisons,

32. **furbished:** scoured.
36. **sooth:** truth.
37. **cracks:** charges of gunpowder.
38. **So they:** they so.
39. **Except:** unless.
40. **memorize another Golgotha:** make the battle as memorable as the Biblical Golgotha ("the place of the skull"), where Christ was crucified (Mark 15:22).
45. **Thane:** a landowner and chief of a clan, equivalent to an English earl.
46. **looks through:** appears in.
47. **seems to:** seems about to.
50. **Fife:** county on the east coast of Scotland.
51. **flout:** mock.
52. **fan . . . cold:** make . . . afraid.
53. **Norway:** the King of Norway (Sweno).
55. **dismal:** ominous.
56. **Bellona:** Roman goddess of war (imagined as wife to Macbeth, the **bridegroom**); **lapped in proof:** (1) wearing proven armor; (2) wrapped in experience.

Point against point, rebellious arm 'gainst arm,
Curbing his lavish spirit. And to conclude,
The victory fell on us—
KING   Great happiness!—
ROSS   That now Sweno,   60
The Norways' king, craves composition.
Nor would we deign him burial of his men
Till he disbursèd at Saint Colme's Inch
Ten thousand dollars to our general use.
KING No more that Thane of Cawdor shall deceive   65
Our bosom interest. Go pronounce his present death,
And with his former title greet Macbeth.
ROSS I'll see it done.
KING What he hath lost noble Macbeth hath won.

Exeunt.

1.3

Thunder. Enter the three WITCHES.

FIRST WITCH Where hast thou been, sister?
SECOND WITCH Killing swine.
THIRD WITCH Sister, where thou?
FIRST WITCH A sailor's wife had chestnuts in her lap,
And munched, and munched, and munched.   5
"Give me," quoth I.
"Aroint thee, witch!" the rump-fed runnion cries.
Her husband's to Aleppo gone, master o' the *Tiger*,
But in a sieve I'll thither sail,

---

57. **self-comparisons**: powers comparable to his own.
59. **lavish**: wild.
61. **Norways'**: Norwegians'; **composition**: agreement, peace treaty.
62. **deign**: grant.
63. **Saint Colme's Inch**: Inchcolm, an isle near Edinburgh. **Colme's** is disyllabic, derived from St. Columba (521–97), who preached, worked miracles, and converted the Northern Picts to Christianity (see 2.4.33n.).
64. **dollars**: silver coins, probably German *thalers*, used throughout Europe.
66. **bosom interest**: heart's trust; **present**: immediate.
1.3. **Location: a heath.**
6. **quoth**: said.
7. **Aroint**: begone; **rump-fed**: (1) fed on rump meat; (2) fat-rumped; **runnion**: woman (an abusive term).
8. **Aleppo**: trading city in Northern Syria; *Tiger*: name of a ship.
9. **sieve**: Witches were commonly thought to sail in sieves.

And like a rat without a tail, 10
I'll do, I'll do, and I'll do.
SECOND WITCH I'll give thee a wind.
FIRST WITCH Thou'rt kind.
THIRD WITCH And I another.
FIRST WITCH I myself have all the other, 15
And the very ports they blow,
All the quarters that they know
I'th' shipman's card.
I'll drain him dry as hay.
Sleep shall neither night nor day 20
Hang upon his penthouse lid;
He shall live a man forbid.
Weary sennights nine times nine
Shall he dwindle, peak, and pine.
Though his bark cannot be lost, 25
Yet it shall be tempest-tossed.
Look what I have.
SECOND WITCH Show me, show me.
FIRST WITCH Here I have a pilot's thumb,
Wrecked as homeward he did come. 30

Drum within.

THIRD WITCH A drum, a drum!
Macbeth doth come!
ALL [*dancing in a circle*] The weïrd sisters, hand in hand,
Posters of the sea and land,
Thus do go, about, about, 35
Thrice to thine, and thrice to mine,
And thrice again to make up nine.
Peace, the charm's wound up.

10. **rat . . . tail:** Transformed witches sometimes had bodily defects.
11. **do:** (1) act; (2) have sexual intercourse.
16. And I control the ports where the winds blow.
17. **quarters:** directions.
18. **shipman's card:** nautical map.
19. By sexual intercourse, presumably, as a succubus (demon in female form).
21. **penthouse lid:** eyelid (projecting over the eye like a **penthouse**).
22. **forbid:** cursed.
23. **sennights:** weeks (seven nights).
24. **peak:** waste away.
25. **bark:** ship.
30. **SD** *Drum:* a signal for the entrance of military characters.
33. **weïrd:** fateful (from **wyrd**, "fate"), pronounced disyllabically, with a suggestion of the uncanny. Audiences might have heard "wayward" too, which appears elsewhere in the play (3.5.11).
34. **Posters of:** travelers over.

Enter MACBETH *and* BANQUO.

MACBETH So foul and fair a day I have not seen.

BANQUO How far is't called to Forres? What are these,   40
So withered and so wild in their attire,
That look not like th'inhabitants o'th' earth,
And yet are on't? —Live you? Or are you aught
That man may question? You seem to understand me
By each at once her choppy finger laying   45
Upon her skinny lips. You should be women.
And yet your beards forbid me to interpret
That you are so.

MACBETH   Speak, if you can. What are you?

FIRST WITCH All hail, Macbeth! Hail to thee, Thane of Glamis!

SECOND WITCH All hail, Macbeth! Hail to thee, Thane of Cawdor!   50

THIRD WITCH All hail, Macbeth, that shalt be king hereafter!

BANQUO Good sir, why do you start and seem to fear
Things that do sound so fair? —I'th' name of truth,
Are ye fantastical or that indeed
Which outwardly ye show? My noble partner   55
You greet with present grace and great prediction
Of noble having and of royal hope
That he seems rapt withal. To me you speak not.
If you can look into the seeds of time
And say which grain will grow and which will not,   60
Speak then to me, who neither beg nor fear
Your favors nor your hate.

FIRST WITCH Hail!

SECOND WITCH Hail!

THIRD WITCH Hail!   65

FIRST WITCH Lesser than Macbeth, and greater.

SECOND WITCH Not so happy, yet much happier.

THIRD WITCH Thou shalt get kings, though thou be none.
So all hail, Macbeth and Banquo!

FIRST WITCH Banquo and Macbeth, all hail!   70

---

40. **called:** said to be; **Forres:** Scottish town.
43. **aught:** anything.
45. **choppy:** chapped.
49. **All hail:** Shakespeare associated this phrase with Judas's betrayal of Jesus (Matthew 26.49) in *3 Henry VI* (5.7.33–34) and *Richard II* (4.1.169–71).
52. **start:** flinch, recoil.
54. **fantastical:** creatures of fantasy.
56. **grace:** honor.
58. **rapt:** entranced; **withal:** with it.
68. **get:** beget.

MACBETH Stay, you imperfect speakers, tell me more.
    By Finel's death I know I am Thane of Glamis,
    But how of Cawdor? The Thane of Cawdor lives,
    A prosperous gentleman, and to be king
    Stands not within the prospect of belief,   75
    No more than to be Cawdor. Say from whence
    You owe this strange intelligence, or why
    Upon this blasted heath you stop our way
    With such prophetic greeting. Speak, I charge you.

                                   WITCHES *vanish.*

BANQUO The earth hath bubbles as the water has,   80
    And these are of them. Whither are they vanished?
MACBETH Into the air. And what seemed corporal
    Melted as breath into the wind. Would they had stayed.
BANQUO Were such things here as we do speak about?
    Or have we eaten on the insane root   85
    That takes the reason prisoner?
MACBETH Your children shall be kings.
BANQUO   You shall be king.
MACBETH And Thane of Cawdor too. Went it not so?
BANQUO To th'selfsame tune and words. —Who's here?

    Enter ROSS *and* ANGUS.

ROSS The King hath happily received, Macbeth,   90
    The news of thy success; and when he reads
    Thy personal venture in the rebels' fight,
    His wonders and his praises do contend
    Which should be thine or his. Silenced with that,
    In viewing o'er the rest o'th' selfsame day,   95
    He finds thee in the stout Norwegian ranks,

71. **imperfect:** unfinished.
72. **Finel:** Macbeth's father.
73–74. An apparent contradiction (explicable as an oversight or an incomplete revision) to 1.2.54–58, which describes Macbeth's victory over Cawdor.
75. **prospect:** possibility.
77. **owe:** own; **intelligence:** news.
78. **blasted:** blighted, often by a supernatural agent.
79. **SD** *vanish*: Probably by use of the trap door or smoke from burning resin.
82. **corporal:** bodily.
85. **insane root:** plant causing insanity (probably henbane).
91. **reads:** considers.
93–94. **His . . . his:** His astonishment strikes him into awed silence but also stimulates the conflicting impulse to praise and reward.

Nothing afeard of what thyself didst make,
Strange images of death. As thick as hail
Came post with post, and every one did bear
Thy praises in his kingdom's great defense   100
And poured them down before him.
ANGUS   We are sent
    To give thee from our royal master thanks,
    Only to herald thee into his sight,
    Not pay thee.
ROSS And for an earnest of a greater honor,   105
    He bade me, from him, call thee Thane of Cawdor;
    In which addition, hail, most worthy thane,
    For it is thine.
BANQUO   What, can the devil speak true?
MACBETH   The Thane of Cawdor lives. Why do you dress me
    In borrowed robes?
ANGUS   Who was the thane lives yet,   110
    But under heavy judgment bears that life
    Which he deserves to lose.
    Whether he was combined with those of Norway,
    Or did line the rebel with hidden help
    And vantage, or that with both he labored   115
    In his country's wrack, I know not.
    But treasons capital, confessed and proved,
    Have overthrown him.
MACBETH [aside]   Glamis, and Thane of Cawdor!
    The greatest is behind. —Thanks for your pains.
    [aside to BANQUO] Do you not hope your children shall be kings,   120
    When those that gave the Thane of Cawdor to me
    Promised no less to them?
BANQUO [aside to MACBETH] That trusted home
    Might yet enkindle you unto the crown.
    Besides the Thane of Cawdor. But 'tis strange,

97. Not at all afraid of what you yourself created.
98. **hail:** Some defend Folio's "Tale," but "thick as hail" is proverbial.
99. **post with post:** messenger after messenger.
103. **herald:** usher.
105. **earnest:** token payment.
107. **addition:** title.
114. **line the rebel:** fortify Macdonald.
116. **wrack:** ruin.
117. **capital:** punishable by death.
119. **behind:** still to come.
122. **home:** all the way.

And oftentimes to win us to our harm, 125
The instruments of darkness tell us truths,
Win us with honest trifles, to betray's
In deepest consequence.
—Cousins, a word, I pray you.

[*He converses apart with* ROSS *and* ANGUS.]

MACBETH [*aside*]   Two truths are told,
As happy prologues to the swelling act 130
Of th'imperial theme. —I thank you, gentlemen.
[*aside*] This supernatural soliciting
Cannot be ill, cannot be good. If ill,
Why hath it given me earnest of success
Commencing in a truth? I am Thane of Cawdor. 135
If good, why do I yield to that suggestion
Whose horrid image doth unfix my hair
And make my seated heart knock at my ribs
Against the use of nature? Present fears
Are less than horrible imaginings. 140
My thought, whose murder yet is but fantastical,
Shakes so my single state of man
That function is smothered in surmise,
And nothing is but what is not.
BANQUO Look how our partner's rapt. 145
MACBETH [*aside*] If chance will have me king, why, chance may
    crown me
Without my stir.
BANQUO   New honors come upon him,
Like our strange garments, cleave not to their mold
But with the aid of use.

126. **darkness:** evil, especially demonic.
128. **deepest consequence:** gravest outcome.
129. **Cousins:** fellow lords.
130. **swelling act:** developing drama.
131. **imperial theme:** the subject of kingship.
132. **soliciting:** urging.
137. **horrid:** bristling; **unfix:** make stand.
139. **use:** custom.
141. **whose:** in which; **fantastical:** imaginary.
142. **single . . . man:** weak human condition.
143. **function:** ability to act; **surmise:** speculation.
144. Nothing exists in the present but thoughts about the future.
147. **stir:** acting; **come:** having come.
148. **cleave . . . mold:** do not fit the body's form.

MACBETH [*aside*]   Come what come may,
  Time and the hour runs through the roughest day.   150
BANQUO Worthy Macbeth, we stay upon your leisure.
MACBETH Give me your favor. My dull brain was wrought
  With things forgotten. Kind gentlemen, your pains
  Are registered where every day I turn
  The leaf to read them. Let us toward the King.   155
  [*aside to* BANQUO] Think upon what hath chanced, and at more
      time,
  The interim having weighed it, let us speak
  Our free hearts each to other.
BANQUO [*aside to* MACBETH]   Very gladly.
MACBETH [*aside to* BANQUO] Till then, enough. —Come, friends.

                                              Exeunt.

                    1.4

  Flourish. Enter KING, LENNOX, MALCOLM, DONALDBAIN,
  and Attendants.

KING Is execution done on Cawdor? Or not
  Those in commission yet returned?
MALCOLM   My liege,
  They are not yet come back. But I have spoke
  With one that saw him die, who did report
  That very frankly he confessed his treasons,   5
  Implored your highness' pardon, and set forth
  A deep repentance. Nothing in his life
  Became him like the leaving it. He died
  As one that had been studied in his death

149. **Come . . . may:** Let whatever will happen happen, a proverbial expression.
150. Even the roughest days come to an end.
152. **favor:** goodwill.
154. **registered:** recorded (in my mind).
155. **leaf:** page.
157. **The . . . it:** having considered the matter in the meantime.
1.4. **Location: the King's camp or palace.**
0.1. SD *Flourish:* a trumpet signal indicating the entrance or exit of royal authority. Flourishes honor King Duncan and later King Malcolm (5.7.64.4 SD, 89 SD) but never the usurper Macbeth.
1. **Or not:** or are not; **in commission:** commissioned (to execute Cawdor); **liege:** superior to whom one owes service.
8. **Became:** graced, befitted.
9. **studied:** prepared by study.

To throw away the dearest thing he owed   10
As 'twere a careless trifle.

KING   There's no art
To find the mind's construction in the face.
He was a gentleman on whom I built
An absolute trust.

>   *Enter* MACBETH, BANQUO, ROSS, *and* ANGUS.

                                    —O worthiest cousin!
The sin of my ingratitude even now   15
Was heavy on me. Thou art so far before
That swiftest wing of recompense is slow
To overtake thee. Would thou hadst less deserved,
That the proportion both of thanks and payment
Might have been mine. Only I have left to say,   20
More is thy due than more than all can pay.

MACBETH The service and the loyalty I owe
In doing it pays itself. Your highness' part
Is to receive our duties, and our duties
Are to your throne and state, children and servants,   25
Which do but what they should by doing everything
Safe toward your love and honor.

KING   Welcome hither.
I have begun to plant thee and will labor
To make thee full of growing.—Noble Banquo,
That hast no less deserved nor must be known   30
No less to have done so, let me enfold thee
And hold thee to my heart.

BANQUO   There if I grow,
The harvest is your own.

KING   My plenteous joys,
Wanton in fullness, seek to hide themselves
In drops of sorrow.—Sons, kinsmen, thanes,   35

---

10. **owed:** owned.
11. **careless:** uncared for.
16. **before:** ahead (in time and in deserving).
19. **proportion:** just and satisfactory reckoning.
23. **it:** my duty.
24–25. **and . . . servants:** We owe duty to your throne and high rank just as children owe duty to their parents, and servants to their masters.
27. **Safe toward:** to make safe.
28. **plant:** nurture.
31. **enfold:** embrace.
34. **Wanton:** profuse.

And you whose places are the nearest, know
We will establish our estate upon
Our eldest, Malcolm, whom we name hereafter
The Prince of Cumberland; which honor must
Not unaccompanied invest him only,   40
But signs of nobleness, like stars, shall shine
On all deservers. [*to* MACBETH] From hence to Inverness,
And bind us further to you.
MACBETH   The rest is labor which is not used for you.
I'll be myself the harbinger and make joyful   45
The hearing of my wife with your approach.
So humbly take my leave.
KING   My worthy Cawdor!
MACBETH [*aside*]   The Prince of Cumberland! That is a step
On which I must fall down or else o'erleap,
For in my way it lies. Stars, hide your fires,   50
Let not light see my black and deep desires;
The eye wink at the hand; yet let that be
Which the eye fears, when it is done, to see.   *Exit.*
KING   True, worthy Banquo, he is full so valiant,
And in his commendations I am fed;   55
It is a banquet to me. Let's after him,
Whose care is gone before to bid us welcome.
It is a peerless kinsman.

> *Flourish. Exeunt.*

1.5

Enter Macbeth's Wife [LADY MACBETH] *alone with a letter.*

LADY MACBETH [*reads*]   "They met me in the day of success, and I
have learned by the perfect'st report they have more in them than
mortal knowledge. When I burned in desire to question them

---

37. **establish . . . upon:** name as heir to the throne. (The monarchy was not hereditary.)
39. **Prince of Cumberland:** an honorific title designating the next king.
40. **Not unaccompanied invest:** not alone adorn.
42. **Inverness:** "Mouth of the River Ness," the city where Macbeth's castle is located.
44. **rest:** repose.
45. **harbinger:** forerunner.
52. **The . . . hand:** Let the eye see not what the hand does.
54. **full so valiant:** fully as valiant (as you say).
55. **his commendations:** praises of him.
1.5. **Location:** Inverness. Macbeth's castle.
2. **perfect'st report:** most reliable evidence.

further, they made themselves air, into which they vanished. Whiles I stood rapt in the wonder of it came missives from 5 the King, who all-hailed me 'Thane of Cawdor,' by which title before these weïrd sisters saluted me and referred me to the coming on of time with 'Hail, king that shalt be!' This have I thought good to deliver thee, my dearest partner of greatness, that thou mightst not lose the dues of rejoicing by being ignorant 10 of what greatness is promised thee. Lay it to thy heart, and farewell."

Glamis thou art, and Cawdor, and shalt be
What thou art promised. Yet do I fear thy nature;
It is too full o'th' milk of human kindness 15
To catch the nearest way. Thou wouldst be great,
Art not without ambition, but without
The illness should attend it. What thou wouldst highly,
That wouldst thou holily; wouldst not play false.
And yet wouldst wrongly win. Thou'dst have, great Glamis, 20
That which cries "Thus thou must do" if thou have it,
And that which rather thou dost fear to do
Than wishest should be undone. Hie thee hither,
That I may pour my spirits in thine ear
And chastise with the valor of my tongue 25
All that impedes thee from the golden round,
Which fate and metaphysical aid doth seem
To have thee crowned withal.

    Enter MESSENGER.

                                  What is your tidings?
MESSENGER The King comes here tonight.
LADY MACBETH   Thou'rt mad to say it!
Is not thy master with him, who, were't so, 30

5. **missives:** messengers; **all-hailed:** greeted.
10. **dues:** due measure.
15. **milk . . . kindness:** compassion natural to humankind.
18. **illness:** evil that; **wouldst highly:** would have or do greatly.
20–21. **Thou'dst . . . it:** You must have, great Glamis, a voice that cries "Thus you must do" (i.e., kill the king), if you would attain the crown.
22–23. **And . . . undone:** And you would rather have Duncan dead (even though you fear killing him) than wish him alive again after he is gone.
23. **Hie:** hurry.
24. **spirits:** supernatural assistants to evil (see 36ff.).
25. **valor:** power.
26. **round:** crown.
27. **metaphysical:** supernatural.
28. **withal:** with.

Would have informed for preparation?

MESSENGER So please you, it is true. Our thane is coming.

One of my fellows had the speed of him,

Who, almost dead for breath, had scarcely more

Than would make up his message.

LADY MACBETH   Give him tending;   35

He brings great news.   *Exit* MESSENGER.

                          The raven himself is hoarse

That croaks the fatal entrance of Duncan

Under my battlements. Come, you spirits

That tend on mortal thoughts, unsex me here,

And fill me from the crown to the toe top-full   40

Of direst cruelty! Make thick my blood,

Stop up th'access and passage to remorse,

That no compunctious visitings of nature

Shake my fell purpose nor keep peace between

Th'effect and it. Come to my woman's breasts   45

And take my milk for gall, you murd'ring ministers,

Wherever in your sightless substances

You wait on nature's mischief. Come, thick night,

And pall thee in the dunnest smoke of hell,

That my keen knife see not the wound it makes,   50

Nor heaven peep through the blanket of the dark

To cry "Hold, hold!"

Enter MACBETH.

                          Great Glamis, worthy Cawdor,

Greater than both by the all-hail hereafter!

Thy letters have transported me beyond

31. **informed for preparation**: sent us word so that we could prepare for the visit.
33. **had . . . him**: traveled more quickly than he.
34. **more**: more breath.
36. **raven**: a bird of evil portent.
37. **fatal**: (1) directed by fate; (2) deadly to Duncan.
39. **mortal**: (1) human; (2) murderous; **here**: At this word actresses have sometimes gestured to breast or groin.
41. **Make . . . blood**: Thickened blood supposedly blocked the operation of emotions like pity and fear.
43. **compunctious visitings**: feelings of compassion or guilt.
44. **fell purpose**: cruel intention; **keep peace**: intervene.
45. **Th'effect and it**: the consequence (i.e., the King's murder) and **my fell purpose**.
46. **take . . . gall**: (1) replace my milk with gall, i.e., bile, associated with envy and hatred; (2) take evil from my breasts by nursing at them.
47. **sightless substances**: invisible presences.
48. **wait on**: attend, aid.
49. **pall**: cover (as with a funeral cloth); **dunnest**: darkest.
53. **all-hail hereafter**: the future in which everyone will salute you as king.

This ignorant present, and I feel now   55
The future in the instant.
MACBETH   My dearest love,
    Duncan comes here tonight.
LADY MACBETH   And when goes hence?
MACBETH   Tomorrow, as he purposes.
LADY MACBETH   Oh, never
    Shall sun that morrow see!
    Your face, my thane, is as a book where men   60
    May read strange matters. To beguile the time,
    Look like the time; bear welcome in your eye,
    Your hand, your tongue. Look like th'innocent flower,
    But be the serpent under't. He that's coming
    Must be provided for. And you shall put   65
    This night's great business into my dispatch,
    Which shall to all our nights and days to come
    Give solely sovereign sway and masterdom.
MACBETH   We will speak further.
LADY MACBETH   Only look up clear.
    To alter favor ever is to fear.   70
    Leave all the rest to me.

                                            Exeunt.

                          1.6

Hautboys and torches. Enter KING, MALCOLM, DONALDBAIN,
BANQUO, LENNOX, MACDUFF, ROSS, ANGUS, *and Attendants.*

KING This castle hath a pleasant seat.
    The air nimbly and sweetly recommends itself
    Unto our gentle senses.
BANQUO   This guest of summer,
    The temple-haunting martlet, does approve

61. **beguile the time:** deceive present observers.
62. **Look . . . time:** Act the way people now expect you to act.
65. **provided for:** prepared for (as guest and as murder victim).
66. **dispatch:** management.
69. **look up clear:** look calm.
70. To change expression (**favor**) is always to show fear.
1.6. **Location:** before Macbeth's castle.
0.1. **SD** *Hautboys:* woodwind instruments, ancestors of the softer-toned oboe.
1. **seat:** site.
4. **martlet:** name used for a number of birds, especially the swallow and house-martin; **approve:** confirm.

By his loved mansionry that the heavens' breath   5
Smells wooingly here. No jutty, frieze,
Buttress, nor coign of vantage, but this bird
Hath made his pendent bed and procreant cradle.
Where they must breed and haunt, I have observed,
The air is delicate.

> *Enter* LADY MACBETH.

KING   See, see, our honored hostess!   10
—The love that follows us sometime is our trouble,
Which still we thank as love. Herein I teach you
How you shall bid God 'ield us for your pains,
And thank us for your trouble.
LADY MACBETH   All our service
In every point twice done and then done double   15
Were poor and single business to contend
Against those honors deep and broad wherewith
Your majesty loads our house. For those of old,
And the late dignities heaped up to them,
We rest your hermits.
KING   Where's the Thane of Cawdor?   20
We coursed him at the heels and had a purpose
To be his purveyor; but he rides well,
And his great love, sharp as his spur, hath holp him
To his home before us. Fair and noble hostess,

5. **loved mansionry:** beloved nest-building.
6. **wooingly:** enticingly; **jutty:** projection (from a building); **frieze:** painted or carved band above or at the top of a wall.
7. **coign of vantage:** a projecting corner, affording a good observation point.
8. **pendent:** hanging; procreant: for breeding.
10. **delicate:** pleasant.
11–12. **The love . . . love:** The attentions of others can sometimes be a nuisance, but we still appreciate the love that motivates them. (The King graciously acknowledges the trouble of hosting him but hopes that he is still welcome.)
13. **bid . . . pains:** ask God to reward me (**God 'ield us**) for putting you to trouble (because my visit is motivated by love).
16. **single business:** slight exertion ("busy-ness").
16–17. **contend Against:** match, vie with.
18. **those of old:** the former honors you bestowed.
19. **late:** recent.
20. **rest your hermits:** remain faithful petitioners to God on your behalf (like hermits, i.e., beadsmen who offered prayers for benefactors).
21. **coursed:** pursued.
22. **purveyor:** domestic officer who preceded the King or other great personages and arranged for lodging and supplies.
23. **holp:** helped.

We are your guest tonight.

LADY MACBETH   Your servants ever   25
    Have theirs, themselves, and what is theirs in count
    To make their audit at your highness' pleasure,
    Still to return your own.

KING   Give me your hand;
    Conduct me to mine host. We love him highly
    And shall continue our graces towards him.   30
    By your leave, hostess.

Exeunt.

1.7

*Hautboys. Torches. Enter a Sewer, and divers Servants
with dishes and service over the stage.*

Then enter MACBETH.

MACBETH If it were done when 'tis done, then 'twere well
    It were done quickly. If th'assassination
    Could trammel up the consequence and catch
    With his surcease success—that but this blow
    Might be the be-all and the end-all!—here,   5
    But here, upon this bank and shoal of time,
    We'd jump the life to come. But in these cases
    We still have judgment here, that we but teach
    Bloody instructions which, being taught, return
    To plague th'inventor. This even-handed justice   10

---

26. **Have theirs:** have their servants; **what is theirs:** whatever they own; **count:** trust (from the King).
27. **make their audit:** render an account.
28. **Still . . . own:** always to render back to you as truly yours (since whatever they own they only have in trust from you).
1.7. **Location: Inverness. Macbeth's castle.**
0.1. **SD** *Sewer:* chief waiter.
0.2. **SD** *service:* a meal and the accompanying equipment.
1–2. **If . . . quickly:** If the whole business of murder could end with the killing itself, then it would be good to kill the King quickly.
3. **trammel . . . consequence:** catch (as in a net) the effects and results.
4. **his surcease:** (1) Duncan's death; (2) the cessation of consequence; **success:** (1) whatever follows; (2) a favorable outcome; (3) succession of heirs; **that but:** if only.
6. **bank and shoal:** riverbank or sandbank and shallows.
7. **jump:** risk.
8. **judgment:** punishment; **that:** in that.

Commends th'ingredients of our poisoned chalice
To our own lips. He's here in double trust:
First, as I am his kinsman and his subject,
Strong both against the deed; then, as his host,
Who should against his murderer shut the door,   15
Not bear the knife myself. Besides, this Duncan
Hath borne his faculties so meek, hath been
So clear in his great office, that his virtues
Will plead like angels, trumpet-tongued, against
The deep damnation of his taking-off;   20
And Pity, like a naked newborn babe
Striding the blast, or heaven's cherubim horsed
Upon the sightless couriers of the air,
Shall blow the horrid deed in every eye,
That tears shall drown the wind. I have no spur   25
To prick the sides of my intent, but only
Vaulting ambition, which o'erleaps itself
And falls on th'other—

    Enter LADY MACBETH.

                      HOW now? What news?
LADY MACBETH He has almost supped. Why have you left the chamber?
MACBETH   Hath he asked for me?
LADY MACBETH   Know you not he has?   30
MACBETH We will proceed no further in this business.
    He hath honored me of late, and I have bought
    Golden opinions from all sorts of people,
    Which would be worn now in their newest gloss,
    Not cast aside so soon.
LADY MACBETH   Was the hope drunk   35
    Wherein you dressed yourself? Hath it slept since?

---

11. **chalice:** drinking goblet, also used for the celebration of the Eucharist.
17. **faculties:** powers.
18. **clear:** blameless.
20. **taking-off:** murder.
22. **Striding the blast:** riding the wind; **cherubim:** an order of angels, sometimes represented as babies, sometimes as huge winged creatures (Ezekiel 10, Psalms 18).
23. **sightless couriers:** invisible messengers, i.e., the winds.
25. **That . . . wind:** so that the resulting tears, thick as rain, shall still the wind.
28. **other:** other side (Ambition overleaps and falls down on the other side of the horse); **How now:** How is it now?
32. **bought:** acquired.
34. **gloss:** luster.

And wakes it now to look so green and pale
At what it did so freely? From this time
Such I account thy love. Art thou afeard
To be the same in thine own act and valor   40
As thou art in desire? Wouldst thou have that
Which thou esteem'st the ornament of life,
And live a coward in thine own esteem,
Letting "I dare not" wait upon "I would,"
Like the poor cat i'th' adage?

MACBETH   Prithee, peace!   45
I dare do all that may become a man;
Who dares do more is none.

LADY MACBETH   What beast was't, then,
That made you break this enterprise to me?
When you durst do it, then you were a man;
And to be more than what you were, you would   50
Be so much more the man. Nor time nor place
Did then adhere, and yet you would make both.
They have made themselves, and that their fitness now
Does unmake you. I have given suck and know
How tender 'tis to love the babe that milks me;   55
I would, while it was smiling in my face,
Have plucked my nipple from his boneless gums
And dashed the brains out, had I so sworn as you
Have done to this.

MACBETH   If we should fail?

LADY MACBETH   We fail?
But screw your courage to the sticking-place,   60
And we'll not fail. When Duncan is asleep—

37. **green and pale:** sickly, as if hung over.
42. **ornament of life:** chief acquisition and good, i.e., the crown.
44. **wait upon:** attend.
45. **cat . . . adage:** The proverb, "The cat would eat fish but she will not wet her feet" (Dent C144, see Resources), exhorted the idle or timorous to action; **Prithee:** I pray thee, please.
48. **break:** disclose.
49. **durst:** dared.
50. **to be:** if you were to be.
52. **adhere:** suit; **would make both:** resolved to make time and place suit the deed.
53. **that their fitness:** the very suitability of time and place (for murder).
58. **dashed . . . out:** Psalms 137:9, anticipating the destruction of Babylon, may have contributed to this horrific image: "Blessed shall he be that taketh and dasheth thy children against the stones."
59. **We fail?:** Folio's punctuation ("?") can represent a question mark or exclamation point and the actress must here choose among various inflections and emotions (incredulity, resignation, scorn).
60. **But:** only; **sticking-place:** the notch or place that holds the string taut on a crossbow or a musical instrument.

Whereto the rather shall his day's hard journey
Soundly invite him—his two chamberlains
Will I with wine and wassail so convince
That memory, the warder of the brain, 65
Shall be a fume, and the receipt of reason
A limbeck only. When in swinish sleep
Their drenchèd natures lies as in a death,
What cannot you and I perform upon
Th'unguarded Duncan? What not put upon 70
His spongy officers, who shall bear the guilt
Of our great quell?
MACBETH   Bring forth men-children only,
For thy undaunted mettle should compose
Nothing but males. Will it not be received,
When we have marked with blood those sleepy two 75
Of his own chamber and used their very daggers,
That they have done't?
LADY MACBETH   Who dares receive it other,
As we shall make our griefs and clamor roar
Upon his death?
MACBETH   I am settled, and bend up
Each corporal agent to this terrible feat. 80
Away, and mock the time with fairest show;
False face must hide what the false heart doth know.

Exeunt.

62. Whereto the rather: to which all the sooner.
63. **Soundly invite him:** induce him to sleep deeply; **chamberlains:** bedroom servants.
64. **wine and wassail:** drink in abundance (a wassail is a drink and drinking toast); **convince:** conquer.
65. **warder:** guardian.
66. **fume:** vapor; **receipt:** receptacle.
67. **limbeck:** the cap of a distilling apparatus, which receives the vapors. The elaborate chemical metaphor says that the vapors rising from drink will overpower the memory and subdue the reason.
71. **spongy:** absorbent (having soaked up drink).
72. **quell:** murder.
73. **mettle:** spirit, courage. There is also a pun on "metal" and another on males (74) and "mails," i.e., armor.
77. **other:** otherwise.
80. **corporal agent:** bodily part.
81. **mock:** delude.

2.1

Enter BANQUO *and* FLEANCE, *with a torch before him.*

BANQUO How goes the night, boy?

FLEANCE The moon is down; I have not heard the clock.

BANQUO And she goes down at twelve.

FLEANCE   I take't 'tis later, sir.

BANQUO Hold, take my sword. There's husbandry in heaven;
  Their candles are all out. Take thee that, too.   5
  A heavy summons lies like lead upon me,
  And yet I would not sleep. Merciful powers,
  Restrain in me the cursèd thoughts that nature
  Gives way to in repose.

Enter MACBETH *and a Servant with a torch.*

                 Give me my sword!
  —Who's there?   10

MACBETH A friend.

BANQUO What, sir, not yet at rest? The King's abed.
  He hath been in unusual pleasure
  And sent forth great largesse to your offices.
  This diamond he greets your wife withal,   15
  By the name of most kind hostess, and shut up
  In measureless content.

[He gives a diamond.]

MACBETH   Being unprepared,
  Our will became the servant to defect,
  Which else should free have wrought.

BANQUO   All's well.
  I dreamt last night of the three weïrd sisters.   20
  To you they have showed some truth.

2.1. Location: Macbeth's castle or courtyard.

4. **husbandry:** good management, thrift.

5. **candles:** i.e., stars; **that:** perhaps a dagger.

6. **heavy summons:** urge to sleep.

7. **powers:** an order of angels that resists demons.

14. **largesse . . . offices:** gifts to your household quarters.

15. **greets . . . withal:** salutes . . . with. He honors her with the diamond and with the title (**name**) of **most kind hostess** (16).

16. **shut up:** (1) concluded (his remarks); (2) went to bed (amidst closed curtains).

18. **will:** good will (to entertain the King); **defect:** deficient means, caused by late notice of the visit.

19. **free:** freely.

MACBETH   I think not of them.
Yet, when we can entreat an hour to serve,
We would spend it in some words upon that business,
If you would grant the time.
BANQUO   At your kind'st leisure.
MACBETH If you shall cleave to my consent, when 'tis,   25
It shall make honor for you.
BANQUO   So I lose none
In seeking to augment it, but still keep
My bosom franchised and allegiance clear,
I shall be counseled.
MACBETH   Good repose the while.
BANQUO Thanks, sir; the like to you.   30

                          Exit BANQUO [*with* FLEANCE].

MACBETH Go bid thy mistress, when my drink is ready,
She strike upon the bell. Get thee to bed.   *Exit* [*Servant*].
Is this a dagger which I see before me,
The handle toward my hand? Come, let me clutch thee.
I have thee not, and yet I see thee still.   35
Art thou not, fatal vision, sensible
To feeling as to sight? Or art thou but
A dagger of the mind, a false creation,
Proceeding from the heat-oppressèd brain?
I see thee yet in form as palpable   40
As this which now I draw.

     [*He draws a dagger*]

Thou marshall'st me the way that I was going,
And such an instrument I was to use.
Mine eyes are made the fools o'th' other senses,
Or else worth all the rest. I see thee still,   45

22. **entreat . . . serve:** find a suitable time.
25. **cleave . . . consent:** agree with my opinion, i.e., go along with me; **'tis:** (1) it is my leisure; (2) it is
achieved (and I am king).
26. **honor:** external honor, i.e., wealth and station. Banquo, however, understands the term to
mean internal honor, or virtue.
28. **franchised:** free (from guilt); **clear:** stainless.
36. **sensible:** perceptible.
42. **marshall'st:** guide.
44–45. **Mine . . . rest:** My eyes are reporting a delusion, unverifiable by the other senses, or else my
eyes alone perceive truly.

And on thy blade and dudgeon gouts of blood.
Which was not so before. There's no such thing.
It is the bloody business which informs
Thus to mine eyes. Now o'er the one half world
Nature seems dead, and wicked dreams abuse   50
The curtained sleep. Witchcraft celebrates
Pale Hecate's off'rings, and withered Murder,
Alarumed by his sentinel the wolf,
Whose howl's his watch, thus with his stealthy pace,
With Tarquin's ravishing strides, towards his design   55
Moves like a ghost. Thou sure and firm-set earth,
Hear not my steps, which way they walk, for fear
Thy very stones prate of my whereabout
And take the present horror from the time,
Which now suits with it. Whiles I threat, he lives;   60
Words to the heat of deeds too cold breath gives.

                                              A bell rings.

I go, and it is done. The bell invites me.
Hear it not, Duncan, for it is a knell
That summons thee to heaven or to hell.   *Exit.*

                              2.2

Enter LADY MACBETH.

LADY MACBETH That which hath made them drunk hath made me bold;
    What hath quenched them hath given me fire.

    [*An owl shrieks.*]

---

46. **dudgeon:** handle; **gouts:** drops.
48–49. **informs Thus:** shapes this fantasy.
50. **abuse:** deceive.
52. **Pale Hecate's off'rings:** deeds done by or sacrifices to Hecate, traditionally goddess of sorcery and the moon (thus **pale**), leader of the witches on stage in 3.5 and 4.1.
53. **Alarumed:** signaled.
54. **his watch:** Murder's signal (like the watchman's cry).
55. **Tarquin:** a Roman tyrant who raped Lucrece. Shakespeare dramatized the incident in a narrative poem, *The Rape of Lucrece.*
59–60. **take . . . it:** break the silence appropriate to the horror of the moment.
61. Words are weak and cold substitutes for the heat of real deeds.
63. **knell:** sound of a struck bell.
2.2. **Location:** Macbeth's castle.
2. **quenched:** (1) satisfied their thirst; (2) rendered them unconscious.
2. **SD** *owl:* a bird of ill omen.

Hark! Peace!

It was the owl that shrieked, the fatal bellman
Which gives the stern'st good-night. He is about it.
The doors are open, and the surfeited grooms   5
Do mock their charge with snores. I have drugged their possets
That death and nature do contend about them
Whether they live or die.

    Enter MACBETH [*with bloody daggers*].

MACBETH   Who's there? What ho!
LADY MACBETH [*to herself*] Alack, I am afraid they have awaked,
   And 'tis not done. Th'attempt and not the deed   10
   Confounds us. Hark! I laid their daggers ready;
   He could not miss 'em. Had he not resembled
   My father as he slept, I had done't.—My husband?
MACBETH I have done the deed. Didst thou not hear a noise?
LADY MACBETH I heard the owl scream and the crickets cry.   15
   Did not you speak?
MACBETH When?
LADY MACBETH Now.
MACBETH As I descended?
LADY MACBETH Ay.   20
MACBETH Hark, who lies i'th' second chamber?
LADY MACBETH Donaldbain.
MACBETH This is a sorry sight.
LADY MACBETH A foolish thought to say a sorry sight.
MACBETH There's one did laugh in's sleep, and one cried "Murder!" 25
   That they did wake each other. I stood and heard them.
   But they did say their prayers and addressed them
   Again to sleep.
LADY MACBETH There are two lodged together.
MACBETH One cried "God bless us!" and "Amen" the other,

---

3. **bellman:** night watchman.
4. **Which . . . good-night:** i.e., who tolls the bell to announce death.
5. **grooms:** servants.
6. **charge:** responsibility (to guard the King); **possets:** drinks made of hot milk, liquor, and spices.
8. **SD:** Editors usually have Macbeth speak the next line while off-stage, or less frequently from above in the gallery, and move this entrance to 13. But his entrance here, as indicated by the Folio, has them miss each other (visually and auditorily) in the dark while on stage, together but each alone.
11. **Confounds:** ruins.
27. **addressed them:** prepared themselves.

As they had seen me with these hangman's hands.   30
List'ning their fear, I could not say "Amen"
When they did say "God bless us!"

LADY MACBETH Consider it not so deeply.

MACBETH But wherefore could not I pronounce "Amen"?
I had most need of blessing, and "Amen"   35
Stuck in my throat.

LADY MACBETH   These deeds must not be thought
After these ways; so, it will make us mad.

MACBETH Methought I heard a voice cry "Sleep no more!
Macbeth does murder sleep"—the innocent sleep,
Sleep that knits up the raveled sleeve of care,   40
The death of each day's life, sore labor's bath,
Balm of hurt minds, great nature's second course,
Chief nourisher in life's feast—

LADY MACBETH   What do you mean?

MACBETH Still it cried "Sleep no more!" to all the house;
"Glamis hath murdered sleep, and therefore Cawdor   45
Shall sleep no more! Macbeth shall sleep no more!"

LADY MACBETH Who was it that thus cried? Why, worthy thane,
You do unbend your noble strength to think
So brainsickly of things. Go get some water
And wash this filthy witness from your hand.   50
Why did you bring these daggers from the place?
They must lie there. Go, carry them and smear
The sleepy grooms with blood.

MACBETH   I'll go no more.
I am afraid to think what I have done.
Look on't again I dare not.

LADY MACBETH   Infirm of purpose!   55
Give me the daggers. The sleeping and the dead
Are but as pictures; 'tis the eye of childhood

---

30. **hangman's hands:** executioner's hands, hence bloody from cutting up bodies.
34. **wherefore:** why.
37. **so:** thinking so.
40. **raveled sleeve:** frayed sleeve (the part of a garment that covers the arm and wrist). Some prefer "raveled sleave," i.e., a tangled filament or thread, indistinguishable in sound but less likely in sense, given the idea of repair by knitting.
42. **second course:** the main course.
48. **unbend:** slacken (as one does a bow).
50. **witness:** evidence, i.e., the blood.

That fears a painted devil. If he do bleed,
I'll gild the faces of the grooms withal,
For it must seem their guilt.   *Exit [with the daggers].*

     Knock within.

MACBETH   Whence is that knocking?   60
How is't with me, when every noise appalls me?
What hands are here? Ha, they pluck out mine eyes!
Will all great Neptune's ocean wash this blood
Clean from my hand? No, this my hand will rather
The multitudinous seas incarnadine,   65
Making the green one red.

     Enter LADY MACBETH.

LADY MACBETH   My hands are of your color, but I shame
To wear a heart so white. (*Knock.*) I hear a knocking
At the south entry. Retire we to our chamber.
A little water clears us of this deed.   70
How easy is it then. Your constancy
Hath left you unattended. (*Knock.*) Hark, more knocking.
Get on your nightgown lest occasion call us
And show us to be watchers. Be not lost
So poorly in your thoughts.   75
MACBETH   To know my deed 'twere best not know myself.
(*Knock.*) Wake Duncan with thy knocking. I would thou couldst!

               Exeunt.

58. **he:** the King. Corpses of victims were thought to bleed in the presence of their murderers.
59. **gild:** cover with gold, a synonym for red (see 2.3.106). **Gild** here sets up the pun on **guilt** (60).
60. SD *within:* behind the stage façade (representing the outside of the castle).
60. **Whence:** from where.
63. **Neptune:** Roman god of the ocean.
65. **multitudinous:** many and vast; **incarnadine:** turn red.
66. **green one red:** green color of the oceans a pervasive red.
68. **white:** cowardly.
72. **left you unattended:** deserted you.
74. **watchers:** awake.
75. **poorly:** dejectedly.
76. If I fully admit to this crime, I would be better off if I were someone else. I no longer know who I am.

2.3

Enter a PORTER. *Knocking within.*

PORTER Here's a knocking indeed! If a man were porter of
hell gate, he should have old turning the key. (*Knock.*)
Knock, knock, knock. Who's there, i'th' name of Beelzebub?
Here's a farmer that hanged himself on th'expectation of
plenty. Come in time! Have napkins enough about you; here   5
you'll sweat for't. (*Knock.*) Knock, knock. Who's there, in
th'other devil's name? Faith, here's an equivocator that could
swear in both the scales against either scale, who committed
treason enough for God's sake, yet could not equivocate to
heaven. Oh, come in, equivocator. (*Knock.*) Knock, knock, knock.   10
Who's there? Faith, here's an English tailor come hither
for stealing out of a French hose. Come in, tailor. Here you
may roast your goose. (*Knock.*) Knock, knock. Never at quiet?
What are you? But this place is too cold for hell. I'll devil-porter
it no further. I had thought to have let in some of all professions   15
that go the primrose way to th'everlasting bonfire. (*Knock.*)
Anon, anon. [*He opens the gate.*]—I pray you, remember the
porter.

Enter MACDUFF *and* LENNOX.

MACDUFF Was it so late, friend, ere you went to bed,
That you do lie so late?   20
PORTER Faith, sir, we were carousing till the second cock, and drink, sir,
is a great provoker of three things.

2.3. **Location: the courtyard of Macbeth's castle.**
2. **hell gate:** the door to hell, imagined as a castle; **old:** frequent.
3. **Beelzebub:** the devil.
3–4. **farmer . . . plenty:** The porter introduces imaginary residents of hell, beginning with the
farmer who, expecting plenty but disappointed, hanged himself.
5. **Come in time:** You have come in good time; **napkins:** handkerchiefs (to wipe away sweat).
7. **Faith:** in faith (a mild oath); **equivocator:** one who uses deceitful language. Shakespeare alludes
to the doctrine of equivocation, associated with Jesuits including Henry Garnet, recently executed
(1606) for alleged complicity in the Gunpowder Plot (1605), a plan to blow up Parliament. In his
Treatise on Equivocation Garnet justifies various types of verbal deceit, including, for example, the
telling of a partial truth (see below, 218–19).
8. **both . . . scale:** argue either side (perhaps with an allusion to the scales of Justice).
11–12. **English . . . hose:** The tailor has skimped on the fabric when making stylish French leggings
or breeches.
13. **roast . . . goose:** (1) heat your tailor's smoothing iron; (2) have sex with a prostitute; (3) suffer
from venereal disease.
16. **primrose . . . bonfire:** the pleasant path to hell.
18. **remember:** i.e., tip.
21. **second cock:** 3:00 A.M., when the cock crowed for the second time.

MACDUFF What three things does drink especially provoke?

PORTER Marry, sir, nose-painting, sleep, and urine. Lechery, sir, it
provokes and unprovokes: it provokes the desire but it takes away the 25
performance. Therefore, much drink may be said to be an equivocator
with lechery: it makes him and it mars him; it sets him on and it takes
him off; it persuades him and disheartens him, makes him stand to
and not stand to; in conclusion, equivocates him in a sleep and, giv- 30
ing him the lie, leaves him.

MACDUFF I believe drink gave thee the lie last night.

PORTER That it did, sir, i'the very throat on me. But I requited him for
his lie and, I think, being too strong for him, though he took up my 35
legs sometime, yet I made a shift to cast him.

MACDUFF Is thy master stirring?

Enter MACBETH.

Our knocking has awaked him. Here he comes.

[PORTER *may exit.*]

LENNOX Good morrow, noble sir.

MACBETH   Good morrow, both.

MACDUFF Is the King stirring, worthy thane?

MACBETH   Not yet.

MACDUFF He did command me to call timely on him.   40
I have almost slipped the hour.

MACBETH   I'll bring you to him.

MACDUFF I know this is a joyful trouble to you,
But yet 'tis one.

MACBETH The labor we delight in physics pain.
This is the door.

MACDUFF   I'll make so bold to call,   45

FOR 'tis my limited service.   *Exit* MACDUFF.

LENNOX Goes the King hence today?

---

24. **Marry:** a mild oath ("By the Virgin Mary," originally); **nose-painting:** nose-reddening from
excessive drink.
29. **stand to:** become erect.
30. **equivocates . . . sleep:** tricks him into falling asleep; **giving . . . lie:** (1) deceiving him; (2) making him lie down.
32. **gave . . . lie:** (1) called you a liar; (2) made you sleep.
33. **i' . . . throat:** deeply, egregiously. (Drink accused the porter of serious, deliberate lying.)
35–36. **took . . . legs:** lifted me (as a wrestler would); **made a shift:** managed; **cast:** (1) toss him as in
wrestling; (2) vomit.
40. **timely:** early.
41. **slipped:** let slip.
44. **physics:** relieves.
46. **limited:** appointed.

MACBETH He does; he did appoint so.

LENNOX The night has been unruly. Where we lay,
    Our chimneys were blown down and, as they say,   50
    Lamentings heard i'th' air, strange screams of death,
    And prophesying with accents terrible
    Of dire combustion and confused events,
    New hatched to th'woeful time. The obscure bird
    Clamored the livelong night. Some say the earth   55
    Was feverous and did shake.

MACBETH   'Twas a rough night.

LENNOX My young remembrance cannot parallel
    A fellow to it.

      Enter MACDUFF.

MACDUFF Oh, horror, horror, horror!
    Tongue nor heart cannot conceive nor name thee!   60

MACBETH *and* LENNOX What's the matter?

MACDUFF Confusion now hath made his masterpiece!
    Most sacrilegious murder hath broke ope
    The Lord's anointed temple and stole thence
    The life o'th' building!

MACBETH   What is't you say? The life?   65

LENNOX Mean you his majesty?

MACDUFF Approach the chamber and destroy your sight
    With a new Gorgon. Do not bid me speak.
    See, and then speak yourselves.

              Exeunt MACBETH *and* LENNOX.

         —Awake, awake!

Ring the alarum bell! Murder and treason!   70
Banquo and Donaldbain, Malcolm, awake!
Shake off this downy sleep, death's counterfeit,
And look on death itself! Up, up, and see

---

52. **accents:** utterances.
53. **combustion:** (1) fire; (2) tumult.
54. **obscure bird:** bird of darkness, the owl.
55. **livelong:** long-lived.
57–58. **parallel A fellow:** recall a similar one.
60. The subjects and verbs are out of order (the **tongue** names, the **heart** conceives) to suggest the disorder and emotion.
62. **Confusion:** destruction.
68. **Gorgon:** a mythical monster whose face turned beholders to stone.
72. **counterfeit:** likeness.
74. **great doom's image:** a sight of doomsday, the Last Judgment.

The great doom's image! Malcolm, Banquo,
As from your graves rise up and walk like sprites   75
To countenance this horror!—Ring the bell!

    Bell rings. Enter LADY MACBETH.

LADY MACBETH What's the business
    That such a hideous trumpet calls to parley
    The sleepers of the house? Speak, speak!
MACDUFF O gentle lady,   80
    'Tis not for you to hear what I can speak.
    The repetition in a woman's ear
    Would murder as it fell.

    Enter BANQUO.

    —O Banquo, Banquo! Our royal master's murdered!
LADY MACBETH Woe, alas! What, in our house?   85
BANQUO Too cruel anywhere.
    Dear Duff, I prithee, contradict thyself,
    And say it is not so.

    Enter MACBETH, LENNOX, *and* ROSS.

MACBETH Had I but died an hour before this chance,
    I had lived a blessèd time, for from this instant   90
    There's nothing serious in mortality.
    All is but toys. Renown and grace is dead.
    The wine of life is drawn, and the mere lees
    Is left this vault to brag of.

    Enter MALCOLM *and* DONALDBAIN.

DONALDBAIN What is amiss?
MACBETH   You are and do not know't.   95
    The spring, the head, the fountain of your blood
    Is stopped, the very source of it is stopped.
MACDUFF Your royal father's murdered.
MALCOLM   Oh! By whom?

---

75. On doomsday the spirits (**sprites**) of the dead will rise to be judged; see John 5.28: "The hour is coming, in the which all that are in the graves shall hear his voice."
76. **countenance:** (1) face; (2) act in accordance with.
78. **parley:** conference, generally between enemies.
89. **chance:** occurrence.
91. **mortality:** human life.
93. **lees:** dregs.
94. **vault:** (1) wine cellar; (2) earth, with its vault, the sky.

LENNOX Those of his chamber, as it seemed, had done't.
    Their hands and faces were all badged with blood; 100
    So were their daggers, which unwiped we found
    Upon their pillows. They stared and were distracted;
    No man's life was to be trusted with them.
MACBETH Oh, yet I do repent me of my fury
    That I did kill them.
MACDUFF   Wherefore did you so? 105
MACBETH Who can be wise, amazed, temp'rate and furious,
    Loyal and neutral in a moment? No man.
    Th'expedition of my violent love
    Outran the pauser, reason. Here lay Duncan,
    His silver skin laced with his golden blood, 110
    And his gashed stabs looked like a breach in nature
    For ruin's wasteful entrance; there the murderers,
    Steeped in the colors of their trade, their daggers
    Unmannerly breeched with gore. Who could refrain
    That had a heart to love, and in that heart 115
    Courage to make's love known?
LADY MACBETH [*faints*]   Help me hence, ho!
MACDUFF Look to the lady!
MALCOLM [*aside to* DONALDBAIN] Why do we hold our tongues,
    That most may claim this argument for ours?
DONALDBAIN [*aside to* MALCOLM] What should be spoken here,
    where our fate,
    Hid in an auger-hole, may rush and seize us? 120
    Let's away. Our tears are not yet brewed.
MALCOLM [*aside to* DONALDBAIN] Nor our strong sorrow upon the
    foot of motion.
BANQUO Look to the lady.

---

100. **badged:** marked as if with a badge or emblem.
106. **amazed:** shocked out of one's wits.
108. **expedition:** speedy expression.
109. **pauser:** controller.
110. **golden:** red.
111. **breach:** gap (in fortifications).
114. **Unmannerly . . . gore:** indecently clothed in blood on his thighs (as if wearing red breeches).
120. **auger-hole:** a hole made by an auger, or carpenter's pointer; here, a place of ambush.
122. **upon . . . motion:** ready to act.

[LADY MACBETH *may exit, attended.*]

And when we have our naked frailties hid,
That suffer in exposure, let us meet   125
And question this most bloody piece of work
To know it further. Fears and scruples shake us.
In the great hand of God I stand, and thence
Against the undivulged pretense I fight
Of treasonous malice.
MACDUFF   And so do I.
ALL   So, all!   130
MACBETH Let's briefly put on manly readiness,
    And meet i'th' hall together.
ALL   Well contented.

               Exeunt [all but MALCOLM *and* DONALDBAIN].

MALCOLM What will you do? Let's not consort with them.
    To show an unfelt sorrow is an office
    Which the false man does easy. I'll to England.   135
DONALDBAIN To Ireland, I. Our separated fortune
    Shall keep us both the safer. Where we are,
    There's daggers in men's smiles. The nearer in blood,
    The nearer bloody.
MALCOLM   This murderous shaft that's shot
    Hath not yet lighted, and our safest way   140
    Is to avoid the aim. Therefore, to horse,
    And let us not be dainty of leave-taking,
    But shift away. There's warrant in that theft
    Which steals itself when there's no mercy left.

                                                        Exeunt.

124. **naked frailties:** (1) unclothed bodies; (2) vulnerabilities.
126. **question:** examine.
128. **thence:** from there.
129. **undivulged pretense:** unrevealed purpose (of the traitor).
131. **briefly:** quickly.
134. **office:** function.
138–39. **The nearer . . . bloody:** The nearer one is to Duncan in blood, the closer he is to being killed.
140. **lighted:** landed.
142. **dainty of:** particular about.
143. **shift:** leave stealthily; **warrant:** justification.
144. **steals:** steals away.

2.4

Enter ROSS *with an* OLD MAN.

OLD MAN Threescore and ten I can remember well,
　　Within the volume of which time I have seen
　　Hours dreadful and things strange, but this sore night
　　Hath trifled former knowings.
ROSS 　　　　　　　　　　　　Ha, good father,
　　Thou seest the heavens, as troubled with man's act,　　　　　5
　　Threatens his bloody stage. By th'clock 'tis day,
　　And yet dark night strangles the traveling lamp.
　　Is't night's predominance or the day's shame
　　That darkness does the face of earth entomb
　　When living light should kiss it?
OLD MAN 　　　　　　　　　　　'Tis unnatural,　　　　　10
　　Even like the deed that's done. On Tuesday last
　　A falcon, tow'ring in her pride of place,
　　Was by a mousing owl hawked at and killed.
ROSS And Duncan's horses—a thing most strange and certain—
　　Beauteous and swift, the minions of their race,　　　　　15
　　Turned wild in nature, broke their stalls, flung out,
　　Contending 'gainst obedience, as they would
　　Make war with mankind.
OLD MAN 　　　　　　　　　'Tis said they ate each other.
ROSS They did so, to th'amazement of mine eyes
　　That looked upon't.

　　　　Enter MACDUFF.

　　　　　　　　　　　Here comes the good Macduff.　　　　　20
　　How goes the world, sir, now?
MACDUFF 　　　　　　　　　　Why, see you not?

2.4. **Location: outside Macbeth's castle.**
1. **Threescore and ten:** 70, the biblical allotment of human life; see Psalms 90:10: "The days of our years are threescore years and ten."
3. **sore:** severe, violent.
4. **Hath . . . knowings:** has made other experiences seem trivial; **father:** old man.
6. **stage:** the earth. The metaphor continues the theatrical imagery of **heavens,** the decorated roof over the stage, and **act** (5).
7. **traveling lamp:** the sun.
8. **predominance:** superiority.
12. **tow'ring:** soaring; **pride of place:** pre-eminent position.
13. **mousing owl:** an owl that preys on mice; **hawked at:** attacked in flight.
15. **minions:** darlings.
16. **flung out:** kicked and bucked violently.

ROSS Is't known who did this more than bloody deed?

MACDUFF   Those that Macbeth hath slain.

ROSS   Alas, the day!
What good could they pretend?

MACDUFF   They were suborned.
Malcolm and Donaldbain, the King's two sons,   25
Are stol'n away and fled, which puts upon them
Suspicion of the deed.

ROSS   'Gainst nature still!
Thriftless ambition that will ravin up
Thine own life's means! Then 'tis most like
The sovereignty will fall upon Macbeth.   30

MACDUFF He is already named and gone to Scone
To be invested.

ROSS   Where is Duncan's body?

MACDUFF Carried to Colmekill,
The sacred storehouse of his predecessors
And guardian of their bones.

ROSS   Will you to Scone?   35

MACDUFF No, cousin, I'll to Fife.

ROSS   Well, I will thither.

MACDUFF Well may you see things well done there. Adieu,
Lest our old robes sit easier than our new.

ROSS Farewell, father.

OLD MAN God's benison go with you and with those   40
That would make good of bad and friends of foes.

                                        Exeunt all.

                        3.1

Enter BANQUO.

BANQUO Thou hast it now—King, Cawdor, Glamis, all
As the weïrd women promised, and I fear

---

24. **pretend:** put forward as a pretext; **suborned:** bribed.
28. **Thriftless:** wasteful; **ravin up:** devour hungrily.
31. **Scone:** ancient royal city of Scotland.
32. **invested:** formally crowned and robed as king.
33. **Colmekill:** small island (now Iona) off the West of Scotland, home of St. Columba (see 1.2.63).
34. **storehouse:** burial place.
36. **Fife:** land ruled by Macduff.
40. **benison:** blessing.
3.1. **Location:** Forres. The palace.

Thou play'dst most foully for't. Yet it was said
It should not stand in thy posterity
But that myself should be the root and father   5
Of many kings. If there come truth from them—
As upon thee, Macbeth, their speeches shine—
Why by the verities on thee made good
May they not be my oracles as well
And set me up in hope? But hush, no more.   10

> *Sennet sounded. Enter* MACBETH *as King,* LADY [MACBETH
> *as Queen,*] LENNOX, ROSS, LORDS *and Attendants.*

MACBETH Here's our chief guest.
LADY MACBETH   If he had been forgotten,
   It had been as a gap in our great feast,
   And all-thing unbecoming.
MACBETH Tonight we hold a solemn supper, sir,
   And I'll request your presence.
BANQUO   Let your highness   15
   Command upon me, to the which my duties
   Are with a most indissoluble tie
   Forever knit.
MACBETH   Ride you this afternoon?
BANQUO Ay, my good lord.
MACBETH We should have else desired your good advice,   20
   Which still hath been both grave and prosperous,
   In this day's council; but we'll take tomorrow.
   Is't far you ride?
BANQUO As far, my lord, as will fill up the time
   Twixt this and supper. Go not my horse the better,   25
   I must become a borrower of the night
   For a dark hour or twain.
MACBETH   Fail not our feast.
BANQUO My lord, I will not.

---

4. **stand:** remain.
7. **shine:** shed light (of good fortune).
10. SD *Sennet*: a distinctive set of notes on a trumpet or cornet signaling a ceremonious entrance.
13. **all-thing:** completely.
14. **solemn:** formal.
16. **the which:** which commandments.
21. **still:** always.
22. **take:** take it (Banquo's advice).
25. **Go . . . better:** unless my horse goes faster than I expect.
27. **twain:** two.

MACBETH We hear our bloody cousins are bestowed
    In England and in Ireland, not confessing   30
    Their cruel parricide, filling their hearers
    With strange invention. But of that tomorrow,
    When therewithal we shall have cause of state
    Craving us jointly. Hie you to horse. Adieu,
    Till you return at night. Goes Fleance with you?   35
BANQUO Ay, my good lord. Our time does call upon's.
MACBETH I wish your horses swift and sure of foot,
    And so I do commend you to their backs.
    Farewell.   *Exit* BANQUO.
    —Let every man be master of his time   40
    Till seven at night. To make society
    The sweeter welcome, we will keep ourself
    Till supper-time alone. While then, God be with you.

        Exeunt Lords [and all but MACBETH *and a* SERVANT].

    —Sirrah, a word with you: attend those men
    Our pleasure?   45
SERVANT They are, my lord, without the palace gate.
MACBETH Bring them before us.   *Exit* SERVANT.
    To be thus is nothing, but to be safely thus.
    Our fears in Banquo stick deep,
    And in his royalty of nature reigns   50
    That which would be feared. 'Tis much he dares;
    And to that dauntless temper of his mind
    He hath a wisdom that doth guide his valor
    To act in safety. There is none but he
    Whose being I do fear, and under him   55
    My genius is rebuked, as it is said

29. **bestowed:** lodged.
31. **parricide:** father-killing.
32. **invention:** falsehood (i.e., that Macbeth killed the King).
33. **therewithal:** besides that.
33–34. **cause . . . jointly:** state business requiring our joint attention.
38. **commend:** entrust.
41. **society:** company of friends.
43. **While:** till.
44. **Sirrah:** a form of address to a social inferior.
48. **but:** unless.
49. **stick deep:** pierce deeply.
50. **royalty of nature:** natural royalty.
52. **to:** in addition to; **dauntless temper:** fearless temperament.
56. **genius:** attendant spirit; **rebuked:** abashed.

Mark Antony's was by Caesar. He chid the sisters
When first they put the name of king upon me,
And bade them speak to him; then, prophet-like,
They hailed him father to a line of kings.   60
Upon my head they placed a fruitless crown
And put a barren scepter in my grip,
Thence to be wrenched with an unlineal hand.
No son of mine succeeding. If't be so,
For Banquo's issue have I filed my mind,   65
For them the gracious Duncan have I murdered,
Put rancors in the vessel of my peace
Only for them, and mine eternal jewel
Given to the common enemy of man
To make them kings, the seeds of Banquo kings!   70
Rather than so, come fate into the list,
And champion me to th'utterance!—Who's there!

     Enter SERVANT *and two* MURDERERS.

[to SERVANT] Now go to the door, and stay there till we call.

                                   Exit SERVANT.

—Was it not yesterday we spoke together?
MURDERERS It was, so please your highness.
MACBETH   Well, then; now,   75
Have you considered of my speeches? Know
That it was he in the times past which held you
So under fortune, which you thought had been
Our innocent self. This I made good to you
In our last conference, passed in probation with you   80
How you were borne in hand, how crossed, the instruments,

---

57. **Caesar:** Octavius Caesar (Augustus), who eventually defeated Mark Antony in a battle Shakespeare dramatized in *Antony and Cleopatra*.
63. **unlineal hand:** a descendant from another family line.
65. **filed:** defiled.
66. **gracious:** virtuous, filled with divine grace.
67. **rancors:** bitter feelings (imagined as poison added to a vessel, or cup).
68. **eternal jewel:** immortal soul.
69. **common enemy:** the devil.
71. **list:** combat area, originally, jousting lanes.
72. **champion me:** (1) fight with me; (2) support me; **to th'utterance:** to the end, to death (French *à l'outrance*).
78. **under:** out of favor with.
80. **passed . . . with:** proved to.
81. **borne in hand:** manipulated; **crossed:** thwarted; **instruments:** means.

Who wrought with them, and all things else that amight
To half a soul and to a notion crazed
Say "Thus did Banquo."
FIRST MURDERER   You made it known to us.
MACBETH I did so, and went further, which is now   85
    Our point of second meeting. Do you find
    Your patience so predominant in your nature
    That you can let this go? Are you so gospeled
    To pray for this good man and for his issue,
    Whose heavy hand hath bowed you to the grave   90
    And beggared yours for ever?
FIRST MURDERER   We are men, my liege.
MACBETH Ay, in the catalogue ye go for men,
    As hounds and greyhounds, mongrels, spaniels, curs,
    Shoughs, water-rugs, and demi-wolves are clept
    All by the name of dogs. The valued file   95
    Distinguishes the swift, the slow, the subtle,
    The housekeeper, the hunter—every one
    According to the gift which bounteous nature
    Hath in him closed, whereby he does receive
    Particular addition from the bill   100
    That writes them all alike; and so of men.
    Now, if you have a station in the file.
    Not i'th' worst rank of manhood, say't,
    And I will put that business in your bosoms
    Whose execution takes your enemy off,   105

82. **wrought:** worked.
83. **To . . . crazed:** to a half-wit and unsound mind.
88. **gospeled:** influenced by gospel teachings, especially Matthew 5:44: "But I say unto you, love your enemies, bless them that curse you, do good to them that hate you, and pray for them which despitefully use you, and persecute you."
91. **beggared yours:** made your family poor.
92. **catalogue:** list (of human types).
93. **curs:** watch dogs or sheep dogs, sometimes used as a term of contempt.
94. **Shoughs:** lapdogs; **water-rugs:** shaggy water-dogs; **demi-wolves:** dogs that are half wolf; **clept:** named.
95. **valued file:** list that records the qualities of each breed.
97. **housekeeper:** watchdog.
99. **closed:** enclosed.
100. **Particular addition:** distinguishing characteristics.
100–101. **the bill . . . alike:** the general qualities common to all dogs.
102. **station . . . file:** place in the list (of humans).
105. **takes . . . off:** removes, kills.

Grapples you to the heart and love of us,
Who wear our health but sickly in his life,
Which in his death were perfect.

SECOND MURDERER   I am one, my liege,
Whom the vile blows and buffets of the world
Have so incensed that I am reckless what   110
I do to spite the world.

FIRST MURDERER   And I another,
So weary with disasters, tugged with fortune,
That I would set my life on any chance
To mend it or be rid on't.

MACBETH   Both of you
Know Banquo was your enemy.

MURDERERS   True, my lord.   115

MACBETH   So is he mine, and in such bloody distance
That every minute of his being thrusts
Against my near'st of life. And though I could
With barefaced power sweep him from my sight
And bid my will avouch it, yet I must not   120
For certain friends that are both his and mine,
Whose loves I may not drop, but wail his fall
Who I myself struck down. And thence it is
That I to your assistance do make love,
Masking the business from the common eye   125
For sundry weighty reasons.

SECOND MURDERER   We shall, my lord,
Perform what you command us.

FIRST MURDERER   Though our lives—

MACBETH Your spirits shine through you. Within this hour, at most,
I will advise you where to plant yourselves,
Acquaint you with the perfect spy o'th' time,   130

---

106. **Grapples:** seizes and attaches firmly. Grappling irons held ships to each other during nautical battles.
107. **in his life:** while he (Banquo) lives.
113. **set:** risk.
114. **on't:** of it.
116. **distance:** (1) enmity; (2) striking range.
118. **near'st of life:** vital organs.
119. **barefaced:** open, without excuses.
120. **And . . . it:** And use my royal will as justification enough for Banquo's murder.
122. **wail:** I must lament.
124. That I request your help.
130. **perfect spy o'th'time:** (1) best time and place for spying; (2) the best spy for the job, i.e., the Third Murderer of 3.3.

The moment on't, for't must be done tonight,
And something from the palace, always thought
That I require a clearness. And with him—
To leave no rubs nor botches in the work—
Fleance, his son that keeps him company,   135
Whose absence is no less material to me
Than is his father's, must embrace the fate
Of that dark hour. Resolve yourselves apart.
I'll come to you anon.
MURDERERS   We are resolved, my lord.
MACBETH I'll call upon you straight; abide within.   140

                                        Exeunt [MURDERERS].

It is concluded. Banquo, thy soul's flight,
If it find heaven, must find it out tonight.   [*Exit.*]

3.2

     Enter LADY MACBETH *and a* SERVANT.

LADY MACBETH Is Banquo gone from court?
SERVANT Ay, madam, but returns again tonight.
LADY MACBETH Say to the King I would attend his leisure
     For a few words.
SERVANT   Madam, I will.   *Exit.*
LADY MACBETH   Naught's had, all's spent,
     Where our desire is got without content.   5
     'Tis safer to be that which we destroy
     Than by destruction dwell in doubtful joy.

     Enter MACBETH.

How now, my lord? Why do you keep alone,
Of sorriest fancies your companions making,

131. **on't:** for the murder.
132. **something:** some distance; **thought:** borne in mind.
133. **clearness:** freedom from suspicion.
134. **rubs nor botches:** rough spots nor flaws.
136. **material:** important.
138. **Resolve . . . apart:** (1) determine your course of action in private; (2) gather your courage in private.
3.2. **Location: the palace.**
4. **Naught:** nothing.
7. **doubtful:** (1) uncertain; (2) worried.
9. **sorriest fancies:** most wretched imaginings.

Using those thoughts which should indeed have died   10
With them they think on? Things without all remedy
Should be without regard. What's done is done.
MACBETH We have scorched the snake, not killed it.
   She'll close and be herself, whilst our poor malice
   Remains in danger of her former tooth.   15
   But let the frame of things disjoint, both the worlds suffer,
   Ere we will eat our meal in fear and sleep
   In the affliction of these terrible dreams
   That shake us nightly. Better be with the dead,
   Whom we, to gain our peace, have sent to peace,   20
   Than on the torture of the mind to lie
   In restless ecstasy. Duncan is in his grave.
   After life's fitful fever he sleeps well.
   Treason has done his worst; nor steel, nor poison,
   Malice domestic, foreign levy, nothing   25
   Can touch him further.
LADY MACBETH   Come on, gentle my lord,
   Sleek o'er your rugged looks. Be bright and jovial
   Among your guests tonight.
MACBETH   So shall I, love,
   And so, I pray, be you. Let your remembrance
   Apply to Banquo; present him eminence   30
   Both with eye and tongue—unsafe the while that we
   Must lave our honors in these flattering streams
   And make our faces vizards to our hearts,
   Disguising what they are.
LADY MACBETH   You must leave this.
MACBETH Oh, full of scorpions is my mind, dear wife!   35
   Thou know'st that Banquo and his Fleance lives.
LADY MACBETH But in them nature's copy's not eterne.

11. **them . . . on:** the subject of your thoughts, i.e., the murdered King; **all:** any.
13. **scorched:** slashed.
14. **close:** heal; **poor:** weak.
15. **her former tooth:** her fang, just as before.
16. **frame . . . disjoint:** structure of the universe collapse; **both the worlds:** heaven and earth.
22. **ecstasy:** frenzy.
25. **domestic:** civil; **levy:** troops.
26–27. **gentle . . . looks:** My noble lord, smooth over your rough look of concern.
29. **remembrance:** reminder.
30. **eminence:** favor.
31–32. **unsafe . . . streams:** We are unsafe during this time in which we must cover ourselves with this display of flattering cordiality.
33. **vizards:** masks.
37. **copy:** copyhold, i.e., lease (on life); **eterne:** eternal.

MACBETH There's comfort yet; they are assailable.
   Then be thou jocund. Ere the bat hath flown
   His cloistered flight, ere to black Hecate's summons   40
   The shard-born beetle with his drowsy hums
   Hath rung night's yawning peal, there shall be done
   A deed of dreadful note.
LADY MACBETH   What's to be done?
MACBETH Be innocent of the knowledge, dearest chuck,
   Till thou applaud the deed. Come, seeling night,   45
   Scarf up the tender eye of pitiful day,
   And with thy bloody and invisible hand
   Cancel and tear to pieces that great bond
   Which keeps me pale! Light thickens,
   And the crow makes wing to th'rooky wood;   50
   Good things of day begin to droop and drowse,
   Whiles night's black agents to their preys do rouse.
   —Thou marvel'st at my words, but hold thee still.
   Things bad begun make strong themselves by ill.
   So, prithee, go with me.   55

                                          Exeunt.

                        3.3

   Enter three MURDERERS.

FIRST MURDERER But who did bid thee join with us?
THIRD MURDERER   Macbeth.

40. **cloistered**: through dark buildings and enclosures.
41. **shard-born**: born in dung.
42. **Hath . . . peal**: has (with its **hums**) announced the arrival of night and sleep. (The image derives from the ringing of the curfew bell.)
43. **note**: notoriety.
44. **chuck**: a term of affection.
45. **seeling**: eye-closing. (Falconers seeled, i.e., stitched shut, the eyes of falcons.)
46. **Scarf up**: blindfold.
48. **bond**: contract (Banquo's lease on life).
49. **thickens**: dims.
50. **rooky**: filled with rooks, i.e., black birds, regarded as ill omens.
52. **rouse**: rouse themselves.
3.3. **Location: outdoors, near the palace.**
0.1. SD *three*: The identity of the Third Murderer has caused speculation; some have proposed Ross, Macbeth himself in disguise, an allegorical abstraction like Destiny, or, most probably, an unnamed extra whom Macbeth sent to make sure the others carry out the murder.

SECOND MURDERER [*to* FIRST MURDERER]
    He needs not our mistrust, since he delivers
    Our offices and what we have to do
    To the direction just.
FIRST MURDERER [*to* THIRD MURDERER]   Then stand with us.
    The west yet glimmers with some streaks of day.   5
    Now spurs the lated traveler apace
    To gain the timely inn, and near approaches
    The subject of our watch.
THIRD MURDERER   Hark, I hear horses.
BANQUO (*within*) Give us a light there, ho!
SECOND MURDERER   Then 'tis he. The rest
    That are within the note of expectation   10
    Already are i'th' court.
FIRST MURDERER   His horses go about.
THIRD MURDERER Almost a mile, but he does usually.
    So all men do from hence to th'palace gate
    Make it their walk.

        Enter BANQUO *and* FLEANCE, *with a torch.*

SECOND MURDERER A light, a light!   15
THIRD MURDERER 'Tis he.
FIRST MURDERER Stand to't.
BANQUO It will be rain tonight.
FIRST MURDERER   Let it come down!

      [*They attack.* FIRST MURDERER *puts out the light.*]

BANQUO Oh, treachery!
    Fly, good Fleance, fly, fly, fly!   20
    Thou mayst revenge.—O slave!

      [BANQUO *dies.* FLEANCE *escapes.*]

THIRD MURDERER Who did strike out the light?
FIRST MURDERER   Was't not the way?

---

2. **He:** the Third Murderer.
2–3. **delivers Our offices:** explains our duties.
4. **To . . . just:** exactly according to Macbeth's instructions.
6. **spurs:** hurries; **lated:** belated; **apace:** quickly.
7. **timely:** arrived at in good time.
10. **note of expectation:** list of invited guests.
11. **about:** another route, being led or ridden to the stable.
17. **Stand to't:** get ready.
18. **It:** i.e., the rain and the attack.
22. **way:** right way to proceed.

THIRD MURDERER There's but one down. The son is fled.

SECOND MURDERER We have lost best half of our affair.

FIRST MURDERER Well, let's away and say how much is done.   25

Exeunt [with BANQUO's *body].*

3.4

Banquet prepared. Enter MACBETH, LADY MACBETH, ROSS, LENNOX, LORDS, *and Attendants.*

MACBETH You know your own degrees; sit down.
  At first and last, the hearty welcome.

LORDS Thanks to your majesty.

MACBETH Ourself will mingle with society
  And play the humble host.   5
  Our hostess keeps her state, but in best time
  We will require her welcome.

LADY MACBETH Pronounce it for me, sir, to all our friends,
  For my heart speaks they are welcome.

Enter FIRST MURDERER *[and stands aside].*

MACBETH See, they encounter thee with their hearts' thanks.   10
  Both sides are even. Here I'll sit, i'th' midst.
  Be large in mirth; anon we'll drink a measure
  The table round.

[He converses apart with the FIRST MURDERER.]*

                      There's blood upon thy face.

FIRST MURDERER 'Tis Banquo's, then.

MACBETH 'Tis better thee without than he within.   15
  Is he dispatched?

FIRST MURDERER My lord, his throat is cut. That I did for him.

MACBETH Thou art the best o'th' cutthroats.
  Yet he's good that did the like for Fleance;

3.4. **Location: a room in the palace.**
1. **degrees:** ranks, and, therefore, places at the table.
2. **At . . . last:** to all.
4. **mingle with society:** mix with the guests (and not remain in his special chair).
6. **keeps her state:** remains in her special chair; **in best time:** at the right time.
10. **encounter:** respond to.
11. **Both . . . even:** (1) Both sides of the table have equal numbers; (2) The guests' gratitude matches Lady Macbeth's welcome.
12. **anon:** straightway.
12–13. **measure . . . round:** toast for the whole table.
15. **thee . . . within:** on you than in him.

If thou didst it, thou art the nonpareil.   20

FIRST MURDERER Most royal sir, Fleance is scaped.

MACBETH Then comes my fit again. I had else been perfect,
  Whole as the marble, founded as the rock,
  As broad and general as the casing air,
  But now I am cabined, cribbed, confined, bound in   25
  To saucy doubts and fears. But Banquo's safe?

FIRST MURDERER Ay, my good lord, safe in a ditch he bides,
  With twenty trenchèd gashes on his head,
  The least a death to nature.

MACBETH   Thanks for that.
  There the grown serpent lies; the worm that's fled   30
  Hath nature that in time will venom breed,
  No teeth for th'present. Get thee gone. Tomorrow
  We'll hear ourselves again.   *Exit* FIRST MURDERER.

LADY MACBETH   My royal lord,
  You do not give the cheer. The feast is sold
  That is not often vouched, while 'tis a-making,   35
  'Tis given with welcome. To feed were best at home;
  From thence the sauce to meat is ceremony:
  Meeting were bare without it.

     Enter the Ghost of BANQUO *and sits in* MACBETH'*s place.*

MACBETH   Sweet remembrancer.
  —Now, good digestion wait on appetite,
  And health on both.

LENNOX   May't please your highness, sit.   40

MACBETH Here had we now our country's honor roofed,
  Were the graced person of our Banquo present,

---

20. **nonpareil:** one without equal.
23. **founded:** securely established.
24. **broad and general:** free and omnipresent; **casing:** encasing.
25. **cribbed:** enclosed in a narrow space.
26. **saucy:** sharp, insolent.
30. **worm:** small serpent.
31. **nature:** such a nature.
33. **hear ourselves:** converse together.
34–36. **The . . . welcome:** The feast seems a mere duty, as if sold for a price, if not often accompanied with assurances of welcome while the guests are eating.
36. **To . . . home:** Simply eating is best done at home.
37. **From thence:** away from home; **meat:** food; **ceremony:** courtesy.
38. **Meeting were bare:** social gathering would be unadorned.
39. **wait on:** serve, follow.
41. **roofed:** under one roof.

Who may I rather challenge for unkindness
Than pity for mischance.
ROSS His absence, sir, 45
    Lays blame upon his promise. Please't your highness
    To grace us with your royal company?
MACBETH [*seeing his place occupied*] The table's full.
LENNOX Here is a place reserved, sir.
MACBETH Where?
LENNOX Here, my good lord. What is't that moves your highness?
MACBETH Which of you have done this?
LORDS What, my good lord? 50
MACBETH [*to Ghost*] Thou canst not say I did it. Never shake
    Thy gory locks at me!
ROSS Gentlemen, rise. His highness is not well.
LADY MACBETH Sit, worthy friends. My lord is often thus
    And hath been from his youth. Pray you, keep seat. 55
    The fit is momentary; upon a thought
    He will again be well. If much you note him,
    You shall offend him and extend his passion.
    Feed, and regard him not.

    [*She converses apart with* MACBETH.]

Are you a man?
MACBETH Ay, and a bold one that dare look on that 60
    Which might appall the devil!
LADY MACBETH Oh, proper stuff!
    This is the very painting of your fear;
    This is the air-drawn dagger which you said
    Led you to Duncan. Oh, these flaws and starts,
    Impostors to true fear, would well become 65
    A woman's story at a winter's fire,
    Authorized by her grandam. Shame itself!
    Why do you make such faces? When all's done,

---

43. **challenge:** rebuke.
45. **Lays blame:** calls into question.
49. **moves:** affects (an implied stage direction, as Macbeth recoils at the sight of the Ghost).
52. **gory locks:** bloody hair.
56. **upon a thought:** as quick as a thought.
61. **proper stuff:** nonsense.
63. **air-drawn:** imagined in, or moved through, the air.
64. **flaws:** outbursts of passion; **starts:** sudden nervous movements.
65. **to:** compared to.
67. **Authorized:** originally told and validated.

You look but on a stool.

MACBETH   Prithee, see there!
Behold, look, lo! How say you?   70
Why, what care I? [*to Ghost*] If thou canst nod, speak too.
If charnel houses and our graves must send
Those that we bury back, our monuments
Shall be the maws of kites.   [*Exit Ghost.*]

LADY MACBETH What, quite unmanned in folly?   75

MACBETH If I stand here, I saw him.

LADY MACBETH   Fie, for shame!

MACBETH Blood hath been shed ere now, i'th' olden time,
Ere humane statute purged the gentle weal;
Ay, and since, too, murders have been performed,
Too terrible for the ear. The times has been   80
That, when the brains were out, the man would die,
And there an end. But now they rise again,
With twenty mortal murders on their crowns,
And push us from our stools. This is more strange
Than such a murder is.

LADY MACBETH   My worthy lord,   85
Your noble friends do lack you.

MACBETH   I do forget.
—Do not muse at me, my most worthy friends.
I have a strange infirmity, which is nothing
To those that know me. Come, love and health to all;
Then I'll sit down. Give me some wine; fill full.   90

          Enter Ghost.

I drink to th'general joy o'th' whole table
And to our dear friend Banquo, whom we miss.
Would he were here! To all and him we thirst,
And all to all.

LORDS   Our duties and the pledge.

---

70. **lo:** look.
71. **nod:** an implicit stage direction for the ghost.
72. **charnel houses:** repositories for bones or corpses.
73–74. **monuments . . . kites:** burial places will be the stomachs of scavenging birds.
78. Before law (human and kindly) cleansed and civilized the commonwealth.
80. **times has been:** it used to be.
83. **mortal murders:** deadly wounds; **crowns:** heads.
93. **thirst:** long for.
94. **all to all:** let all drink to all.
94. **Our . . . pledge:** We offer our respect (**duties**) and this toast (**pledge**).

[*They drink.*]

MACBETH [*to Ghost*] Avaunt, and quit my sight! Let the earth hide thee! 95
    Thy bones are marrowless, thy blood is cold;
    Thou hast no speculation in those eyes
    Which thou dost glare with.
LADY MACBETH   Think of this, good peers,
    But as a thing of custom; 'tis no other,
    Only it spoils the pleasure of the time. 100
MACBETH What man dare, I dare.
    Approach thou like the rugged Russian bear,
    The armed rhinoceros, or th'Hyrcan tiger!
    Take any shape but that, and my firm nerves
    Shall never tremble. Or be alive again, 105
    And dare me to the desert with thy sword.
    If trembling I inhabit then, protest me
    The baby of a girl. Hence, horrible shadow,
    Unreal mock'ry, hence!   [*Exit Ghost.*]
               Why, so. Being gone,
    I am a man again. —Pray you, sit still. 110
LADY MACBETH You have displaced the mirth, broke the good meeting
    With most admired disorder.
MACBETH   Can such things be,
    And overcome us like a summer's cloud,
    Without our special wonder? You make me strange
    Even to the disposition that I owe, 115
    When now I think you can behold such sights
    And keep the natural ruby of your cheeks
    When mine is blanched with fear.
ROSS   What sights, my lord?
LADY MACBETH I pray you, speak not; he grows worse and worse.

95. **Avaunt:** go away.
97. **speculation:** sight.
99. **thing of custom:** common occurrence.
103. **armed:** armor-plated; **Hyrcan:** Hyrcanian, i.e., an ancient region on the Caspian sea, noted for its wildness.
104. **nerves:** tendons.
107. If I tremble then proclaim me.
108. **baby:** infant or doll.
112. **admired:** amazing.
113. **overcome:** come over.
114–15. **You . . . owe:** You make me feel estranged from my natural courageous self (**owe** means "own").
118. **blanched:** whitened.

Question enrages him. At once, good night.   120
Stand not upon the order of your going,
But go at once.
LENNOX   Good night, and better health
Attend his majesty.
LADY MACBETH   A kind good night to all.

                    Exeunt LORDS [*and Attendants*].

MACBETH It will have blood, they say; blood will have blood.
Stones have been known to move and trees to speak;   125
Augurs and understood relations have
By maggot-pies and choughs and rooks brought forth
The secret'st man of blood. What is the night?
LADY MACBETH Almost at odds with morning, which is which.
MACBETH How say'st thou that Macduff denies his person   130
At our great bidding?
LADY MACBETH   Did you send to him, sir?
MACBETH I hear it by the way, but I will send.
There's not a one of them but in his house
I keep a servant fee'd. I will tomorrow—
And betimes I will—to the weïrd sisters.   135
More shall they speak, for now I am bent to know
By the worst means the worst. For mine own good
All causes shall give way. I am in blood
Stepped in so far that, should I wade no more,
Returning were as tedious as go o'er.   140
Strange things I have in head that will to hand,
Which must be acted ere they may be scanned.

121. Don't insist on an orderly, ceremonious exit (cf. the ordered entrance 3.4.1).
124. Macbeth recalls the proverb "Blood will have blood"; the idea occurs in Genesis 9:6: "Whoso sheddeth man's blood, by man shall his blood be shed."
126. **Augurs:** predictions; **understood relations:** comprehended correspondences, as between cause and effect, for example.
127. **maggot-pies . . . rooks:** magpies, jackdaws, and crows (three types of birds that mimicked human speech); **brought forth:** revealed.
128. **secret'st . . . blood:** best-hidden murderer; **the night:** the time of night.
130. **How sayst thou:** what do you think.
132. **by the way:** casually; **send:** send a messenger.
133. **them:** the Scottish nobles.
134. **fee'd:** paid (to spy).
135. **betimes:** (1) speedily; (2) early in the morning.
136. **bent:** determined.
140. **go o'er:** going all the way over.
141. **will to hand:** demand to be acted out.
142. **scanned:** analyzed.

LADY MACBETH You lack the season of all natures, sleep.
MACBETH Come, we'll to sleep. My strange and self-abuse
    Is the initiate fear that wants hard use.   145
    We are yet but young in deed.

Exeunt.

3.5

Thunder. Enter the three WITCHES, *meeting* HECATE.

FIRST WITCH Why, how now, Hecate? You look angerly.
HECATE Have I not reason, beldams, as you are
    Saucy and overbold? How did you dare
    To trade and traffic with Macbeth
    In riddles and affairs of death,   5
    And I, the mistress of your charms,
    The close contriver of all harms,
    Was never called to bear my part,
    Or show the glory of our art?
    And, which is worse, all you have done   10
    Hath been but for a wayward son,
    Spiteful and wrathful, who, as others do,
    Loves for his own ends, not for you.
    But make amends now. Get you gone,
    And at the pit of Acheron   15
    Meet me i'th' morning. Thither he
    Will come to know his destiny.
    Your vessels and your spells provide,
    Your charms and everything beside.
    I am for th'air. This night I'll spend   20
    Unto a dismal and a fatal end.
    Great business must be wrought ere noon.
    Upon the corner of the moon

---

143. **season:** seasoning, preservative.
144. **strange and self-abuse:** unusual violation of who I am.
145. **initiate:** new; **wants hard use:** lacks experience.
3.5. **Location: a heath.** Most scholars agree that this scene and parts of 4.1 were written by another author, perhaps Thomas Middleton. See below, 295–305.
1. **angerly:** angrily, angry.
2. **beldams:** hags, witches.
7. **close:** secret.
11. **wayward:** self-willed, disobedient.
15. **Acheron:** a river in Hades.
21 **dismal:** disastrous.

There hangs a vap'rous drop profound;
I'll catch it ere it come to ground.   25
And that, distilled by magic sleights,
Shall raise such artificial sprites
As by the strength of their illusion
Shall draw him on to his confusion.
He shall spurn fate, scorn death, and bear   30
His hopes 'bove wisdom, grace, and fear.
And you all know security
Is mortals' chiefest enemy.

    Music and a song.

Hark, I am called. My little spirit, see,
Sits in a foggy cloud and stays for me.   [*Exit.*] 35

    Sing within: "Come away, come away," etc.

FIRST WITCH Come, let's make haste. She'll soon be back again.

                                               Exeunt.

3.6

    Enter LENNOX *and another* LORD.

LENNOX My former speeches have but hit your thoughts,
    Which can interpret farther. Only I say
    Things have been strangely borne. The gracious Duncan
    Was pitied of Macbeth; marry, he was dead.
    And the right valiant Banquo walked too late,   5
    Whom you may say, if't please you, Fleance killed,
    For Fleance fled; men must not walk too late.
    Who cannot want the thought how monstrous

---

24. **vap'rous drop:** lunar foam, supposedly gathered for enchantments; **profound:** with deep, hidden properties.
26. **sleights:** tricks.
27. **artificial:** constructed by art.
29. **confusion:** destruction.
32. **security:** spiritual overconfidence and complacency.
3.6. **Location: somewhere in Scotland.**
1. **hit:** touched upon.
2. **interpret:** draw the logical conclusions (without me saying more).
3. **borne:** (1) endured; (2) represented.
4. **of:** by.
8. **cannot . . . thought:** can help thinking.

It was for Malcolm and for Donaldbain
To kill their gracious father? Damnèd fact, 10
How it did grieve Macbeth! Did he not straight
In pious rage the two delinquents tear,
That were the slaves of drink and thralls of sleep?
Was not that nobly done? Ay, and wisely, too,
For 'twould have angered any heart alive 15
To hear the men deny't. So that I say
He has borne all things well. And I do think
That had he Duncan's sons under his key—
As, an't please heaven, he shall not—they should find
What 'twere to kill a father. So should Fleance. 20
But peace. For from broad words and 'cause he failed
His presence at the tyrant's feast, I hear
Macduff lives in disgrace. Sir, can you tell
Where he bestows himself?
LORD   The son of Duncan,
From whom this tyrant holds the due of birth, 25
Lives in the English court and is received
Of the most pious Edward with such grace
That the malevolence of fortune nothing
Takes from his high respect. Thither Macduff
Is gone to pray the holy King, upon his aid, 30
To wake Northumberland and warlike Siward,
That by the help of these, with Him above
To ratify the work, we may again
Give to our tables meat, sleep to our nights,
Free from our feasts and banquets bloody knives, 35
Do faithful homage, and receive free honors—

10. **fact:** crime.
13. **thralls:** prisoners.
17. **borne:** (1) carried out; (2) represented.
18. **under his key:** in his control.
19. **an't:** if it.
21. **from broad words:** for plain speaking.
24. **son of Duncan:** Malcolm.
27. **Edward:** Edward the Confessor (King of England, 1042–66).
28–29. **nothing Takes:** does not detract.
30. **upon his aid:** with his assistance.
31. **Northumberland:** an earl, or a northern English county; **Siward:** the family name of some Northumberland earls.
33. **ratify:** approve.
35. Free our feasts and banquets from bloody knives.
36. **free:** untainted.

All which we pine for now. And this report
Hath so exasperate the King that he
Prepares for some attempt of war.

LENNOX Sent he to Macduff?   40

LORD He did, and with an absolute "Sir, not I,"
The cloudy messenger turns me his back
And hums, as who should say, "You'll rue the time
That clogs me with this answer."

LENNOX   And that well might
Advise him to a caution, t'hold what distance   45
His wisdom can provide. Some holy angel
Fly to the court of England and unfold
His message ere he come, that a swift blessing
May soon return to this our suffering country
Under a hand accursed.

LORD   I'll send my prayers with him.   50

Exeunt.

4.1

Thunder. Enter the three WITCHES.

FIRST WITCH Thrice the brinded cat hath mewed.
SECOND WITCH Thrice, and once the hedge-pig whined.
THIRD WITCH Harpier cries, "'Tis time, 'tis time!"
FIRST WITCH Round about the cauldron go;
In the poisoned entrails throw.   5
Toad, that under cold stone

---

37. **this report:** (1) news of Macduff's flight (though this is in apparent contradiction with Macbeth's surprise at 4.1.141); (2) news of Malcolm's reception and purpose in England.
38. **exasperate the King:** exasperated Macbeth. Those who do not emend the Folio's "their" to **the** take "their" to refer to Northumberland's and Siward's King, Edward; in this reading the report (37) refers to Malcolm's report of Scotland's troubles to Edward. But the **he** (40) following, which must refer to Macbeth, argues strongly for emendation.
41. **absolute:** certain, unconditional; **Sir . . . I:** In these words Macduff refuses Macbeth's request (to return?).
42. **cloudy:** gloomy; **turns me:** turns ("me" is colloquial).
44. **clogs:** burdens.
45. **t'hold:** to keep.
47. **unfold:** reveal.
4.1. **Location: an interior space, perhaps a cavern.**
1. **brinded:** streaked or spotted.
2. **hedge-pig:** hedgehog.
3. **Harpier:** perhaps a familiar spirit.

Days and nights has thirty-one
Sweltered venom sleeping got,
Boil thou first i'th' charmèd pot.

ALL   Double, double, toil and trouble;   10
Fire burn, and cauldron bubble.

SECOND WITCH   Fillet of a fenny snake
In the cauldron boil and bake;
Eye of newt and toe of frog,
Wool of bat and tongue of dog,   15
Adder's fork and blind-worm's sting,
Lizard's leg and owlet's wing,
For a charm of powerful trouble,
Like a hell-broth boil and bubble.

ALL   Double, double, toil and trouble;   20
Fire burn, and cauldron bubble.

THIRD WITCH   Scale of dragon, tooth of wolf,
Witches' mummy, maw and gulf
Of the ravined salt-sea shark,
Root of hemlock digged i'th' dark,   25
Liver of blaspheming Jew,
Gall of goat, and slips of yew
Slivered in the moon's eclipse,
Nose of Turk and Tartar's lips,
Finger of birth-strangled babe   30
Ditch-delivered by a drab,
Make the gruel thick and slab.
Add thereto a tiger's chawdron,
For th'ingredients of our cauldron.

ALL   Double, double, toil and trouble;   35
Fire burn, and cauldron bubble.

7–8. For thirty-one days and nights has exuded venom like sweat while sleeping.
12. **Fillet:** slice; **fenny:** inhabiting fens or swamps.
16. **fork:** forked tongue; **blind-worm:** a small venomous snake.
17. **owlet:** a small owl.
23. **mummy:** mummified human flesh; **maw and gulf:** throat and stomach.
24. **ravined:** (1) ravenous; (2) glutted with prey.
26. **blaspheming:** Jews were so called for denying Christ's divinity.
27. **slips:** cuttings.
29. **Turk:** In the popular imagination the Turk threatened Europe and Christian civilization and often appeared as a figure of evil; **Tartar:** inhabitants of Central Asia, often considered as Turks or violent pagans.
31. **drab:** whore.
32. **slab:** semi-solid.
33. **chawdron:** entrails.

SECOND WITCH Cool it with a baboon's blood;
  Then the charm is firm and good.

  Enter HECATE *and the other three* WITCHES.

HECATE Oh, well done. I commend your pains,
  And every one shall share i'th' gains.   40
  And now about the cauldron sing,
  Live elves and fairies in a ring,
  Enchanting all that you put in.

  Music and a song, "Black spirits," etc.

SECOND WITCH By the pricking of my thumbs,
  Something wicked this way comes.   45
  Open, locks, whoever knocks!

  Enter MACBETH.

MACBETH How now, you secret, black, and midnight hags!
  What is't you do?
ALL WITCHES   A deed without a name.
MACBETH I conjure you by that which you profess,
  Howe'er you come to know it, answer me.   50
  Though you untie the winds and let them fight
  Against the churches, though the yeasty waves
  Confound and swallow navigation up,
  Though bladed corn be lodged and trees blown down,
  Though castles topple on their warders' heads,   55
  Though palaces and pyramids do slope
  Their heads to their foundations, though the treasure
  Of nature's germens tumble all together
  Even till destruction sicken, answer me
  To what I ask you.
FIRST WITCH   Speak.
SECOND WITCH   Demand.
THIRD WITCH   We'll answer.   60

39–43. Most consider these lines non-Shakespearean.
49. **conjure:** invoke.
52. **yeasty:** frothy.
54. **bladed corn:** leafed grain (**corn** is a generic term); **lodged:** laid on the ground (by the wind).
55. **warders:** guards.
56. **slope:** bend.
58. **nature's germens:** seeds from which all life springs.
59. **sicken:** gets sick from excess.

FIRST WITCH   Say if thou'dst rather hear it from our mouths,
   Or from our masters.
MACBETH   Call 'em; let me see 'em.
FIRST WITCH Pour in sow's blood that hath eaten
   Her nine farrow; grease that's sweaten
   From the murderer's gibbet throw   65
   Into the flame.
ALL WITCHES   Come high or low,
   Thyself and office deftly show!

    Thunder. FIRST APPARITION, *an armed head.*

MACBETH   Tell me, thou unknown power—
FIRST WITCH   He knows thy thought.
   Hear his speech, but say thou naught.
FIRST APPARITION Macbeth, Macbeth, Macbeth. Beware Macduff,   70
   Beware the Thane of Fife. Dismiss me. Enough.

                               He descends.

MACBETH Whate'er thou art, for thy good caution, thanks;
   Thou hast harped my fear aright. But one word more—
FIRST WITCH He will not be commanded. Here's another,
   More potent than the first.   75

    Thunder. SECOND APPARITION, *a bloody child.*

SECOND APPARITION Macbeth, Macbeth, Macbeth.
MACBETH Had I three ears, I'd hear thee.
SECOND APPARITION Be bloody, bold, and resolute; laugh to scorn
   The power of man, for none of woman born
   Shall harm Macbeth.   *Descends.* 80
MACBETH   Then live, Macduff. What need I fear of thee?
   But yet I'll make assurance double sure
   And take a bond of fate. Thou shalt not live,
   That I may tell pale-hearted fear it lies

64. **nine farrow:** litter of nine; **sweaten:** sweated (rhymes with **eaten**).
65. **gibbet:** gallows, from which criminals were hanged.
67. **office:** function.
67. SD **armed head:** helmeted head, foreshadowing Macbeth's decapitation by Macduff.
71. SD **descends:** The stage had a trap-door for such effects.
73. **harped:** given voice to; **aright:** exactly.
75. SD **bloody child:** This image suggests the infanticides in the imagery (1.7.54–58) and the action (4.2), and also the retribution in the person of Macduff, untimely ripped from his mother's womb.
79. **of woman born:** a human being. The phrase echoes biblical pronouncements (see Job 14:1, 15:14, 25:4).
83. **take . . . fate:** get a guarantee from fate; **Thou:** Macduff.

And sleep in spite of thunder.

> *Thunder.* THIRD APPARITION, *a child crowned, with a tree in his hand.*

What is this   85
That rises like the issue of a king,
And wears upon his baby brow the round
And top of sovereignty?
ALL WITCHES   Listen, but speak not to't.
THIRD APPARITION Be lion-mettled, proud, and take no care
Who chafes, who frets, or where conspirers are.   90
Macbeth shall never vanquished be until
Great Birnam Wood to high Dunsinane Hill
Shall come against him.   *Descends.*
MACBETH   That will never be.
Who can impress the forest, bid the tree
Unfix his earth-bound root? Sweet bodements, good.   95
Rebellious dead, rise never till the Wood
Of Birnam rise, and our high-placed Macbeth
Shall live the lease of nature, pay his breath
To time and mortal custom. Yet my heart
Throbs to know one thing: tell me, if your art   100
Can tell so much, shall Banquo's issue ever
Reign in this kingdom?
ALL WITCHES   Seek to know no more.
MACBETH   I will be satisfied. Deny me this,
And an eternal curse fall on you! Let me know.

> [*The cauldron descends.*] *Hautboys.*

Why sinks that cauldron? And what noise is this?   105
FIRST WITCH Show!
SECOND WITCH Show!
THIRD WITCH Show!
ALL WITCHES Show his eyes, and grieve his heart;

---

85. SD *child*: This figure may represent Malcolm, true heir to the throne, or Banquo's issue, future heirs. The tree suggests Birnam Wood.
87–88. **round And top:** crown.
89. **lion-mettled:** as fearless and fierce as a lion.
94. **impress:** draft into service.
95. **bodements:** omens, prophecies.
96. **Rebellious dead:** i.e., Banquo and his ghost.
98. **lease of nature:** natural lifespan.
99. **mortal custom:** the custom of mortality.

Come like shadows, so depart.   110

> *A show of eight Kings, and* BANQUO *last;* [*the eighth King*]
> *with a glass in his hand.*

MACBETH Thou art too like the spirit of Banquo. Down!
Thy crown does sear mine eyeballs! And thy heir,
Thou other gold-bound brow, is like the first.
A third is like the former. —Filthy hags,
Why do you show me this? —A fourth! Start, eyes!   115
What, will the line stretch out to th'crack of doom?
Another yet? A seventh! I'll see no more.
And yet the eighth appears, who bears a glass
Which shows me many more; and some I see
That two-fold balls and treble scepters carry.   120
Horrible sight! Now, I see 'tis true,
For the blood-boltered Banquo smiles upon me,
And points at them for his.   [*The apparitions vanish.*]
                     What, is this so?
FIRST WITCH Ay, sir, all this is so. But why
Stands Macbeth thus amazedly?   125
Come, sisters, cheer we up his sprites,
And show the best of our delights.
I'll charm the air to give a sound,
While you perform your antic round,
That this great king may kindly say   130
Our duties did his welcome pay.

> *Music. The* WITCHES *dance and vanish.*

MACBETH Where are they? Gone? Let this pernicious hour
Stand aye accursèd in the calendar!
Come in, without there.

---

110. SD: The eight kings represent descendants of Banquo, the ancestors of the Stuart line culminating in King James (1603–1625), reigning at the time of the play.
110.2. SD *glass*: mirror.
113. **other**: second.
115. **Start**: bulge from eye sockets.
116. **crack of doom**: thunder at the end of world and Last Judgment.
120. **two-fold . . . scepters**: two orbs and three scepters, symbolic accoutrements of royalty, perhaps alluding to James I, King of Scotland and Ireland. The three scepters may refer to James's assumed authority over Great Britain, France, and Ireland.
122. **blood-boltered**: having hair matted with blood.
124–31. Usually regarded as non-Shakespearean.
129. **antic round**: fantastic circle dance.
133. **aye**: ever.

Enter LENNOX.

LENNOX   What's your grace's will?
MACBETH   Saw you the weïrd sisters?
LENNOX   No, my lord.   135
MACBETH   Came they not by you?
LENNOX   No, indeed, my lord.
MACBETH Infected be the air whereon they ride,
    And damned all those that trust them! I did hear
    The galloping of horse. Who was't came by?
LENNOX   'Tis two or three, my lord, that bring you word   140
    Macduff is fled to England.
MACBETH   Fled to England?
LENNOX Ay, my good lord.
MACBETH [*aside*]   Time, thou anticipat'st my dread exploits.
    The flighty purpose never is o'ertook
    Unless the deed go with it. From this moment   145
    The very firstlings of my heart shall be
    The firstlings of my hand. And even now,
    To crown my thoughts with acts, be it thought and done.
    The castle of Macduff I will surprise,
    Seize upon Fife, give to th'edge o'th' sword   150
    His wife, his babes, and all unfortunate souls
    That trace him in his line. No boasting like a fool;
    This deed I'll do before this purpose cool.
    But no more sights. —Where are these gentlemen?
    Come, bring me where they are.   155

                                                          Exeunt.

4.2

Enter Macduff's WIFE, *her* SON, *and* ROSS.

WIFE What had he done to make him fly the land?
ROSS You must have patience, madam.

---

143. **anticipat'st:** foresee (and thus prevent).
144–45. **The . . . it:** The fleeting resolution to do something never amounts to anything unless accompanied by action.
146. **firstlings:** first children. Macbeth promises to turn immediately his impulses to deeds.
149. **surprise:** attack unexpectedly.
152. **trace . . . line:** follow him in his family line.
154. **these gentlemen:** the two or three messengers (140).
4.2. **Location:** Fife. Macduff's castle.

WIFE He had none;
His flight was madness. When our actions do not,
Our fears do make us traitors.

ROSS You know not
Whether it was his wisdom or his fear. 5

WIFE Wisdom? To leave his wife, to leave his babes,
His mansion, and his titles in a place
From whence himself does fly? He loves us not;
He wants the natural touch. For the poor wren,
The most diminutive of birds, will fight, 10
Her young ones in her nest, against the owl.
All is the fear and nothing is the love,
As little is the wisdom, where the flight
So runs against all reason.

ROSS My dearest coz,
I pray you, school yourself. But, for your husband, 15
He is noble, wise, judicious, and best knows
The fits o'th' season. I dare not speak much further.
But cruel are the times when we are traitors
And do not know ourselves; when we hold rumor
From what we fear, yet know not what we fear, 20
But float upon a wild and violent sea,
Each way and none. I take my leave of you;
Shall not be long but I'll be here again.
Things at the worst will cease or else climb upward
To what they were before. [*to the* SON] My pretty cousin, 25
Blessing upon you.

WIFE Fathered he is, and yet he's fatherless.

ROSS I am so much a fool, should I stay longer
It would be my disgrace and your discomfort.
I take my leave at once. *Exit* ROSS.

WIFE Sirrah, your father's dead. 30

3–4. **When . . . traitors:** Even when we commit no acts of treason, our fears can make us treasonous or appear treasonous. (By running away, Macduff has betrayed his family and country or he has made himself look guilty of treason.)
9. **wants:** lacks.
14. **coz:** cousin, kinswoman (a term of affection).
15. **school:** discipline.
17. **fits . . . season:** violent conditions of the time.
19. **know ourselves:** know ourselves to be such (traitors); **hold:** believe.
20. About what we fear, though we don't know what we fear exactly.
22. **Each . . . none:** in every direction at once and in none specifically.
29. My staying (and weeping) would disgrace me and distress you.
30. **Sirrah:** an affectionate form of address to a child.

And what will you do now? How will you live?

SON As birds do, mother.

WIFE   What, with worms and flies?

SON With what I get, I mean, and so do they.

WIFE Poor bird, thou'dst never fear the net nor lime,
The pitfall nor the gin.   35

SON Why should I, mother? Poor birds they are not set for. My father
is not dead, for all your saying.

WIFE Yes, he is dead. How wilt thou do for a father?

SON Nay, how will you do for a husband?

WIFE Why, I can buy me twenty at any market.   40

SON Then you'll buy 'em to sell again.

WIFE Thou speak'st with all thy wit, and yet, i'faith, with wit enough
for thee.

SON Was my father a traitor, mother?

WIFE Ay, that he was.   45

SON What is a traitor?

WIFE Why, one that swears and lies.

SON And be all traitors that do so?

WIFE Every one that does so is a traitor and must be hanged.

SON And must they all be hanged that swear and lie?   50

WIFE Every one.

SON Who must hang them?

WIFE Why, the honest men.

SON Then the liars and swearers are fools, for there are liars and swearers 55
enough to beat the honest men and hang up them.

WIFE Now, God help thee, poor monkey! But how wilt thou do for a
father?

SON If he were dead, you'd weep for him; if you would not, it were a good 60
sign that I should quickly have a new father.

WIFE Poor prattler, how thou talk'st!

Enter a MESSENGER.

MESSENGER   Bless you, fair dame. I am not to you known,
Though in your state of honor I am perfect.

34–35. **net . . . gin:** These are all traps for birds. **lime:** birdlime, a sticky substance; **gin:** snare or trap.

36. **they:** traps. (The traps are set for superior or game birds.)

47. **swears and lies:** swears an oath to a sovereign (or wife) and breaks it.

59–60. **if . . . father:** The son suggests that the mother's lack of tears would indicate a new love interest.

63. Though I know well your nobility.

I doubt some danger does approach you nearly.
If you will take a homely man's advice,   65
Be not found here; hence with your little ones.
To fright you thus, methinks, I am too savage;
To do worse to you were fell cruelty,
Which is too nigh your person. Heaven preserve you.
I dare abide no longer.   *Exit* MESSENGER.
WIFE   Whither should I fly?   70
I have done no harm. But I remember now
I am in this earthly world, where to do harm
Is often laudable, to do good sometime
Accounted dangerous folly. Why, then, alas,
Do I put up that womanly defense,   75
To say I have done no harm?

    Enter MURDERERS.

                        What are these faces?
MURDERER Where is your husband?
WIFE I hope in no place so unsanctified
Where such as thou mayst find him.
MURDERER   He's a traitor.
SON Thou liest, thou shag-haired villain!
MURDERER [*stabbing him*]   What, you egg!   80
Young fry of treachery.
SON   He has killed me, mother.
Run away, I pray you! [*He dies.*]

                  Exit [WIFE] *crying* "Murder!"
              [*followed by* MURDERERS *with* SON's *body*].

4.3

    Enter MALCOLM *and* MACDUFF.

MALCOLM Let us seek out some desolate shade and there
Weep our sad bosoms empty.
MACDUFF   Let us rather

64. **doubt:** fear.
65. **homely:** plain (speaking).
68. **fell:** vicious.
69. **Which . . . person:** such cruelty is too near you now.
81. **fry:** offspring (of fish).
4.3. **Location: England. Before King Edward's palace.**

Hold fast the mortal sword and like good men
Bestride our downfall birthdom. Each new morn
New widows howl, new orphans cry, new sorrows   5
Strike heaven on the face, that it resounds
As if it felt with Scotland and yelled out
Like syllable of dolor.

MALCOLM   What I believe, I'll wail;
What know, believe; and what I can, redress;
As I shall find the time to friend, I will.   10
What you have spoke, it may be so, perchance.
This tyrant, whose sole name blisters our tongues,
Was once thought honest. You have loved him well;
He hath not touched you yet. I am young, but something
You may deserve of him through me, and wisdom   15
To offer up a weak, poor, innocent lamb
T'appease an angry god.

MACDUFF   I am not treacherous.

MALCOLM   But Macbeth is.
A good and virtuous nature may recoil
In an imperial charge. But I shall crave your pardon.   20
That which you are my thoughts cannot transpose;
Angels are bright still though the brightest fell.
Though all things foul would wear the brows of grace,
Yet grace must still look so.

MACDUFF   I have lost my hopes.

MALCOLM Perchance even there where I did find my doubts.   25
Why in that rawness left you wife and child,
Those precious motives, those strong knots of love,
Without leave-taking? I pray you,

---

3. **mortal:** deadly.
4. **Bestride . . . birthdom:** stand over and protect our fallen native land.
6. **that:** so that.
8. **Like . . . dolor:** the same cry of pain.
10. **friend:** befriend me, be favorable.
12. **sole:** mere.
15. **deserve . . . me:** get from him as a reward for betraying me; **wisdom:** it is wise.
19–20. **recoil . . . charge:** give way, or go in a reverse motion, because of imperial force or command. (The image is of a gun springing back by force of the firing.)
21. **transpose:** transform.
22. **the brightest:** i.e., Lucifer.
23. **brows:** appearance.
24. **look so:** like grace. Though foul things put on good appearances, good things must still appear good and may be trusted.
25. **there:** in the general climate of suspicion and fear.
26. **rawness:** (1) vulnerable position; (2) rudeness (referring to Macduff's abrupt departure).

Let not my jealousies be your dishonors
But mine own safeties. You may be rightly just,   30
Whatever I shall think.
MACDUFF   Bleed, bleed, poor country!
Great tyranny, lay thou thy basis sure,
For goodness dare not check thee; wear thou thy wrongs,
The title is affeered.—Fare thee well, lord.
I would not be the villain that thou think'st   35
For the whole space that's in the tyrant's grasp
And the rich East to boot.
MALCOLM   Be not offended.
I speak not as in absolute fear of you.
I think our country sinks beneath the yoke;
It weeps, it bleeds, and each new day a gash   40
Is added to her wounds. I think withal
There would be hands uplifted in my right,
And here from gracious England have I offer
Of goodly thousands. But, for all this,
When I shall tread upon the tyrant's head   45
Or wear it on my sword, yet my poor country
Shall have more vices than it had before,
More suffer and more sundry ways than ever,
By him that shall succeed.
MACDUFF   What should he be?
MALCOLM It is myself I mean, in whom I know   50
All the particulars of vice so grafted
That, when they shall be opened, black Macbeth
Will seem as pure as snow, and the poor state
Esteem him as a lamb, being compared
With my confineless harms.

29–30. **Let . . . safeties:** Assume that I voice my suspicions not for your dishonor but for my safety.
32. **basis sure:** foundation securely.
33. **check:** restrain, rebuke; **wear:** display (as on a heraldic shield).
34. **title is affeered:** Tyranny is confirmed.
38. **absolute fear:** complete mistrust.
41. **withal:** in addition.
42. **in my right:** in support of my claim to the throne.
43. **England:** the King of England.
44. **goodly:** considerable in respect to size.
49. **succeed:** follow as king.
51. **grafted:** implanted into his character.
52. **opened:** revealed (as a bud opens).

MACDUFF   Not in the legions   55
   Of horrid hell can come a devil more damned
   In evils to top Macbeth.
MALCOLM   I grant him bloody,
   Luxurious, avaricious, false, deceitful,
   Sudden, malicious, smacking of every sin
   That has a name. But there's no bottom, none,   60
   In my voluptuousness: your wives, your daughters,
   Your matrons, and your maids could not fill up
   The cistern of my lust, and my desire
   All continent impediments would o'erbear
   That did oppose my will. Better Macbeth   65
   Than such an one to reign.
MACDUFF   Boundless intemperance
   In nature is a tyranny. It hath been
   Th'untimely emptying of the happy throne
   And fall of many kings. But fear not yet
   To take upon you what is yours. You may   70
   Convey your pleasures in a spacious plenty
   And yet seem cold; the time you may so hoodwink.
   We have willing dames enough. There cannot be
   That vulture in you to devour so many
   As will to greatness dedicate themselves,   75
   Finding it so inclined.
MALCOLM   With this there grows
   In my most ill-composed affection such
   A stanchless avarice that, were I king,
   I should cut off the nobles for their lands,
   Desire his jewels and this other's house,   80
   And my more-having would be as a sauce

---

55. **confineless:** limitless.
58. **Luxurious:** lecherous.
59. **Sudden:** rash, impetuous.
63. **cistern:** water tank.
64. **continent:** containing, restraining.
65. **will:** lust.
67. **nature:** human nature.
69. **yet:** nevertheless.
71. **Convey:** manage in secret.
72. **cold:** chaste; **hoodwink:** blindfold, deceive.
77. **ill-composed affection:** (1) evil disposition; (2) poorly managed passion.
78. **stanchless:** insatiable.
80. **his:** one man's.
81. **more-having:** gains and greed for more.

To make me hunger more, that I should forge
Quarrels unjust against the good and loyal.
Destroying them for wealth.
MACDUFF   This avarice
 Sticks deeper, grows with more pernicious root   85
 Than summer-seeming lust, and it hath been
 The sword of our slain kings. Yet do not fear;
 Scotland hath foisons to fill up your will
 Of your mere own. All these are portable,
 With other graces weighed.   90
MALCOLM But I have none. The king-becoming graces—
 As justice, verity, temp'rance, stableness,
 Bounty, perseverance, mercy, lowliness,
 Devotion, patience, courage, fortitude—
 I have no relish of them, but abound   95
 In the division of each several crime,
 Acting it many ways. Nay, had I power, I should
 Pour the sweet milk of concord into hell,
 Uproar the universal peace, confound
 All unity on earth.
MACDUFF   O Scotland, Scotland!   100
MALCOLM If such a one be fit to govern, speak.
 I am as I have spoken.
MACDUFF   Fit to govern?
 No, not to live. O nation miserable,
 With an untitled tyrant, bloody-sceptered!
 When shalt thou see thy wholesome days again, 105
 Since that the truest issue of thy throne
 By his own interdiction stands accused

---

85. **pernicious:** evil, destructive.
86. **summer-seeming:** (1) seeming like summer, i.e., hot and transitory; (2) summer beseeming, i.e., appropriate to youth.
87. **sword . . . slain:** sword that slew our.
88. **foisons:** resources.
89. **Of . . . own:** from your royal supplies alone; **portable:** endurable.
90. **graces weighed:** virtues considered.
91. **king-becoming graces:** virtues suitable to a king.
93. **lowliness:** humility.
95. **relish:** enjoyment of the taste.
96. **division:** variations; **several:** distinct.
99. **Uproar:** throw into confusion.
104. **untitled:** usurping.
107. **interdiction:** declaration of incompetency.

And does blaspheme his breed? Thy royal father
Was a most sainted king; the queen that bore thee,
Oft'ner upon her knees than on her feet,   110
Died every day she lived. Fare thee well.
These evils thou repeat'st upon thyself
Hath banished me from Scotland.—O my breast,
Thy hope ends here.

MALCOLM   Macduff, this noble passion,
Child of integrity, hath from my soul   115
Wiped the black scruples, reconciled my thoughts
To thy good truth and honor. Devilish Macbeth
By many of these trains hath sought to win me
Into his power, and modest wisdom plucks me
From over-credulous haste. But God above   120
Deal between thee and me. For even now
I put myself to thy direction and
Unspeak mine own detraction, here abjure
The taints and blames I laid upon myself
For strangers to my nature. I am yet   125
Unknown to woman, never was forsworn,
Scarcely have coveted what was mine own,
At no time broke my faith, would not betray
The devil to his fellow, and delight
No less in truth than life. My first false speaking   130
Was this upon myself. What I am truly
Is thine and my poor country's to command,
Whither, indeed, before thy here-approach,
Old Siward with ten thousand warlike men
Already at a point was setting forth.   135

108. **blaspheme:** slander.
111. **Died . . . lived:** died to this world by daily religious practices.
112. **repeat'st upon:** declare against.
113. **banished me:** made it impossible for me to return (with you).
116. **scruples:** doubts.
118. **trains:** tricks.
119. **plucks:** restrains.
123. **mine own detraction:** my former self-condemnation.
125. **For:** as.
126. **Unknown to women:** a virgin.
131. **this upon:** this false witness against.
133. **Whither:** to which place; **here-approach:** arrival here.
134. **warlike:** armed.
135. **at a point:** prepared.

Now we'll together, and the chance of goodness
Be like our warranted quarrel. Why are you silent?
MACDUFF Such welcome and unwelcome things at once
'Tis hard to reconcile.

Enter a DOCTOR.

MALCOLM Well, more anon, [*to the* DOCTOR] Comes the King
forth, I pray you?   140
DOCTOR Ay, sir. There are a crew of wretched souls
That stay his cure. Their malady convinces
The great assay of art, but at his touch—
Such sanctity hath heaven given his hand—
They presently amend.
MALCOLM   I thank you, Doctor.   *Exit* [DOCTOR]. 145
MACDUFF What's the disease he means?
MALCOLM   'Tis called the Evil.
A most miraculous work in this good King,
Which often since my here-remain in England
I have seen him do. How he solicits heaven
Himself best knows; but strangely-visited people,   150
All swoll'n and ulcerous, pitiful to the eye,
The mere despair of surgery, he cures,
Hanging a golden stamp about their necks,
Put on with holy prayers; and, 'tis spoken,
To the succeeding royalty he leaves   155
The healing benediction. With this strange virtue,
He hath a heavenly gift of prophecy,
And sundry blessings hang about his throne
That speak him full of grace.

Enter ROSS.

136. **we'll:** we'll go; **the . . . goodness:** may the chance of our success.
137. **Be . . . quarrel:** match the justice of our cause.
142. **stay:** await; **convinces:** conquers.
143. **assay of art:** attempts of medical science.
146. **Evil:** scrofula, the chronic enlargement of the lymphatic glands and ulcers, supposedly cured by the royal touch.
148. **here-remain:** stay.
150. **visited:** afflicted.
152. **mere:** absolute.
153. **stamp:** coin. (Elizabeth and James gave a gold coin to those they touched.)
154. **Put on with:** accompanied by.
155. **succeeding royalty:** following monarchs.
156. **healing benediction:** this power to heal; **virtue:** power.
159. **speak him:** declare him to be.

MACDUFF   See who comes here.

MALCOLM My countryman, but yet I know him not.   160

MACDUFF My ever gentle cousin, welcome hither.

MALCOLM I know him now. Good God, betimes remove
> The means that makes us strangers.

ROSS   Sir, amen.

MACDUFF Stands Scotland where it did?

ROSS   Alas, poor country,
> Almost afraid to know itself. It cannot   165
> Be called our mother but our grave, where nothing
> But who knows nothing is once seen to smile;
> Where sighs and groans and shrieks that rend the air
> Are made, not marked; where violent sorrow seems
> A modern ecstasy. The deadman's knell   170
> Is there scarce asked for who, and good men's lives
> Expire before the flowers in their caps,
> Dying or ere they sicken.

MACDUFF   Oh, relation
> Too nice and yet too true!

MALCOLM   What's the newest grief?

ROSS That of an hour's age doth hiss the speaker;   175
> Each minute teems a new one.

MACDUFF   How does my wife?

ROSS Why, well.

MACDUFF   And all my children?

ROSS   Well too.

MACDUFF The tyrant has not battered at their peace?

ROSS No, they were well at peace when I did leave 'em.

MACDUFF Be not a niggard of your speech. How goes't?   180

ROSS When I came hither to transport the tidings

---

160. **countryman:** Malcolm recognizes Ross as a Scot by his dress.
162. **betimes:** immediately.
163. **means . . . strangers:** cause of our separation, i.e., Macbeth.
166. **nothing:** nobody.
167. **who:** one who; **once:** ever.
169. **marked:** noticed.
170. **modern ecstasy:** common frenzy.
170–171. **The deadman's . . . who:** No one in Scotland bothers to ask who died when the funeral bell tolls (because death is so common).
173. **or . . . sicken:** before they become ill; **relation:** report.
174. **nice:** precise.
175. A report only one hour old is hissed as old news.
176. **teems:** brings forth.
180. **niggard:** miser.

Which I have heavily borne, there ran a rumor
Of many worthy fellows that were out,
Which was to my belief witnessed the rather
For that I saw the tyrant's power afoot.   185
Now is the time of help, [*to* MALCOLM] Your eye in Scotland
Would create soldiers, make our women fight
To doff their dire distresses.
MALCOLM   Be't their comfort
We are coming thither. Gracious England hath
Lent us good Siward and ten thousand men—   190
An older and a better soldier none
That Christendom gives out.
ROSS   Would I could answer
This comfort with the like. But I have words
That would be howled out in the desert air,
Where hearing should not latch them.
MACDUFF   What concern they?   195
The general cause, or is it a fee-grief
Due to some single breast?
ROSS   No mind that's honest
But in it shares some woe, though the main part
Pertains to you alone.
MACDUFF   If it be mine,
Keep it not from me; quickly let me have it.   200
ROSS Let not your ears despise my tongue forever,
Which shall possess them with the heaviest sound
That ever yet they heard.
MACDUFF   Hum—I guess at it.
ROSS Your castle is surprised, your wife and babes
Savagely slaughtered. To relate the manner   205
Were, on the quarry of these murdered deer,
To add the death of you.

183. **out:** in the field, in arms.
184. **witnessed the rather:** made more credible.
185. **power afoot:** army mobilized for action.
186. **eye:** person, i.e., yourself.
188. **doff:** take off (like clothing).
189. **England:** King Edward.
191. **none:** is no one.
192. **gives out:** tells of.
195. **latch:** catch.
196–97. **fee-grief . . . breast:** grief belonging to a particular person. (The phrase derives from legal language about property inheritance.)
206. **Were:** would be; **quarry:** heap of slaughtered deer (with a pun on "dear").

MALCOLM   Merciful heaven!
  What, man, ne'er pull your hat upon your brows.
  Give sorrow words. The grief that does not speak
  Whispers the o'er-fraught heart and bids it break.   210
MACDUFF My children too?
ROSS   Wife, children, servants—
  All that could be found.
MACDUFF   And I must be from thence?
  My wife killed too?
ROSS   I have said.
MALCOLM   Be comforted.
  Let's make us med'cines of our great revenge
  To cure this deadly grief.   215
MACDUFF He has no children. All my pretty ones?
  Did you say all? Oh, hell-kite! All?
  What, all my pretty chickens and their dam
  At one fell swoop?
MALCOLM   Dispute it like a man.
MACDUFF I shall do so.   220
  But I must also feel it as a man.
  I cannot but remember such things were
  That were most precious to me. Did heaven look on
  And would not take their part? Sinful Macduff,
  They were all struck for thee. Naught that I am,   225
  Not for their own demerits but for mine
  Fell slaughter on their souls. Heaven rest them now.
MALCOLM Be this the whetstone of your sword. Let grief
  Convert to anger; blunt not the heart, enrage it.
MACDUFF Oh, I could play the woman with mine eyes   230
  And braggart with my tongue. But, gentle heavens,
  Cut short all intermission. Front to front
  Bring thou this fiend of Scotland and myself.

210. **Whispers:** whispers to; **o'er-fraught:** overburdened.
212. **from thence:** away from home.
216. **He . . . children:** 1) Macbeth has no children (and therefore cannot suffer a fitting retribution); 2) Malcolm has no children (and therefore cannot understand this pain).
217. **hell-kite:** kite (bird of prey) from hell.
218. **dam:** mother.
219. **Dispute:** fight against.
225. **Naught:** wicked man.
226. **demerits:** faults.
228. **whetstone:** sharpening stone.
230. **play . . . eyes:** weep.
232. **intermission:** delay; **Front to front:** face to face.

Within my sword's length set him. If he scape,
Heaven forgive him too.
MALCOLM   This tune goes manly.   235
Come, go we to the King. Our power is ready;
Our lack is nothing but our leave. Macbeth
Is ripe for shaking, and the powers above
Put on their instruments. Receive what cheer you may;
The night is long that never finds the day.   240

Exeunt.

5.1

Enter a DOCTOR *of physic and a waiting* GENTLEWOMAN.

DOCTOR I have two nights watched with you but can perceive no truth in
your report. When was it she last walked?

GENTLEWOMAN Since his majesty went into the field, I have seen her
rise from her bed, throw her nightgown upon her, unlock her closet,
take forth paper, fold it, write upon't, read it, afterwards seal it, and   5
again return to bed, yet all this while in a most fast sleep.

DOCTOR A great perturbation in nature, to receive at once the benefit of
sleep and do the effects of watching. In this slumb'ry agitation, besides
her walking and other actual performances, what at any time have you
heard her say?   10

GENTLEWOMAN That, sir, which I will not report after her.

DOCTOR You may to me, and 'tis most meet you should.

GENTLEWOMAN Neither to you nor anyone, having no witness to confirm my speech.

Enter LADY MACBETH *with a taper.*

LO, you, here she comes. This is her very guise and, upon my life, fast 15
asleep. Observe her; stand close.

DOCTOR How came she by that light?

237. **Our . . . leave:** We have only to take leave of the English King.
239. **Put . . . instruments:** (1) arm themselves for action; (2) take us as their agents.
5.1. **Location: Dunsinane Hill. Macbeth's castle.**
0.1. SD *physic:* medicine; *waiting* GENTLEWOMAN: personal servant.
4. **closet:** cabinet.
6. **fast:** deep.
8. **do . . . watching:** act as if she were awake.
12. **meet:** fitting.
14. SD *taper:* candle.
15. **very guise:** exact manner or conduct.
16. **close:** concealed.

GENTLEWOMAN Why, it stood by her. She has light by her continually;
'tis her command.

DOCTOR You see her eyes are open.   20

GENTLEWOMAN Ay, but their sense are shut.

DOCTOR What is it she does now? Look how she rubs her hands.

GENTLEWOMAN It is an accustomed action with her to seem thus washing her hands. I have known her continue in this a quarter of an hour.

LADY MACBETH Yet here's a spot.   25

DOCTOR Hark, she speaks. I will set down what comes from her to satisfy
my remembrance the more strongly.

LADY MACBETH Out, damned spot! Out, I say! One, two, why, then, 'tis
time to do't. Hell is murky. Fie, my lord, fie, a soldier and afeard?
what need we fear? Who knows it when none can call our power to 30
account? Yet who would have thought the old man to have had so much
blood in him?

DOCTOR Do you mark that?

LADY MACBETH The Thane of Fife had a wife. Where is she now?
What, will these hands ne'er be clean? No more o'that, my lord, no 35
more o'that. You mar all with this starting.

DOCTOR Go to, go to. You have known what you should not.

GENTLEWOMAN She has spoke what she should not, I am sure of that.
Heaven knows what she has known.

LADY MACBETH Here's the smell of the blood still. All the perfumes of 40
Arabia will not sweeten this little hand. Oh, oh, oh!

DOCTOR What a sigh is there! The heart is sorely charged.

GENTLEWOMAN I would not have such a heart in my bosom for the
dignity of the whole body.

DOCTOR Well, well, well.   45

GENTLEWOMAN Pray God it be, sir.

DOCTOR This disease is beyond my practice. Yet I have known those
which have walked in their sleep who have died holily in their beds.

LADY MACBETH Wash your hands, put on your nightgown, look not
so pale. I tell you yet again, Banquo's buried; he cannot come out on's grave. 50

DOCTOR Even so?

---

21. **their . . . shut:** they are unseeing.
26. **set:** write; **satisfy:** confirm.
34. **Thane of Fife:** Macduff.
36. **starting:** flinching.
37. **Go to:** come on (a mild reprimand).
41. **Arabia:** exotic land known for its spices.
44. **dignity:** high rank (as queen).
50. **on's:** of his.

LADY MACBETH To bed, to bed. There's knocking at the gate. Come, come, come, come, give me your hand. What's done cannot be undone. To bed, to bed, to bed.

Exit LADY MACBETH.

DOCTOR Will she go now to bed? 55
GENTLEWOMAN Directly.
DOCTOR Foul whisp'rings are abroad. Unnatural deeds
  Do breed unnatural troubles. Infected minds
  To their deaf pillows will discharge their secrets.
  More needs she the divine than the physician. 60
  God, God, forgive us all. Look after her;
  Remove from her the means of all annoyance,
  And still keep eyes upon her. So, good night.
  My mind she has mated, and amazed my sight.
  I think but dare not speak. 65
GENTLEWOMAN   Good night, good Doctor.

Exeunt.

5.2

Drum and colors. Enter MENTEITH, CAITHNESS, ANGUS, LENNOX, *Soldiers.*

MENTEITH The English power is near, led on by Malcolm,
  His uncle Siward, and the good Macduff.
  Revenges burn in them, for their dear causes
  Would to the bleeding and the grim alarm
  Excite the mortified man.
ANGUS   Near Birnam Wood 5
  Shall we well meet them; that way are they coming.
CAITHNESS Who knows if Donaldbain be with his brother?
LENNOX For certain, sir, he is not. I have a file
  Of all the gentry. There is Siward's son

60. **divine:** clergyman.
62. **annoyance:** harm. (The Doctor seeks to prevent suicide.)
64. **mated:** stupefied.
5.2. **Location: country near Dunsinane Hill.**
0.1. SD *Drum and colors*: Drummers and flag-carriers.
3. **dear:** deeply felt.
4–5. **Would . . . man:** would stir a dead (**mortified**) man to bloody (**bleeding**) and grim battle.
8. **file:** list.

And many unrough youths that even now   10
Protest their first of manhood.
MENTEITH   What does the tyrant?
CAITHNESS   Great Dunsinane he strongly fortifies.
   Some say he's mad; others that lesser hate him
   Do call it valiant fury, but for certain
   He cannot buckle his distempered cause   15
   Within the belt of rule.
ANGUS   Now does he feel
   His secret murders sticking on his hands;
   Now minutely revolts upbraid his faith-breach.
   Those he commands move only in command,
   Nothing in love. Now does he feel his title   20
   Hang loose about him, like a giant's robe
   Upon a dwarfish thief.
MENTEITH   Who then shall blame
   His pestered senses to recoil and start,
   When all that is within him does condemn
   Itself for being there?
CAITHNESS   Well, march we on   25
   To give obedience where 'tis truly owed.
   Meet we the med'cine of the sickly weal,
   And with him pour we in our country's purge
   Each drop of us.
LENNOX   Or so much as it needs
   To dew the sovereign flower and drown the weeds.   30
   Make we our march towards Birnam.   *Exeunt, marching.*

---

10. **unrough:** unbearded, young.
11. **Protest:** assert publicly; **first:** first evidence.
15. **distempered:** diseased and swollen. (The image of failing to buckle a belt around a bloated stomach suggests that Macbeth cannot legally or morally justify his disordered regime.)
18. **minutely:** every minute; **upbraid:** rebuke; **faith-breach:** violation of faith and trust.
19. **in command:** out of obligation.
23. **pestered:** tormented.
24. **all . . . him:** Macbeth's conscience.
25. **there:** illegitimately in power.
27. **weal:** commonweal.
28. **him:** Malcolm (the medicine for sick Scotland); **pour we:** we pour ourselves (as part of the bloodletting, or **purge** of the country).
30. **sovereign** (1) royal; (2) curative. Malcolm is the sovereign flower.

5.3

Enter MACBETH, DOCTOR, *and Attendants.*

MACBETH Bring me no more reports. Let them fly all.
   Till Birnam Wood remove to Dunsinane
   I cannot taint with fear. What's the boy Malcolm?
   Was he not born of woman? The spirits that know
   All mortal consequences have pronounced me thus: 5
   "Fear not, Macbeth. No man that's born of woman
   Shall e'er have power upon thee." Then fly, false thanes,
   And mingle with the English epicures!
   The mind I sway by and the heart I bear
   Shall never sag with doubt nor shake with fear.   10

   Enter SERVANT.

   The devil damn thee black, thou cream-faced loon!
   Where gott'st thou that goose look?
SERVANT There is ten thousand—
MACBETH   Geese, villain?
SERVANT   Soldiers, sir.
MACBETH Go prick thy face and over-red thy fear,
   Thou lily-livered boy. What soldiers, patch?   15
   Death of thy soul! Those linen cheeks of thine
   Are counselors to fear. What soldiers, whey-face?
SERVANT The English force, so please you.
MACBETH Take thy face hence.   [*Exit* SERVANT.]
              —Seyton! —I am sick at heart,
   When I behold—Seyton, I say!—This push   20
   Will cheer me ever or disseat me now.

5.3. Location: Dunsinane Hill. Macbeth's castle.
1. **them:** deserting thanes.
3. **taint:** become weak.
5. **mortal consequences:** human eventualities.
8. **epicures:** soft lovers of pleasure.
9. **sway:** rule.
11. **black:** the color of damned souls; **loon:** idler.
12. **goose:** stupid.
14. **over-red:** redden over. The servant is pale with fear (**cream-faced,** 11; having **linen cheeks,** 16).
15. **lily-livered:** cowardly. Blood has vacated the servant's liver, seat of passions like courage; **patch:** fool.
16. **of thy:** on thy.
17. **Are . . . fear:** advise others to fear; **whey:** pale (as milk).
20. **behold:** Macbeth does not finish this thought; **push:** enemy advance.
21. **disseat:** dethrone.

I have lived long enough. My way of life
Is fall'n into the sere, the yellow leaf,
And that which should accompany old age,
As honor, love, obedience, troops of friends,   25
I must not look to have, but in their stead
Curses, not loud but deep, mouth-honor, breath,
Which the poor heart would fain deny and dare not.
—Seyton!

    Enter SEYTON.

SEYTON   What's your gracious pleasure?
MACBETH   What news more?   30
SEYTON All is confirmed, my lord, which was reported.
MACBETH I'll fight till from my bones my flesh be hacked.
    Give me my armor.
SEYTON   'Tis not needed yet.
MACBETH I'll put it on.
    Send out more horses, skirr the country round,   35
    Hang those that talk of fear. Give me mine armor.
    —How does your patient, doctor?
DOCTOR   Not so sick, my lord,
    As she is troubled with thick-coming fancies
    That keep her from her rest.
MACBETH   Cure her of that.
    Canst thou not minister to a mind diseased,   40
    Pluck from the memory a rooted sorrow,
    Raze out the written troubles of the brain,
    And with some sweet oblivious antidote
    Cleanse the stuffed bosom of that perilous stuff
    Which weighs upon the heart?
DOCTOR   Therein the patient   45
    Must minister to himself.
MACBETH Throw physic to the dogs! I'll none of it.
    —Come, put mine armor on; give me my staff.
    —Seyton, send out. —Doctor, the thanes fly from me.

23. **sere:** withered.
27. **mouth-honor:** honors given only with the mouth (and not the heart).
28. **fain:** gladly.
35. **skirr:** scour.
42. **Raze out:** erase.
43. **oblivious:** causing forgetfulness.
47. **physic:** medicine.

—Come, sir, dispatch. —If thou couldst, Doctor, cast   50
The water of my land, find her disease,
And purge it to a sound and pristine health,
I would applaud thee to the very echo
That should applaud again. —Pull't off, I say.
—What rhubarb, senna, or what purgative drug   55
Would scour these English hence? Hear'st thou of them?
DOCTOR   Ay, my good lord. Your royal preparation
   Makes us hear something.
MACBETH   —Bring it after me.
   I will not be afraid of death and bane
   Till Birnam forest come to Dunsinane.   60

                            Exeunt [all but the DOCTOR].

DOCTOR   Were I from Dunsinane away and clear,
   Profit again should hardly draw me here.   [*Exit.*]

                              5.4

   *Drum and colors. Enter MALCOLM, SIWARD, MACDUFF, YOUNG
   SIWARD, MENTEITH, CAITHNESS, ANGUS, and SOLDIERS,
   marching.*

MALCOLM   Cousins, I hope the days are near at hand
   That chambers will be safe.
MENTEITH   We doubt it nothing.
SIWARD   What wood is this before us?
MENTEITH   The Wood of Birnam.
MALCOLM   Let every soldier hew him down a bough
   And bear't before him. Thereby shall we shadow   5
   The numbers of our host and make discovery
   Err in report of us.
SOLDIER   It shall be done.

---

50. **dispatch:** hurry, finish the job (of arming me).
50–51. **cast . . . land:** discover the disease of Scotland. To "cast water" was to diagnose by the inspection of urine.
55. **rhubarb, senna:** medicinal plants.
56. **scour:** clear out, purge.
58. **it:** the armor, not yet put on.
59. **bane:** destruction.
5.4. Location: **country near Birnam Wood.**
2. **chambers:** bedchambers, i.e., the homes of citizens; **nothing:** not at all.
5. **shadow:** conceal.
6. **discovery:** scouting information.

SIWARD We learn no other but the confident tyrant
    Keeps still in Dunsinane and will endure
    Our setting down before't.
MALCOLM   'Tis his main hope.   10
    For where there is advantage to be given,
    Both more and less have given him the revolt,
    And none serve with him but constrainèd things
    Whose hearts are absent too.
MACDUFF   Let our just censures
    Attend the true event, and put we on   15
    Industrious soldiership.
SIWARD   The time approaches
    That will with due decision make us know
    What we shall say we have and what we owe.
    Thoughts speculative their unsure hopes relate,
    But certain issue strokes must arbitrate—   20
    Towards which, advance the war.   *Exeunt, marching.*

5.5

Enter MACBETH, SEYTON, *and Soldiers, with drum and colors.*

MACBETH Hang out our banners on the outward walls.
    The cry is still, "They come!" Our castle's strength
    Will laugh a siege to scorn. Here let them lie
    Till famine and the ague eat them up.
    Were they not forced with those that should be ours,   5
    We might have met them dareful, beard to beard,
    And beat them backward home.

    A cry within of women.

                    What is that noise?

8. **other:** other news.
9. **Keeps still:** remains yet.
10. **setting down before't:** besieging the castle.
11. **advantage . . . given:** opportunity (to escape).
12. **more and less:** soldiers higher and lower in rank.
14–15. **Let . . . event:** Let our impartial judgment await the actual outcome.
18. What is truly ours and what we owe to another.
19–20. Thoughts now can relate only our hopes; blows must decide the real outcome.
21. **war:** army.
5.5. **Location: Dunsinane Hill. Macbeth's castle.**
4. **ague:** fever.
5. **forced:** reinforced.
6. **dareful:** boldly.

SEYTON   It is the cry of women, my good lord.

[*Exit.*]

MACBETH   I have almost forgot the taste of fears.
The time has been my senses would have cooled   10
To hear a night-shriek, and my fell of hair
Would at a dismal treatise rouse and stir
As life were in't. I have supped full with horrors.
Direness, familiar to my slaughterous thoughts,
Cannot once start me.

[SEYTON *re-enters.*]

Wherefore was that cry?   15
SEYTON   The Queen, my lord, is dead.
MACBETH   She should have died hereafter;
There would have been a time for such a word.
Tomorrow and tomorrow and tomorrow
Creeps in this petty pace from day to day   20
To the last syllable of recorded time,
And all our yesterdays have lighted fools
The way to dusty death. Out, out, brief candle.
Life's but a walking shadow, a poor player
That struts and frets his hour upon the stage   25
And then is heard no more. It is a tale
Told by an idiot, full of sound and fury,
Signifying nothing.

Enter a MESSENGER.

Thou com'st to use thy tongue; thy story quickly.
MESSENGER   Gracious my lord,   30

10. **my . . . cooled:** I would have felt cold fear.
11. **fell:** covering, i.e., the hair on my head.
12. **dismal treatise:** dreadful story.
14. **Direness:** horror.
15. **start:** startle; **Wherefore:** why.
17. **should have:** (1) ought to have (at some better time); (2) would have (anyway).
21. **syllable:** bit; **recorded time:** recordable time.
23. **dusty death:** perhaps echoing Genesis 3:19: "for dust thou art, and unto dust shalt thou return"; **candle:** a traditional symbol of life (see Job 18:6, 21:17).
24. **Life's . . . shadow:** There are many classical and biblical precedents for the idea, including Job 8.9: "We are but of yesterday and know nothing because our days upon earth are a shadow."
25. **stage:** The world as stage is another common metaphor; **frets:** (1) worries; (2) wears out; (3) consumes.

I should report that which I say I saw,
But know not how to do't.
MACBETH   Well, say, sir.
MESSENGER As I did stand my watch upon the hill,
I looked toward Birnam, and anon methought
The wood began to move.
MACBETH   Liar and slave!   35
MESSENGER   Let me endure your wrath if't be not so.
Within this three mile may you see it coming,
I say, a moving grove.
MACBETH   If thou speak'st false,
Upon the next tree shall thou hang alive
Till famine cling thee; if thy speech be sooth,   40
I care not if thou dost for me as much.
I pull in resolution and begin
To doubt th'equivocation of the fiend
That lies like truth. "Fear not, till Birnam Wood
Do come to Dunsinane" —and now a wood   45
Comes toward Dunsinane. Arm, arm, and out!
If this which he avouches does appear,
There is nor flying hence nor tarrying here.
I 'gin to be aweary of the sun,
And wish th'estate o'th' world were now undone.   50
Ring the alarum bell! Blow, wind, come, wrack!
At least we'll die with harness on our back.

Exeunt.

5.6

Drum and colors. Enter MALCOLM, SIWARD, MACDUFF, *and their
army, with boughs.*

MALCOLM   Now near enough. Your leafy screens throw down
And show like those you are. You, worthy uncle,

40. **cling:** shrivel; **sooth:** truth.
42. **pull in:** rein in.
47. **avouches:** reports.
49. **'gin:** begin.
50. **estate:** order.
51. **wrack:** ruin.
52. **harness:** armor.
5.6. **Location: Dunsinane Hill. Before Macbeth's castle.**
2. **show:** show yourselves; **uncle:** Siward (a term of respect).

Shall with my cousin, your right noble son,
Lead our first battle. Worthy Macduff and we
Shall take upon's what else remains to do,   5
According to our order.
SIWARD   Fare you well.
Do we but find the tyrant's power tonight,
Let us be beaten if we cannot fight.
MACDUFF   Make all our trumpets speak. Give them all breath,
Those clamorous harbingers of blood and death!   10

Exeunt. Alarums continued.

                              5.7

Enter MACBETH.

MACBETH   They have tied me to a stake. I cannot fly,
But bear-like I must fight the course. What's he
That was not born of woman? Such a one
Am I to fear, or none.

Enter YOUNG SIWARD.

YOUNG SIWARD   What is thy name?
MACBETH   Thou'lt be afraid to hear it.   5
YOUNG SIWARD   No, though thou call'st thyself a hotter name
Than any is in hell.
MACBETH   My name's Macbeth.
YOUNG SIWARD   The devil himself could not pronounce a title
More hateful to mine ear.
MACBETH   No, nor more fearful.
YOUNG SIWARD   Thou liest, abhorrèd tyrant! With my sword   10
I'll prove the lie thou speak'st.

Fight, and YOUNG SIWARD *slain.*

MACBETH   Thou wast born of woman.
But swords I smile at, weapons laugh to scorn,

---

4. **battle:** battalion.
6. **order:** battle plan.
7. **power:** army.
10. **harbingers:** forerunners.
5.7. **Location: Dunsinane Hill. Before Macbeth's castle.**
2. **course:** a round in bearbaiting, the blood sport wherein dogs attacked a bear tied to a stake (1).
11. **prove . . . speak'st:** prove that you speak a lie.

Brandished by man that's of a woman born.

Exit [with the body].

Alarums. Enter MACDUFF.

MACDUFF That way the noise is. Tyrant, show thy face!   15
    If thou beest slain and with no stroke of mine,
    My wife and children's ghosts will haunt me still.
    I cannot strike at wretched kerns, whose arms
    Are hired to bear their staves. Either thou, Macbeth,
    Or else my sword with an unbattered edge   20
    I sheathe again, undeeded. There thou shouldst be;
    By this great clatter one of greatest note
    Seems bruited. Let me find him, Fortune,
    And more I beg not.   *Exit. Alarums.*

    Enter MALCOLM *and* SIWARD.

SIWARD This way, my lord. The castle's gently rendered.   25
    The tyrant's people on both sides do fight;
    The noble thanes do bravely in the war;
    The day almost itself professes yours,
    And little is to do.
MALCOLM   We have met with foes
    That strike beside us.
        SIWARD   Enter, sir, the castle.   30
                            Exeunt. Alarums.

    Enter MACBETH.

MACBETH Why should I play the Roman fool and die
    On mine own sword? Whiles I see lives, the gashes
    Do better upon them.

---

17. **still:** ever.
18. **kerns:** light-armed foot soldiers.
19. **staves:** lances.
21. **undeeded:** having done nothing.
22. **note:** reputation.
23. **bruited:** noised, indicated.
25. **rendered:** surrendered.
28. **itself professes:** proclaims itself.
30. **strike beside:** (1) fight on our side; (2) miss intentionally.
30. **SD:** The action is continuous but the cleared stage has led editors to indicate a change in scene, perhaps to another part of the battlefield or to a place within the castle.
31. **play . . . fool:** imitate those foolish Romans who commit suicide to avoid dishonor.
32. **lives:** living enemies.

Enter MACDUFF.

MACDUFF   Turn, hellhound, turn!
MACBETH   Of all men else I have avoided thee.
    But get thee back. My soul is too much charged   35
    With blood of thine already.
MACDUFF   I have no words.
    My voice is in my sword, thou bloodier villain
    Than terms can give thee out!

    Fight. Alarums.

MACBETH   Thou losest labor.
    As easy mayst thou the intrenchant air
    With thy keen sword impress as make me bleed.   40
    Let fall thy blade on vulnerable crests.
    I bear a charmèd life which must not yield
    To one of woman born.
MACDUFF   Despair thy charm,
    And let the angel whom thou still hast served
    Tell thee, Macduff was from his mother's womb   45
    Untimely ripped.
MACBETH   Accursèd be that tongue that tells me so.
    For it hath cowed my better part of man.
    And be these juggling fiends no more believed,
    That palter with us in a double sense,   50
    That keep the word of promise to our ear
    And break it to our hope. I'll not fight with thee.
MACDUFF   Then yield thee, coward,
    And live to be the show and gaze o'th' time.
    We'll have thee, as our rarer monsters are,   55
    Painted upon a pole and underwrit,

35. **charged:** (1) burdened; (2) accused.
38. **terms:** words; **give . . . out:** describe.
39. **intrenchant:** incapable of being cut.
40. **impress:** leave a mark on.
41. **crests:** heads.
43. **charm:** magic.
44. **angel:** evil spirit (said ironically).
46. **Untimely:** prematurely, by Caesarean section.
48. **better . . . man:** courage.
49. **juggling:** deceiving.
50. **palter:** equivocate.
51–52. **to . . . hope:** verbally but not in deed.
54. **gaze:** spectacle.
56. Macbeth's picture will be painted on a pole and displayed with an accompanying description.

"Here may you see the tyrant."
MACBETH   I will not yield,
  To kiss the ground before young Malcolm's feet,
  And to be baited with the rabble's curse.
  Though Birnam Wood be come to Dunsinane,   60
  And thou opposed, being of no woman born,
  Yet I will try the last. Before my body
  I throw my warlike shield. Lay on, Macduff,
  And damned be him that first cries, "Hold, enough!'"

                              Exeunt fighting. Alarums.
          Enter [MACBETH and MACDUFF] fighting, and Macbeth slain.
                    [Exit MACDUFF with MACBETH's body.]
          Retreat and flourish. Enter, with drum and colors, MALCOLM,
          SIWARD, ROSS, Thanes, and Soldiers.

MALCOLM I would the friends we miss were safe arrived.   65
SIWARD Some must go off; and yet, by these I see
  So great a day as this is cheaply bought.
MALCOLM Macduff is missing, and your noble son.
ROSS Your son, my lord, has paid a soldier's debt.
  He only lived but till he was a man,   70
  The which no sooner had his prowess confirmed
  In the unshrinking station where he fought,
  But like a man he died.
SIWARD   Then he is dead?
ROSS Ay, and brought off the field. Your cause of sorrow
  Must not be measured by his worth, for then   75
  It hath no end.
SIWARD   Had he his hurts before?
ROSS Ay, on the front.
SIWARD   Why, then, God's soldier be he.
  Had I as many sons as I have hairs,
  I would not wish them to a fairer death.
  And so, his knell is knolled.
MALCOLM   He's worth more sorrow,   80

59. **baited:** attacked (as by dogs).
62. **last:** (1) my last reserves of strength and courage; (2) the last battle.
64.4. **SD:** The *Retreat* is a sound from a trumpet or drum signaling the concluding stage of battle. Some editors indicate a new scene here.
66. **go off:** die; **these:** the survivors present.
71. **prowess:** courage.
72. **unshrinking station:** place where he refused to back down.
76. **before:** on his front (from facing the enemy).
80. **knolled:** rung.

And that I'll spend for him.

SIWARD He's worth no more.
They say he parted well and paid his score,
And so, God be with him. Here comes newer comfort.

Enter MACDUFF *with* MACBETH's *head.*

MACDUFF Hail, King, for so thou art. Behold where stands
Th'usurper's cursèd head. The time is free. 85
I see thee compassed with thy kingdom's pearl,
That speak my salutation in their minds,
Whose voices I desire aloud with mine:
Hail, King of Scotland!
ALL Hail, King of Scotland!

Flourish.

MALCOLM We shall not spend a large expense of time 90
Before we reckon with your several loves
And make us even with you. My thanes and kinsmen,
Henceforth be earls, the first that ever Scotland
In such an honor named. What's more to do,
Which would be planted newly with the time, 95
As calling home our exiled friends abroad
That fled the snares of watchful tyranny,
Producing forth the cruel ministers
Of this dead butcher and his fiend-like queen—
Who, as 'tis thought, by self and violent hands 100
Took off her life—this, and what needful else
That calls upon us, by the grace of grace,
We will perform in measure, time, and place.
So, thanks to all at once and to each one
Whom we invite to see us crowned at Scone. 105

Flourish. Exeunt all.
Finis.

---

82. **score:** reckoning.
85. **time is free:** a proclamation of liberty from tyranny and the restoration of order in Scotland.
86. **compassed . . . pearl:** surrounded by the treasures of your kingdom, the Scottish nobles.
91. **reckon:** settle accounts.
95. **planted . . . time:** established in this new age.
98. **Producing forth:** leading to justice; **ministers:** agents.
100. **self and violent:** her own violent.
102. **grace of grace:** favor of divine grace.
103. **measure:** due proportion.

DISCUSSION QUESTIONS

1. *What role do the witches play in Macbeth's decision-making process?*

2. *Why doesn't Banquo respond to the prophecy the same way Macbeth does?*

3. *Who is the more disciplined character: Macbeth or Lady Macbeth?*

4. *What are Macbeth's most and least admirable traits?*

5. *How are ambitious members of your organization or institution generally regarded?*

ALBUM
Art of the Story

> Whether I shall turn out to be the hero of my own life, or whether
> that station will be held by anybody else, these pages must show.
>
> —CHARLES DICKENS, *David Copperfield*

We live in an age at once cynical and credulous about the story: we endure a lightning-quick news cycle and a barrage of spin from image consultants and strategic communicators. Somehow, the power of the story endures, and we need not share all the anxieties of a David Copperfield to wonder what the story of our lives might be and whether we shall end the hero or the villain of the piece. As Aristotle long ago noted, history tells us what happened, poetry what might. Perhaps that's why he gave his pupil Alexander the Great his annotated copy of Homer's *Iliad*. It was a poem that would help shape the narrative of Alexander's life.

As his epithet attests, Alexander the Great hardly seems to have suffered from a public relations problem over the centuries, yet he evidently brooded enviously over Achilles's good luck in finding a Homer to immortalize his deeds. In Plutarch's account, Alexander's anxiety about his fame, or *kleos*, is apparent from the very beginning of his campaign in 334 BCE, when a cypress-wood statue of Orpheus in Macedonia began "to sweat in great abundance, to the discouragement of many" of his followers. The seer Aristander immediately alleviated Alexander's concern by claiming that the portent "signified he should perform acts so important and glorious as would make the poets and musicians of future ages labour and sweat to describe and celebrate them." Aristander knew his man. He understood precisely the sort of vanity Alexander possessed: there could be nothing more gratifying to it than poetic fame. The urgency with which Alexander felt his lack of a herald becomes even clearer in Plutarch's account of the episode at Troy when the king and his friend Hephastion placed wreaths at the tombs of their heroes, Achilles and Patroclus:

> [Alexander] passed the Hellespont, and at Troy sacrificed to Minerva, and honoured the memory of the heroes who were buried there, with solemn libations; especially Achilles, whose gravestone he anointed, and with his friends, as the ancient custom is, ran naked about his sepulchre, and crowned it with garlands, declaring how happy he esteemed him, in having while he lived so faithful a friend, and when he was dead, so famous a poet to proclaim his actions.

This scene encapsulates Alexander's ardor for epic models as well as his anxiety that his own career would be incomplete without a Homeric tribute. Modern scholars endorse the idea that Alexander connived at the cultivation of his own heroic image.

If it is true that a desire to equal the exploits of a literary model animated at least in part Alexander's immense undertaking of global conquest, we might well ask what role his own example has served for subsequent leaders. What, in other words, did it mean to dream of Alexander as Alexander dreamed of Achilles? Julius Caesar reportedly wept when he reached the age at which Alexander died to think that he had accomplished so little in comparison.

The contemplation of Alexander prompted very different thoughts in Shakespeare's Hamlet. In the graveyard scene in act 5, when Hamlet imagines Alexander, he is led to the conclusion that the corpses of the great also reek and that even "noble dust" serves the basest uses. Horatio tries to temper Hamlet's speculations—to pull him back from the catechism provoked by the *memento mori* of the skull—but Hamlet presses on, turning his attention next to "Imperious Caesar," whose person once "kept the world in awe" yet whose dust now patches a hole in a wall. This, then, is what an exceptional Renaissance boy might make of his humanist education. Nevertheless, as the end of the play suggests, the tale Hamlet has to tell after thus sounding glory's emptiness will be drowned out by "[t]he soldiers' music and the rite of war" that the unimaginative Fortinbras demands "speak loudly" for Hamlet, the erstwhile rival whom he profoundly misunderstands. How could it be otherwise? We already know that Fortinbras is eager to fight over a strip of land for which one of his own captains would not "pay five ducats" for the privilege of farming. Hamlet, by contrast, once returned to Denmark from his strange, time-bending voyage with the pirates, has brought himself face to face with the "undiscovered country" about which he could only tentatively speculate earlier in the play. It is this possession—intellectual, not territorial—that spurs Hamlet's ambition.

The graveyard scene in *Hamlet* could be said to crystallize the tension infusing the play between the public responsibilities of the prince and the private hungers of the man. Hamlet wants to live another kind of life, but "all occasions do inform against" him. His tragedy is that he is trapped within a plot of vengeance and aggression in which he no longer believes but to which family, custom, and tradition condemn him. Hamlet needs someone who will tell his story. The yearning for such stories is the subject of this album. Joan Didion explores the possible consequences of this desire in the following passage from her essay "The White Album." The next selection, Montaigne's essay "Of the Inconsistency of Our Actions," invites us to consider the difficulty of weaving a coherent story out of all the many contradictory actions we might take over the course of a lifetime. Finally, Walter Kirn investigates the mythology surrounding the American investor Warren Buffett.

RECOMMENDED READING AND VIEWING

Katharine Graham, *Personal History* (1997)

Sima Qian, *Records of the Grand Historian*, translated by Burton Watson (second–first century BCE)

William Shakespeare, *Hamlet* (1600)

Stranger Than Fiction (2006), directed by Marc Forster

Virginia Woolf, *Moments of Being* (1972)

Joan Didion
(b. 1934)

,

JOAN DIDION, ONE of the foremost writers and cultural critics of twentieth-century America, was born in Sacramento, California. She has devoted an important part of her work, including the essay collections *Slouching Toward Bethlehem* (1968) and *The White Album* (1979), to analyzing California counterculture as an embodiment of the dark complexities of the American dream. Didion attended the University of California at Berkeley, and went to work for *Vogue* after graduation. After several years in New York City, Didion returned to California, where she and her husband, John Gregory Dunne, lived for several decades while producing journalism and collaborating on screenplays. Didion also continued to write novels. In 2005, in response to her husband's death and her daughter's grave illness, Didion wrote *The Year of Magical Thinking*, which won a National Book Award. She followed this meditation on grief with *Blue Nights*, an exploration of her daughter's subsequent death. The brief selection that follows comes from the beginning of Didion's essay "The White Album," which charts a period of dislocation she experienced not long after moving to Los Angeles.

We Tell Ourselves Stories
from *The White Album*

We tell ourselves stories in order to live. The princess is caged in the consulate. The man with the candy will lead the children into the sea. The naked woman on the ledge outside the window on the sixteenth floor is a victim of accidie, or the naked woman is an exhibitionist, and it would be "interesting" to know which. We tell ourselves that it makes some difference whether the naked woman is about to commit a mortal sin or is about to register a political protest or is about to be, the Aristophanic view, snatched back to the human condition by the fireman in priest's clothing just visible in the window behind her, the one smiling at the telephoto lens. We look for the sermon in the suicide, for the social or moral lesson in the murder of five. We interpret what we see, select the most workable of the multiple choices. We live entirely, especially if we are writers, by the imposition of a narrative line upon disparate images, by the "ideas" with which we have learned to freeze the shifting phantasmagoria which is our actual experience.

Or at least we do for a while. I am talking here about a time when I began to doubt the premises of all the stories I had ever told myself, a common condition but one I found troubling.

Michel de Montaigne
(1533–1592)

IN HER *NEW YORKER* essay "Me, Myself, and I," Jane Kramer captures the achievement of Montaigne's three volumes of essays: "However you read them, Montaigne's books were utterly, if inexplicably, original. They were not confessional like Augustine's, nor were they autobiographical. You could call them the autobiography of a mind." Montaigne wrote about many subjects, yet he claimed always to be writing about himself: presenting himself, in his words, as close to naked as custom permitted before his reader. In this essay he concludes that the lives of individuals are full of contradictions and that it is a fool's errand to attempt to knit the whole together. (The following selection is translated by Donald Frame.)

Of the Inconsistency of Our Actions
from *Essays* (1588)

Those who make a practice of comparing human actions are never so perplexed as when they try to see them as a whole and in the same light; for they commonly contradict each other so strangely that it seems impossible that they have come from the same shop. One moment young Marius is a son of Mars, another moment a son of Venus. Pope Boniface VIII, they say, entered office like a fox, behaved in it like a lion, and died like a dog. And who would believe that it was Nero, that living image of cruelty, who said, when they brought him in customary fashion the sentence of a condemned criminal to sign: "Would to God I had never learned to write!" So much his heart was wrung at condemning a man to death!

Everything is so full of such examples—each man, in fact, can supply himself with so many—that I find it strange to see intelligent men sometimes going to great pains to match these pieces; seeing that irresolution seems to me the most common and apparent defect of our nature, as witness that famous line of Publilius, the farce writer:

> Bad is the plan that never can be changed.
> PUBLILIUS SYRUS

There is some justification for basing a judgment of a man on the most ordinary acts of his life; but in view of the natural instability of our conduct and opinions, it has often seemed to me that even good authors are wrong to insist on fashioning a consistent and solid fabric out of us. They choose one general characteristic, and go and arrange and interpret all a man's actions to fit their picture; and if they cannot twist them enough, they go and set them down to dissimulation. Augustus has escaped them; for there is in this man throughout the course of his life such an obvious, abrupt, and continual variety of actions that even the boldest judges have had to let him go, intact and unsolved. Nothing is harder for me than to believe in men's consistency, nothing easier than to believe in their inconsistency. He who would judge them in detail and distinctly, bit by bit, would more often hit upon the truth.

In all antiquity it is hard to pick out a dozen men who set their lives to a certain and constant course, which is the principal goal of wisdom. For, to comprise all wisdom in a word, says an ancient [Seneca], and to embrace all the rules of our life in one, it is "always to will the same things, and always to oppose the same things." I would not deign, he says, to add "provided the will is just"; for if it is not just, it cannot always be whole.

In truth, I once learned that vice is only unruliness and lack of moderation, and that consequently consistency cannot be attributed to it. It is a maxim of Demosthenes, they say, that the beginning of all virtue is consultation and deliberation; and the end and perfection, consistency. If it were by reasoning that we settled on a particular course of action, we would choose the fairest course—but no one has thought of that:

> He spurns the thing he sought, and seeks anew
> What he just spurned; he seethes, his life's askew.
> HORACE

Our ordinary practice is to follow the inclinations of our appetite, to the left, to the right, uphill and down, as the wind of circumstance carries us. We think of what we want only at the moment we want it, and we change like that animal which takes the color of the place you set it on. What we have just now planned, we presently change, and presently again we retrace our steps: nothing but oscillation and inconsistency:

> Like puppets we are moved by outside strings.
>
> HORACE

We do not go; we are carried away, like floating objects, now gently, now violently, according as the water is angry or calm:

> Do we not see all humans unaware
> Of what they want, and always searching everywhere,
> And changing place, as if to drop the load they bear?
>
> LUCRETIUS

Every day a new fancy, and our humors shift with the shifts in the weather:

> Such are the minds of men, as is the fertile light
> That Father Jove himself sends down to make earth bright.
>
> HOMER

We float between different states of mind; we wish nothing freely, nothing absolutely, nothing constantly. If any man could prescribe and establish definite laws and a definite organization in his head, we should see shining throughout his life an evenness of habits, an order, and an infallible relation between his principles and his practice.

Empedocles noticed this inconsistency in the Agrigentines, that they abandoned themselves to pleasures as if they were to die on the morrow, and built as if they were never to die.

This man would be easy to understand, as is shown by the example of the younger Cato: he who has touched one chord of him has touched all; he is a harmony of perfectly concordant sounds, which cannot conflict. With us, it is the opposite: for so many actions, we need so many individual judgments. The surest thing, in my opinion, would be to trace our actions to the neighboring circumstances, without getting into any further research and without drawing from them any other conclusions.

During the disorders of our poor country, I was told that a girl, living near where I then was, had thrown herself out of a high window to avoid the violence of a knavish soldier quartered in her house. Not killed by the fall, she reasserted her purpose by trying to cut her throat with a knife. From this she was prevented, but only after wounding herself gravely. She herself confessed that the soldier had as yet pressed her only with requests, solicitations, and gifts; but she had been afraid, she said, that he would finally resort to force. And all this with such words, such expressions, not to mention the blood that testified to her virtue, as would have become another Lucrece. Now, I learned that as a matter of fact, both before and since, she was a wench not so hard to come to terms with. As the story says: Handsome and gentlemanly as you may be, when you have had no luck, do not promptly conclude that your mistress is inviolably chaste; for all you know, the mule driver may get his will with her.

Antigonus, having taken a liking to one of his soldiers for his virtue and valor, ordered his physicians to treat the man for a persistent internal malady that had long tormented him. After his cure, his master noticed that he was going about his business much less warmly, and asked him what had changed him so and made him such a coward. "You yourself, Sire," he answered, "by delivering me from the ills that made my life indifferent to me." A soldier of Lucullus who had been robbed of everything by the enemy made a bold attack on them to get revenge. When he had retrieved his loss, Lucullus, having formed a good opinion of him, urged him to some dangerous exploit with all the fine expostulations he could think of,

> With words that might have stirred a coward's heart.
> HORACE

"Urge some poor soldier who has been robbed to do it," he replied;

> Though but a rustic lout,
> "That man will go who's lost his money," he called out;
> HORACE

and resolutely refused to go.

We read that Sultan Mohammed outrageously berated Hassan, leader of his Janissaries, because he saw his troops giving way to the Hungarians and Hassan himself behaving like a coward in the fight. Hassan's only reply was to go and hurl himself furiously—alone, just as he was, arms in hand—into the first body of enemies that he met, by whom he was promptly swallowed up; this was perhaps not so much self-justification as a change of mood, nor so much his natural valor as fresh spite.

That man whom you saw so adventurous yesterday, do not think it strange to find him just as cowardly today: either anger, or necessity, or company, or wine, or the sound of a trumpet, had put his heart in his belly. His was a courage formed not by reason, but by one of these circumstances; it is no wonder if he has now been made different by other, contrary circumstances.

These supple variations and contradictions that are seen in us have made some imagine that we have two souls, and others that two powers accompany us and drive us, each in its own way, one toward good, the other toward evil; for such sudden diversity cannot well be reconciled with a simple subject.

Not only does the wind of accident move me at will, but, besides, I am moved and disturbed as a result merely of my own unstable posture; and anyone who observes carefully can hardly find himself twice in the same state. I give my soul now one face, now another, according to which direction I turn it. If I speak of myself in different ways, that is because I look at myself in different ways. All contradictions may be found in me by some twist and in some fashion. Bashful, insolent; chaste, lascivious; talkative, taciturn; tough, delicate; clever, stupid; surly, affable; lying, truthful; learned, ignorant; liberal, miserly, and prodigal: all this I see in myself to some extent according to how I turn; and whoever studies himself really attentively finds in himself, yes, even in his judgment, this gyration and discord. I have nothing to say about myself absolutely, simply, and solidly, without confusion and without mixture, or in one word. *Distinguo* is the most universal member of my logic.

Although I am always minded to say good of what is good, and inclined to interpret favorably anything that can be so interpreted, still it is true that the strangeness of our condition makes it happen that we are often driven to do good by vice itself—were it not that doing good is judged by intention alone.

Therefore one courageous deed must not be taken to prove a man valiant; a man who was really valiant would be so always and on all occasions. If valor were a habit of virtue, and not a sally, it would make a man equally resolute in any contingency, the same alone as in company, the same in single combat as in battle; for, whatever they say, there is not one valor for the pavement and another for the camp. As bravely would he bear an illness in his bed as a wound in camp, and he would fear death no more in his home than in an assault. We would not see the same man charging into the breach with brave assurance, and later tormenting himself, like a woman, over the loss of a lawsuit or a son. When, though a coward against infamy, he is firm against poverty; when, though weak against the surgeons' knives, he is steadfast against the enemy's swords, the action is praiseworthy, not the man.

Many Greeks, says Cicero, cannot look at the enemy, and are brave in sickness; the Cimbrians and Celtiberians, just the opposite; *for nothing can be uniform that does not spring from a firm principle* [Cicero].

There is no more extreme valor of its kind than Alexander's; but it is only of one kind, and not complete and universal enough. Incomparable though it is, it still has its blemishes; which is why we see him worry so frantically when he conceives the slightest suspicion that his men are plotting against his life, and why he behaves in such matters with such violent and indiscriminate injustice and with a fear that subverts his natural reason. Also superstition, with which he was so strongly tainted, bears some stamp of pusillanimity.

And the excessiveness of the penance he did for the murder of Clytus is also evidence of the unevenness of his temper.

Our actions are nothing but a patchwork—*they despise pleasure, but are too cowardly in pain; they are indifferent to glory, but infamy breaks their spirit* [Cicero]—and we want to gain honor under false colors. Virtue will not be followed except for her own sake; and if we sometimes borrow her mask for some other purpose, she promptly snatches it from our face. It is a strong and vivid dye, once the soul is steeped in it, and will not go without taking the fabric with it. That is why, to judge a man, we must follow his traces long and carefully. If he does not maintain consistency for its own sake, *with a way of life that has been well considered and preconcerted* [Cicero]; if changing circumstances makes him change his pace (I mean his path, for his pace may be hastened or slowed), let him go: that man goes before the wind, as the motto of our Talbot says.

It is no wonder, says an ancient [Seneca], that chance has so much power over us, since we live by chance. A man who has not directed his life as a whole toward a definite goal cannot possibly set his particular actions in order. A man who does not have a picture of the whole in his head cannot possibly arrange the pieces. What good does it do a man to lay in a supply of paints if he does not know what he is to paint? No one makes a definite plan of his life; we think about it only piecemeal. The archer must first know what he is aiming at, and then set his hand, his bow, his string, his arrow, and his movements for that goal. Our plans go astray because they have no direction and no aim. No wind works for the man who has no port of destination.

I do not agree with the judgment given in favor of Sophocles, on the strength of seeing one of his tragedies, that it proved him competent to manage his domestic affairs, against the accusation of his son. Nor do I think that the conjecture of the Parians sent to reform the Milesians was sufficient ground for the conclusion they drew. Visiting the island, they noticed the best-cultivated lands and the best-run country houses, and noted down the names of their owners. Then they assembled the citizens in the town and appointed these owners the new governors and magistrates, judging that they, who were careful of their private affairs, would be careful of those of the public.

We are all patchwork, and so shapeless and diverse in composition that each bit, each moment, plays its own game. And there is as much difference between us and ourselves as between us and others. *Consider it a great thing to play the part of one single man* [Seneca]. Ambition can teach men valor, and temperance, and liberality, and even justice. Greed can implant in the heart of a shop apprentice, brought up in obscurity and idleness, the confidence to cast himself far from hearth and home, in a frail boat at the mercy of the waves and angry Neptune; it also teaches discretion and wisdom. Venus herself supplies resolution and boldness to boys still subject to discipline and the rod, and arms the tender hearts of virgins who are still in their mothers' laps:

> Furtively passing sleeping guards, with Love as guide,
> Alone by night the girl comes to the young man's side.
>
> TIBULLUS

In view of this, a sound intellect will refuse to judge men simply by their outward actions; we must probe the inside and discover what springs set men in motion. But since this is an arduous and hazardous undertaking, I wish fewer people would meddle with it.

Walter Kirn
(b. 1962)

A NOVELIST, ESSAYIST, and reviewer, Walter Kirn grew up in Minnesota and attended Princeton University and later Oxford. His early ambition was to be a poet, but today Kirn is known for his prose. He has written two novels, *Up in the Air* (2001) and *Thumbsucker* (2005). *Up in the Air* centers on the alienation of a downsizing specialist who is also a frequent flyer. The novel and the 2009 film adapted from it struck a particular chord with an audience living through an economic downturn. Kirn has also written a memoir, *Lost in the Meritocracy*. In this 2004 essay, which originally appeared in the *Atlantic Monthly*, he attempts to locate the man behind the myth of Warren Buffett as barometer, oracle, and seer.

American Everyman: Portrait of Warren Buffett
Atlantic Monthly (November 2004)

On a Sunday afternoon in May of last year Warren Buffett, America's second richest man and, some feel, the greatest investor in its history, was meeting the press in an Omaha hotel when a dark-suited man—a bodyguard, apparently—hustled up onto the platform where Buffett was seated and whispered into his ear. The multibillionaire listened without expression while the man in the seat beside him, Charlie Munger, the vice-chairman of their company, Berkshire Hathaway, stared ahead through a pair of horn-rimmed glasses whose lenses weren't merely thick but virtually spherical, like a pair of crystal Ping-Pong balls. Buffett and Munger are quite a duo, with the conversational timing and style of a vaudeville comedy team—Buffett dry and jovial and extroverted, and Munger even drier but blunt and mordant. For an hour or so, until this interruption, the two—both native Nebraskans—had been answering questions on everything from corporate-governance scandals to the likelihood that a major act of terrorism would bankrupt the insurance industry. It's their gift to be able to talk about such subjects so plainly, incisively, and honestly that the reporters had been laughing the whole time.

Now, though, it seemed that something dire was happening. The bodyguard looked concerned—a little panicky, even. When the guard left the platform, Buffett looked up and spoke. The hotel, he informed us, was advising everyone to take shelter immediately in a windowless safe room located in the center of the building: tornadoes had been sighted in western Omaha, and radar indicated that they were headed this way.

For his part, however, he intended to keep on taking questions until no one had anything more to ask or the whole building blew away. He sipped from a can of Cherry Coke and exchanged a look with his straight man Munger, whose myopic self-containment seemed impregnable. Moments later sirens started to wail. A few reporters scuttled out, but most of them took up Buffett's stoic challenge to ignore the warnings and carry on.

The reporters who had done their research knew that this was how Buffett always operates—not only in the face of violent winds but in the face of turbulent markets. He sits tight. He keeps his head while others are losing theirs, and then he moves in, if he wishes, and buys those heads (meaning large blocks of stock or entire companies) at an advantageous price. And then he keeps them. He rolls them into Berkshire Hathaway's almost comically diverse portfolio (the company's wholly owned properties, to list just a few, include a chocolate-candy retailer, an underwear manufacturer, a furniture store, a chain of ice-cream restaurants, a maker of cowboy boots, and an insurance firm that insures insurance firms) and watches his wealth, and that of his shareholders, grow and grow. He watches it grow while the fortunes of other investors—more-excitable types with more fashionable holdings, which they tend to think about selling the moment they buy them—rise and fall and gyrate and go sideways and eventually, in all too many cases, are ground down between the twin millstones of fear and greed.

The weekend of that stormy Sunday was dedicated to celebrating Buffett's success, or what the business writer Robert Hagstrom has called "the Warren Buffett way"—as though there were some sort of wizardry behind what may be the most thoroughly explained investment method in recent history. Every May, Buffett, Munger, and attending shareholders, whom the two like to refer to as "our partners," gather for Berkshire Hathaway's annual meeting: two hectic days of capitalist frolicking, featuring exhibition Scrabble games, hot-dog feeds, and shareholders-only sales at Borsheim's Jewelers and the Nebraska Furniture Mart, two of the company's retail properties. Though Buffett's personal thrift is the stuff of legend (he still lives in the fairly modest house that he bought in the 1950s), he isn't shy about encouraging shareholders to break out their credit cards for diamonds and carpets. At the end of the weekend he totals the receipts and makes the figures public.

The annual meeting's main event, which took place on a Saturday in 2003, is a freewheeling question-and-answer session with Buffett and Munger, held in a cavernous downtown sports arena. Among the thousands of adoring fans are scores of millionaires who owe their net worth to Berkshire's lofty stock price, which hit a three-year low on March 10, 2000, on the same day the NASDAQ reached its all-time high, and then reversed course while the NASDAQ sank and sank. In the 1990s highfliers derided Buffett for sitting out the run-up in high-tech and dot-com stocks (he once famously said that he simply "didn't understand" them), but this contrarian feat provided sweet vindication.

The May 2003 session began with a short movie in which Buffett poked fun at his rumpled, down-home image while reminding the cheering audience of his unique celebrity—an unquantifiable but valuable asset that he has never been shy about exploiting but that financial writers tend to overlook when analyzing his character and accomplishments. In one segment Buffett appeared as Daddy Warbucks alongside Bob Kerrey, the former Nebraska senator and now the president of New School University, and belted out the song "Tomorrow," from *Annie*. In another Ron Insana, a balding, huggable CNBC reporter, summarized Berkshire's recent performance by cracking, "While the rest of the market was taking it in the shorts, Mr. Buffett was buying the shorts" (a reference to Berkshire's acquisition of Fruit of the Loom). At one point the singer Jimmy Buffett, a distant relative of the tycoon's, strummed a guitar and crooned, "I bought Berkshire back when it was cheap." For the finale, CEOs from various Berkshire-owned companies put new words to a familiar Coca-Cola jingle: "It's the real thing, Berkshire Hathaway. What the world wants today. Berkshire Hathaway." When Buffett joined in at the close, and urged the audience members to sing along from their seats, they did so, heartily, swaying to the music and clapping in the dreamy, loose-wristed manner of old ladies feeling the spirit at a gospel service.

With its roster of grinning well-known faces letting Buffett upstage them at every turn (Tiger Woods made a cameo appearance too, pretending to coach Buffett on his creaky golf swing), the movie revealed at least as much about the so-called Oracle of Omaha as did his refusal to bow to the tornado warning. Buffett is a conscious, sophisticated performer, the inventor and caretaker of a rare persona that has no equivalent in American business. Not since Samuel Goldwyn, perhaps, has a tycoon functioned in the culture as both a first-class entertainer and the embodiment of his industry. Buffett's

Will Rogers folksiness and Mark Twain wit ("Never ask the barber if you need a haircut"; "Price is what you give; value is what you get"; "Predicting rain doesn't count; building arks does") aren't merely colorful secondary traits but stylized expressions of his very being. They represent more than that, in fact. Buffett's attitudes and mannerisms now stand for American capitalism itself—or at least for its more positive aspects. He is what's good about the free market, in human form—akin to what Joe DiMaggio was to baseball. Bill Gates may be richer, and Donald Trump (the anti-Buffett) flashier, but compared with Buffett they're mere character actors. The role of the straight-shooting leading man, trusted by all, belongs to Buffett alone.

He understands this. Others know it too—particularly ambitious politicians in search of instant economic credentials and an air of humane financial probity. Not long after last year's annual meeting, when more than 10,000 dazzled shareholders shot to their feet as Buffett finally took the microphone, and then hung on his every word for hours afterward, the financier was recruited by Arnold Schwarzenegger to advise his gubernatorial campaign on budget issues. It takes a leading man to know one, and although their relationship foundered over the question of property taxes (Buffett suggested that California raise them), Buffett's decision to even be seen with Schwarzenegger solemnized the muscle man's candidacy. This year John Kerry is looking for the same magic: he teamed up with Buffett early on, and will surely be dropping his name until Election Day.

All of which is to say that the popular business media have for some time now been missing the big story when it comes to the country's second richest man. Buffett's fortune—and the oft told tale of how he made it and continues to add to it—has become the least interesting thing about him. It's Buffett the symbol that matters now, Buffett the folk hero, Buffett the communicator. As a successful investor, he merely moved markets; but as the charismatic, reassuring, quotable prototype of the honest capitalist (a sort of J. P. Morgan with a moral sense), he's capable of influencing elections, galvanizing rock-concert-size crowds, and in general defining how we Americans feel about the system that underlies our wealth.

That Sunday afternoon in Omaha the system was sorely in need of a defender. The violent storm cells approaching from the west, whose dangers Buffett chose to ignore, were nothing compared with the financial cyclones whose winds could still be felt across the country. The Enron and WorldCom scandals, the NASDAQ crash, the post-9/11 recession, and the run-up to the Iraq War had shaken the faith of millions. Buffett, Coke in hand, seemed sobered too. He spoke at length against the lax accounting standards that had enabled so much corporate fraud. He mocked the pseudo-scientists of Wall Street who had led so many investors to believe that a market bubble can grow to infinite size. He made a persuasive statistical case, backed by

his experience in the insurance world, for a future terrorist attack employing weapons of mass destruction. As usual, he spoke vividly and succinctly,
cutting through complexities to the commonsense core of every issue and
neither lightening harsh realities nor unduly darkening them. Buffett seemed
ever mindful of the role he'd been cultivating for decades: the voice of playful,
tempered reason. His most memorable line of the day was not his wittiest, but
it typified his understated style, and resonated with authority—an authority
derived partly from his investment record, but also from what deserves now
to be viewed as his cultural, artistic record.

In response to a question about the prospects of a country beset by
war and scandal, Buffett eyed his nearsighted sideman and said simply, as
civil-defense sirens sounded in the background and reporters readied their
pens and notebooks, "We think America will do pretty well over time."

Pure Omaha poetry.

THERE IS A line of self-made, iconoclastic, pragmatic, larger-than-life American Everymen that begins in the popular mind with Benjamin Franklin, and
runs through Mark Twain, Will Rogers, and Harry Truman, but also shows up
in such far-flung characters as Walt Whitman, Henry Ford, and Ernest Hemingway. They are the fresh-air paragons of democratic self-invention—the
anti-phonies who tell it like it is and, with their grassroots words and ways,
rebuke the pretentious sophistication of Europeanized elites. Even when they
hold liberal political views, they sometimes come off as reactionary cornballs,
because of the way they extend our native mythology of salty, slightly cranky
individualism.

Warren Buffett, as much as anyone else alive right now, belongs to this
indispensable tradition of truth-telling Americans so square and forthright
that they end up seeming subversive. His "true" identity—the stuff about
him that can be discovered by interviewing his family and associates or digging through his garbage—doesn't really matter, finally, compared with the
reputation he has created, and which the public has chosen to embrace, even
idolize. This outward self is a literary artifact. It's a *book*, not a life. It cries
out to be *read*.

The best way to start reading Warren Buffett is to gather up ten or twenty
years' worth of his annual letters to Berkshire Hathaway shareholders (these
"Chairman's letters" make up the bulk of the company's annual reports, and
copies are available on the Internet), which may be the only documents of their
type whose prose is worth poring over even for those who have no stake in
the appended balance sheets. Buffett's choice of such a dreary medium as the
primary showcase for his thoughts has always sent a message in itself. While
the Trumps and Iacoccas of the world prefer to present themselves in garish

books with jackets featuring large color photos of their own faces, Buffett, the legendary midwestern cheapskate with a knack for discovering hidden value in cookware clubs (The Pampered Chef) and encyclopedia publishers (World Book), has reclaimed a form of junk mail for his collected works.

Buffett's penny-pinching persona doesn't allow for lavish photos or graphics; the reports are all text, and they're printed in black-and-white. They customarily open with a few sentences on the corporation's financial performance, which is almost always dazzling. Any other CEO would trumpet such numbers with eye-catching graphs, but Buffett tends, if anything, to play them down. Year after year, and especially in his best years, he warns the shareholders that Berkshire's results are not likely to be repeated. When they are repeated, which happens more often than not, he expresses no surprise, just gratitude, and then slips back into his chronic pessimism. In 1992, for example, after citing an increase in Berkshire's per-share book value of more than 20 percent, Buffett made a gloomy general market prediction that couldn't have been more wrong: "The return over the next decade from an investment in the S&P index will be far less than that of the past decade." He went on to remark that his firm's own rate of growth, which continued to be superb, had a perverse dark side: "The drag exerted by Berkshire's expanding capital base will substantially reduce our historical advantage relative to the index."

Such are the boring parts of the reports, composed in the dusty language of the business page. They do exhibit a certain buttoned-down wit, though. Like a multibillionaire Jack Benny, the thrifty Buffett just can't stop worrying. He can't stop finding the bad news in the good. Because we know how well he's done and how well he'll do, his nervousness is amusing and disarming. And by avoiding emotion in his expression at moments when others in his position would be euphoric, he also caricatures his well-known suspicion of moody reactions to short-term market swings. When things look up, he doesn't celebrate, and when things look down, he's not surprised—that's the pose, at least. The truth, we suspect, is that such a cautious outlook is a luxury of the financially untouchable, and that Buffett fully understands this. For himself he feels no anxiety at all—he only pretends to, out of compassion for us, the vulnerable public. The hidden message is a subtle one: I, who don't have to, am keeping my guard up as a way of reminding all of you that you can't afford to let yours down.

Such gestures betray an underlying arrogance. Biographers and magazine writers love to detail Buffett's austerity—his middle-class house, his bare-bones corporate headquarters, his decision to stay put in Omaha—but they make a mistake when they accuse him of modesty. In a man worth tens of billions of dollars, self-deprecation is a boast. When, after returning from a high-profile rescue mission at the scandal-plagued bond firm Salomon Brothers, Buffett joked in his 1992 report that Berkshire "didn't miss me while I was gone," he was complimenting himself for creating a company so successful, so replete with its founder's systems, methods, and attitudes, that it could beat the Street on autopilot.

Buffett's false modesty would be annoying if it weren't so clearly an act—an act meant to instruct rather than to deceive, and one that his followers are eager to learn from in the hope of getting rich themselves. By calling himself "your Chairman" in the reports, by endlessly dissecting his own investment mistakes even when they've done his firm no damage, and by constantly pointing up the unattractiveness of the stock that accounts for his stupendous $40 billion net worth, Buffett is using a form of show-and-tell—exaggerated, dramatic, humorous—to teach lessons about humility, skepticism, and other qualities that he believes are crucial to profitable long-term investing. That is, he's playing the part of Warren Buffett, and a lot of the time he's hamming it up, one senses, in the spirit of Clemens playing Twain.

Once he has dispensed with reporting on Berkshire's performance, Buffett likes to spread out as a writer and indulge his flair for aphorism. "Fear is the foe of the faddist," he wrote in the 1994 report, "but the friend of the fundamentalist." This is the soul of the Buffett program: Stay cool. Exploit the follies of the crowd. It's the oldest investment advice there is, but Buffett has personalized it over the years by showing a certain contempt for the financial markets themselves, which he likes to portray as dens of waste and vanity rather than basically efficient systems for allotting capital. It's one of the reasons he's adored: he treats his shareholders as fellow members of a morally solid, wised-up in crowd surrounded by ethically wayward crazy people. It's us against them, the sane versus the mad, the prudent versus the greedy, and it's our right, perhaps even our duty, to grab the money from their trembling, sweaty hands. After all, left to their own unsound devices, they'd only fritter it away.

To be both an overlord and an underdog, an opportunist and a populist, is quite a trick, but Buffett manages to pull it off by implying that contemporary capitalism has fallen into a self-indulgent decadence that requires a puritan resistance movement led by the likes of Berkshire and its subsidiaries, whose CEOs he loves to praise as exemplars of uncorrupted, old-school enterprise. In 2002 he singled out the founder of The Pampered Chef, Doris Christopher, relating the Horatio Alger tale of how she parlayed $3,000 she had borrowed against a life-insurance policy into a business with annual revenues of $700 million, and fondly noting that Christopher had started her operation in her own basement. For Buffett, the ideal corporate leader is someone who grabs hold of his own bootstraps and never stops pulling up, no matter how far he rises.

Bracing stories of Buffett's clear-eyed managers stand in contrast to his chronic warnings about the dangerous softheadedness of almost everyone else. "Nothing sedates rationality like large doses of effortless money," he observed in the 2000 report, in an essay on the difference between investment and speculation. With the S&P 500 down almost 10 percent for the year, after a prolonged bull run that Buffett had been mocked for missing out on, and with Berkshire showing a 6.5 percent gain, the time had come for the old man to gloat. His 1999 letter had predicted an imminent comeuppance for the markets, and payback had arrived as if on schedule. He shamed everyone involved, but especially the promoters of hyped-up tech stocks, whom he accused first of running a con game and then of suffering from a disease. "It was as if some virus, racing wildly among investment professionals as well as amateurs, induced hallucinations," he wrote.

Mental illness is one of Buffett's pet metaphors. (Indeed, his fixation on it makes one wonder if losing his own mind is his deepest fear.) Again and again in his letters he compares—by implication, at least—his own stability with the manic-depression displayed by Wall Street, which Buffett and his mentor Benjamin Graham, of Columbia University—the author of *The Intelligent Investor*, the classic primer on value-based stock picking—have famously personified as the flighty "Mr. Market." According to this conceit, investing success is a matter not of intelligence, social position, or inside information but of simple common sense and psychological self-control—an encouraging message for the average person, and perhaps the best reason for Buffett's popularity with the aspiring middle class. Suppressing emotion is the key to wealth, he preaches; the dull and steadfast will inherit the earth from the fancy and neurotic.

Not many people have Bill Gates's IQ, Donald Trump's brazenness, or Tom Cruise's looks, but almost anyone—with a bit of discipline—can have Warren Buffett's temperament. That, at least, is the promise he holds out: unlike most tycoons, he can be imitated, because he's just like the rest of us, only more so.

BUFFETT'S PUBLIC IMAGE represents a singular cultural accomplishment whose difficulty is hard to overstate. Until Buffett came along, the notion of a folk-hero investor was an oxymoron in America. Before the 1920s, buying and selling corporate securities was regarded by ordinary people as an occult activity practiced by a shadowy elite acting in nobody's interest but its own. This view changed, of course, when a prolonged bull market, widely promoted as unstoppable, started sucking in the Main Street masses. It was a golden moment. Then came the Crash. Suddenly the denizens of Wall Street seemed even more sinister, selfish, and cynical than they had before—an impression that lingered for decades. When the markets recovered a portion of their lost honor in the 1950s and 1960s, ordinary Americans kept their distance, intimidated by a Brahmin hauteur. The leading investment personality of the 1970s, Louis Rukeyser, for more than thirty years the host of TV's *Wall Street Week*, had the patrician profile of a Founding Father, the flowing hair of a concert pianist, and the clubby nasal voice of a Harvard English professor. He was a true blue blood or a smooth fraud or some of both. What he wasn't was one's neighbor. Identifying with Rukeyser was impossible; this marble bust could only be *beheld*.

The market's next media star was less pretentious, but his affect and appearance were equally odd. The Street-beating mutual-fund manager Peter Lynch, of Fidelity Investments, had prematurely white hair, a pink complexion, a face and body nearly devoid of flesh, and a nerdy, asexual demeanor that seemed to mark him as a sheltered prodigy who had lived indoors all his life to spare his allergies, and had researched stocks while soaking in the tub. Lynch's message was not dissimilar to Buffett's: buy shares in firms whose products you like and use; don't get the willies when prices drop, or succumb to euphoria when they go up; and turn a deaf ear to tipsters, sharpies, and analysts. But the messenger resembled a friendly alien possessed of uncanny intuitive gifts that seemed normal only to him. Lynch insisted that any earthling could use his methods, but one sensed that he overestimated us. The best bet was to buy into his fund, Magellan—which, by the time most Americans had heard of Lynch, had risen so high that its potential seemed spent. And then, abruptly, Lynch gave up his post and faded inexorably from the public's view, despite Fidelity's decision to send him around as its roving corporate ambassador. He had stopped making money for people, so who cared?

Lynch's exit, in 1990, left Buffett alone in the arena. He'd been raising his profile for some time by then (the business press had been raising it for him, actually), but his fame was largely limited to money mavens. He hadn't yet become a semi-official national treasure—the last honest capitalist as conceived by Frank Capra, pitting his provincial integrity against the big boys' metropolitan guile, and sharing the spoils with the folks back home. His breakthrough into superstardom, sometime in the early nineties, was precipitated by a lucky cluster of events over which Buffett had no direct control. The economic weather was right. Growing doubts about the Social Security system, and the widespread embrace of IRAs and other tax-deductible retirement-savings plans, caused the stock-owning population to balloon just as the tech-led bull market was starting to look like a wealth-creating perpetual-motion machine. All one needed to ride it was a computer and a discount brokerage account; to monitor its movements, track its chatter, meet its VIPs, and learn its language, one had only to watch CNBC. The country was turning into one big trading desk.

In the turbulent news stream that flowed across this desk, Buffett's name was a tidal presence. Stocks rose on rumors of his interest in them, and quickly fell back when the rumors were dispelled. When he bought a company outright—any company, no matter how pedestrian or obscure), the talking heads dissected his decision and ritually concluded that it showed genius. When the NASDAQ retreated for two or three days running, Buffett's disdainful statements about tech stocks were deemed prophetic; and when the index climbed to a new high, his negative comments were talked about in a way that reaffirmed his legend but set it in the past tense. America's greatest, most influential investor (almost everyone acknowledged that he'd earned the title) was said by the experts to have lost his touch and dwindled into an "old economy" has-been. All the traits that have earned him tens of billions—his long-term outlook, his midwestern probity, his practice of buying on the dips and closing his checkbook during the advances, his total lack of interest in the Next Big Thing, and, most important, his belief that the market is just a running opinion poll that prices stocks by assigning the same weight to whims, hallucinations, and wild guesses as it does to rational judgments—were now recast as crippling prejudices, or even symptoms of creeping senility. My own go-go broker told me over lunch one day (after touting a glamour stock named Nortel, whose balance sheet would have made Buffett laugh out loud, but whose price seemed to double every couple of months), "The man's defunct. He's in denial. We're living in a new age, and he can't handle it."

To be canonized, one must first die. With the Oracle of Omaha's portfolio underperforming the average Toledo schoolteacher's, Buffett was declared dead by the financial world in the late 1990s and then, after a pause for schadenfreude, fondly elevated to sainthood. The eulogies served a hidden purpose. By remembering Buffett as nearly infallible and making him the great icon of traditionalism, the children of perpetual motion affirmed their new faith. The twisted syllogism went like this: If Buffett, who knew almost everything, was wrong, then investors who know almost nothing must be right. Or: If Buffett can lose, then anyone can win.

As in Twain's case, the rumors of Buffett's death proved to be greatly exaggerated. And like Tom Sawyer, who attended his own funeral in disguise and snickered at the solemn goings-on there, Buffett probably took some secret pleasure in imagining the effect his resurrection (which his sense of history told him was inevitable) would have on the people who were just pretending to miss him.

In the meantime, he sent letters from the tomb to his true disciples: Berkshire's shareholders. In 1999, the stock's worst year ever both in absolute terms and in comparison with the S&P, Buffett assured them that his philosophy—a liberalized version of his old professor Graham's "value" approach—hadn't changed and wasn't going to change, even if the world itself did. He also reminded the panicky and the depressed that the stock represented all but one percent of his personal assets ("We eat our own cooking," Buffett and Munger often like to say). He wound up by conceding that the new technologies would probably "transform" society, but said it was his prerogative as an old codger who'd done pretty well for himself over the years to tend his own garden while others built Utopia. "We just stick with what we understand," he wrote, lumping himself with his fellow Luddite, Munger. They knew nothing about geology, either, he wrote, or about several other important industries, but it hadn't prevented them from getting rich backing businesses they *did* know something about.

In the hyperbolic climate of the tech boom, with the media loudly lamenting Buffett's demise while it heralded the coming wired paradise, this sensible, understated rationale for declining to join the party was a brilliant rhetorical gesture. "I would prefer not to," says Melville's Bartleby, when asked why he refuses to leave his desk even though he no longer has a job. Buffett's response to his critics was just as memorable, just as disarming. Fiber-optic switches? Waveplex multipliers? Don't understand them. (And, truthfully, who did?) Buffett's indifference to cyberspace made fools of millions of panting investors who'd staked their retirements on gear and gizmos they probably wouldn't recognize if crateloads of them were dumped on their doorsteps.

The following year, as mentioned earlier, brought a modest gain for Buffett and a beating about the head for his antagonists. The NASDAQ, whose tech listings embodied the whiz kids' futuristic aspirations, crashed, got up again, fell down the stairs, and staggered around like a sloppy waterfront drunk. But aside from a pointed homily on the difference between investment and speculation, the 2000 letter went light on the I-told-you-sos. It talked business, and one business especially: the almost invisible reinsurance field, led by the obscure but mammoth Gen Re, the largest of Berkshire's wholly owned subsidiaries, the foundation of its financial structure, and the key to understanding Buffett's true character as opposed to the character the public assigns him. Buffett the straight-talking conscience of capitalism is, at bottom, a casino operator, and his casino is the whole world.

Gen Re is a vehicle for accepting bets, enormous bets, for the very highest stakes. A comparatively small bet, cited in Buffett's 2000 letter, involved Grab. com, an Internet firm that hoped to draw traffic to its site by offering visitors a chance to win a billion dollars. The odds were low that anyone would take the prize, but not so low that Grab.com wasn't willing to pay Gen Re to accept responsibility for paying it. Gen Re bet that it wouldn't have to, and won.

But this was a quirky, small-potatoes wager compared with the bets Gen Re is used to making on the likelihood of major earthquakes, killer hurricanes, and other shattering catastrophes, known as "mega-cats." It makes these bets with other insurance companies, which, should a mega-cat occur, might buckle from having to pay the overload of claims. To put it simply, Gen Re earns its fees by backing other gamblers' biggest gambles, and then uses these fees (the so-called "float") to bankroll yet other bets on the behavior of stocks and bonds and so on. Buffett views the float as essentially a low-cost loan, though, borrowed against the potential mega-cats—or perhaps the single super-mega-cat—that could oblige Gen Re to pay it back.

Buffett, the incomparable simplifier of arcane financial concepts, explained the reinsurance game with a streetwise candor befitting a Brooklyn bookie: "We receive a modest premium, face the possibility of a huge loss, and get good odds."

Those "modest" premiums add up, providing Buffett with the enormous pool of virtually no-cost liquid capital that lets him make cash offers for whole companies within fifteen minutes (or so he often boasts) of getting an asking price. The losses he risks in exchange for this rare privilege aren't just huge, however; they're monumental. And the good odds are merely that—good odds. It's hard to exaggerate the nerve involved here. Instead of the thousands of short-term fears faced by lesser investors—stock X will fall on disappointing earnings news; stock Y will stagnate owing to flattening sales; the market itself will plummet on rumors of war—Buffett faces a vast and long-term terror: the mega-cat of mega-cats, whatever it might prove to be. Although Gen Re reserves plenty of money for rainy days, its owner has written that "there is nothing symmetrical about surprises in the insurance business." All of which raises an inevitable question: Who insures the reinsurer? Jehovah?

On September 11, 2001, the question was answered: No one does. Buffett was hosting a golf tournament in Omaha when the mega-cat hit Manhattan. According to someone who was at the tournament, a top officer at a major bank, the magnates and CEOs out on the course first panicked about the act of terrorism and then began fretting about the possibility of insulting Buffett by leaving early and rushing home. The source wouldn't talk about Buffett's own demeanor, but left the impression that he remained composed—at least in comparison with his guests.

In his 2001 letter Buffett was still composed, despite having suffered, through Gen Re, a healthy portion of the largest loss in the history of the insurance industry. He wrote that he had "overlooked" the possibility that the next mega-cat would be man-made, and he scolded himself as an underwriter for "focusing on experience, rather than exposure." Buffett's superbly impersonal formulation describes a universal human weakness—our blockheaded blindness to the unfamiliar—that he needn't have apologized for sharing. Still, it was sporting of him to do so, considering that most people don't earn billions of dollars by estimating the likelihood of mega-cats.

Buffett went on in the letter to analyze the probability of an attack—nuclear, biological, or chemical—large enough to bankrupt the insurance industry and, as a consequence, Berkshire and himself. The risk was low, he asserted, but it was rising, and in any event it would never reach zero. "The best the nation can achieve is a series of stalemates," he concluded. He called on the government to absorb the risk of what might be a trillion-dollar loss, and he warned the public that unless this happened, it was on its own. "Fear may recede with time," he wrote, "but the danger won't." He summed up by telling Berkshire's shareholders that the company was in a better position than most firms to survive another such catastrophe.

He added, in what could be his epitaph: "At Berkshire, we retain our risks and depend on no one."

No wonder he doesn't cower before tornadoes. No wonder his mere presence in a political campaign is enough to inspire voters' confidence. And no wonder he can speak humorously and simply about delusional securities markets, scandalous accounting practices, corrupt corporate management structures, and other troublesome topics that his peers would rather not discuss at all and that the press can only shriek about. No wonder he seems so calm, so cool, so dry, so patient, so fluent, and so darn . . . reassuring.

It's Warren Buffett versus the apocalypse, and until the apocalypse arrives (he understands the odds; he probably calculates them in his sleep), the charming old gambler can afford to kid around.

DISCUSSION QUESTIONS

1. *Does Montaigne's theory of human personality accord with your own observation and experience?*

2. *When, as in the case of Warren Buffett, does the myth become more important than the facts?*

3. *What is your story?*

CODA: LETTING GO

Now my charms are all o'erthrown,
And what strength I have's mine own . . .

—PROSPERO,
William Shakespeare, *The Tempest*

You may take your leave with a good dinner and a gold watch, or you may exit with millions in stock options, but letting go is never easy. This is as true for plant managers, professors, and small business owners as it is for CEOs and kings. The tensions inherent in succession—in the passing of knowledge, responsibility, and authority from one leader to another—produce dramatic situations ripe for literary exploitation.

Ailing in body and mind, his conscience troubled by the "bypaths and indirect crook'd ways" by which he seized the throne from Richard II, Shakespeare's Henry IV awakens on his deathbed in *2 Henry IV* to discover that the crown—the symbol of both his power and his guilt—has disappeared. It is his son, Prince Hal, who has removed it from the pillow sincerely believing that its owner has died. "Dost thou so hunger for my empty chair," the outraged king demands, "That thou wilt needs invest thee with mine honors / Before thy hour be ripe?" The fretful king's reaction, especially his insistence that the prince has impatiently grasped at a "greatness that will overwhelm" him, also expresses the fear of many leaders on finding themselves nearer the end than the beginning: dubious about the ability of their successors; unwilling to relinquish control to a younger leader with new ideas and methods; reluctant to share the information that would ease transition; so closely and intensely identified with position, title, or uniform that they can no longer imagine a life without the trappings of office. Whatever the scope of one's authority and the sphere of one's responsibility, the rhythms and requirements of leadership, acquiring an almost physiological dimension, can grow to define a leader. As a result, contemplating the drift of life in their absence can seem daunting to even the most self-aware among us.

In this closing section of the anthology three lyric poems address aspects of letting go: retiring from the hurly-burly of public office to the isolation of solitary retreat (Wang Wei's "In Reply to Vice-Magistrate Chang"), withdrawing from the public arena to the secluded world of the family (Gjertrud Schnackenberg's "Darwin in 1881"), and surrendering to the embrace of death itself (Lucie Brock-Broido's "Inevitably, She Declined").

Whether negotiated with grace and elegance or mightily resisted, whether the occasion for rewarding reflection or debilitating crisis, the passage from office, authority, and power into a world unbounded by an explicit charter or an urgent, all-encompassing mission can prove as challenging as the practice of leadership itself.

FURTHER READING

Horace, *The Odes of Horace*, translated by David Ferry (1997)
Meng Chiao, *The Late Poems of Meng Chiao*, translated by David Hinton (1996)
William Shakespeare, *The Tempest* (1611)
Rebecca Solnit, *A Field Guide to Getting Lost* (2005)
Alfred, Lord Tennyson, "Ulysses" (1842)

Wang Wei
(ca. 699–ca. 761)

POET, PAINTER, MUSICIAN, bureaucrat, Wang Wei was a remarkable polymath. Together with his near contemporaries Li Bai and Du Fu, he is generally regarded as one of the most accomplished poets of the High Tang period, a golden age of Chinese intellectual and cultural life, which has been compared in its energy and achievement to that of Elizabethan England. Although certain details of Wang Wei's life remain obscure, we do know that he was born in Shanxi province and descended on both sides from influential families involved in government and the arts. His first official post was that of assistant minister of music at the court of Emperor Xuanzong, whose support of artists through government positions helped to fuel the age's creative exuberance. Wang Wei served in a variety of posts, culminating in that of grand secretary of the imperial chancellery, for the rest of his life. His career in the capital, Ch'ang-an, was interrupted by voluntary retreats to his nearby estate at Wang River but also, on occasion, by longer periods of banishment to remote posts and by brief imprisonment after he sided with the rebels during the An Lushan Rebellion in 755. The exile's peripatetic existence became the great subject of Wang Wei's poetry, which often juxtaposes the frenetic movement of city life with the contemplative dwelling of rural retreat. Heavily influenced by Zen (*Ch'an* in China) Buddhist spiritual practice, to which he turned after the death of his wife, Wang Wei was, as his translator David Hinton observes, "the quintessential poet of recluse solitude." Yet Wang remained, like the Augustan poet Horace, who appraised the political landscape of Rome from the tranquillity of his Sabine Farm, always a man of the world, the vicissitudes of which he contemplated with a perceptive clarity made possible by the achievement of the "empty consciousness," or "no-mind," that is the quest of *Ch'an* meditation. Representative of the High Tang's imagistic style and embrace of a highly personal, occasionally confessional mode, Wang Wei's poetry is also distinguished by what Burton Watson calls its "impartiality," which Watson regards as a measure of the poet's extraordinary "level of enlightenment." Wang Wei's poetry has strongly influenced American poets ranging from Ezra Pound to the Beats. The late poem "In Reply to Vice-Magistrate Chang" reflects on a career in public service from the perspective of retirement. (The poem appears here in a translation by David Hinton, who in 2007 won the PEN Award for Poetry in Translation for *The Selected Poems of Wang Wei*. The *ch'in* referred to in the poem is a stringed musical instrument.)

In Reply to Vice-Magistrate Chang

In these twilight years, I love tranquility
alone. Mind free of all ten thousand affairs,

self-regard free of all those grand schemes,
I return to my old forest, knowing empty.

Soon mountain moonlight plays my *ch'in*
and pine winds loosen my robe. Explain this

inner pattern behind failure and success?
Fishing song carries into shoreline depths.

Gjertrud Schnackenberg
(b. 1953)

GJERTRUD SCHNACKENBERG IS the author of several collections of poetry, among them *A Gilded Lapse of Time* (1992); *The Throne of Labadacus* (2000), a long-form poem recounting the Oedipus myth from alternate perspectives; and *Supernatural Love: Poems 1976–1992* (2000). Born in Tacoma, Washington, and educated at Mount Holyoke College in Massachusetts, Schnackenberg has won fellowships from the National Endowment for the Arts, the John Simon Guggenheim Foundation, and the Radcliffe Institute. Her honors and awards also include the Rome Prize of the American Academy and Institute of Arts and Letters and the 2011 Griffin Poetry Prize for her book *Heavenly Questions*. Much of Schnackenberg's work investigates the intersections of familial relationships, history, and myth. This is the case with "Darwin in 1881," a poem set in the year before the death of the celebrated and controversial nineteenth-century naturalist Charles Darwin, during a time when he had begun to write his memoirs for his children. In a review of her work in the *New York Times*, Adam Kirsch called attention to Schnackenberg's "desire to treat history as something more than a stage setting, to make it the medium of thought and feeling." In this poem, history is interwoven with the imaginary as Schnackenberg parallels Darwin with Prospero, the magician-protagonist of Shakespeare's final play, *The Tempest*. Prospero and Darwin, Schnackenberg explains, each retreated from the larger world into a private universe of books and ideas: Prospero from his dukedom in Milan to a remote island, Darwin from his scientific writing to autobiography. This "withdrawal from society and politics" presents Schnackenberg with an ideal vantage point from which to contemplate the two figures' shared preoccupation with mutability: with "the metamorphosis of living creatures." In an interview with her editor Jonathan Galassi, Schnackenberg proposed a fundamental relationship between poetry and the scientific practice of someone like Darwin: "I think that poetry tells us, intuitively, insufficiently perhaps, but compulsively, that we are made of *this*. As does science."

Darwin in 1881
(1982)

Sleepless as Prospero back in his bedroom
In Milan, with all his miracles

Reduced to sailors' tales,
He sits up in the dark. The islands loom.
His seasickness upwells,
Silence creeps by in memory as it crept
By him on water, while the sailors slept,
From broken eggs and vacant tortoise shells.
His voyage around the cape of middle age
Comes, with a feat of insight, to a close,
The same way Prospero's
Ended before he left the stage
To be led home across the blue-white sea,
When he had spoken of the clouds and globe,
Breaking his wand, and taking off his robe:
Knowledge increases unreality.

He quickly dresses.
Form wavers like his shadow on the stair
As he descends, in need of air
To cure his dizziness,
Down past the ship sunk emptiness
Of grownup children's rooms and hallways where
The family portraits stare,
All haunted by each other's likenesses.

Outside, the orchard and a piece of moon
Are islands, he an island as he walks,
Brushing against weed stalks
By hook and plume
The seeds gathering on his trouser legs
Are archipelagoes, like nests he sees
Shadowed in branching, ramifying trees,
Each with unique expressions in its eggs.
Different islands conjure
Different beings; different beings call
From different isles. And after all
His scrutiny of Nature
All he can see
Is how it will grow small, fade, disappear,
A coastline fading from a traveler
Aboard a survey ship. Slowly,
As coasts depart,
Nature had left behind a naturalist

Bound for a place where species don't exist,
Where no emergence has a counterpart.

He's heard from friends
About the other night, the banquet hall
Ringing with bravos—like a curtain call,
He thinks, when the performance ends,
Failing to summon from the wings
An actor who had lost his taste for verse,
Having beheld, in larger theaters,
Much greater banquet vanishings
Without the quaint device and thunderclap
Required in Act 3.
He wrote, Let your indulgence set me free,
To the Academy, and took a nap
Beneath a *London Daily* tent,
Then puttered on his hothouse walk
Watching his orchids beautifully stalk
Their unreturning paths, where each descendant
Is the last—
Their inner staircases
Haunted by vanished insect faces
So tiny, so intolerably vast.
And while they gave his proxy the award,
He dined in Downe and stayed up rather late
For backgammon with his beloved mate,
Who reads his books and is, quite frankly, bored.

Now done with beetle jaws and beaks of gulls
And bivalve hinges, now, utterly done,
One miracle remains, and only one.
An ocean swell of sickness rushes, pulls,
He leans against the fence
And lights a cigarette and deeply draws,
Done with fixed laws,
Done with experiments
Within his greenhouse heaven where
His offspring, Frank, for half the afternoon
Played, like an awkward angel, his bassoon
Into the humid air
So he could tell
If sound would make a Venus's-flytrap close.

And, done for good with scientific prose,
That raging hell
Of tortured grammars writhing on their stakes,
He'd turned to his memoirs, chuckling to write
About his boyhood in an upright
Home: a boy preferring garter snakes
To schoolwork, a lazy, strutting liar
Who quite provoked her aggravated look,
Shushed in the drawing room behind her book,
His bossy sister itching with desire
To tattletale—yes, that was good.
But even then, much like the conjurer
Grown cranky with impatience to abjure
All his gigantic works and livelihood
In order to immerse
Himself in tales where he could be the man
In Once upon a time there was a man,

He'd quite by chance beheld the universe:
A disregarded game of chess
Between two love-dazed heirs
Who fiddle with the tiny pairs
Of statues in their hands, while numberless
Abstract unseen
Combinings on the silent board remain
Unplayed forever when they leave the game
To turn, themselves, into a king and queen.
Now, like the coming day,
Inhaled smoke illuminates his nerves.
He turns, taking the sand walk as it curves
Back to the yard, the house, the entranceway
Where, not to waken her,
He softly shuts the door,
And leans against it for a spell before
He climbs the stairs, holding the banister,
Up to their room: there
Emma sleeps, moored
In illusion, blown past the storm he conjured
With his book, into a harbor
Where it all comes clear,
Where island beings leap from shape to shape
As to escape

Their terrifying turns to disappear.
He lies down on the quilt,
He lies down like a fabulous-headed
Fossil in a vanished riverbed,
In ocean drifts, in canyon floors, in silt,
In lime, in deepening blue ice,
In cliffs obscured as clouds gather and float;
He lies down in his boots and overcoat,
And shuts his eyes.

Lucie Brock-Broido
(b. 1956)

LUCIE BROCK-BROIDO IS a Pittsburgh, Pennsylvania, native who received her B.A. and M.A. from Johns Hopkins University and an M.F.A. from Columbia University. Before becoming the poetry director in the Writing Program of Columbia's School of the Arts, she taught at Princeton, Bennington, and Harvard. Brock-Broido is the author of several collections of poetry, including *A Hunger* (1988), *The Master Letters* (1995), and *Trouble in Mind* (2004). Among the honors and prizes she has received are the Witter Bynner Prize for Poetry, given by the Academy of American Arts and Letters; the Harvard Phi Beta Kappa Teaching Award; and a John Simon Guggenheim Fellowship. In a *New York Times* review of *Trouble in Mind*, Maureen N. McLane proposes that Brock-Broido's "poems etch a series of unsought, inflexible transformations." This characterization also aptly describes "Inevitably, She Declined" (1991), an elegiac sonnet on the death of Elizabeth I of England, who would not lie down during her final illness, gripping at a certain upright majesty and refusing to surrender to the inevitable decline forecasted by the poem's title. Harold Bloom selected the poem for inclusion in the tenth anniversary edition of the *Best American Poetry* annual, in the notes to which Brock-Broido explains, "I had the heats of history, a narrative, an ostensible purpose, a politic—& I chose to crowd all these heats into the densest song. So I concocted the whole Ordeal in the sonnet form, bending the form, Carrying On in the hellish embrace of the confines of the fourteen lines. The sonnet—a marriage of Hysteria & Haiku—seemed the perfect crowded Room for the overwrought, swollen, declining, bedecked, embellished rendition of Elizabeth—bastard of Henry, girl-child, *Idea*—of Anne [Boleyn]." "Inevitably, She Declined" marks the end of a forceful monarch's forty-five-year reign (1558–1603), an end whose certainty the heirless queen herself refused to discuss. The succession was, as her biographer Alison Weir notes, a "taboo" subject among the queen's councilors, for Elizabeth feared to inflame factions at court by naming an heir. While the queen's condition deteriorated, her secretary, Robert Cecil, worked behind the scenes to engineer the succession, and the crown passed peacefully to James, the son of Elizabeth's onetime rival Mary, Queen of Scots. Brock-Broido's theory that poetry is "a thing that wounds," as she phrased it in a 1995 interview in *BOMB* magazine, "this kind of poking, needling, a tampering . . . to peer inside," is encapsulated in this sonnet's unsentimental consideration of the queen's decay.

Inevitably, She Declined
(1991)

On a bishop's backless chair, inevitably, upright she declined
Watching an empire flicker & die out. Morning, an anodyne
Of undrugged sleep, her attendant files the wedding ring embedded
In her flesh for half a century, an unhinged sapphire unmarrying
A monarch to this life of beautiful bastard sovereignty, unwedding
England's bloated hand. By evening an heirless country waits to bury
A distended queen with hawthorn boughs, bonfires blazing majusculed
Letters in the streets. She will go on watching them, upright & inevitable.
When Elizabeth sat dying, she would not lie down, for fear
She would never rise again, her high neck propped with molecules
Of lace, circling a countenance decked with the small queer
Embellishments of monarchy. In a breathless hour, her virguled
Breath, a speechless pilgrim grateful for a little death, minuscule
Between moments, squall of air reclining, upright bolt, declining vertical.

DISCUSSION QUESTIONS

1. *How does one know when it is time to let go?*

2. *What are the most difficult aspects of a leadership transition?*

3. *What is the most important legacy a leader can leave?*

Permissions Acknowledgments

Lucie Brock-Broido: "Inevitably, She Declined," by Lucie Brock-Broido. Originally printed in the *Michigan Quarterly Review*, 30.1 (Winter 1991). Reprinted by permission of the author.

Alvar Núñez Cabeza de Vaca: From *Chronicle of the Narváez Expedition: A Norton Critical Edition*, by Alvar Núñez Cabeza de Vaca, edited by Ilan Stavans, translated by David Frye. Copyright © 2013 by W. W. Norton & Company, Inc. Used by permission of W. W. Norton & Company, Inc.

Rachel Carson: "The Obligation to Endure" and "The Other Road," from *Silent Spring*, by Rachel Carson. Copyright © 1962 by Rachel L. Carson, renewed 1990 by Roger Christie. Reprinted by permission of Houghton Mifflin Harcourt Publishing Company and by permission of Pollinger Limited (www.pollingerltd .com) on behalf of the Estate of Rachel Carson.

Baldesar Castiglione: Excerpt from *The Book of the Courtier*, by Baldesar Castiglione. Copyright © 1959 by Charles S. Singleton and Edgar de N. Mayhew. Copyright renewed © 1987 by William B. Dulany (Estate of Charles S. Singleton) and Edgar Mayhew. Used by permission of Doubleday, an imprint of the Knopf Doubleday Publishing Group, a division of Random House LLC. All rights reserved.

Miguel de Cervantes: From *Don Quijote: A Norton Critical Edition*, by Miguel de Cervantes, edited by Diana de Armas Wilson, translated by Burton Raffel. Copyright © 1999 by W. W. Norton & Company, Inc. Used by permission of W. W. Norton & Company, Inc.

Marilyn Chin: "Blues on Yellow," from *Rhapsody in Plain Yellow*, by Marilyn Chin. Copyright © 2002 by Marilyn Chin. Used by permission of W. W. Norton & Company, Inc.

Christine de Pizan: From *The Book of the City of Ladies*, by Christine de Pizan, translated by Rosalind Brown-Grant (Penguin Classics, 1999), pp. 82–85. Translation © by Rosalind Brown-Grant, 1999. Reproduced by permission of Penguin Books Ltd.

Chuang Tzu: From *Inner Chapters*, Book 2, Chapter 22, pp. 33–34, translated by David Hinton (1998). Copyright © 1998, 2002 by David Hinton from *Four Chinese Classics*. Used by permission of Counterpoint Press.

Winston Churchill: Winston S. Churchill's "The Lights are Going Out" Speech, 16 October 1938. Reproduced with permission of Curtis Brown, London, on behalf of the estate of Sir Winston Churchill. Copyright © by Winston S. Churchill.

Carl von Clausewitz: From *On War*, Chapter 3, pp. 100–112, translated by Michael Howard. Copyright © 1976 by Princeton University Press, 2004 renewed PUP. Reprinted by permission of Princeton University Press.

Joan Didion: Excerpt from "The White Album," by Joan Didion. Copyright © 1979 by Joan Didion. Reprinted by permission of Farrar, Straus & Giroux, LLC and by permission of the author via Janklow and Nesbit.

Friedrich Engels: "On Authority," from *The Marx-Engels Reader*, 2nd ed., edited by Robert C. Tucker. pp. 730–33 (1978).

Anne Fadiman: "The Arctic Hedonist" from *At Large and At Small*, by Anne Fadiman (Penguin Books, 2007, 2008). Copyright © 2007 by Anne Fadiman. Reprinted by permission of Farrar, Straus & Giroux, LLC and Penguin Books Ltd.

Abolqasem Ferdowsi: "The Reign of Sekandar," from *Shahnameh: The Persian Book of Kings*, by Abolqasem Ferdowsi, foreword by Azar Nafisi, translated by Dick Davis. Copyright © 1997, 2000, 2004 by Mage Publishers, Inc. Used by permission of Viking Penguin, a division of Penguin Group (USA) LLC.

Janet Flanner: From *Paris Was Yesterday*, edited by Irving Drutman, pp. 28–35 (1972). Originally published in *The New Yorker*, January 1, 1927. Copyright © by The New Yorker Magazine / Janet Flanner / Condé Nast. Reprinted by permission of Condé Nast.

Gavin Flood and Charles Martin (trans.): From *The Bhagavad Gita: A New Translation*, translated by Gavin Flood and Charles Martin. Copyright © 2012 by Gavin Flood and Charles Martin. Used by permission of W. W. Norton & Company, Inc.

Atul Gawande: "Personal Best," by Atul Gawande. Originally published in *The New Yorker*, October 3, 2011. Reprinted by permission of the author.

Malcolm Gladwell: "Open Secrets," by Malcolm Gladwell. Originally published in *The New Yorker*, pp. 44, 46–53, January 9, 2007. Reprinted by permission of the author.

Woody Guthrie: "Do Re Mi." Words and music by Woody Guthrie. WGP/TRO-© Copyright 1961 (renewed), 1963 (renewed) by Woody Guthrie Publications, Inc. and Ludlow Music, Inc., New York, NY, administered by Ludlow Music, Inc. International copyright secured. Made in USA. All rights reserved including public performance for profit. Used by permission.

Husain Haddawy (trans.): From *The Arabian Nights: The Thousand and One Nights*, translated by Husain Haddawy. Copyright © 1990 by W. W. Norton & Company, Inc. Used by permission of W. W. Norton & Company, Inc.

Dashiell Hammett: Excerpts from *The Maltese Falcon*, by Dashiell Hammett. Copyright © 1929, 1930 by Alfred A. Knopf, Inc. and renewed 1957, 1958 by Dashiell Hammett. Used by permission of Alfred A. Knopf, an imprint of the Knopf Doubleday Publishing Group, a division of Random House LLC. All rights reserved.

Index